COUNSELING RESEARCH AND PROGRAM EVALUATION

M000209677

ROBERT G. HADLEY
CALIFORNIA STATE UNIVERSITY, LOS ANGELES

LYNDA K. MITCHELL
CALIFORNIA STATE UNIVERSITY, LOS ANGELES

BROOKS/COLE
CENGAGE Learning

Australia • Brazil • Japan • Korea • Mexico • Singapore • Spain • United Kingdom • United States

BROOKS/COLE
CENGAGE Learning™

Counseling Research and Program Evaluation
Robert G. Hadley,
Lynda K. Mitchell

Sponsoring Editor:
Claire Verduin

Marketing Team:
Connie Jirovsky,
Jean Vevers Thompson

Marketing Representative:
Diana Rothberg

Editorial Associate: Patsy
Vienneau

Production Editor: Nancy
L. Shammas

Manuscript Editor: Kay Mikel

Permissions Editor: Elaine Jones

Interior Design: Vernon T. Boes

Interior Illustration: LM
Graphics

Cover Design: Katherine
Minerva

Art Coordinator: Lisa Torri

Indexer: Do Mi Stauber

Typesetting: Bookends
Typesetting

For product information and
technology assistance, contact us at **Cengage Learning
Customer & Sales Support, 1-800-354-9706**

For permission to use material from this text or product,
submit all requests online at **www.cengage.com/permissions**
Further permissions questions can be emailed to
permissionrequest@cengage.com

Library of Congress Control Number: 94036135

ISBN-13: 978-1-111-82893-6

ISBN-10: 1-111-82893-8

Brooks/Cole
20 Davis Drive
Belmont, CA 94002
USA

Cengage Learning is a leading provider of customized learning solutions with office locations around the globe, including Singapore, the United Kingdom, Australia, Mexico, Brazil, and Japan. Locate your local office at **www.cengage.com/global**

Cengage Learning products are represented in Canada by Nelson Education, Ltd.

To learn more about Brooks/Cole, visit
www.cengage.com/brookscole

Purchase any of our products at your local college store or at our preferred online store **www.cengagebrain.com**

Printed in the United States of America
2 3 4 5 6   16 15 14 13 12

FD010

We dedicate this book to our respective spouse-colleagues,
Patricia A. Hadley and Donald C. Butler,
for their ideas and for the many ways they have enriched our lives,
and to our students, who, more than any other source, have given us
a reason for writing.

CONTENTS

CHAPTER FOUR
PROGRAM EVALUATION: PROCESS AND PRODUCT QUESTIONS; DISSEMINATION AND UTILIZATION 78

CHAPTER FIVE
ETHICAL RESEARCH PRACTICES 98

CHAPTER SIX
FORMULATING THE MISSION 134

CHAPTER SEVEN

PLANNING THE PROJECT 163

CHAPTER EIGHT

DESIGN PRINCIPLES 183

CHAPTER NINE

DESIGN RISKS AND REMEDIES 221

CHAPTER FOURTEEN
DRAWING INFERENCES AND REPORTING THE PROJECT 378

APPENDIX A
POTENTIAL LITERATURE SOURCES 406

APPENDIX B
SAMPLE GOAL AND OBJECTIVES 413

APPENDIX C
DOCUMENTS PERTINENT TO ETHICAL RESEARCH PRACTICES 418

APPENDIX D
SUGGESTIONS FOR MANAGING LITERATURE REVIEW MATERIALS 423

APPENDIX E
SAMPLE TIME LINES 427

APPENDIX F
RANDOM NUMBER TABLES AND INSTRUCTIONS FOR THEIR USE 430

APPENDIX G
SUGGESTIONS FOR DEVELOPING A CONTENT ANALYSIS SYSTEM 432

PREFACE

This book has been written to serve as a sole or main text in research methodology courses in counselor education or counseling psychology programs. The text offers a specialized focus on *counseling* research, as distinct from other areas of research in behavioral sciences such as sensation, perception, social groups, and animal behavior. "Counseling" is construed broadly, including psychotherapy and other specialties such as school, career, employee assistance, and rehabilitation counseling.

Our main goal in writing this book was to provide adequate coverage of research design and program evaluation and to make the material interesting through the use of many practical examples and literature from the field. We have attempted to present the material in such a way that upon completion of the course students will be able to:

- read and comprehend most of the research literature in counseling,
- envision how the results of various projects might apply to their own work in counseling,
- understand the requirements for program evaluation that would apply in their own professional counseling workplace,
- find additional information when aspects of research or evaluation projects exceed their immediate understanding,
- participate as a co-investigator with a more experienced principal investigator in the formulation, planning, and execution of research and program evaluation projects in counseling, and
- progress to more advanced research courses in counselor education or psychology programs that offer them.

These goals represent the knowledge and skills students should acquire as a result of mastering the information in the text. It is also our intent to present the material in a manner as interesting as possible for counseling students. Counseling students tend to be people-oriented rather than data-oriented. This orientation often leads them to view courses in research design with suspicion or active dislike (probably because of their frequent association with statistics).

We have therefore attempted to engage the interest of students through numerous examples relevant to counseling practice. Thorough discussion of the reasons counselors need to both understand and be able to conduct research and practical exercises at the end of each chapter are designed to provide students with interesting and engaging learning experiences related to the concepts presented in the text.

The feature that most distinguishes this book from others currently available is its *program evaluation* content. We know of no other book that includes this content in a text suitable for a research methods course in counseling. We have made it a point to include this material because our sense of the field is that counselors can increasingly expect to be called upon to evaluate the programs in which they work, and these evaluations will be expected to meet increasingly higher standards. Certainly most counseling programs funded by federal and state sources include an evaluation component as part of their accountability requirements. Since such programs are where many professional counselors work, we believe program evaluation represents important knowledge and skills for counselors to have.

We envision a secondary use for this text. Practicing counselors with long-unused research skills are sometimes expected to assume research responsibilities. Such new responsibilities often include program evaluation, which may or may not have been included among the research skills originally studied. Practitioners in such situations may find this text helpful as a refresher.

Content

The book consists of 14 chapters plus appendixes and a glossary. Chapter 1 provides an introduction to the text, covering such issues as the nature of research, the reasons for counselors to know about and be able to conduct research (including the scientist-practitioner model), and an explanation of what is meant by the "mission" of a research project. Chapter 2 introduces the varieties of research commonly used in counseling, including descriptive (for example, case and field, correlational, qualitative), experimental and quasi-experimental (both group and time series), developmental, and other types not often mentioned in traditional research texts, such as trend and product research.

Chapters 3 and 4 cover the basic concepts of planning and conducting program evaluation. These chapters include such issues as why program evaluation is conducted (for example, for feedback and accountability purposes) and various pitfalls that await program evaluators. Pitfalls discussed include the interests of stakeholders in certain outcomes and their ability to sabotage evaluation projects that do not appear to be producing the desired findings.

Chapter 5 covers ethical issues in conducting research, including the issue of informed consent. It also includes issues unique to counseling research, such as confidentiality of findings about clients and the ethical requirements of conducting research on programs providing therapeutic interventions.

Chapter 6 covers formulating the mission of a research or evaluation project, and Chapter 7 covers its detailed planning. Chapter 8 then treats basic design principles for the varieties of research discussed in Chapter 2.

Chapter 9 discusses threats to internal and external validity and provides various suggestions for addressing those threats as rigorously as possible within the requirements of the project's research questions and circumstances.

Chapter 10 covers sampling, and Chapters 11 and 12 cover measurement issues. Chapter 13 discusses analyzing the data from research and evaluation projects. This chapter does not cover basic statistics but rather assumes that students know both descriptive and inferential statistics to the extent usually covered in a one-semester or one-quarter upper division course in education or behavioral science. The statistical knowledge assumed consists of concepts rather than computation. For example, students should know that a t test is used to evaluate the significance of difference between two means and what the idea of "significance" entails but need not know how to carry out the computations. Students should also know that a Pearson correlation coefficient represents the degree of relationship between two variables, that its values may range from -1.00 to 1.00, and what positive and negative values mean; they do not need to know the formula.

The final chapter (Chapter 14) discusses drawing inferences from a research project and various concerns in reporting the results of a project, such as the selection of reporting media appropriate to the audience.

Except for the program evaluation content (Chapters 3 and 4), the book's chapters follow a relatively traditional sequence. The first five chapters are introductory; then Chapters 6 through 14 follow the research process as a project is formulated and planned, data are collected and analyzed, and results are interpreted and reported.

We placed the program evaluation content in Chapters 3 and 4 for two reasons. First, this material continues the varieties of research idea of Chapter 2. We view program evaluation as applied research distinguished by its relationship with service programs. Second, many of our students were working in counseling agencies while taking the research course. A number of them told us that the program evaluation content helped make the remaining chapters more meaningful because they could see how the research process might be applied in their agencies. One of our course assignments is to formulate and plan a research project. Since many employers had asked students to develop an evaluation project to meet agency needs, the early introduction of this material profoundly enhanced their motivation and learning. Some instructors may prefer to teach the program evaluation content after the remaining material rather than according to our organization plan. We have provided for this preference by writing Chapters 5 through 14 without assuming that students have previously mastered Chapters 3 and 4.

Features and Learning Aids

Each chapter begins with an outline and set of "Questions to Guide Your Reading" to help students organize and understand the material as they read. The questions are especially useful in helping students recognize material they do not understand so they can seek clarification either in class or during office hours.

Practical exercises are included at the end of each chapter. These exercises will allow students to work individually or in groups to apply their knowledge of the concepts in that chapter to realistic situations involving research in counseling. It is our intention that these exercises will allow some latitude in teaching style. We have attempted to write so that the chapters are comprehensible with a minimum of lecture support, depending on the instructor's preference. If an instructor so chooses, a significant portion of class time can be spent discussing the practical exercises and encouraging the students to be actively engaged in problem solving. If, on the other hand, an instructor prefers a traditional lecture format, these exercises can serve as outside assignments.

Eight appendixes follow the main text. They provide a wealth of detailed information that augments materials provided in text chapters. And finally, an extensive glossary is presented at the back of the book.

Supplementary Materials

An unusually detailed instructor's manual is available. Its primary purpose is to provide a large bank of multiple-choice, short answer, and essay items, organized by chapters, for use in constructing examinations. A unique feature of the instructor's manual is that answers are provided for all short answer and essay items.

Feedback for the practical exercises in the text is also included and is printed in such a way that those pages can be duplicated from the instructor's manual and given directly to students.

Acknowledgments

Development of this book began in 1987, and the book was used in our research classes as a main text in unpublished manuscript form between 1987 and 1994. Many changes were introduced based on our experience teaching from it throughout these years, and we are grateful to all the students who suggested valuable ideas for revision and addition. Additionally, a number of indispensable people made this book possible. Don Butler, Roy Mayer, and Sam Moss carefully critiqued each chapter. Constructive reviews of the manuscript were provided by Stanley B. Baker, Pennsylvania State University; L. DiAnne Borders, University of North Carolina at Greensboro; John Corazzini, Virginia Commonwealth University; Joshua M. Gold, Fairfield University; Wayne Lanning, University of Nevada at Las Vegas; Nancy Murdock, University of Missouri at Kansas City; and Norman R. Stewart, Michigan State University. Thanks are also in order for the people at Brooks/Cole: Claire Verduin, publisher; Nancy Shammas, production editor; Vernon Boes, art director; Lisa Torri, art coordinator; and Elaine Jones, permissions editor.

ROBERT G. HADLEY
LYNDA K. MITCHELL

CHAPTER ONE

WHAT IS RESEARCH AND WHY IS IT IMPORTANT TO COUNSELORS?

QUESTIONS TO GUIDE YOUR READING

Defining Research
1. What features distinguish research from other activities?
2. What is meant by the phrase *publicly observable?*
   a. Why do researchers focus on what is publicly observable?
   b. Is it possible to do research on unobservable events?
3. What is a definition of research?

Reasons for Counselors to Know about Research
4. Why is knowing about research important for counselors?
5. Why do some counselors and counseling students prefer to avoid research activities?

Reasons for Conducting Research
6. What is meant by the term *scientist-practitioner* with respect to the counseling profession?
7. What benefits does the scientist-practitioner model offer?
8. What factors may interfere with the conduct of research by counselors?
9. What additional reasons, apart from their acknowledged professional responsibilities, may counselors have for conducting research?

Conducting Research
10. What is meant by *the scientific method?*
11. Why is it often difficult to be confident in the answer suggested by research results?
12. What controversy surrounds the idea that research questions should be drawn systematically from a body of theory?

Variables
13. What is a variable?
14. What is the difference between an independent and a dependent variable?
15. What are input, process, and outcome variables?

Hypotheses
16. What is a hypothesis?
17. What is meant by the terms *null hypothesis, directional hypothesis,* and *nondirectional hypothesis?* (Use of examples may help to clarify your answer.)

Other Ways to Seek Answers to Questions
18. Why is it impossible to answer some questions with data?
19. Why are values important to the research endeavor?
20. Why must we often rely on authorities for answers to questions?

21. Why is it dangerous to accept the pronouncements of authorities uncritically?
22. What is the difference between data acquired through ordinary experience and data acquired through research?
23. How is the concept of common sense similar to that of the scientific method? How is it different?

The Mission of a Research Project
24. What is the mission of a research project?
25. What are the essential components of formulating a research project effectively?
26. What is the difference between the mission of a research project and its purpose as often expressed in research reports?
27. How does a research program differ from a research project?

Research as Process, Industry, and Product
28. What are the six steps in the research process?
29. Explain the sequential and recycling features of the research process.
30. What factors, other than the mission of a research project, influence its planning?
31. What is meant by the term *research industry*?
32. What are the products of research activity?

WHAT IS RESEARCH?

Any discussion of what **research** is, whether among researchers or people without research training, will reveal as many answers to this question as there are people to discuss it. How, then, is research different from any other sphere of human activity? And how can we define it? A number of similarities appear among the various definitions offered. These ideas are included in most definitions of research:

- The purpose of research is to increase knowledge.
- Researchers seek to increase knowledge by gathering data to answer questions.
- Research addresses some questions but not others. The questions addressed concern events directly or indirectly observable. Such events either take place in the objective, observable world (for example, overt behavior) or are represented in an observable way (for example, feeling states represented by verbal report).
- Research questions are formulated carefully so that it is clear what sort of data will satisfactorily answer them.
- Research data are collected, analyzed, and interpreted systematically to maximize confidence in the answers they provide.

Using these ideas as a base, we offer the following definition of research: Research is an activity conducted to increase knowledge by systematically collecting, analyzing, and interpreting data to answer carefully formulated questions about publicly observable phenomena.

Much of the objective world in counseling research consists of publicly observable verbal and nonverbal behavior. This objective world contrasts with the private, unobservable world of thoughts, senses, and emotions. For example, if we (as many counselors do) wish to do research on feelings of love and hostility, we must decide what publicly observable behaviors accompany these emotions, such as angry and loving comments and gestures. Whatever is observable to one researcher should also be observable to others with the necessary knowledge, skill, and equipment. This emphasis on the observable world is necessary so that researchers can share a common body of knowledge and replicate and verify each other's work.

The emphasis on the observable world does not mean that research concerning unobservable events cannot be conducted, however. Counselors conduct much research on unobservable events, such as attitudes and emotions. It simply means that we must find some way to translate the unobservable (for example, attitudes) into the observable (for example, responses on an attitude questionnaire).

WHY SHOULD COUNSELORS KNOW ABOUT RESEARCH?

Counseling students often ask why they should know about research when they feel they could better spend their time and efforts learning the knowledge and skills more directly applicable to the work they plan to do as counselors. Furthermore, Holland (1973) has noted that counselors tend to be people-oriented, not data-oriented. Many who choose the profession of counseling do so because they are drawn to an occupational environment that involves social interaction and helping others. By the same token, they tend to avoid abstract, analytical, and data-oriented environments. The idea of conducting research often evokes images of the very activities many counselors prefer to avoid. Nonetheless, it is important to remember that aversion to research is not a necessary qualification for a good counselor. Nor does the fact that you enjoy helping people necessarily imply a lack of skill or interest in research.

Counseling exists as a profession partly because of the work of individuals who are recognized as both great researchers and great counselors. For example, we know of Carl Rogers, Donald Super, John Holland, and Virginia Satir not from their counseling activities alone but because they conducted research and published their findings. In the process, they changed the course of our profession.

Even if you have no intention of becoming famous by publishing research, you should know about the research process most fundamentally because this knowledge helps counselors provide better services to clients.

A number of additional reasons flow from this main idea. We will discuss several of these reasons without implying that they are the only ones.

It is necessary to know something about research to keep abreast of research literature in your field of professional practice. One of the distinguishing characteristics of professions versus other occupations is that professional practitioners are expected to keep their knowledge current as their specialty advances and to apply the findings from research to their specialty (Anderson & Heppner, 1986).

Studying research cultivates a systematic, rigorous mode of thinking that should help counselors to:

- teach clients to identify and remedy their own faulty thinking patterns,
- conduct counseling activities so that their results are more clearly demonstrable than they would otherwise be, and clearly and objectively evaluate the claims of others, whether they be clients, colleagues, or advertisers of products for counselors' use.

For example, an advertisement recommends a product because there is "none better" on the market. Research training helps you recognize immediately that this statement is fully consistent with the idea that all similar products on the market are equally effective. A claim that this product is "better than all others" would risk legal action for false advertising unless supported by research data. Further, research training helps you spot unsupportable claims such as statements that something is "better" or "faster," or offers "more" without saying to what it is being compared: more, better, faster than what? Studying research alerts you to such unsupportable claims, because the essence of research is to answer questions with data.

The professional responsibilities of some counselors include conducting research, whether as principal investigator or as collaborator in the research activities of colleagues. For example, some counselors in schools and agencies must evaluate the service programs in which they work or other programs to which they refer clients.

With a knowledge of research, the scientist-practitioner idea (Barlow, Hayes, & Nelson, 1984; Pepinsky & Pepinsky, 1954) can be better understood. The **scientist-practitioner model** requires that counselors (and other human service professionals) conduct and publish research while providing direct client service. This idea appears sufficiently often in the professional counseling literature, and in some counselors' work environments, that counselors can reasonably be expected to be familiar with it. The scientist-practitioner concept can be applied as a model in counselor training and practice (Claiborn, 1987; Haring-Hidore & Vacc, 1988; Hoshmand & Polkinghorne, 1992). (This idea is discussed in greater detail in the next section.)

Research content appears on professional certifying examinations administered by such bodies as the National Board for Certified Counselors (NBCC) and the Commission on Rehabilitation Counselor Certification (CRCC), and on most state licensing examinations. Further, bodies that accredit professional counselor preparation programs include research coverage in the standards they expect these programs to meet. Examples include the Commission on Accreditation of Counseling and Related Educational Programs (CACREP), the American Association of Marriage and Family Therapists (AAMFT), and the Council on Rehabilitation Education (CORE).

WHY DO COUNSELORS CONDUCT RESEARCH?

Some counselors' responsibilities include collecting data about the effectiveness of the programs in which they work. Further, the scientist-practitioner idea recommends that practitioners have training in the methods of scientific research and that their professional activities include both research and direct client service. These activities are viewed not as "based on disparate modes of reasoning" but as "a unified, interactive system of purposeful inquiry and action . . . uniting knowledge, thought and theory with professional skills, action and practice" (Hoshmand & Polkinghorne, 1992). The benefits of this combination of knowledge and action are numerous.

Research offers the best available means for counselors to know which kinds of interventions are most effective and which do not merit continued use with certain types of clients. Research reduces the likelihood that ineffective interventions will be continued based on a belief that they *might* work. In Anderson's (1992) recommendation for clinical outcome evaluation and research, he noted, "Minimal standards of clinical practice . . . should include periodic appraisal of counselor effectiveness" (p. 24).

The experience of serving clients yields ideas for research that are more relevant to counseling than they would be if developed without this experience.

Conducting research requires counselors to keep abreast of related literature more than practice alone does; this knowledge benefits both research and practice.

A counselor who conducts research can put the findings immediately into practice; research reports written by others often reach readers after a long delay.

Conducting research encourages counselors to think rigorously. In turn, such thinking (a) helps identify clients' faulty logic, and (b) encourages counselors to conduct service activities so that their results are clearly demonstrable.

Being skilled at conducting research helps counselors make good decisions about whether existing knowledge is sufficient for the tasks at hand or whether new research needs to be carried out.

Conducting and publishing in the professional literature expands opportunities for two-way communication with other scientist-practitioners, thus enriching the professional knowledge base of all participants in the counselor's network.

Discovering new knowledge is fun. It is exhilarating to have an idea for a new way to work with clients, test it out, and see the data confirm its validity. Further, researchers are often fascinated when unanticipated features are discovered in the data, such as cultural or gender differences. This exhilaration and fascination energize both research and counseling activities.

Practicing counselors vary in the extent to which their professional activities fit the scientist-practitioner model. Heppner and Anderson (1985) noted that "relatively few counselors and counseling psychologists publish (research findings) after they leave graduate school," and "research is seemingly continually criticized for not being relevant" (p. 545). These authors cited several factors as contributors to this lack of research activity, including:

- Current research methods often seem simplistic in relation to the complexity of human behavior counselors must address.
- Graduate schools often treat research as a training hurdle future practitioners must undergo to get their degree rather than as a lifelong, rewarding endeavor in which one study builds upon another.
- Many counselors' work environments present pressures to do more than the available time allows. Counselors feel driven to meet daily needs of client service, with neither time nor encouragement to plan or conduct research about their activities and results. Similarly, Martin (1992) noted that his day-to-day responsibilities as a counselor education faculty member led to "progressive distraction from scholarship"; therefore he did less than he wished toward redressing a prevailing "neglect" of "empirical and conceptual work in counseling" (p. 563).

In addition to these professional responsibilities, counselors usually have other reasons for conducting research that are omitted from most research textbooks. We refer to personal, political, and career concerns. These concerns include: meeting academic course or degree requirements, getting grant funds, getting professional recognition, influencing or justifying administrative decisions, influencing legislation, or advancing their careers.

Motivations such as these are expressed in very few research reports, although they profoundly affect planning, execution, and reporting of most projects. We recommend, therefore, that researchers have these goals clearly and honestly in mind as each project is formulated, planned, and conducted. Even if a researcher's professors, supervisors, or colleagues disdain such motivations and therefore discourage their open expression, we contend that it is advantageous to be honest with oneself about such matters. Many of the problems clients bring to counselors include self-defeating behaviors based on conflicting motivations or on desires repressed or unacknowledged because they are socially disapproved. Most beginning researchers encounter their fair share of obstacles to surmount without adding others based on their own self-defeating behavior.

HOW DO COUNSELORS CONDUCT RESEARCH?

We introduced this chapter with four principles that define research. As a reminder, we review them here:

- Researchers seek to increase knowledge, to answer questions with data.
- Researchers investigate publicly observable and verifiable phenomena with procedures that can be repeated given like conditions.
- Research questions are formulated carefully so it is clear what kinds of data will answer them.
- Research data are collected and analyzed systematically to maximize confidence in their answers to the questions asked.

The Scientific Method

The above four principles are part of a concept commonly referred to as **the scientific method**. Although the language of this term implies otherwise, it refers to a concept or idea rather than a single method.

To illustrate research that adheres to the concept of the scientific method, we offer a fictitious example. Ms. Hernandez is a counselor in a junior high school. In response to a debate among her colleagues about the attitudes of 9th grade students toward their school, she decided to seek better information than the anecdotes offered by her debating colleagues. This decision fulfilled the first principle: *Researchers seek to increase knowledge, to answer questions with data.*

To continue with the scientific method, Ms. Hernandez had to decide what kind of observable and publicly verifiable data would reveal the students' attitudes toward their school. She discussed her idea with the district's research director, then conducted a library search and found the *School Attitude Scale,* which students answer by circling numbers 0 through 4 to indicate their agreement or disagreement with a number of statements. Possible scores range from 0 to 100, with 0 indicating that the respondent detests school and 100 indicating a highly favorable attitude. A sample of 9th grade students from several other schools had an average score of 75, with the middle two-thirds of this group scoring between 60 and 90. Based on this information, Ms. Hernandez decided to find out whether her students' *School Attitude Scale* scores were comparable to those from the other schools or higher or lower. By this decision, she fulfilled the second and third principles: *Researchers investigate publicly observable and verifiable phenomena with procedures that can be repeated given like conditions,* and *Research questions are formulated carefully so it is clear what kinds of data will answer them.*

Ms. Hernandez administered the *School Attitude Scale* to all 114 9th grade students in her school, and found their average score was 30, much lower than that of the earlier sample. She was inclined to conclude that her 9th grade students strongly disliked school. Has she fulfilled Principle 4: *Research data are collected and analyzed systematically to maximize confidence in their answers to the questions asked?* To sustain her original interpretation, Ms. Hernandez must first rule out any rival interpretations, any one or more of which might be true instead of the favored one. We list some possibilities without suggesting they are the only ones:

- The scale did not measure the attitudes of the students toward school but measured something else, such as the attitudes they thought their peers expected of them.
- The scale was too difficult for the students because of features such as vocabulary, sentence structure, size and clarity of print, or the way responses were to be recorded. As a result, the students became frustrated and their answers expressed their dislike of the scale rather than the school.
- While answering the scale, the students gave too little effort to provide a good measure of their attitudes.
- The conditions under which the students answered the scale influenced their responses (for example, unclearly read instructions, noisy room, interruptions, feelings about answering the scale instead of whatever activity it displaced).

As we hope you can readily see from the above discussion, Principle 4 is often the most difficult to meet. That is why most research textbooks, including this one, emphasize planning research studies so that plausible rival interpretations can be ruled out. Ruling out such plausible rival interpretations almost always requires that more complex studies than Ms. Hernandez's be designed, and much of the remainder of this text discusses the means of doing so.

Most writers about the scientific method include the four principles we listed, but some controversy surrounds a fifth component idea: that *the questions asked are drawn systematically from a body of theory, and the answers obtained support, expand, or refine that body of theory.* As Strong (1991) put it, "Scientific work cycles from theory to observation and back to theory in an unending effort to evolve robust and useful concepts (p. 217). Some writers include this idea as a required component of the scientific method; others omit it.

The scientific career of B. F. Skinner has been cited as an example in support of both sides of this controversy. Skinner (1953) developed a set of theoretical propositions about human behavior based in part on a series of experiments. These experiments were logical outgrowths of the original propositions, and their results added to the explanatory power of those propositions. Thus, development of these theoretical propositions has been said to illustrate this last suggested component of the scientific method. To a casual observer at least, it appeared that he reasoned in orderly, systematic steps from theory to experiment, and then from experimental results back to theory.

Nonetheless, Skinner's (1956) account of his own behavior as a scientist includes some dramatic departures from this tradition. As a "principle not formally recognized by scientific methodologists," he suggested, "When you run onto something interesting, drop everything else and study it" (p. 223). Rather than being ideas systematically derived from theory and confirmed by experiment, many of his most important discoveries resulted from accidents (such as apparatuses breaking down) or his searches for easier ways to do something. Similarly, much research in counseling has been spawned by practitioners' curiosity about phenomena noted during their professional experience.

Formulating theory is one task scientists perform, whether "partial theories" or "grand unified theories" (Hawking, 1988, p. 156). Theories permit making connections among many observations and achieving a deeper and more satisfying understanding of the phenomena studied than is possible from empirical observation alone. Counselors, for example, would find their profession much more difficult if there were no theories of personality or human behavior but only unrelated observations of individuals. Strong (1991) makes a convincing case for the idea that "useful concepts of the underlying realities" are necessary to "understand what makes counseling special" (p. 218). Nonetheless, these points do not justify concluding that any project must bear on theory to qualify as "scientific." Counseling **research questions** come from many sources, including theory, practitioners' experience, and agencies' accountability for their service programs. We find no merit in claiming that some projects are more scientific and, therefore, presumably more worthy than others solely because their questions are drawn from theory.

We also caution against taking the term *the scientific method* to mean that only one research method qualifies as scientific. Many methods have yielded both valid and invalid research results. The methods of choice for each project depend on the questions it seeks to answer and the context in which it is carried out. A theoretical basis contributes to a project's worth if, and only if, these factors require this component.

Some university degree programs require their students to conduct research projects investigating theory-based questions. Such requirements are usually justifiable and fully consistent with the viewpoint we have expressed. Deriving research questions from theory is a valuable skill, one much more likely to be learned in the university environment than elsewhere. Equally valuable to counseling researchers are skills to formulate research missions derived from contexts other than theory, such as counseling experience and the need for counseling programs to maintain accountability.

The Role of Variables in Research

Clear statements of the questions a research project seeks to answer must include the variables being investigated. A **variable** is a characteristic of people, environments, physical objects, tasks, behavior, or anything else in which the researcher is interested. Here are a few examples in random order:

age	counseling technique used
grade point average	language(s) spoken
gender of interviewer	drug metabolites in urine
gender of subject or participant	ethnic identity
education completed	score (on any test, inventory, or scale)
occupation	
clarity of instructions	sound level (db)
task complexity	speed of presentation of stimulus material
dosage of medication given	
degree of disablement	years of professional experience as a counselor
attitude (toward any issue)	
intelligence	physical distance between respondent and interviewer
interviewer's style of dress	
marital status	number of "I" statements in verbal material
knowledge (about any topic)	
blood-alcohol level	

A complete list would be almost endless. The counseling research literature uses many descriptive adjectives with the term *variable*. Some of these pertain to the phenomena being studied, others to the role of variables in research projects.

Variables related to counseling phenomena. Hill (1991, pp. 85–88) classified variables according to aspects of counseling to which they refer:

- *input variables,* present at the time counseling begins:
  - *client variables* (for example, background, presenting problem),
  - *counselor/therapist variables* (for example, theoretical orientation, training, experience),
  - *setting variables* (for example, agency versus private practice, fees charged);
- *process variables,* what happens within sessions (for example, verbal behaviors, covert behaviors, content, strategies);
- *extratherapy events,* happenings outside of counseling but concurrent with it;
- *outcome variables:*
  - *immediate outcome,* change immediately following specific interventions (for example, counselor self-disclosure) within the process,
  - *outcome of a counseling event,* change following a series of therapeutic transactions,
  - *session outcome,* change following a specific session, and
  - *treatment outcome,* change from the entire treatment.

Though Hill's (1991) language reflects a primary interest in what is commonly called psychotherapeutic counseling, we find her classification system equally applicable to other kinds of counseling. Further, not all categories in this system are mutually exclusive; increased client openness occurring in the same session as a counselor's self-disclosure is both an *immediate outcome* and a *process variable*.

Role of variables in the research project. Some variables are deliberately administered, managed, or "manipulated" by a researcher (for example, counselors may be instructed to use certain techniques with clients according to specifications contained in a research plan, or clients may be asked to wait in waiting rooms that differ in planned ways). Other variables are observed or measured, as when a researcher notes the grades or attendance records of a project's participants or rates the clarity with which clients express what they want from counseling.

All research projects involve at least one observed or measured variable. In an experimental project, a researcher manages or manipulates an **independent variable** and observes or measures a **dependent variable**. For example, a researcher might offer three different styles of counseling (independent variable) for career indecision and then measure the ease with which clients make career decisions (dependent variable) during or after counseling. Though managed by the researcher, an independent variable is "independent" in its relationship with other factors in the project; it is hypothesized to be "cause" rather than "effect." A dependent variable is "dependent" in that the research project seeks to determine whether it depends upon the independent variable as an effect. The cause idea has been the subject of some controversy. Chapter 2 discusses this idea and other differences between experiments and other kinds of research. Additional roles variables may take in research projects are discussed in Chapter 8.

The Role of Hypotheses in Research

When research questions are drawn systematically from a body of theory, they are usually refined until they can be stated in the form of hypotheses. A **hypothesis** is a statement that expresses the researcher's best prediction about the outcome of the research project. To state it another way, a hypothesis is a prediction about what the answer to a research question will be. For example, Ms. Hernandez's research question was, "What is the attitude of our 9th graders toward school?" Based on her prediction about what the 9th graders' attitudes would be, she had several alternative hypotheses available to her:

- Our 9th grade students have roughly the *same* attitudes toward school as students in comparable schools, as measured by the *School Attitude Scale* (SAS).
- Our 9th grade students have *more favorable* attitudes toward school than students in comparable schools, as measured by the SAS.
- Our 9th grade students have *less favorable* attitudes toward school than students in comparable schools, as measured by the SAS.

Hypotheses and tests of their accuracy will be discussed in more detail in a later chapter. Suffice it to say for now that hypotheses that predict no difference between comparison groups (as does Ms. Hernandez's first hypothesis) are called **null hypotheses.** The term *null* is used because the hypothesis predicts the null, or zero difference, state. When hypotheses predict a difference between comparison groups, as do the second and third hypotheses, they can be either directional or nondirectional. The term *directional* means that a difference is predicted in some direction (for example, attitudes will be more favorable or less favorable than attitudes of comparable students). A nondirectional hypothesis in this project would predict that the students studied would have different attitudes from comparable students, without saying which group's will be the more favorable.

OTHER WAYS TO SEEK ANSWERS TO QUESTIONS

The scientific method has a long and illustrious history as a contributor to human knowledge. However, people use many other ways of seeking answers to questions, including (a) faith, (b) authority, (c) the vast amount of unsystematically collected and analyzed data represented by everyday life experiences, and (d) reasoning based on premises from one or any combination of the above sources, sometimes with and sometimes without additional premises from research findings. This latter process is often called "common sense."

Faith

Some questions cannot be answered with data. Many of these concern matters such as life values, which do not have factual answers. Or they may pertain only to the researcher's private experience. Other questions cannot be answered with data because, for technical or other reasons, the necessary data cannot be collected. For example, it is currently impossible to directly ascertain the conditions at the center of the earth. When important questions cannot be answered with data, people often seek guidance from authority or hold their answers on faith.

Albert Einstein (1954) noted that most scientists' research activities are guided not only by researchable questions and findings but also by many propositions accepted on faith. One of these is a "profound faith" (p. 46) in the orderliness and rational understandability of natural phenomena. Another is the idea that we should aspire toward truth and understanding. People hold their answers to questions of values and the meaningfulness of life largely on faith, whether these answers are drawn from religious denominations or elsewhere. We would add to Einstein's observations that even adherence to the scientific method is to some extent a matter of faith in the likelihood that it will produce findings of the most useful sort. Although that faith is primarily based on a long and illustrious history including many applications of the scientific method, the scientific method itself arises from philosophical beliefs such as logical positivism (Kuhn, 1962) that are driven by values.

In Einstein's (1954) view, science and faith work together; to hold them at odds is to defeat them both. In this context, our sense of Einstein's meaning is that without values and a sense of meaningfulness based largely on faith people would not generate the energy and sustained commitment good science requires. In turn, knowledge gained through science can enrich and enlighten these values as they develop throughout life.

Some religious groups include in their doctrines not only life value issues but answers to factual questions research has already addressed or future research data will likely address. When science provides data relevant to such questions, we have the option of accepting science's answers to replace doctrine-based answers, formerly held on faith, without compromising our faith in life values. For example, some creationists who once believed in the Bible's literal truth with regard to the time period in which the Earth was created have accepted science's evidence regarding that time period without abandoning their faith. To replace a belief based on doctrine with one based on data does not mean abandoning our faith as a whole; faith still answers value questions, which data cannot. Nonetheless, many people experience discomfort when new information contradicts long-held beliefs. People vary widely in their readiness to change beliefs under such circumstances. The 19th century philosopher Charles Pierce noted that some people tenaciously cling to old beliefs, resisting information contrary to them; this tenacity is "a species of faith" (Buchler, 1966, p. 66), whether or not the beliefs are religious. Einstein held that to keep on faith beliefs about matters of fact, and to seek to resolve value questions through scientific means, are both "fatal errors" (1954, p. 45).

Authority

Enough people uncritically accept celebrities as authorities that the statements of famous athletes and entertainers are very valuable to advertisers of commercial products even when the celebrity knows little about the product. As a second illustration of an unfortunate reliance on authority as a way of knowing, we like a story recounted by Gay (1987):

> According to the story, . . . Aristotle caught a fly and carefully counted and recounted its legs. He then announced that flies have five legs. No one questioned the word of Aristotle. For years his finding was uncritically accepted. (pp. 3–4)

People did not recognize the possibility that his specimen had a leg missing.

This story illustrates the further point that in many instances the pronouncements of authorities are based on data. In each instance, the data may support the offered conclusions strongly, moderately, minimally, or not at all.

To live in a complex society such as ours, we must often rely on authorities because the knowledge needed for daily activities requires data beyond the capacity of any individual to collect and interpret. Two key ideas in the 5-legged fly story are that no one questioned the word of Aristotle and that his finding was accepted uncritically. Our society now includes individuals and groups whose major role is to add to the data on which earlier conclusions were based and to change these conclusions when new data so indicate. These people are usually called scientists or researchers. We can question the extent to which authorities' conclusions are supported by their data insofar as our knowledge and sophistication will allow. Even without such knowledge and expertise, we can evaluate a claimed authority's background or credentials. The scientist-practitioner concept, discussed earlier in this chapter, includes the idea that a practitioner who has sufficient research training can make sound decisions whether to rely on existing data or to carry out new research projects.

Some people's background and credentials indicate authoritative expertise in some areas of knowledge. We rely on meteorologists to forecast the weather and physicians to help us manage health conditions without having to collect the necessary data ourselves. Difficulties can arise when people are regarded uncritically as authorities on issues outside their expertise. This process permits commercial exploitation of celebrities, as noted earlier. We regard Steven Hawking and Kareem Abdul Jabbar as authorities on physics and basketball, respectively, but not vice versa. We know of no basis to regard either as an authority on chewing gum, motor oil, or breakfast cereal.

Authorities are not necessarily individuals but may be groups or written materials. The Bible is often cited as an authority about many issues. The traditions of our families, our social groups, and our subculture are also often treated as authorities. We suggest that it is at best a risky business to accept the propositions or suggestions of authority without considering the extent to which they are based on data.

Ordinary Experience

Every waking moment humans acquire vast amounts of data from ordinary experience. A myriad of factors determine which of these data are noticed, remembered, combined in various ways, and interpreted. The conclusions reached are used to guide life's many decisions. This process differs from research in that it is relatively unsystematic. Research data are collected, analyzed, and interpreted systematically so as to maximize the confidence with which the data support interpretations and, in turn, the researcher's mission. To return to Aristotle's 5-legged fly, examining one specimen many times provided for the possibility that he might have made an error in counting but did not provide for the possibility that the specimen being examined might have been atypical of the species about which he wanted to make a statement. As another example, experience as practitioners has led us to the idea that clients who react defensively to discussing alcohol use are more likely than others to have alcohol dependence problems. However, we have much less confidence in this idea than we would if it were supported by systematically collected research data.

Common Sense

Common sense is both similar to the scientific method and different from it. Both involve reasoning from data to interpret phenomena. In this respect, science has been interpreted as an extension of common sense. Further, as scientific knowledge becomes widely shared, it becomes a basis for commonsense interpretations. Two examples of such knowledge are the findings that the earth is round and that smoking causes lung cancer. But common sense and the scientific method are also different, and we will discuss some of these differences in detail.

Common sense includes the idea that we would expect an ordinary person, without specialized knowledge or unusual intelligence, to arrive at interpretations similar to our own. For example, if you have driven a long time without refueling and the engine stops, it takes no specialized mechanical knowledge to suspect an empty fuel tank as the most likely culprit, even if the fuel gauge does not work. Science, on the other hand, often relies on specialized knowledge when interpreting data. The evaluation of scientific conclusions does not include the issue of whether people without specialized knowledge would agree with them. For example, a developmentally disabled client was frequently observed pulling out her hair. A commonsense interpretation might be that she was experiencing excessive stress. In contrast, a systematic analysis of her behavior revealed that she enjoyed the attention her hair pulling elicited and needed something to do with her hands in an understimulating environment. The validity of this analysis did not depend on whether it agreed with a commonsense explanation.

Scientific research addresses a more limited range of questions. As noted earlier in this chapter, scientific methods do not apply to value questions or to phenomena entirely within the researcher's private experience. Common sense does not observe these limits.

Science ideally relies only on reasoning from data and theory to interpret phenomena. In contrast, common sense may use reasoning based on premises derived from faith, authority, or both, in addition to data. Sometimes these premises represent widely held social stereotypes or other beliefs of a sort anthropologists call folklore. The pervasive beliefs of many people in ghosts and extrasensory perception, despite researchers' consistent failure to demonstrate that such phenomena exist, clearly illustrate beliefs derived from a combination of faith, authority, and misinterpretation of ordinary experience (Moss & Butler, 1978). Even scientists do not always follow scientific methods perfectly in this respect. Denmark, Russo, Frieze, and Sechzer (1988) noted that some projects are flawed because interpretive logic included social stereotypes as premises. Among other examples, these authors list: "Differences in male and female nurturing behavior are assumed to be biologically based because women give birth and breast-feed, even though research has determined that nurturing behavior is strongly influenced by culture and previous experience" (p. 584).

Science proceeds more carefully and systematically than does commonsense reasoning. In the scientific method, questions to be answered are carefully formulated, a research plan is prepared, and then data are systematically collected, analyzed, and interpreted according to the plan. This process is designed to rule out plausible rival interpretations and answer the questions asked with maximum confidence. Scientific projects usually lead to a record of their procedures and results in the professional literature. Data underlying commonsense interpretations are drawn largely from ordinary experience, interpreted without any special plan, and usually are not represented in any formal record.

THE MISSION OF A RESEARCH PROJECT

At the beginning of this chapter we discussed reasons for conducting research in general. Reasons for conducting any particular project usually include more than one of the reasons we recounted, and often additional ones. We think of the entire set of reasons why any project is being carried out as its **mission**.

To formulate a research project effectively, it is essential to clearly identify the questions it seeks to answer, the variables included in these questions, and the role of each such variable in the project. Sometimes variables not part of a research question must nonetheless be identified and taken into account in planning so results will answer the research questions with maximum clarity. For example, a study of clients' satisfaction with counseling services must take into account their verbal ability and the amount of time they have available to give to the research process.

A project's mission contains more than its research questions. Many research reports contain statements such as, "The purpose of this project was to . . .," followed by an expression of the research questions. Definitions of purpose in such reports often focus on the research questions exclusively; reasons why answers to these questions were sought are usually found in the supporting discussion of a project's purpose. We introduce the mission concept to emphasize the fact that every project has not only one or more questions the researcher is seeking to answer but also reasons (usually several) why answers to these questions are being sought. These reasons and the research questions together make up the project's mission.

Effective planning requires that these reasons be kept in central focus along with the research questions rather than being limited to a supporting role.

Reasons for Asking and Answering Research Questions

As noted earlier in this chapter, some of the reasons for seeking answers to questions come from the professional context in which the project's questions were developed; other reasons concern the researcher's personal goals, such as getting grant funds, advancing a career, or fulfilling academic requirements.

Researchers seek to answer questions with data. Clear statements of research questions form an important part of any project's mission. These questions, however, are not developed in a vacuum. For example, a college dean wants to determine how many students have physical disabilities and what services these students believe would help reduce the extent to which their disabilities interfere with their studies. Answers to these research questions are sought to help college officials decide whether to open a disabled student services office and, if so, what services this office should provide. This particular research mission comprises these latter issues and the questions to be answered.

As a second example, a learning theory predicted that toddlers trained to choose the smaller of two balls would more quickly learn to choose the smaller ball in a second set (with both balls different from the first in size) than toddlers trained to make a different kind of discrimination, such as choosing a ball versus a cube. The project's mission included testing this hypothesis to support or refine this body of theory; it was not limited to testing the hypothesis.

As a third example, a faculty member and a graduate student in a counselor education program conducted a survey of its graduates. They wanted to determine the extent to which the graduates were working in their field of specialization and how well prepared they felt in the essential knowledge and skills of their profession. This project's mission included these research questions along with these additional factors:

- The faculty would use the results to help decide whether to make any changes in the program's required courses.
- The university required every program to conduct a self-evaluation process every five years. The survey results were to be included in the documents that fulfilled this accountability requirement.
- The program was being evaluated for accreditation. The survey results were to be submitted in support of its application.
- The faculty member was preparing an application for a grant to fund another project she had planned. The survey results were to be included in support of this application.
- The faculty member planned to use the survey results as part of an article she and the student were jointly preparing for journal

publication. A publication would improve her chances of being promoted and granted tenure.

- A journal publication would strengthen the student's professional resume.
- The survey was part of the student's master's thesis project.

In some environments where researchers work, theory-based projects are regarded more highly than applied ones. Tracey (1991) illustrates this viewpoint:

> Counseling research, due to its focus on application and the "fuzzy" variables examined, will never "bootstrap" itself up to be a more basic scientific branch of psychology. (p. 26)

In contrast, some counseling agencies require applied projects and consider theoretical issues academic. Such workplace attitudes profoundly shape the missions researchers choose for their projects.

Research Programs

A **research program** is a set of related projects that have some aspects of their missions in common. The program as a whole has a mission, which in turn forms part of each individual project's mission. On May 25, 1961, President Kennedy proposed to Congress a major component of the mission for a very large research program: "before this decade is out, . . . landing a man on the moon and returning him safely to earth." This program included many projects, each with its own mission. Each project sought to answer its own set of research questions; all their missions were alike in that they were derived from this program.

In the field of counseling, numerous research programs have contributed to the knowledge base counselors use. Some examples are:

- the work of Bandura (1969; 1977) and his colleagues, which led to the development of social learning theory and the interventions derived from it;
- the research of Beck (1976) and his colleagues, which led to a cognitive-behavioral treatment for depression; and
- the research program of Holland (1966; 1973) and his colleagues, which led to the modal personal style theory of career choice, which led in turn to construction or revision of several interest inventories.

The Role of a Project's Mission

Formulating the mission is the first stage in any research project. This mission serves as a reference point or guidepost for all the remaining phases, from planning to reporting. Decisions in these latter phases involve choosing the course of action expected to fulfill this mission best.

Research as Process, Industry, and Product

We now repeat the definition of research offered earlier in this chapter:

> Research is an activity conducted to increase knowledge by systematically collecting, analyzing, and interpreting data to answer carefully formulated questions about publicly observable phenomena.

Common usage suggests two subdivisions: (a) the processes by which each project or program proceeds from beginning to end and by which new projects build on older ones, and (b) all research activities of the society as a whole or any segment within it. Further, research often refers to the accumulated results of these activities.

The Research Process

Any activity takes place over time and can therefore be viewed as a process. Thus, each research project has a process as it moves from beginning to end. This **research process** comprises six steps in sequence:

1. formulation,
2. planning,
3. data collection,
4. data analysis,
5. interpretation, and
6. reporting.

These steps are sequential in that earlier steps must be accomplished satisfactorily before later ones can succeed. If a project's mission is incompletely or vaguely formulated, the researcher will lack a sufficient basis for deciding how to conduct the other phases. Careless planning may lead to faulty data collection, to data the researcher does not have the resources to analyze appropriately, or to a completed project with no reporting outlet. When data are collected or analyzed carelessly, their meaning is seldom clear, and wrong conclusions often follow. There is little reason to report data that cannot be meaningfully interpreted.

Not only is the relationship among the six steps sequential, it also has a recycling feature. Midway in the planning process, researchers often recognize unclear formulations that must be revised before the project can proceed satisfactorily. To reduce the risk of having to abandon a large study because of unanticipated problems, researchers often conduct **pilot studies**. A good pilot study includes planning, data collection, data analysis, and **interpretation**—all carried out on a smaller scale. The experience of conducting a pilot study, and the resulting data, often reveal faults in planned procedures. Plans can then be revised before the main study is conducted. Planning a research project encompasses all subsequent steps in symbolic form and is discussed in greater detail in Chapter 7.

Figure 1.1 illustrates the research process. The large clockwise arrows in Figure 1.1 are from Drew and Hardman (1985, p. 9). A research mission leads to a plan by which a project is designed and data are collected and analyzed. Inferences from the results lead to a report containing descriptive statements; these, in turn, trigger further research missions.

The upper left corner of the figure represents the idea that research missions can come not only from previous research but also from theory and practice, whether directly, in combination with earlier research results, or as represented in the professional literature. The upper right portion of the figure depicts the professional literature as a source not only of research missions but also of ideas for collecting, analyzing, and reporting data. A small reverse arrow shows that the experience of designing a project can lead to changes in its mission. Another small reverse arrow shows what often happens in a pilot study; early data or experiences of data collection lead to changes in plans for the main study or in its mission.

The right-hand side of the figure shows two additional details. The planning of a project is influenced not only by its mission but also by outside forces, such as supports and constraints in the setting in which the project is to be carried out. For example, the funding policies of federal agencies strongly influence the kinds of projects planned and conducted. Second, research data are often considered together with data from other sources (including but not limited to the professional literature) when researchers draw inferences from a project's results. Hill (1991) noted that it is unrealistic to expect any one project to "answer questions definitively"; rather, "confidence in our findings" will require "a number of studies conducted by different researchers at different sites" (p. 89).

The Research Industry

The **research industry** refers collectively to all research activity being carried out by the society as a whole or any part of it. Industry is used similarly in such expressions as "insurance industry" and "health care industry." Like the health care industry, the research industry spans both public and private sectors of the economy, involves many professional disciplines, and includes many programs and projects. Some of these programs and projects are related, and others are carried out independently of each other.

Research is a growing industry. Early research projects contribute their findings and raise questions for later ones, which in turn do likewise for still more projects to follow. This process not only feeds on itself but incorporates many outside influences from its context, such as practical questions to be answered, funding contingencies, and political supports and constraints. Some of these relationships are depicted in Figure 1.1. Much more research is being conducted now than throughout most of human history. In fact, more than half of the scientists who ever lived are alive today.

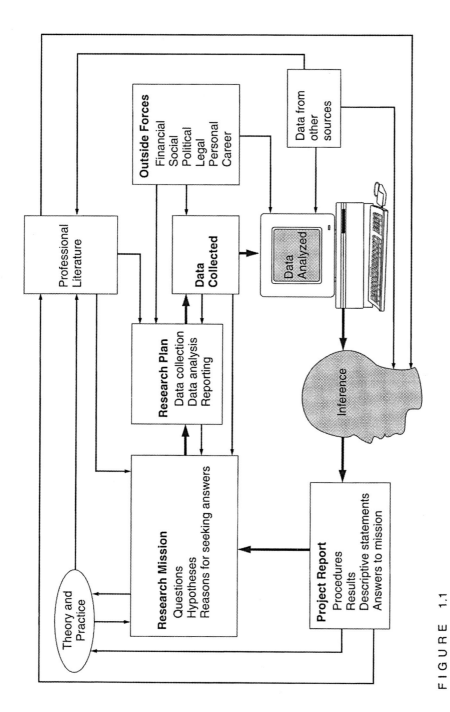

F I G U R E 1.1

An open feedback loop model of the research process and relationships within the research industry.

SOURCE: From *Designing and Conducting Behavioral Research*, by Clifford J. Drew and Michael L. Hardman. Copyright © 1985 by Allyn & Bacon. Adapted by permission.

As an analogy, we are reminded of Hawking's (1988) view of the physical universe expanding through time. The universe comprises an unknown number of bodies, most of them related to some other bodies through structures such as solar systems and galaxies. Some of these bodies and structures are expanding, others collapsing, while the universe as a whole expands. New research projects and programs are being formed; some existing ones are being expanded and others phased out. Meanwhile, the research industry as a whole is expanding.

Research as Product

The **research product** is an extensive body of formal and informal records. The formal part is contained in a voluminous professional literature. Each project contributes one or more reports to this literature, which grows at an accelerating rate as the research industry expands. Various parts of this literature are discussed in Chapter 7; preparing a research report is discussed in Chapter 14. Some journals, annual reviews, computerized **databases,** and professional organizations are listed in Appendix A.

The research product also contains a large informal component. Each project not only adds to the professional literature but contributes to the experience of the researcher and any other people who may have participated in the project. Most researchers discuss these experiences in informal networks involving other researchers and perhaps also consumers of research results. A cumulative collective experience results, analogous to what has been called a "corporate culture" in some work organizations (Deal & Kennedy, 1982). Both the formal and informal components of the research product at any one time influence the research process as it continues.

CHAPTER SUMMARY

Research is an activity conducted to expand knowledge by systematically collecting, analyzing, and interpreting data to answer clearly formulated questions. The scientific method differs from other ways of answering questions, such as faith, authority, and common sense. Knowing about research helps counselors read the professional literature with more understanding, identify and choose more effective techniques, and conduct their activities with more demonstrable results than they might without this knowledge.

The scientist-practitioner model involves conducting and publishing research while providing direct client service. This combination helps counselors formulate more relevant research questions than they might without practitioner experience. It helps them choose service activities more wisely and maintain a wider professional communication network than they likely would if working only as practitioners. The entire research activity of a society, comprising many programs and projects, may be thought of as its research industry. Each new project builds on older ones as this industry expands. Each project has a process consisting of six sequential and recyclable steps. These activities yield a research product with both formal and informal components, namely, a formal professional literature and an informal researcher subculture.

PRACTICAL EXERCISES

1. At the beginning of Chapter 1, it was noted that "research questions concern events that take place in the objective, observable world." For the following examples of research questions, consider whether they concern objective, observable events or unobservable events. If the questions are stated in a way that the phenomena with which they are concerned appear unobservable, can they be restated so that they are concerned with observable phenomena?
   a. Do people have immortal souls?
   b. Can old dogs be taught new tricks?
   c. Is it true that "What's good for General Motors is good for the country"?
   d. Can middle-aged adults change their behavior as easily as adolescents?
   e. How many angels can dance on the head of a pin?
   f. Is it possible for two people to communicate telepathically?
   g. Do role playing and modeling increase the effectiveness of assertion training?
   h. Does reincarnation occur?
   i. In state rehabilitation agencies, would the number of successful closures per thousand clients increase if all intake interviewers inquired about the use of alcohol and other drugs?
   j. Is this a productive set of discussion questions?
2. The maker of an interest inventory sends out a flyer to practicing career counselors announcing that this particular inventory "has an unbeaten track record" in helping counselors to assist their clients and "is preferred to all other inventories on the market." What questions arise in your mind about the research justification for these statements?
3. In Chapter 1 we quote Heppner and Anderson's (1985) three reasons why few counselors conduct research after leaving graduate school. Imagine that you must debate Heppner and Anderson, taking the point of view that despite their arguments the research endeavor and the scientist-practitioner model are still worthwhile. What points will you include in your response to their three arguments?
4. It was noted in Chapter 1 that in an experiment variables may be independent (managed or manipulated by the experimenter and hypothesized to be causally related to the phenomena of interest) or dependent (presumed to arise from the effect of the independent variable). Several

brief descriptions of fictitious experiments follow. For each, identify the independent and dependent variables.

a. Three counselors sharing office space were offered the opportunity to have their session rooms repainted. They were unable to agree on one color for all three rooms due to their different hypotheses about the effect of color on client mood. Counselor No. 1 chose light blue, Counselor No. 2 chose red, and Counselor No. 3 chose yellow. To determine whether the different colors had different effects on client mood, they asked clients to fill out a rating scale after they had sat in the session room for 5 minutes. The rating scale assigned a score of "4" to "agitated, anxious, or excited" and a score of "0" to "calm and relaxed."

b. Patients in a drug rehabilitation program were required to give a urine sample from time to time on a random schedule. The urine sample was tested chemically for drug metabolites. A pharmaceutical company donated to the program a supply of a new medication, "LDX-2," which was designed to reduce both the craving for a wide range of commonly used addictive drugs and withdrawal symptoms related to these drugs. Half of the patients were given LDX-2 and the other half were not, and urine sample testing continued as before.

c. A counselor at a large, urban university noted that many of her college student clients reported doing poorly on tests because of "test anxiety." She had experienced success reducing these clients' symptoms through systematic desensitization. She had also read that cognitive restructuring was supposed to be quite effective with anxiety-related problems and decided to try both methods with some of her clients. Accordingly, she used cognitive restructuring as the major therapeutic mode with half of the clients who came to her complaining of test anxiety. With the remaining half of her clients, she used systematic desensitization. She collected data on all her clients' GPAs two quarters before and two quarters after they presented themselves for and completed her treatment program.

d. Two peer counselors at the same community counseling agency disagreed about the "best" counseling style for the agency's clientele. Connie insisted that clients must be "confronted" about their "games." Sue insisted they needed "a warm place" where they could "be free to be themselves." The director of the counseling agency suggested a means to help them come to some conclusions about the effectiveness of their different styles. After each session, Connie and Sue gave their clients a one-page questionnaire asking if the client was "very satisfied, generally satisfied, neutral, generally dissatisfied, or very dissatisfied" with the session, and why.

e. The director of a residential facility for developmentally disabled boys felt that the boys were being punished excessively and was very concerned about the effect on the boys of this punishment. Accordingly, he asked a specialist in behavior management to train the staff of one house in the use of positive discipline approaches. These approaches stress reinforcing appropriate behavior and ignoring inappropriate behavior as much as possible. He then compared the behavior problems of the boys residing in that house with the average number of behavior problems in other houses in the facility.

5. In an earlier practical exercise, the question was asked, "Is this a productive set of discussion questions?" Using the structure presented in Figure 1.1 of Chapter 1, try to design a research study to answer that question. Consider how you might try to carry out each of the steps of (1) formulating the mission, (2) developing the research plan, (3) collecting the data, (4) analyzing the data, (5) interpreting the results, and (6) reporting the results and conclusions.

6. We listed several reasons we believe counselors should be able to understand and do research, and several reasons counselors often prefer to avoid doing research. Now that you have read all these pros and cons, we would like you to examine your own thoughts and feelings on the subject. List and discuss the reasons you, personally, would like to do research, and any reasons you would prefer to avoid doing research.

7. Interview two or more practicing counselors to find out how much they incorporate the scientist-practitioner model in their working lives and their reasons for these decisions. Of their reported reasons for choosing work activities, which reasons are similar to and which are different from the pros and cons discussed in the text?

8. We mentioned some major research programs from both counseling (for example, Holland's work) and other fields (for example, the space program). Describe at lease three other major research programs currently being conducted in the field of counseling or elsewhere.

CHAPTER TWO
VARIETIES OF RESEARCH

QUESTIONS TO GUIDE YOUR READING

A Research Taxonomy
  1. What is meant by the term *taxonomy*?
     a. What other term do researchers sometimes use as a synonym for taxonomy?
     b. Why is a taxonomy of research approaches desirable?
  2. On what does a research project's approach primarily depend?

Causality
  3. Why is it so difficult to be certain that you have ascertained the cause of a given phenomenon?
  4. What do researchers mean by saying that two variables are *functionally related*?

Descriptive Approaches
  5. What do the missions of descriptive studies have in common?
  6. What can be described using survey research?
  7. What is the purpose of most case studies?
  8. What is the distinction between process and outcome studies?
  9. What does developmental research attempt to investigate? What kinds of developmental processes can be investigated?
  10. What are follow-up studies?
  11. How do the purposes of trend studies differ from those of developmental studies?
  12. What does correlational research seek to investigate?
      a. What kinds of relationships may exist between variables?
      b. Why should a relationship between two variables not be interpreted to mean one variable causes the other? For example, if spousal abuse is more common in families with an alcoholic member than in those without, why should you not conclude that alcoholism causes spousal abuse?

Historical, Action, and Product Development Approaches
  13. What do historical studies seek to accomplish?
  14. What distinguishes historical from descriptive approaches?
  15. What is the mission of most action research projects?
  16. What is product development research?
  17. What other kinds of research are usually conducted as part of product development?

Passive Causal Approaches
  18. What three approaches are used for passive studies concerned with cause questions?
  19. How are the ex post facto and experimental approaches similar? How do they differ?

20. Why is it difficult to base causal statements on studies of external phenomena as causes?
21. Why is the causal-correlational approach weak?

Experimental Approaches
22. What is meant by analogue research?
23. What are the four essential features of experiments?
24. What is meant by traditional group experimentation? Provide an example different from any in the text.
25. What is a time series experiment? Again, provide an example different from any in the text.
26. When should the term *quasi-experiment* be applied to a research project?
27. What are constructed controls?
28. When would a time series experiment be considered a true experiment? When would a quasi-experiment?

Other Issues
29. What is the difference between basic and applied research?
30. What is program evaluation? Why is it becoming increasingly important in the counseling profession?
31. What is qualitative research?
32. In what ways do most qualitative projects differ from other types of projects?

A RESEARCH TAXONOMY

This chapter introduces a classification system, or taxonomy, that defines different types of research. The similarities and differences among various projects are so numerous that studying them would be extremely difficult without a classification system. In a like manner, biologists have developed a taxonomy, albeit a much more complex one, on which to base their study of life forms. Our taxonomy defines the **research approaches** represented by most projects in counseling.

A research approach depends primarily on the project's mission, defined as the entire set of reasons for carrying out the project, and secondarily on the methods used to conduct it. The literature contains many lists of research approaches; each list has its similarities with, and its differences from, each of the others. One of the differences is that some authors use the term *methods* instead of *approaches*. We prefer the term *approaches* to convey the idea that the distinctions among these approaches depend more on what projects seek to accomplish than on the methods used, in other words, more on mission than method.

No list of research approaches is "right" or "wrong" in the sense of correspondence with objective fact. We view the entire set of approaches as a conceptual framework that helps us think about research projects and

T A B L E   2.1
A Taxonomy of Research Approaches

Descriptive approaches
a. Survey research
b. Case studies
c. Process studies
d. Developmental research
e. Follow-up studies
f. Trend studies
g. Correlational research

Historical approach

Action approach

Product development approach

Passive casual approach
a. Ex post facto research
b. External phenomena studies
c. Causal-correlational research

Experimental approaches
a. True experiment
   i. Group experiment
   ii. Time series experiment
b. Quasi-experiment

SOURCES: Adapted from Ary, Jacobs, & Razavieh,
1985; Drew & Hardman, 1985; Isaac & Michael,
1981.

communicate our thoughts. Table 2.1 displays the full taxonomy of research approaches, with the order representing a more or less consistent progression of research approaches from those that simply attempt to describe *what is* (descriptive) or *what was* (historical) to those that attempt to ascertain *causes* of observed phenomena (experimental). Before discussing these approaches in detail, however, it is important to clarify the issue of causality as it pertains to research.

CAUSALITY

People often conduct research to answer "why" questions. Such studies seek to discover the causes of observed phenomena, for example, the causes of poor performance on high school achievement tests by students with high grade point averages (GPAs).

Philosophers have debated whether it is ever reasonable to regard one phenomenon as causing another (see Gleick, 1987; Kuhn, 1962; Popper, 1982). Two underlying concerns are: (a) most phenomena probably have multiple causes stretching back over a long period of time, and (b) because all reality is filtered through human experience, the complete objectivity required to be certain that the cause has accurately been determined probably does not exist.

In some experiments, Sulzer-Azaroff and Mayer's (1991) **functional relationship** concept offers a workable criterion for inferring causation: A dependent variable has a functional relationship with an independent variable if it "changes reliably *when and only when*" certain conditions, defined by the independent variable, are present (p. 299, emphasis in original).

Many practical decisions involve variables that do not meet the definition of functional relationship, yet the cause idea is useful despite philosophers' concerns. For example, some smokers live long lives without developing lung cancer, and some people have lung cancer even though they have never smoked. Cancer risk changes not only with changes in smoking but also with changes in other factors, such as exposure to environmental pollutants. Nonetheless, the idea that smoking causes cancer has supported many people's decision to reduce their cancer risk by not smoking. Within some experiments studying only these two variables, smoking and cancer risk meet the definition of functional relationship: In the larger context in which people decide to smoke or not to smoke, they do not.

Similarly, we say that drunk driving causes accidents, though drunk drivers sometimes reach their destinations without accident and some vehicle accidents do not involve alcohol. Drunk driving and accidents do not fulfill Sulzer-Azaroff and Mayer's (1991) definition of functional relationship except perhaps within specific experiments (for example, with participants operating a simulator in drunk and sober conditions). Nonetheless, wise drivers reduce their risk of accidents by driving only when sober.

Demonstrating a functional relationship within an experiment is often sufficient to answer a research question about cause in this practical sense. (And similar findings in numerous experiments over a long period of time provide much stronger evidence.) Wherever the cause idea appears throughout this book, we intend it in this practical sense rather than as the ultimate cause the philosophical debate addresses. Because most phenomena have multiple causes, it is rarely if ever reasonable to formulate a research question about "the cause" of anything.

Research is also conducted for reasons other than to support causal inferences. It may be conducted for purely **descriptive** reasons. Before trying to determine causes of poor performance, a researcher might seek to discover how many students with high GPAs actually perform poorly on high school achievement tests. This would be a purely descriptive study. Of all the research approaches listed in Table 2.1, only the experimental approaches are designed to enable a researcher to answer questions about causes of observed phenomena. We sometimes use other types of research to raise questions about cause or to choose which of several possible questions to study, but in these cases causal inferences are speculative. Only experimental research allows speculations to be tested in such a way that causation can be inferred, as will be discussed in more detail later in this chapter.

DESCRIPTIVE APPROACHES

Ary, Jacobs, and Razavieh (1985) succinctly noted that the purpose of descriptive studies is "to tell what is" (p. 26). The idea of cause is always absent from the research questions in a purely descriptive study and is usually absent from its entire mission. Sometimes a question of causation appears elsewhere in the mission of a descriptive study, such as one that is carried out to help researchers make decisions about future experiments. Subcategories of descriptive approaches include:

- survey research,
- case studies,
- process studies,
- developmental research,
- follow-up studies,
- trend studies, and
- correlational research.

Next we will examine the merits of each of these approaches in more detail.

Survey Research

Most **surveys** describe defined sets of people, such as the inhabitants of a particular geographic area, employees in a company, students in one or more schools, or members of an organization. The U.S. census is an example of a survey. A poll of people's political views and affiliations is another. An investigation of clients' opinions about the quality of counseling services is a third example. The people studied are described according to the variables stipulated by the research questions. A survey is not necessarily a study of people; surveys have studied sets of things, organizations, animals, curriculum topics, and documents, to name just a few of the innumerable possibilities. Examples of the kinds of variables that could be studied in survey research include:

- makes and ages of automobiles in an employee parking lot,
- eligibility criteria for clients of a city's counseling agencies,
- kinds of animals kept as pets in a city's households,
- journal articles addressed to gender issues in counseling,
- employment opportunities for newly trained counselors,
- accreditation status of counselor education programs in the nation's universities,
- tasks counselors perform in their jobs,
- themes appearing in alcoholic beverage advertising (for example, social status, athletics, sex, feelings of belonging),
- political candidates for whom people intend to vote,
- occupations of characters with disabilities in published fiction and films,

- consequences of drug use identified by addicts as determined by an interview study, and
- clients' reactions to their counseling experiences as determined by a questionnaire study.

Although many surveys use questionnaires, interviews, or both to collect data, the presence of these methods does not necessarily represent a survey project. Some studies use these methods with other approaches, such as experiments. Surveys seek to describe defined sets (usually of people) according to clearly specified variables, regardless of the method used to collect the data. As stated previously, we give *mission* more importance than *methods* in defining research approaches.

Case Studies

Case studies are sometimes referred to by the more inclusive designation of *case and field*; their purpose is to study intensively a given social unit such as an individual, group, institution, school, workplace, or community. These projects are carried out to generate ideas that might apply in similar situations. For example, Brooks (1983) discussed case studies of independent living programs for people with physical disabilities.

It is important to distinguish between case studies for research purposes and case studies to support service activities. The mission of a service-oriented case study is limited to the specific individual or group studied and does not include generalizing to a wider population. In contrast, most researchers have interests that extend beyond the specific individuals studied. Part of the case study research mission is exploratory, to generate ideas that can be used in program planning or tested through later research with more rigorous sampling methods. For example, a case study of a counseling client with acquired immune deficiency syndrome (AIDS) provides information only about that client. Such a case study might be conducted to yield a better understanding of the client and therefore enable better services to be provided to him or her. This purpose does not go beyond these particular services for this individual. However, a study of the same case could be carried out with a research mission to generate ideas for services to other clients with AIDS or for testing with further research involving wider samples.

Case studies support only tentative, exploratory generalization to conclusions about a wider population than the individuals studied. To generalize to such wider conclusions with confidence, it is necessary to study a **sample** of a population of individuals. Case study results offer little confidence that the one particular case being observed is not somehow very different from the rest of the population, as was the 5-legged fly observed by Aristotle. As a second example, a case study on the effectiveness of color coded pill dispensers for an elderly woman has limited value toward generalization if the woman is later discovered to be color blind. When single case studies are repeated a number of times, with similar findings from different individuals (**replicated**, in common research parlance), the results can be generalized with more confidence. However, careful consideration needs to be given to the extent to which the individuals in these replicated studies represent the population to which the researcher wants to generalize the conclusions. Examples of case study research include:

- the case history of a child with an above average IQ but severe learning disabilities,
- an intensive study of a counseling group composed of adolescents on probation for substance abuse,
- a study of a group of workers about to be displaced by sale of the company for which they work who collectively plan to buy and run the company,
- a study of a community counseling agency's response to major changes in its funding sources and clientele, and
- a study of a rural school's treatment of its first Asian immigrant child.

Process Studies

The distinction between **process** and **outcome** studies appears frequently in the counseling research literature. Most process studies of counseling address what takes place during sessions with clients. Outcome studies address what happens after the entire counseling process or some specified part of it is completed. Some studies address both process and outcome. For instance, a study may show a relationship between certain kinds of client behavior within counseling sessions (process) and outcome measures such as grade point average, job performance ratings, or use of available medical services. Some examples of process studies include:

- examining clients' "I" statements in early and later phases of counseling to determine if clients are more likely to self-disclose in later phases of counseling,
- investigating relationships between clients' stated counseling goals and selected personality inventory scores,
- studying clients' responses to counselors' homework assignments, and
- studying words used by counselors to refer to pleasant and unpleasant feelings.

Process and outcome *variables* were discussed in Chapter 1.

Developmental Research

Developmental research is used to investigate change over time. The studies arising from the research of Piaget in cognitive development (1952, 1972) and Kohlberg in moral development (1963) readily come to mind. Developmental studies of people are not limited to children and adolescents;

human development continues throughout the lifespan. The phenomena studied may be psychosocial, physical, or both and may be regarded as progress, deterioration, or neither. These phenomena may, but need not, pertain to the development of individuals; researchers study developmental processes in organizations as well as those in interpersonal relationships. The time span studied may range from very long to very short. Examples of developmental research topics include:

- lives of adults who attained high intelligence test scores as children,
- gender–role differentiation in children of different ages,
- blood-alcohol changes after a dose of alcohol,
- social behavior changes during recovery from heroin addiction,
- changes in eye contact during the first 10 minutes of encounters between strangers, and
- group cohesiveness among staff during a new agency's first several years.

Some developmental studies of people collect much information about their past experiences. The research questions, however, do not concern descriptions of the past but inferences about developmental processes. Interest in describing changes over time characterizes the developmental approach.

Developmental studies can also be process studies, seeking to describe a process as it takes place over time. An example is provided by a study of clients' "I" statements in early and later phases of the counseling relationship.

Follow-Up Studies

Follow-up studies are descriptive studies of outcome. These studies examine the people who have experienced a process, such as education, counseling, or medical treatment. The measures taken refer to their behavior or experience, or both, after the process has been completed. An example is provided by a follow-up study of clients who received career counseling. Six months after the counseling was completed the researchers attempted to determine the nature of the career decisions these clients had reached during this intervening time. Missions of some follow-up studies include comparisons between follow-up data and earlier data; others address follow-up data alone.

Like other descriptive approaches, follow-up research questions do not include the idea of cause. Studying changes in people between the time they began counseling and a time after they completed it does not by itself answer the question of whether counseling caused any of the changes found. An outcome study designed to answer such questions would use an experimental approach, perhaps combining it with descriptive follow-up. Examples of descriptive follow-up studies include:

- grade point averages of college students are examined after counseling,
- post-closure employment status of rehabilitation clients is investigated,

- driving records of traffic violators before and after attending a traffic school are examined,
- clients' use of other agencies to which they had been referred is investigated, and
- assignments completed by a student in all classes are examined after an intervention to increase the number of completed assignments in one class.

Trend Studies

Trend studies examine the same variables over a period of time, including the present, to predict at least one of these variables in the future. Most trend studies examine relatively large social units, such as the population of a city, a state, or a nation. Both trend studies and developmental studies examine changes over time. They differ in that developmental studies seek to describe these changes while trend studies use them to predict the future. This interest in predicting the future also distinguishes trend studies from historical studies, which focus on reconstructing the past, and from surveys, which seek to describe the groups of people or other subjects studied as they are at present. Here are two examples of trend studies:

- To predict future educational needs of a community, the school district examined its population and school enrollment records over the previous several years along with recent building permit applications.
- A community counseling agency examined the changing ethnic mix of its catchment area and its clientele along with the presenting problems of different ethnic groups to plan staff training activities.

Correlational Research

Correlational research is used to investigate relationships among the variables studied. Do variations in one factor correspond with variations in one or more factors? If so, how large is the relationship, and is it positive or negative? For example, students' grades are positively correlated with their scholastic aptitude scores; students who have high scholastic aptitude scores also tend to have high grades. On the other hand, students' grades are negatively correlated with the amount of time they spend watching television; low grades are associated with more television viewing.

Relationships between variables may be **rectilinear** (fitting a straight line) or **curvilinear** (not fitting a straight line.) Shedler and Block (1990) found that marijuana use among adolescents was curvilinearly related to subjective distress. The lowest level of marijuana use was found among adolescents who had moderate levels of subjective distress; adolescents whose subjective distress was either very low or very high reported using the most marijuana.

Careful reading of these descriptions will reveal that they do not include the idea of cause. This omission is deliberate; like other descriptive data, correlational data alone do not support inferences about causes.

For example, if a researcher finds a relationship between the incidence of depression and divorce, it is tempting to conclude that divorce causes depression. However, the reverse causal relationship may hold; feelings of depression may lead people to seek divorce. Or perhaps a third factor, such as difficulty maintaining personal relationships, causes both depression and divorce. Similarly, if a researcher notes a relationship between teacher attention and grades of pupils, it is difficult to say whether increased attention improves grades or good grades result in increased attention. Perhaps both these effects operate in a feedback loop. Another possibility is that neither grades nor attention causes the other, with both being results of a third factor such as student effort. When two variables are related, knowing which causes which is only possible if experiments are conducted to establish the causal chain.

Definitions of correlational studies often include the idea that these studies use **correlation coefficients** as the method for studying covariations. Since we define research approaches primarily according to their missions rather than their methods, we recognize that some studies of relationships among variables use other statistical methods and that this choice is sometimes an arbitrary one. Examples of correlational studies include:

- an investigation of the relationship of reading achievement scores with measures of scholastic aptitude, achievement motivation, and social class;
- a study of the relationship between college grades and extracurricular activities in high school;
- a study of relationships between clients' stated counseling goals and selected personality inventory scores; and
- a study of the extent to which scores on a civil service examination predict employee job performance ratings.

HISTORICAL APPROACH

Historical studies are used to reconstruct the past. Missions of some historical projects include hypothesis testing; others do not. Most historical projects rely heavily on documentary records as data sources. Other common sources are memories of people who lived during the time period studied as expressed through interviews and questionnaires. Some examples of historical research include:

- tracing the history of civil rights legislation in the United States since the Civil War,
- testing the hypothesis that Francis Bacon wrote the works usually attributed to William Shakespeare,

- studying the time relationships of counseling theorists' ideas with events in their personal and professional lives, and
- examining changes in gender-based role expectations from 1900 to the present, as expressed in published fiction.

ACTION APPROACH

Action research is employed when the researcher seeks to develop new skills or new methods for doing something or to improve existing skills. In a counseling agency, this "something" is usually delivering service to clients. These new skills or methods must be evaluated or developing them would not qualify as a research project. Program evaluation projects often include action research, alone or in combination with other approaches. The data from action research often generate hypotheses or questions that stimulate descriptive or experimental research. Some examples of action projects are:

- a school offers an in-service training program to help teachers develop new skills in facilitating class discussions,
- a counselor tries new ways to motivate reluctant clients to participate, and
- a counselor uses a new system for inviting underachievers to come in for counseling.

PRODUCT DEVELOPMENT APPROACH

Developing new tests and inventories and revising existing ones require much research activity. The mission of **product development research** is much like that of engineers who develop new and improved automobiles and household appliances. Product development projects may include many research approaches but usually include descriptive survey and correlational research; however, these approaches differ fundamentally in their missions. Correlational studies describe relationships (for example, correlations between test items or between test scores and other variables). Surveys describe populations of potential users and, for achievement tests, domains of subject matter to be tested. Product development projects bring such diverse data together to produce a tangible product such as a new or improved test or inventory.

PASSIVE CAUSAL APPROACHES

Cook and Campbell (1979) used the term *passive* for studies in which the researcher does not administer **treatment conditions** to manipulate variables. A project studying the effects of waiting time on clients' interview behavior will serve as an example. As discussed more fully later in this chapter, an experiment represents the strongest research approach for such projects. In an experiment, the researcher might manipulate the *waiting time* variable by requiring some clients to wait 30 minutes before being seen and other clients to wait two minutes, with each client's waiting time chosen according to the research plan. These waiting times represent treatment conditions in common research parlance. In an agency with policies prohibiting researchers from administering such treatment conditions, a **passive** approach may be the only available choice. Passive studies concerned with cause questions are represented by a family of three approaches:

- **ex post facto** studies, which seek to generate hypotheses about "cause and effect relationships by observing some existing consequence and searching back through the data for plausible causal factors" (Isaac & Michael, 1981, p. 42);
- **external phenomena studies,** which involve events beyond the researchers' control, such as earthquakes and new laws; and
- **causal-correlational** studies, which seek to answer questions of cause by examining a systematic set of relationships between variables.

Ex Post Facto Research

Ex post facto is from Latin and means "from after the fact." The ex post facto approach is similar to the **experimental** approach in the sense that both are concerned with cause-and-effect relationships. Researchers use ex post facto studies, however, to help them create causal hypotheses or to explore or choose among them. Experiments seek to test causal hypotheses or answer cause-and-effect questions. Researchers often use results from ex post facto studies as a basis for formulating and planning experimental ones.

The ex post facto approach to research is another about which the literature offers differing definitions. Isaac and Michael's (1981) definition, quoted above, involves a search for "plausible causal factors," without reference to any prior hypotheses the researcher may have in advance. As an illustration of their different concept of ex post facto research, Heppner, Kivlighan, and Wampold (1992) discussed a project that examined the fit between descriptive data and the researchers' hypotheses. The researchers used existing data to explore their hypotheses rather than to create new ones.

Despite a fundamental difference in mission, most ex post facto studies involve the same kinds of data as do descriptive studies. If a researcher is not interested in cause-and-effect relationships among the variables studied, the project is descriptive. An exploratory search for possible causes represents an ex post facto mission.

To generate hypotheses about possible causal relationships, descriptive follow-up could be combined with an ex post facto approach. The following examples illustrate ex post facto projects:

- A rehabilitation administrator examined files of former clients who were placed on jobs quickly and contrasted these files with those of clients whose placements were slow to search for possible reasons placement was delayed.
- A high school kept careful records of the academic and "citizenship" performance of students with and without automobiles to decide whether or not to experiment with new parking regulations.
- A marriage and family counselor examined files of former clients from blended families and from families in which second and later marriages were not involved to form hypotheses about problems family blending causes.
- A researcher examined the records of former students who dropped out of high school in a search for possible causes.

Studies of External Phenomena as Causes

In this context, "external" means outside the control of the researcher. A study of reactions to the 1980 eruption of Mt. St. Helens in Washington (Shore, Tatum, & Vollmer, 1986) illustrates this approach. A small community near the volcano was contrasted with a community near Mt. Hood in Oregon that had been carefully selected for similarity in size and other characteristics. Our interpretation of the report is that the researchers sought to make inferences about the eruption as a cause of psychiatric symptoms, though this point is less clear from the report than we might wish. If the authors had only described differences between these two communities, without inferring causation, we would have classified this project as descriptive.

A study conducted by Deutsch and Alt (1977) and discussed in Cook and Campbell (1979) provides a second illustration of this approach. These researchers noted that a city experienced a sharp decline in armed robberies after the state enacted a gun control law. Did the new law reduce this type of crime? The authors drew an affirmative answer from their analysis, which showed the observed decline to be more than expected within month-to-month variation.

At best, studies of external phenomena offer weak support for inferences about causes. Regardless of how carefully they were selected, the communities studied by Shore et al. (1986) differed in other ways in addition to the volcano eruption and psychiatric symptoms experienced by residents. To infer that the eruption influenced these symptoms, other differences between the communities must be ruled out as possible causes. Some differences could probably be reasonably dismissed on a priori grounds (for example, the fact that Washington had a sales tax and Oregon did not).

Others might be ruled out from data the project collected. But to infer that the new gun control law was effective, it must be established that robberies declined more sharply than would be expected within normal variation. In addition, other possible influences must also be ruled out. For example, suppose enactment of the gun control law was followed by a period of unseasonably severe weather of a sort in which robberies are rare. Or perhaps a private organization carried out a publicity campaign to educate the public about robbery prevention at about the same time the gun control law was enacted. These are but two examples of the many events that might have coincided with the phenomena under study. As you can see, it is difficult to base causal statements on this research approach.

Causal-Correlational Research

Earlier in this chapter we discussed the difficulties of inferring causation from one correlation between two variables. In some situations, a set of correlations can provide more information about a causal chain than one correlation can. This is called the causal-correlational approach. Cook and Campbell (1979) discuss two techniques based on this approach: **path analysis** and **cross-lagged correlations.**

Path analysis.   Ideally, a researcher begins this technique by constructing a model of causal relationships among the variables being studied. The model includes three or more variables and must specify the direction, strength, and sign of influence (if any) between each pair. Cook and Campbell (1979) offered an example involving educational advantage (EA), Head Start (HS) attendance, and achievement (ACH) in first grade. Their model includes the following influences. (The numbers are path coefficients expressing the strength with which one variable increases or decreases the other.)

- EA influences HS (−.7); Head Start accepts only disadvantaged students, though not all of them are enrolled.
- EA influences ACH (.7); experience and previous research show high achievement among advantaged students.
- HS influences ACH (.3); Head Start attendance is expected to improve achievement.

Constructing such models from experience, theory, and previous research helps researchers clarify their thinking about the phenomena being studied.

A model can generate correlations to be expected among the variables; these expected correlations can then be compared with observed correlations after data are collected. Researchers can expect that their first models will be oversimplified. Comparing the model with obtained results often points to possible improvements in the model; the improved model can then be compared with new results. Hackett (1985) used this kind of model to examine the role of mathematics self-efficacy and previous math courses taken on students' choice of math-related majors.

Cross-lagged panel correlations.   This method relies on repeated measures of the variables being studied: at least two variables measured at least twice. Inference about a causal relationship between two variables is based on the idea that if Variable A influences Variable B (but not the reverse) A will show higher correlations with later than with earlier measures of B. In an example discussed by Cook and Campbell (1979), data from 81 cities were interpreted to support the idea that air pollution (AP) increases the mortality rate (M); AP was more highly correlated with future M than with past M. The idea that M might have increased AP was rejected a priori, assuming "bodies have been properly buried and cremation is rare" (p. 319).

Support for inference of cause is strengthened if the variables have been measured many times rather than only twice and if the pattern of correlations is stable over time.

Weaknesses of the causal-correlational approach.   At the beginning of our discussion of this approach, we noted that a set of correlations can often provide more information about a causal chain than one correlation can. Although this approach can determine whether obtained data are consistent with a favored interpretation or model, it does not have the same capacity as do experiments to rule out competing alternative possible explanations. In the mortality study, for example, economic activity might not only have increased air pollution but also increased immigration from areas where infectious diseases are prevalent. Then increased mortality, which the study attributed to air pollution, might have been caused by infectious diseases instead.

Cook and Campbell (1979) cautioned that omitting an important variable from a model can lead to seriously wrong conclusions in path analysis. For example, omitting educational advantage from the Head Start model might have led to a conclusion that Head Start influenced achievement adversely rather than favorably.

These observations underscore the importance of the researcher's judgment in model building and in evaluating causal possibilities consistent with the data. Experience and common sense provide a satisfactory basis for doing so in some instances. For example, the idea that a higher stork population increased human births was dismissed as an unreasonable interpretation of the correlation between the stork population and the human birthrate in Holland at the beginning of this century. If an old folk tale were more widely believed, however, this interpretation might not be so easily dismissed.

Though the researcher's judgment is a necessary part of the interpretation phase in all research, it has a much more prominent role in causal-correlational projects than in any other research approach used to answer questions about causes. We consider this prominent role a weakness because of the high risk that wrong conclusions will result from interpretations shaped by prevailing social attitudes and beliefs. For example, a few decades ago many researchers would have quickly dismissed the idea that psychosocial variables might influence the course of cancer, but data now show strong evidence for such influence (Adler, 1991). The history of ideas about the relationship between race and educational achievement provides another example. Over the last several decades, the emphasis has shifted from genetics to social disadvantagement as the likely cause of differences in educational achievement. When considering causal possibilities in correlational data, researchers must exercise extreme care to prevent prevailing social attitudes and beliefs from unduly influencing interpretations.

These influences also occur in some other approaches such as ex post facto and case studies. However, we consider them a less serious problem in these types of studies than when answers to causal questions are sought. Other things being equal, we see a wrong answer to a research question as a more serious risk than overlooking some possibilities in a project designed to generate ideas.

These weaknesses represent one reason we recommend that beginning researchers avoid the causal-correlational approach. In addition, both path analysis and cross-lagged panel correlation methods involve complex analysis procedures. Since our discussion of this approach is too brief to provide a practical guide for prospective researchers who might choose it, we include it here primarily to help you understand reports of studies that use this approach.

EXPERIMENTAL APPROACHES

Experimental research provides stronger support for inferences about causal relationships among variables than does any other research approach. Four essential features of experiments follow:

- The mission includes the idea of cause.
- The researcher manages or manipulates one or more independent variables.
- Measures are taken of one or more dependent variables.
- The research plan controls extraneous factors that might contaminate the results to minimize unwanted influences of such factors and strengthen the inferences made about causal relationships between independent and dependent variables.

Experimental approaches frequently used in counseling research include analogue research, traditional group experiments, and time series experiments. Sometimes circumstances do not permit controlling extraneous factors to the degree that true experiments require. Quasi-experiments represent a compromise in such instances.

Analogue Research

Counseling is a very complex process. This complexity, and ethical considerations, limit researchers' ability and freedom to study counseling techniques through experiments. Though direct experiments with the counseling process are feasible in many instances, in others they are not. However, research questions about specific aspects of counseling can sometimes be studied with laboratory procedures carefully contrived to represent those aspects. For example, Lyddon and Adamson (1992) exposed participants to "scripted materials designed to reflect a rationalist, constructivist, or behavioral counseling approach" (p. 43). Other possibilities include use of client surrogates or tape recordings of counseling interactions. Experiments of this kind are referred to as **analogue research.**

In analogue research, the laboratory procedures are considered analogous to the counseling phenomena of interest. Such analogues may approximate counseling closely, moderately, or remotely, depending on many factors related to the client, the counselor, the process, and the setting. See Heppner, Kivlighan, and Wampold (1992) for a more detailed discussion of analogue research in counseling.

Many experiments in counseling do not use analogues. The remainder of this section applies to both analogue studies and other kinds of experiments.

Traditional Group and Time Series Experiments

Two approaches for conducting experiments have achieved wide acceptance. The first approach is commonly called **traditional group experimentation.** "Traditional" refers to the fact that most experiments in behavior science over the past several decades have been of this type; "group" refers to the fact that these experiments involve groups or samples, with each sample comprising a number of subjects. Some projects compare two or more samples treated differently; others compare results from the same sample under different conditions. These comparisons enable researchers to rule out extraneous factors as possible causes and to infer that the different treatment conditions caused the observed results.

To illustrate traditional group experimentation, imagine a school district in which 50 elementary teachers each complained about disruptive student behavior in their classrooms. This disruptive behavior persisted despite pleading, scolding, and punitive measures. The district's head counselor wanted to test the idea that the teachers could change student behavior by treating the students differently.

The counselor began by asking each teacher to keep careful daily records of one problem student's disruptive behavior for a week but to make no other changes in the classroom. The counselor then chose 25 teachers at random and asked each to ignore his or her chosen student's disruptive behavior and comment on this student's desirable behavior at least once every 10 minutes. The other 25 teachers were asked to continue treating their problem students the same as before. Meanwhile, all 50 teachers continued to record disruptive incidents. These incidents declined sharply in the classrooms where the teachers changed their response to the problem students but did not change in the other classrooms. The counselor thus concluded that the teachers' new treatment of the problem students changed the students' disruptive behavior.

If all 50 teachers had been asked to change their behavior toward the students, the counselor would have no way to know whether the observed changes in the students' disruptive conduct resulted from the different treatment or from something else that might have been happening at the same time. However, some of the teachers changed the way they treated their disruptive students and others did not, and only the former teachers' students became less disruptive. Comparing these two randomly chosen groups of students gives reasonably strong support for the conclusion that the teachers' different behavior caused changes in their students' behavior.

When only one or a few participants are available for study, a researcher can make similar inferences about causality by carefully managing the time sequence in which treatment conditions are administered. This approach is commonly called **time series, single-subject,** or **N = 1 research.** These latter two terms refer to the fact that time series experiments typically include one or very few participants and represent the only appropriate experimental approach under these conditions.

To illustrate this approach, imagine a small school in which four students in one classroom exhibited the same problems as some of the 50 students in the previous example. The counselor suggested that their teacher (Mr. Jones) begin by keeping daily records of their disruptive behavior for a week, without changing his treatment of them. He was then asked to select one student (James) and ignore his disruptive behavior and comment on his desirable behavior at least once every 10 minutes for the next two weeks, while continuing to record disruptive incidents for all four students. Incidents of disruptive behavior became much less frequent for James but stayed the same for the other three students. The counselor then suggested that Mr. Jones select a second student (Susie) and follow the same procedure used with James. After two more weeks, Susie and James were both models of comportment, but the remaining two students continued to be disruptive. After two additional weeks, these procedures were implemented with the third student, and then after two more weeks, with the fourth student. In each case, disruptive incidents decreased shortly after Mr. Jones began to ignore them and began to comment on desirable behaviors. Now Mr. Jones and the counselor could be reasonably confident that the different treatment condition rather than some extraneous factor was causing the students' changed behavior.

This example implemented the treatment condition at chosen times to achieve the same purpose as the control sample (students whose teachers continued to treat them as before) in the previous example. Chapter 8 discusses additional methods of managing the independent variable, some of which are used in traditional group experiments and some in time series experiments.

True Experiments and Quasi-Experiments

The two imaginary projects just described are true experiments. In both, the researcher wanted to answer questions of cause and managed the independent variable under investigation (teacher behavior) by deliberately instructing teachers to behave differently toward the students. In the first project, the researcher assigned students to experimental conditions according to the research plan to create comparable groups before they were treated differently. In the second project, the counselor used only four students and administered experimental conditions in a carefully predesigned sequence. These procedures determine a **true experiment.**

A **quasi-experiment** represents a compromise between the controls required for a true experiment and the constraints imposed by prevailing conditions. When a true experiment would be the ideal choice for the project's mission but circumstances severely limit the researcher's ability to control risks of contamination by randomly assigning subjects to groups and managing variables, a quasi-experiment is often the best available choice.

The professional literature contains differing definitions of the quasi-experiment concept. We apply this term whenever:

- a true experiment would best serve the project's mission, and
- the researcher administers treatment conditions to subjects, but
- circumstances prevent the researcher from composing the research samples at the outset or administering experimental conditions in a sequence that would minimize contamination risk.

In some quasi-experiments, treatment conditions are administered to preexisting groups of subjects because the ideal plan of composing equivalent groups is not feasible. For example, some offices of a state rehabilitation agency might be assigned a designated placement specialist, while in other offices counselors assist their own clients with placement. Despite researchers' best efforts to choose such existing groups so they are as alike as possible, these groups usually differ in some systematic ways before they are treated differently. Rossi and Freeman (1989) refer to such control samples as "**constructed controls**" (p. 310). For example, some offices might have clients with more severe disabilities than those of other offices, and this factor could have a considerable impact on the ease and outcome of placement. In a true experiment involving group comparisons, the groups are deliberately composed, usually by random assignment, so as to be presumably equivalent. To do so in this instance would seriously disrupt the ongoing work of the agency; therefore, such a plan would not be feasible. Because it is impossible to ensure that the client compositions of offices with and without separate placement specialists would be approximately equivalent at the outset, any inference about the different effects of these arrangements is weakened. Nonetheless, studying the outcomes of offices with these different arrangements would yield more information than not doing so. A quasi-experiment is therefore accepted as the best available approach for this project.

Some time series designs may also be quasi-experiments. In our example of the experiment with Mr. Jones, we noted that the treatment condition was implemented four different times with four different students. If the counselor had simply suggested that Mr. Jones select only one student, the resulting experiment would have implemented the treatment condition only once. Without the staggered implementation of the treatment program with several students, any inference that the experimental (independent) variable produced the desired change in behavior would be weakened.

Our definition of a quasi-experiment can be contrasted with that offered by Drew and Hardman (1985). These authors defined a quasi-experiment as one in which nature, not the researchers, administered the experimental variable. This definition of quasi-experiment is illustrated by the previously discussed study of reactions to the 1980 eruption of Mt. St. Helens in Washington (Shore, Tatum, & Vollmer, 1986).

Some authors have classified some or all of the kinds of projects discussed in the section on passive causes as quasi-experiments (for example, Cook & Campbell, 1979; Heppner, Kivlighan, & Wampold, 1992). Passive studies of causes bear a number of similarities to quasi-experiments. Important among these is that these approaches offer only weak support for inferences about causality, and these weaknesses are accepted because stronger approaches are not feasible under prevailing circumstances. In addition, many passive projects use the same kinds of data analyses experiments use. For example, if the state had been the researcher in the "gun control" project discussed earlier in this section, enacting a new law and studying its effects, we would agree with Cook and Campbell (1979) in calling this project a quasi-experiment. Similarly, if researchers conducted a mental health campaign in one of two small communities while withholding it from the other and carried out the same kinds of data collection and analysis procedures Shore et al. (1986) used, such a project would be a quasi-experiment in our taxonomy.

Despite these differences, the various definitions of quasi-experiment are all alike in a number of ways. A quasi-experiment's mission includes one or more research questions concerning a causal relationship between variables studied. This mission would be served ideally by a plan in which the researcher assigns subjects to presumably equivalent groups and then treats the groups differently, or implements a time series design with procedures that clarify whether the experimental variable is producing the observed effect. Whenever prevailing circumstances make such plans in-feasible, this limitation weakens any inferences about causal relationships involving the treatment variables. These weaknesses are accepted because a quasi-experiment is considered the strongest feasible research approach for the project's mission in view of existing circumstances.

OTHER ISSUES

Any taxonomy of research projects would be incomplete without consider-ing five related issues in addition to research approaches: (1) basic versus applied research, (2) qualitative research, (3) program evaluation, (4) ex-ploratory research, and (5) multiple approaches in the same project.

Basic versus Applied Research

Basic research answers questions of theory, regardless of whether or not the results can be expected to serve any immediate practical purpose. **Ap-plied research** solves practical problems, whether or not the results have any bearing on theoretical issues. Many projects originally conceived with purely basic missions have produced findings that were used later to solve practical problems in ways unanticipated at the time the projects were carried out. Researchers often cite this fact to justify basic projects. For ex-ample, the Science Directorate of the American Psychological Association "will . . . continue to make the case for the importance of basic psychological research . . . by building a compendium of examples of purely basic research that have led to unanticipated applications or far-reaching applied or strategic outcomes" (Gladue, 1994, p. 8).

   Not every project is either basic or applied. A researcher who seeks to answer both theoretical and practical research questions combines both basic and applied components in the project mission. Both action and product development approaches as discussed in this chapter are applied ap-proaches; all the other approaches may be used in both basic and applied projects and in projects that are difficult to classify.

Program Evaluation

Program evaluation is applied research carried out to make or support deci-sions regarding one or more service programs. All research approaches may be used in program evaluation. Like qualitative procedures, program evalua-tion is receiving increasing attention in the counseling literature as counselors are called upon to evaluate the programs in which they work and meet in-creasingly higher standards in conducting these evaluations. Most counseling programs funded by federal and state sources include an evaluation component as part of their accountability requirements. for these reasons, Chapters 3 and 4 of this text are devoted to program evaluation.

Exploratory Research

Exploratory research furnishes data helpful in generating hypotheses or other ideas, usually in the formulation phase of a future project. For example, a counseling agency may interview potential clients to identify the issues of greatest concern to them and use the results to formulate and plan a questionnaire survey of the incidence of problems related to these issues. In this example, the interview study is exploratory. We regard legitimate use of the ex post facto approach as limited to exploratory projects. Most case study research projects have an exploratory component in their mission. Exploratory projects may use any of the approaches listed in this chapter. Descriptive and action studies often have exploratory missions; few experiments and product development projects do.

Qualitative Research

The core idea of qualitative research is that projects do not need to collect data in numerical form or use quantities or numbers to analyze the data. Quantitative expressions need not be entirely absent, though other means of description are emphasized (Best & Kahn, 1989). As a descriptor for research, **qualitative** represents a matter of emphasis rather than a separate and distinct category. Ideas and methods have been drawn from anthropology (ethnographic field methods), sociology (participant observation), and phenomenology (studying people's verbal reports of internal experience). Many case studies are qualitative in nature.

Based on a number of sources (Denton, 1981; Fielding & Fielding, 1986; Filstead, 1970; Glaser & Strauss, 1967: Heppner, Kivlighan, & Wampold, 1992; Patton, 1987; Polkinghorne, 1991; Smith, 1981), we offer the following descriptions of qualitative research. We emphasize that these are typical features, which are not present in every instance. Qualitative research missions:

- are descriptive,
- are exploratory,
- concern people's internal experiences,
- include general rather than specific research questions, and
- are vague at first and evolve as data are collected and analyzed.

Qualitative research projects:

- collect data by **naturalistic** observation,
- use many different kinds of data, and
- impose special kinds of demands on researchers.

Some of these points bring to mind aspects of what Shepherd (1993) called "the feminine face of science." The feminine face includes three components:

- receptivity, or viewing phenomena "without preconceived ideas" such as hypotheses;
- subjectivity, or paying attention to the researcher's own experiencing, and
- relatedness, or viewing phenomena as integrated wholes rather than reduced to parts.

The next eight subsections discuss typical features of qualitative research.

Descriptive mission.   "The purpose of research using qualitative procedures is to produce full and integrated descriptions of an experience under study" (Polkinghorne, 1991, p. 163). As discussed earlier in this chapter, descriptive research uses a number of different approaches to tell what is (Ary, Jacobs, & Razavieh, 1985) rather than to reconstruct the past, predict the future, answer questions about causes, or create a new product. However, qualitative projects may include other research questions in addition to descriptive ones. For example, a researcher might define a "full and integrated description" of an experience as including its history and some hypotheses about possible causes; the resulting project might therefore combine descriptive, historical, and ex post facto approaches. As a second example, a large state agency might conduct a quasi-experiment, setting up several branch offices with different staffing patterns, and then use naturalistic (Smith, 1981) methods to study their day-to-day operation.

Exploratory mission.   Most qualitative research has an exploratory mission. Some entire projects are exploratory. Other projects begin with an exploratory mission and in later phases seek answers to questions raised through this initial exploration. This kind of evolving mission is discussed more fully in a later subsection.

The development of **grounded theory** depends on exploratory research. Applying this concept to program evaluation projects, Patton (1987) defined the researcher's task as "to generate . . . theory from holistic data gathered through naturalistic inquiry" (p. 39) to understand how and why the program functions as it does. In short, grounded theory uses exploratory research to generate theory.

Internal experience.   Polkinghorne (1991) and Heppner et al. (1992), among other authors, noted that qualitative research studies *experience*. **Phenomenology** is a common term for this process. As noted in Chapter 1, research relies on phenomena that are publicly observable, either directly or indirectly. Most studies of internal experiences rely on the verbal reports of these experiences. These reports are sometimes produced at a researcher's request and sometimes produced spontaneously in response to other life events. Because verbal reports are publicly observable, they can be studied through research, although how well they represent the underlying experience cannot be known.

Much has been written about the usefulness of self-report data. Laing (1988) noted that this literature is inconsistent, with some authors saying such data are reliable and trustworthy while other authors say the opposite. She suggested, as did Pace, Barahona, and Kaplan (1985), that the credibility of self-reports depends primarily on the quality of the data collection instruments and the questions that elicited them. She further suggested that self-report data are reliable and credible only if:

- the respondent clearly understands what information is requested,
- the respondent has that information,
- the respondent is willing to provide that information, and
- the researcher can interpret the responses.

Osgood (1989) extended Laing's work with additional recommendations. He noted that it is important to:

- examine clients' own level of confidence in their self-reports,
- encourage clients to attend to their past behavior to enhance the accuracy of self-reports, and
- assess clients' level of introspectiveness to determine whether reliance on self-report is appropriate.

The Dalai Lama (1984) has argued that some confidence in the reports of Tibetan monks is justified by the long hours they spend examining their experiences through meditation. A premise underlying this argument applies not only to Buddhist religious practices but also to the practice of research in Western societies: People can learn to report their experiences validly. Phenomenological researchers need to feel reasonably comfortable that their informants can do so. When reporting their experiences, respondents are asked to set aside "accustomed perceptual sets and interpretive frameworks" (Denton, 1981, p. 597). This idea has a long history in relation to the search for self-understanding, both in Asian thought (for example, Krishnamurti, 1968) and through counseling.

Qualitative research questions are not necessarily limited to experience but may include accompanying behavior, not only what people think and feel but also what they do. Studying experience and behavior together often provides a better understanding of both than would studying either alone.

General versus specific research questions.   Patton (1987) suggested that qualitative evaluation research is appropriate when goals are "vague, general and nonspecific" (p. 42). Such generality is often appropriate when the goal of evaluation is to study as much of the context and richness of a program as possible. For example, Murray, Levitov, Castenell, and Joubert (1987) used qualitative procedures (interviews and observations) to determine the extent of intraorganizational perception and trust among administrators, counselors, and teachers involved in a high school counseling center. As a second example, Gysbers, Hughey, Starr, and Lapan (1992) used qualitative research procedures to evaluate an 11th grade guidance and language arts career unit; these procedures facilitated the understanding of the impact of the unit, raised new questions, and offered new insights. A third example is Burrello and Reitzug's (1993) qualitative study that sought to understand how the organizational culture of a school (the underlying shared values, assumptions, beliefs, and ideology held by staff) would be likely to affect attempts at school restructuring. Borders and Drury (1992a) noted that qualitative procedures are especially relevant to school counseling programs as they examine student needs, goals, and resources for change.

Ponterotto and Casas (1991) emphasized the value of qualitative research when "not much is known about a particular topic." They pointed out that "qualitative methods can be of great value in exploring the topic and raising more specific questions and hypotheses to be pursued in subsequent research" (p. 138). For example, Skovholt and Ronnestad (1992) used qualitative procedures to develop hypotheses regarding a stage model of therapist–counselor development and suggested that future empirical research be conducted to support or refute those hypotheses. Froehle and Rominger (1993) noted that qualitative procedures are especially appropriate for documenting and understanding the complexities of a consultation relationship and suggesting hypotheses to test through future research. Martin (1988) has recommended that qualitative procedures be used to study the relationship between the scientific and personal theories of counseling researchers and between the personal theories of counselors and clients. Such qualitative studies could then generate hypotheses for additional research on the relationship between scientific and practical knowledge in counseling. Ponterotto and Casas (1991) noted that qualitative procedures could be especially fruitful in conducting counseling research with racial/ethnic minority clients, as such research allows in-depth examination of clients in a sociocultural context.

Some inexperienced researchers are tempted to embrace qualitative procedures too quickly as a means of generating or clarifying research questions. Qualitative procedures may not be required for this purpose, however. Before deciding to pursue qualitative research to clarify research questions, we recommend that an inexperienced researcher first conduct a thorough literature review, make a concerted effort to refine his or her ideas, and consult with more experienced researchers.

Evolving mission. Many qualitative projects begin with vague and general research questions. Examining the phenomena to be studied helps the researcher decide what aspects of these phenomena require further study. Not every qualitative project stops with the first refinement of its research questions; instead, the researcher may continue to collect data and develop and investigate more specific research questions as the project proceeds. For example, McKenzie (1986) collected qualitative data on nine black, male, West Indian-American youths to understand their culture, family, and peer group interactions. These data yielded themes and rudimentary guides for the collection of a second set of data from which McKenzie drew implications for counseling such youths. As a second example, Smith (1981) described a fictitious situation in which a researcher spent a year observing a career information service as she looked for "patterns," developed "numerous questions, issues and working hypotheses," and "maintained a list of these hypotheses and modified them as she [collected] data" (pp. 586–587). In terms of the six-part model of the research process offered in Chapter 1, she recycled repeatedly through formulation while data collection was under way. Though Smith's (1981) account is not explicit on this point, our model leads us to expect that this recycling also included planning, such as making decisions about whether to observe, conduct interviews, or both. In short, many qualitative projects begin data collection with a rather vaguely formulated mission and use the first data to refine research questions and plans. These questions may then be answered with later data.

Naturalistic observation.   In addition to the term *naturalistic*, the qualitative research literature includes the concepts **ethnographic** and *naturalistic-ethnographic* to refer to a method often used in anthropological field studies. This method "involves the researcher's entering the participants' environment and either recording verbatim or through notes the interactions" (Heppner, Kivlighan, & Wampold, 1992, p. 196). If the researcher is both an observer and at the same time participating in the process being observed, the term **participant observer** describes this role. Patton (1987) noted that a participant observer may be a "full participant" or not, according to limitations inherent in the setting. For example, an observer who is not chemically dependent but is participating as a client in a chemical dependency program cannot be a full participant. Similarly, a person admitted to a prison as an observer without being incarcerated will "never . . . know what it's like from the inside." The ideal degree of participation is that "which will yield the most meaningful data given the characteristics of the participants, the . . . questions to be studied, and the sociopolitical context of the setting" (p. 76).

An important feature of naturalistic observation is that the research plan does not call for any attempt to change the process being observed, as would be required in an experiment. For example, in her qualitative study of women in crisis in the lesbian community, Hunnisett (1986) stressed the importance of capturing the participants' experience rather than imposing her own values and experience on them. Nonetheless, the researcher must build "a collaborative working relationship with the subject" (Heppner, Kivlighan, & Wampold, 1992, p. 196). Participant observers necessarily influence any process in which they are participants; accordingly, they must take care to influence the process only as participants and not as if they were experimenters.

Many kinds of data.   In searching for patterns, most qualitative projects use data of many different types; Polkinghorne (1991) listed interviews, naturalistic observation, previous case studies, videotapes, transcripts of counseling sessions, and previous research reports. Additional types of data noted by Heppner, Kivlighan, and Wampold (1992) include oral history and critical incident reports. If different sorts of data are consistent in the conclusions they support, increased confidence in these conclusions is justified unless the different types of data contain the same biases (Fielding & Fielding, 1986).

Demands on the researcher.   Heppner, Kivlighan, and Wampold (1992) cautioned against expecting qualitative research to be "easier or less involved . . . than quantitative research"; rather, it "can be quite time-consuming and expensive" (p. 201). As additional cautions, these authors noted that qualitative research must often be conducted without "concrete guidelines" or experienced advisers and that few editorial reviewers are experienced with qualitative studies (pp. 201–202). The researcher often feels "like he or she is operating in a vacuum" (p. 201). In addition, qualitative research relies heavily on the researcher's judgment, not only when data are interpreted for the project's final report but also when the formulation and planning phases are repeatedly revisited after data collection has begun.

Based on these observations, we recommend that qualitative research is a wise choice only for researchers who have the ability, experience, temperament, and resources to carry out their projects relatively independently or for those who are in one of the few special situations that offer appropriate support. In the future, we expect that these situations will become less rare as more and more qualitative projects are conducted and reported.

Multiple Approaches

As noted in the preceding section, qualitative projects often combine more than one descriptive approach. It is unwise to assume that any project, qualitative or not, must represent one and only one approach. Shakespeare (*Hamlet*, Act II, Scene 2) offers an analogy: Polonius describes the players as able to perform not only "tragedy, comedy, history, pastoral" but also "pastoral-comical, historical-pastoral, tragical-historical, tragical-comical-historical-pastoral." Similarly, some research projects represent only one of the approaches discussed in this chapter while others combine more than one. Some projects involve more than one phase, each with a different approach, such as a survey and an experiment. Sometimes the same data are collected for more than one purpose, such as:

- to describe a process (process study),
- to examine the relationship of that process to various client characteristics (correlational research),

- to examine the evolution of that process over time (developmental approach),
- to generate hypotheses about causal relationships (ex post facto research), or
- to develop ways to improve the process (action approach).

Sometimes experiments are carried out within action or product development projects. A combination of experimental and historical approaches is represented when archaeologists break animal bones by several methods and compare the results with exhumed fragments to infer practices of extinct societies.

CHAPTER SUMMARY

This chapter offers a system for classifying research approaches that is based primarily on a project's mission or purposes, and secondarily on its methodology. A system of classification (a taxonomy) represents a conceptual framework that functions as a helpful tool to enable researchers to think and communicate about research projects. Any single project may use only one or several of the various research approaches.

The various approaches differ with regard to their concern with questions of cause and effect. True experiments offer the strongest support for inferences about cause-and-effect relationships between variables. Quasi-experiments offer somewhat weaker support but are used when true experiments are desirable but not feasible. The experimental approach is the only appropriate approach for testing hypotheses about cause and effect. Ex post facto and action projects can generate and explore cause-and-effect hypotheses for later testing through experiments. Descriptive studies and most product development studies are uninterested in questions of cause.

Basic research studies theoretical questions; applied research seeks to solve practical problems. Evaluation research is distinguished by its relationship to a service program. Exploratory research generates hypotheses rather than testing them. Qualitative research emphasizes descriptions that do not require quantities or numbers; the mission of many qualitative projects evolves as the formulation, planning, and data collection phases are repeatedly revisited as the project proceeds.

PRACTICAL EXERCISES

1. The following studies are drawn or adapted from the research literature in counseling. For each, select the research approaches (case and field, ex post facto, experiment, and so on) that you believe the study represents. Justify your answers by describing the specific features of the study that represent the research approach you selected.

a. Philips, Friedlander, Kost, Spectermas, and Robbins (1988) were in-
    terested in determining the relationship between client satisfaction
    with counseling and type of counseling (personal or vocational). They
    examined the case notes of 22 counselors who had seen 46 adult clients
    at a community counseling center for an average of eight sessions
    each. They also sent questionnaires to former clients asking them how
    satisfied they had been with their counseling. Their results suggested
    that client satisfaction was related only to the counselor's length of
    experience.
b. Bolk (1983) was interested in adolescents' reactions to bereavement.
    He interviewed 33 adolescents, ages 14–19, at 4 and 84 months after
    their siblings' deaths and found that the emotions present during
    the first and second interviews were shock (88%, 30.3%), anger (75%,
    27.3%), confusion (88%, 3.1%), depression (81.8%, 45.5%), fear (57.5%,
    24.2%), and loneliness (66.7%, 33.3%).
c. Two counselors who frequently worked with bulimic clients read an
    article by Bauer and Anderson (1989) that presented a set of maladap-
    tive beliefs the authors suggested were common among bulimic clients.
    The two counselors then asked all their bulimic clients to fill out a
    questionnaire that asked if they agreed with these beliefs, on a scale
    from 1, "disagree completely," to 5, "agree completely."
d. A study by Jones, Gorman, and Schroeder (1989) sought to compare
    the effect of two different career interest inventories on the amount
    of time spent on occupational exploration in the career library. The
    participants were 68 college students who responded to a career center
    invitation to take an interest inventory to help them with their career
    choices. When the students appeared for their appointments at the
    career center, a research assistant gave them, at random, one of the
    two inventories to fill out. Each inventory was followed by identical
    instructions to feel free to explore the resources in the career library.
    After the students had filled out the inventory, the research assis-
    tant unobtrusively recorded how much time each student spent ex-
    ploring the resources of the library.
e. Gordon and Shontz (1990) intensively studied a 21-year-old male who
    had tested positive for the AIDS virus but had no AIDS symptoms.
    The initiating investigator collected behavioral and projective data as
    well as dream reports and spontaneously produced artistic material
    from the client/participant. A narrative was produced to describe the
    study, and the data were integrated in terms of five themes: feeling
    infected and infectious, facing death and dying, ambivalence, un-
    certainty, and secrecy.
f. A study was conducted in a large northern state to examine the ex-
    tent to which public school counselors were functioning in accordance
    with professional guidelines and whether or not they considered it
    important to do so (Tennyson, Miller, Skovholt, & Williams, 1989).
    A questionnaire listing 58 counselor functions was developed by a

committee composed of the research team and the counseling practitioners. The functions were classified under four broad categories of services: counseling, consulting, career development, and administrative support. Counselors were asked to respond to two questions about each function: (1) How often do you perform each function? and (2) How important is each function for school counselors? Responses were recorded on a 5-point scale ranging from "never" to "frequently" for the first question and "unimportant" to "crucially important" for the second.

g. Paradoxical intention (PI) is a form of therapy in which clients are encouraged to deliberately engage in the problematic or maladaptive behaviors or cognitions for which they are seeking treatment. The rationale for this therapy is that much of the pathology associated with such problems is "due to the increase of compulsion and anxieties caused by the very effort to fight them" (Debord, 1989, p. 394). Wright and Strong (1982) examined the effects of PI on 30 college students who all complained of debilitating effects of procrastination on their study behaviors. Ten of the students were told to deliberately continue procrastinating as they had been; another ten were told to deliberately procrastinate only some of the time. A third group of ten students received no intervention whatsoever except for the administration of measuring instruments. The researchers found that both groups that had received instructions to procrastinate reduced their procrastination while the group that had received no intervention did not improve.

2. Imagine that it is your task to design a process study of some feature of either clients' or counselors' behavior during counseling sessions. Give three examples of variables that might be examined in such a study that are different from any examples in the text.

3. A professional counseling organization studied its distinguished members (those with more than 25 years of professional and research contributions to the field) to find out whom they had mentored from the succeeding generation of counseling professionals. This second generation was also studied to determine the nature of their mentoring patterns. What major research approaches does this study represent? Provide the rationale for your answer.

4. From a recent issue of a counseling journal, select an article describing a research study that exemplifies one of the approaches discussed in Chapter 2. Bring the article to class and be prepared to discuss why the study exemplifies this particular approach.

5. A correlational study of more than 6,000 men participating in company sponsored health promotion programs ("Couch Potato," 1989) found that a strong relationship existed between watching television two to three hours a day and obesity. The researchers labeled this finding the "couch potato phenomenon." The authors pointed out that it was impossible to causally link the variables of television watching and obesity despite

the strong relationship between them. In light of the discussion of causality presented in Chapter 2, explain why neither of these variables can be presumed to cause the other.

6. Read the following study and decide whether it represents a true experiment or a quasi-experiment. Discuss the rationale for your answer.

A college counselor who was responsible for counseling student athletes on campus was interested in the effects of stress-inoculation training on athletic performance. (Stress inoculation is a procedure whereby individuals are taught a systematic means of conceptualizing, acquiring skills for, rehearsing, and following through with their responses to stressful tasks.) To assess the effects of stress inoculation, the counselor conducted a training workshop on its use with all the football players but deliberately avoided discussing stress inoculation principles with the basketball players. He then compared the win–loss record of both teams for the remainder of the season.

PROGRAM EVALUATION: A VARIETY OF APPLIED RESEARCH; CONTEXT AND RESOURCE QUESTIONS

QUESTIONS TO GUIDE YOUR READING

An Overview of Program Evaluation
1. What is program evaluation?
   a. Why has it become increasingly important in the counseling profession?
   b. What is a service program? Give some examples in your response.
2. What kinds of decisions does program evaluation address?

Evaluation and Other Research
3. What are the similarities between evaluation and other research?
4. What are the differences between evaluation and other research?
5. What research skills and techniques are unique to evaluation?
6. How does the concept of generalizability apply to evaluation?
7. What is the role of cause-and-effect relationships in evaluation projects?
8. What is the role of theory in evaluation?
9. What political considerations must evaluation researchers be sensitive to?
10. What time pressures exist in most evaluation projects?
11. Why is a lower standard of scientific rigor acceptable for most evaluation projects than for other research?
12. Why do evaluation researchers incur greater risk of being severely criticized for their work than do other researchers?
13. What is evaluability assessment?

Formulation: Program Goals and Objectives
14. What do we mean by a service program's mission?
15. What does a service program's formal mission statement include?
16. If a service program does not have a formal mission statement, how is its mission expressed?
17. What are goals and objectives?
18. How does the mission of an evaluation project differ from that of the service program being evaluated?

A Conceptual Model
19. Why is a conceptual model useful to evaluation researchers?
20. What does the acronym CIPP stand for?
   a. What sorts of questions are addressed in context evaluation?
   b. What information does input evaluation seek?
   c. What is studied in process evaluation?
   d. Why is product evaluation carried out?
21. What is a needs assessment?
22. What issues should be considered when formulating the questions to be answered with needs assessment data?
23. Why is it so important to assess community attitudes in most context evaluations?

24. Why must service program planners understand prevailing constraints and resources?

An Overview of Program Evaluation

As noted in Chapter 2, program evaluation is applied research that addresses decisions about service programs. This chapter and the next are given to this topic, which is increasingly prominent in the counseling literature. Counselors are now being called upon more than ever before to evaluate the programs in which they work and to meet increasingly higher standards in conducting those evaluations (Bishop & Trembley, 1987; Gysbers, Hughey, Starr, & Lapan, 1992). Further, most counseling programs funded by federal and state sources must have an evaluation component as an accountability requirement.

In this chapter we will discuss program evaluation as a variety of applied research in general and then examine evaluation questions concerning the context in which a planned program is to operate and the resources at its disposal. In Chapter 4 we will address evaluation of a program's day-to-day operations and its results and then discuss dissemination and utilization of evaluation data. Both chapters emphasize evaluation of programs that provide counseling services.

A **service program** can be any size, from very large to very small. For example, this term might apply to the entire federal–state public rehabilitation system or to a small community agency's activities with a few local high school students who have special needs or even to one counselor's work with one client. (Evaluating your work with a client is not the same as evaluating the client.) Program evaluation can and should be distinguished from program development. Evaluation research often furnishes answers to questions important to administrative and policy decisions about program development.

Program evaluation involves collecting, analyzing, and interpreting data to make or support decisions about a service program. These decisions may concern one or more of the following:

- planning a new program;
- establishing a new program;
- conducting an existing program by
  - determining the ways the program is and is not operating according to plan and
  - fine-tuning (Rossi & Freeman, 1989) (that is, changing versus keeping unchanged one or more details while leaving the program's basic concept intact), sometimes undertaken because sponsors, staff, or service recipients are dissatisfied, sometimes to meet sponsors' or accrediting bodies' routine requirements;

- supporting a program (for example, in the role of a parent organization, grant-awarding agency, or accrediting body);
- establishing or continuing other relationships with a program, such as sending or accepting referrals and subcontracting for services (for example, job placement); and
- continuing versus discontinuing a program.

Program evaluation to answer context and resource questions may be addressed to any one of these decisions. Usually, however, context and resource questions are addressed to planning or establishing new programs.

The conceptual and technical development of program evaluation as a discipline can be traced from the 1930s. Since then it has become a large enterprise. Rossi and Freeman (1985) estimated that annual federal expenditures for evaluation research during the 1970s ranged from $.5 billion to $1 billion. In the early 1980s, there was little change in the amount of evaluation research being done, though a smaller proportion was supported directly by the federal government. For the 1990s, Rossi and Freeman (1989) predicted further growth. Much of this development has been carried out by specialists in public affairs and public policy; nonetheless, most of the ideas and techniques they developed can be used to evaluate counseling programs in both the public and the private sectors. Within the counseling profession, the employee assistance specialty and counseling programs in the public schools have carried out much of the program evaluation work. We predict that increasing demands for accountability will require counseling service agencies to carry out more program evaluation research than they now do. Naisbitt and Aburdene (1990) have noted the increasing concern with cost effectiveness throughout the industrially developed nations of the world.

EVALUATION AND OTHER RESEARCH

We defined program evaluation as a form of applied research distinguished by its relationship to a service program. In addition to these defining features, program evaluation projects differ generally in some ways from other research projects, although individual contrary instances may be found. Drew and Hardman (1985) believe "the gap between the two appears to be widening . . . and may be even more notable in the future" (p. 17). We see evaluation as sufficiently maturing in its technology and conceptualization to be considered a discipline in its own right. This idea seems fully consistent with the proposition that evaluation is a form of applied research. To note an analogy, psychiatry is both a discipline in its own right and a medical specialty. Like other research, program evaluation follows the six sequential and recyclable steps discussed in Chapter 1. In addition, program evaluation has other similarities to and differences from other kinds of research, including:

- a program evaluation project may use any of the general research skills and techniques discussed throughout this book plus others unique to this specialty;
- the kind of generalizability sought in evaluation is often somewhat different from that of other research;
- like other research, some evaluation projects include issues of cause and effect in their missions and some do not;
- as is true with other research, some evaluation projects' missions include theory and others do not, and when theory has a role, it is often a somewhat different one, such as linking findings to practical applications;
- political considerations are more important to evaluation projects than they are to other types of research projects;
- evaluation projects are more subject to time pressures than are other projects;
- a lower standard of scientific rigor is usually acceptable in evaluation projects; and
- evaluation projects have a higher risk of being severely criticized if results disagree with the sponsors' wishes.

Skills and Techniques

The skills and techniques required to formulate a research mission, plan a project, collect and analyze the data, interpret the findings, and report the results apply to all research, including evaluation. Other skills and techniques are unique to the evaluation specialty and stem from its relationship to the service program evaluated. The mission of an evaluation project is derived from all, or a portion of, the mission of the program to be evaluated. In Chapter 1, the mission of a research project was defined as comprising its research questions and the reasons answers to these questions are being sought. In program evaluation projects, these reasons have to do with program decisions. Research questions are usually based on the program's service mission. If the service program has a vague or incompletely formulated mission, the evaluator may need to work with program sponsors and staff to clarify this service mission before the evaluation project's mission can be formulated. In some instances, evaluation data are sought to make decisions about a program's service mission; in such cases the decisions that need to be made must be clearly defined.

Evaluation projects are more likely than other research projects to involve a complex network of people with vested interests in the service program, the evaluation project, or the project's results. Rossi and Freeman

(1989) used the term **stakeholders.** To carry out an evaluation project successfully, the researcher must formulate, plan, conduct, and report it while taking into account all these interests. The cooperation of program decision-makers and staff is often essential. For these reasons, evaluation usually makes heavy demands on researchers' organizational, administrative, and negotiating skills.

Evaluation is a discipline in its own right. We base this judgment in part on the fact that this specialty has a growing professional literature separate from that of its progenitor disciplines such as education, political science, psychology, sociology, counseling, social work, and business. Evaluation researchers are well advised to have some familiarity with this literature. (Several specific sources from this literature are listed in Appendix A and in the references.)

Generalizability

Most researchers seek generalizable results. Researchers often study samples to understand phenomena that occur not only in the samples studied but in the wider populations these samples represent. Most evaluation projects are more concerned with the specific programs being evaluated than with generalizing their findings to a wider population of programs. As Rossi and Freeman (1985) noted, it is nonetheless an oversimplification to state that other research seeks generalizability while evaluation does not. Evaluation projects usually seek results that can be generalized to similar programs or to the same program's future. To base operational decisions on evaluation results represents such generalization. To do so, the researcher usually assumes that the people who were studied are reasonably representative of those to be affected by the decisions. This assumption permits the results to be generalized.

Cause and Effect

It is also an oversimplification to say that other research is concerned with cause-and-effect relationships while evaluation is not. Experimental research supports inferences about a causal relationship between treatment conditions and outcomes. Ex post facto research generates hypotheses about causes, sometimes to explore which of several possible explanations might be more plausible than others. Descriptive research does not involve cause-and-effect inferences. Some evaluation projects are concerned only with discovering the extent to which expected outcomes have occurred, without asking why. Deciding upon operational changes based on evaluation data, however, implies that the changes are expected to cause differences in a program's results. Some evaluation projects are explicitly concerned with causal relationships between program features and outcomes. The **impact assessment** concept discussed in the next chapter contains this idea.

Theory

A third oversimplification found in the literature asserts that other research tests ideas drawn from theory while evaluation does not. It was noted earlier in this chapter that theory often plays a different role in evaluation than it does in other research. Basic research draws its research questions from theory. Applied research draws its questions from practice and sometimes also from theory. Gottfriedson (1984) proposed that integrating "theory testing with the development and evaluation of action programs" will "(a) develop stronger programs . . ., (b) increase the clarity of projects' theoretical rationales, (c) identify and measure the most appropriate variables, and (d) increase the strength and fidelity of the interventions." He proposed "an adaptation of the action research paradigm . . . to increase the theoretical and practical relevance of evaluation research" (p. 1101).

Political Considerations

All researchers need to take into account the interests of participants or clients and other involved persons when planning a project. In most research projects, these interests concern the time and effort the project will ask of them in view of other activities and commitments that may compete or conflict with the project. Administrators of service programs must be concerned not only with their own time commitments but also with those of the people responsible to them. Evaluation researchers must take into account stakeholders' added concerns that stem from their vested interests in the program being evaluated. People cannot be expected to cooperate with an evaluation project if they fear it may lead to decisions adverse to their own interests. These fears are particularly likely among people who have been excluded from the planning process. Stakeholders often extend far beyond the people whose efforts and resources are required to carry out the project. For example, students who need counseling assistance are likely to feel threatened by an evaluation of the program that provides them this service if they believe the evaluation is a ploy to justify reducing the program's budget; so might faculty who rely on the program for assistance with troubled students. Even if based entirely on false beliefs, such feelings can result in vigorous protests, leading administrators to cancel an evaluation project or demand changes that weaken it. Rossi and Freeman's (1989) term **evaluability assessment** refers to approaching these problems systematically as part of planning an evaluation project. Patton (1987) noted that qualitative research methods are often appropriate for evaluability assessment.

Time Pressures

Almost all researchers face time pressures. Organizations that award grant funds impose deadlines for proposals. After funds are awarded and the project is under way, timely reports must be submitted. Universities have deadlines for students' dissertations and theses that partially fulfill degree requirements. To be presented at a conference, a research report must be submitted by a deadline.

Evaluation projects usually face additional pressures that may be even more severe. Program sponsors and policy-makers often need information about a program's operations and results to make decisions, and most decisions have deadlines. These deadlines often come much too soon to allow the best methods to be used to collect the required data.

In many organizations, long planning and procurement procedures make it difficult to conduct timely studies. Often, a planned project and its procedures must be approved at several levels and by several important stakeholders. Agreement must be established regarding the evaluation questions and design. All these processes take time. So do legal requirements related to contracting when a project involves more than one organization. For example, "the typical evaluation done under contract to the U.S. Department of Education requires three years from conception to completion." During this period, decision-makers' needs sometimes lead them to ask evaluators "to release preliminary results" and "impressions" despite the evaluators' concerns that such impressions are likely "to be useless in the absence of firm results" (Rossi & Freeman, 1985, p. 380). Planners of large projects relying on external funds are well advised to consider all these time pressures. Small projects carried out without external funds avoid bureaucratic delays arising from relationships with funding sources. Nonetheless, such projects usually must face decision-makers' urgent need for information, even when this urgency conflicts with the time requirements of sound methodology. Rossi and Freeman (1985) advised evaluators to (a) "confine technically complex evaluations to pilot or prototype projects . . . implemented on a small scale" before the programs studied "appear on the agendas of decision-making bodies," and (b) "anticipate the direction of programs . . . rather than be forced, within tight time constraints, to respond to the demands of other parties" (p. 382).

Rigor

A lower standard of scientific **rigor** than that usually required of other research is acceptable for most evaluation projects. Unlike much other research, evaluation must always adjust to the requirements of a service setting. These requirements often include, but are not limited to, time pressures. Further, rigorous control of variables through laboratory procedures is not an option. In Chapter 2 we discussed quasi-experiments in which constructed controls are used because random assignment to treatment groups is not possible. Constructed controls are untreated or differently treated persons "selected by nonrandom methods to be comparable in crucial respects to . . . intervention groups" (Rossi & Freeman, 1989, p. 310). When even constructed controls are impracticable, some evaluation projects substitute **shadow controls**, "expert and participant judgments" in lieu of controls (Rossi & Freeman, 1989, p. 310). Most research journals would reject as insufficiently rigorous an article describing a project with shadow controls; researchers who wish to publish in such outlets should choose projects more amenable to the level of rigor required.

Program evaluators often cannot achieve the rigor other research requires and still meet feedback and accountability demands within deadlines. In addition, service settings present many more possibilities for plausible rival interpretations than laboratories do, despite researchers' best efforts at control. However, these considerations should never be used as an excuse for an evaluation project to be less rigorous than prevailing constraints permit. As UCLA athletic coach John Wooden was heard to remark, "Don't let what you can't do interfere with what you can do."

Risk of Criticism

Compared to other researchers, authors of evaluation projects incur a greater risk of being severely criticized for results that "contradict the policies and programs" their sponsors or other important stakeholders advocate (Rossi & Freeman, 1989, p. 425). We discuss a related problem in Chapter 6: Projects' procedures are often accepted uncritically by reviewers who like the conclusions and criticized harshly by reviewers who do not. It might be argued that this issue should have been discussed under political considerations on the premise that a project's overall success includes the way its results are received. Nonetheless, we find this issue important enough to deserve separate attention. Rossi and Freeman (1989) referred to an instance in which project staff had "naively expected" its prestigious sponsors to receive its contrary results "as peers and colleagues." However, they reacted "like most disappointed sponsors" and "hired technical experts to go over the report in great detail to uncover possible technical errors. Severe (and perhaps unwarranted) criticisms were leveled at the research design, writing style, vocabulary, and even the format for statistical tables" (p. 426).

To reduce the risk of such scenarios, we recommend being very clear about a project's mission. If a sponsor expects a project to support a plan already decided but evaluators expect it to determine what plan best deserves support, the stage is set for just such a process. To avoid it, sponsors and evaluators need to confer and reach agreement about (a) exactly what goals the project is to serve, and (b) how potentially uncomfortable results are to be treated. Related ethical issues are discussed in Chapter 5.

FORMULATION: PROGRAM GOALS AND OBJECTIVES

This section concerns the goals and objectives (mission) of a service program as distinct from the mission of any research project as discussed in Chapter 1.

As these terms are defined in the evaluation literature, a **goal** is a broad, general statement of a desired outcome. A program may have one goal or several. From each goal, several **objectives** are derived. These objectives are specific and much narrower than the parent goal. Most good statements of objectives specify the data by which their attainment can be measured (for example, "Students will receive one hour per week of group counseling on topics related to social skills as verified by counselor log sheets"). Objectives in this context are different from clients' educational and vocational "objectives," which often appear in counseling records. The entire set of a service program's goals and objectives constitutes its mission. A **formal mission statement** is a written document comprising the program's goals and the objectives related to each goal. Appendix B includes an example of a formal mission statement from a funding proposal.

It is essential to distinguish the mission of an evaluation project from that of the program being evaluated. A program's mission has to do with services; an evaluation project's mission has to do with data for decision making. In Chapter 1 we discussed the idea of a research project's mission; evaluation projects represent a special case rather than an exception. Evaluation for program planning often supplies data to shape a program's mission. When evaluation is connected with establishing or conducting a program, the evaluation project's mission is usually based on questions stemming from the program's mission. When one program evaluates another, the evaluator program's goals usually determine the project's mission.

Some service programs have formal statements of goals and objectives. A few have missions that exist as vaguely articulated understandings among the people who carry out program activities. Sometimes such vague understandings conflict with one another (Boschen, 1984). Most service programs have formulated their missions with a degree of explicitness between these extremes. When clear mission statements exist, formal or not, they sharply reduce the remaining work of formulating an evaluation project that draws its research questions from the stated goals and objectives. Often, the researcher must merely choose which objectives are to be evaluated. Absent such statements, the mission of any program evaluation project must be formulated anew.

A CONCEPTUAL MODEL

A conceptual model of anything is a systematic way of thinking about it. The evaluation literature offers a number of such models, which differ from one another to varying degrees in the aspects of the evaluation enterprise chosen for attention. Kaufman and Thomas (1980) discussed eight models, stating that "the ultimate goal of all the models is to support and assist in useful decision making (not to make the decisions for you)" (p. 108). We find such models helpful in two major ways. First, models offer a framework that helps bring order to what seems initially like a chaotic mass of issues, problems, data, and decision points. Second, models reduce the likelihood that anything will be overlooked.

A comparative review of program evaluation models is beyond the scope of this text. If you wish to study different models, we suggest Kaufman and Thomas's (1980) Chapter 6 and the sources cited at the end of that chapter. If you are particularly interested in the evaluation of counseling programs in public schools, Borders and Drury (1992b) offer an extensive list of suggestions. Our discussion will focus on a single model.

CIPP is an acronym in which the letters represent four different types of evaluation research questions: context, input, process, and product. The **CIPP model** is a systematic way of viewing the relationship between the mission of an evaluation project and the service program it is evaluating. It was developed under the auspices of Phi Delta Kappa for evaluating educational programs but appears applicable to program evaluation generally. Our summary is based primarily on three sources: Isaac and Michael (1981, Chapter 1), Phi Delta Kappa (1971), and Stufflebeam and Shinkfield (1985, Chapter 6). We have chosen the CIPP model for discussion here because we think this model offers the best fit with program evaluation in the field of counseling. Let's begin by examining the four aspects of the CIPP model.

Context Evaluation

What unmet needs exist? "What is desired relative to certain value expectations, areas of concern, difficulties, and opportunities, in order that goals and objectives may be formulated?" (Isaac & Michael, 1981, p. 10). What is the nature of the organizational and community context in which the planned program will operate? Are "existing goals and priorities attuned to the needs of whoever is supposed to be served?" (Stufflebeam & Shinkfield, 1985, p. 169). **Context evaluation** seeks answers to questions such as these, usually to serve planning decisions of concern in planning a new program or in planning changes in an existing program.

Input Evaluation

Input evaluation carries the exploration of the environment one step further. It asks: What "human and material resources" does the program have at its disposal? (Isaac & Michael, 1981, p. 11). What "barriers" and "constraints" in the "environment . . . ought to be considered in the process of activating the program?" (Stufflebeam & Shinkfield, 1985, p. 173). This and other information enables the researcher to identify and assess "relevance and capabilities of designs, strategies, and procedures . . . for achieving . . . objectives" (Isaac & Michael, 1981, p. 11).

It is noteworthy that both context and input evaluations call for study of a program's environment. Context evaluation studies it in a general way, and input evaluation seeks to identify the resources, barriers, and constraints this environment offers.

Process Evaluation

Process evaluation studies a program's day-to-day operations. Are activities being carried out as planned? Are they on schedule? Are unforeseen obstacles or delays being encountered? As they implement "previously chosen procedures," the "personnel responsible" for them monitor information collected while the program is operating "so that its strong points can be preserved and its weak points eliminated" (Isaac & Michael, 1981, pp. 10–11). "Implement" in this context refers both to starting new procedures and to carrying out established ones. Stufflebeam and Shinkfield (1985, p. 176) note several uses for process evaluation:

- Mainly, it produces "feedback that can aid staff to carry out a program as it was planned or if the plan is found to be inadequate, to modify it as needed."
- "Regularly scheduled process evaluation feedback sessions" can help keep "staff . . . abreast of their responsibilities."
- Results show consumers of accountability information the extent to which people conducting a program "did what they had proposed."
- Results tell "external audiences . . . what was done in the program in case they want to conduct a similar one."
- When interpreting product evaluation results, knowing "what was actually done in carrying out the program plan" helps in understanding "why program outcomes turned out as they did."

In Chapter 2, we noted that process studies of counseling investigate what takes place within counseling sessions. Analogously, a process evaluation project studies what takes place as a service program carries out its day-to-day activities.

Product Evaluation

Product evaluation is similarly analagous to outcome studies of counseling. To what extent are objectives being achieved? Product evaluation is carried out "to measure, interpret and judge the attainments of a program" (Stufflebeam & Shinkfield, 1985, p. 176). It refers to what is often called the "bottom line" (for example, number of clients who were placed on jobs, dollars saved through reduction in employee health benefit claims, number of new students enrolled through a recruitment program). Evaluation for accountability usually includes product evaluation, which serves "recycling decisions" (that is, "deciding to continue, terminate, modify, or refocus" a program's activity, Isaac & Michael, 1981, p. 13). Stufflebeam and Shinkfield (1985) recommended product evaluation "both during a program cycle and at its conclusion." Further, "product evaluation often should be extended to assess long-term effects" (p. 177). Not only should a program's desirable intended outcomes be studied but evaluation should include "intended and unintended effects and positive and negative outcomes. Judgments of the program's success" should be sought from "a broad range of people associated with the program" (p. 177).

An Example: The CIPP Model in Action

Tom, an ABC Co. executive who believed the company should have an employee counseling program, conducted a questionnaire survey of employees throughout the company's local plants and offices to determine: (a) employee attitudes toward such counseling programs, (b) the number of employees who believed they would use the program if it were established, (c) the kinds of problems employees believed they would bring to such a program, and (d) whether employees believed these problems interfered with their job performance. This first survey illustrates context evaluation; it studied the need for the proposed program and the context within which it would operate.

Next, Tom surveyed personnel records to identify individuals who might have the background to qualify them to work as employee counselors. He also visited offices about to be left vacant by a growing department moving to new space. He learned that the company's weekly personnel newsletter printed announcements of new programs and would be available for articles describing a new counseling program. These activities addressed resources questions and illustrate input evaluation.

After the program was announced, Tom listed the departments from which clients had been referred, rated the attitudes of each department's manager and union steward with regard to making referrals, and noted the time elapsing from referral to first appointment for each client. This procedure illustrates process evaluation.

At the end of the project's first year, Tom supplied top management with a report containing (a) the number of employees seen as clients, (b) the average job performance ratings before and after employees were seen, (c) the absenteeism and tardiness rates of employees before and after they were seen, (d) the average number of visits per month to the company physician for illnesses and injuries before and after they were seen, and (e) a translation of b, c, and d into dollar-cost differences. This report, and the data on which it was based, represent product evaluation.

Using the CIPP Model

How might an evaluator use the CIPP model to be helpful in planning or conducting an evaluation of a service program? By carefully applying the model, the evaluator can reduce the chances of overlooking important research questions. Early in the formulation phase, we suggest asking which one or more of the CIPP components the evaluation is to address: context, input, process, or product. (Context and input evaluation are discussed in greater detail later in this chapter, process and product evaluation in the next.) As each of these components is considered in turn, related research questions often come to mind. A researcher can then decide whether or not to include each such question in the project. Then we recommend examining the paragraphs discussing each component to be included to see if any important aspect of that component is being overlooked.

For example, an evaluator is considering carrying out a **needs assessment** concerning a proposed substance abuse treatment clinic. In the CIPP model, a needs assessment represents context evaluation. The model reminds the evaluator to consider any input (resource), process, or product questions that may also need to be asked. Context evaluation includes the organizational and community context in which the planned program will operate. The evaluator is reminded to decide deliberately whether to include this context in the planned evaluation in addition to the needs assessment. If this context does not need to be studied, well and good. But if it does, the model has reduced the evaluator's chances of overlooking it. In the example of the substance abuse treatment clinic, the evaluator is well advised to consider the impact of such a clinic on its neighbors. Some people object to known substance abusers entering and exiting their area throughout the day.

Applying the CIPP model can be particularly helpful in formulating the kind of thorough, multifaceted evaluation some authors call an **audit**, or in understanding such a project after it has been completed. For example, Roman (1992) illustrated the audit concept with an **employee assistance program** (EAP) experiencing a decline in referrals from supervisors. Interviews revealed that its caseload had increased, management had denied a request for an additional staff person, and therefore the EAP decided to "sharply curtail" routine supervisor training activities. In the CIPP model, the declining referrals, increased caseload, and reduced training activities represent process evaluation findings; the refusal of new staff resources is an input finding. The CIPP model reminds the researcher to decide whether to add context and product questions to the evaluation. Respectively, two such questions are:

- What factors in this workplace led management not to provide the requested additional staff?
- What changes have taken place in cost savings from clients' improved job behavior?

Context Evaluation

We noted previously that context and input evaluation are usually conducted to serve decisions about program planning. We use "planning" in its broad sense, encompassing the entire set of activities preparatory to implementation. Our discussion of context and input evaluation for program planning addresses planning for new programs and for changes in existing programs. Context evaluation for program planning may include but is not necessarily limited to needs assessment and context evaluation of other issues, such as community attitudes.

Needs Assessment

Whether a new program or a changed existing program is envisioned, program planning usually represents a response to a perceived need. Perceived needs that are clearly defined and well understood offer a good basis for program planning. For example, in 1988, the California legislature set forth explicit new criteria any education program must meet to enable its graduates to qualify for licensure as marriage and family counselors. Among other requirements, the education program must be specifically designated by its institution as a marriage and family counseling program and must include a minimum number of hours of internship under the supervision of a licensed professional. Program planning could be based on these needs without defining them more explicitly. In contrast, program planners often begin with a general sense of an unmet need that is too vague to use as a basis for defining or changing a program's goals and objectives. A needs assessment is a tool for clarifying and defining vaguely sensed needs. Tom, the company executive who believed his company needed a counseling program, provides an example. Beginning with a vague sense that his company needed an employee counseling program, Tom conducted a needs assessment to confirm and clarify this need.

A needs assessment project seeks data to answer questions about needs so that effective program planning can proceed. To be answered clearly, questions related to needs must first be formulated accurately and specifically. Doing this often requires the researcher to think through a vague, general sense of an unmet need. Based on the work of Stufflebeam, McCormick, Brinkerhoff, and Nelson (1985), we recommend having clear ideas about the following points in mind when formulating the questions to be answered with needs assessment data:

> Does the need represent a discrepancy between a state of affairs as it now exists and as it is envisioned in an ideal? If so, who holds the ideal on which the need is based?
>
> Does the need represent a change desired by a majority of some particular group? If so, what group? How is this need different from a preference, in the ordinary meaning of these words?

Is the need based on anticipated future circumstances or events? For example, high school students need to learn mathematics and English to compete successfully for some kinds of jobs after graduation.

Would the absence of what is needed be harmful, and if so, to whom? In this sense, infants need not only food, shelter, and oxygen but also the caring attention of other people.

Does the need represent a "defensible purpose" in that individuals' rights are not abridged, the environment is not harmed, and meeting the need would yield an identifiable benefit to society? (Stufflebeam et al., 1985, p. 13).

Clarifying these issues sometimes brings a general sense of unmet need into sufficiently sharp focus that a needs assessment project can be formulated and planned. When it does not, a second step is often helpful—conducting unstructured or semistructured interviews with a few key people. These key people should be carefully chosen to represent knowledge and a variety of viewpoints about the issues being considered. It is often wise to include people whose help will be required in carrying out the needs assessment project. Such interviews often yield a list of needs that can form the basis of a questionnaire or interview study with a larger sample. These respondents can be asked to prioritize the needs on this list by rating or ranking them and to add other needs they see as important. The results of this process offer a more substantial basis for formulating program goals and objectives than a planner's general sense of unmet needs.

Other Context Issues

In addition to unmet needs, other context factors must also be considered in designing a service program. Of these, community attitudes are among the most important. To illustrate, we offer a hypothetical example. The director of a community health clinic noted an increasing number of teen pregnancies. She conducted a formal needs assessment, with pregnant teen-aged girls and their parents as **targets** (persons to receive services). This process identified birth control information as a high-priority need. However, the community contained a politically powerful constituency that opposed birth control on religious and philosophical grounds. Given this fact, it was extremely unlikely that the health clinic could successfully mount a birth-control information program, especially if it involved city funds. When uninformed about important features of their programs' social-political context, planners risk wasting large amounts of time, effort, and money on avoidable failures.

In the CIPP model, context evaluation addresses the surrounding community, and input evaluation addresses the "barriers and constraints" it offers. Relatively informal exploration of such factors (for example, through unstructured interviews) often helps the researcher make an informed decision on whether a more systematic study of them is desirable.

INPUT EVALUATION

In the CIPP model, input evaluation is used to identify available resources and constraints for a service program. Chapter 7 develops the idea that researchers need to identify and secure the required resources and understand prevailing constraints as part of the planning phase of any research project. Service program planners have a similar responsibility. For example, planners of a university-based clinic offering counseling services to the community would need to consider such resources and constraints as (a) whether space, office furniture, and video- and audiotaping equipment are available; (b) the procedure for charging fees and establishing nonprofit status; (c) how to best recruit a qualified staff of counselors; (d) how to advertise the clinic's services; and (e) what rules should govern training of student counselors.

While available fiscal and material resources and constraints can usually be assessed through other methods, the techniques discussed here are often helpful in assessing human resources. Questionnaires, interviews, tests, and records are the most common data sources in such studies. Formal job descriptions can be written for the positions envisioned in a program, and questionnaires, interviews, tests, or records can be used to identify people with the required skills and assess their availability to the program.

CHAPTER SUMMARY

Program evaluation is a form of applied research sufficiently specialized to be considered a discipline in its own right. It is represented by a rapidly growing professional literature. Its distinguishing feature is its relationship to service programs. Though evaluation projects as a group differ in several ways from other research projects, individual contrary examples will be found. The CIPP model offers a systematic conceptual framework for viewing the evaluation of counseling service programs. Evaluation research can contribute to many phases of a service program: planning or implementing a new program, carrying out or fine-tuning an existing program, supporting a program, deciding whether to continue or discontinue a program, and deciding upon other relationships with a program such as referring, subcontracting, or accreditation. Context and resource (input) evaluation projects are usually used to help plan and implement program activities and study one or more of: (a) the needs the program is to address, (b) the context in which it is to operate, (c) the resources at its disposal, or (d) the constraints it must operate within or overcome. Evaluation is an increasingly important research activity in counseling programs, and this trend will probably continue in decades to come.

PRACTICAL EXERCISES

1. Imagine for a moment that you are one of a group of marriage and family counselors in practice together. Your group has a thriving practice located in a downtown office building. One of your fellow counselors recently suggested that the group should consider opening another office in a rapidly growing suburb. What kinds of evaluation data would you recommend collecting to decide whether to open the new office? Base your answers on the CIPP model.
2. Examine some issues of research journals in the counseling field. Find an article you consider to be the report of an evaluation project (for example, the article by Barnette, 1989, reported in the *Journal of Counseling and Development*).
   a. Explain why you think the project you have chosen is an evaluation project as opposed to some other kind of research.
   b. What one or more parts of the CIPP model are included in the project you chose? To justify your answer, link specific points from the report's discussion of the project's mission with specific points from the descriptions of the four parts of the CIPP model.
3. A college counseling center has recently decided to include a variation of family systems therapy among the counseling approaches it uses with student clients. This therapeutic approach involves working with students' "significant others" as well as actual family members. Imagine that you have been requested to evaluate this new service program. Referring to the discussion of the skills and techniques unique to evaluation research, what skills and techniques would you need to carry out this evaluation? Use examples specific to this project in your answer.
4. Chapter 3 frequently referred to the interests of "stakeholders" in its discussion of evaluation research. Imagine that you are responsible for evaluating an outplacement counseling center, funded by a large automotive firm, designed to counsel employees who lost their jobs when robots were introduced into the manufacturing process. Who do you think the "stakeholders" interested in this evaluation project are likely to be, and why?
5. Read the following description of the establishment of a community service counseling clinic and decide which of the activities described represent context, input, process, and product evaluation. Explain the rationale for each of your decisions.

   A counselor education program at a large urban university wanted to establish a clinic that would offer services to the community and also serve as a training and practicum site for the program's advanced graduate students. The researchers first surveyed residents in the university's immediate service area to see how many people might avail themselves of such a clinic if one existed. They also asked if people would be more likely to avail themselves of services if they were offered in languages other than English, and if so, what languages. Finally, they inquired as to which counseling services people saw as most potentially useful.

Representatives from the counseling program then consulted with university administrators about the resources available to such a clinic (for example, space, office furniture, video- and audiotaping equipment, a telephone answering machine, funding for a clerical assistant, faculty released time for supervision of students). They also consulted with the university's attorney and accounting office concerning how fees could legally be charged to clients and how to form a nonprofit organization. They then interviewed several graduate students in counseling who had indicated interest in being among the first group of student counselors for the clinic and discussed with local newspapers and radio stations the possibility of advertising the clinic's services through those venues.

The clinic was ultimately funded and opened its doors to clients. During its operation, the faculty member who directed it prepared quarterly evaluation reports including (1) the number of calls requesting information about the clinic, (2) the number of persons who made appointments for counseling services, (3) the average number of people on the clinic waiting list at any time, (4) the kinds of counseling services requested, (5) the number of sessions attended by clients, (6) the ratings of client satisfaction with counseling immediately, 6 months, and 1 year after services were completed, (7) the ratings of student counselor satisfaction with the quality of their supervision, (8) the average fee paid per session, and (9) the gross and net income of the clinic.

CHAPTER FOUR

PROGRAM EVALUATION: PROCESS AND PRODUCT QUESTIONS; DISSEMINATION AND UTILIZATION

Questions to Guide Your Reading

Process Evaluation
1. Why are process evaluations conducted?
2. What kinds of data are useful in process evaluation?

Product Evaluation
3. What kinds of questions does product evaluation address?
4. What is meant by program utility?
5. How does impact assessment relate to the concept of causality?
6. What is the distinction between cost–benefit and cost-effectiveness evaluation?
7. What kinds of factors may be included when considering costs?
8. Why is it important to consider benefits and costs that cannot be quantified in monetary terms?
9. Why are formal efficiency analyses sometimes impractical or unwise?

Feedback, Accountability, and Evaluation of Other Programs
10. What three kinds of decisions are ordinarily addressed in process and outcome evaluation?
11. What is feedback evaluation?
12. What types of accountability information are most pertinent to process evaluation?
13. What types of accountability information are most pertinent to product evaluation?
14. What type of accountability information pertains importantly to both process and product evaluation?
15. Why do programs evaluate each other? Illustrate your answer with an example different from those used in the text.

Phasing and Subcomponents of Evaluation Activities
16. When is one-shot evaluation likely to be carried out?
17. How are evaluation data most efficiently collected? What kind of advance planning is required to ensure efficiency?
18. What subcomponents should a service program's overall evaluation component include?

Dissemination and Utilization of Evaluation Results
19. What is meant by direct, conceptual, and persuasive utilization of evaluation results?
20. Why must evaluators often choose multiple reporting media?
21. How should a report be prepared so that it is acceptable to its receivers?
22. Why is it important to assess utilization of evaluation results?
23. When an evaluation project's results are underutilized, what more should a utilization evaluation include?

Chapter 3 introduced the concept of program evaluation as an applied research specialty and discussed the CIPP model as a conceptual tool for evaluation to answer context and resources questions. This chapter begins with a discussion of evaluation addressed to process and product questions and ends by discussing dissemination and utilization of evaluation results.

PROCESS EVALUATION

Carefully monitoring a program's activities can provide a wealth of evaluation data. Feedback about the daily operation of a program often reveals ways to make large improvements in efficiency through small changes in a program's operation. For example, an agency's counselors were reluctant to use the personality inventories they regarded as most appropriate for their clients because mail-out scoring service took three weeks; however, it was discovered that commercially available software would enable these inventories to be scored much more rapidly with the agency's computer. A second example is provided by a rehabilitation agency that found that client service was often delayed because requests for medical examinations had to wait their turn for clerical processing. Management established a priority system for clerical work, and client service delays were reduced. In a third example, an employee counselor received many referrals of employees who often arrived late for work. Most of them complained that the early morning bus schedule left them no choice but to arrive a few minutes late or almost an hour before the front gate opened. Examination of records revealed that all who expressed this complaint, and many who had not been referred, were checking in within five minutes after a particular bus line stopped in front of the plant. Employee tardiness substantially declined after management changed the official starting time to fit the city bus schedule. In a fourth example, counselors at a public school found themselves unable to respond to student counseling needs because they were required to process a heavy volume of routine class changes. This task was transferred to the clerical staff, and counselors were once again able to respond to student needs. We resist the temptation to add endlessly to this list.

In each of these cases, knowledge about the program's operation enabled management to make changes to increase efficiency. Process evaluation provides the information on which such decisions can be based. We offer the following system as one idea among many possibilities for process evaluation in a counseling agency:

1. Construct a flowchart representing the sequence of client services and decision points (the client pathway). Figure 4.1 presents an example.

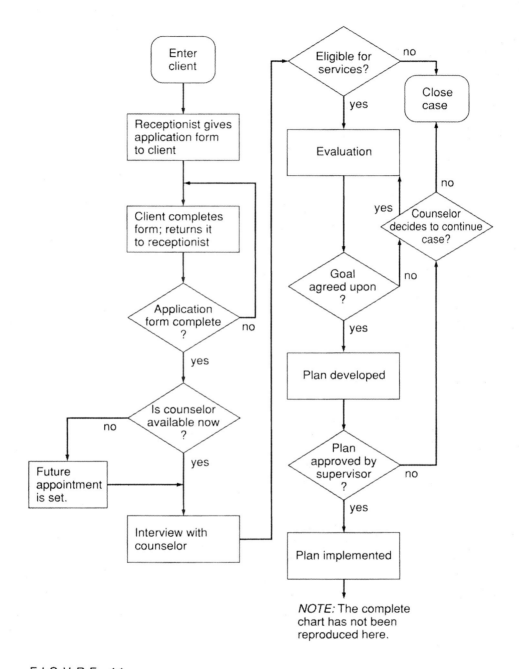

F I G U R E 4.1

Flowchart representing first part of a client pathway. Rectangular forms represent service procedures; rhombus forms (◇) represent decision points.

2. For each client, note the date and, if appropriate, also the time of day that each service procedure was
   - requested,
   - initiated, and
   - completed.
3. Develop a system for routinely compiling and storing this data in a manner readily accessible without searching individual client files. Computer programs exist that can execute these storage and retrieval functions in large agencies (Backer & Trotter, 1986; Walz, Bleuer, & Maze, 1989).
4. Review the flowchart periodically for needed revisions. People who record the data required for step 2 will probably recommend improvements from time to time because the flowchart as originally prepared skips some steps or linkages or because the program changes make an existing flowchart obsolete.
5. Periodically examine the data generated in step 2. One obvious analysis is to compile a frequency distribution and calculate a mean elapsed time between initiation and completion at each step. It is also desirable to determine the extent to which elapsed times may have been affected by weekends, holidays, and agency events such as staff meetings.
6. Combine the elapsed time data with other data to estimate the cost of each step.
7. When a step takes longer or costs more than seems reasonable, discuss the matter with the people involved to get some ideas about possible reasons.
8. Review the data accumulated, looking for ways the process can be made more efficient without sacrificing service quality.

PRODUCT EVALUATION

Product evaluation addresses outcome questions, and these questions usually concern a program's utility: How effectively, and at what cost, did the program accomplish what it set out to do? Such evaluation not only provides valuable feedback but accountability demands often require it. Rossi and Freeman (1989) defined **program utility assessment** as comprising two components: **impact assessment** and **efficiency assessment.**[1] In turn, efficiency may be measured in two ways: cost–benefit and cost-effectiveness analyses.

---

[1]Scattered excerpts on this and subsequent pages are from *Evaluation: A Systematic Approach,* 3rd and 4th editions, by P. H. Rossi & H. E. Freeman. Copyright © 1985, 1989 by Sage Publications, Inc. Reprinted by permission of the publisher.

Impact Assessment

Impact assessment refers to evaluation of "the extent to which a program causes changes in the desired direction" (Rossi & Freeman, 1989, p. 49). It is noteworthy that this definition contains the explicit idea of cause, contrary to some writers' notion that evaluation is uninterested in cause-and-effect relationships. As noted earlier in this chapter, program evaluators cannot control extraneous variables to the degree possible in many other research contexts. More often than not, conditions prohibit true experiments. Sometimes even quasi-experiments are not feasible, and evaluators must use descriptive or action approaches when experiments would more ideally suit their mission. Therefore it is often not possible to rule out all plausible rival hypotheses to account for desired conditions that follow interventions. Evaluators must often be content to argue for the idea that the program interventions caused these conditions (whether as sole or contributing cause) because it is the most reasonable among a number of plausible rival possibilities.

In contrast, it is often sufficient for accountability purposes to show that the conditions sought by program interventions are more prevalent after than before these interventions, without addressing the cause question. To be most effective, feedback must do more. Wise decisions require some idea about what features of a program cause its results. Experience as educators leads us to predict that accountability requirements will become more rigorous as evaluators, managers, granting agencies, accrediting bodies, and other consumers of evaluation data become more sophisticated. We expect that more careful attention to cause questions will be required in the future than is usual now.

Cost–Benefit and Cost-Effectiveness Analyses

These two related ideas concern the relationship between program outcomes and costs, usually but not necessarily in monetary terms. **Cost–benefit** and **cost-effectiveness analyses** represent two ways of measuring a program's efficiency. Relevant concepts are cost–benefit analysis, cost-effectiveness analysis, and opportunity costs.

To measure a program's efficiency, the researcher must quantify both its desired outcomes and its costs. Some desired outcomes may be quantified in monetary terms, such as income earned or expenditures avoided. Other desired outcomes are best quantified in other ways, such as students' improved grades or achievement scores. Costs may include any one or more of the following items, but are not necessarily limited to these:

- dollars;
- time;
- human effort;

- buildings, equipment, and other facilities used;
- unwanted outcomes or risks of unwanted outcomes; or
- opportunities foregone.

A program's direct dollar expenditures and some other costs are easy to quantify from the organization's fiscal records (staff salaries and fringe benefits, office space, supplies, mileage). But it is important not to overlook costs that may be present though much more difficult to quantify, such as unwanted reactions by people important to the organization.

Opportunity costs (Rossi & Freeman, 1989) are too often forgotten. Some of these are easy to quantify and some are not. For example, if an agency re-allocates some of its counseling staff from their regular duties to a special program, desirable outcomes foregone because of this reassignment should be estimated and counted among the program costs. If an agency did not apply for a large grant because staff were too busy carrying out an intervention, this missed opportunity should be counted among the intervention costs. But this cost was not the entire amount of the grant that might have been awarded if applied for; rather, this cost is limited to a lost opportunity to apply.

Opportunity costs can only be estimated rather than precisely calculated. Let's use the grant example to illustrate two ways of including opportunity costs in an efficiency analysis. If the program evaluator can estimate with sufficient confidence both the amount of the possible grant and the probability it would be awarded if applied for, the dollar value of this opportunity cost might be estimated by multiplying the amount of the grant by the probability it would be awarded. This estimate could then be added to other program costs for purposes of efficiency analysis.

Such estimates are often dubious, however. When the evaluator has little confidence in quantitative estimates of opportunity costs, these costs can be excluded from efficiency analysis computations and reported as an addendum instead. For example, the evaluator might accompany the efficiency analysis with a statement that the demands of the program left insufficient staff time to prepare an application for a $100,000 grant for which the agency was eligible but that the likelihood such an application would have been successful is unknown.

Rossi and Freeman (1989) distinguished between cost–benefit analysis and cost-effectiveness analysis on the basis that the former quantifies both costs and desired outcomes in the same terms, usually monetary, while the latter does not. Reports issued annually by the California Department of Rehabilitation illustrate both of these ways of expressing costs in relation to outcomes. These reports give an average dollar cost per rehabilitated client, both for the agency as a whole and subdivided by disability groups. Such reporting illustrates cost-effectiveness analysis because costs are indicated in monetary terms while outcomes are indicated only by the information that clients are rehabilitated.

The California Department of Rehabilitation reports also illustrate cost–benefit analysis: Costs to the tax-supported agency are balanced against taxes rehabilitants will probably pay on income earned and reductions in payments of public funds to them through such programs as welfare. These dollar amounts are then converted into an estimated number of years required for the body politic to recover the agency's rehabilitation expenditures, a **payback period.**

Smith and Mahoney's (1989) evaluation of a corporation's employee assistance program (EAP) also illustrates cost–benefit analysis. Medical claim costs of employees served by the EAP were compared with those incurred by similar employees who were not served. Combining these differences with "the value of working days saved" yielded conservative estimates of $5.1 million saved over four years and a final **cost-offset ratio** of 4:1 (p. 26). This ratio means that the company's investment in costs of conducting the EAP yielded savings of four times the amount invested. A third cost–benefit project (Coffler & Hadley, 1973) compared pretreatment and posttreatment arrest and incarceration records of all public drunkenness offenders referred to a specific treatment facility in lieu of jail during a specified time period (while jailing of these persons was still common practice). These records were converted to estimated dollar costs to the criminal justice system. Cost reductions between the pretreatment and posttreatment periods were compared with the dollar costs of treatment. The cost-effectiveness idea is further illustrated by Moore's (1977) observation that hospital programs for treating alcoholics were less cost-effective than other alternatives because the types of programs did not differ significantly in success rates, though hospital programs cost more. Success rates were not expressed in monetary terms.

Efficiency analyses in monetary terms have some strong advantages. Decision-makers in both profit-making businesses and social programs must consider money matters such as whether an activity is earning its keep or how best to allocate a limited budget. To be maximally helpful, evaluation data must address these concerns. Further, Rossi and Freeman (1989) pointed out that efficiency analyses encourage evaluators "to become knowledgeable about program costs," which are "very salient to many of the stakeholder groups important to program acceptance and modification." Evaluators' attention to these costs "often increases cooperation and support from such groups" (p. 386).

Nonetheless, we caution against overlooking important desirable and undesirable outcomes (benefits and costs, respectively) solely because they cannot be quantified in monetary terms. The cost–benefit idea can be applied not only formally, as Rossi and Freeman (1989) did, but also informally. Smith and Mahoney's (1989) and Coffler and Hadley's (1973) projects represent formal cost–benefit analyses: EAP clients incurred lower medical claim costs than did similar clients who did not receive services, and drunkenness offenders cost the justice system less for arrest and incarceration after treatment than before. In addition, these differences were presumably also accompanied by other desirable outcomes such as a better quality of life.

In a study limited to such nonmonetary benefits and costs, Hadley and Hadley (1970) composed an intervention group entirely of Native Americans in a residential alcoholism treatment facility. This project achieved its service mission in that more of this group than of a similar untreated group were discharged to training or employment. However, there were also some undesirable outcomes, one of which was that more of the treatment group than of the other group were discharged for disciplinary reasons. It appears that the treatment group's increased cohesiveness and sense of identity led some of its members to increased disruptive behavior. Administrative staff became concerned that the group might become militant. Even when such undesirable outcomes cannot be measured in monetary terms, they should be considered among a program's costs. They represent important risks planners of similar programs are well advised to consider. Balancing desired outcomes against unwanted ones, without necessarily quantifying either, represents informal cost–benefit analysis.

To summarize the concepts discussed in this section:

Two types of efficiency assessment are formal cost–benefit analysis and cost-effectiveness analysis.

Cost-effectiveness analysis quantifies both desired outcomes and costs, but not in the same terms. For example, such an analysis might yield an average dollar cost per contact hour or per rehabilitated client.

Formal cost–benefit analysis quantifies both desired outcomes and costs in the same terms, usually monetary. For example, dollar costs of operating a public rehabilitation agency are balanced against taxes its rehabilitated clients pay and welfare payments they do not collect because they are employed.

Informal cost–benefit analysis examines both desired outcomes and costs to reach a decision, without necessarily quantifying costs or desired outcomes.

Opportunity costs are opportunities forgone because of program activities. When part of the computations in an efficiency analysis, they must be quantified; they need not be quantified when part of an informal cost–benefit analysis.

Informal cost–benefit analysis is recommended not only as part of product evaluation but also as part of program planning. The outcomes sought through a program or intervention should be weighed against its anticipated costs, even when educated guesses are the most reliable measures available for these costs and outcomes. Such an **ex ante efficiency analysis** (Rossi & Freeman, 1989, p. 377) forces planners' systematic attention to anticipating desirable and undesirable outcomes, reducing the likelihood that important outcomes will be overlooked.

Some Caveats

Efficiency analyses can serve some important purposes in program evaluation. Nonetheless, we recommend that evaluators address several questions before undertaking such analyses. We base the following list on Rossi and Freeman's (1989) reasons why "in many evaluations formal, complete efficiency analyses are either impractical or unwise" (p. 381).

Does an efficiency analysis help fulfill the evaluation project's mission? If impact assessment fails to show that the service program did what it was intended to do, an efficiency analysis is futile. If an evaluation project was conducted only to convince decision-makers to support a program and impact assessment reveals an effect large enough to do so without showing its relation to costs, efficiency analysis is redundant.

Does the project have at its disposal the methodological expertise necessary to carry out the planned efficiency analysis? If staff do not have this expertise, consultants might be used.

Would placing economic value on certain input and outcome measures arouse adverse stakeholder attitudes or political controversies that might impair the progress or the utilization of the evaluation project? For example, some readers criticized Coffler and Hadley (1973) for implying that it was more important to reduce the dollar costs of arrest and incarceration than to reduce the adverse social and emotional effects of these procedures on people's lives.

Would some stakeholders fail to understand the accounting perspective implied in an efficiency analysis and therefore impair the evaluation project's progress or utilization?

Are sufficient data available to carry out a meaningful efficiency analysis? For example, Smith and Mahoney (1989) could get medical claim data for their clients who had fee-for-service medical coverage but not for those served by a health maintenance organization. We agree with the judgment of these authors that the available data permitted a meaningful analysis, though having all client data would have permitted a better one.

Do the monetary values attached to cost and outcome variables rest on unreasonable or insufficiently supportable assumptions? For example, the early EAP literature contains an often repeated estimate that alcoholism reduces employee job performance efficiency by 25%. Though the literature also notes that this amount may vary widely from one employer and one kind of work to another, many EAP evaluations adopted the 25% figure uncritically as a basis for estimating pretreatment to posttreatment gains by recovered workers.

FEEDBACK, ACCOUNTABILITY, AND EVALUATION OF OTHER PROGRAMS

Process and outcome evaluation are ordinarily conducted to address three kinds of decisions:

- a researcher collects data about his or her own program to use in internal decision making (**feedback evaluation**),
- a researcher collects data about his or her own program to influence decisions by others or to meet external requirements (**accountability evaluation**), and
- a researcher collects data about another program for use in deciding its relationship to the researcher's program.

In each of these instances, "collects data" is construed broadly; the people who conduct the program may collect the data themselves or may hire external contractors to do this job. The distinctions among these three types of mission rest on the reasons for collecting the data, not who performs this work.

Feedback Evaluation

In feedback evaluation, a researcher collects data about the program so the people who operate the program can make better decisions than they could without the data. Feedback does not necessarily involve sharing the data with people outside the program, though sometimes an outside organization is engaged to perform part of the evaluation task. To offer an analogy, a student counselor may arrange to have videotapes made of his or her sessions with clients to identify opportunities to improve counseling skills. The student may or may not decide to share those tapes with a faculty member for additional feedback.

Accountability

Sometimes the people who operate a program collect data to influence others' decisions. These others might be higher management, a funding organization, a board of directors, accrediting bodies, legislators, political constituents, referral sources, clients (past, present, or potential future), or the general public, to name a few possibilities. Sometimes the people conducting a program want those receiving the evaluation data to decide that the program has met the formal requirements for some action by the receivers, such as funding or accreditation. In the absence of any formal requirements, the researcher may provide data about the program being evaluated in support of recommended action on the part of the people receiving the data. To return to the analogy in the previous section, the student counselor might supply the videotapes to meet the formal requirements of an application for advancement from a master's to a doctoral program, or show them to a prospective employer.

An accountability evaluation may consider data about a program's feedback process. The Commission on the Accreditation of Counseling and Related Educational Programs (CACREP) and the Council on Rehabilitation Education (CORE) both include this component in the requirements their accredited programs must meet. In accredited programs, the responsible officials must indicate how they use the information gathered from students, professors, and the public they serve to improve or modify their programs' offerings. In both accountability and feedback evaluation, a researcher collects, analyzes, and interprets data about the program or contracts with others to do all or part of this work.

Seven types of **accountability** can be distinguished, some of which are more relevant to process evaluation and some of which are more relevant to product evaluation. The following list (with the exception of ethical accountability) is from Rossi and Freeman (1989, pp. 157–158). The types of accountability that pertain primarily to process evaluation include:

Service delivery accountability. To what extent does the program operate according to plans, with services delivered by appropriately qualified staff?

Legal accountability. To what extent does the program meet legal responsibilities such as informed consent, protection of privacy, community representation on decision-making boards, equity in provision of services, and cost sharing? Some legal requirements are codified in law; others are specified by contracts. For example, many grant-supported programs operate under contracts that include cost sharing as a legal requirement.

Ethical accountability. To what extent and by what means does the program meet its ethical responsibilities, particularly those not codified in law or specified by contract? The American Counseling Association (1988, formerly the American Association of Counseling and Development) has set forth several responsibilities that apply to counselors.

Coverage accountability. To what extent does the program reach the people it is intended to serve and provide the intended services to them? What are the number and characteristics of the people served, partially served, and not served?

Accountability information pertaining most to product evaluation includes:

Impact accountability. Does the program bring about the desired changes in the target population?

Efficiency accountability. How are the impacts of the entire program and its component elements related to costs?

Accountability information pertaining importantly to both process and product evaluation includes:

Fiscal accountability. Do fiscal reports adequately document use of funds? How much do services provided cost per client? What does each kind of service cost? If service levels were to be increased or decreased, how much would such changes raise or lower costs? How much do costs vary as a function of such factors as program site, time of year, and introduction of any competing programs?

Evaluation of Other Programs

To fulfill a third kind of program evaluation mission, researchers from one program evaluate another program. People from Program A analyze and interpret data about Program B and use the results to make decisions about Program A's relationship with Program B. The necessary data may be collected by either program or by both. For example, employee assistance counselors often refer clients to other agencies for services not offered by the EAP. To do this responsibly, a counselor must select agencies that provide an acceptable quality of service at an acceptable cost (Myers, 1984). Evaluation data provide a basis for these selections. Some other examples include rehabilitation agencies that evaluate the schools to which they refer clients for training, accrediting bodies that evaluate programs to decide which ones they will recognize, and counselors who evaluate therapists to whom they refer clients for further treatment.

Historical Trends

The political climate influences program evaluation more strongly than it does other types of research. Rossi and Freeman (1989) have noted

a change in emphasis in the evaluation field, [particularly] increased concern with documenting the worth of social program expenditures in comparison to their costs and increased attention to fiscal accountability and the management effectiveness of programs. Paradoxically, fiscal and political conservatives, often skeptical of social science methods, joined the advocates of social action programs in pressing for the types of information that evaluations provide. (p. 35)

In short, accountability emphasis has increased. This emphasis has been felt in counseling programs both within and outside the social action context. For example, 54.8% of Fairchild and Zins's sample of school counselors reported collecting "some type of accountability information" (1986, p. 197); these authors recommended that counselor education programs should give more attention to this matter.

Though we have not collected any systematic supporting data, our experience suggests another trend, increasing activity involving evaluation of one program by another. Two recent phenomena seem to represent both of these trends: (1) an increasing number of accrediting bodies within counseling and related fields, and (2) an increasing number of counseling programs that refer clients to other programs for services outside their own specializations.

The accrediting arm of the American Association of Marriage and Family Therapists (AAMFT), the Commission on the Accreditation of Rehabilitation Facilities (CARF), CORE, and CACREP have all emerged within the past two decades. Accrediting bodies develop and publicize program standards and evaluate individual programs' compliance with these standards. Accreditation represents a concise way to document program compliance. In addition, one who demands accountability can lighten his or her workload by asking for a program's accreditation status rather than the detailed information on which this accreditation status is based.

As noted earlier in this chapter, employee assistance programs (EAPs) and public school counseling programs often refer clients for services these programs do not offer. EAPs especially have become much more numerous since the 1960s (Myers, 1984). Such programs vary widely in the services they offer; most provide short-term counseling, though some offer only assessment and referral. Typically, such a program must maintain a "comprehensive and continually updated file of local resources that offer help" (Lewis & Lewis, 1986, p. 83). To have continually updated information about a comprehensive array of such agencies, an EAP must carry out systematic evaluation activity.

PHASING OF EVALUATION ACTIVITIES

Evaluation activity may be carried out one time only, recurrently, or continuously. Recurrently occupies the entire continuum between the two extremes of one time only and continuously. Intervals between recurrent evaluation activities may be regular or irregular, long or short. Franklin and Thrasher (1976) called recurrent evaluation with regular intervals **periodic evaluation.**

One-shot evaluation is often carried out as part of planning or establishing a new program, or "in response to a perceived crisis or particularly difficult policy situation" (Franklin & Thrasher, 1976, p. 27). Most ongoing service programs are evaluated recurrently. Often, evaluation data are collected continuously and analyzed recurrently to meet needs for feedback, demands for accountability, or both. It is usually more efficient to collect evaluation data routinely as part of regular service activities than to search through files later when evaluation time comes around. To do so, however, one must plan sufficiently in advance to know what data will be required. An appropriate **management information system (MIS)** can then be devised or selected. Most MISs are computerized systems for collecting and analyzing service delivery and outcome information on an ongoing basis and providing timely access to this information as required to meet management needs. Ideally, an MIS provides both managers and evaluators with needed program information. Backer and Trotter (1986) listed and briefly described 13 computer-based systems applicable to rehabilitation programs. Their descriptions suggest that some of these systems are equally suitable for other counseling programs. Walz, Bleuer, and Maze (1989) listed additional computer programs applicable to a broad range of counseling-related functions: the "client records" section briefly describes 18 programs; the "database systems" section, 16 programs. The usefulness of any computer program can be expected to vary widely from agency to agency.

Parts of an Evaluation Component

Some accrediting bodies expect service programs to conduct evaluation as a regular part of their service activities (in common parlance, to have an evaluation component). Other service programs do not need to meet accreditation requirements but contain an evaluation component because it is in the organization's best interest to do so. Even though each service program, accrediting body, and program sponsor has a unique set of needs and specific requirements, some generally desirable subcomponents of an evaluation component can be specified. The following list is drawn from a survey of rehabilitation programs (Flynn, Glueckauf, Langill, & Schacter, 1984); we have rephrased the statements to express their applicability to service programs generally rather than to rehabilitation specifically:

- written documents defining program goals and objectives (formal mission statement as defined earlier in Chapter 3);
- written documents describing the need for the agency's programs in its community or region;
- written documents showing evidence that program activities are relevant to known needs;
- written documents defining criteria for evaluating the extent to which program objectives are being met;
- standardized instruments or tests measuring client status at admission, status at discharge, satisfaction with services, and status at follow-up;

- staff persons who collect, tabulate, and report evaluation data as their primary or secondary job;
- written reports showing how much clients change between admission and discharge;
- written reports showing how much clients change between discharge and follow-up;
- written reports showing how much programs cost;
- written reports showing the relationship between costs and outcomes (efficiency analysis, discussed earlier in this chapter); and
- modification of service programs based on information derived from evaluation activities.

Many of these elements are also included in Borders and Drury's (1992a) recommended standards for evaluating school counseling programs. We add another desirable component to the above list: written documents showing costs and time requirements of various program activities, particularly any activities that form part of a series. This idea was discussed in greater detail under the "process evaluation" heading earlier in this chapter.

DISSEMINATION AND UTILIZATION

"Evaluative studies are worthwhile only if they are used" (Rossi & Freeman, 1989, p. 468). Earlier in this chapter, accountability and feedback purposes for evaluation projects were distinguished. Rossi and Freeman (1989) define direct, conceptual and persuasive utilization of evaluation results. **Direct utilization** refers to use of evaluation results to influence program decisions. Feedback use is direct; so is use of evaluations for such purposes as making accreditation decisions or deciding what programs will be used as referral resources. **Conceptual utilization** refers to "the use of evaluations to influence thinking about issues in a general way. These uses range from simply sensitizing persons and groups about current and emerging social problems to influencing program and policy development by examining the results of a series of evaluations together" (p. 455). In **persuasive utilization,** someone other than evaluators or sponsors uses the evaluation results to support or attack a political position. For example, the Reagan administration defended cutting social programs by noting that evaluations of major social programs failed to produce clear findings of desired impact.

Reporting Evaluation Projects

Unless the people who conduct an evaluation project are also responsible for applying its results, utilization requires dissemination. This section addresses reporting issues of particular importance to evaluation projects. Chapter 14 discusses research reporting in general.

To use a project's findings, a decision-maker must learn about them. The usual means of learning are to receive a report and read it or to hear a report at a meeting. An evaluator's first dissemination task is to decide who is to receive the project's reports. If the evaluation project's mission was well formulated, these receivers have already been identified. Some receivers may be identified by name, such as Jack Jones, President, Jones Mfg. Co.; others may be identified as a group, such as mental health counselors in Ohio or counselor supervisors throughout the state-federal rehabilitation system or voters in Chicago.

Second, an evaluator must decide what media to use to deliver the project's reports to these receivers. The media must be suited to the intended receivers. For example, many busy directors of counseling agencies would reject unread a technical report long enough to include the detail required by an evaluator's academic colleagues. Such a report would require too much time for most directors to read and contain too much material outside their interest or beyond their understanding. In contrast, some directors expect material to be presented in a way many of the evaluator's academic colleagues might disdain as gaudy and slick. When evaluators report to diverse stakeholder groups to fulfill a project's mission, they often must choose several reporting media.

Third, a report must be prepared in a manner acceptable to its receivers, or it will go unread and unused. To do this effectively, the report must address receivers' needs and take into account their commitments. It must contain the information they need, and not too much of what they don't need. A decision-maker already committed to a line of action may be inclined to reject an entire report if it recommends actions contrary to his or her existing commitments.

The report's language must be understandable to its receivers, without requiring excessive effort on their part. An important caution to report writers is that consumers often react with strong aversion to technical jargon they do not understand. Such jargon is therefore twice counterproductive: it fails to convey its intended meaning and arouses emotional reactions that make consumers less receptive to the remainder of the report.

The report must be of an acceptable length. Busy receivers often reject overlong reports unread. And receivers must have the report when they need it. A report does no good if it arrives after the deadline for decisions it was designed to help. As noted earlier in this chapter, this need for timeliness often conflicts with the time requirements of sound methodology. Evaluators "must therefore balance timing and accessibility of findings with thoroughness and completeness of analysis, [even at the risk of] criticism from some of their academic colleagues, whose standards of scholarship cannot always be met because of the need for rapid results and crisp reporting" (Rossi & Freeman, 1985, p. 392).

Evaluators must often prepare multiple reports of the same project to meet the needs of these diverse stakeholder groups.

Utilization Evaluation

"Evaluations should include an assessment of utilization. Evaluators and decision makers must . . . agree on criteria by which . . . successful utilization may be judged" (Rossi & Freeman, 1989, p. 460); data may then be collected concerning the extent to which the project's reports served their intended purposes. When evaluation results are little used or unused it is important to identify barriers to satisfactory utilization. When barriers are identified, they can often be avoided or surmounted in future evaluation activities.

For example, an evaluation revealed serious weaknesses in the procedures yielding data on which television ratings were based and suggested more scientifically sound procedures (Tomlinson, 1992). The evaluators noted that some decisions involving thousands of dollars might have been different if a few participants had more faithfully pushed buttons on electronic measuring devices attached to their TV sets, or if samples had been different within expected margins of sampling error. Earlier practices continued nonetheless. Tomlinson (1992) delineated two major barriers to applying this project's results: (1) it was easier to continue existing practices, though flawed, than to change them; and (2) networks and advertisers disagreed about who should pay the costs of changes.

A second example is drawn from Ireland's (1992, pp. 56–58) account of political compromises in translating "what nutritional scientists actually know" into dietary guidelines issued by the U.S. Department of Agriculture (USDA). Although research results indicated that "lifestyle measures could reverse heart disease on a diet containing 10 percent of total calories from fat," the USDA recommended "no more than 30 percent of calories from dietary fat." The reasons for compromise included: (a) the influence of "the meat and dairy industries," (b) doubts that people would follow recommendations if they were "too extreme," and (c) concerns that current scientific knowledge was insufficient. Utilization evaluation of research on nutrition and health is not limited to USDA recommendations. Ireland (1992) noted that "consumers are beginning to demand more healthful products," and various nongovernment organizations are "spreading the latest nutritional information" (p. 63). This example establishes that **utilization evaluation** is not necessarily limited to program evaluation results per se but can be applied to all research findings. Discovering barriers to utilization may be part of a context evaluation project for purposes of planning a new program or changing an existing one.

Utilization evaluation can involve a formal research process in and of itself or no more than an informal follow-up contact between evaluators and decision-makers. When evaluation is being conducted continuously or recurrently, this follow-up contact can be carried out as part of planning for the next cycle of program evaluation activity. Whether done as part of planning or separately, utilization evaluation often yields important information so that future plans can continue earlier effective strategies and change less effective ones. For example, if an evaluation report arrived too late to help decision-makers as intended, future plans can provide for more timely reports. As a second example, evaluation reports sometimes contain recommendations inconsistent with commitments decision-makers have agreed to after the evaluation study was planned. In such cases, future plans can provide for keeping evaluators better informed of decision-makers' agreements.

Utilization evaluation has a role even in one-shot program evaluation projects with no future plans that utilization information might improve. Knowing the extent to which an evaluation project's results were used and identifying any barriers to better utilization help evaluators improve their skills. Analogously, a counselor who experiences a failure with one client can carefully examine the relationship with that client and identify barriers to more effective work. This process often enhances the counselor's skills, permitting more effective work with future clients.

Chapter Summary

Evaluation addressed to questions of a program's own operating process and its outcomes or results may be carried out to serve internal decision making (feedback) or to influence decisions by others (accountability). One program may evaluate another so officials can make decisions about the relationship between them. Evaluation activity may be carried out one time only, recurrently, or continuously. Program utility assessment (outcome or product evaluation) includes impact, cost–benefit, and cost-effectiveness evaluations. To fulfill its mission, an evaluation project must be reported to the receivers who will use its results, and it must contain information these consumers need. The report's timing, media, and style should be well chosen to maximize chances that it will be accepted and used. Follow-up data concerning use of one project's results (utilization evaluation) often helps researchers and practitioners plan future evaluation activities more effectively.

Practical Exercises

1. Suppose that the Department of Health and Human Services has expended $3 million in grant funds for programs offering counseling services for weight control. Each funded program has now been operating for one year, and the department needs to decide which ones, if any, should be refunded for an additional year. You have been told that the department is particularly interested in refunding programs that have had the greatest impact on their clientele. You are the counselor in charge

of one of the programs. What data would you have collected this past year to prepare your application for refunding?

2. In practical exercise 5 at the end of Chapter 3, a community counseling clinic operated by a university was described. Drawing on the discussion of process evaluation in Chapter 4 and the flowchart in Figure 4.1, outline how that clinic might monitor its activities to get feedback about its daily operation.

3. Read the following description of a study conducted by Coursey, Ward-Alexander, and Katz (1980) examining alternative methods of providing insurance benefits to mentally ill persons. Does this study represent cost–benefit analysis, cost-effectiveness analysis, or both? Justify your answer by indicating which kind of data collected represents either or both approaches.

   Thirty-two hospitalized mentally ill persons were released to halfway houses and provided with 120 days of insurance benefits. (Prior to the study, insurance benefits were only available while patients were hospitalized.) Data collected during 14 months of halfway house treatment were compared to data collected for the same individuals during the 42 prior months. The researchers found no significant deterioration among patients after hospital release except for an increase in somatization. Further, (a) the cost of placement in a halfway house was only 59% that of hospitalization, (b) only 29% of patients were returned to the hospital as opposed to 79% who had required more than one hospitalization during the previous 42 months, and (c) the mean length of hospitalization per year per patient decreased from 83 to 18 days for a 78% reduction in hospital costs.

4. Imagine that you are one of the researchers who conducted the evaluation project described in practical exercise #3. The project has just been completed, and it is time to report the results. The various stakeholder groups interested in the findings include the insurance company providing benefits, the owners of the halfway houses, the patients, and the staff of the hospital. In addition, you wish to prepare a formal report of the findings for publication in a professional journal. What issues will you consider when preparing reports that are acceptable to these diverse groups?

5. Imagine that you are the principal investigator for a large, grant-funded high school dropout prevention project. One of your responsibilities in that role is to prepare quarterly reports for the Department of Education. Each quarterly report must provide data on several topics of interest to the Department of Education, including the number of students from your project who remain in high school. You have been told that your next report must focus on accountability evaluation. What kinds of information will you provide the Department of Education? Use examples specific to this kind of project.

CHAPTER FIVE

ETHICAL RESEARCH PRACTICES

Questions to Guide Your Reading

The Social Context of Ethical Research Practices

1. What trends in the larger society have required counselors and researchers to give increasing attention to the ethical aspects of their work?
2. What individual rights are recognized by the laws of the United States and its political subdivisions? What limits these rights?
3. How have counseling and research relationships come to be viewed differently in recent decades?
4. What ethical standards documents are most relevant to counselors?
5. Who bears the ultimate responsibility for ethical behavior in a given research situation?

Setting Priorities

6. What are the arguments for and against conducting research in a service setting?
7. How can informal cost–benefit analysis be helpful in making decisions about whether or not to conduct research?
8. When the role of counselor conflicts with that of researcher, which role is generally given higher priority?
9. How might counselor-researchers resolve conflicting or competing demands between their employment situation and their professional ethical duties?

Protecting Participants from Harm

10. How can informal cost–benefit analysis be helpful in determining what risk of harm to clients is acceptable in a research setting?
11. What precautionary steps should be taken so that research subjects are exposed to a minimum of discomfort, harm, and danger?
12. What is meant by the term *debriefing*?
    a. What situations require debriefing?
    b. When might debriefing be delayed?
13. What is meant by the term *remediation*? When might remediation be necessary as part of a research project?

Informed Consent

14. What rights of individuals must researchers protect according to the principle of informed consent?
15. What steps should be followed to ensure informed consent?
16. For what kinds of projects is informed consent probably not necessary?
17. What is a free agent adult?
18. What special considerations must be taken into account when obtaining consent from children or from adults with diminished capacity?
19. What procedures should researchers follow when they wish to obtain information about participants from third parties?

20. Why is it sometimes not advisable to obtain consent before participation begins?
21. What kind of information do participants need to help them make decisions about whether to grant or withhold consent?
22. What are the pros and cons of seeking written versus oral consent?
23. How should a written consent form be constructed?
24. What kinds of situations are likely to result in coercion rather than free consent?
25. What conditions must instructors meet to defend the ethics of a class requirement that students participate in research as subjects?
26. What are the limits to confidentiality in research settings?

Professional Competence
27. What safety precautions help ensure that counselors do not exceed the limits of their competence in research settings?

Reporting Research Projects
28. What problems arise when reported results tenuously rather than strongly support inferences that have significant implications for practice?
29. What kinds of circumstances have led some researchers to compromise their integrity?
30. How might responsible administrators shape researchers' work environments to promote integrity?
31. How can a cost–benefit perspective be useful in deciding whether to report findings that might be misused by consumers?
32. When several researchers have worked together on a project, how should they decide in what order to list their names as authors?

Social Consequences of Research Projects
33. What kinds of research projects are likely to lead to controversy? How should researchers deal with such controversy?

THE SOCIAL CONTEXT OF ETHICAL RESEARCH PRACTICES

For the past several decades, both counselors and researchers have been required to give increasing attention to the ethical aspects of their endeavors. The increasing attention to ethical issues by counselors and other professionals appears to be part of ongoing trends in the larger society toward increasing recognition of individual rights, increasing demands for accountability, and changing views of counseling and research.

People have rights as citizens, customers, employees, students, and parents, and in many other life roles. The laws of the United States and its political subdivisions explicitly or implicitly recognize a number of individual rights, including:

- *self-determination*—the right to decide for themselves what they will do and what is to happen to them;
- *privacy*—the right to choose what information to disclose and what to withhold about themselves, their activities, and their communications with others;
- *freedom from harm*—the right not to be harmed by the activities of others; and
- *fair treatment*—the right to be treated honestly and equitably.

Any one individual has all of these rights, but they are limited to an extent by the rights of others. For example, employers' freedom to hire and fire at will is limited by applicants' and employees' rights to fair treatment. Rights are further limited if an individual lacks the capacity to exercise them responsibly. Children's self-determination is limited by parental authority because children are judged less able than adults to use that freedom responsibly. Parents who abuse their children, however, are likely to lose some of their rights of self-determination based on the court's judgment that such parents cannot use this freedom responsibly and that the children have a right not to be harmed.

People with professional or official authority have responsibilities to observe the rights of individuals. Professionals have always been accountable to higher authorities, and they are now increasingly accountable also to those over whom they have authority and to their peers. For example, university faculty are accountable not only to their deans and department chairpersons but also to their students and colleagues.

Both counseling and research relationships have come to be viewed differently than they were in earlier decades. Fewer people expect counselors to know what is best for their clients. Instead, the counselor and the client usually join together in a process of exploration and growth. The people from whom research data are collected no longer have a role analogous to inanimate specimens being manipulated and examined as the researcher sees fit. Rather, they are participants (APA, 1992) with the researcher in an activity designed to produce knowledge: a "granting agency . . . granting researchers time instead of money" (Blanck, Bellack, Rosnow, Rotheram-Borus, & Schooler, 1992, p. 963).

Ethics and Professional Organizations

The rights of **clients,** colleagues, research **participants,** and research **consumers** confer certain responsibilities on counselors and researchers. So do the rights and responsibilities of people who financially and administratively support the work of counselors and researchers. To meet these responsibilities, counselors and researchers must do much more than comply with applicable law.

Counseling and research frequently require decisions in complex situations characterized by many interconnecting and possibly conflicting loyalties and commitments. A counselor conducting an externally funded research project in a community mental health agency serves as an example. This counselor-researcher's several roles involve responsibilities to a number of people, as summarized in Table 5.1.

Various professional organizations and certifying bodies have produced ethical standards documents designed to help counselors and researchers with this decision making. The ethical standards most immediately relevant to most counselors are those published by the American Counseling Association (1988, formerly the American Association for Counseling and Development). Other ethical standards documents exist, however, that may also be relevant depending on a counselor's field of specialization (for example, those published by the American Association of Marriage and Family Therapists, 1991). For a more complete list of organizations that publish ethics documents, see Appendix C of this book.

Projects supported with federal funds are legally required to observe provisions of the Family Educational Rights and Privacy Act (Buckley Amendment) and other federal rules related to privacy such as the Code of Federal Regulations, Title 45, Subtitle A, Part 46. Agencies receiving federal funds for rehabilitation of people dependent on alcohol or other drugs must observe confidentiality standards more restrictive than those that apply to most other federally funded programs (Blume, 1987; Royce, 1989). And states have various laws and regulations affecting research activities conducted within their borders. Professional ethical standards provide that counselors and researchers must comply with legal requirements pertaining to them.

Some professional organizations have standing ethics committees that offer consultation to members and regularly examine their ethics documents to decide whether revisions are needed. The Committee on Standards in Research of the American Psychological Association monitors and discusses emerging ethical issues (Grisso et al., 1991). Many large organizations that provide counseling services or fund research projects have ethics **review committees** that evaluate research proposals before granting financial support or permission to carry out a project. Research planners must seek to resolve "unclear" ethical issues through consultation (APA, 1992, Standard 6.06). However, consultation and review committee approval do not replace individual researchers' ethical responsibilities.

All ethical standards documents known to us explicitly state or implicitly follow the principle that an individual bears the ultimate moral responsibility for his or her own behavior. Individual counselors bear responsibility for ethical counseling practice; individual researchers bear responsibility for ethical research practice. Counseling practitioners who carry out research have ethical responsibilities both as counselors and as researchers. Some ethical issues important in studies of counseling are common to research

T A B L E   5.1
Summary of Counselor-Researcher Roles and People to Whom Responsible

In the role of:	Counselor-researcher is responsible to:
Counselor	Own clients
Representative of agency	Own clients
	Other counselors' clients
	Third parties (for example, insurance carriers) who fund agency services
	Other agencies from which referrals are received
	Community with which agency is affiliated
Researcher	Own clients
	Other counselors' clients
	Other counselors in the agency
	Other persons who may participate in a project
	Readers of project's reports
Employee	Professional and administrative supervisors
Professional colleague	Fellow counselors in and outside the agency
	Other members of own professional organizations
Provider of paid services	Research project's funding source
	Insurance carriers who fund agency services
	Sources from which agency receives referrals
License/certificate holder	Bodies issuing licenses and certificates held

Note: This list is not exhaustive.

on human behavior generally. Additional ethical issues become important when the same people have a counselor-client relationship and a research relationship simultaneously.

SETTING PRIORITIES

A counselor-researcher has two roles in relation to clients who are also research participants, that of counselor and that of researcher. In some contexts, these roles are complicated by administrative responsibilities. In state rehabilitation agencies, for example, counselors conduct the first steps in the approval process for rehabilitation plans. In addition, counselor-researcher responsibilities include collecting and analyzing data according to a research plan. The demands of these various roles can lead to concern regarding setting priorities, allocating resources (Hadley, 1972), and conflicting and competing obligations. The best research plans permit fulfilling all these obligations. Sometimes this joint fulfillment is not possible, however, and compromises must be made.

Allocating Resources

To be or not to be both counselor and researcher? This question faces individual counselors and counseling agencies alike. How much of the available human and economic resources should be allocated to service versus research? When resources are limited, conducting research usually means offering less service than you otherwise might, at least temporarily. On the other hand, not conducting research often means continuing to offer the same services in the same old way without benefit of the knowledge research could provide along with the consequent opportunities to improve services.

Ethical standards of the American Counseling Association (1988) require counselors to "maintain the highest levels of professional services offered to the individuals to be served" (Standard A2), to try to "improve professional practices, teaching, services, and research" (Standard A1), and to "gather data on their effectiveness and be guided by the findings" (Standard A1). What is a counselor to do when available human and financial resources are insufficient to support all these activities? "In the time it takes to do . . . research, agency personnel can be seeing clients, producing income, or reducing waiting lists" (Meara, 1990, p. 68). None of the ethical standards documents we examined addresses this question.

One approach to such decisions is based on the cost–benefit idea developed in Chapter 4. A counselor can apply informal cost–benefit analysis when deciding whether to conduct a research project. Is the project likely to yield results that justify allocating to it the required resources, perhaps depriving other people or activities of these resources? Such decisions are similar to those most of us make daily as professionals and as citizens: How do we best use available time, space, energy, property, and money?

Evaluating Conflicting Obligations

As noted earlier in this chapter, a person who conducts both research and counseling activities incurs ethical obligations stemming from both roles. A research plan that permits both sets of obligations to be fulfilled without compromising either is a goal well worth the considerable effort it often requires. When it is not possible to fulfill both goals, we generally give the highest priority to a counselor-researcher's duties as a counselor.

Some planned projects must be abandoned as ethically infeasible. More often, a researcher can acceptably fulfill both the project's mission and the ethical requirements for the project by changing the research approach or details of the research plan. For example, a study of client reactions to overt sexual advances from counselors could not use an experimental approach deliberately subjecting clients to such experiences. However, a survey might locate present and former clients who say they have experienced this unethical behavior from their counselors; these clients could be asked to report their reactions.

Although it is not ethically feasible to determine experimentally whether overt sexual advances by counselors caused their clients' reported reactions, it may be feasible to find out what their reported reactions are and what the clients believe the causes to be. As a second example, it would be unethical to use suicidal clients as subjects in an experiment to study the effects of offering versus refusing services on client outcome. Emergency cases should be deleted from studies requiring delay or refusal of services. These clients should be served without restrictions from the research plan. The resultant sampling bias is an acceptable price to pay for fulfillment of a counseling agency's obligation to serve such clients.

As a third example, English (1987) compromised the methodological rigor of her single-subject experiment by beginning an intervention earlier than the ideal time for her research plan. She made this choice because the subject was an employee at risk of losing her job because of inappropriate social behavior in the workplace. Any delay would have substantially increased this risk. Further, this subject had an emotional disability, and the employer would probably have become less willing to hire people with similar disabilities if this employee were to be discharged for her behavior.

Ethical standards of the American Counseling Association (ACA) (1988, Standard A2) and the American Psychological Association (APA) (1992, Standard 8.03) both address the possibility that an employing organization might demand unethical behavior from a practitioner. Based on both documents, we offer the following recommendations to counselors-researchers in this situation:

- Adopt the goal of seeking resolution to the conflict by finding an ethically acceptable way to meet the legitimate needs of all concerned.
- "Clarify the nature of the conflict" (APA, 1992, Standard 8.03) between the organization's demands and professional ethical requirements.
- Assert your personal commitment to the ethical standards of your profession.
- "If, despite concerted efforts," you "cannot reach agreement . . ., then terminating the affiliation should be seriously considered" (ACA, 1988, A2).

As a case in point, a management executive asked an employee assistance program (EAP) director to reveal the names of the individual employees represented in a routine program evaluation report. The EAP director knew management was reducing the company's work force and suspected that EAP clients would be selected for termination if they were identified. The EAP director refused, asserting his obligation to respect EAP client confidentiality. The EAP director vigorously sought an ethically acceptable resolution. The executive was nonetheless adamant. The EAP director thus resigned, leaving the clients' names in locked files to which he kept the key. A short time later, the executive also was working elsewhere. We suggest that scenarios such as this can often be avoided if the written employment contract of any counselor or researcher includes responsibility to comply with professional ethical standards.

An additional source of possible ethical conflict is the large number of organizations representing different counseling specialties that independently issue ethical standards. Many individuals belong to several organizations. We have found no specific points on which ethical standards of various counseling specialties require incompatible behavior, though some standards are more lenient than others on the same points. However, an increasing number of specialty organizations, each with its own set of standards, increases the likelihood that such a conflict will eventually develop. When it does, we suggest that affected individuals call the conflict to the attention of the organizations involved and work through them toward a resolution.

PROTECTING PARTICIPANTS FROM HARM

Counselors and researchers have a responsibility to observe the rights of clients and research participants not to be harmed (APA, 1992, Standards 1.14, 6.06b, 6.13, 6.18c). An earlier document develops some of the underlying ideas more fully:

> The investigator protects the participant from physical and mental discomfort, harm and danger. If risks of such consequences exist, the investigator informs the participant of that fact. Research procedures likely to cause serious and lasting harm to a participant are not used unless failure to use these procedures might expose the participant to greater harm or unless the research has great potential benefit and fully informed and voluntary consent is obtained from each participant. (APA, 1990, p. 395)*

This issue is much more complex than it may seem at first reading. Among related questions are:

- What degrees of discomfort, harm, and danger deserve attention?
- Must all projects involving risk of discomfort, harm, and danger be disallowed, or are there circumstances under which it is ethically justified to expose participants to these risks?
- If such risks are deliberately accepted during planning or discovered while a project is under way, what are the researcher's responsibilities?

The first of these questions is the one least discussed in the ethics documents we reviewed. Short of "likely to cause serious and lasting harm," it is entirely a matter of judgment how serious these risks must be to merit a researcher's attention. We believe most researchers would agree that

---

*APA cautions that this document is no longer current.

deliberate administration of pain warrants their attention as an ethical issue, while few would give much thought to the risks and discomforts to participants from driving their automobiles through heavy traffic to the research site. To researchers who find this decision difficult, we suggest consultation with professional colleagues or institutional research review committees.

To address questions of justifiability and the researcher's responsibilities, we suggest that researchers undertake an informal cost-benefit analysis, institute precautionary steps to minimize risks to participants, provide on-site debriefing for participants at completion of the project, and include remediation counseling in the project plan to address undesirable consequences that may result from participation. Throughout these processes, participants' privacy and confidentiality must be protected.

Cost–Benefit Analysis

This principle was developed in Chapter 4 and applied earlier in this chapter to allocation of resources issues. The same idea can be applied to decisions concerning what risks of discomfort, harm, and danger to participants are acceptable. Some research likely to yield important human benefits cannot be carried out without such risks. Many examples can be found among studies of physical and mental stress. These risks are ethically acceptable only when all of these conditions are met:

- the anticipated risks have been carefully considered with regard to the probability, intensity, and expected duration of any uncomfortable or harmful effects;
- the benefits expected from the project are judged to be sufficient to justify exposing participants to the anticipated risks; and
- after concerted efforts to seek alternative approaches and procedures, the anticipated risks are judged necessary to achieve these benefits.

Precautionary Steps to Limit Risks

To fulfill researchers' responsibilities to "implement appropriate protections for the rights and welfare of human participants" (APA, 1992, Standard 6.06), plans for any project that exposes participants to risks of discomfort, harm, and danger should provide steps to minimize these risks. Some examples of such precautionary steps are:

- screening out susceptible participants (APA, 1982),* such as children in a study administering pain, people with heart disease in a study

---

*APA cautions that the guidelines and information contained in the 1973 and 1982 *Ethical Principles in the Conduct of Research with Human Participants* are not enforceable as such by the APA Ethics Code of 1992 but may be of educative value to researchers, courts, and professional bodies.

evoking strong emotional stress, and alcoholics in a study administering alcohol;

- ensuring that any equipment used to administer uncomfortable stimuli, such as electric shocks, is functioning properly;
- ensuring that people administering research procedures are thoroughly trained in the use of any equipment involved and in dealing with emergencies that might result from participants' unusual reactions to their experience; and
- avoiding the creation of more discomfort or danger than necessary to achieve the project's mission (for example, if a moderate level of stress will suffice, a higher level should not be evoked).

Privacy and Confidentiality

Within limits, people have the right to choose whether to disclose or withhold information about themselves and their activities. This right affects research in two ways: the kinds of information a researcher should ask for from participants and the ways the information is handled after it has been collected.

Certain kinds of information are customarily regarded as more private than others. For example, to ask casually about someone's intelligence scores, religious views, or sexual practices is usually considered an invasion of privacy; to ask "How are you today?" is not. Researchers need to take such customs into account when planning projects. If the research mission requires asking participants for information commonly regarded as private, participants need to clearly understand both the importance of this information for the project and their right to withhold the information if they so choose, even if doing so means withdrawing from the project. If participants do not clearly understand the importance of any requested private information, they will likely feel offended that their privacy is being invaded. If participants do not clearly understand their right to withhold this information, the researcher is intentionally or inadvertently practicing coercion.

Because much research in counseling concerns experiences, behavior, and personal information often considered private, the privacy issue should be routinely considered in planning each project. Researchers should never ask participants for information customarily considered private unless it is essential to the project's mission, although such disclosures are quite common in counseling. Counselor-researchers need to keep these two roles clearly in mind and help their clients avoid confusing what is asked of them as counseling clients with what is asked of them as research participants.

Both counselors and researchers have a responsibility to prevent unauthorized disclosure of information about clients and research participants.

> Counseling records are to be considered professional information for use in counseling, . . . not . . . records of the institution in which the counselor

is employed unless specified by state statute or regulation. Revelation to others of counseling material must occur only upon the expressed consent of the client. Researchers have a responsibility to take due care so that participants can not be individually identified unless their specific authorization to do otherwise has been obtained (ACA, 1988, B-5, D-10). [This authorization must be in writing (APA, 1992, Standard 5.08).]

Many research projects draw data from counseling records. To do so creates no **confidentiality** problem if counseling staff, who routinely have access to these records, enter the data into research records with all possibility of identifying individuals deleted. One common method is to replace individual names with code numbers; a list linking names with numbers is maintained in a separate locked file accessible only to counseling staff. Except when the research plan requires identifying individuals, numbers that might permit doing so, such as Social Security numbers or institutional identifying numbers, should not be used.

In some projects, people who handle the data need to be able to identify individual participants. For example, it might be necessary to arrange second appointments with participants who gave certain kinds of responses in their first session. If counseling clients are also research participants and people other than counseling staff will be able to link them individually with their data, informed consent to this process is required.

Clients and participants have a right to know the limits to confidentiality. For example, courts have the authority to require researchers' testimony in trials and to issue subpoenas requiring them to disclose information. In one instance, researchers anticipating such a requirement divested themselves of the list linking individual names with code numbers. They sent it to a colleague in a foreign country for safekeeping, despite risk of contempt proceedings (APA, 1973, p. 93). When data collection is complete and it is no longer necessary to link individuals with the data, the safest procedure is to destroy any list that does so.

Appelbaum and Rosenbaum (1989) raised an additional issue related to confidentiality and informed consent. To what extent do researchers have a duty to protect potential victims when data lead to a reasonable prediction that a research participant will likely commit violence? In some such cases, strict confidentiality can be maintained only at considerable risk of harm to third parties. In others, it is possible to intervene constructively without breaching confidentiality. If a participant is also the researcher's counseling or psychotherapy client, the duty to protect third parties may be specified by statute or case law in the location where the project is taking place. In 1976, the California Supreme Court decided in the *Tarasoff* case that psychotherapists have a duty to take "whatever steps are reasonably necessary to protect potential victims of their patients' violent acts" (Appelbaum & Rosenbaum, 1989, p. 885). Subsequently, many other U.S. jurisdictions have imposed a similar duty on mental health workers.

To date, the courts have not held researchers to this obligation. Nonetheless, it is strongly recommended that researchers and institutional

review boards address this matter in planning. Appelbaum and Rosenbaum (1989) give two reasons for this recommendation. First, "professional associations' . . . ethics [permit] disclosures to be made to protect third parties in therapeutic and research contexts; ethical grounds alone [justify recommending that researchers] consider building provisions for the protection of potential victims into their protocols" (p. 889). Second, future court actions may hold researchers to such duties. Because such actions may come at any time, to overlook this possibility when planning a project risks having to weaken it by making changes after it is under way. Researchers studying populations at high risk of violence, such as violent criminals or parents who have abused their children, can expect that from time to time they will need to act to protect third parties. Though other researchers expect to face this need less frequently, the duty to protect issue deserves the attention of all researchers studying humans.

Debriefing Participants

After data are collected, the investigator provides participants with

> a prompt opportunity . . . to obtain information about the nature of the study and ... attempt[s] to remove any misconceptions that participants may have.... If scientific or humane values justify delaying or withholding this information, [the investigator must] take reasonable measures to reduce the risk of harm. (APA, 1992, Standard 6.18)

Debriefing should be conducted before participants leave the research setting whenever data collection procedures involve any of these features:

- withholding important information,
- deceiving participants (providing misinformation),
- evoking strong emotional reactions, or
- evoking self-doubt or reduced self-esteem.

Of particular concern are procedures that might lead participants to base life decisions or long-term emotional reactions on false impressions elicited during the project. For example, one project induced stress by giving college students false feedback that they were not intelligent enough to be in college (APA, 1973, p. 84). It is easy to recognize the risk that some students might decide to withdraw from college based on such misinformation.

In some projects the research mission might be best served by delaying debriefing beyond the time participants leave the data collection setting. For example, early participants in a study on a small college campus might discuss the project with classmates, reducing the effectiveness of the procedure with later participants. As a second example, some projects call for several sessions with the same participants on different days. Rather than maintain false impressions under such circumstances, a researcher should consider changing the design or abandoning the project. Whenever debriefing is required, it should not be delayed. If a participant chooses to leave the project prematurely after experiencing a procedure that requires debriefing, a debriefing session should be conducted immediately.

When planning the debriefing procedure and the project of which it is a part, researchers need to recognize that the experience of being misled or deceived often elicits feelings of embarrassment, resentment, anger, mistrust, and loss of self-esteem. These feelings may be directed toward the researcher, the project, the institution, the researcher's profession in general, research in general, or any combination of these. It is the researcher's responsibility to all these potential targets to minimize the risk that such reactions might persist beyond the debriefing session. The best means of doing so is often an alternative design that permits full disclosure at the beginning of the project; a debriefing session may then become unnecessary.

Debriefing is sometimes conducted individually, sometimes in a group. The process should include informing participants that help is available to cope with long-term aftereffects if any are experienced.

Remediation

"Reasonable steps to implement appropriate protections for . . . participants" (APA, 1992, Standard 6.06) include provisions to correct undesirable consequences participants may experience from research procedures. Continuing counseling or psychotherapy may need to be made available at no cost in some instances, such as studies in which strong emotional reactions are elicited or in which participants' experiences bring to their attention undesirable personal qualities. For example, Milgram's (1963) participants knew they had obeyed instructions to administer painful electric shocks to another person, although they learned through debriefing that the victim was the experimenter's accomplice and experienced no shocks. Participants felt "extraordinary tension" (p. 377) during the experiment. Debriefing included "procedures . . . to assure that the subject would leave the laboratory in a state of well-being. A friendly reconciliation was arranged between the subject and the victim, and an effort was made to reduce any tensions that arose as a result of the experiment" (p. 374). Because deliberately inflicting pain conflicts with many people's personal values, some participants might have later experienced emotional turmoil in response to their behavior during the experiment. Milgram's (1963) report describes no provisions for responding to this possibility; ethical standards at that time did not explicitly require such provisions. In contrast, the American Counseling Association's (1993) ethical standards draft requires counselor-researchers to "detect and remove or correct" undesirable consequences for participants, "including where relevant, long-term aftereffects" (p. 22).

INFORMED CONSENT

Participants need to understand the risks involved in their participation, to accept these risks freely without coercion, and to be free to discontinue their participation at any time. In some projects that have been carried out, the researchers believed their research goals justified deceiving participants or withholding information participants needed to make an informed decision to participate. Other writers have criticized these practices as unethically violating participants' rights. **Informed consent** is based primarily on the right of self-determination, which requires that research participation be voluntary. Informed consent means individuals have the right to:

- decide for themselves whether or not to participate in any given project;
- have sufficient information about the project and the probable consequences of participating in it to make a sound decision in their own interests; and
- discontinue their participation after having begun, if they so choose.

To the extent possible, participants have a right to base this decision on accurate information.

According to Bersoff (1978) and the American Counseling Association (1993), prospective participants need a "fair explanation of the purpose and procedures to be followed," including identification of any procedures that are "experimental" (in the sense of being relatively untried, *not* in the sense of being an experimental treatment in the project's design). Any "attendant discomforts and risks" and any "benefits or changes in individuals or organizations that might reasonably be expected" should be described. The researcher should disclose any "appropriate alternative procedures that may be advantageous" to the participant and offer to answer any inquiries concerning the procedures. Prospective participants should be instructed that they are "free to withdraw their consent and to discontinue participating in the project at any time" (ACA, 1993, p. 21).

Informed consent may be regarded as a complex family of issues rather than a single issue. Related issues include:

- Do all projects require informed consent?
- Whose consent is required?
- When should consent be sought?
- What information about the project must client-participants have to protect their rights?
- Does participation in the research project compromise the services clients are likely to receive?
- In what ways is information likely to bias clients' response to counseling?
- Should consent be obtained orally or in writing?
- Are clients entitled to counseling services whether or not they agree to participate in a research project?

- Does participation in the research project place clients' privacy and confidentiality at greater risk than if they did not participate?
- Does the organizational context in which the research takes place include features that limit participants' informed, autonomous decision making?
- How well will prospective participants understand the information presented in a contemplated procedure to request consent?
- Does a contemplated consent procedure ask for more time and effort from prospective participants than is warranted by the degree of protection it would afford them?

A Universal Requirement?

ACA standards state, "All research subjects must be informed of the purpose of the study except when withholding information or providing misinformation is essential to the investigation" (1988, p. 6). Diener and Crandall (1978) have argued that when research is entirely harmless and does not expose participants to risks or compromise their personal rights, mandatory consent is probably unrealistic and unnecessary. ACA standards include this same idea: "Involuntary consent is appropriate only when it can be demonstrated that participation will have no harmful effects on subjects and is essential to the investigation" (1988, p. 6). For example, a rehabilitation agency might examine files of closed cases for a correlational study to predict outcome from intake variables without trying to contact every former client individually to request consent. Before deciding consent is unnecessary, the researcher should first reach a considered judgment that the research does not place clients' privacy and confidentiality at additional risk beyond that which may already exist through their relationship with the agency.

Further, to request people's consent is to ask for their time and attention to consider and respond to the request. Researchers need to evaluate this demand in relation to the degree of protection a consent procedure will afford to participants. In the above example, we suspect the project posed so little risk to former clients' rights that many would have felt a request for consent was a waste of their time.

The following fictitious example, which closely parallels many experiments conducted in social psychology, illustrates the point that a request for consent may both seriously weaken the value of the data and introduce ethical issues of its own. Imagine an experiment taking place in a large international airport in which an actor hired for a research project asks passing strangers for the time. In the experimental condition, he adopts clothing and an accent associated with a politically controversial immigrant group. In the control condition, he wears ordinary clothes and uses unaccented speech. By counting floor tiles, an unobtrusive observer measures how closely each respondent approaches the actor. On the average, respondents approach the actor more closely in the control condition than in the feigned immigrant condition. It is easy to envision how an advance informed consent procedure would probably weaken such data.

Researchers conducting such studies judge that the knowledge to be gained from these projects justifies their momentary intrusion, without advance consent, into the lives of the people approached as potential respondents. Such researchers also assume that the deception and the lack of consent procedure pose no risk of harm to respondents. Regarding the airport project, we agree with these judgments, believing that leaving subjects with this deception would entail less risk of harm than asking them to take time for debriefing. The data provide no possibility that respondents could be identified later, their experience is well within bounds of what might be expected in such a public place, and a debriefing could make some of them late. This opinion is expressed by Diener and Crandall (1978):

> The investigator could scarcely justify waylaying people in a public place to describe a study that had little or no effect on their lives and of which they were totally unaware. (p. 39)

Decisions regarding consent and related procedures should never be made lightly, but only after careful thought. Photographing respondents in this fictitious project rather than counting floor tiles, for example, would increase the risk to privacy enough to be ethically questionable. "Applicable regulations and institutional review board requirements" (APA, 1992, Standard 6.12) need to be considered.

Must service agencies and schools secure informed consent from their clients and students before implementing and evaluating program changes? For example, schools may change their textbooks or teaching methods, or counseling agencies may change their intake and counseling procedures. When research procedures in such institutions exceed the bounds of reasonable variations in the normal program or the research requires participant data not normally collected for service purposes, participants have a right to know what is being asked of them and why and to grant or withhold their consent. Under such conditions, researchers have a responsibility to consider this right along with other ethical issues and the requirements of the research mission.

Is informed consent required in studies within such reasonable variations of the normal service program based on data ordinarily collected for service purposes? The American Counseling Association's (1988) and the American Psychological Association's (1992) ethical standards do not address this issue in such cases, although an earlier document (APA, 1982) stated: "there would seem to be no compelling case for insisting absolutely on the informed consent of the participants" in these circumstances (p. 39). As discussed in Chapters 3 and 4, schools, counseling agencies, and similar organizations often routinely collect data of considerable research value in the course of their service activities.

Whose Consent Is Required?

Much counseling research uses **free agent adult** participants (Keith-Spiegel, 1976). Free agent adults are of legal age and have the legal capacity to give or withhold consent on their own behalf. Except when otherwise evident, free agent adults are presumed to have the functional capacity to do so. With such participants, their own consent is usually sufficient. Consent becomes a more complex question when a project involves children or others whose diminished "physical, mental, legal, and social power" requires "special considerations" (Keith-Spiegel, 1976, pp. 54–55). These special considerations include the rights, responsibilities, and capabilities of the participants themselves and the people legally authorized to act on their behalf.

When participants are minors or otherwise "legally incapable of giving informed consent," a project that requires consent must "provide an appropriate explanation, . . . obtain the participant's assent, . . . [and] obtain appropriate consent from a legally authorized person, if such substitute consent is permitted by law" (APA, 1992, Standard 6.11).

Keith-Spiegel (1976) proposed securing consent from all participants old enough to give or withhold it, "even if they can only understand that they may refuse to participate" (p. 56). Even when a child's full understanding of information about a project is doubtful, a refusal to participate should be accepted without questioning its basis. She acknowledged that some participants may be lost because they refuse consent for "seemingly irrelevant reasons" but stressed that it is essential for participants "themselves to decide to enroll in a participatory system they have not designed for themselves" (p. 36). Only preverbal children need not be asked for their consent.

The same principles apply to adult participants with diminished capacities who are not free agents because of characteristics such as "institutionalization, physical illness, mental disability or the like" (Keith-Spiegel, 1976, p. 53). Consent, when required, must be obtained from whoever has legal authority to give it. Legal guardians must have sufficient information to support a wise decision. In addition, participants with sufficient capacity must have the opportunity to grant or withhold consent. Insofar as possible, researchers must provide potential participants with sufficient information, in a manner understandable to them, to support a wise decision.

When participants are children or adults with diminished capacity, securing the required consent does not fulfill the researchers' responsibilities to protect the rights of participants to the same extent as it does the rights of free agent adults. Parents and other legal guardians do not always act in the best interests of their minor children, as cases of child abuse and neglect repeatedly show. Nor do legal guardians of adults with diminished capacity always act in the best interests of their charges. Further, children cannot be assumed to have the same capacity as free agent adults to act in their own interests. Therefore, a researcher studying such populations has an added responsibility to protect participants' rights, particularly those pertaining to privacy, confidentiality, and freedom from harm and coercion.

An additional complication to the consent question arises when information about participants is sought from third parties, such as counselors, psychotherapists, teachers, employers, supervisors, friends, or neighbors. In such projects, the researcher should obtain from the person being studied consent to contact the intended informants, and then obtain each informant's informed consent. These informants, not only the persons studied, are participants.

As noted above, consent from participants with diminished capacity does not always sufficiently protect their "rights and welfare" (APA, 1992, Standard 6.06). For example, contact with employers was desirable in "a follow-up study of retarded adults" but was not included in the research plan "because in certain cases the informant would have learned for the first time of the subject's retarded status and institutional history" (APA, 1973, p. 34). In such situations, researchers have added responsibilities beyond securing the explicitly prescribed informed consent.

Informed consent must be secured not only from participants but also "from host institutions . . . prior to conducting research" (APA, 1992, Standard 6.09). Many such host institutions (for example, universities) have institutional review boards that are specifically charged with reviewing research projects conducted under their auspices to ensure that participants' rights are protected.

When to Seek Consent

Ordinarily, prospective participants are told about a project and asked for their consent before their participation begins. However, consent procedures introduced prior to participation can have a "range of complicating effects" in laboratory studies (Adair, Dushenko, & Lindsay, 1985). In some studies of counseling, an advance informed consent process is not desirable because it might adversely affect either the counseling service or the meaningfulness of the research results, or both.

When a troubled person asks a counselor for help, the counselor must address the client's concerns. Counselors are ethically obligated to provide quality service. Research is usually the counselor-researcher's agenda, not the client's. Delaying attention to a client's concerns to conduct a research consent procedure, which clients often see as an irrelevant formality, compromises quality of service. The extent of the compromise depends on many factors including the nature of the client's problem and the length and complexity of the consent process.

In addition, information given when requesting consent might affect clients' participation in counseling or their response to it. For example, if clients are told that their counselors' techniques are being assigned at random rather than based on professional judgment of what is best for the client's specific concerns, they might react to this information by participating less actively in counseling or expecting less benefit from it.

Any effect of advance information on client response to counseling influences not only the value of the service provided but also the value of the research results. Many researchers studying counseling process and outcome hope to apply the findings to later counseling services not introduced by research-oriented consent procedures. This generalizability is reduced if the counseling sessions studied have such introductory procedures, and the procedures influence clients' participation in counseling or their response to it.

When ethical obligations conflict with each other or with requirements for sound research, a researcher must find the best solution to the conflict. As noted earlier in this chapter, informed consent may not be necessary in projects that involve only "reasonable variations in the normal program of organizations" (APA, 1982, p. 39) with no special data collection procedures introduced for research purposes. In some projects, experimental conditions represent "reasonable variations in the normal program" even though clients are asked to complete a questionnaire or participate in a research interview after counseling is completed. Under such circumstances, it is satisfactory to proceed without consent for research until counseling is completed, and then request consent to participate in a data collection procedure.

Researchers need to consider carefully whether clients' participation in a project reduces their freedom to make choices regarding the services they are to receive or places their privacy at greater risk than if they did not participate. If involvement in a research project has either of these consequences, clients need to know and have the opportunity to grant or withhold consent before their participation begins. In some settings, a skilled receptionist is available who can inform clients about a project and request consent as part of an administrative intake process, freeing counselors to attend fully to their clients' concerns.

Needed Information

Prospective participants need to have the information that will enable them to make sound decisions whether to grant or withhold their consent to participate in a project. Prospective participants ordinarily need to know:

- the kinds of tasks they will be asked to do;
- the amount of time they will be asked to contribute;
- any risks of harm or substantial discomfort, either physical or psychological;
- reasons why the project is being conducted;
- rewards for their participation, if any; and
- planned uses for the data, including any risks to confidentiality.

In studies of counseling, clients need to know which tasks, time demands, and data analysis are part of the counseling relationship and which tasks are added for research purposes. Some limits to confidentiality are already present in the counseling situation (for example, counselors are legally required to report child abuse). Does participation in the research project increase risks to confidentiality? For example, the research plan might require that tape recordings or case records be kept longer or examined by more people than would be needed for counseling purposes alone.

Clients need to know whether or not they are entitled to counseling services if they do not consent to participate in research. If eligibility for counseling requires participation in the research project, clients need to be informed of this requirement at intake. Any who choose not to participate in the research should be referred elsewhere for service. If participation is not a requirement, clients should not be led to feel that they will be given better service if they agree to participate.

The information given needs to be understandable to participants. Often a researcher is aware of complex issues related to consent that are beyond participants' probable understanding. Researchers must decide what information participants need to protect their rights and what they will probably be able to understand. Perhaps researchers should consider participants' probable understanding more carefully than many do now; Stanley, Sieber, and Melton (1987) reported that "in general . . . comprehension of consent information is relatively poor" (p. 736).

Written or Oral Consent

When requesting consent, researchers must choose whether consent is to be given orally or in writing. Usually, either will satisfactorily protect participants' rights. Sometimes researchers ask for consent orally to create a less formal emotional atmosphere. However, it may be necessary to have consent in writing to provide for the counselor's or the agency's accountability. Occasionally, researchers are asked to respond to challenges concerning compliance with ethical standards, in which case a written record is necessary to prove that participants' consent was secured. Informed consent must be "appropriately documented" (APA, 1992, Standard 6.11); this documentation may take many forms ranging from an entry in the researcher's daily log to a formal written agreement signed by participant and researcher. The most appropriate form for any project depends on prevailing conditions.

Similarly, the information given in support of a request for consent may be given orally, in writing, or both. When the information is long or difficult to understand, a combination often works best, such as a one-page fact sheet supplemented by an oral explanation. When a written consent form is used, it must be short, clear, nonthreatening in appearance, and written in simple language. A generic example of a consent form useful for counseling research is reproduced in Appendix C.

Coercion

To be voluntary, consent must be secured without coercion; research participation must not be "an offer he can't refuse," as expressed in the *Godfather* films. Ethical researchers respect individuals' freedom to "decline to participate or to withdraw from the research" (APA, 1992, Standard 6.11). This freedom must not only be real but must be correctly perceived by the participants; researchers must "explain the foreseeable consequences of declining or withdrawing" (APA, 1992, Standard 6.11).

This principle requires special care when the researcher has a role of power in relation to the participant, such as counselor, professor, renowned expert, employer, military officer, or prison official. In this context, power refers to more than the authority to command or the capacity to administer tangible rewards or punishments. People also have power if you hold them in high regard, if you greatly value their opinion of yourself, or if you believe you should do as they ask. It is coercive to create a false impression that research participation is a job assignment or to imply that refusal to participate will lead to diminished regard from one or more persons with power. If participation in research is a job requirement, employees should understand this fact at the time of hiring.

Coercion does not necessarily represent the researcher's intention. Some organizational contexts in which research takes place include features that limit participants' informed, autonomous decision making. Robinson and Gross (1986) noted that hierarchical organizations, such as are common in business and industry, often do so. "Employees are often required to participate . . . because they are employees of the organization" (pp. 331–332). Counselors' freedom to approach these people as individuals may be severely limited. Researchers must "take special care to protect the prospective participants from adverse consequences of declining or withdrawing from participation" (APA, 1992, Standard 6.11). These observations hold even more strongly in penal, hospital, and military settings. An earlier document offers additional detail:

> The safeguard of ethical consultation to protect the interests of the participants [is] especially important. . . . The coercive implications of the power relationship between participant and staff [require] exceptional care in protecting the participants' interests. [The idea] that prisoners and patients should be required to cooperate in therapeutic or corrective programs . . . and, by extension, in research toward improving the program . . . is too readily available as a rationalization for exploitation" (APA, 1982, pp. 45–46).

Counselors are also responsible for not compromising the quality of their service as a reaction to clients' refusal to participate in research. This requirement is sometimes difficult to meet, especially when the counselor-researcher has strong feelings about a project. For example, a client's withheld consent might imperil timely completion of a thesis on which a job opportunity depends. Such situations are similar to others in which counselors' emotional reactions place quality of service at risk (for example, a counselor strongly dislikes a client's political stand or style of dress). A counselor's responsibility is not to be unfeeling or superhumanly immune to influence from his or her emotions but to be aware of such reactions and to provide the best service he or she can. When such emotional bias is extreme, this "best service" might be referral to another counselor.

Some university courses require students to participate as subjects in research. The ethical merits of this practice have been vigorously debated. Supporters contend that research participation has learning value for students and contributes to scientific knowledge. Critics contend that requiring students to participate in research is self-serving on the part of faculty and coercively exploits student efforts. The APA (1992, Standard 6.11d) requires that such "prospective participant[s be] given the choice of equitable alternative activities." An earlier document includes this idea and some additional conditions (APA, 1982, pp. 47–48):

- "Students are informed about the research requirement before they enroll," including such details as "amount of participation required," kinds of projects among which a student may choose, "the right . . . to drop out of a given research project at any time without penalty," and such consequences as "benefits . . . to be gained from participation" and "any penalties for failure to complete the requirement or for nonappearance after agreeing to take part."
- "Prior approval of research proposals," sometimes by a single faculty member but more often by a departmental committee or institutional review board, ensures that participation has learning value for the students and that their rights as participants are protected.
- "Before beginning participation, the student receives a description of the procedures . . . and is reminded of the option to drop out later without penalty. . . . Participation in any teacher's own research project should be optional for all students."
- Participants are "treated with respect and courtesy."
- "There is a mechanism by which students may report any mistreatment"; for example, one might inform the instructor, the department chair, or an ethics committee.
- "The recruiting procedure is under constant review," based on data such as "assessments of student attitudes toward the requirement . . . obtained at the end of each course having such a requirement each time the course is offered" and investigators' "evaluations of the workability of the procedures."

It is common practice to offer incentives to research participants, although such incentives must not be "excessive or inappropriate" (APA, 1992, Standard 6.14). The boundary between ethically acceptable incentives and coercive ones has been much debated. For example, few would question the acceptability of sending participants a report of the project's results. Under most circumstances, paying participants for their time would also be considered appropriate. However, the issue becomes more controversial when prospective participants are in dire financial need such as "a prisoner without money" who "might agree to participate in a hazardous experiment for a very small sum." Under such conditions, which is to be ethically preferred (APA, 1982, p. 43), "exploitation of the prisoner's special situation" or "diminishing the prisoner's freedom by withholding the opportunity"? Two major factors to be considered are the strength of the participant's need for the offered incentive and the degree of discomfort or risk incurred by participating in the project.

PROFESSIONAL COMPETENCE

Ethical standards (ACA 1988, A1, A4, B15) require counselors to:

- recognize their boundaries of competence;
- provide only those services and use only those techniques for which they are qualified by training and experience;
- accept only positions for which they are professionally qualified;
- neither claim nor imply professional qualifications "exceeding those possessed";
- "influence the development of the profession by continuous efforts to improve professional practices, services and research"; and
- clearly indicate to prospective recipients any experimental treatments and follow safety precautions. (In this context, *experimental* refers to new and relatively untried methods, not to "experimental treatments" versus "control conditions" as discussed in Chapter 2 and elsewhere.

Despite these warnings, however, counselors are clearly expected to try out new methods or techniques to expand not only their own skills but also the knowledge on which professional counseling practice is based. When considering a new technique, become informed about the technique before you employ it. If it has been discussed in the professional literature, read enough about it that you understand the kinds of experiences other workers have had with this technique. Such literature review should routinely be included in research planning regardless of its value as a safety precaution. If you don't find the technique reported in the literature, discuss it with knowledgeable fellow professionals. Perhaps your idea contains components that have been tried by others. Perhaps a method you thought was experimental really isn't. Consult with other knowledgeable professionals who are familiar with your work concerning your own skills to carry out the techniques you plan to use.

The requirement to stay within your area of competence applies not only to counseling techniques and experimental procedures but also to measurement methods. With regard to standardized tests, the American Educational Research Association (1985, Standard 6.6) stated:

> Responsibility for test use should be assumed by or delegated only to those individuals who have the training and experience necessary to handle this responsibility in a professional and technically adequate manner. Any special qualifications for test administration or interpretation noted in the manual should be met.

Sometimes a project includes a test, counseling technique, or other procedure with which the principal investigator or project director is underskilled. In such instances, responsibility for this test or procedure can be delegated to another member of the research team who has the necessary competence. This responsibility extends throughout all phases of the project, from formulating the contribution this test or procedure makes to the project's mission through preparing the final report.

REPORTING RESEARCH PROJECTS

After having conducted a study, should the findings be reported? If so, when, how, and where? These questions also have ethical aspects. Related issues include the usefulness of findings, integrity, authorship, and protecting the privacy of participants.

Usefulness of Findings

ACA ethical standards (1988, D13) require reporting results "judged to be of professional value." We interpret "professional value" to refer to the probable contribution of the findings to science or service and the soundness with which the data support meaningful interpretations. We do not extend this meaning to include a researcher's need to publish to support personal or career goals.

What is a counselor-researcher's reporting responsibility when results tenuously rather than strongly support inferences that have significant implications for practice? One option is to report the results and tentative conclusions, along with the researcher's reservations. Colleagues who know enough about research methodology will probably understand such a report correctly. But some counselors, and most lay readers, lack this sophistication. Such readers often understand but uncritically accept conclusions offered as tentative, poorly understand the author's caveats and reservations, and therefore overlook or discount them. In short, inferences offered as tentative are accepted as conclusive. Because to invite such misunderstanding is to be misleading, we recommend that you bear this matter in mind when making reporting decisions such as:

- whether results are clear enough in their meaning to deserve being reported,
- whether preliminary results from an ongoing project should be reported immediately or held pending further data, and
- through what outlet results should be reported.

As Chapters 3 and 4 noted, time pressures of sponsors and other consumers sometimes complicate these decisions.

Integrity

Consumers of research have a right to honesty in the reports they read and hear. Counselor-researchers, therefore, "must be responsible for conducting and reporting investigations in a manner that minimizes the possibility that results will be misleading" (ACA, 1988, D8). Breaches of this responsibility may be deliberate or inadvertent, may vary in importance from trivial to crucial, and may take place at any phase of the research process from planning to reporting. The preparer of a research report has a responsibility to know enough about what took place earlier in the project that any carelessness or fraud in earlier phases is not allowed to mislead the report's consumers. This responsibility typically requires no more than careful record keeping when a researcher carries out a project alone but may become quite difficult when a large research team is involved.

Diener and Crandall (1978) discussed several circumstances that can lead researchers to "transgressions of the mores of science" (p. 152):

- Researchers feel under pressure to publish.
- Researchers want results to come out a particular way for various reasons, such as to support their own theory, to satisfy "the usual practice of journals to publish only positive results," or "to help the scientist" for whom they are working (pp. 152–153).
- Data collection procedures are difficult, embarrassing, tedious, or boring.
- Assistants do not understand the importance of honest data.
- A researcher strongly believes he or she knows ahead of time how the data will come out.

Transgressions may range from minor carelessness to outright falsification of data (Diener & Crandall, 1978). Falsification sometimes consists of recording the results as you want them to be rather than as they were observed; sometimes people make up fictitious data without conducting the research procedures, a process known as "dry labbing."

Incidents of scientific fraud have received significant attention not only in the professional literature but also in the popular press. For example, a *U.S. News and World Report* article states that studies were reported that "apparently were never done," and an assistant "faked key results to cover up failure" of an experiment (Greenberg, 1987, p. 72). In another example, discovery of "faked data" in a large federally funded cancer study eroded public trust, though findings were essentially unchanged when the falsified cases were removed (Stolberg, 1994, p. A1). Though these specific events concern medical research, the underlying issues deserve the attention of all researchers regardless of discipline. Among federal agencies, the National Science Foundation and Public Health Service have issued "requirements for grantee institutions to have guidelines for dealing with fraud" (Holzman, 1991, p. 50). Meanwhile, debate continues about whether "science" can and will police itself against both fraud and careless error. This debate includes concern about whether misconduct will be reduced enough to justify the effort required for policing and whether publicizing misconduct would decrease public confidence in scientific work generally (Holzman, 1991).

All members of a research team have a responsibility to conduct their own activities with integrity so that the project report when issued is not misleading. The principal investigator has the added responsibility to create a working climate that encourages the other team members to do so.

A significant challenge faces administrators, committee members, and credentialers who shape the professional environments wherein researchers work. We construe "researchers" much more broadly than its traditional meaning to include counselors and others who collect program evaluation data for accountability or accreditation purposes. Greenberg (1987) suggested that

> the science establishment isn't keen about cleaning house or even looking closely for malfeasance. Varying consequences follow for the society at large. . . . Some hoked-up papers deal with scientific trivia and have no consequences. [Others, for example, have affected treatment practices in] institutions for the retarded throughout the country, [and wasted very large amounts of money by] faked and inexcusably sloppy research that sends honest scientists down false trails. (p. 73)

We suggest that increased vigilance to discover and stop malfeasance is treating the symptom rather than the cause. When people face pressures for obtaining funding and career advancement opportunities they believe they cannot meet by honest means, we can expect that some of them will choose dishonest means. One challenge facing responsible administrators and committee members is to change the professional environment wherein researchers work so that ethical practices will get them more of what they want than will unethical ones. The underlying principle is not new: The Koran holds that one who leaves something where it is tempting to steal shares the guilt for its theft.

Additional integrity issues concern planning and issuing project reports. Ideas and information drawn from the work of others should not be misleadingly presented as the researcher's own but credited to the appropriate sources. Whether your report is written or oral, and whether or not the material drawn from others has been published, their contributions should be acknowledged with specific citations (APA, 1990, p. 31). Ethical research reports "give credit where credit is due" (ACA, 1988, D11).

A researcher must decide how many reports are needed to communicate the results. Some large projects may need several articles to convey all the necessary information. A project of interest to several distinct readerships (for example, employee assistance professionals, marriage and family counselors, and applied behavior analysts) may need a separate article for each group. But to prepare several articles for a project that needs only one is to waste journal space and create unnecessary difficulties for readers. "It is unethical to fragment a study into several articles simply to gain additional authorships" and lengthen the researcher's list of publication credits (Diener & Crandall, 1978, p. 169).

Because most journals copyright their material, it would be a violation of copyright to knowingly publish the same article in another journal without permission and acknowledgment. Authors, therefore, must

> not submit the same manuscript or one essentially similar in content for simultaneous publication consideration by two or more journals. In addition, manuscripts published in whole or in substantial part in another journal or published work should not be submitted for publication without acknowledgement and permission from the previous publication. (ACA, 1988, Standard D15)

It is common practice, however, to submit the same material simultaneously for consideration both by a journal for publication and by a conference committee for presentation. If it is accepted by both, it will probably be presented at the conference before it appears in the journal because most journals take longer to review and process material than most conference committees do. If the material has been presented at a conference, this fact should be acknowledged in the published report. If it has been accepted for publication when presented at a conference, this fact too should be acknowledged at that time.

Many researchers promise a report of the project's results to people who contribute their efforts to the project, such as participants and anyone who gives technical or administrative support. Ethical researchers honor these commitments.

Authorship

Whose names should be given as authors of research reports? If a report has more than one author, in what order should their names be listed? How should a report recognize contributions to the project by people other than authors? These decisions need to take into account the right to fair treatment of the project's contributors and the report's consumers.

Credit should be in accordance with "scientific contributions" (Diener & Crandall, 1978, p. 164). Authorship, footnotes, and acknowledgment within the text are three recognized means of expressing credit in a project report.

Customarily, authorship represents a major contribution to the project in one or more of the formulation, planning, interpretation, and reporting phases. Authors are listed in order of their relative contributions. The person who makes the greatest contribution is called the **senior author** or **principal author** and is listed first,

> regardless of . . . status. Mere possession of an institutional position, such as Department Chair, does not justify authorship credit. . . . A student is usually listed as principal author of any multiple-authored article that is substantially based on the student's dissertation or thesis. (APA, 1992, Standard 6.23)

Exceptions to this general rule may be found in three situations. First, some projects have two or more equal major contributors. In such situations, the order in which they are listed should be determined by lot or in some other mutually agreeable and fair manner, preferably with an accompanying footnote that the authors contributed equally to the project. Higher professional status should never be used to intimidate people with lower status into accepting a disadvantageous arrangement. Second, some professional conferences have a rule that the person listed in the program as the first author must be a member of the organization; others require that the presenter of the report must be listed first. When a person other than the major contributor is listed first to comply with such a rule, the major contributor should be listed as second author and his or her major role acknowledged in the presentation. Third, some researchers work under an agreement that the employing organization is listed as sole author of any reports of projects conducted under its auspices. Such reports should recognize individual contributors in another way, such as a listing on a separate page or acknowledgment in the text.

Footnote credit is usually used to acknowledge such contributions as (a) ideas with a minor role in the project, (b) major financial or administrative support, and (c) a major share of any task consisting primarily of executing the research plan.

We emphasize two distinctions regarding who should be listed as an author, who should get footnote credit, and who is ordinarily not listed. First, a major versus a minor contribution is a matter of judgment rather than a boundary easy to define explicitly. Contributors of major ideas in formulation, planning, interpreting data, and preparing the report should be listed as authors, while an individual who contributes a minor idea should be given footnote credit. Major sources of funding, such as granting agencies, should be recognized in a footnote; individual minor contributors might be listed in an appendix or given no recognition.

A second distinction concerns contributing ideas versus carrying out plans developed by others. Formulating a project's mission, developing its plans, interpreting its results, and preparing a report all require substantial contributions of ideas. Tasks such as routine data collection, entering data into a computer, and copyediting the report represent executing the project's plans. Such tasks alone do not merit recognition as an author, regardless of how much time an individual spends on them. If an author carries them out, no separate recognition is ordinarily given for these tasks. A person who performs a major portion of any of these executing tasks should be given thanks in a footnote; minor contributions are ordinarily not recognized.

Protecting Privacy of Participants

Researchers have a responsibility to ensure when reporting results that no participants can be individually identified unless their specific authorization to do otherwise has been obtained (ACA, 1988, D10). Sometimes a study of clients from different groups (such as race or national origin) includes one or more categories containing one or very few persons who could be identified if data about them were reported. For example, a study sample might include one male subject of mixed Cherokee and Greek ancestry who had worked as a missionary in Africa. To identify this person by ancestry and employment history would be to identify him as an individual for anyone who knows of his participation in the project. We hold that a counselor-researcher's obligation to protect the privacy of participants supersedes any scientific duty to report obtained data.

SOCIAL CONSEQUENCES OF RESEARCH PROJECTS

To what extent do researchers have an ethical obligation to consider how the knowledge they produce will be used? As impartial scientists, should researchers limit themselves to producing new knowledge and leave decisions about its use to others? Is there some knowledge that might be so dangerous that it should not be reported? These issues were discussed at length among scientists who developed nuclear technology during World War II.

Byck (1987) took one side of this controversy in an article on the effects of cocaine: "There is certain research which is dangerous to the public welfare. . . . The potential for abuse of cocaine is too great to find out anything favorable about the drug" (p. 11). On the other hand, what are the risks of not finding out? Is ignorance ever the wisest course in the long run? Should concerns such as Byck's limit a counselor's obligation to produce research and improve professional practice?

ACA's (1988) ethical standards do not take a stand on this issue; the APA (1992, Principle F) requires researchers to "strive to advance human welfare and . . . try to avoid misuse of their work." These broad directives leave each counselor-researcher the task of basing such choices on personal beliefs and values from his or her perspectives as a professional and as a citizen. We disagree strongly with the view that certain scientific knowledge should be stifled. Images from 1930s newsreels showing Nazi book-burnings come to mind. To whom belongs the task of judging what knowledge is acceptable and what is too dangerous? We believe society has more to fear from abuse of this kind of political authority than from an individual's abuse of cocaine or any other drug. We offer this viewpoint not as doctrine to which we hope everyone will agree but as a position we hope fellow researchers will think about as they develop their own standards.

Sieber and Stanley (1988) noted an additional aspect of the issue of whether any topic is "too dangerous" to investigate:

> Socially sensitive investigations, by their very nature, are likely to draw the attention of other [researchers], the media, and the general public. Ethical analysis relating to the research question, the research process, and the potential application of findings is particularly important under these circumstances. (p. 49)

A researcher who studies a controversial topic needs to be prepared to face controversy. Scarr (1988) noted that institutional review boards disapprove proposals to study "positive racial and gender discrimination and reverse discrimination . . . at a much higher rate than more neutral proposals . . . though they met ethical guidelines" (p. 59). Chapter 4 includes an example in which researchers faced harsh criticism when the results of their project displeased its sponsors. As another example, a researcher who finds "anything favorable" about the effects of cocaine can expect to encounter a broad range of opinions, from views such as Byck's (1987) to the contrary idea that the findings should be used to support long-needed liberalization of drug laws. Such a researcher can expect to encounter many views expressed with strong emotion and to be vehemently pressed to undertake greatly differing and mutually incompatible courses of action. A researcher who would find such a prospect a personal or professional threat is well advised to consider this fact in the formulation or planning phase, before collecting data.

ACA standards obligate counselor-researchers to "communicate to other members the results of any research judged to be of professional value. Results reflecting unfavorably on institutions, programs, services, or vested interests must not be withheld for such reasons" (1988, D13). Recently, a major tobacco company was criticized in Congress for suppressing results showing nicotine to be addictive (Eaton, 1994).

However, "reflecting unfavorably" is sometimes the least of a researcher's concerns. Brooks (1983) discussed a related dilemma researchers sometimes face with regard to reporting their findings. Though her remarks were addressed specifically to studies of independent living programs for people with physical disabilities, we find them much more broadly relevant. What should a researcher do if findings are discovered that, if known, might lead legislative, regulatory, or administrative bodies to act against participants' interests? Gathering "behind the scenes information . . . has the potential for exposing unexpected data that might have serious impact on policies and programs" (p. 304). After participants have been helpful by supplying data for a project, it hardly seems decent to place them at such risk as a result. In contrast, "selective reporting is not in keeping with standard research principles" (p. 304).

Other examples concern findings about racial and religious groups that might be misused to support actions that exclude or otherwise discriminate against them. Brooks (1983) offered no cut-and-dried solution, but rather a principle: "Neither whitewashing nor muckraking will be beneficial to science or subjects" (p. 304). She took a cost–benefit perspective, advising researchers to ask themselves whether revelation can be expected to "produce enough long-term benefit to warrant any immediate damage to persons or programs" (p. 304).

"As part of the process of development and implementation of research projects, [researchers] consult those with expertise concerning any special population under investigation or most likely to be affected" (APA, 1992, Standard 6.07). We suggest that this duty to consult extends to the reporting phase of a project whenever decisions about reporting place a researcher in conflict between the obligation to contribute to knowledge and the obligation to protect participants from harm.

A similar problem occurs when powerful stakeholders try to suppress research results. Wheelwright (1991) noted that political, financial, and legal concerns led public and corporate employers to place severe restrictions on scientists investigating the major oil spills in Alaska and the Persian Gulf. "Gag orders" forbade them from sharing their methods and results; preliminary findings were publicized; definitive results were suppressed. Though we know of no similar experiences among researchers in counseling, the risk of their occurrence increases as socially important issues (such as drugs and criminal behavior) are investigated. We suggest clear, written agreements between researcher and employer as one important safeguard.

MEETING ETHICAL STANDARDS

After reading so many pages of warnings and descriptions of unethical practices, you may wonder if it is possible to conduct research in an ethical manner. We assure you that ethical research is indeed possible. Pope and Vetter's (1992) study of ethically troubling incidents reported by psychologists suggests such difficulties are more likely to arise in client relationships than in research. The "research" category accounted for only 4% of the reported incidents, and "publishing" another 2%.

We share Blanck et al.'s (1992) "view of research ethics not as a hindrance to . . . sound research, but as an opportunity for rewards in . . . research with human participants" (p. 960). Many aspects of the research process must be painstakingly learned at first, but then come quite naturally over time. Ethical aspects are no exception. With practice, researchers learn to see quickly if proposed plans (a) comply with ethical standards, (b) contain flagrant violations that render them ethically infeasible, or (c) involve ethical issues that require further careful attention before decisions are made as to whether plans need to be modified to fulfill ethical guidelines.

To help beginning researchers plan ethically sound studies, we provide an "Ethical Issues Checklist" in Appendix C. This checklist covers the major ethical requirements that should be considered in each phase of a research project (planning, data collection, data analysis, and reporting). We intend this checklist to serve as a guideline for counselor-researchers in designing research projects. However, we emphasize that such a checklist should be used in conjunction with a thorough understanding of ethical principles and the rationale for their existence.

CHAPTER SUMMARY

To protect the rights of the many people the research process touches, researchers must consider an increasing variety of requirements. These requirements are influenced by the larger society's concern with individual rights and professional accountability. Laws and the regulations implementing them express these concerns, as do ethical standards published by the professional organizations to which counselors belong. Counselor-researchers must often set priorities when allocating resources and resolving conflicts between competing commitments. They have a responsibility to protect their clients and research participants from being harmed by the counseling and research relationships. In general, people to be studied in research have a right to grant or withhold their consent to do so, and to have sufficient information about the project to make this decision in their best interest. This principle of informed consent represents a complex family of related issues. Both counselors and researchers need to know the limits of their own competence and function within those limits. Decisions concerning whether, when, and how to report results have their ethical aspects too. A researcher's decisions about what to investigate may be based partly on judgments about how the knowledge produced will be used and how society will react to it.

PRACTICAL EXERCISES

1. Imagine that you are a graduate student in a program leading to the master's degree in counseling. While waiting outside the door for an appointment with your adviser one day, you overhear a conversation between your adviser and another individual, whom you had assumed had already graduated from your program. You made this assumption because this person works in the family counseling clinic where you are doing your internship, and which frequently conducts research on the

effectiveness of the interventions its counselors use. While serving as a co-counselor for one of these research investigations, you had heard the other individual tell clients that he was a graduate of the master's degree program and held the master's degree.

The conversation you overhear is one in which the other individual asks your adviser to fill out the final paperwork necessary to apply to the state for a counseling license. Your adviser refuses to do so, pointing out that this individual still has "Incompletes" in two courses required for the master's degree and has not yet passed the comprehensive examination, which the program requires of all students.

After hearing this conversation, you are concerned about the professional ethics of this individual, especially in regard to the deception of clients in the ongoing research investigations at the clinic where you both work. What steps, if any, would you take to resolve this situation?

2. Consider a situation in which a researcher studied financial coping behavior among people of limited income. The study was based on interviews with people from a local senior citizens center. Center staff and "members" cooperated fully, based on assurances of confidentiality. Some gave considerable time and effort without compensation. In the course of the interviews, widespread abuses of government-funded entitlement programs were discovered. The researcher had reason to predict that reporting these discoveries (even without identifying the center or any respondent individually) would probably lead responsible administrators to substantially cut the funds of this and similar senior centers, more vigorously enforce the entitlement programs' rules, and perhaps seek out past violators to file legal charges against them. As viewed by a number of the study participants, such actions would work considerable hardship on them; their quality of life was substantially enhanced by their abuse of these entitlement programs. Further, any punitive actions would probably raise suspicions that the researcher had not maintained confidentiality as promised. On the other hand, knowing about the discovered abuses would help the research report's consumers understand the participants' financial coping behavior. Should the researcher include these abuses in the project's report to fulfill its mission or withhold them to protect the participants? Give reasons for your decision.

3. The following is a subject consent form that was used in a study comparing three different methods of counseling for career indecision. Based on the discussions of informed consent presented in Chapter 5 and Appendix C, evaluate the strengths and weaknesses of this form.

Workshop on Career Decision Making
In return for the opportunity to receive free instruction in career decision making as part of a research project, I agree that if I am selected for instruction I will:

- attend all five sessions of the Workshop on Career Decision Making and will remain a maximum of two hours each session if required,

- devote a maximum of five hours per week to "homework" to be completed between sessions, and
- devote a maximum of one-half hour per week and two hours at the end of the workshop series to filling out conscientiously the evaluation forms given to me.

In the event that I am not scheduled to receive instruction, I understand that I will receive $25.00 when I complete the evaluation forms described above.

I also:

- affirm that I have had the nature of this research project explained to me,
- understand that all evaluation forms I complete for this project will remain completely confidential and my anonymity will be protected at all times,
- understand that if I am dissatisfied with any aspect of the Workshop on Career Decision Making at any time I may report grievances anonymously to the Sponsored Projects Office, and
- understand that I may withdraw from this project at any time.

Signature _____

PLEASE PRINT: Name _____

Address _____

Telephone Number _____

4. Some participants in an interview study had been convicted of violent crimes. A written consent form signed by all participants assured them of confidentiality. During an interview, the researcher learned of a participant's plans to kill his estranged wife, their children, and her lover. The researcher had no counselor–client relationship with this participant and therefore *Tarasoff* legal duties did not apply. Should the researcher violate confidentiality to protect these intended victims? The researcher believed doing so would entail substantial risk that this participant would commit violence against the researcher and the agency conducting the project.

5. Five doctoral students in counseling psychology had for three years been engaged in conducting a series of research investigations on pain management, supervised by a professor. Two of the doctoral students had conducted two of the studies as their dissertations. After the data from all the studies were analyzed, it was determined that four articles should be written to report the project results. The supervising professor said that she would be the first author on all publications. Each doctoral student was given second authorship on one publication, regardless of his or her actual contribution to that particular study. The remaining three doctoral students were given authorship on each study in the order of

their seniority in the counseling psychology program. The doctoral student who was most familiar with any given study was assigned the task of writing the entire first draft of the article. Based on the discussion of authorship issues in Chapter 5, what is your opinion of how these issues were decided in this situation? Be specific about any changes you recommend and your reasons for these changes.

CHAPTER SIX

FORMULATING THE MISSION

Questions to Guide Your Reading

Formulating a Research Project

1. To what should the process of formulation lead? What does good formulation specify?
2. How can researchers maximize the likelihood that they will persevere and eventually succeed with a research endeavor?
3. From where are the most satisfying ideas for research projects likely to come?
4. What activities are carried out as part of the problem distillation phase?

Feasibility and Related Issues

5. When is a project inherently unresearchable?
6. How do you determine technical feasibility?
7. What questions should you ask to determine whether a project is fiscally and administratively feasible?
8. How does fiscal *justifiability* differ from fiscal *feasibility*?
9. What is the distinction between *legal* feasibility and *ethical* feasibility?
10. What issues should be considered with regard to selection of a journal as the reporting outlet of choice?
11. What other reporting outlets are usually available to researchers?
12. How does the principle of triangulation apply to formulation of a research project?
13. How can researchers select a good set of dependent variables for an experiment?
14. How is the term *population* defined?
15. What is a representative sample? How do representative samples differ from subpopulations?

Kinds of Answers to Research Questions

16. What are qualitative descriptions? Give two examples different from those provided in the text.
17. What is the difference between frequencies and proportions?
18. What are the mean, median, and mode? Which is most often presented in counseling research?
19. What two measures of variability are most often presented in counseling research? How do they differ?
20. Distinguish between independent groups comparisons and related groups comparisons.
21. What are repeated measures comparisons?
22. What are within-group comparisons?
23. How are related groups, repeated measures, and within-group comparisons alike?
24. Distinguish between predictor variables and criterion variables.

25. Describe a direct relationship between two variables. How does such a relationship differ from an inverse relationship?
26. What kind of correlation coefficient should you expect from a strong inverse relationship? From a weak relationship?
27. What kinds of curvilinear relationships might be found in research projects?
28. When are research hypotheses likely to enhance a project? When are they likely to be irrelevant?
29. On what characteristics are social stereotypes likely to be based?
30. When do social stereotypes cause problems for research projects? When are they appropriate topics to investigate?

Reviewing the Literature

31. For what five reasons should researchers be knowledgeable about related work that others have done?
32. What factors determine the extent to which the literature review is discussed in a project's final report?
33. What can researchers do to increase the likelihood that they will evaluate other researchers' work objectively?
34. What should be the final formulation step before planning is begun?

The six major phases of any research project are formulation, planning, data collection, data analysis, interpretation, and reporting. This chapter addresses the first phase, **formulation.** As noted in Chapter 1, this process should lead to a clear statement of the project's mission (the set of reasons why a project is being carried out, including its research questions). For example, in Chapter 1 we referred to a study in which a faculty member and a graduate student conducted a survey of a counselor education program's graduates. The project's mission included its research questions and the planned use of the results; one of these uses was to help decide whether to make any changes in the program's required courses. Good formulation clearly specifies both the research questions and these additional aspects of the project's mission.

In the next step, **planning,** a researcher develops a detailed written or mental representation of how the four remaining steps will proceed: data collection, data analysis, interpretation, and reporting. Planning a research project is discussed in Chapter 7.

Some projects begin with one or more research questions already at hand. Occasionally such questions are clear and specific enough that no further formulation is necessary. For example, a researcher might be interested in determining how many counselors left the employ of a certain agency within a given time period. This research question is clear with little or no additional formulation. At first, however, most research questions are too broad, too general, or too vague to permit planning to proceed satisfactorily without further formulation. For instance, to find out why counselors left the employ of the agency, considerable formulation would be necessary before the researcher could reasonably expect accurate and meaningful answers to that research question. Drew and Hardman called this work "problem distillation" (1985).

In contrast, some projects begin with no research questions decided at the outset; rather, the researcher's primary concern is with some other aspect of the project's mission, such as fulfilling a thesis requirement or publishing an article to advance personal career goals. In this circumstance, the problem to be studied must first be chosen. Problem distillation follows.

Choosing a Problem

Isaac and Michael (1981) recommended that a researcher "select a problem that engages your attention and begs for a solution" (p. 32). A problem may contain one or more research questions. Most counseling research projects require considerable effort over a period of time and involve more obstacles and difficult issues than researchers expect at first. To maximize the likelihood that a researcher will persevere and eventually succeed in such an endeavor, we strongly recommend choosing a problem of more than perfunctory interest.

Whether or not research questions must be based on theory often depends on the policies of the institution for which a thesis or dissertation is being planned or the requirements of the journal to which the project's report will be submitted for publication. In either case, defining a research question is a significant challenge. At this stage, many students experience an "idea desert" (Drew & Hardman, 1985) or, in contrast, a bewildering forest of possibilities with so many factors to consider that they do not know where or how to begin. Among our students, the most satisfying ideas have come from their workplaces or internship sites. Issues addressed in coursework or reading are also sources of possible research problems.

Rubin and Rice (1986) recommended that rehabilitation researchers consult with practitioners, administrators, and consumers (people with disabilities) "in groups formed to generate meaningful research questions" (p. 35). We extend this recommendation to all counseling specialties. Counselors, administrators, clients, employers, and other researchers are all potential sources of research questions. In addition, projects that require external support (for example, grant funds) must address research questions compatible with the priorities of the supporting sources.

Problem Distillation

When first identified, most research problems are very broad and expressed in rather general terms; these problems must be narrowed down and specified more precisely before planning can proceed very far. For example, a researcher might at first decide to investigate communication styles of couples experiencing marital difficulties, and then narrow the project down to a content analysis of such couples' statements to each other in response to specific conflict situations. To decide exactly what categories to consider in the content analysis and what couples to include as participants for the study, the researcher must specify the project's mission even more precisely.

A project's scope must fit within the researcher's ability to plan and execute it. Hill (1991) recommended that students "pick a narrow focus" to avoid being "overwhelmed with the plethora of details" (p. 114). More experienced researchers will be able to manage broader projects more effectively; nonetheless, they may expect similar consequences if they reach beyond their grasp.

Distillation addresses one of the requirements of the scientific method discussed in Chapter 1: Research questions are formulated carefully, so it is clear what kinds of data will answer them. In this phase, a researcher:

- answers several feasibility-related issues;
- decides what population and what variables to study and what kinds of answers are sought (for example, qualitative descriptions, proportions, averages, comparisons, relationships between variables);
- expresses the project's research questions precisely, along with any hypotheses it is to test, without bias based on social stereotypes;
- explores the possibility that additional research questions might enrich the project with little or no added work;
- reviews the relevant literature and brings it to bear on the project's mission; and
- considers carefully the relevance of each research question and hypothesis to other aspects of the project's mission and decides which to retain and which to discard based on these considerations.

The remainder of this chapter addresses these issues. The last refinements of a project's mission are made during the planning process as ambiguities become apparent. Although some qualitative projects begin data collection with relatively vague research questions, in most projects problem distillation involves repeatedly revisiting the formulation, planning, and data collection phases of the research process.

Feasibility and Related Issues

We recommend that a researcher consider a series of questions about any project and have affirmative answers to most of them before beginning the planning phase. Answering these questions in advance makes it easier to develop a clear and workable research plan.

- Is each question inherently researchable?
- Is the project technically feasible?
- Is the project fiscally and administratively feasible?

- Is the project fiscally justifiable?
- Is the project legally and ethically feasible?
- Is the project consistent with other plans of the researcher and any co-workers whose help may be required?
- Will the researcher have an appropriate outlet for reporting the project when it is completed?
- Will answering the research questions satisfactorily fulfill other aspects of the project's mission?

All of these questions should be affirmatively answered before data collection in the main study begins; one or more pilot studies may be required to provide some needed answers.

Inherent Researchability

Chapter 1 noted that researchers seek to answer questions with data and investigate publicly observable and verifiable phenomena with procedures that can be repeated given like conditions. Questions that cannot be answered with data are not researchable. If a question concerns private experience (such as thoughts and feelings), the experience must be expressed in publicly observable form (such as verbal behavior) to be researchable. Each research question for a prospective project should be examined from this standpoint. It is futile to waste planning effort on unresearchable questions. Here are some examples of unresearchable questions:

- How many angels can sit on the point of a pin?
- Is there one God?
- "Whether 'tis nobler in the mind to suffer
  The slings and arrows of outrageous fortune,
  Or to take arms against a sea of troubles,
  And by opposing end them" (*Hamlet*, Act 3, Scene 1).

We reemphasize that unresearchable questions are not necessarily unworthy. Albert Einstein (1954) noted that for most scientists research activities are guided not only by researchable questions and findings but also by many unresearchable propositions arising from personal values. For example, a counselor investigating the emotional impact of abortion is likely to develop different research questions depending on whether he or she views abortion as murder or as a woman's right.

Technical Feasibility

When developing any new project, a researcher needs to consider each of its research questions from a technological standpoint. It is possible to investigate these questions only if the technology exists to collect the data that will answer them. We draw an example from space research. Until recently, scientists could not say what materials Neptune's moons consist of even though they could easily specify what data would be required to answer this question. A Voyager space vehicle has changed this inherently researchable question from technically infeasible to technically feasible. A researcher formulating a new project will not necessarily be able to answer the feasibility question at the beginning of the distillation phase; the needed technology is sometimes discovered during the literature review. For example, a researcher formulating an anxiety-management project might first learn of some relevant biofeedback technology during such a review.

Fiscal and Administrative Feasibility

Will the necessary financial, material, and human resources be available? Will the researcher likely have the authority to carry out the data collection procedures? Will the needed resources and authority continue to be available throughout the anticipated duration of the project? These issues were discussed as "political considerations" in relation to program evaluation projects in Chapter 3. Although these issues are more often troublesome in program evaluation than in other research, they need to be addressed in all research projects.

Current social and political forces strongly shape the policies and priorities of the various sources from which most research projects derive their support. Topics that evoked strong interest at one time may arouse no interest at a later date, and vice versa. For example, Adler (1991) quoted David Spiegel regarding his study of support groups for cancer patients: "Three years ago we would have been laughed out of the study section of any of these agencies" that support cancer research (p. 9). As a second example, abortion-related controversy about research with fetal tissue led President Bush to veto 1992 legislation reauthorizing the National Institutes of Health budget even though such research would likely have represented a very small portion of that agency's funded activity.

Government agencies are not the only sources of research support. Many private nonprofit organizations and for-profit businesses also fund research projects that fit their interests. These organizations can be expected to vary much more widely in their interests than government agencies, and each will be shaped by its own mix of social and political influences.

Similar social and political influences often affect decisions of institutional review boards that may grant or withhold a project's authority to proceed. Scarr (1988) pointed out the bias boards may have against proposals to study "positive racial and gender discrimination and reverse discrimination" (p. 59).

We do not recommend abandoning all potentially controversial projects in favor of what may be popular or considered politically correct at the time. Rather, we suggest formulating and planning every project so it can be carried out with the support and authority likely to be available. To do so, a researcher must identify and appropriately solicit the necessary support and authority; to do otherwise is wasteful and frustrating.

Fiscal Justifiability

Do the project's anticipated outcomes justify allocating to it the necessary financial and human resources? This matter was discussed under setting priorities in Chapter 5 and is different from the question of fiscal and administrative feasibility. Although consultation with fellow professionals is recommended, researchers are personally responsible for deciding the ethical issue of justifiability. In contrast, administrative feasibility usually rests on the decisions of others. Some projects were obviously feasible because they have been completed, though their justifiability may be long debated. Senator Proxmire's Golden Fleece Awards were designed to call public attention to government-funded projects he judged to be fiscally unjustifiable. For example, the National Institute on Alcohol Abuse and Alcoholism spent $102,000 to discover whether sunfish became more aggressive after drinking gin or tequila; the National Institute of Mental Health spent $97,000 to study social interactions in a Peruvian bordello. These brief descriptions provide insufficient information for any judgment about the merits of these projects. We offer them only as examples to illustrate the fact that fiscal justifiability is often debated.

Legal and Ethical Feasibility

We have chosen the phrase "legal and ethical" despite its internal redundancy; ethical standards require counselors and researchers to comply with applicable law. We emphasize, however, that some procedures are not feasible because they are illegal, while other procedures the law permits must still be considered for compliance with professional ethical standards. Ethical feasibility includes consistency not only with professional ethics but also with the personal values of the researcher and others whose efforts are necessary to carry out a given project. This question is also separate from administrative feasibility. Administrative authorities sometimes sanction unlawful and ethically questionable procedures, as became painfully evident during the Watergate investigation in the early 1970s and again during the Iran-Contra hearings in the 1980s.

Other Plans

A single project is rarely if ever a researcher's only life activity. Good planning takes into account the project's place among whatever else the researcher and any co-workers will be doing while it is under way. For example, a researcher who is 13 weeks pregnant should not begin a project without taking into account her probable absence for a period of time six months hence. We regard this issue as part of fiscal and administrative feasibility but list it separately because we have seen many student researchers omit their own efforts from their accounts of fiscal and human resources.

Reporting Outlets

Reporting is the last of the six phases that make up any research project. If a suitable outlet for reporting results does not exist, any project's mission will remain unfulfilled. For a project that serves only to meet a course assignment, a report submitted to the professor is usually sufficient. Similarly, some projects need to be reported only to an organization's management or to a designated committee. In contrast, many researchers envision presenting their results at a conference or publishing them in a journal, or both. During the review of the literature, beginning researchers are well advised to explore possible conferences and journals that could serve as reporting outlets.

If journal publication is the outlet of choice, we recommend considering the following issues in the problem distillation phase:

- the kinds of projects usually published in the chosen journals, including subject matter, length, methodology, and basic versus applied research;
- the acceptance rate (proportion of manuscripts submitted that the journal accepts in present form, accepts after revision, and rejects);
- **publication lag,** or the usual time elapsing between submission and publication of accepted articles; and
- the relationship of these factors to your reasons for conducting the project.

If a desired promotion depends on getting the project published by a given date, for example, these matters can be crucial to planning. It is a good idea to identify several journals as possible outlets and to seek information about their acceptance rates and publication lag in advance.

Researchers seeking to be included in conferences need to consider the same issues as prospective journal authors, although project reports and waiting time are usually both shorter and conferences usually have higher acceptance rates than journals. A researcher should have in mind several possible journals, conferences, or both, if these are the chosen media for reporting a project. As alternatives, some large organizations (for example, metropolitan school districts, government agencies, unions, and major corporations) have internal newsletters or other publications that report projects of interest. Such media are often called "house organs." We strongly recommend addressing these reporting issues during problem distillation, because they can profoundly affect decisions about the kind and size of problem chosen for investigation.

TRIANGULATION

Denzin (1978) introduced the idea of **triangulation** with a recommendation to "combine multiple data sources, research methods, and theoretical schemes" (p. 21). Isaac and Michael (1981) advocated measuring "a given concept or attribute" in more than one way (p. 90). As an example, they noted a study of the effect of praise or blame on the outcome of reading instruction; no significant differences were found with regard to the one dependent variable chosen, "gain in reading." They suggested that "a highly significant treatment difference might have been found" if a second dependent variable such as "attitudes toward reading" had been added (p. 90). To continue this example, suppose the results showed little difference in reading skill among students experiencing praise versus blame from their teachers, although students who were praised had a substantially more favorable attitude toward reading. This twofold result might lead the researchers to expect praise to produce a delayed gain in reading skill through increased independent reading activity.

The triangulation idea is a metaphor based on a method used by surveyors and others to determine distances when direct measurement is difficult. For example, a surveyor might establish two markers in line with a mountaintop a known distance from each other and at a known elevation. The surveyor then sights the mountaintop through an instrument at both markers, measuring the angle between the line of sight and the horizontal. Knowledge of these angles and the horizontal distance between the markers allows the surveyor to calculate the height of the mountain. Knowing either the horizontal distance between the markers or the sighting angles alone does not permit calculating the vertical distance to the top; knowing both does. In this instance, collecting the data for one or two questions would answer one or two questions only; adding the data for a carefully chosen third question permits a fourth to be answered with little further work.

To generalize this principle, answering a set of research questions usually provides a richer understanding of the phenomena studied than does answering one question alone. Counseling can be expected to have more than one outcome worth investigating. As an example, consider an agency that wishes to conduct a follow-up study of its former clients to examine the effectiveness of its counseling services. Client satisfaction with the services they received is one obvious possibility. However, Gladstein (1969) questioned "using client satisfaction as a major criterion of counseling success" because "clients are too easily satisfied" (p. 481). The researcher might develop additional questions such as:

- How do clients rate the competence of their former counselors?
- To what extent have the problems for which clients sought counseling been resolved?
- Have clients sought other therapy?
- How do clients rate their interpersonal functioning in different settings, such as on the job and in the marital relationship?

Fleming and Baum (1987) applied the triangulation idea in their recommendations for studies of job stress. And Comings (1991) used it as a basis for combining several different findings to derive a conceptual model linking heredity, neurotransmitter processes, and various behavior disorders such as chemical dependency, attention deficit disorder, and depression.

To select a good set of dependent variables for an experiment, we suggest the research team ask itself why the one dependent variable of primary interest is expected to have the hypothesized relationship to the independent variables. This "why" question often leads to ideas for other dependent variables that can be added to a study without greatly increasing its demands on financial and human resources. For example, suppose a researcher is interested in comparing systematic desensitization and participant modeling as methods for treating agoraphobia. (People with agoraphobia experience a pathological fear of going outdoors.) Systematic desensitization involves progressively relaxing tense muscle groups while thinking about the feared stimulus; in participant modeling, clients observe others approaching the feared stimulus and then gradually approach it themselves. Obviously, the dependent variable of immediate interest is the clients' ability to leave their homes. The "why" question may lead to other possibilities for dependent variables, such as the anxiety experienced when outside the home, their willingness to talk to people they may come in contact with when out, the length of time they take to complete the treatment program, and how long the treatment effects last.

This same idea can be applied to generating research questions in other research approaches. When a researcher explores why a particular question is of primary interest, other related research questions often come to mind. The qualitative research literature discusses studying phenomena with many different kinds of data (such as naturalistic observation, interviews, case studies, videotapes, and transcripts) as a form of triangulation. However, triangulation is not limited to qualitative projects.

The triangulation metaphor emphasizes the idea that combining two or more carefully chosen direct measures often permits other characteristics to be inferred though not directly measured. In the reading example discussed earlier, skill and attitude were directly measured, permitting a third characteristic (independent reading activity) to be inferred. Most research is like the surveyor's use of triangulation in this respect. An important difference is that the surveyor could infer the height of the mountaintop as if it were directly measured; in most studies of human behavior, such as education and counseling, inferences from triangulation lead to hypotheses rather than indirect measures. A second important difference is that the surveyor's direct measurements (sighting angles and distance between the markers) were not important in themselves; they were valuable only because they enabled the height of the mountain to be inferred. In contrast, including more than one direct measure enriches most behavioral research projects not only because of what may be indirectly inferred from the combination but because the direct measures are important in themselves. Including several related research questions in a project can reduce a researcher's chances of interpreting findings in a manner similar to one of the blind men who investigated an elephant in a popular fable. (In the fable, each of six blind men examined a different part of an elephant and reached a different conclusion about the nature of the animal. For example, one man examined a leg and inferred the elephant was like a tree; another examined a side and concluded the elephant was like a wall.) Despite these differences, the triangulation metaphor provides a convenient label for the idea that having a set of research questions or several different kinds of data rather than only one enriches a project.

To formulate a research project effectively, you must clearly identify the research questions you seek to answer, the variables included in these questions, and the role of each such variable in the project. A project's mission includes not only its research questions but also the reasons these questions are asked. We suggest that researchers routinely apply the triangulation principle as part of every project's problem distillation process. Doing so can create opportunities to achieve a richer understanding of the phenomena studied and better fulfill the project's mission.

CHOOSING A POPULATION

A clear statement of any research question includes the populations to which it applies. In this context, a **population** consists of all "members of any well-defined class of people, events or objects" (Kerlinger, 1973, p. 52) to which the research question refers. A few projects collect data from the entire population of interest without generalizing conclusions to other people, events, or objects than those studied. For example, all students in a high school could be surveyed as to how often they see their counselor. Most projects, however, collect data from samples to draw inferences about a wider population than the individuals studied. A sample consists of a few members of a population selected as representative of the population as a whole. **Representative** means that studying the sample yields approximately the same results as you would get if the entire population were studied.

Election polls are probably the most familiar example. Approaching elections bring abundant news reports of polls concerning candidates and issues on which voters will vote. In such polls, the population of interest is usually the entire electorate of a geographic area, such as a city, county, state, or nation. Studying such populations in their entirety is almost always unnecessarily expensive if not entirely infeasible. Satisfactory results can be obtained much more cheaply and easily by using samples. However, pollsters must define their populations of interest carefully to decide how to select their samples. This is equally true for all researchers who use samples. A population may be as broad as all 4th grade students nationwide or as narrow as all 4th grade students in a particular school.

The population of primary interest should be decided as part of problem identification. When confronting feasibility issues during problem distillation, some compromises with this choice may be necessary. A researcher may decide that sampling from the population of primary interest is too difficult, too expensive, or otherwise impractical and choose a more limited population for the research question.

Here is a fictitious example of how a project's study population may be progressively more explicitly defined and limited as problem distillation proceeds. A researcher from a health insurance company wanted information regarding all clients nationwide whose psychotherapy fees were paid by insurance. Selecting a representative sample from this population would be difficult and require more time and money than the researcher had available. Clients whose fees were paid by the researcher's own company, however, could be identified and studied much more easily. The research question was therefore changed by specifying the study population as all clients with psychotherapy fees paid by this company's insurance instead of all clients nationwide with psychotherapy fees paid by insurance. While deciding how to select a sample, the researcher recognized the need to clarify the study population further by specifying its time limits. The study population was then further limited to all clients with psychotherapy fees paid by this company's insurance, billed during the past 12 months.

We emphasize that the decision to study insurance-supported psychotherapy clients from one company's files rather than in general represents a change in the research question to pertain to a different population. Clients supported by one insurance company are a **subpopulation** of insurance-supported clients as a whole, not a sample. A subpopulation is not chosen so as to be representative of the wider population. Nonetheless, the research question of primary interest (pertaining to insurance-supported psychotherapy clients in general in this example) is not lost because the new research question addresses the original question of primary interest insofar as the phenomena studied are the same in the population of primary interest as in the subpopulation. The idea that these phenomena are similar in the two populations is an essential link in drawing inferences from the data to the research question of primary interest. The extent of this similarity is usually not known but must be inferred from the literature and from the researcher's judgment.

KINDS OF ANSWERS TO RESEARCH QUESTIONS

Clear formulation of research questions includes clear ideas about the kinds of statements sought as answers to them. These statements may involve qualitative descriptions, frequencies, proportions, central tendencies, variabilities, comparisons, relationships between variables, or any combination of these. Each of these kinds of statements is useful in particular circumstances. Let's take a closer look at the explanatory value of each type of statement.

Qualitative Descriptions

Many **qualitative** research questions can be answered without numbers. Some examples are:

- What reasons did dropouts give for leaving school?
- What kinds of problems did clients present in initial sessions?
- What reasons did applicants list for leaving their former jobs?
- What sources referred new clients to this counseling center?

These questions can be answered by listing reasons, kinds of problems, or referral sources without presenting quantitative information. However, adding information such as frequencies or percentages fulfills the missions of many projects better than qualitative statements alone.

As discussed in Chapter 2, qualitative projects generally seek patterns involving many different kinds of data. The simple examples listed here illustrate single research questions that can be answered with qualitative descriptions, but most qualitative research projects are much more complex than these examples suggest.

Frequencies and Proportions

Frequencies are determined by counting. For example, a list answering the last of the above qualitative questions might be enhanced by showing that 50 of the last 130 clients were referred by schools, 31 by other counselors, 20 by churches, 17 by family or friends, and 12 by physicians.

The same information could be expressed as **proportions**: 38% of the 130 clients were referred by schools, 24% by other counselors, 15% by churches, 13% by family or friends, and 9% by physicians. (As is common in such lists, these proportions do not add to exactly 100% because of rounding.) Proportions are particularly useful for comparing corresponding frequencies in a sample and a population, or in two samples of different size. For example, the referral data from these 130 clients might be compared with similar data from 400 clients in another agency. Comparisons are discussed more fully later in this chapter.

Central Tendencies

Most statistics texts discuss the **mean** (the arithmetic average of a set of scores), the **median** (the point that divides the ordered scores into two equal halves), and the **mode** (the most common score) as representing the central tendency of any group's distribution of scores. However, means are presented much more often in counseling research reports than are medians or modes; reasons for this choice usually have to do with data analysis issues discussed in Chapter 13. Here are a few examples:

- the average age of new clients,
- the average length of time from intake to closure,
- the average scholastic aptitude score of students dropping out, and
- the average blood-alcohol concentration at time of arrest of clients referred by the courts for alcoholism treatment.

Variabilities

Few research questions in counseling directly ask how widely the members of a group differ from one another on the variables being studied. However, measures of variability are often reported because they enhance consumers' understanding of central tendencies. The **standard deviation** (a measure of the dispersion of scores around the mean) and the **range** (the difference between the highest and lowest scores) are the most often reported. We list a few examples:

- New clients ranged in age from 16 to 79.
- GRE scores of applicants to the M.S. program had a mean of 508 and a standard deviation of 96.
- Rehabilitated clients' case costs ranged from $125 to $5,897.

Comparisons

Many research questions require comparisons. Four kinds can be distinguished: comparisons between independent groups, comparisons between related groups, comparisons between repeated measures from the same group, and comparisons between similar but different measures within the same group. **Related-groups, repeated-measures,** and **within-group comparisons** are alike in that the measures being compared may be correlated. For example, pretest and posttest scores (repeated measures) are correlated if high and low pretest scorers tend to score high and low, respectively, at posttest, whether or not the average score changes from pretest to posttest. Collectively, these three types of comparisons may be called **correlated-measures comparisons.** To develop a better understanding of the various types of comparisons, we will discuss them and provide examples of fictitious results representing each type.

Independent-groups comparisons.   In independent-groups comparisons the same measures are taken from two or more groups comprising different participants, and the groups are compared with respect to these measures. "Independent" in this context means that the composition of any one group did not determine the composition of any other group. Persons randomly assigned to two different treatment groups, for example, represent independent groups in this sense as do students in two different classrooms or men and women voters in an electorate. Husbands and their wives are not independent groups. Examples of results of such comparisons are:

- Clients experiencing career indecision who were randomly assigned to a decision-making skills treatment program were more successful in completing the career decision-making process than were clients randomly assigned to a nondirective counseling program.
- A higher proportion of men than women students dropped out.
- Average case costs were higher among clients referred by public agencies than among self-referred clients.
- This year's graduating seniors expressed more scholarly interest than this year's entering freshmen.

Related-groups comparisons.   Sometimes the groups to be compared comprise different participants even though the composition of the two groups is not independent. These kinds of groups are related groups. Workers and their supervisors represent related groups. Husbands and their wives are related groups not only in this sense but also in the usual social sense. Careful attention is sometimes necessary to avoid confusing these meanings. Some examples of results are:

- Among married high school students, wives planned to continue their formal education longer than their husbands did.
- Employees rated their company as a more desirable place to work than their immediate supervisors did.

Repeated-measures comparisons.   Many projects compare measures of the same variables taken at two or more different times from the same participants (in single-subject projects, from the same person). These are repeated-measures comparisons. Repeated-measures comparisons are common in developmental projects and in experiments studying changes. Some examples of results are:

- EAP clients' job performance ratings improved after counseling.
- Tom's absenteeism rate declined when the token economy was introduced, rose when it was discontinued, and declined again when it was reintroduced.
- The graduating seniors expressed more scholarly interest this year than they did when they entered as freshmen.

Within-group comparisons.   A project might compare measures of the same group on two or more different variables (for example, language achievement and mathematics achievement), whether at the same time or at different times. These are within-group comparisons. Some examples of results include:

- Students with part-time jobs earned higher grades in courses directly related to their jobs than they did in other courses.
- Employees expressed more satisfaction with their job duties than with their salaries or promotional opportunities.

Combining types of comparisons.   Many projects combine comparisons of more than one type. For example, many experiments compare two or more samples (independent groups or related groups) with regard to their changes from pretest to posttest (repeated measures). Most traditional group experiments involve independent-groups comparisons, either alone or in combination with other types. All time series experiments involve repeated-measures comparisons. The following two fictitious examples illustrate findings that involve more than one type of comparison:

- Among couples seeking relationship counseling, partners of two-career couples expressed more similar views of the presenting problem than did partners of couples with only one person earning income.
- The frequency with which students spoke out of turn in class declined more rapidly when the experimental intervention was introduced than did their frequency of aggressive acts against classmates.

The first of these examples combines a related-groups comparison (partners within couples) and an independent-groups comparison (two-career versus one-earner couples). The second example includes a repeated-measures comparison (declined) and a within-group comparison (speaking out of turn versus aggressive acts).

Covariation Between Variables

Covariation refers to two or more variables varying together, regardless of any causal relationship. To name a few possibilities, either of two variables may cause the other, or they may have a third variable as a common cause, or they may have no causal connection whatever. Correlational projects study such relationships, whether or not correlation coefficients are used in the statistical analysis. Covariation is sometimes expressed with comparisons rather than as correlations. For example, a researcher might ask a question about the relationship of gender to preferred recreational activities and answer it by comparing the preferences of males versus females. The following statements express covariation between variables:

- Shedler and Block's (1990) study, discussed in Chapter 2, found marijuana use curvilinearly related to subjective distress; adolescents with very high and very low distress used the most marijuana, while those with moderate distress used less.

- Scores on the Scholastic Aptitude Test were moderately correlated with freshman grade point average.
- Driving performance was inversely related to blood-alcohol level; participants who had consumed the most alcohol performed worst.

Some research questions concern differences between groups regarding the extent to which variables are related. The following statement expresses such a difference: Among new employees with little experience, the job aptitude test predicted work performance ratings strongly; among new employees hired with extensive experience, the predictive value of the job aptitude test was close to zero.

A relationship between variables may be described according to its strength, direction, shape, and role within the project. Precise word choices are often required to avoid confusion when describing such relationships. In the next four subsections we discuss these descriptors and define the terms we have found most troublesome in the work of students and colleagues.

Strength of a relationship.   A high **degree of relationship** (or a strong relationship) means that almost all instances follow the indicated trend; contrary examples, if any, are few. For example, Figures 6.1 and 6.2 indicate relatively strong relationships. If the degree of relationship is low (weak relationship), contrary examples are many, as represented by the fictitious data in Figure 6.3. High (near 1.00 or −1.00) and low (near zero) correlation coefficients represent strong and weak relationships, respectively. Correlation coefficients of 1.00 and −1.00 represent perfect direct and inverse relationships. In scatter graphs of such data, all points fall on a straight line.

Direction of a relationship.   In a **direct relationship,** high, moderate, and low values on one variable are associated with high, moderate, and

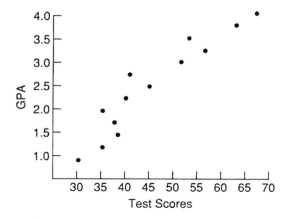

F I G U R E   6.1
Scatter graph representing a strong direct relationship (*r* = .96) between test scores and grade point averages. Data are fictitious.

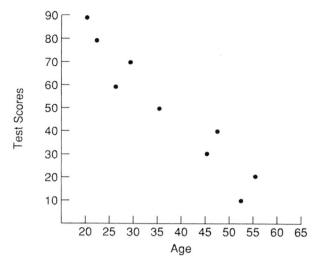

F I G U R E   6.2
Scatter graph representing a strong inverse relationship ($r = -.97$) between age and scores on a speeded ability test. Data are fictitious.

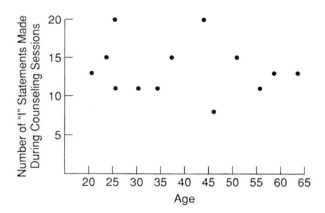

F I G U R E   6.3
Scatter graph representing a weak relationship ($r = -.17$) between client age and number of "I" statements in a session. Data are fictitious.

low values (respectively) on the other. For example, most studies of scholastic aptitude tests show a direct relationship with grades. Students with high scores can earn high grades on the average, while students with low scores earn low grades, and students with intermediate scores earn intermediate grades. Figure 6.1 graphically presents fictitious data indicating a direct relationship. The term *direct relationship* refers only to the direction in which variable values are associated. It says nothing about the strength of

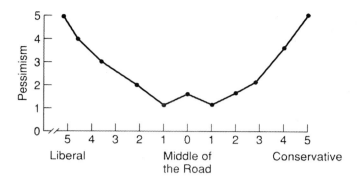

F I G U R E   6.4
Line graph illustrating a U-shaped curvilinear relationship. The data are fictitious, representing mean self-ratings of pessimism among respondents with various ratings on a liberalism–conservatism scale. According to the graph, respondents with the most extreme political views, either conservative or liberal, expressed the most pessimism; respondents with middle-of-the-road ratings were least pessimistic.

relationship. A positive correlation coefficient (between zero and 1.00) represents a direct relationship.

In an **inverse relationship,** high, moderate, and low values on one variable are associated with low, moderate, and high values on the other, respectively. For example, adult performance on many speeded ability tests is inversely related to age; young adults perform best on the average, old people worst, and middle-aged people at intermediate levels. Figure 6.2 graphically presents fictitious data representing such an inverse relationship. A negative correlation coefficient (between zero and −1.00) represents an inverse relationship.

Correlations are precisely described as positive and negative, but relationships are not. The careless expressions "positive relationship" and "negative relationship" are best avoided.

Shape of a relationship.   A relationship is rectilinear if its graph approximates a straight line and curvilinear if its graph is a curve. One kind of curvilinear relationship is illustrated by Shedler and Block's (1990) study of marijuana use related to subjective distress (noted in Chapter 2 and earlier in this chapter). Their participants with very high and very low distress used the most marijuana, while those with moderate distress used less. A graph of this relationship would have a U shape similar to the fictitious data in Figure 6.4. In contrast, some curvilinear relationships, such as age and physical strength, take the form of an inverted U as illustrated by the fictitious data in Figure 6.5. Young and middle-aged adults are stronger on the average than are preschool children and very old people. A relationship is also described as curvilinear if its graph is steeper at low than at high levels of one of the variables, a **decelerating curve** (see Figure 6.6), or the reverse, an **accelerating curve** (see Figure 6.7).

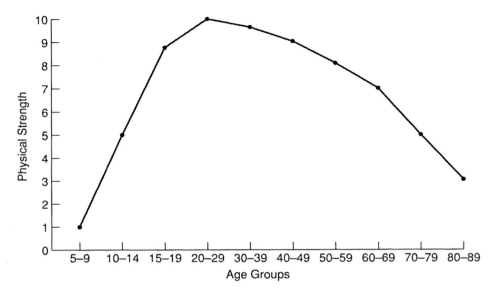

F I G U R E   6.5

Line graph illustrating a curvilinear relationship with an inverted-U shape. The data are fictitious, representing mean physical strength scores of respondents of different ages. The graph shows that the 20–29 and 30–39 age groups were strongest, with both younger and older respondents showing less strength.

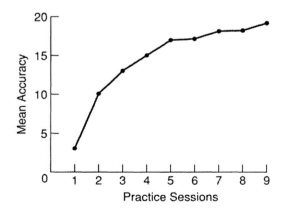

F I G U R E   6.6

Line graph illustrating a decelerating curvilinear relationship. The data are fictitious, representing mean accuracy scores of respondents as they repeated a task. The graph shows that most improvement took place in the first few sessions, with little improvement thereafter.

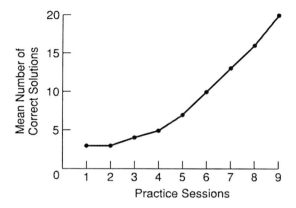

F I G U R E   6.7

Line graph illustrating an accelerating curvilinear relationship. The data are fictitious, representing mean number of correct solutions as respondents performed similar sets of problem-solving tasks during nine sessions. The graph shows little change during the first few sessions, with increasingly greater improvement thereafter. Such data would be consistent with a hypothesis that respondents worked largely by trial and error at first but with increasing practice learned strategies they successfully applied to later problems.

Role within the project.   When measures on one variable are used to predict another, the former is a **predictor variable** and the latter a **criterion variable.** For example, aptitude test scores (predictor variables) are often used to predict individuals' grades in school or performance at work (criterion variables). We prefer to reserve criterion variable for this use, although some writers use criterion measure synonymously with dependent variable. When a project studies a relationship between variables without using either variable to predict the other, predictor and criterion are best avoided as imprecise terms.

As noted in Chapter 2, we recommend reserving the expressions *independent variable* and *dependent variable* for experiments. When used in purely correlational projects, these terms often cause confusion. An independent variable is managed or manipulated by the researcher; the term dependent variable implies an independent variable is present.

HYPOTHESES

A **research hypothesis** expresses an expectation about the outcome of a research project; a **statistical hypothesis** concerns the populations from which a project's samples came. This section discusses research hypotheses; Chapter 13 discusses statistical hypotheses. When research questions are drawn from theory, it is customary to state one or more research hypotheses. Sometimes different lines of reasoning from theory produce conflicting hypotheses and the research question concerns which hypothesis the data will support. When research questions are not based on theory, it is sometimes but not always helpful to express them in hypothesis form.

Chapter 1 lists three possible hypotheses in the example of Ms. Hernandez's study of her 9th grade students' attitudes toward school. Experience often gives researchers a basis for choosing some of a project's possible outcomes as more likely than others. If the Ms. Hernandez example were real rather than fictitious, she no doubt could have expressed such a hypothesis before collecting her data. In contrast, researchers sometimes have no basis for choosing which possible outcome to expect. In many such instances, a researcher can express all meaningful possible outcomes in hypothesis form. If Ms. Hernandez had been totally unfamiliar with the students being studied, she might have written all three hypotheses listed in Chapter 1.

We have noted previously that research questions are formulated carefully, so it is clear what data will answer them. Good research hypotheses require similar care. For illustration, we express Ms. Hernandez's research question in hypothesis form:

> Our 9th grade students have roughly the same attitudes toward school as students in comparable schools, as measured by the School Attitude Scale.

This hypothesis can be further refined so that it more explicitly expresses a possible outcome in terms of the data:

> Our 9th grade students' average score on the School Attitude Scale will be approximately the same as that reported for students in comparable schools.

Such refinement is part of the problem distillation task when a project's mission requires one or more hypotheses.

Even when not required by the mission, research hypotheses enhance the quality of some projects. They may be irrelevant to others, however, such as purely fact-finding or descriptive projects. In the problem distillation phase of each new project, we recommend that beginning researchers routinely ask themselves whether preparing one or more research hypotheses would strengthen the project. If it would, the hypotheses should be written for learning value and for reference in the planning phase regardless of whether they are included in the project's report. If preparing one or more research hypotheses would not be helpful, none is necessary; absence of a hypothesis does not by itself mean a faulty project.

BIASES AND SOCIAL STEREOTYPES

Various authors have cautioned researchers against allowing research questions to be biased by social stereotypes concerning characteristics such as age (Schaie, 1993), gender (Denmark, Russo, Frieze, & Sechzer, 1988), and sexual orientation (Herek, Kimmel, Amaro, & Melton, 1991). As examples,

Schaie (1993) noted "reliance on biological models of decrement or decline" and "age assumed to be the cause of differences . . . with little consideration of alternative explanations" (p. 49–50). Similarly, Herek and his co-workers (1991) noted that "phenomena should not be assumed to result from sexual orientation simply because they are observed in the gay community" (p. 959). Nor should disabilities themselves be regarded as causing phenomena (such as employment discrimination) that result from social reactions to disabilities (Hadley & Brodwin, 1989). As precautions, we recommend examining each research question for implicit assumptions containing social stereotypes (for example, that women are passive or gay males artistic) and for language reflecting social stereotypes (for example, wheelchair-bound). A list of the many other characteristics on which social stereotypes are based would include these descriptors: race, religion, national origin, gender, language spoken, marital status, occupation, social class, living arrangements (for example, homeless), age, sexual orientation, and disability. It is important to eliminate social stereotypes as implicit assumptions in research questions. Nonetheless, it is quite legitimate to investigate the extent to which these stereotypes represent true group differences. For example, a research question should not assume gay males are artistic, but it might legitimately ask whether a disproportionate number of gay males work in artistic occupations. Many stereotyped beliefs are applied to all individuals in a category (for example, all women, all Hispanics); in contrast, very few true group differences hold for every individual. Though more men than women enjoy mechanical activities, it is wrong to assume that all men do or that no women do. Another legitimate kind of research question concerning social stereotypes asks the extent to which they are present in the thinking or behavior of a population. For example, a researcher might ask what proportion of high school students believe gay males are artistic.

In short, propositions based on social stereotypes may lead to good research questions about group differences or about people's beliefs. But research questions that contain social stereotypes as implicit assumptions need to be changed to eliminate this bias.

REVIEWING THE LITERATURE

A good job of formulation requires some knowledge about related work others have done. A researcher needs to know about this work to carry out the problem distillation process satisfactorily. The reasons are several.

- It is not desirable to unknowingly repeat a project others have done.
- The literature may contain or suggest related questions to consider when applying the triangulation principle discussed earlier in this chapter.

- Other researchers' techniques, results, and experiences may suggest changes or additional research questions for the project at hand. For example, another project's use of a particular test may raise questions about possible uses of this test.

While these reasons apply to all projects, two additional reasons apply to some but not all projects.

- If a project is formulated in response to other researchers' results, its research questions need to take into account any additional supporting and conflicting results that exist in the literature.
- A theory-based project's report needs to express the reasoning leading from theoretical propositions to research hypotheses.

Researchers usually choose projects concerning topics about which they have some prior knowledge. Some of this knowledge is based on reading relevant literature. However, most projects require detailed knowledge of the professional literature closely related to the specific research questions being studied. An intensive literature search usually begins in the problem distillation phase and continues well into the planning phase. Creating a good plan often requires excursions into the literature addressing such matters as measuring instruments and procedures for collecting and analyzing the data. Further, some attention to the professional literature is advisable throughout the duration of the project, since some relevant items may have earlier escaped the researcher's attention or may emerge while the project is under way. This section discusses the role of literature review as part of formulation; Chapter 7 includes a more detailed discussion of the literature review process, including its contributions to planning a project.

The extent to which literature reviews appear in projects' final reports varies widely. Most journal articles take little if any space to review previous work. Some students infer from this fact that they need to read correspondingly little to formulate and plan their own projects. Ordinarily, a researcher who publishes a journal article has read quite widely about the topic and cited only a very small portion of the material read. "It is not necessary for authors to document their knowledge of the subject matter in the introduction" (Boor, 1986, p. 721), although professors often require students to write literature reviews in class assignments. A thesis or dissertation usually allocates an entire chapter to a literature review. Whatever its value to readers, such a chapter represents a learning exercise for its writer. The skills learned in this task often prove very valuable in later research activities. Some publications (for example, annual reviews) are devoted entirely to literature reviews, and articles in some other journals have a review of the literature as a major purpose.

A thorough literature review is a time-consuming task. How thorough a review must be depends upon the project. A thesis, dissertation, or annual review chapter requires a more thorough review than most class assignments. A brief review may help when choosing a problem; problem distillation usually requires a more thorough review.

Evaluating Other Projects

The literature review process includes evaluating the material found. Other researchers' findings must be evaluated not only for their relevance to your own project but also with regard to the strength with which results support the offered conclusions. These evaluations often suggest research questions for the project at hand.

We have known reviewers to apply widely different standards when evaluating others' work, depending on the reviewers' agreement or disagreement with reported conclusions. Minor methodological shortcomings are severely criticized in projects with disliked conclusions; when conclusions are more acceptable, much more serious flaws escape comment. In the words of a popular expression, this practice is "to strain at a gnat and swallow an elephant whole."

It is an understandable human tendency to seek support for your own position by looking carefully for flaws in a project with unpalatable conclusions. In contrast, if a reviewer likes the conclusions, it is easy to accept the whole project at face value with an "of course" attitude. We recommend that researchers guard against this tendency when reviewing others' work; be alert to the possibility that reviews found in the literature may reflect this tendency, especially when the topic is controversial; and never rely entirely on other authors' evaluations of the projects they cite—when possible, read the primary sources yourself. To see direct evidence of the phenomenon to which we refer, conduct a brief literature review on either of two topics: psychic phenomena (such as extrasensory perception) or controlled drinking as a treatment goal for alcoholics.

Summarizing the Literature Review

It is often helpful to write a summary of the literature review in the researcher's own words. This summary should note the major issues and findings discovered and express the ways in which this material bears on the present project's research questions. Such a summary can be very useful as research questions are formulated, particularly if the formulation phase must be revisited to revise research questions after planning has begun. Such a summary is required in some project reports, particularly theses and dissertations.

A Final Formulation Step

Before planning is begun, it is often helpful to put in writing the project's entire mission: all its research questions and all the reasons answers to these questions are being sought. Researchers' personal reasons (for example, to add publication credits to their personnel files) should not be omitted. This informal record, kept conveniently at hand, can be consulted from time to time during planning and later phases of the project. This step may be unnecessary for an experienced researcher conducting a small project with a simple mission that is easy to keep in mind. Nevertheless, we recommend a written statement of mission for every project of a beginning researcher, and whenever the project is large or its mission complex, however experienced the researcher may be. Portions of this mission statement can usually be incorporated into the project's report when the time comes to prepare this report.

Chapter Summary

Formulating a research project includes choosing a problem and clearly specifying the project's mission (its research questions and the reasons these answers are sought). Researchable questions must be clear and specific enough to lead to a feasible plan. Formulating several research questions rather than one usually produces more meaningful results. Clear research questions specify the variables and populations involved and the kinds of data to be collected. Some projects specify hypotheses about the outcomes. Data may be qualitative, quantitative, or both. Quantities may include frequencies, proportions, central tendencies, variabilities, relationships, comparisons, or any combination of these. A literature review is necessary for both formulation and planning. A project's research questions are often shaped by material from the literature. As most projects proceed, a written expression of the entire mission is a useful guide.

Practical Exercises

1. Examine the following research questions. For each, decide if it is inherently researchable. If the answer is yes, decide whether or not the project is:
   - technically feasible,
   - legally and ethically feasible (within what limits, if any),
   - administratively feasible, and
   - fiscally justifiable.

   If a question is so vaguely formulated that you cannot decide, say what needs to be clarified so you can decide. In some instances, you may be able to give affirmative answers to researchability and feasibility issues, though further clarification would be necessary to carry out the project.

a. Do people have immortal souls?

b. How do clients usually respond when counselors make overt sexual overtures to them in the initial session?

c. Does severe childhood toilet training produce anal retentive adults?

d. Can middle-aged adults learn as easily as adolescents?

e. How many angels can dance on the head of a pin?

f. Among students taking multiple-choice final examinations, does immediate feedback about correctness of responses improve performance?

g. Does reincarnation occur?

h. Is sexual behavior among elephants affected by the weightless environment of an orbiting space vehicle?

i. What are the most closely guarded secrets of the world's heads of state?

j. Are counselors more effective with clients who are of their own gender and ethnicity?

k. What is the temperature at the core of the North Star?

l. Is this a productive set of discussion questions?

2. In Chapter 6 we discuss the principle of triangulation as it applies to selecting a set of research questions for a project. In an experiment, the several questions often involve a set of dependent variables and the same independent variables.

a. Keeping triangulation in mind, what would you suggest as dependent variables for an experiment investigating the impact of two forms of child therapy (behavioral versus play) on children's disruptive behavior in the home?

b. Again, keeping triangulation in mind, what would you suggest as a set of research questions for a survey of counselors' comfort in working with multicultural populations?

3. Classify the following studies according to whether they involve independent groups, related groups, repeated measures, within-group comparisons, or some combination of these types.

a. A school counselor consulted with a classroom teacher about methods of improving the climate of his classroom by paying attention only to students who were on task. Records were made at 10 and 40 minutes into the period for several consecutive days concerning the percentage of students on task at those times.

b. Counselors at a youth services agency met with pregnant adolescent girls and their boyfriends in separate groups to encourage feelings of responsibility for the unborn children. All clients' feelings of responsibility were ascertained via the administration of a questionnaire after a one-month period.

c. A counselor at a hospital offering psychological services randomly divided his clients with eating disorders into two groups. Both groups were asked to keep daily records of the number of calories they consumed. One group was asked to share those records during group counseling sessions; the other group did not.

d. A clinic offering couples counseling distributed a questionnaire to its clients regarding their impressions of the effectiveness of the counseling services. Responses were analyzed to test whether partners in same-sex couples or opposite-sex couples agreed with each other more about several different issues.

4. Examine some recent issues of counseling journals and find an article describing a study involving comparisons of related groups, independent groups, repeated measures, or different measures within a group. Bring the article to class and be prepared to discuss why the study used the kinds of comparisons it did.

5. Imagine that you want to design a study to investigate the extent to which counselors in private practice adhere to the ethical guidelines of the American Counseling Association. Try to develop a complete list of the issues you would need to consider during the formulation phase of such a study.

CHAPTER SEVEN

PLANNING THE PROJECT

QUESTIONS TO GUIDE YOUR READING

The Planning Process: Steps and Components
1. What five major steps usually make up the planning process?
2. What components of the project must be considered throughout all five planning steps?
3. Why is a review of the literature a crucial aspect of the planning process?
4. What three important functions are served by conducting pilot studies?
5. What administrative steps are likely to be necessary before a main study can proceed?
6. Why is it important that a project be thoroughly planned?
7. What does a good plan specify with regard to sampling?
8. What decisions must be made during planning with regard to measures?
9. What strategy is recommended for determining whether data analysis procedures have been planned properly?
10. What issues should be addressed when planning for report preparation and dissemination?

Review of the Literature
11. What people are likely to know where more material about a topic may be found?
12. How can you best find books related to a topic?
13. What sources other than books and people are likely to be helpful in a literature search?
14. What four expectations are likely to hold for any new literature review?

Pilot Studies, Fine-Tuning, and Administrative Arrangements
15. What are the two types of pilot studies?
16. What are the three major advantages of carrying out pilot studies?
17. Why must participants in a pilot study not be used in the main study?
18. Why is it improbable that a project will proceed with as few flaws as possible?
19. What planning strategies are useful for dealing with problems that arise as projects are carried out?
20. What three issues are researchers wise to consider while mentally rehearsing the administrative arrangements necessary to carry out a research project?
21. What issues must be resolved in the selection of participants for a research project? In addition to the researcher and participants, who else must be considered?

Measures and Timing
22. What are the most frequent errors students make in choosing tests and inventories for research projects?
23. Under what circumstances are informal tests an appropriate choice of measuring instruments?
24. Why is it useful to mentally rehearse a project's entire procedure in detail during the planning stage?

Planning is the second major phase of a research project and involves a representation of all the subsequent phases: data collection, data analysis, interpretation, and reporting. For the simplest projects, a mental representation often suffices; plans for more complex projects need to be expressed wholly or partly in writing so that details are not forgotten as the remaining phases proceed.

THE PLANNING PROCESS: STEPS AND COMPONENTS

Viewed chronologically, the planning process comprises five major steps:

- literature review;
- preliminary planning, often called an "armchair" phase;
- one or more pilot studies;
- fine-tuning; and
- administrative arrangements to conduct the main study.

Planning for any project can be expected to follow these steps in approximately the order listed. The literature review usually begins during formulation, continues very actively during the early parts of the planning process, and overlaps much of the remaining work of the project, although it requires less of the researcher's effort as the project continues. The literature review and preliminary planning steps are often interactive in that some of the earliest planning ideas may be changed as relevant literature is encountered. Some small projects omit pilot studies and do any needed fine-tuning while administrative arrangements are being made. In very complex projects, some administrative arrangements must be made far in advance, even though earlier planning steps have not yet been completed.

Throughout all five planning steps, a researcher needs to consider the project's various components: design, people, sampling, experimental procedures (if any), measures (both instruments and procedures), statistical analysis, report preparation, and report dissemination.

Combined, these steps and components may be viewed in a two-dimensional model such as that depicted in Table 7.1. The horizontal dimension represents the five major planning steps in an approximate time sequence. The vertical dimension represents the various components of the plan to be considered at each of these five steps. In the following subsections we briefly discuss each of these steps and components as a part of the planning process. In later sections in this chapter we will discuss some of these steps and components in greater detail.

The Five Steps

Planning a research project has many similarities with planning any other activity. For example, you may have gotten some ideas about a particular place by reading about it before planning a visit. Preliminary plans come

T A B L E   7.1
A Two-Dimensional Model of the Planning Process

	Steps				
Components	*Literature review*	*Preliminary plans*	*Pilot studies*	*Fine-tuning*	*Administrative arrangements*
Research approach					
Design					
People					
Sampling					
Experimental procedures					
Measurement					
Statistical analysis					
Reporting					
Timing					

from thinking, more reading, and usually writing and consultation with other people. Some parts of a plan may be tried out in advance (for example, Can everything I want to take be packed into a flight bag?). Plans are refined as more information is accumulated. Finally, administrative arrangements (for example, reservations) must be made. These activities are analogous, respectively, to literature review, preliminary planning, pilot studies, fine-tuning, and administrative arrangements in research planning. We will introduce these activities next, followed by a discussion of the components that make up these five steps.

Literature review.   A **literature review** is an important part of a research plan because the professional literature contains many ideas for the various components listed in the vertical dimension of Table 7.1. Almost always, these ideas offer ways to improve a project's quality or to make it easier to conduct. The process of conducting a literature review is discussed in greater detail later in this chapter.

Preliminary plans.   Planning a research project, even a small one, requires many decisions. The matters to be decided vary widely in scope, from the most minuscule to those that affect the entire project. For example, a researcher's decision to conduct an experiment rather than a survey affects almost everything else about the project; which question to ask first in an interview is a much less far-reaching decision. While reviewing the literature for a project, a researcher usually considers several possibilities for most of the necessary decisions of large and moderate scope, and for many of the smaller decisions as well. Before conducting pilot studies, a researcher must decide most of these matters at least provisionally, with the expectation that some (perhaps many) decisions will be changed later.

Pilot studies.   A pilot study is a small research project carried out to provide answers helpful in planning a larger main study. Pilot studies can serve three important functions. The most common is to enable a researcher to test plans before putting them into action. A pilot study can also provide information the researcher needs to make effective plans, such as information about the participants or the institutional environment in which the project will be conducted. Third, pilot studies give researchers the opportunity to practice planned procedures before using them in the main study.

Fine-tuning.   Information from pilot studies enables researchers to revise plans before proceeding further. This process is called **fine-tuning.** If faults are discovered, the researcher can correct them. This process is analogous to fine-tuning a service program as discussed in Chapter 3. If this step involves any major changes, a new pilot study may be wise before proceeding with the main study.

Administrative arrangements.   Before most main studies can proceed, the researcher must carry out many preparatory steps. For example, the cooperation of crucial people or organizations must be secured, space must be arranged in which to conduct project activities, and supplies must be ordered. An application for external funding is among the early steps for many projects.

If any materials or equipment must be purchased or leased, arranging for procurement is part of planning. Likewise, planning includes recruiting and arranging to hire any personnel who must be employed specifically for the project. Many projects draw their equipment, supplies, and staff from a host organization such as a school or agency; others operate as fiscally independent entities. Preparatory administrative steps are discussed in more detail later in this chapter.

Components

In each of the five planning steps, a researcher needs to consider several components of the project as it is to be carried out. These components, represented by the vertical dimension in Table 7.1, are introduced next along with a brief explanation of their value to the research planning process.

Research approaches.   As discussed in Chapter 2, some projects represent only one research approach while other projects represent more than one, such as a survey and an experiment. Probably the most far-reaching decisions in planning any project concern which of the various research approaches will be used. First, researchers decide which approach best suits each research question in a project, and then they consider each of these approaches for feasibility. For example, a researcher might want to study the effects of counselors' sexual overtures to their clients. Because this research question includes the idea of cause, an experiment would be the strongest research approach. However, counselors cannot ethically make sexual overtures to clients. Therefore, alternative research approaches must be considered, such as a survey of clients who say they have experienced such overtures.

Design. **Design** includes most of the other components listed in Table 7.1. Despite this redundancy, we include design in the list to emphasize the idea that these components of a plan are not separate bits and pieces but must form a unified whole. Good design maximizes the chances that a project's data will provide clear rather than equivocal answers to its research questions. This complex concept is discussed more fully in Chapters 8 and 9.

People. Whose efforts will be required to carry out the project? A few projects can be carried out by a single researcher working alone. For example, a person who has free access to an agency's records can examine these records for research purposes. At the other extreme, a very large project might involve an entire organization established solely to conduct the project. A project's people also include its participants. Sometimes participants are asked to furnish new data; at other times these data already exist in the form of records.

Sampling. As noted in Chapter 6, good formulation specifies the populations included in the project's research questions. A good plan specifies how one or more samples will be recruited and selected so that each population will be appropriately represented. In some projects, sampling issues apply to other populations in addition to participants, such as agencies, counselors, teachers, or workplaces. Chapter 10 discusses sampling issues in detail.

Experimental procedures. Plans for an experiment must specify what procedures will be administered as experimental treatments and as control conditions. These procedures must represent the one or more independent variables specified by the project's research questions.

Measures. A good formulation specifies what variables will be measured. Planning includes decisions about how to measure them. This "how" includes both instruments (for example, tests, questionnaires, rating scales, observation schedules) and procedures. Some **measures** may be based on data from documents or other sources rather than directly from participants.

The measurement aspects of planning are discussed further later in this chapter. Chapters 11 and 12 provide detailed discussion of issues related to measures.

Statistical analysis.   How are the data to be processed, both to answer the research questions and for presentation in the project report? **Statistical analysis** may include tabulation, graphing, descriptive statistics, tests of significance, or any combination of these. These procedures are discussed in greater detail in Chapter 13.

Beginning researchers often have difficulty planning data analysis in sufficient detail to serve as a satisfactory guide when the analysis must be carried out. We suggest the following technique for determining whether statistical methods have been planned clearly enough. Choose a reader who is relatively naive about this specific project and who understands the statistical methods to be used. Ask this person to read a description of the planned data collection and statistical analysis, then answer this question: "If I handed you the data from this project and all the necessary tools (for example, computer, statistical software package, calculator, significance tables), could you carry out the analysis based on this written plan?" If the answer is negative, ask why. Unclear procedures are often identified immediately. If they are not, give the person time to think about it. If the answer is still negative, gaps remain in the plan.

A good plan identifies not only the methods to be used and the data to which they are to be applied but also the people who are responsible for carrying out the analysis. Will it be done by computer or by hand? If by computer, the software and computer system to be used should be identified in planning and conditions of access should be determined.

Report preparation and dissemination.   Beginning researchers often overlook reporting as a project activity when preparing research plans. Clear formulation specifies why answers to research questions are sought. From these reasons, it is often possible to infer whom some of the project report's consumers should be. Identifying these consumers usually points to one or more reporting outlets likely to reach them. Familiarity with the requirements of these outlets and the kinds of reports they usually present may offer ideas about how the present project's report should be prepared. How long should it be? How much detail should it include? Also, the researcher should bear in mind any stakeholder interests when designing the report. Although this idea was introduced in Chapter 4 in connection with program evaluation, it applies to other research projects as well. In large projects involving a research team, responsibility for report preparation should be assigned as part of planning. Reporting is discussed in detail in Chapter 14.

Timing.   This component of a research plan considers all the others. Every project activity must take place at some time and in some order in relation to the other activities. Carefully planning the sequence and timing of these various activities increases the likelihood that the project will proceed smoothly. This careful planning is more important with large, complex projects than with small, simple ones.

REVIEW OF THE LITERATURE

As noted in Chapter 6, an intensive literature search usually begins in the formulation phase and continues through the planning phase and at reduced intensity throughout the remainder of the project. Creating a good plan often requires excursions into the literature addressing such matters as measuring instruments and procedures for collecting and analyzing the data. The literature review for many projects includes journals and other possible outlets for reporting the project at hand.

Literature Sources

Many students approach a literature review in a frame of mind similar to the "idea desert" Drew and Hardman (1985) discussed in connection with choosing a problem. How can you find out whether anything has been written about this topic? If so, where could it be found? Possibilities for starting the process include people, books, professional journals, conferences, abstracts, indexes, annual reviews, the popular press, government publications, and computerized databases. Here are some questions and recommendations for researchers to consider when formulating and planning new projects.

People. Who among your colleagues, friends and acquaintances, or people you have had recent contact with would likely know where you might find more material about your topic? These people may be experts with helpful knowledge (about the matter being investigated, about the methodological choices being considered, or about the institutional environment in which the project is to be carried out), or they may be people whose administrative cooperation the study will require. Did any courses you have taken recently include related material? If so, ask the instructor. If you work in a school or an agency, think about your supervisor's and colleagues' special interests and areas of expertise. Talk over your ideas with people who have relevant interest and knowledge, and ask them where you might find published material. Some service agencies and self-help groups can provide leads to literature or to people with special expertise related to their areas of interest.

Books. Look over the texts you have used in recent courses or other books that have come to your attention. If a book gives even brief attention to a topic related to your project, it may cite a reference. If you identify a relevant book, find it in the library. Examine other books shelved nearby. Many libraries use the Library of Congress catalog system by which books with similar call numbers have related content. The "subject" catalog in the library will probably reveal other books that bear on your topic. Examine the reference list in each reasonably recent book to locate other materials you can use. When you find a good book, look up others by the same author. The author and subject indexes of the current issue of *Books in Print* (available in most libraries) may lead you to books your library does not have. So might the computer-based catalog access systems in some large libraries. Given sufficient time, you may be able to get important books through interlibrary loan or by direct order from the publisher.

Journals.   Appendix A lists a number of journals related to counseling. Find several of the recent issues and scan the table of contents in each issue for articles related to your project. Some journals have a subject index covering a year's articles. When you find a good article, look over its list of references as you did with books.

Abstracts and indexes.   These are usually housed in the reference section of a large library. Most reference guides search a large segment of professional literature and have author and subject indexes. Appendix A lists a few that cover materials related to counseling. The *Readers' Guide to Periodical Literature* covers the popular press.

Annual reviews.   Each year an annual review contains several chapters that review the literature on different topics. Chapter topics vary from year to year. If you find a chapter on your topic, it will likely contain much relevant information. However, we recommend bearing in mind that the references cited will probably not include the most recent. For example, a chapter one of us co-authored (Hadley & Hadley, 1983) covering the 1970s decade was begun in 1980, largely completed in late 1981, and published in 1983. In addition, we recommend following up an annual review chapter by getting as many primary sources as you can; do not assume the chapter author reported the various sources completely and accurately. Sources may contain material of interest to you that was outside the chapter author's interest and therefore omitted from the chapter. Additionally, annual review authors, like other humans, occasionally make mistakes. The *Annual Review of Psychology* and the *Annual Review of Rehabilitation*, among others, contain chapters related to counseling.

Conferences.   Most large professional organizations, and some smaller ones, hold regularly scheduled conferences in which professional issues are discussed and information is exchanged. Gruber's *Encyclopedia of Associations* is available in the reference section of many large libraries and lists forthcoming conferences. Some counseling-related organizations are listed in Appendix A. Conferences vary widely in the extent to which they yield documentary records. Conferences may record presentations in their entirety in a journal or a set of proceedings, produce a booklet with abstracts of the presentations, provide a schedule distributed to attendees listing presenters and titles, or simply provide access to copies of individual papers distributed by the authors. If you identify a relevant paper, you may be able to get a copy by writing to the author or accessing it via a database. All content presented in conference sessions is part of the professional literature whether or not it is reflected in a documentary record.

Popular press. Newspapers and magazines occasionally publish articles related to counseling. Most libraries have the *Readers' Guide,* which has a subject index for accessing this very large body of published material. If you find the name of a prominent person with expertise in your topic, look it up in the author index of *Books in Print* and the author catalog of your library; you may find one or more books.

Government publications. Some activities of the U.S. Congress and state legislatures concern settings or problems with which counselors work, such as education, rehabilitation, mental health, family relations, employee relations, and abuse of alcohol and other drugs. Many government agencies at federal, state, and local levels publish reports. Most large libraries have a special room or specialized staff for government publications. The U.S. senators in your state and the congressional representative and state legislators from your district probably have local offices with staff who can inform you of activities in your area of interest. These activities might include recent or pending legislation or reports from committees or agencies. If you find an item you can use, ask for a copy; if it is not available from the legislator's office, ask how you might get it.

Computerized databases. ERIC, REHABDATA, and PsycINFO cover education, rehabilitation, and psychology literature respectively. If you have access to a large library, ask the reference librarian how you might use these systems. A user fee may be required. Appendix A lists mailing addresses from which more information about these systems may be obtained.

Managing the Information Found

Our experience leads us to four expectations for any new literature review:

- many more sources will be identified than are eventually used,
- some sources will at first appear irrelevant and later be found useful,
- different sources will bear on different aspects of the project (for example, some may concern theoretical issues, some design, some sampling, some measurement methods, some counseling techniques, some statistical analysis), and
- the final report will require an alphabetized list of references including **bibliographic data.**

Researchers need to bear these points in mind while conducting a literature review and managing the material found.

Once the relevant information has been found and read, it must be summarized, evaluated, and stored so it is readily available when needed. The researcher will rely on this material when pursuing leads to further relevant sources, planning the project, and preparing the project report. Sampson (1991) noted that commercially available "reference management software" enables researchers to use computers in this process (p. 263). Appendix D offers some practical suggestions for managing reference lists without this aid and provides a sample summary of one reference source. This sample is based on these suggestions and the ideas offered in this chapter.

Pilot Studies

A pilot study may be either of two types. Most commonly, it is a miniature of the main study; all or part of its procedures are tried out with a few participants. The second type of pilot study is conducted when researchers need additional information about a prospective project's participants or the context in which the project is to be carried out. A small project is thus conducted to collect the needed data. For example, the best choice among several available forms of an achievement test, an interest inventory, or an attitude scale might depend on participants' reading skills. In a pilot study, the researcher might administer a reading test to a sample from the intended study population.

There are three major advantages to be gained from trying out a planned project's entire procedure with a small sample before beginning to collect data for the main study. These advantages stem partly from the experience of collecting data on a trial basis, partly from the data collected.

First, as noted in Chapter 6, a pilot study permits a preliminary test of the project; pilot data often permit faulty research questions or hypotheses to be improved or dropped. If pilot results suggest that the project will likely be unproductive when carried out in full, the researcher may choose to discontinue it at this stage with much time, effort, and money saved. In short, a pilot study sometimes indicates that a researcher needs to revisit the formulation phase.

Second, carrying out planned data collection and analysis procedures on a trial basis often leads to improvements. In a pilot study, it is possible to try out several alternative instruments or procedures and to then choose the best one for the main study. Flaws in the procedures can be identified and corrected before data collection for the main study is begun. Comments from research participants and support people often contain or stimulate ideas for improving a project. Even when planned procedures work as intended, ideas for better ones may come to mind. As noted earlier in this chapter, a pilot study permits fine-tuning a project's plans.

And third, practicing a project's procedures in a pilot study often allows a researcher to carry out procedures more skillfully and confidently in the main study than would otherwise be possible. This practice opportunity may be especially important with any procedures that are both unfamiliar and complex, such as counseling techniques new to the project staff.

How large a pilot study should be depends upon many factors, including the size of the planned main study. If the main study is a project for a one-term university class, a tryout with four or five participants will probably suffice as a pilot. In contrast, a master's thesis project may serve as a pilot study for a large grant-funded research program or doctoral project. Pilot studies are not necessarily limited to one per major project. Rather, several pilot studies might be conducted as successive planning refinements are made before data collection for the main study begins.

Whatever the size of a pilot study, its participants should not be used in the main study, although they should be as much like the main study's participants as is feasible. Any refinements of procedure need to be made before data collection for the main study is begun. Mixing pilot data with data from the main study would be equivalent to omitting the pilot study and making procedural refinements while data collection is under way. Also, inexperienced researchers sometimes recycle pilot participants by re-administering the project's procedures to them in the main study. This practice is inadvisable because these participants' experiences in the pilot study are likely to influence their responses to the project's procedures in the main study.

FINE-TUNING THE PLAN

A research plan should be carefully reviewed for possible improvements after pilot data are collected and analyzed and before data collection for the main study begins. A thorough job of planning minimizes the difficulties likely to occur later in the project. Nonetheless, flawless progress is extremely improbable. We note two reasons for this prediction. First, unpredictable and uncontrollable events occur. Crucial people become ill or injured; staff get reassigned; promised deliveries of important equipment or materials get delayed; budgets get cut. Second, unexpected events occur that hindsight says the researcher should have been able to predict and avoid. For example, a crucial piece of equipment breaks down and then the researcher notices its frayed electric cord or lapsed maintenance schedule. Researchers, like other people, have finite abilities to recognize and correctly interpret the large volume of information that surrounds us. "Information overload" affects us all. An old homily alleges that "the course of true love never did run smooth"; experienced researchers expect the same of their projects. As Murphy's Law notes, "Anything that can go wrong will go wrong."

Good, thorough planning is a first line of defense against Murphy's Law. Even with a good first line of defense, it is wise to have a backup system; events requiring further fine-tuning may occur throughout the duration of the project. As the foundation for a backup system, we recommend two ideas. First, difficulties are not only obstacles but also opportunities for learning. Information gained from such experiences sometimes enables the researcher to improve an ongoing project; sometimes it stimulates ideas for new projects. We refer you once again to Skinner's (1972) account of his own career as a scientist. Second, research plans are not cast in concrete or etched in stone. Paper and floppy diskettes are much cheaper and more flexible media. When difficulties arise, think divergently and creatively about the possibilities for coping with them. The brainstorming strategy is sometimes helpful: generate ideas first; then analyze, criticize, and choose among them.

If some of these possibilities involve changes in the research plan, examine each such change carefully from an informal cost–benefit perspective. How effectively would this change address the difficulties at hand? What new difficulties (if any) would this change likely bring about? Would this change compromise the value of data already collected? Would the change violate any agreements already made with support people or other stakeholders? Would the change make the data more difficult to interpret with regard to the project's mission? We suggest that you ask such questions as these about each change you think might be helpful. Modify project plans or keep them unchanged based on your answers. Sometimes difficulties encountered in planning require that the formulation phase be revisited before planning can continue satisfactorily. If so, accept that setback and revise both the mission and the plan accordingly.

ADMINISTRATIVE ARRANGEMENTS

What steps must be taken to assure that the researcher has the needed **authority** and resources to collect, analyze, interpret, and report the data? Authority refers to official permission to collect the data and report the project according to plan. Resources may be subdivided into three categories: human, material, and fiscal. In the formulation phase, a researcher asks an all-important feasibility question: Are needed authority and resources available? To complete the planning phase, the researcher must take whatever steps are necessary to assure that authority and resources are at hand when needed.

Mentally rehearsing the entire procedure in detail while planning a project affords a good opportunity to generate "to do" lists of administrative arrangements necessary to collect, analyze, and report the data. During this mental rehearsal, we suggest making three lists:

- authority and funding,
- human resources, and
- material resources.

Begin the authority and funding list by noting whether any organization involved with the project (for example, university, counseling service agency) has an institutional review committee that must approve the project. Next, note whether any special funds are to be sought. Then, as each data collection step is mentally rehearsed, ask yourself whose permission, if any, is required. From this list, decide what steps must be taken to get the necessary permission and funds.

As each data collection step is mentally rehearsed, note who will do it. When this human resources list is complete, review it and identify each person who must be specially hired for the project or asked for his or her help. Then decide what must be done to recruit, hire, and solicit the cooperation of these people. If any of these people must be paid or if their work in the project is part of their jobs, check the authority and funding list to be sure you have included whatever must be done to secure the necessary funds or the permission of their supervisors. If any of your own activities must be rearranged to allow you to devote the necessary time to the project, list what must be done to accomplish that rearrangement.

Finally, prepare a material resources list. As each data collection, analysis, and reporting step is mentally rehearsed, note what facilities, equipment, and supplies, if any, are required. Facilities are often easy to overlook, such as a room in which to conduct tests or interviews, a chair for an observer in a classroom, a telephone for conducting interviews, a computer, and a compatible software package for analyzing data. When this list is complete, decide what must be done to ensure that facilities, equipment, and supplies are available when needed, with equipment in good working order. Revisit the authority and funding list to be sure you have included the permission and finances necessary to provide these material resources.

From these three lists, the researcher can make a master list containing each administrative step and the time when it should be carried out. As each step is taken, we suggest keeping a dated record of it. Dated records of this process can be very helpful when the project report must be prepared.

PEOPLE

Participants and researchers are usually the first to come to mind as you think of the people involved in a project. Most research projects in counseling involve data from participants, whether newly collected specifically for the project or drawn from preexisting records. Many questions about participants must be considered. Think about these questions when planning the project.

- For purposes of interpretation, are the study's participants to be regarded as representative samples of one or more populations or do they themselves constitute one or more meaningful groups?
- How are participants to be recruited, selected, and assigned?
- Are certain people to be excluded or deleted from the project? If so, what rules will govern the decisions about whom to exclude or delete?

- How will participants' cooperation be enlisted?
- What are participants to be told about the project?

Additional questions will probably come to mind. Most research projects in counseling require the efforts of other people in addition to researchers and participants. For want of a better name, we call these individuals **support people.** We include counselors, psychometrists, receptionists, survey interviewers, raters, and observers, to name a few. Most of the questions asked about participants in the previous paragraph also apply to support people. In a study of counseling methods, for example, is it desirable to generalize beyond the specific counselors who applied the methods in this project? If so, it is desirable to sample a meaningful population of counselors who are to apply the techniques, in addition to sampling the clients to whom they are applied. Issues related to observers and raters are discussed in connection with behavioral observation and rating scales in Chapter 12. Most researchers are not concerned with sampling issues in connection with psychometrists, receptionists, and survey interviewers, although the researcher must often select and instruct these individuals carefully to be assured of their competent cooperation and to reduce bias. In some experimental projects, such people need to be assigned carefully to reduce the risk of confounding treatment effects with the persons who administer the treatments. Confounding is discussed in detail in Chapter 8.

To the list of support people, we add the administrators and officials who confer the authority to conduct a project and who provide the needed material and financial resources. Some projects draw fiscal and administrative support from the same sources, some from different sources. Such people usually have interests of their own in relation to a project; these interests are often expressed in agreements on which their support is conditional. For example, a researcher may have agreed to issue timely reports, to exclude emergency cases, or to observe a room-use schedule. It is necessary but not sufficient that such agreements be ethically acceptable. The researcher must consider the terms of these agreements during the planning phase to provide for their fulfillment.

Many support people have other duties in addition to their activities with any given research project. Further, few if any support people will match the researcher's enthusiasm for his or her project. These matters must be considered in the planning phase to avoid placing unrealistic demands and expectations on support people whose cooperation is essential. For example, a project may call for observers in wards of a hospital to record patients' behavior before and after a counseling intervention. Planning must take into account the needs and regularly scheduled activities of these wards so observers can be present at appropriate times.

To the extent possible, a researcher should seek to identify in the planning phase:

- every support person whose efforts are expected or desired in connection with the project;
- what each person is expected to do in relation to the project;

- what each person has to gain from participation in the project;
- any agreements that have been made or will probably be made related to each person's participation; and
- other commitments, interests, and needs of each person that should be taken into account as the project is conducted.

MEASURES

Some variables in research projects are measured with instruments such as tests, inventories, rating scales, observation schedules, and polygraphs. Alternatively, measures may be based on data from other sources such as records or other documents.

Instruments and Procedures

Whether or not **instruments** are used, measures require procedures. For example, tests and inventories must be administered and scored; observations must be recorded. If records are a data source, they must be examined and the data recorded.

Each instrument to be used must be chosen from among existing ones or constructed anew. Each instrument chosen may be used as is or revised to fit the project at hand. Similarly, procedures for collecting data can be designed anew or adopted (with or without revision) from earlier work. These decisions are part of planning a project. When planning is complete, a researcher has in hand all measures and instruments to be used in the main study (as distinguished from pilot studies discussed earlier in this chapter) in a form ready to use and knows what participants and support people involved in the data collection will be asked to do.

Any standardized tests and inventories to be used are chosen from among many that have been published. When planning is complete, a researcher knows why the particular instruments chosen are preferred over other possibilities. Isaac and Michael (1981) suggest a "form for evaluating tests" that lists 26 points to consider. In our experience, the most frequent errors students make in choosing tests and inventories for research projects are that the instruments chosen are too loosely related to the project's mission and ill-suited to the project's participants (for example, contain words too difficult for some respondents). Ordinarily, standardized tests and inventories should not be revised to suit a research project. To do so destroys their standardization; results cannot be meaningfully compared with existing normative data, and such modified instruments lose their advantages over informal ones.

If informal tests are to be used, reasons for this choice should be clear. Two common reasons are: (1) a thorough literature review reveals no existing standardized tests sufficiently suited to the project, or (2) the project is to be carried out in a setting such as a classroom in which informal tests are to be used for other purposes.

Usually, questionnaires must be written specifically for a project. In rare instances, a questionnaire found in the literature suits a planned project so well as to need no revision. Even these should be carefully examined for possible improvements in general quality. Just because a questionnaire is published or has been used in a published project, it should not be assumed to be free from flaws. Flawless questionnaires are the exception rather than the rule, even among published projects. When a new questionnaire is to be developed, existing ones often offer a good point of departure.

Research interviews require written instructions. Usually these include an **interview guide** (also sometimes called an **interview schedule** or an **interview protocol**) and a system for recording the data obtained. Planning includes writing and the preliminary tryout of any interview guides to be used. The observations about adopting or adapting questionnaires of other researchers apply equally to interview guides.

If **content analysis** is to be applied to the responses, a researcher should decide in the planning phase whether content categories or **rating scales** are to be decided in advance or developed after some or all of the data have been collected. If rating scales are to be decided in advance, they should be developed during planning. If rating scales are to be developed later, planning should determine what rules and considerations are to be used to guide their development.

Behavioral observation, like interviews, requires a written guide and a system for recording the observations. These materials should be developed during planning.

If any mechanical apparatus is to be used, planning includes its selection and justification. Why is this particular apparatus to be preferred over other possibilities (if any competing possibilities exist)? Often these reasons are simple, such as being conveniently at hand rather than having to be procured. When procurement is necessary, it is part of planning.

Data Collection from Documents

Many projects draw all or part of their data from existing written sources such as case files, official records, correspondence, books, and periodicals—in short, from **documents.** For example, one of us remembers a project conducted by a fellow student when we were in graduate school that was based in part on ratings of mystery stories' violence. As a second example, Matkin and Riggar (1986) reported the "number of articles containing information about private sector topics in five rehabilitation journals" during the years 1978–1984 (p. 51). We consider the distinction between data collection and literature review an important one to bear in mind, even though the same sources might serve both functions in some projects.

In some projects, the researcher can specify in advance exactly what documents will be used (for example, the files of all clients seen in the Student Counseling Center during the Spring 1993 term). When documents cannot be specified in advance, plans should include the rules by which they will be selected. For example, Byrd, Williamson, and Byrd (1986) studied all characters with disabilities who were listed in the *Cyclopedia of Literary Characters*. As part of their rules for selecting documents, these authors defined the term *disability* and distinguished this concept from acute illness.

Good plans also provide for access to required documents. Sometimes this access is easy. A project carried out in an agency by its own staff should present little or no problem regarding access to the agency's client files. In contrast, if a researcher wants to study old correspondence kept locked in a private collection, access might be the most difficult issue in the entire planning phase of the project.

TIMING

In discussing the issue of timing, Drew and Hardman (1985) recommended that researchers "mentally rehearse the entire procedure in detail" (p. 63). This idea includes both identifying the activities to be carried out and specifying their sequence and timing. We further suggest doing this rehearsal from the perspective of each significant person (or category of persons) involved in the project. It is often helpful to prepare one or more **time lines** to express the sequence and timing of the project. Most proposals prepared for grant support include a general time line for the project (see Appendix E for examples). However, each person has his or her own time line that may cover all or part of the project's entire time span. In a complex project, to "mentally rehearse the entire procedure in detail" may be extremely difficult without expressing most if not all of it in writing.

As an example, let's look at a project that might take place in a university counseling center. The receptionist assigns clients/participants at random to counselors who are offering one of two different counseling programs, informs clients about their role in the project, secures their consent, administers a questionnaire to each one before and after the first session, and keeps a record of each session's length. When all interviews have been held and all questionnaires administered, the receptionist gives them to judges (graduate students in counseling) for rating. Her role in the project ends when all the ratings are returned. A client sees the receptionist to schedule an appointment, reads and listens to a description of the project, signs the consent form, completes a questionnaire, and attends counseling sessions as agreed upon with the counselor; after the first session, he or she completes a second questionnaire.

The activities of each person involved should be mentally rehearsed in similar fashion. If a group of people (for example, all experimental group participants) are alike in their sequence of activities, one representative will suffice for the lot. Activities of support persons should be considered in light of each person's interests and other commitments. Such thorough mental rehearsal often enables a researcher to identify and correct flaws in a project before the plan is put into action even tentatively as in a pilot study.

In a project using documents as data sources, access to some documents, such as library books, may be time limited. Planning must provide for use of documents during the times they are available. It is sometimes possible and highly desirable to schedule document usage in advance, especially if certain documents are best examined first and others later.

Good planning provides for the time and resources required to prepare the intended reports of the project, taking into account the requirements of the outlets to which the reports will be directed.

CHAPTER SUMMARY

A research plan ensures that the project (a) has access to the necessary technology and resources, (b) anticipates outcomes that warrant the necessary effort and expense, (c) observes legal and ethical standards, (d) fits the researcher's other plans, and (e) has an outlet for reporting the findings. Planning a research project envisions all future phases in some detail: data collection, analysis, interpretation, and reporting. The planning process may be viewed as comprising two dimensions: a sequence of steps and the aspects of the project that must be considered. Most projects' planning steps include literature review, preliminary planning, one or more pilot studies, fine-tuning, and administrative arrangements. A literature review begun during formulation continues during planning and usually offers ideas for preliminary plans. One or more pilot studies permit fine-tuning project plans and increase researchers' skill and confidence with planned procedures. Administrative arrangements must ensure access to the necessary authority and resources. A plan must consider the people, the measuring instruments, and the statistical procedures to be involved. Participants (and also support persons in some projects) must be selected, recruited, and possibly assigned to treatments. Measuring instruments must be chosen or constructed. The sequence and timing of all procedures must be decided. All projects encounter some difficulties; careful planning minimizes these difficulties.

PRACTICAL EXERCISES

1. Imagine that you want to design a study to investigate the extent to which counselors in private practice adhere to the ethical guidelines of the American Counseling Association. An exercise for Chapter 6 called for you to develop a complete list of the issues you would need to consider

for such a study during the formulation phase. For this exercise, develop a list of issues you would need to consider for the components of the planning phase of such a study.

2. Chapter 7 and Appendix D include suggestions for conducting a review of the literature. Based on the suggestions offered, prepare a summary of a reference source you found in the literature using the sample summary in Appendix D as a model. The reference source should describe a research project.

3. Practical Exercise 1 asked you to consider several components of planning for a research project to investigate the extent to which counselors in private practice adhere to the ethical guidelines of the American Counseling Association. For this exercise, try to determine how you would ensure that you have the needed authority and resources to conduct such a project. Whose permission would be required to collect the data and report the project according to plan? What human, material, and fiscal resources would be required to carry out such a project?

DESIGN PRINCIPLES

QUESTIONS TO GUIDE YOUR READING

An Overview of Design

1. What aspects of any research project's plan are specified by the design?
2. What additional aspects of an experiment's plan does the design specify?
3. What may constitute a subject in counseling research?
4. How may assignment of subjects differ in different research plans?
5. Why are treatment and control conditions important to experiments?
6. What decisions are involved in the timing of treatment conditions?
7. How may the number and sequence of measures and kinds of statistical analyses differ from project to project?
8. Define independent, dependent, classification, control, stratification, predictor, criterion, developmental, and extraneous variables.
9. Explain the concept of confounding. What is the relationship between control and confounding?
10. How can you control a potentially confounding variable by holding it constant? By varying it systematically and deliberately within the project? By randomizing it? Give examples of each type of control.

Choosing Designs

11. What two major types of designs do researchers use when they wish to feel confident about conclusions pertaining to causality?
12. What synonyms exist for the term *time series*?
13. What is meant by the term *functional relation*?
14. What kinds of conclusions do time series designs support that group designs do not support?
15. Why is the AB design considered weak?
16. Distinguish between withdrawal and reversal time series designs.
17. Explain how withdrawal and reversal operate in ABAB designs. Why are ABAB designs considered so much stronger than AB designs?
18. Why was the multiple baseline design developed? How are functional relations demonstrated in this design?
19. Under what conditions is a multiple baseline design preferable to an ABAB design? When is an ABAB design preferred?
20. When is the use of group designs especially appropriate?
21. How do no-treatment and differential treatment control groups differ? Why is the term *control condition* preferred to *no treatment* when describing control groups' experiences?
22. What is the simplest traditional group design? What is the simplest repeated-measures design? Why are both considered weak?
23. What is the distinguishing feature of own-control designs? How does this type of design differ from the one-group pretest–posttest design?
24. What is counterbalancing, and how is it used in own-control designs?
25. What is the distinction between factorial and mixed designs?
26. What kinds of variables may serve as factors in a factorial design?

27. What do we mean by the phrase *the levels of a factor*? Give an example.
28. How many independent groups would be required in a factorial experiment with 3 factors and 2 levels of each factor?
29. What is an interaction effect in a factorial experiment? Create an example of an interaction in a two-factor experiment with two levels of each factor that is different from any used in the text.
30. Distinguish between repeated-measures, related-groups, and within-group factors in a mixed design, and give examples of each. What general term is used to describe these three types of factors?
31. What is the simplest possible mixed design? What variations of this design are possible?
32. What advantage does the pretest–posttest control-group design offer over the posttest-only control-group design? Under what conditions is the posttest-only design preferable?
33. What is the Solomon four-group design? How does this design measure the effects of pretesting?
34. What problems may arise when a wait-control design is used? What solutions may be possible for those problems?
35. Define single-blind and double-blind design features.
36. What is the difference between convenience sampling and probability sampling?
37. Describe the basic features of cohort, longitudinal, and retrospective developmental designs.
38. What are the weaknesses of the three designs in question 37? How can a combination approach help counteract these weaknesses?
39. How can ex post facto designs be used to help researchers choose variables to be tested for causal relations in experiments?

What Is Design?

This rather complex concept refers to a major part of any research plan. Based on the discussion of design by several authors (for example, Ary, Jacobs, & Razavieh, 1985; Drew & Hardman, 1985; Isaac & Michael, 1981; Kerlinger, 1986), we offer this definition: Design is that aspect of a research project's plan that specifies:

1. what subjects are to be used,
2. the number of variables considered and the role of each variable in the project (for example, independent, dependent, control, classification, stratification, predictor, criterion),
3. whether and how subjects are divided into groups to be studied,
4. the choice and timing of measurements taken on subjects, and
5. the general type of analysis to be applied.

The design of experiments includes three additional aspects of the project's plan that do not apply to other research approaches:

6. the number of **experimental treatment** and **control conditions,**
7. the sequence and timing of experimental and control conditions, and
8. the method of assigning these conditions to subjects.

By means of design, researchers seek to **control** various factors that might otherwise be **confounded** with the phenomena being studied and cloud the meaning of the results.

Writers often refer to basic designs; these are commonly used patterns of choices. The Solomon four-group design and the wait-control design, among others, are discussed later in this chapter.

When no previously described designs fulfill the needs of a particular project, a researcher might change an existing design or develop a new one. Few projects use newly developed designs; most use existing designs combined in various ways. Some issues that must be considered when choosing a design are: the subjects, assignment to groups, treatment conditions, timing, measures, analysis, and variables.

Subjects.   A **subject** is a person or other entity upon whom (or which) a research project makes observations or measures. In counseling research, most subjects are people. Some projects use other kinds of subjects, such as agencies, families, literary productions, or interview statements. When people are used as subjects in counseling research, they are usually called participants. Many participants are clients; some are other people, such as counselors, students, teachers, employees, or supervisors. In experiments, treatment conditions are administered to participants or other subjects.

Assignment.   Some research plans require subjects to be assigned to groups that are to be studied. Others use existing groups; in this case, the **assignment** process has already taken place before the research planning begins. In experiments, subjects must be assigned to the experimental and control conditions in an unbiased manner prescribed by the research plan. Some plans assign them in groups, others individually.

Treatment conditions.   Experiments involve treatment conditions administered according to the research plan; other approaches do not. An experiment may involve one or more treatment conditions. Most experiments also include one or more control conditions; some compare two or more conditions without designating any as a control.

Timing.   Timing involves decisions about when treatment conditions are administered and measures taken, in what order, and whether any of them are repeated. This order may differ among subjects. Some designs require a waiting period for one or more subjects but not for others.

Measures.   The simplest projects involve one measure; most projects involve several. In some projects, measures are taken once; in others, they are repeated. Chapter 10 discusses various kinds of measures in detail.

Analysis.   Some project plans call for statistical analysis; others do not. Some statistical analyses involve only a tabular or graphic presentation of data or calculation of descriptive statistics; others involve significance tests ranging from the very simple to the very complex. Some significance tests compare central tendencies or variabilities. Others test the extent to which two or more variables are related. We include these issues in the design concept but not the exact statistical techniques to be employed; some designs can be analyzed appropriately using any one of several techniques. Some writers discuss choice of specific statistical techniques as part of design. Statistical procedures are discussed more fully in Chapter 13.

Variables.   As noted in Chapter 1, a researcher conducting an experiment manipulates or manages an independent variable and observes or measures a dependent variable. Some writers reserve the terms *independent variable* and *dependent variable* for experimental projects only; other writers also apply these terms to some correlational projects. We prefer the former because we have observed that the terms *independent* and *dependent variable* in correlational studies tempt some readers to make improper causal inferences from the results, as was discussed in Chapter 2.

Several kinds of variables are identified in research reports. These variables are not limited to experiments but may appear in projects of any research approach. Classification, control, and stratification variables are used to manage the composition of the group.

> *Classification.* If a researcher deliberately compiles participant groups so that they differ on some preexisting characteristic such as age, gender, or intelligence scores, this characteristic is called a **classification variable**. For example, a project could be designed in which one group consisted of all males and another of all females. Groups might also be composed of persons with below average, average, and above average intelligence scores, respectively. Sometimes participants are assigned to such groups based on preexisting data before the project's new data are collected. Alternatively, participants may be divided according to a classification variable after the data collection is fully or partially completed.
>
> *Control variables.* If a researcher assigns participants to groups so that the groups are as alike as possible in some ways, the characteristics considered in this assignment process are called **control variables**; for example, one might compose two groups so that they contain exactly the same proportion of males and females and the same distribution of previous professional experience.

Stratification variables. In **stratified sampling,** the population to be sampled is subdivided according to one or more variables before participants are selected and the resulting subdivisions are sampled rather than the whole population at once. Variables used for subdividing a population in this way are called **stratification variables.** One common purpose for stratified sampling is to ensure that the stratification variables are distributed in a sample exactly as they are in the population sampled. For example, a sample of university students might be chosen to have exactly the same proportion of freshmen, sophomores, juniors, seniors, and graduate students as the entire student body. Class level is a stratification variable in this case. If the researcher compared these class levels among the project's participants, class level would be both a stratification variable and a classification variable. Stratified sampling is discussed in greater detail in Chapter 10.

Students sometimes confuse control variables, classification variables, and stratification variables, since all are used to manage the composition of groups of participants. The difference is that stratification variables are used to make samples of participants match the populations they are intended to represent, control variables are used to make these participant groups similar to each other, and classification variables are used to divide groups of participants into subgroups that differ from one another in planned ways. Some other kinds of variables mentioned in reports include:

Predictor and criterion variables. As noted in Chapter 2, correlational studies investigate the extent to which variables are related without manipulating variables as is done in experiments. Some correlational studies test the extent to which one or more predictor variables correctly predict one or more criterion variables. For example, researchers who develop scholastic aptitude tests study the extent to which scores on these tests predict grades in school. It is misleading to substitute the terms *independent variable* and *dependent variable* in such studies.

Developmental variables. In developmental studies, **developmental variables** usually refer to time or to variables such as age or grade level, which are a function of time.

Extraneous variables. Factors in which the researcher is not interested but which may weaken the project if they are not controlled are often called **extraneous variables.** For example, a researcher might attribute an outcome such as increased self-esteem to the results of a treatment program but later discover that the treatment group contained a greater number of highly educated individuals than did the control group. Such a difference, rather than the treatment, could also account for the outcome. When extraneous variables are identified during the formulation or planning phase, it is often possible to compose study groups so that they are alike with reference to these variables. In our example, the treatment and control groups would be composed so as to have the same distribution of educational levels among participants. In such instances, the extraneous variables are also control variables.

CONFOUNDING AND CONTROL

Researchers want to answer research questions as unequivocally as possible, ruling out alternative explanations for obtained results. Possible alternative explanations can cloud the meaning of results when extraneous variables influence the phenomena being studied. An extraneous variable is said to be confounded with an independent variable if the two are acting together so that results cannot be clearly interpreted; a researcher cannot say whether either variable, or the two in combination, produced the effect obtained. In such situations, extraneous variables are sometimes called confounding variables.

To interpret results unequivocally, the researcher must control extraneous influences: either protect the phenomena being studied from influence by extraneous variables or isolate these unwanted influences to separate them from the phenomena being studied.

This idea was first developed in agricultural research. To study the effect of added fertilizer on crop yield, for example, some plots were planted with added fertilizer and others without; the plots were kept as alike as possible with regard to other factors such as water, soil conditions, and sunlight exposure. The research plan controlled these "other factors," plus additional ones that may not have been identified. This strategy, to **hold constant** other variables, is one way to avoid confounding.

A different answer to possible confounding is illustrated in the project discussed in Chapter 2, in which some teachers changed their treatment of problem students and others did not. The aspect of teacher behavior being studied was changed for an experimental group and left unchanged for a control group. Instead of deliberately keeping these groups as alike as possible in other ways, the researcher randomly assigned teachers to the two conditions. Presumably, extraneous factors that might influence the results operated similarly for both groups. Random assignment to equalize influences of extraneous variables represents one way to control these factors. In a second project discussed in Chapter 2, Mr. Jones introduced a change in his behavior toward one problem student, waited a specified period of time before introducing the change toward a second, then repeated this procedure with a third and fourth student. This process of **systematic variation** represents a third way to control unwanted influences on results.

To develop the discussion of confounding further, we offer a fantasy. Imagine that Molly Fye and Ann Tagonist were counselors at the same elementary school. The principal wanted them to teach a new social skills program to students referred to counseling for peer-relationship problems. Molly and Ann both liked the same cartoon-based test of social skill development but disagreed strongly about which of two methods to use to teach these skills. They decided each would give the test to her own counselees; then each would try out her own preferred teaching method for two months. At the end of two months, each would give the test again. Teaching method is the independent variable; two methods are deliberately administered according to the research plan. The dependent variable is the students' scores on the social skills test given before and after the two months of teaching. Molly and Ann will note the difference between each student's score before and after the two-month instructional period.

Several extraneous variables are confounded with the independent variable, while other potentially confounding factors are controlled. One of the most blatant confounding problems stems from the differences in the counselors' personalities. As you might guess, we deliberately invented their names to emphasize this point. The two groups of students are treated differently not only in the methods used to teach social skills but also in many other ways due to the counselors' different temperaments. If Molly and Ann also differ in teaching experience or talent, these factors are also confounded with the independent variable in this example.

Another confounding problem stems from whatever differences may have existed between the two groups of students at the outset. In many schools, students are assigned to counselors based on nonrandom factors, such as students' preferences or an administrator's judgment regarding the best counselor choice for each individual student. For example, if the principal had systematically assigned rebellious students to Ann and compliant ones to Molly, this difference would also be confounded with teaching method. Additional confounding problems are discussed in Chapter 9. Even if one group was found to show a much larger average gain in social skills test scores than the other, the counselors could not reasonably infer that the different teaching methods caused this result. It might have been due to any one or more of these confounded extraneous variables acting alone or in combination with the different teaching methods.

For all the above reasons, control of potentially confounding extraneous variables is crucial. Three ways to control such a variable are:

- to hold it constant,
- to vary it deliberately and systematically within the project, or
- to randomize it.

Each strategy has unique advantages and limitations that fit some projects well and others poorly.

Holding Constant

In Molly and Ann's project, several factors are held constant: (a) all students are fourth graders, (b) all students are in the same school, (c) both counselors are women, and (d) the experimental classes take place during the same term. Perhaps you can identify other factors that are also held constant. None of these factors is confounded with the independent variable because both groups are alike in all these respects. However, solving potential confounding problems in this way imposes a limitation: This project's results cannot be directly generalized to other grades, other years, other schools, or male counselors.

Any such generalization would require a premise that the phenomena studied in this project would operate similarly under these different conditions. Such a premise might come from expert judgment or previous research results but does *not* come from this project. If the researcher is uninterested in such generalizations or has sufficient support for them from outside the project, holding extraneous factors constant is the most efficient control procedure. Considerations such as these underlie much controversy concerning the value of laboratory research. Laboratories enable researchers to hold constant many more variables than would be possible in the contexts where most people live and work. However, this very advantage often makes laboratory results more difficult to generalize to the practical problems of everyday-life situations. To return to our example, the project could be made more generalizable by adding other grades, other schools, other years, and male counselors; such changes would also make it more complex and laborious.

Systematic Variation

To illustrate systematic variation as a control tactic, imagine that Molly and Ann in the example wanted to generalize their results to other grades and other schools while holding counselor gender and project term constant. They might select four women counselors serving students from each grade in each of their district's six elementary schools; multiplying four counselors by six grades by six schools gives 144 samples. Statistical analysis could then separate out differences attributable to grade levels and schools.

Randomization

Randomization is the easiest way to control any factors the researcher cannot explicitly identify as well as those easy to identify. Because of the procedures involved in random assignment (discussed in greater detail in Chapter 10), potentially confounding extraneous variables, identified and unidentified, are usually similarly distributed across experimental and control groups. Random assignment generally results in all groups having approximately the same distribution of ages, genders, intelligence levels, and prior education, among other variables. In the project discussed here, four counselors are used in each school. In each of the many schools, two counselors might be randomly assigned to one teaching method and two to the other.

This procedure would eliminate confounding due to counselor characteristics and preexisting differences in the counselors' caseloads. It would probably also eliminate other confounding problems not explicitly identified. (Chapter 9 discusses confounding due to selection and assignment at length.)

CHOOSING DESIGNS

A major part of the task of planning a project consists of deciding which one or more designs will best answer the research questions so as to fulfill the remainder of the project's mission. To return to the project in Chapter 2 in which some teachers changed their treatment of problem students and others did not, a pretest–posttest control group design (discussed later in this chapter) was used. The issues listed in the definition of design at the beginning of this chapter were addressed as follows:

1. The participants were students.
2. One independent and one dependent variable were used.
3. The researcher randomly divided the students into two groups, keeping existing classrooms intact.
4. One measure was taken twice: once before and once after the experimental and control conditions were administered.
5. The two groups of participants were compared with regard to their average change in the measure.
6. One experimental treatment condition and one control condition were used.
7. Experimental and control conditions were administered once, simultaneously, to different groups.
8. The experimental treatment condition was randomly assigned to one group; the other group experienced the control condition.

It should be noted that as researchers commonly use the word **group** (for example, independent group, experimental group, control group) it does not necessarily refer to a group in any social sense; such groups often comprise people who do not communicate with each other in any way. An **experimental group** is a set of participants to whom a project applies one or more experimental treatments or conditions; some projects use one or more control groups to estimate what the experimental groups would have done without the experimental treatments.

Some Experimental Design Features

Experiments represent the appropriate research approach for answering questions about the causes of various phenomena. For example, does one teaching method cause elementary school students to learn social skills more reliably than another? Sulzer-Azaroff and Mayer (1991) defined a functional relation between independent and dependent variables: Changes in the dependent variable occur when, and only when, changes are introduced in the independent variable. Demonstrating a functional relation indicates that the independent variable, and not some extraneous variables, produced a change in the dependent variable.

There are two general categories of experimental designs that researchers use when they wish to feel confident about conclusions pertaining to causes. They are time series and traditional group designs. Both types of designs attempt to control for extraneous factors that may influence the dependent variables in order to demonstrate a functional relationship between the independent and dependent variables. Time series designs rely on repeated measures, usually with one subject or very few. Traditional group designs may use one or any combination of the various types of comparisons discussed in Chapter 6: independent groups, related groups, repeated measures, or within-group. The next two sections discuss time series and traditional group designs, respectively.

TIME SERIES EXPERIMENTAL DESIGNS

The term *time series* is often used interchangeably with $N = 1$, *single case, single subject,* and *intensive.* These terms refer to various aspects of this category of designs, which generally relies on only one or a very few participants studied intensively over a long period of time (usually weeks or months). These designs have become increasingly popular because they allow the impact of a treatment to be assessed for *each individual* to whom it is applied; in contrast, group designs do not permit conclusions to be drawn about the effect of any treatment program on individual members of the group (Sulzer-Azaroff & Mayer, 1991). Group designs rely on an average change within the group as a means of assessing treatment impact; averages sometimes mask contrary or neutral effects of the treatment on some members. Further, behavior changes constantly; a single pre- or posttest, as used in group designs, does not assess behavior as fully as does the ongoing assessment used in time series designs. Finally, if a treatment is not having the desired effect, a time series design will indicate this lack of effect rapidly. In traditional group designs, a lack of effect may not be evident until a posttest is administered.

AB Design

The **AB design** is the simplest time series design, with A and B referring to **phases** (periods of time) in which repeated observations are taken on a participant under different conditions. For example, for several days an observer could count how many times a day a child acts aggressively toward a sibling. The **A phase** corresponds to a control condition. In the A phase,

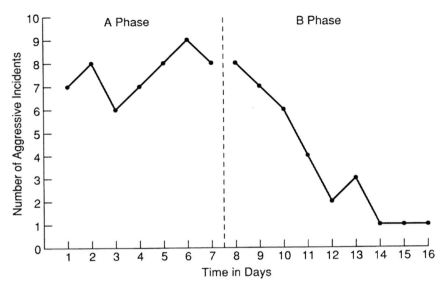

F I G U R E   8.1
AB design illustrated. Data are fictitious.

observations are taken without any attempt to change the behavior. The period of time represented by this initial A phase is usually called the **base-line period.** In the **B phase,** an experimental treatment is implemented, such as asking the parents to respond to any nonaggressive interactions with the sibling with praise and affection and to remove the child to her room for 5 minutes when aggressive interactions occur. If the incidence of aggressive behavior toward the sibling changes shortly after the experimental treatment is introduced, the result suggests that the treatment is producing the change in behavior. Figure 8.1 graphs fictitious behavioral observations from such an experiment, with the vertical axis (**ordinate**) showing the number of aggressive incidents and the horizontal axis (**abscissa**) showing the passage of time.

The AB design is considered very weak because a number of extraneous variables could be confounded with the introduction of the experimental treatment. For example, what if the aggressive sibling were taught a lesson in school on respecting others' rights just as the parents began the B phase? Because of this weakness, the AB design represents a quasi-experiment and is rarely used for experiments. Instead, researchers prefer the **ABAB design.**

ABAB Design

Withdrawal and reversal.   The ABAB design applies the AB series twice in succession. One version of the ABAB design uses the principle of **with-drawal** to demonstrate a functional relationship between the independent

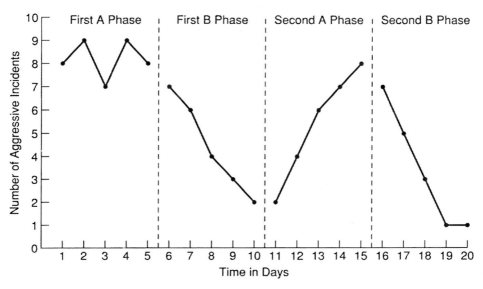

F I G U R E   8.2
ABAB design illustrated. Data are fictitious.

and dependent variables; another variation uses **reversal** for this purpose. In the example of the aggressive child, we noted that in the B phase of the AB design the parents were asked to reinforce any instances of nonaggressive behavior and remove the child to her room when she was aggressive. In an ABAB design, the researchers would ask the parents to withdraw this new response pattern in the second A phase. In other words, the parents would be asked to return to whatever they were doing in the first A phase; they would discontinue reinforcing nonaggressive incidents and removing the child to her room when she behaved aggressively. If the independent and dependent variables are functionally related, we would expect this second A phase to bring an end to the reduction in aggressive incidents that occurred in the first B phase. Instead, the number of aggressive incidents would be expected to increase toward their earlier level because the parents are no longer behaving in a way that reduces aggressive incidents. In the second B phase, the parents would be asked to resume reinforcing non-aggressive behavior and removing the child to her room when she was aggressive. Changes in the dependent variable (aggressiveness) with each change in the independent variable (parent behavior) represent a functional relationship, evidence of cause and effect. Figure 8.2 presents fictitious observations from this ABAB design.

A design employing reversal is similar, but rather than withdrawing the treatment in the second A phase, the researcher reverses the treatment in the second A phase. To apply reversal in our example, the parents could reinforce aggressive incidents during the second A phase by paying attention to them while ignoring appropriate behavior. If the independent variable is functionally related to the dependent variable as hypothesized, the child should increase the number of aggressive incidents during the second A phase; in other words, when the treatment is reversed, the behavior produced in the first B phase should also reverse itself.

Similar results might be expected with either withdrawal or reversal procedures; the choice between them depends on circumstances. Some dependent variable behaviors may respond more clearly to reversal than to the more benign withdrawal. Obviously, reversal is appropriate only when it is ethically responsible to reverse a behavior. For this reason, we chose withdrawal in the aggression example just discussed. Reversal designs are used more often in laboratory situations than in field settings. In most applied projects, withdrawal designs are the preferred choice. Sulzer-Azaroff and Mayer (1991) report the use of reversal designs with the dependent variables of imitating others and using grammatically correct sentences.

Some past writers have used the term *reversal design* to refer to withdrawal projects. This usage is now obsolete or careless, given Sulzer-Azaroff and Mayer's (1991) distinction between withdrawal and reversal designs.

Advantages and limitations.   The ABAB design is a substantial improvement over the AB design. As noted earlier in this section, the AB design represents a quasi-experiment. There is some controversy whether the ABAB design represents a true experiment, with some authors (Cook & Campbell, 1979) asserting that it does not and others (Drew & Hardman, 1985) asserting that it does. At the least, it can be considered to be a very strong quasi-experiment.

The ABAB design has an important limitation in that it is suitable only when these three conditions are fulfilled:

- baseline conditions can be tolerated long enough to provide a meaningful first A phase,
- the intervention introduced in the first B phase can and should be withdrawn or reversed in the second A phase, and
- the dependent variable represents a behavior change that is not expected to continue when the intervention is reversed or withdrawn in the second A phase (for example, unlearning a newly learned skill).

In our example of the aggressive child, any of the following conditions would rule out an ABAB design:

- immediate intervention is necessary because the child's aggressive behavior threatens the sibling's safety,
- the parents are so reluctant to return to the chaotic conditions of the A phase that they refuse to return to their old ways of interacting with her despite pleas from the researchers, or
- the child finds interacting pleasantly with her sibling so intrinsically rewarding that she continues this new behavior even when her parents stop reinforcing it.

An ABAB design would also be ruled out if the dependent variable were learning to read, because the newly learned reading behavior could not be "unlearned" and returned to baseline levels.

Multiple Baseline Design

Researchers using time series designs often face situations in which the treatment cannot or should not be withdrawn or reversed, or in which the dependent variable represents a behavior expected to continue when the intervention is withdrawn or reversed. Such situations led to the development of the **multiple baseline design.** This design is essentially composed of a number of AB designs with baselines of varying lengths. The functional relation is demonstrated by the change in the dependent variable, which occurs maximally only when the independent variable is introduced. The term *multiple* in multiple baseline may refer to any one of three possibilities:

- multiple participants,
- multiple behaviors of the same participants, or
- the same behavior of the same participant in multiple situations.

Using multiple behaviors, situations, or participants allows the functional relationship to be demonstrated without relying on withdrawal or reversal of the independent variable. Figure 8.3 shows an example of observations from a multiple baseline design using the same behavior with multiple participants.

A multiple baseline design like the one illustrated in Figure 8.3 could also be used with one person and several dependent variables. For example, suppose staff in a sheltered workshop wanted to reduce the frequency with which a client used foul language, fought with other clients, and stopped working at unauthorized times. Figure 8.4 illustrates this application. Fighting behavior would probably be chosen for intervention first after the initial baseline period because it is the most objectionable.

In the ABAB design discussed previously, experimental control is demonstrated because the dependent variable varies systematically as the treatment is instituted, then reversed or withdrawn, and then reinstituted. A functional relationship is demonstrated between the presence of the independent variable (treatment) and fluctuations in the dependent variable. In multiple baseline designs, that functional relationship is demonstrated not by withdrawing or reversing the treatment but rather by instituting the treatment program at different times for each participant, behavior, or situation. The functional relationship is demonstrated by the variation in the dependent variable that occurs whenever the independent variable is introduced for the different participants or behaviors or situations.

Multiple baseline designs are true experiments; the ABAB design is a very strong quasi-experiment at the least. And the AB design is a

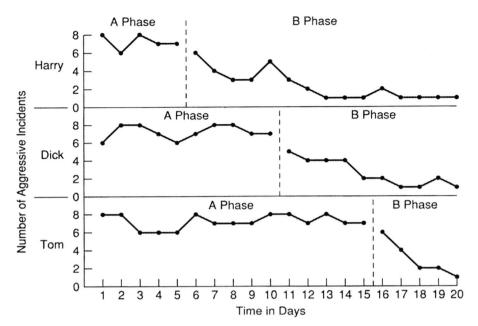

FIGURE 8.3
Multiple baseline design employing the same behavior with multiple participants. Data are fictitious.

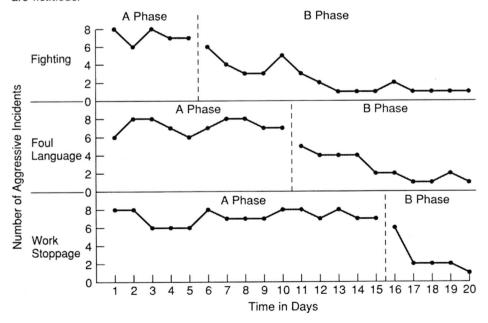

FIGURE 8.4
Multiple baseline design employing multiple behaviors with the same participant. Data are fictitious.

quasi-experiment. The basis for experimental control in the ABAB and multiple baseline designs, particularly for other events occurring at the same time as and thereby being confounded with treatment, comes from the fact that the dependent variable changes predictably in response to the application of the independent variable on at least two occasions. Therefore, a minimum of two participants, behaviors, or situations must be used in any multiple baseline design. Additional participants, behaviors, or situations strengthen the design.

Numerous variations on these and other time series designs exist. Alternating treatments designs, in which two or more treatments are rapidly alternated either within or between observational sessions, allow analysis of more complex behaviors and comparison of the effects of more than one treatment. These designs are discussed in detail in Barlow and Hersen (1984) and Sulzer-Azaroff and Mayer (1991).

TRADITIONAL GROUP EXPERIMENTAL DESIGNS

Group designs have a long history in behavioral research and are especially appropriate when studying a whole population or making inferences about a larger population from which participants are sampled. For example, a researcher might wish to study a university's entire student body (a population) or generalize from a sample to all depressed clients seeking services in mental health clinics or all dysfunctional families seeing marriage and family counselors. Using many participants, rather than only a few, supports such generalization if sampling procedures are sound. As noted previously, however, the statistical analysis of data generated by these designs, while telling us about the average performance of groups, does not tell us about the performance of any individual.

Independent Groups Designs

The **posttest-only control-group design** is the simplest independent groups design. Participants are assigned to two groups. One group is administered an experimental treatment, the other a control condition. During or after administration of these treatment conditions, participants are measured on the dependent variable. An independent groups comparison evaluates the results. Figure 8.5 summarizes the simplest form of this design.

No-treatment control is the simplest version of the control group idea. An experimental treatment is administered to one group of participants and is withheld from the other. Isaac and Michael (1981) caution against careless use of "do nothing" control groups. Insofar as possible, a control group "should experience *all things* in common with the treatment group *except* the critical factor, per se. Control groups that 'do nothing' are apt to differ from the treatment groups in more ways" than the identified independent

Experimental Group:	Experimental Treatment	Posttest
Control Group:	Control Condition	Posttest

F I G U R E 8.5
Posttest-only control-group design in its simplest form.

variable (p. 88). For example, a researcher might plan to provide counseling to some applicants (an experimental group) and withhold it from others (a control group). Such a plan not only arouses ethical concerns, as discussed in Chapter 5, but under conditions prevailing in most practical service environments at least some of the rejected applicants could be expected to know that others are being served. The control group is not only unserved but denied a service that is provided to others, probably with at least some of them feeling unfairly treated. Based on survival rates in breast cancer studies, LeShan (1992) argued that being in a control group might affect participants adversely in some projects. Cook and Campbell (1979) used the term *resentful demoralization* to describe this phenomenon. Analogously, if the experimental participants know they are receiving a service being denied to others, this knowledge is confounded with the counseling intervention per se.

These considerations led us to represent control groups' experiences with **control condition** rather than blank spaces in Figure 8.5. A control condition should be thought of as a total experience for the participants, not mere absence of the experimental treatment. If experimental participants experience observers, interruptions, or special equipment, so should the control participants. When a biological study injects experimental animals with drugs, for example, control animals are usually injected with physiological saline solution.

Differential treatment control is involved when projects compare two or more different treatments rather than a treatment with its absence. For example, Lauver, Kelley, and Froehle (1971) arranged interviews between counselors and a coached client. The client systematically varied the latency of her responses: about 15 seconds in the "long" condition and about one second in the "short" condition. Sobell and Sobell (1973) compared the post-treatment drinking behavior of alcohol abusers treated with two kinds of goals: abstinence versus nonproblem drinking. Rogers and Dymond (1954) compared client-centered counseling with other approaches. Possible variations are many; we list a few:

Two or more experimental treatments are compared, with none designated as "control."

Two or more experimental groups are each given a different treatment, and an additional control group is used.

| **Experimental Group:** | Pretest | Experimental Treatment | Posttest |

F I G U R E 8.6
One-group pretest–posttest design.

More than one control group is used (for example, one group is given a no-treatment control condition and another group a differential-treatment control condition).

The best choice for any project depends on the research questions of that project.

Repeated-Measures Designs

One-group pretest–posttest design. Using this type of design, one group of participants is tested, then given an experimental treatment, and then retested. A repeated-measures comparison evaluates any change that may have taken place. The repeated-measures comparison is necessary because the pretest and posttest measures are from the same group of participants, unlike the independent groups comparison. This design is useful in some nonexperimental projects, such as descriptive follow-up, that do not require inferences about causes. For experiments, the one-group pretest–posttest design is considered very weak because it offers insufficient support for an inference that the independent variable influenced the dependent variable. It offers no control for the possibility that the dependent variable might have changed in the observed direction without the treatment (similar to the problem with the time series AB design previously discussed). However, we discuss it here because it offers a helpful comparison for understanding the more complex designs discussed in the remainder of this chapter. Figure 8.6 summarizes this design.

Own-control designs. Sometimes it is more practical to expose every participant to all treatment conditions than to administer each treatment to a different group of participants. One example of an **own-control design** was represented in a demonstration broadcast on television: Volunteer drivers drove the same slalom course several times after having ingested different amounts of alcohol. The required turns were marked with flexible plastic cones, and the number of cones each driver left standing provided a measure of the dependent variable. Experience with his or her own performance in the no-alcohol condition gave each driver a basis for judging the effects of the drinks consumed. In another example, Sheehan, Hadley, and Gould (1967) asked stutterers to read standard passages to listeners who were dressed and introduced so as to represent different degrees of authority. Each participant read to an "authority" listener and to a "peer" listener;

Group	First Session	Second Session	Third Session	Fourth Session
1	Romantic Fiction	Science Fiction	Political Commentary	Medical Information
2	Science Fiction	Medical Information	Romantic Fiction	Political Commentary
3	Political Commentary	Romantic Fiction	Medical Information	Science Fiction
4	Medical Information	Political Commentary	Science Fiction	Romantic Fiction

F I G U R E   8.7
Plan for counterbalancing clients' exposure to four types of reading material in the waiting room before four counseling sessions. This plan provides only partial control for sequence effects; complete counterbalancing would require 24 sequences.

observers counted the number of stuttering blocks as the dependent variable.

Some students have unwittingly perverted the own-control idea to a one-group pretest–posttest design. They represented the control condition by absence of a treatment before the pretest; the treatment was then to be administered, followed by a posttest. Own-control designs require more than one experimental group and usually work better with the differential-treatment control than the no-treatment control design feature.

Caution is required with own-control designs. If several treatments are to be administered to the same person, they must be given in some order. This order can lead to confounding problems. It is possible that experience with treatment conditions administered earlier could affect responses to treatment conditions given later. To administer them in the same order to every participant confounds order and sequence effects with treatment differences. For example, the drinking slalom drivers all experienced the no-alcohol condition first and had increasingly more alcohol on each successive trial. They might have learned the slalom task a little more on each trial, and this practice effect could have partially obscured the effects of their drinks.

Counterbalancing provides one answer to this problem. For example, the independent variable might be the kind of reading material available in a counseling center's waiting room and the dependent variable some aspect of client behavior in sessions. Four types of reading material are at hand: romantic fiction, science fiction, political commentary, and medical information. Clients are seen for at least four sessions. Which kind of reading material should they encounter while waiting for the first, second, third, and fourth sessions? To counterbalance this order of exposure, participants are divided into four groups, preferably by random assignment. The groups are then scheduled so that their available waiting room reading material will follow a plan such as the one in Figure 8.7.

The term **Latin square** is often applied to such plans. The important features of the plan in Figure 8.7 are that each group experiences all treatment conditions and that each treatment appears once in each sequence position (first, second, third, fourth). See Isaac and Michael (1981) for some additional discussion of counterbalancing. Winer, Brown, and Michels (1991) offer additional plans; some of them are quite complex, counterbalancing more than one variable simultaneously. A *Graeco-Latin square* plan simultaneously counterbalances two variables.

Although counterbalancing requires that participants be divided into independent groups, dividing them serves a different purpose than in the independent groups designs discussed earlier in this chapter. In an independent groups design, comparing the results from differently treated groups directly addresses the research question. In an own-control design, the research question is answered by comparing results of the same participants under different conditions (repeated-measures comparisons); the independent groups differ only in the order in which treatment conditions are administered.

Factorial and Mixed Designs

Many research projects simultaneously investigate either more than one independent variable with the same dependent variables or an independent variable and one or more classification variables with the same dependent variables. Any such design that includes only **independent groups comparisons** is called a **factorial design.** If independent groups comparisons are used together with any other types of comparisons (repeated-measures, related-groups, within-group), the design is referred to as a **mixed design.** As noted in Chapter 6, we refer collectively to the latter three types of comparisons as correlated-measures comparisons.

Factorial designs. A study by Grantham (1973) illustrates the simplest possible factorial design. African American and Caucasian student clients were randomly assigned to counselors. Counselor race (African American, Caucasian) and gender were the two independent variables. A factorial design evaluated the effects of these variables on expressed client satisfaction as a dependent variable. Figure 8.8 illustrates a customary way of representing such designs graphically.

		Race	
		African American	Caucasian
Gender	Male	African American Male	Caucasian Male
	Female	African American Female	Caucasian Female

FIGURE 8.8
Factorial design with two factors and two levels of each factor.

		Race	
	African American	Caucasian	Asian
Male	African American Male	Caucasian Male	Asian Male
Female	African American Female	Caucasian Female	Asian Female

Gender (label to the left, spanning Male and Female rows)

FIGURE 8.9
Factorial design with two factors: two levels of one factor and three levels of the other.

Adding a third racial group of counselors (such as Asian) would not change the number of factors. Rather, the design would have three levels of one factor (race) and two levels of the other (gender), as in Figure 8.9; six groups of participants would be used rather than four.

Subdividing the results from the design in Figure 8.9 according to client gender would create a three-factor design with 12 groups of participants, as illustrated in Figure 8.10. The design in Figure 8.10 illustrates two additional important points.

First, the factors in a factorial design may be all independent variables, all classification variables, or any combination of these, so long as only independent groups comparisons are involved. In this example, client gender represents a classification variable, while counselor gender and counselor race are independent variables. The researcher randomly assigned clients to counselors but could do nothing about client gender except classify the participants. A project with no independent variables is not an experiment; a factorial design based only on classification variables represents one or more descriptive approaches.

Second, increasing the number of factors greatly increases the complexity of the project. One reason for this fact is that factorial designs study not only the different factors separately but also the interaction between them. **Interaction,** in this sense, refers to the influence of one variable on the effect of another. For example, difficulty of material to be learned interacts with amount of practice; if material is so easy as to be fully learned in one exposure, mastery does not improve with added practice, while mastery of more difficult material does. The two-factor designs in Figures 8.8 and 8.9 address three questions:

1. Did counselor race affect client satisfaction?
2. Did counselor gender affect client satisfaction?
3. Was the influence of counselor race on client satisfaction the same among male and female counselors? Alternatively phrased, is the influence of counselor gender on client satisfaction the same among the different races studied?

The third of these questions represents the interaction of counselor race and counselor gender on client satisfaction. In contrast, the three-factor

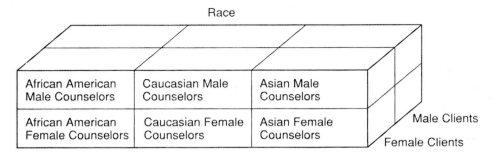

FIGURE   8.10
Factorial design with three factors: two factors with two levels each and one factor with three levels. This design requires 12 groups of participants.

design in Figure 8.10 addresses seven questions, the above three plus four additional ones:

4. Were male and female clients equally satisfied with counseling?
5. Was the influence of counselor race on client satisfaction the same among male and female clients?
6. Was the influence of counselor gender on client satisfaction the same among male and female clients?
7. Was the interaction of counselor race and gender, as influences on client satisfaction, the same among male and female clients?

Adding a fourth factor would raise the number of questions addressed to 15, with some of them sufficiently complex to challenge the interpretation skills of many experienced researchers. It is our experience that beginning researchers often have difficulty with designs involving more than two factors.

Mixed designs.   A design with two or more factors is a mixed design if it has at least one factor based on independent-groups comparisons and at least one factor based on correlated-measures comparisons. For illustration, we return to the project mentioned in Chapter 2 in which teachers changed their treatment of an experimental group of students with problem behavior but not of a control group of similar students. Each teacher kept records of one student's problem behavior for a week before the different treatment was introduced to the experimental group and continued keeping these records afterward. The design is illustrated in Figure 8.11.

This mixed design differs from the factorial design shown in Figure 8.8 in that it involves two independent groups with repeated measures, while the design in Figure 8.8 has four independent groups.

A variation of this design (Figure 8.12) illustrates additional points:

• A mixed design may have more than two levels of any factor.
• The number of levels need not be the same for every factor.

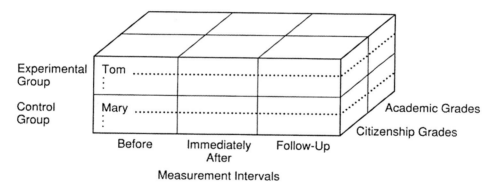

F I G U R E 8.11
Mixed design with two factors and two levels of each factor. The gaps in the lists of names represent omission of 21 names from each list. Each group had 25 participants, but only four are listed by name.

F I G U R E 8.12
Mixed design with three factors: one independent-groups factor with two levels, one repeated-measures factor with three levels, and one within-group factor with two levels.

- A correlated-measures factor may represent any of the three types (repeated-measures, related-groups, within-group).
- A mixed design may have more than one correlated-measures factor.
- Correlated-measures factors need not be all of the same type.

For the example illustrated in Figure 8.12, suppose that this project also noted the students' academic and citizenship grades during three grading periods: immediately before the treatment was introduced to the experimental group, immediately after it was introduced, and later in the academic year for follow-up. This design has two correlated-measures factors: the grading periods (a repeated-measures factor with three levels) and academic versus citizenship grades (a within-group factor with two levels).

In earlier decades, factorial and mixed designs with many factors and many levels of each factor required so much computational labor that most researchers kept these designs small and simple. Now, available software has largely eliminated these concerns for researchers having access to a computer, even a personal computer with moderate memory capacity. Instead, researchers are well advised to think carefully in the planning stage about how results will be interpreted after the analysis is complete. If factors unnecessary to a project's mission are carelessly added to these designs, the interpretation task can be made enormously more complex and difficult than it needs to be.

For a more detailed discussion of these designs, we refer you to Keppel and Zedeck (1989), who offer several examples representing a wide range of complexity.

Three commonly used mixed designs are the **pretest–posttest control-group design,** the **Solomon four-group design,** and the **wait-control design.** Because of their special features, we give each of these designs a subsection of its own though they all qualify as mixed designs.

Pretest–posttest control-group design. This is the simplest possible mixed design. It uses two groups of participants, one of which experiences an experimental treatment and the other a control condition. It differs from the posttest-only design in that a measure of the dependent variable is obtained twice: both before and after the experimental or control condition. Procedures for this design in its simplest form are:

1. Compose two groups of participants.
2. Pretest both.
3. Expose one group to the experimental treatment and the other group to the control condition.
4. Test both groups a second time.

This simple form is presented graphically in Figure 8.13.

As with the posttest-only control group design, several variations are possible, such as:

- more than one experimental group,
- more than one control group,
- no group designated as control,
- more than one dependent variable (repeated-measures factor), or
- more than one posttest (one immediate and one or more follow-up).

Both independent groups and repeated-measures comparisons are used to evaluate the results. Repeated-measures comparisons evaluate changes from pretest to posttest in the two groups. Independent groups comparisons show whether one group changed more than the other and whether the groups differed in their posttest scores.

Experimental Group:	Pretest	Experimental Treatment	Posttest
Control Group:	Pretest	Control Condition	Posttest

F I G U R E 8.13
Basic pretest–posttest control-group design.

This design has both advantages and disadvantages in comparison to the posttest-only control group design. One obvious difference is that participants are tested twice using this design. However, when the testing procedure is difficult or time-consuming, the pretest–posttest design places much greater demands on participants than does the posttest-only design.

With both designs, the usual practice is to begin by assigning participants at random to the experimental and control groups. The resulting groups cannot be expected to be identical; they usually differ by small amounts. Pretesting the groups enables group differences to be measured; in the posttest-only design, such differences remain unknown. Both designs compare the groups at posttest; the pretest–posttest design also compares their *changes* from pretest to posttest. Other things being equal, a larger difference between the groups is usually required to achieve statistical significance with the posttest-only design. To achieve statistical significance, a difference between the groups at posttest must be large enough to outweigh the small differences usually found at the outset between groups assigned at random. A comparison of changes does not have this hurdle to surmount. In short, the pretest–posttest design is statistically more powerful than the posttest-only design. The concept of statistical power is developed more fully in Chapters 10 and 13.

The pretest-posttest design has a serious weakness when the experience of responding to a pretest might influence participants' reactions to the treatment conditions. For example, a researcher might pretest participants by asking them about their racial attitudes and then show them a film involving characters from different racial groups. It is reasonable to suspect that this pretest experience might lead participants to be more alert to racial issues in the film than they would be without the pretest. Further, the film might exert more (or less) influence on their answers to this inquiry when it is repeated as a posttest than if they were not so alerted. Because the posttest-only design includes no pretest, it avoids this potential problem. If the researcher has sufficient reason to expect that the pretest experience will not influence participants' reactions to the treatment conditions, the pretest–posttest design may be preferable because it is more powerful statistically.

In short, any of the following conditions may make the posttest-only design preferable to the more powerful pretest–posttest design:

- Undergoing a long or difficult testing procedure twice would be excessively burdensome for participants.

Pretested Experimental Group:	Pretest	Experimental Treatment	Posttest
Pretested Control Group:	Pretest	Control Condition	Posttest
Unpretested Experimental Group:		Experimental Treatment	Posttest
Unpretested Control Group:		Control Condition	Posttest

F I G U R E   8.14
Solomon four-group design.

- The experience of pretesting is expected to influence participants' reactions to the treatment conditions.
- Pretesting is infeasible or undesirable for any other reason.

A pilot study is sometimes necessary to evaluate these points when choosing the best design.

Solomon four-group design.   This design (Solomon, 1949; Van Dalen, 1979) combines the posttest-only and the pretest–posttest control-group design features. As its name indicates, it requires four groups of participants: pretested experimental, pretested control, unpretested experimental, and unpretested control. Figure 8.14 illustrates this design.

Researchers often choose the Solomon four-group design when they suspect that the experience of pretesting will influence participants' reactions to the treatment conditions. The posttest-only design eliminates such effects; the Solomon four-group design enables evaluation of these effects. If the pretested experimental and control groups differ from one another at posttest significantly more (or less) than their unpretested counterparts do, the researcher can infer that pretesting influenced the results. Although the Solomon four-group design has this advantage, it usually requires more participants than either the posttest-only or pretest–posttest design used alone. Subdividing two small groups into four may make the resulting subgroups too small to produce interpretable results.

Wait-control design.   When practical or ethical considerations require that all participants be treated, a researcher can sometimes solve the problem of control by requiring some of the participants to wait longer than others. The immediate treatment group is pretested, treated, and posttested. The wait group is pretested, required to wait, posttested, and then treated. In some projects, both groups are posttested again after the wait group has been treated. Figure 8.15 represents this optional possibility by enclosing the second posttest in brackets.

Independent-groups and repeated-measures comparisons are both used to evaluate the results of wait-control designs. These designs have a major potential weakness in that emergency cases must be excluded. To require

Immediate Group:	Pretest	Treatment	Posttest	[Wait]	[Second Posttest]
Wait Group:	Pretest	Wait	Posttest	Treatment	[Second Posttest]

F I G U R E   8.15
Wait-control design. Brackets indicate that the second posttest is an optional variation rather than a universal requirement for this design.

them to wait for the sake of the research plan would be ethically suspect; to assign them all to the immediate treatment group would confound clients' urgency with the independent variable. The results, therefore, can be generalized only to nonemergency cases. When this limitation is of little or no consequence, a wait-control design is often the best solution to a difficult set of problems.

Gelso (1979) questioned the ethics of requiring applicants for service to wait too long, "e.g., beyond 12 weeks" (p. 23). In addition, long waiting periods tend to lead clients to defect from waiting lists, sometimes seeking other sources of help and sometimes deciding not to accept professional help even when it is offered. Methodologically, these defections introduce extraneous variables into the difference between the immediate group and the wait group, confounding the treatment effect. Such **experimental mortality** problems are discussed in greater detail in Chapter 9. As partial solutions when the treatment period is longer than a defensible waiting period, Gelso suggested three possibilities:

- offer limited treatment to clients during their waiting period,
- contrast a new treatment method with a conventional one, or
- allow the control period to last only as long as is considered ethically or practically feasible (measure participants repeatedly and compare the change patterns of immediately treated and delayed groups).

The first two of these suggestions apply the differential treatment control idea; the third suggestion applies a time series idea.

Single-Blind and Double-Blind Designs

Single-blind and **double-blind** designs were developed to control for the **placebo effect** in medical experiments comparing different medications. In such experiments, it was discovered that a patient's knowledge about what effects should be expected from a medication was often sufficient to produce the effects, even when a chemically inert substance (**placebo**) was given. Therefore, participants (usually patients) in a single-blind plan do not know what medication they are being given so the physical effects of the medication are not confounded with patients' expectations about these effects. In a double-blind study, this information is withheld not only from participants who are taking the medication but also from the staff who dispense it to them, who may have their own expectations. These expectations can influence staff behavior toward patients (for example, facial expressions) or the observations staff make of patients.

Some counseling and psychotherapy researchers have extended the placebo effect idea to refer to the possibility that clients might improve not because of the particular features of a treatment program but because of the attention they receive and their expectations for improvement (Critelli & Neumann, 1984). In a single-blind study, clients would not be told why their particular treatment is expected to work or how it differs from treatments other clients may be receiving. In a double-blind study, neither clients nor counselors would be told why the treatment would be expected to work or which treatments are control versus experimental. These restrictions are often impractical, however. The placebo effect is discussed in greater detail in Chapter 9.

SOME DESCRIPTIVE DESIGN FEATURES
Designing Surveys

The research questions of a survey are usually concerned with describing a defined set of people (for example, the inhabitants of a city, state, or nation; clients seeking counseling; students in one or more schools). Some surveys seek to describe other sets, such as organizations, work tasks, curriculum topics, or documents, to name a few of many possibilities. Most of the work of designing a survey concerns choosing participants and developing or choosing the instruments for collecting data. A survey is a research approach or a project based on this approach, not an instrument for data collection such as a questionnaire or interview. To call such an instrument a survey is careless usage.

For example, suppose voters in a coming election were to approve or defeat a bond issue to provide funds enabling the school district to hire additional counselors. To help a campaign committee plan its campaign, the district might want to conduct a survey to predict the outcome. Two obvious questions to ask participants are how they intend to vote on this issue and the reasons for their choice. However, experience with similar surveys in other districts suggests that the project would probably serve its stated purposes more effectively if it included additional information such as:

- whether and how respondents voted in previous school elections,
- political party affiliation,
- age,
- education,
- occupation,
- number of school-age children, and
- precinct of residence.

Each item in this list represents a research question. Additional research questions concern relationships among these variables. For example, if the highest proportion favorable to the bond issue was found among Democrats living in certain precincts with professional or managerial occupations and several children, the campaign committee might send "get out and vote" literature selectively to these voter segments. Further, if other researchers had improved their predictions by counting only the responses of participants who had voted in at least two of the four previous elections, the present project might include a research question concerning the intentions of this subgroup. This project would probably use a questionnaire or interview, or perhaps both, to collect data. To prepare or choose such an instrument, it is necessary to decide what content to include and how the results are to be analyzed. These topics are discussed more fully in Chapters 11 and 12.

When researchers design projects, they must decide how many variables to consider, the role of each variable in the project, whether and how participants are divided into groups, and the choice and timing of measures. More often in surveys than in other types of research, these design decisions are made as the survey instrument is chosen or developed, with repeated revisiting of the formulation phase to fine-tune the project's set of research questions.

The second major part of designing surveys is deciding what participants are to be used. Some projects study the entire population of interest, such as all students in a particular university at a particular time. Other projects select samples to be representative of the population of interest because the population is so large that collecting data from everyone is impractical. Some methods for selecting representative samples are very simple, others very complex. In the school district example, a sample might be selected very simply by choosing them at random from a list of all registered voters in the district. Many large surveys, such as national public opinion polls, use very complex sampling methods, sometimes involving many stratification variables. Babbie (1973) and Fowler (1988) discuss these methods in detail.

Some small projects with limited resources have missions that can be best fulfilled by collecting data from participants conveniently at hand, whether or not these participants are representative of any meaningful population. Such groups of participants are often called **convenience samples,** though they are not samples in any true sense. When convenience sampling is used, the researcher often has some interest in generalizing to a population, but time or other resources are insufficient for even the simplest true sampling procedures. For example, a researcher might be interested in a community's response to the idea of establishing a new counseling center. Rather than drawing up a list of all citizens and randomly sampling them to determine their opinions about the establishment of the center, a researcher might simply stop passersby in a mall and ask them their opinions. Obviously, such a sample is unlikely to be representative of the community as a whole. Depending on the time of day people are surveyed, the sample might include very few people who are employed full time. Selecting respondents in a mall may overrepresent individuals who live near the mall and have enough money to shop frequently. Can you think of other biases likely to be present in such participant groups? Representative (true) sampling is much to be preferred over convenience sampling unless the project's mission does not include generalizing to a population or available resources are insufficient for true sampling. These and other sampling issues are discussed more fully in Chapter 10.

Last among the nonexperimental design components listed at the beginning of this chapter is the general type of analysis to be applied. As discussed in Chapter 6, clearly formulated research questions specify the kinds of answers sought: qualitative descriptions, frequencies, proportions, central tendencies, variabilities, comparisons, or relationships between variables. In most survey projects, research questions that are clear in these respects lead rather directly to decisions about the best type of analysis; these decisions add little to the design work if the project's formulation has been done well.

Developmental Designs

Developmental studies frequently concern human development through various life stages. However, the same issues pertain to other developmental studies (for example, counseling relationships, employees' attitudes toward employers, or changes in organizations' staff behavior with age of the organization). Three possibilities for developmental designs are:

- Study respondents who differ in the stage of development they have reached.
- Study the same respondents at different times as their development proceeds.
- Ask respondents to report earlier experiences from memory.

Respectively, these design features are called **cohort, longitudinal,** and **retrospective.** Each type of design has its unique strengths and weaknesses; therefore many developmental studies combine more than one of these design features. Much of the material in this section is drawn from Schaie (1965; 1988).

Cohort design.   The cohort design feature uses independent groups comparisons among samples who have reached different stages of development at the time the study is conducted. For example, a researcher might compare samples of people of different ages (20, 30, 40, 50, 60, and 70) and from these comparisons draw inferences about the course of development. Each age group is called a cohort. Another name for this design is **cross-sectional.**

This design confounds the developmental variable (age) with the time period in which participants grew up. Older cohorts differ from younger ones not only because they are older but also because they developed under different conditions. People 30 years old in 1994 were pre-adolescent children during the Vietnam war and the Watergate affair; television, antidiscrimination laws, nuclear weapons, and the feminist movement have been facts of life throughout their entire memories. In contrast, people age 70 in 1994 were children during the Depression and adolescents during World War II; males reached draft age during that war. These people were old enough to vote in the Truman–Dewey presidential election; they remember the emergence of television, antidiscrimination laws, and nuclear weapons as realities. Many political, economic, and attitudinal changes took place in the country between the times these samples grew up (for example, younger people had more educational opportunities after high school and experienced more permissive attitudes about social roles based on gender). To what extent do intercohort differences represent the developmental variable and to what extent do they represent social changes such as these? Used alone, the cohort design offers no answer to this question.

Longitudinal design. In contrast, some developmental projects study the same people at different times. Inferences about the developmental variable are based on repeated-measures comparisons. This design also confounds the developmental variable with history, but in a different way. For example, a sample 70 years old in 1994 might have been interviewed at age 18 during World War II, at age 22 during the postwar period, at age 30 during the McCarthy era, at age 40 during the Vietnam war, and at age 50 during the 1970s energy crisis. People's answers may change not only due to age but also as they react to current events. A longitudinal design confounds these effects. Further, a longitudinal study of a single sample offers limited generalizability in that the researcher cannot say whether similar results would be obtained by studying people developing under different sets of conditions. Third, a longitudinal design confounds practice effect (discussed previously in relation to own-control designs) with the developmental variable. Fourth, most projects that cover long time periods lose some participants before data collection is complete.

Retrospective design. Sometimes a longitudinal design is desirable but not practical because time and resources are insufficient to study the participants over a long time period. With some kinds of measures, it is possible to ask people for their responses under two sets of instructions: (a) in the usual way, representing present time, and (b) remembering their experiences of a previous time, so as to answer as they think they would have then. Questionnaires, interviews, and rating scales are suitable measuring tools (not necessarily the only ones) for this design. Retrospective studies of this sort confound the developmental variable with responding from immediate experience versus responding from memory; participants may remember their earlier experiences and attitudes less completely or less accurately than they report their immediate ones. This problem ranges from inconsequential in some projects to prohibitive in others. Campbell and Stanley (1966) discussed the weaknesses of this design; they also noted evidence supporting the validity of a "retrospective pretest" under some conditions.

A second confounding problem stems from the fact that it is often easier for participants to report their immediate experience and then earlier memories rather than to recall earlier memories first. However, using the same sequence with every participant confounds the developmental variable with practice effect.

A combination approach. Combining the longitudinal and cohort designs to study the same developmental phenomena provides more information than either design alone, although it does not completely eliminate confounding. As an example of the confounding that can result from a cohort design, Anastasi (1982) noted that Wechsler's early cohort studies of age differences in intelligence confounded the developmental variable with historical factors. These studies have been long used as a basis for a belief that intelligence declines significantly with age:

> better-designed studies of adult intelligence strongly suggest that the ability decrements formerly attributed to aging are predominantly intergeneration or intercohort differences, probably associated with cultural changes in our society. (pp. 336–337)

A study by Schaie and Strother (1968) illustrates the combination of longitudinal and cross-sectional design features. The sample comprised 50 people at each five-year age interval from 20 to 70. Those who could be located seven years later were retested at that time. This design permitted independent groups comparisons among the age cohorts and repeated-measures comparisons between the first test and retest. See Schaie (1988) for a more extensive discussion of this type of design.

Ex Post Facto Studies

Ex post facto projects usually use the same kinds of data as do descriptive projects. These two research approaches differ in that ex post facto projects seek to generate or explore hypotheses about causes. Ary et al. (1985) discussed ways in which ex post facto studies can be designed to indicate that some plausible hypotheses are more tenable than others. As an example, they cited a high school that found that students who drove automobiles to school earned lower grades than other students. Did access to a car impair scholastic performance? Did the experience of scholastic difficulty increase students' desire to have a car? Did some common cause such as socioeconomic status or social group membership underlie both auto use and poor grades? Did teachers perceive drivers as uninterested students and assign lower grades than these students deserved? Did a prevailing faculty attitude toward drivers influence these students to do poorer work than they might otherwise? Many causal hypotheses are plausible to account for the difference found. If car users did not have lower grades after they began to drive than before, this additional finding contradicts the idea that car use caused grades to go down. However, this finding does not address the hypothesis that car use prevented grades from rising.

The underlying principle is twofold. First, generate as many plausible hypotheses as you can to account for observed differences or relationships. Next, examine additional differences and relationships to decide which among these hypotheses to investigate further with one or more experiments (for example, with parking regulations as an independent variable in the above example). These additional differences and relationships might involve only existing data, or existing data might suggest new data that should be collected.

Ex post facto projects lack the controls necessary to test hypotheses about causes as experiments do. Nonetheless, well-designed ex post facto studies can satisfactorily fulfill their mission of generating such hypotheses and providing data to help researchers choose which among a number of possible research questions to study with experiments.

CHAPTER SUMMARY

The design of the project is a core component of any research plan. It applies to all varieties of research, experimental and nonexperimental, basic and applied, exploratory and otherwise, program evaluation and otherwise. A project's design specifies what subjects are to be used; the number of variables considered and the role of each variable in the project (for example, independent, dependent, control, classification, stratification, predictor, criterion); whether and how subjects are divided into groups to be studied; the choice and timing of measurements taken on subjects; and the general type of analysis to be applied.

The design of experiments includes three additional aspects of the project's plan that do not apply to other research approaches. These are the number of experimental (treatment) and control conditions, the sequence and timing of experimental and control conditions, and the method of assigning experimental and control conditions to subjects.

Experimental designs include time series and traditional group types. Design issues are discussed for nonexperimental studies including surveys, developmental, and ex post facto projects. Good design minimizes the likelihood and importance of the various risk factors discussed in the next chapter.

PRACTICAL EXERCISES

1. Examine each of the following descriptions of time series experiments and identify its design (AB, ABAB, or multiple baseline).
   a. John and Mary sought marital counseling for a progressively intense series of arguments they were having over household chores since

Mary accepted a full-time job outside the home. They had jointly drawn up a list of household duties and selected the half for which each would be willing to accept responsibility. Mary complained to the counselor that John procrastinated in doing his chores and that she ended up doing more than her fair share every day. The counselor suggested that for two weeks they simply select three chores that were John's daily responsibility and keep a record of whether or not he did them. In the third week he suggested that they select one of these chores, and each day that John did it, John could select what they watched on television during the evening. If he didn't do it, Mary selected what they watched on television. This procedure proved highly effective. The counselor suggested that during the fourth week they select a second chore and add a further chore each week during additional weeks until John was completing all his chores satisfactorily. At the end of ten weeks, John was indeed completing all his chores satisfactorily, and Mary could name all the players in the National Football League.

b. A newly hired high school teacher was having great difficulty controlling his students' classroom behavior. Students spoke out without raising their hands, left their seats without permission, and talked to each other when he was trying to teach a lesson. The teacher sought consultation from the school's counselor, who kept records for several days of the number of infractions observed during the teacher's fifth period class. The counselor then suggested that the teacher draw up a list of classroom rules in concert with the students. The rules were: "Raise your hand before speaking," "Ask permission before leaving your seat," and "Speak to your neighbor only during specified 'visiting' times." On every occasion that students followed a rule they were given a "lottery ticket" good for a drawing held at the end of the period for pencils, markers, paper, and other school supplies. The counselor kept records for an additional week, at the end of which the students were models of comportment.

c. A counselor at a community college counseling center was interested in whether maintaining eye contact with clients during sessions helped clients to be more open about their feelings. For five days he kept a piece of paper in front of him during counseling sessions on which he placed a checkmark each time a client used a "feeling" word (for example, angry, happy, sad). During these days he did not avoid making eye contact with clients but made no special effort to maintain eye contact. On the sixth day he made a special effort to maintain eye contact with clients during the entire session, and he continued these efforts for five days. On the tenth day, he returned to his previous habit of making no special effort to maintain eye contact, and on the 15th day he resumed consistent eye contact. He continued his record keeping during all these periods. He found that the number of feeling words spoken by clients increased by an average of 15% per day during the days on which he made consistent eye contact but stayed about the same during other days.

2. Examine each of the following projects and identify the design it represents: (1) posttest-only control group, (2) one-group pretest–posttest, (3) own-control, (4) factorial, (5) pretest–posttest control group, (6) Solomon four-group, or (7) wait-control.

   a. A counseling center's staff had noted that many couples who called the center requesting therapy for relationship problems were no longer interested in receiving therapy when a counselor was finally available to see them, usually after a two- or three-week period. The staff wanted to determine whether the relationship actually improved during the intervening period or whether the couples simply learned to live with their problems. The staff designed an experiment in which couples were no longer accepted on a first-come, first-served basis. Instead, half of the couples were randomly assigned to appointments within the next two days; the other half were given appointments two weeks later. All couples were asked to complete a "marital problems checklist" immediately after their first phone call to the center. The clients with immediate appointments were then seen for six sessions (three sessions per week), and all couples were again given the checklist. The group with delayed appointments was then offered counseling for six sessions, and all couples were once again given the checklist at the end of those sessions.

   b. An experiment was designed to determine which of two treatments, participant modeling or assertiveness training, was more effective in helping shy people initiate interactions in social settings. Each client experienced both treatments. Half of the clients experienced assertiveness training first and participant modeling second, while the other half experienced the treatments in the reverse order. Clients were asked to keep self-report records of the number of contacts they initiated in social situations throughout the course of both treatments and for six weeks afterward.

   c. An airline company was interested in determining which of two treatment plans was most effective for its new "Fly Without Fear" program for people who were phobic about airplane travel. The program was offered free of charge to interested persons provided they complied with the experimental protocol. Individuals who signed up for the program were randomly divided into four groups. Groups 1 and 2 were taken on a brief (20-minute) flight and asked to record their feelings of subjective distress during the flight. All four groups then experienced a treatment program; Groups 1 and 3 experienced Plan A, while Groups 2 and 4 were given Plan B. All four groups were then taken on a brief flight and asked to record their subjective feelings of distress.

   d. A career counselor at a university counseling center was interested in whether group career counseling would be enhanced by ending each group with 15 minutes of free discussion, with group members allowed to bring up any topics of interest to them, as opposed to the usual group counseling procedure of structuring the groups very tightly around one topic. The center typically offered ten career groups of six sessions each quarter. Accordingly, five of the ten new groups followed the free discussion model, and the other five followed the usual tightly structured model. Clients rated their satisfaction with the group process at the end of the six sessions.

e. Counselors at a large medical complex "Wellness Center" were interested in investigating the impact of a stress management treatment on the psychological distress reported by cancer patients. They were also interested in whether results differed depending on clients' gender and age. Forty-two clients were randomly divided into two treatment groups (stress management or no stress management), with each group composed of 21 males and 21 females. Male and female clients were also categorized according to age levels. There were seven clients of each gender in each age group: 20–35, 36–50, and 51–65. All clients were administered a psychological distress inventory after the treatment program was completed, and results were analyzed to determine the effects of treatment, gender, age, and interactions of these variables.

f. A middle school counselor was interested in whether a curriculum emphasizing an Afrocentric world view would increase the self-esteem of African American 6th graders. With the permission of a teacher who had an entirely African American 6th grade history class, she administered a self-esteem inventory to each student in the class at the beginning of the academic year. The teacher then taught the Afrocentric curriculum, which took ten weeks. At the end of that time the counselor re-administered the self-esteem inventory to the students. Analysis of the inventory results indicated that students' self-esteem had increased by an average of 20 points on the scale.

g. The counselor who investigated the effect of her Afrocentric curriculum reported in (f) presented the results of her analysis to the school's principal and to the PTA group. Several parents questioned whether the increase in self-esteem was actually due to the Afrocentric curriculum. They wondered whether the students' self-esteem increased for other reasons, such as adjustment to the middle school setting over a ten-week period. (Sixth grade students were new to the school at the beginning of the academic year and perhaps felt like they were "at the bottom of the totem pole," thus affecting their self-esteem scores.) The following year, the counselor repeated her experiment, but this time she selected two all–African American 6th grade history classes. Both classes were administered the self-esteem inventory at the beginning of the academic year. The Afrocentric curriculum was taught in only one history class. At the end of the ten weeks, both classes were again administered the self-esteem inventory.

3. Imagine that you are a rehabilitation counselor working in a rehabilitation agency. Your supervisor asks you to begin making daily support phone calls to your clients who are looking for jobs. You would like to design a time series experiment to examine the impact of your phone calls on their daily job seeking activities. Design such an experiment in three ways: AB, ABAB, and multiple baseline formats.

4. Imagine that you are an employee assistance counselor working for a large computer software company. The company is noted for its employee friendly policies, such as on-site exercise facilities employees are encouraged to use for one hour each day, flextime, and on-site day care for children. The company CEO is interested in determining whether employees' attitudes toward the company become more or less favorable with length of time employed. You decide that a developmental study would be appropriate for answering this research question. However, you are uncertain whether a longitudinal, cohort (cross-sectional), retrospective, or combination design would be most appropriate. You therefore decide to present plans for all three designs to the CEO, prepare to discuss the advantages and disadvantages of each, and let him decide which he would prefer. What will you say to your employer? (Include the specific structure of each design in your remarks.)

5. Examine recent counseling journals for examples of any of the time series, independent groups, repeated-measures, mixed, survey, developmental, or ex post facto designs discussed in this chapter. Bring the article describing the research project to class and be prepared to discuss its design features.

CHAPTER NINE
DESIGN RISKS AND REMEDIES

Questions to Guide Your Reading

Design Validity
1. What is meant by the term *design validity*?
2. What is the relationship between design validity and a project's research questions?
3. When is internal validity considered strong?
4. When is external validity considered strong?
5. How does the "bubble" analogy illustrate the relationship between internal and external validity and between rigor and relevance?
6. What is the researcher's task with regard to rigor and relevance?
7. What role can theory play with regard to external validity?
8. How does design validity differ from measurement validity?

Internal Validity
9. How does bias in group composition threaten internal validity?
10. What is the most effective remedy for bias in group composition?
11. How does experimental mortality threaten internal validity?
12. When does experimental mortality not threaten internal validity?
13. How is experimental mortality similar to and different from bias in group composition?
14. What procedures can a researcher carry out to reduce the risk of experimental mortality in a research project?
15. Why is replacement of participants at random an unsatisfactory remedy for experimental mortality?
16. How does history threaten internal validity? Create an example different from any offered in the text.
17. What remedies exist for history as a threat to internal validity?
18. When does maturation pose a threat to internal validity? When does it not pose such a threat?
19. Why does the repeated-measures control-group design offer the best control for maturation as a threat to internal validity?
20. When does practice effect threaten internal validity?
21. How do the pretest–posttest control-group design, the posttest-only control group design, the Solomon four-group design, own-control designs, and time series designs control for practice effect?
22. How does the placebo effect differ in counseling studies as opposed to drug studies?
23. What is the Hawthorne effect? Why does it pose a threat to internal validity?
24. How may the Hawthorne effect interact with an experimental treatment?
25. What is the John Henry effect?
26. Why is experimenter bias sometimes referred to as a self-fulfilling prophecy?
27. What is a remedy for experimenter bias as a threat to internal validity?
28. What are demand characteristics? Why are they a threat to internal validity?

29. Distinguish rater bias, rater drift, raters' use of favorite parts of rating scales, and the halo effect.
30. What are some possible remedies for rater problems?
31. How does instrumentation pose a threat to internal validity?
32. What groups of participants are most vulnerable to statistical regression?
33. What is the best remedy for statistical regression as a threat to internal validity?

External Validity
34. How is external validity defined?
35. How may differences arise between the participants available for a research project and the population of interest?
36. Why does mortality pose a threat to external validity?
37. How do artificial arrangements pose a threat to external validity?
38. How does pretesting participants pose a threat to external validity?
39. What remedy is often used for the problem of multiple treatment influences?
40. What is the best remedy for external validity problems in general?

We begin this chapter by discussing the concept of **design validity,** which includes both **internal validity** and **external validity** and which differs from measurement validity. Next, we discuss the tradeoff relationship internal and external validities have in many projects, as articulated in Mindus's "bubble hypothesis" analogy (Gelso, 1979) and the related issues of rigor and relevance. Third, we list in outline form the major risks to design validity in counseling research. Fourth, we define and discuss each of these risks and indicate ways each can be reduced. In any one project some of these risks may be substantial, others moderate to minimal, and some entirely absent. Each project will have its own unique set of risks to guard against. Likewise, each will have its own unique set of possible remedies.

DESIGN VALIDITY

Design validity refers to the technical soundness of a project's design as it relates to fulfillment of the project's mission. Design was defined at the beginning of Chapter 8 as that aspect of a research project's plan that specifies (among other things) what subjects are to be used, what variables are to be considered, how measurements are to be taken on subjects, whether and how subjects are to be divided into groups to be studied, and the general type of analysis to be applied. Strong design validity generally results in data that strongly support answers to the questions posed in the project's mission. If design validity is weak, these answers are in doubt because rival interpretations are plausible. To return to an example from Chapter 8, elementary school counselors Molly and Ann found differences in social skills gains between groups of students who experienced two different social skills programs. Design validity is weakened because the different gains they found might have resulted not from the different programs but from other factors, such as the counselors' different temperaments or differences between the student groups at the outset. Further, their findings might not hold for the two programs generally but only if applied to 4th graders with women counselors at a particular school.

Internal and External Validities

As Campbell and Stanley (1966) developed these ideas, internal validity is strong to the extent that the researcher has controlled all factors, other than the ones being studied, that might account for the results. An experiment has strong internal validity if the effect of its independent variables on its dependent variables can be interpreted unambiguously. Internal validity in Molly and Ann's experiment is very weak. Molly's results might have differed from Ann's not because these counselors used different programs but because of differences in their temperaments or in their students before the classes began.

In contrast, external validity refers to generalizability. Are the results meaningful not only for the specific people, times, measurement methods, and circumstances studied but also to populations of people in different times or places, to whom different measurement methods might be applied under somewhat different circumstances? External validity is strong if sampling methods, measurement methods, and the research setting enable the researcher to generalize interpretations to other populations, times, places, and circumstances relevant to the project's mission. To return to Molly and Ann, these counselors' results might apply only to 4th graders working with women counselors at this particular school. Their project's external validity is weak because the data do not support generalization beyond their specific participants, school, and circumstances and because their mission was not confined to these specific participants, school, and circumstances. Had their mission been so confined, limited external validity would not be a weakness in their project.

Rigor, Relevance, and the Bubble Hypothesis

Internal validity is relevant to all research projects, external validity to most. Sometimes the very steps necessary to strengthen internal validity will weaken external validity and vice versa. Mindus (Gelso, 1979) used the term *bubble hypothesis* to represent an analogy between conducting research and "placement of a sticker on a car windshield." At that time, such stickers had to be applied wet. During the process, a bubble would appear. The owner pressed the bubble in an attempt to eliminate it, but it reappeared elsewhere. "The only way to get rid of it was to eliminate the entire sticker."

Gelso was addressing the problem that "all experiments are imperfect" (p. 12). So are all nonexperimental research projects. Solving one design problem usually creates others. Tightly controlled laboratory experiments maximize internal validity, though they sacrifice external validity because laboratories differ from the kinds of settings in which counseling takes place. Field studies may maximize external validity, but the kinds of controls necessary for strong internal validity are difficult if not infeasible.

These issues, among others, underlie a "polarization of investigative styles along a rigor–relevance dimension" (Gelso, 1979, p. 8). Some writers have advocated laboratory experiments that offer greater control of variables than most field studies and permit causal inferences correlational and descriptive studies do not support. Other writers have deplored the loss of relevance to counseling practice inherent in laboratory analogues and have recommended regarding less rigorous studies as professionally respectable. Rigor and relevance have a tradeoff relationship; maximizing either usually reduces the other. Nonetheless, this relationship is not all or none. A project totally lacking in either rigor or relevance would be worthless. One of the senior author's professors in graduate school (the late Joseph G. Sheehan) cautioned students not to let "rigor become rigor mortis." Nor should relevance be used as an excuse to abandon concern with rigor. As we view a researcher's task, it is to design the project so that it has the optimal balance of rigor and relevance in view of its mission: to make the project as rigorous as it can be within existing circumstances while keeping it as relevant as it needs to be to meet its goals. The concept of relevance includes, but is not limited to, external validity.

The risks to both internal and external validities should be avoided or reduced to the extent possible and, when unavoidable, chosen so as to be as unimportant as possible in relation to the project's mission. To return to the bubble analogy, we recommend making the bubble as small as possible and placing it where it least impairs the value of the sticker.

A Role for Theory

Much controversy has surrounded the role of theory in research. As noted in Chapter 1, one extreme position holds that research, to be respectable, must be based on hypotheses derived from theory. At the other extreme is the view that theory should be avoided because it biases researchers' observations. A less extreme pro-theory position is that "research is always guided by some assumptions and theories are the means by which these assumptions can be clearly articulated" (Forsyth & Strong, 1986, p. 117). A less extreme position in the other direction holds that it is well and good that some projects address theoretical issues, but we should not demean the value of studies that have purely practical missions. These two moderate positions do not necessarily contradict one another.

Forsyth and Strong (1986) suggested that theory offers a partial solution to generalizability problems and argued for

> the scientific unity of basic and applied research. . . . [M]any laboratory studies certainly involve highly artificial situations, [but] may still be relevant to practical problems if they examine theoretical generalizations that are relevant to these applied problems. (pp. 114, 116)

Examples of laboratory studies relevant to applied problems in counseling include those conducted by Wolpe (1958), who developed systematic desensitization as a treatment program for anxieties and phobias, and those conducted by Bandura (1977), who developed a participant modeling approach for similar problems. Although their experiments were conducted in psychology laboratories, the resulting treatment programs have been used in numerous and varied settings.

Forsyth and Strong (1986) proposed that generalizability of such laboratory results "is determined more by the structure of the theory . . . than by location of the supporting research" (p. 117). A laboratory study may have weak external validity because its conditions are different from a counselor's office. Because of these differences, researchers cannot directly generalize the results across situations, but theory can provide a basis for judging the importance of these differences in view of the generalizations sought by the project's mission. Bryans (1983) expressed a similar idea:

> Across to that-which-is from that-which-seems
> I see a high suspension bridge of dreams.
> Above is endless sky, anonymous.
> Below an unbeginning river streams. (p. 11)

Theories, like the poet's dreams, are built in people's minds and offer metaphorical bridges. Theories can offer bridges for inference when the direct path of design validity is necessarily weak, such as between the carefully controlled world of laboratory research and the much less controllable world of counseling practice. To carry the metaphor a step farther, the poet's "endless sky, anonymous" and "unbeginning river" call attention to two additional points. First, there is much that theories do not address. Hamlet observed, "There are more things in heaven and earth, Horatio, than are dreamt of in your philosophy" (Act I, Scene 5). Second, what theories do not address does not necessarily lose value on that account; the sky and the river remain beautiful to behold even though the bridge does not reach them.

Design Validity and Measurement Validity

In general, **validity** refers to the technical soundness of the procedures used to generate data that support the inferences the researcher wants to make. Design validity refers to the soundness of research designs; in contrast, measurement validity refers to the extent to which the measures chosen reflect the variables the researcher is interested in. For example, a scholastic aptitude test has measurement validity if its scores satisfactorily predict students' grades. A test used to screen job applicants has validity if its scores predict workers' job performance. A mathematics achievement test has validity if it fairly represents the knowledge and skills contained in the curriculum for which it was designed. The idea of measurement validity is introduced here only to distinguish it from design validity. Measurement validity is discussed more fully in Chapter 11.

POTENTIAL RISKS TO DESIGN VALIDITY

Risks to design validity can be divided into two major categories, internal and external. Internal risks include:

- bias in group composition,
- experimental mortality,
- history,
- maturation (includes spontaneous remission),
- practice effects,
- placebo effect,
- Hawthorne effect,
- John Henry effect,
- experimenter bias,
- demand characteristics,
- rater and observer issues,
- instrumentation, and
- statistical regression.

External risks include:

- initial population-sample differences,
- mortality,
- artificial research arrangements,
- pretest influences, and
- multiple-treatment influences.

The following sections discuss these risks to internal and external validity in detail.

INTERNAL VALIDITY

Threats to internal validity are those factors, other than the ones being studied, that may account for results.

Bias in Group Composition

In many experimental projects, independent variables are defined by administering different treatments to different groups. As noted in Chapter 2, traditional group experiments select a sample of participants and assign these participants to treatment groups at random or in some other way to ensure that these groups are approximately the same. Treatment procedures are then administered to these presumably equivalent groups according to the research plan.

If participants are assigned to treatment groups so that these groups are not equivalent, internal validity is weakened. For example, a newly opened counseling center might assign its first 50 clients to one counseling technique and the next 50 to another. Pretreatment differences between these groups would include whatever factors led some clients to learn about the new counseling center and apply for services earlier than others did. Confounding such differences with the independent variable (counseling technique in this example) weakens internal validity.

Sometimes it is not possible to assign participants so as to create equivalent treatment groups. Instead, the researcher is limited to studying preexisting groups. When different treatments are administered to groups that differ systematically in their composition, any such differences become confounded with the treatment effect. Internal validity is weakened, and the researcher has a quasi-experiment rather than a true experiment. In Molly and Ann's project, internal validity was weakened because their students might have differed systematically in important ways at the outset. In many schools, students are assigned to counselors based on nonrandom factors such as counselors' preferences or an administrator's judgment regarding the best counselor for each student. So if Ann and Molly had been allowed to select any of their students, or if the principal had deliberately assigned rebellious students to Ann and compliant ones to Molly, such pretreatment differences would be confounded with the counselors' different methods. Rossi and Freeman (1989) referred to nonrandom comparison groups in experimental studies as "constructed controls."

It is important to distinguish these systematic differences from **random** ones. Whenever a sample is subdivided at random into treatment groups, these groups will differ somewhat due to chance factors. Rarely if ever are two randomly chosen groups exactly alike. However, groups of participants assigned at random from the same population usually differ by small amounts, and the statistical significance tests used to analyze data from group comparisons take into account the magnitude and probability of such differences. When samples are of moderate or larger size, random differences in group composition do not weaken internal validity. With very small samples, randomization offers only limited control of group composition bias.

Regardless of sample size, systematic differences between groups weaken internal validity. How important this weakening is depends on the degree to which the group differences are related to the phenomena under study. For illustration we return to Molly and Ann's project and add some further details. Suppose the principal had assigned rebellious students to Ann and compliant ones to Molly. Rebellious versus compliant student temperament is an extraneous variable. Regardless of its importance, this extraneous variable was confounded with the independent variable: Molly's versus Ann's methods of teaching social skills. If rebellious students responded the same as compliant ones to instructional programs, this confounding variable would not affect the results. However, suppose one program required substantial independent thinking and the other relied heavily on complying with instructions, with this difference defined as part of the independent variable. It is likely that compliant and rebellious students would respond differently to these two programs. In this case, confounding the independent variable with student temperament as an extraneous group composition difference may have substantially influenced the results.

The most effective remedy for the risk of group composition bias is to create comparable groups at the outset by assignment from a single sample of participants, provided such assignment is feasible. Random assignment is usually the simplest method. In designs involving pretests, the groups can be compared for similarity on pretest measures.

When circumstances limit a project to constructed controls for purposes of comparing treatment methods administered to different groups, it is desirable to ensure that the groups are as alike as possible at the outset and that they differ from each other only in ways relatively unrelated to the phenomena under study. Unfortunately, this process is substantially less dependable than random assignment. Freedom to choose constructed control samples is often limited. Also, it is difficult if not impossible to guess what all the factors of potential group composition bias are and to judge how much each is likely to be related to the phenomena being studied. Some projects identify a few such factors while an unknown number go unnoticed. For example, a research study investigating a treatment program designed to improve self-esteem may attempt to have two groups that are as alike as possible on such variables such as age, socioeconomic status, and ethnicity. But there is no guarantee that the two groups do not differ from each other in other important ways or that these variables are the only ones that could affect the project's outcome.

Experimental Mortality

The samples originally selected for a study may change as people withdraw from the project while it is being conducted. This phenomenon is known as experimental mortality. In an experiment with different treatment groups, internal validity is weakened if these groups lose participants in different proportions or for different reasons. These losses create differences in group composition that, in turn, may affect the results. For illustration, we offer a fictitious example. Two groups were created by random assignment; one group was treated with aversive conditioning and the other with a primarily verbal intervention. Each group lost some participants. Some left the verbal intervention group because it offered "all talk and no action." Some left the aversive conditioning group because they felt the staff were insufficiently attentive to their feelings and concerns. After these departures, the groups were no longer equivalent.

Sometimes mortality (leaving treatment versus remaining) is the dependent variable being studied rather than a validity problem. Mortality risks weakening validity when other dependent variables are being studied, such as change in behavior. Suppose, for example, that participants with a high tolerance for talk and a low tolerance for perceived lack of staff concern (likely to remain in the verbal group and leave the conditioning group) were least willing to change their behavior regardless of treatment methods. Under such circumstances, the resulting group composition differences would lead to greater behavior change in the conditioning group; mortality is confounded with the independent variable.

This problem is similar to that discussed in the previous section in that group composition differences are confounded with the independent variable. An important difference is that mortality introduces group composition differences while the project is under way *after* treatment groups have been created; the previous section discussed treatment group differences present at the outset.

Most longitudinal and follow-up studies, whether experimental or descriptive, lose some participants while in progress. In any study involving group comparisons, mortality threatens internal validity if participants lost differ in important ways from those who remain or if the groups being compared lose participants in different proportions or for different reasons.

We know of no fully satisfactory remedy for mortality as a risk to internal validity. However, we recommend reducing this risk as much as possible during the planning phase. Sometimes a researcher can provide incentives to remain with a project until it is completed without compromising the ethical obligation to let participants discontinue their participation if and when they so choose. For example, when participants are paid for their participation in each of several sessions, the researcher can structure the payment schedule so that all or a major portion of the amount earned is paid at the end of the final session. In a longitudinal study involving repeated contacts over several months or years, the researcher can periodically ask participants to update addresses and telephone numbers. This practice retains some participants who might otherwise be lost, such as those who have moved and whose automatic forwarding provisions have not yet expired. If a study involving college or university students can be confined to one academic term, doing so will reduce the risk of losing participants who graduate, transfer, or discontinue their education.

Researchers sometimes replace lost participants by selecting at random from the original pool. If one group loses a substantially greater portion of its original participants than another, any characteristics that led to their departure from the project will be less represented in the group that lost the most participants. When lost participants are replaced by random sampling from the original pool, differences between the two experimental groups are reduced but not eliminated.

To illustrate this principle, we offer a fictitious example with a much larger difference in dropout rates than usually occurs in practice: A project's randomly assigned experimental sample lost 50 of its original 100 participants and its control sample none. As a best guess, we might infer that about 50% of the original participant pool and about 50% of the control sample would also have dropped out if they had experienced the experimental treatment. For convenience, we call these people "potential experimental dropouts" (PEDs). After the experimental sample lost its 50 people, it contained no PEDs, in contrast to the control sample's 50%. If the participants lost to the experimental sample are replaced at random from the original participant pool, we assume that about 50% of the 50 replacements (25% of the sample's 100 people) will be PEDs, in contrast to 50% of the whole control sample. Researchers almost never know what characteristics led participants to leave a project; therefore replacement cannot be planned so as to redress whatever group differences their loss may have caused. The same problem occurs when groups lose participants for different reasons rather than in different proportions.

To the extent that a follow-up study loses participants, it has pretreatment data and follow-up data from different samples. To compare the entire pretreatment sample with the remaining follow-up sample would confound pre-post differences with whatever factors led some participants to discontinue their participation and others to continue. This confounding problem is present even if participants who dropped out do not differ with regard to their pretreatment data from those who remained. The pretreatment data cannot be assumed to include all factors related to dropping out versus remaining. Suppose, for example, that a sample of college students is offered career counseling, and the students' career-related activities are examined 3, 6, and 12 months after counseling. If a number of students have dropped out of the study at these follow-up points, what conclusions are we to draw about them? One possibility is that those who dropped out had career activities that took them out of our purview. Another is that they abandoned career activities for a lifestyle without traditional gainful employment. The point is that our pre- and posttreatment samples are different and these differences are confounded with the treatment effects.

These same considerations apply to developmental studies using a longitudinal design. One common remedy is to delete the participants who dropped out and analyze only the data from the participants who remained with the project from start to finish. Though this practice solves an internal validity problem, it creates an external validity problem if the project's research questions concern a population represented by the pretreatment data. We discuss this matter more fully later in this chapter.

To monitor and guard against mortality as a validity risk, Drew and Hardman (1985) recommended deciding on an a priori caution point before collecting the data. How high this caution point should be will vary from project to project; "decisions are typically based on the experience and clinical judgment of the investigator" (p. 145). For example, a researcher might decide on the basis of previous research reports that the risk to internal validity is excessively high if two groups of participants differ in their dropout rate by 10% or more. This criterion would be reached if one group lost 15% of its participants and the other 25% or more, or if one group lost 5% and the other 15% or more. These authors note that the researcher is faced with some unpleasant decisions if the a priori caution point is reached or exceeded. The researcher can report the problem as a potential weakness in the findings along with the researcher's judgment and supporting arguments that this weakness does not excessively compromise the interpretations offered. To do so requires that "the rationale sustaining the researcher's interpretations must have considerable strength" (Drew & Hardman, 1985, p. 145).

Alternatively, the researcher can decide the risk to internal validity is so great that the project must be discontinued with this sample of participants and begun anew with a new sample. Of course, abandoning the project altogether is another possibility. These latter choices are obviously unpleasant. Before beginning anew with a new sample, we recommend finding out whatever you can about the reasons for mortality problems in the old sample and doing all you can to avoid repeating these problems with the new sample. Further, a caution point relating to different mortality rates in two samples offers no safeguard against samples having similar mortality rates for different reasons.

It is usually possible and desirable to compare lost and remaining participants on all available pretest measures. Such comparisons are often very informative. However, it is rarely defensible to assume that the lost and remaining participants are sufficiently alike merely because these comparisons yield no significant differences. These participants often differ in other important ways not addressed by the pretest measures.

History

In any project involving repeated measures over a period of time (including all pretest–posttest and time series designs), unplanned events outside the researcher's control can influence the dependent variable. Such events may be confounded with one of the variables under study, such as a treatment effect, a classification variable, or a developmental variable.

For example, suppose a pharmaceutical company was studying effects of a new medication designed to reduce depressive symptoms in psychiatric patients. The research plan called for the depressed patients on Ward X to (1) answer a pretest questionnaire, (2) receive medication for a week, (3) answer the questionnaire a second time, (4) continue the medication another week, and (5) answer the questionnaire a third time.

Unknown to the researcher, a nurse well-liked by all Ward X patients was hit by a drunk driver and killed on her way home from work the evening before the third administration of the questionnaire was scheduled. Data from this third administration indicated substantially more depressive symptoms than the previous week's data. With only the Ward X data at hand, the researcher might have concluded that the medication reduced depressive symptoms initially, but symptoms resumed even though the medication was continued. Responses to the third questionnaire were influenced by the combination of medication and an unplanned event. The medication might have substantially mitigated symptoms the patients would have otherwise experienced in reaction to the event, but the researcher would have no way to know from these patients' questionnaire data.

As a second example, suppose a researcher wanted to find out whether college students with different majors responded differently to an intervention designed to improve confidence in their test-taking skills. The study was carried out in a private college that required students to pass a qualifying examination to advance from junior to senior standing. Juniors in each of several majors were pretested with a questionnaire asking how skillful they thought they were at taking tests. A week after they took the qualification test, they answered a similar questionnaire. Juniors from the previous year had answered the same questionnaires at comparable times and served as a control sample. In the "control" year, all qualification test results were released after the last questionnaire. In the year of the intervention (and unknown to the researcher) the Physical Science Department released the results the day before the last questionnaire. In both years, everyone passed. The researcher concluded that the intervention increased students' confidence in their test-taking skills much more strongly among physical science majors than among other majors. Were these students' beliefs in their test-taking skills improved by the intervention, by the news they had passed, or by these two experiences acting together? In this example, history is confounded with both the independent variable and a classification variable.

History also represents a risk to internal validity in descriptive studies, particularly developmental ones. In Chapter 8, we noted that cross-sectional studies of development compare people of different ages. Also noted in Chapter 8 is that older cohorts differ from younger ones not only with respect to age but also with respect to the time period in which they grew up. Many political, economic, and attitudinal changes took place in the country between the times these cohorts grew up. Among these changes were increased educational opportunity for people of college age and more permissive attitudes about male and female social roles. To what extent do intercohort differences represent the effects of aging, and to what extent do differences reflect social changes such as these?

Longitudinal studies of development use repeated measures of the same people at different times; people not only get older but also experience different historical events and conditions. Suppose a sample of people expressed greater optimism in 1946 than in 1931. Were they more optimistic because they were 15 years older or because they had recently experienced the end of World War II, or perhaps for both reasons? The developmental variable (age) is confounded with history in both cross-sectional and longitudinal designs, but the nature of this confounding is different in each design.

We call attention to the special meaning of the word *history* in this discussion. With respect to research design, this term refers to unplanned incidents or changes in conditions experienced by participants that take place before data are collected or between times data are collected. Because the longitudinal research design involves comparisons between data collected at these different times, the unplanned incidents or changes represent risks to internal validity. In the cohort design, unplanned differences in conditions experienced by the participants are confounded with the developmental variable, weakening internal validity. This meaning of history differs from the traditional one, and it is important not to confuse these meanings.

Good design is the best remedy for problems of confounding with history. As noted in Chapter 8, control samples in experiments should experience conditions as close as possible to the ideal of "all things in common with the treatment group except the critical factor per se" (Isaac & Michael, 1981, p. 88). In the hospital example discussed earlier in this section, the researchers might have used a double-blind design, giving the medication under study to some Ward X patients and a placebo to others. If hospital rules required giving every Ward X patient the same medication, the drug under study might have been given to more than one ward and control conditions to several other wards. Repeating this pattern in more than one hospital would strengthen this design further.

After research data have been collected, it is often helpful to ask a few participants or staff people whether any special events occurred that might have affected the dependent variable. The researcher can then judge whether any such events are likely to have influenced the results and whether design controls were sufficient safeguards against risks to validity. Any events or changes in conditions related to either the independent or dependent variables pose risks to validity. If design controls do not offer sufficient safeguards, the researcher should consider either enlarging the project with one or more new samples or discarding the affected results in favor of a new start, despite the delays and expense these courses of action entail. If an event occurred that the researcher judges to have affected the results too little to be concerned about, this event should be included in the project's report along with the researcher's judgment and supporting rationale.

History also poses a severe threat to internal validity in time series designs, especially those of a quasi-experimental nature, such as the AB design. For this reason, the best way to control for the confounding effects of history with time series research is to use either an ABAB (withdrawal or reversal) or multiple baseline design, as discussed in Chapter 8. The ABAB design relies on the low probability that a specific historical event will be confounded with the treatment variable each time it is changed. Similarly, the multiple baseline design across participants or behaviors also relies on the low probability that a confounding historical event will occur more than once at the same times the treatment is introduced. If we return to the example involving Mr. Jones and his students discussed in Chapter 2, the multiple baseline design ensured that his change in attention pattern was responsible for the decrease in his students' disruptive behaviors. When ABAB and multiple baseline designs are inappropriate or impractical, the researcher must rely on repetition of the AB design with as many participants as possible at different times. Such numerous repetitions reduce the probability that introduction of the treatment will be consistently accompanied by a similar confounding event.

Maturation

In some projects, the passage of time is a variable under study (for example, in developmental studies). In others, the passage of time brings about changes in the participants, and these changes can influence their performance on measures of dependent variables. People become hungry and tired with the passage of hours, older with the passage of years. These changes rely only on time rather than specific events or changed conditions in the physical or social environment. For example, do students perform better on tests as seniors than they did as freshmen because of the instruction they received in the meantime or because they are three years older, or for both reasons? Studying only one group of students offers no way to know.

Maturation poses no risk to internal validity when it is the phenomenon under study. In contrast, internal validity is threatened when maturational changes are not the phenomenon of interest but are confounded with an independent variable such as a treatment program. Most outcome studies of counseling or psychotherapy require control of spontaneous recovery as a maturation problem. An old homily observes that a physician is fortunate to come at the height of a disease. Another notes that you can expect to recover from a common cold in about seven days if you treat it carefully, but left untreated, it will probably last a week. A third says, time heals all wounds. If a client leaves a counseling relationship feeling better than when he or she entered it, both counselor and client may be tempted to credit the counseling intervention as the cause of the change. However, neither knows whether similar improvement might have taken place without counseling. When clients credit one of us with having made their lives better, we like to point out their responsibility in the process by noting that they used the counseling relationship to make changes they wanted. Outcome studies need to address the possibility that people without counselors use other resources to help them bring about wanted changes.

To control for maturation as a validity risk, it is rarely if ever satisfactory to rely on preexisting data for estimates of the amount of change to be expected from maturation alone. For example, if a researcher knew that 8-year-old children could be expected to improve their scores on a certain test by an average of 50 points when retested a year later as 9-year-olds, the researcher might attribute to an intervention any pretest–posttest gains exceeding that amount in an experimental sample of similar age. Though many developmental studies are in the literature, particularly regarding children, current researchers' dependent variables (such as a particular test used to measure social skills) often do not correspond exactly with the phenomena previously reported. Even when a previously reported study has addressed the desired variables, there is rarely if ever sufficient basis to believe that the participants in the earlier study are sufficiently like the researcher's own to avoid group composition differences as a serious risk to internal validity.

Maturation is like history in that good design offers the best remedy. Fortunately, the same repeated-measures control-group designs that offer the best control for history also control for maturation. When participants are randomly assigned to groups that experience different conditions over the same period of time, maturational changes usually affect both groups equally. In studies comparing two interventions without a control condition, it is safe to infer that the interventions do or do not differ from each other with regard to the dependent variable, but it is never safe to assume that either intervention produced changes in excess of maturation. In traditional group experiments, this latter inference requires a control condition that estimates changes due only to extraneous variables such as maturation. The ABAB design controls for maturation by withdrawing or reversing and then reinstating the treatment condition under study as maturation changes presumably continue. In multiple baseline designs, the baselines of varying length serve as a control for maturational changes. Treatment effects can be compared to changes, such as maturation, that occur in the absence of intervention.

Practice Effects

People who perform any learnable task repeatedly usually do it better later than earlier provided fatigue or other adverse conditions do not intrude. Many measures of dependent variables in research projects are based on learnable tasks. This learning threatens internal validity when the effects of practice are confounded with a treatment effect or a developmental variable. The most obvious illustrations are pre-post and time series designs without adequate controls. Many projects call for participants to answer an aptitude or achievement test, experience a treatment, and then answer the same test or a similar one again. Participants score better on the second test than on the first not only because of the intervening treatment but also because they have learned something about the test and its content while taking it the first time. Drew and Hardman (1985) noted that practice effect is likely to be particularly strong when the kind of instrument being used is a new and unique experience for the participants. For example, people who take the XYZ Mathematics Test as their very first achievement testing experience will probably improve their scores if retested because of learning from the pretest experience. This learning can be expected to include some general test-taking skills in addition to some particulars of the XYZ Test and some mathematics. In contrast, people who have taken scholastic achievement tests before and experience the XYZ Mathematics Test for the first time will probably improve their retest scores less than their less test-experienced counterparts. Though they can be expected to learn some XYZ Test particulars and some mathematics from the pretest experience, it will probably not improve their general test-taking skills substantially.

Measures such as inventories, questionnaires, interviews, rating scales, and observation schedules are also subject to practice effect, though usually somewhat less so than tests. Practice effect can influence the differences among successive measures drawn from any task that can be affected by learning.

Tasks that yield measures of dependent variables are not the only ones subject to practice effect. With long-term involvement in any research project, participants become more practiced at many tasks incidental to those under investigation. The building and room become easier to find; participants know where the rest room is; a receptionist's face is familiar rather than new. Such practice effects can contaminate studies of counseling, particularly when clients' distress experiences are being investigated. Clients' greater comfort with the surroundings may influence pre-post differences in addition to whatever benefit they derive from counseling.

As with other risks discussed earlier in this chapter, good design offers the best remedy for practice effect. In group experiments, the pretest–posttest control-group design adequately controls for the possibility that practice effect may add to treatment influences. Though much less powerful in a statistical sense, the posttest-only control-group design eliminates practice effects due to pretesting. The Solomon four-group design not only controls for pretest influences but allows measurement of them. In own-control designs, counterbalancing the order in which treatments are administered offers at least partial control of practice effect and is reasonably satisfactory in most instances.

In time series experiments, a baseline of adequate length is the best control for practice effects. The experimental treatment should never be introduced until the behaviors measured in the baseline condition have stabilized into a recognizable pattern without a consistent upward or downward slope over time. With variables that represent learnable skills, practice effects should produce an upward slope until these effects stabilize.

A researcher might be tempted to control for practice effect by giving all participants some practice with the measurement instrument before pretest measures are taken. This procedure might be useful to reduce initial variability among participants if some of them have had experience with this measure and others have not. However, it does not offer satisfactory control of practice effects because the initial "practice" experience with an instrument does not ensure that participants will not learn from further experience with it when pretest measures are taken.

Placebo Effect

When patients are given medications, many physicians tell them what effects to expect. The chemical effects of the medication and the psychosocial effects of the physician's statements are thus combined. Many drug studies approach this problem by giving one group of participants a pharmacologically inert substance (placebo) with the same information and recommendations as are given to the group receiving the drug under study. Ordinarily, participants are not told what medication they are receiving. As noted in Chapter 8, withholding this information from the participants alone is called *single blind.* A single-blind procedure risks confounding if the people who dispense the medication show different facial expressions or other cues to the "drug group" versus the "placebo group." A double-blind design addresses this possibility; neither the patients nor the dispensing staff know who gets the active drug and who gets the placebo.

In studies of counseling and psychotherapy, the placebo effect differs from that in drug studies. Placebos in drug studies are pharmacologically inert. Critelli and Neumann (1984) criticized psychotherapy researchers for extending this inert metaphor to mean therapeutically inert and giving it a negative connotation. These authors further suggested that the placebo idea in psychotherapy research refers to common factors among psychotherapies as opposed to factors specific to particular therapies; "common factors of psychotherapy conform closely to traditional listings of placebo variables . . . such as attention, expectancy of cure and demand for improvement" (Critelli & Neumann, 1984, pp. 34–35). Therefore, studies that contrast a particular form of therapy with a placebo intervention do not address the question of its general effectiveness. Instead, such studies are designed to determine whether the particular therapy's results can be attributed to its specific features rather than to the characteristics it shares with most if not all other therapies. Wilkins (1986) recommended that "the term *placebo* be used sparingly, if at all, when one is describing events in . . . psychotherapy" (p. 553). Rather, he recommended that social-psychological events be investigated as legitimate causes and that researchers use such terms as *artifact, control procedure,* and *control group* or *comparison group* instead of *placebo effect, placebo procedure,* and *placebo group.*

Counseling and psychotherapy ordinarily include as part of treatment the phenomena drug studies identify as placebo effects. When present in a nondrug study of counseling or psychotherapy, the placebo idea is usually an analogy or metaphor. To a researcher inclined to include the placebo idea in such a study, we suggest returning to the formulation of the project's mission and specifying exactly what variables are of interest, what possible phenomena the placebo idea includes, and why it is desirable to separate these phenomena from other treatment effects.

Hawthorne Effect

When participants know they are part of a research study, this knowledge can influence their behavior. "If we pay attention to people, they respond" (Kerlinger, 1964, p. 318). In early studies of production employees at Western Electric Company's Hawthorne plant, experimentally introduced changes in working conditions produced both expected and unexpected changes in output (Roethlisberger & Dickson, 1939). Workers increased their production when environmental conditions such as lighting were improved and further increased it when these environmental changes were reversed. The Hawthorne effect poses a particular risk to internal validity when one group more than another experiences conditions that lead participants to feel special (that is, when these conditions are confounded with a treatment effect). A wide variety of circumstances can contribute to this feeling of being special, including:

- Participants know or believe they have been specially chosen.
- The way participants are introduced to experimental procedures evokes a feeling of being special.
- The research plan changes everyday routines.
- Participants notice that they are treated differently than their counterparts are.
- Participants experience unusual surroundings such as a laboratory.

Although feeling discriminated against elicits different reactions than does feeling special, it poses the same kind of risks to internal validity when confounded with a treatment effect.

Problems with do-nothing control groups were discussed in Chapter 8. This misuse of the no-treatment control design is particularly vulnerable to the Hawthorne effect because one group of participants is treated while the other is ignored. In a placebo control group, on the other hand, participants receive equal attention and are treated in other ways as comparably to the treatment group as possible.

Time series designs attempt to control for the Hawthorne effect in two ways. First, the baseline period allows participants to become accustomed to being observed and the attention paid to them. As was mentioned previously, the treatment variable is not introduced until the baseline measures have stabilized, which means that any changes attributable simply to being observed will have stabilized also. Second, the ABAB design addresses the Hawthorne effect because we assume that the behaviors that changed as a result of introducing the treatment condition should return to their former levels after the treatment condition is withdrawn or reversed. If the Hawthorne effect is operating, any change in conditions should result in continued change in the dependent variable rather than a return to former levels. In fact, the Hawthorne effect was originally discovered because unexpected behavior changes followed withdrawal of experimental conditions.

The Hawthorne effect may not only add to an experimental treatment but may also interact with it. For example, in a project comparing medication and supportive counseling as interventions for emotional distress, feeling special might lead clients to participate more actively in the support condition than they would without this feeling, and therefore derive more benefit. The medication group, meanwhile, feels similarly special, but this feeling does not influence their participation or their reactions to the treatment. In such circumstances, the Hawthorne effect poses a risk to internal validity even though both groups feel similarly special.

John Henry Effect

Participants who know they are in a control group sometimes react with intensified effort in an attitude of determination "to show the experimental group a thing or two" (Isaac & Michael, 1981, p. 86). The John Henry and Hawthorne effects both represent participants' reactions to knowledge that they are in a research project. If experimental and control participants both react with intensified effort, John Henry and Hawthorne effects may partially cancel each other with regard to group differences. However, it is difficult if not impossible for a researcher to know to what extent each effect has influenced results. Either of these effects, with or without the other, limits the researcher's ability to unambiguously attribute group differences in results to the independent variable.

Experimenter Bias

Many factors can influence the manner in which one administers an experimental treatment. One of the most frequent is a preconceived idea about the results desired or expected. For this reason, **experimenter bias** is sometimes referred to as a **self-fulfilling prophecy.** For illustration, imagine a project in a university counseling center in which participants are students with grade point deficiencies who receive official notice of probationary status from the dean. Notices to one group set a specific date and time for an appointment at the Student Counseling Center. The other group are "encouraged" to make their own appointments for academic counseling. The researcher wants to find out if setting specific appointments for counseling leads to better academic performance by these students.

At worst ("worst" from the standpoint of internal validity), counselors might deliberately attempt to influence which practice the university adopts by providing better services to one group than the other, although such practices are ethically suspect. Usually, problems of experimenter bias are less blatant. Differences in counselors' services to two groups are inadvertent more often than deliberate. A counselor who disagrees with the prearranged appointment strategy might unintentionally provide poorer services to students so referred or attempt to compensate for the harsh treatment he or she believes such students have received from the dean. Whatever the direction of such bias, it is confounded with the independent variable and therefore threatens internal validity.

Knowledge of participants' group assignment is not the only factor that can precipitate experimenter bias. Any other knowledge or beliefs that service providers may have about participants will do. For example, Rosenthal and Jacobson (1968) reported a Pygmalion effect in research they carried out in schools. They found that teachers' beliefs about students' ability influenced their classroom behavior toward these students, creating a self-fulfilling prophecy regarding the students' achievement. Though the Pygmalion study has been criticized for methodological flaws, including errors in data analysis, this fact does not reduce researchers' responsibility to minimize the risk of experimenter bias.

One of the most effective remedies for experimenter bias is to ensure that the people who administer services to participants in an experiment do not know what treatment group any individual participant is in, or participants' pretest performance, if any. In the university counseling center project introduced as an example in this section, a receptionist could manage the details concerning appointments and withhold from the counselors all information about how any student's appointment was made. Sometimes this strategy is not feasible, such as when each counselor uses one counseling technique with some clients and other techniques with other clients. While planning a project, researchers need to consider the following:

- Who knows what about the participants?
- Of this knowledge, what is necessary so that people can carry out the project and also fulfill their other obligations?
- How much does this knowledge increase the risk of experimenter bias?
- How might the researcher withhold the knowledge that risks experimenter bias without unduly compromising people's ability to meet their responsibilities?

Demand Characteristics

Any research activity involving interaction between a participant and anyone else is a social situation. Therefore, the researcher can expect the behavior of the people in the research activity to be guided by the social norms and standards our society and its various subcultures offer for such situations. Milgram (1974) induced an unexpectedly high proportion of paid participants to administer painful "shocks" to another person despite their feeling that it was wrong to do so. This project involved deception in that no shocks were delivered; the person allegedly receiving them was the experimenter's accomplice. Among other points, the results demonstrated the powerful influence of experimenters over their participants. Orne (1962) gave further evidence of experimental participants' willingness to give an experimenter what they think he or she wants.

The outcome of the 1989–90 McMartin Preschool child molestation trial offers another illustration. After the trial, some jurors reported that they supported a not guilty verdict despite their belief that the defendants were probably guilty. These jurors expressed concern that testimony was obtained from child witnesses under conditions that diluted the children's credibility or contaminated their testimony (that is, the children said what they thought the adults questioning them wanted to hear), leaving open the possibility that this testimony did not represent a factual account of events as they took place. Therefore, these jurors judged that the evidence was not convincing beyond a reasonable doubt, as is legally required for criminal conviction (Wilkinson & Rainey, 1990).

Many studies of counseling call upon clients to rate or answer questions about services they have received. In so doing, clients comply to varying degrees with the idea that they should be grateful rather than critical of help received, particularly if they believe the help (though less than expected) represents the helper's best efforts.

Demand characteristics such as these are not always confounding or biasing effects; sometimes they are the phenomena being studied. Any research project that relies on data collected from people risks being subject to demand characteristics. In some, these risks seriously impair internal validity; in others, they are inconsequential; in most, their importance lies between these two extremes.

Rater and Observer Issues

Many studies of counseling rely on ratings or observations as a data source. Technical qualities of rating scales are discussed in Chapter 12. This section addresses other potential problems related to raters' and observers' behavior: **rater bias,** the **halo effect, rater drift,** and some individual raters' habitual use of the same sections of a scale (low, high, middle, or extreme) to the exclusion of other sections. Unless otherwise specified, the following comments apply equally to raters and persons who are recording observations other than ratings.

Rater bias. The self-fulfilling prophecy family includes rater bias as well as the previously discussed experimenter bias. If raters or observers know which participants belong to an experimental sample and which to a control sample, this knowledge can influence their judgment. Similarly, raters' other knowledge about participants can also affect their ratings. For example, teachers who know their students' scholastic aptitude scores are sometimes influenced by these scores when they assign grades. In a time series design, "perhaps the experimenters, either knowingly or unknowingly, alter their mindset for data recording because change is expected as a function of the intervention" (Drew & Hardman, 1985, p. 135). Ratings can be biased either deliberately or inadvertently. For example, a rater may deliberately give all "experimental" participants high ratings or all "minority" participants low ratings to cause the results of a project to come out as desired. As discussed in Chapter 5, such practices violate counselors' ethical standards. Inadvertent bias is more common and much harder to identify and control. Despite raters' best intentions to be objective, any knowledge that might bias their ratings can be expected to do so to some extent.

Some students confuse rater bias with experimenter bias. Rater bias affects only ratings and observations; experimenter bias affects the administration of procedures to participants. These procedures may include introduction and orientation to the project, experimental and control treatments, and perhaps counseling or other services. If the same people who administer procedures also make ratings, both experimenter bias and rater bias may occur concurrently.

Halo effect. The halo effect refers to people's tendency to generalize from irrelevant qualities or general impressions to relevant qualities of the person or object they are rating. This generalization may influence a rating in a favorable or unfavorable direction. Here is an example. Jack and Bill are seated in a restaurant. Jack wears dark glasses and has a white cane. A waitress takes Bill's order and asks Bill, "And what would he like to have?" The waitress has observed Jack's dark glasses and white cane; she has good reason to believe he cannot see. However, she has generalized her impression to conclude that he cannot order for himself. Wright (1983) discussed these ideas as part of the "spread" concept. Here is another illustration. If a student gave a particularly good answer to the first question on an essay examination, the grader may form an impression that this is a "particularly good student" and allow this impression to bias ratings of this student's answers to later questions.

Favorite parts of rating scales. Raters differ among themselves as to the portions of a rating scale they habitually use. Some, but by no means all, use the entire range of possible ratings. Some raters are consistently lenient, others consistently strict. Some tend to cluster their ratings in the middle of a scale, avoiding the extremes; other raters tend to avoid the middle. When such individual differences are equally distributed among treatment conditions, they do not threaten the validity of intertreatment comparisons. Care is often required, however, to see that interrater differences are not confounded with treatment conditions. As an illustration, suppose two communities have very different proportions of their licensed drivers convicted for drunk driving. Such a fact is an insufficient basis to conclude that fewer people drive drunk in the town with the lower rate; its police and judges might be less inclined to rate drivers as drunk.

Rater drift. Raters who are involved in a project over a period of time can inadvertently change their approach to the task as the project progresses (Hill, 1991). Some of these possible changes are:

- becoming more strict or more lenient about standards,
- becoming less vigilant (more careless),
- becoming less attentive to subtleties,
- making more snap judgments, or
- making more assumptions about the data.

Different raters can be expected to show different patterns of drift. Drew and Hardman (1985) discussed this matter as a **calibration** issue. If a mechanical measuring apparatus is adjusted while a project is in progress, the change will introduce differences in data collected after versus before the adjustment. Slow changes in calibration while a project is under way have the same effect. The same considerations apply to human judges whenever a project requires some judgments to be made later than others. Judges' experiences between earlier and later ratings may influence their rating standards.

We offer an example from clinical experience. Rehabilitation counselors in a hospital whose entire caseload consisted of psychiatric inpatients rated some patients as ready to return to competitive employment. Such patients were referred to the state rehabilitation agency because hospital counselors were not involved in job placement. The agency, however, judged many of the referred patients too emotionally disturbed to return to work. As the hospital counselors discussed their experience, it became evident that they had slowly shifted their rating standard during their years of hospital experience; they had lost touch with employers' tolerance limits for emotionally disturbed behavior. If these counselors had rated patients' work readiness in a longitudinal research project spanning these years, their changes in rating standards would have been confounded with the developmental variable.

Remedies for rater problems. The variables to be rated must be defined clearly enough that specific rating instructions let raters know what they are to rate. Isaac and Michael (1981) noted that the halo effect influences ratings more strongly when variables are vague and impressionistic than when they are specific and clearly defined. The same principle holds for other rater problems. Clarifying definitions of variables is one of the researcher's formulation tasks, not a rating or judging task. Nonetheless, open communication between researcher and raters often identifies ambiguities previously overlooked.

Raters need to be selected, screened, and trained so they have the necessary skill, temperament, and motivation to perform their tasks satisfactorily. Enough raters must be recruited to allow for attrition and still leave enough to achieve satisfactory reliability. Training of raters should ensure that they sufficiently understand their task and are motivated to carry it out responsibly. Raters need to feel that their contribution to the project is meaningful and valuable. However, they should not know the specific hypotheses being investigated. Hill (1991) provides a detailed discussion of these issues.

Withholding any knowledge that might bias a judge's ratings or observations is the best remedy for rater bias. This knowledge includes but is rarely if ever limited to the researcher's hypotheses. With modifications, we repeat the recommendations that ended the section on experimenter bias. While planning any project involving ratings or observations, a researcher should consider these questions.

- What information will judges have about the participants?
- Of this knowledge, what is necessary for these judges to carry out the project and meet their other obligations?
- How much is this knowledge likely to bias the judges' ratings or observations?
- How might a researcher withhold any knowledge that risks such bias without unduly compromising judges' ability to meet their responsibilities?

As is the case with rater bias, raters' and observers' intentions to be objective usually reduce the halo effect but do not sufficiently ensure against it. It is better that researchers keep raters and observers ignorant, insofar as possible, of any information likely to evoke powerful first impressions.

Hill (1991) offered three recommendations specific to reducing rater drift.

- Raters should meet regularly as a team in order to feel responsible to the team and avoid developing idiosyncratic ways of interpreting items.
- Raters should have and use "standard calibration examples" in order to compare their current ratings with their own earlier ratings and other calibrated sets of raters.
- Raters should be made aware of the problem of rater drift and should be regularly remotivated for the rating task. (p. 109)

Instrumentation

Machines as well as human judges can undergo changes as a project progresses. We refer not only to machines that measure (such as polygraphs, timers, and stopwatches) but also to machines that present stimuli, such as tachistoscopes and audio- or videotape playback equipment. If changes in the quality of presentation are confounded with experimental variables, clear interpretation of results is compromised. Further, if a machine breaks down in the presence of participants, the breakdown becomes part of their experience in the treatment condition in which it occurs.

Researchers use the term **instrumentation** in two senses: instruments used in a project, and the risks to design validity arising from their use. If instruments that present stimuli or measure responses are poorly designed, chosen, or administered, internal validity is weakened. Such measurement issues are discussed in greater detail in Chapter 11.

Statistical Regression

Groups of people chosen for their atypically high or low scores usually have more moderate mean scores when retested. This phenomenon is known as **statistical regression** and occurs because at least part of the reason they scored at the extreme ends of the scale was due to chance factors that favored high scorers or depressed the scores of low scorers. On retest, any group of very high or very low scorers will tend to have an average score closer to the mean of the scale.

To illustrate, suppose a university's freshman class were given an anxiety scale, and the ten highest scorers were given six weeks of therapy and then retested. Even if the therapy had no effect, the average anxiety score of the group given therapy would, in all likelihood, be lower due to the regression effect. This subsection discusses how statistical regression can influence research data and some remedies for this threat to design validity.

Some students confuse statistical regression with a different phenomenon found in some studies of attitude change. If participants are pretested, then given an intervention (such as a film), immediate retesting usually shows a change in mean attitude scores in the direction intended by the intervention. However, if these same participants are retested again weeks later, their mean attitude scores usually revert toward pretest levels. This finding attests to the temporary effect of most attitude interventions; it is not a statistical artifact. In contrast, statistical regression is a statistical artifact that results when groups of participants are selected for their high or low scores.

Statistical regression is not limited to projects in which the researcher selects participants based on pretest measures. Any selection based on high or low scores will do. This point is particularly important to consider when studying atypical groups such as gifted, intellectually disabled, or emotionally disturbed. For example, a community mental health center might use results from an instrument such as the Minnesota Multiphasic Personality Inventory (MMPI) to select clients at intake for a special program and base measures of improvement on post-treatment MMPI scores. Suppose a researcher were to compare such clients' improvement with pretest–posttest differences in MMPI scores among a sample of college students as constructed controls. The risk of statistical regression is very high in the mental health center sample. Though the college students are often selected for high scholastic aptitude and achievement scores, this selection would not likely cause statistical regression in their MMPI results. Therefore statistical regression would pose a serious risk to the validity of any comparison of these two samples with regard to MMPI changes; it would be confounded with a variable being investigated.

Many samples of participants studied in counseling research were formed by selection processes using measures of interest to counseling researchers. We list a few:

- college students chosen for above average scholastic aptitude, achievement, or both;
- psychotherapy clients chosen or assigned to treatments on the basis of personality inventory scores;
- students in public schools assigned to special programs based on scholastic aptitude or achievement measures;
- clients placed in rehabilitation facilities based on a diagnosis of "mental retardation"; or
- students chosen for counselors' special attention because of low scores on measures of vocational maturity.

For participants selected from any such special population, statistical regression poses a substantial risk if the researcher is studying changes in any one or more of the variables by which the population was identified as special.

Statistical regression can also affect variables other than scores on tests, inventories, and attitude scales. Absenteeism from school or work provides an illustrative example.* For ease of discussion, we introduce the medical terms *chronic* and *acute* as analogies. Acute conditions last only a limited time. They are atypical of both the affected individual and most groups of which he or she is a part (such as fellow students or coworkers in the case of absenteeism). In this context, we use *acute* to refer to the temporary nature of a condition, not its severity. In contrast, chronic conditions last longer, usually for an indefinite time. Though typical of the individual, they are atypical of most groups of which he or she is a part. An individual who maintains an unusually high rate of absenteeism is atypical of fellow students or coworkers in this regard. Acutely atypical behavior is usually a response to temporarily changed life circumstances. For example, a family crisis may cause someone to be absent from school or work unusually often; attendance usually returns to the person's customary pattern after the crisis is past.

*We thank Patricia A. Flores of Montebello Unified School District for this idea.

Statistical regression poses a risk to design validity when people are selected for an intervention addressed to chronically atypical behavior, and the selection includes some people whose problem behavior is acutely atypical. For example, a public school counselor administered a special intervention to students selected for high absence records the previous term, in comparison with the student body at large. The intervention was designed to reduce chronic absenteeism. However, the selected students probably included some who were absent more often the previous term than was their personal custom because of temporary circumstances and who would probably return to their more customary attendance pattern with or without a special intervention. Without adequate controls, the counselor could be easily misled into believing that improved attendance by these students was due to the special intervention. It is often difficult for researchers to know whether a participant's desirable behavior change represents a response to an intervention or would have happened without it.

We discuss this matter as a statistical regression problem because most samples of people selected for atypical behavior characteristics (whether scores or anything else) exhibit more typical behavior when reexamined later. Fluctuating circumstances sometimes elicit personally atypical behavior; this behavior often leads to their selection in atypical samples and then reverts to more personally typical levels. In some instances, however, the underlying process may be a maturational one, such as spontaneous remission from problems for which clients seek counseling.

The best protection against statistical regression is prevention. To the extent practical, researchers should avoid any selection or assignment of participants based on atypically high or low scores. If participants are to be selected or assigned on the basis of atypical behavior, the risk can be reduced if the researcher does not mix chronically and acutely atypical participants without knowing which is which. These precautions are particularly important when any selection variable is identical with or closely related to one or more of the variables the project is investigating.

Randomly selecting participants from any population avoids introducing new risk of statistical regression, although it retains whatever such risk the population may already have. Similarly, assigning participants at random to treatment groups does not introduce risk of statistical regression. Rather, random assignment enables a researcher to assume that if any such risk is already present in the original subject pool it will affect all groups about equally rather than confounding group differences. This procedure provides satisfactory control in many projects that cannot prevent statistical regression.

To minimize risk to internal validity from statistical regression, we recommend that researchers ask themselves the following questions during the planning phase of each project. For the design of projects that do not involve group comparisons:

1. Are any of the subject populations of interest to the project composed of people originally selected as atypical of a larger population from which they came?

2. If the answer to #1 is yes, was this selection based on any variables identical with, or closely related to, any of the variables specified in the project's mission?
3. If the answer to #2 is yes, risk of statistical regression is substantial. How important is this risk to the project's mission?

For the design of projects that do involve group comparisons:

1. Does the research plan call for comparing a sample from a population originally selected as atypical with a sample from a population not so selected? Any such comparisons involve confounding observed changes with statistical regression. If the selection was based on any variables identical with, or closely related to, any of the variables specified in the project's mission, this confounding may substantially impair internal validity.
2. Does the research plan call for selecting any samples primarily from either the upper or lower end of the subject pool distribution? In any such samples, risk of statistical regression will be high.
3. If the answer to #2 is yes, does the research plan call for comparing any such samples with any other samples selected by different rules? In any such comparisons, risk of confounding sample differences with statistical regression will be high.
4. If the answer to either #1 or #3 is yes, is any selection variable identical with, or closely related to, any of the variables specified in the project's mission? If so, statistical regression poses a substantial risk to internal validity.

If the answers to these questions indicate statistical regression places internal validity at risk, we recommend that the researcher carefully estimate the importance of this risk to the project's mission. The project's report should then include (a) an acknowledgment that this risk exists, (b) the researcher's judgment concerning its importance, and (c) the facts and the reasoning on which this judgment is based.

EXTERNAL VALIDITY

External validity concerns generalizability. To what extent can a project's findings be applied to people, places, times, or situations other than those studied?

External validity does not include as many different issues regarding both risks and remedies as does internal validity. Nonetheless, issues of external validity are equally important to consider, especially because projects vary widely in the extent of their concern with such generalization. At one extreme, some projects are concerned only with the people and situations investigated; the project's mission does not require external validity. For example, an employee counseling firm's consulting contract provides for a fee determined by cost savings calculations based on the job performance of the employees counseled during a specified time period. Data are therefore collected from the records of these employees. For purposes of setting the counselor's fee, no one cares whether similar results could be expected with other people in other times or places. Such generalization issues become crucially important, however, when a project is carried out to test a scientific hypothesis or guide long-term agency policy. In such projects, external validity is part of relevance; a degree of external validity is necessary if the data are to be relevant to the project's mission.

Initial Population-Sample Differences

Most projects collect data from one or more samples of participants, with each sample intended to represent a much larger population. The project's mission is concerned with the larger populations rather than the specific people from whom data are collected. In these circumstances, any systematic factors making the sample unrepresentative of the population will weaken external validity. Two major factors affect representativeness:

- the extent to which the participants available to the project for study are like the populations of interest to its mission, and
- the methods by which the participants studied are sampled from those available.

The first of these factors is discussed in this section, the second in the next chapter.

Differences between the participants available and the populations of interest can arise in a number of ways. As noted in Chapter 6, research questions often specify populations different from researchers' populations of primary interest. For example, a researcher may be interested in phenomena affecting college and university students throughout the United States yet be limited to one or a few local campuses due to fiscal restraints or other practicalities. If research procedures are difficult, long, or uncomfortable, many prospective participants may refuse to participate. Participants who respond when volunteers are sought cannot be presumed representative of the population from which they were solicited, even when the tasks asked of them are easy, short, and benign. The way research procedures must be scheduled may limit available participants to people who are free during certain hours or days of the week.

Rossi and Freeman (1989) noted that bias results when subgroups of a target population participate in a project in different proportions or in different ways. To illustrate this principle, we offer an example much more extreme than is usually encountered in practice. Suppose we select at random from all students at our university a list of names for a sample; the upper-division students we approach all readily consent to participate, but half of the freshmen refuse. Our sample is no longer representative of the university's general student body. We might increase the number of freshmen in the project by approaching additional ones; however, such a step would only partially solve the external validity problem because the freshmen who agree to participate are less representative of their class as a whole than are the upper-division students. Even when much less severe, such bias can seriously threaten external validity.

Blanck et al. (1992) suggested an additional partial solution in clinical studies: Obtain detailed descriptive comparisons of both the participants selected and the nonvolunteers. These descriptions could then be compared to estimate probable effects of bias from "exclusion of refusers." These authors regarded such comparisons as "too rare in clinical literature" (p. 963).

Mortality

This problem was discussed earlier in this chapter as a threat to internal validity. Mortality also affects external validity because participants who leave a project while it is under way usually differ from those who remain. Therefore, their loss changes the sample composition. For example, a longitudinal study might keep the participants who remain at the same addresses and lose those who move out of town. If a project's sample was representative of a population at the beginning, it is made less so by losing such a subset of its members. The effect of mortality on external validity does not depend on differences between experimental samples (for example, between experimental and control groups) in proportion of participants lost, although it does depend on the total proportion of participants lost and the extent to which lost participants differ in important ways from those who remain.

Artificial Research Arrangements

Not only the sample but the circumstances in which participants provide their data should be representative of those to which findings are to be generalized. People may not respond the same in a psychology laboratory or counseling clinic with two-way mirrors and videotape recorders as they would in a counseling office, classroom, workplace, or other settings of interest to the project's mission. To the extent that such differences of setting are present and influence the phenomena being studied, external validity is weakened. Gelso (1979) regarded laboratory procedures in counseling research as "analogues" to the counseling situation. (This idea was discussed in Chapter 2.) Sometimes such laboratory analogues are to be preferred as the best approach to a project's mission because of the rigorous controls they allow despite the risks they pose to external validity. The tradeoff relationship between rigor and relevance was discussed earlier in this chapter, as was the use of theory as a bridge to generalization when external validity is weak.

A special case of this problem occurs not only in laboratories but often in field settings: A project's circumstances permit studying only short-term results, although long-term recommendations are to be based on these results. For illustration we return to Molly and Ann's project. Suppose these researchers had redesigned their project and conducted it again with satisfactory solutions for all the validity problems discussed so far. Based on their results, they might then be tempted to recommend that their school adopt one social skills training program instead of the other. However, their results consisted of immediate pretest–posttest differences, and their recommendation appears to assume longer-lasting effects. For example, they might have offered the opposite recommendation if the gains from one program were largest immediately afterward but lasted only a month while the other program showed small but longer-lasting gains. Making long-term generalizations from short-term results requires adequate support from outside the project. For example, such support might come from theory (Forsyth & Strong, 1986) or from other researchers' work.

Pretest Influence

Pretesting participants may alter them so that they are no longer representative of the population of interest. If experimental treatments are applied to pretested participants, can the results be generalized to unpretested individuals receiving similar treatments?

In the earlier discussion of practice effect, we noted that a pretesting experience might sensitize participants so that they react differently to a treatment procedure, such as a persuasive communication or film, than they would without the pretest. Such sensitization weakens internal validity if it affects group differences. It also weakens external validity if the project's mission calls for generalization to people who have not been pretested. For example, in an experiment on the impact of different types of career counseling on occupational exploration, participants may be asked to answer questions about recent occupational exploration activities as a pretest. Such questions may by themselves stimulate occupational exploration on the part of all participants, thereby reducing external validity if the different forms of career counseling would not ordinarily begin with such questions.

Drew and Hardman (1985) noted that some researchers use a warm-up task so that learning to respond has taken place before the actual experimental procedures begin. Because such "preresearch activity may . . . increase or decrease . . . subjects' sensitivity to the variable under study . . . , the results may not be representative of performance by subjects who were not pretested" (p. 150). Whether pretesting or warm-up tasks weaken external validity depends on two factors:

- whether the project's mission includes generalization to people who have not experienced the pretest or warm-up tasks, and
- the extent to which these experiences influence the phenomena being studied.

Multiple Treatment Influences

When a project administers more than one treatment condition to the same participants, as in own-control designs, the experience of earlier treatments and testing may affect participants' response to later ones, just as pretests and warm-up tasks sometimes do. Participants are presumably naive when they begin the first treatment condition. But when they begin the second, they have experienced the first; they approach all subsequent treatment conditions after having experienced all previous ones. As noted in Chapter 8, counterbalancing largely removes the influence of this factor on comparisons between treatments, since each treatment condition appears in every sequence position. For illustration, we suggest reexamining the counterbalanced design depicted in Figure 8.7. Each type of reading material is experienced first by 25% of the participants when they are presumably naive, and by 75% of the participants after they have experienced at least one other condition. The dependent variable might be influenced by an interaction among types of reading material (for example, romantic fiction evokes a different response if science fiction versus medical information is read first) or by a change in reading material, and not just the type available on the day of each session. In either event, external validity is weakened if the project's mission calls for generalizing to people who have not experienced a different kind of waiting room reading material on previous appointment days.

With regard to both pretest influence and multiple treatment interference, we refer readers to earlier sections of this chapter that discuss pretest and multiple treatment issues in relation to internal validity. Carefully comparing these influences on external versus internal validity will contribute to an understanding of both.

Remedies for Threats to External Validity

The best remedy for external validity problems is to ensure that the subjects and conditions used in a project are as representative as possible of the populations and conditions of interest to the project's mission with respect to the variables specified in this mission. As noted earlier in this chapter, reality constraints almost always require some compromises with ideal representativeness in studies of counseling. As a partial remedy for population-sample differences, Bracht and Glass (1968) proposed that researchers thoroughly know both their populations of accessible subjects and the total population of interest to their projects' missions. Researchers can then use this knowledge to judge the representativeness of accessible subjects. This thorough knowledge is often not available, however. Other authors have proposed defining the study population to fit the sample, generalizing the results to a population of which the study sample is representative. We suggest that this choice usually represents the point of view that the populations to which conclusions apply is relatively unimportant to the project's mission. The exceptions are a few situations in which the entire population of interest is accessible for sampling.

As discussed earlier in this chapter with regard to internal validity, theory often provides a partial remedy. Theory can provide an inferential bridge between laboratory findings and the counseling process about which the researcher wishes to draw conclusions (Forsyth & Strong, 1986). We emphasize that this remedy does not improve the representativeness of the data, although it may help strengthen the links between the data and the project's mission.

Remedies for mortality as a risk to internal validity were discussed earlier in this chapter. Much of this discussion applies equally to external validity. Steps to prevent loss of participants can often be built into the project during the planning phase. Comparing lost and retained participants on pretest measures provides valuable information, but the absence of significant pretest differences does not ensure that the retained participants are as representative of the parent population as was the entire original sample. Replacing lost participants with new ones randomly chosen from the parent population reduces but does not eliminate whatever unrepresentativeness mortality may have caused.

Chapter Summary

Good design validity generally results in data that strongly support answers to the questions posed in the project's mission. If design validity is weak, these answers are in doubt because rival interpretations are plausible. Internal validity is strong to the extent that the researcher has controlled all factors, other than the ones being studied, that might account for the results. External validity is strong if sampling methods, measurement methods, and the research setting enable the researcher to generalize interpretations to other people, times, places, and circumstances than the ones studied, as required to fulfill the project's mission. A researcher's task is to design projects so that the risks to both internal and external validities are avoided or reduced to the extent possible and, when unavoidable, are chosen so as to be as unimportant as possible in relation to the project's mission. Many factors pose risks to design validity; the relative importance of each will vary from project to project. Each of these risk factors has several possible remedies of varying effectiveness. Effective planning includes deciding which of these risks are most important to the project and which remedies offer the best protection under prevailing circumstances.

Practical Exercises

For exercises 1 through 3, read the following descriptions of studies conducted by counselors in various settings. What problems with internal and external validity do you see in these studies? Decide how each study might be changed to remedy these problems.

1. A counselor in a large urban area in California prone to earthquakes was interested in the effectiveness of systematic desensitization as a treatment program for "earthquake phobia." He had several clients who professed to be debilitated by fear of earthquakes, and several of his colleagues also mentioned that they had clients who complained of fears about earthquakes. He thus decided to design an experiment that would compare systematic desensitization to a "control" treatment, which consisted of encouraging clients to discuss their fears but limited the counselor's responses to active listening strategies such as paraphrasing and reflection of feeling.

   At intake, he randomly assigned 16 clients to receive either systematic desensitization or the control treatment. The systematic desensitization program consisted of teaching progressive relaxation skills and helping clients to use those skills to deliberately relax in response to imagining events associated with earthquakes. These events were arranged on a hierarchy from relatively nonthreatening, such as hearing about a mild earthquake in a foreign country, to very threatening, such as actually experiencing a severe earthquake while at home or work. All clients filled out an "Earthquake Phobia Inventory" both before and after experiencing the treatment programs. Clients were seen individually, with each program consisting of five sessions. All sessions were conducted by the counselor in his private office. An analysis of the results from the "Earthquake Phobia Inventory" showed that the systematic desensitization clients were significantly less fearful about earthquakes at the end of the treatment programs than were clients who experienced the control treatment. The counselor thus concluded systematic desensitization was an effective treatment program for earthquake phobia.

2. A state rehabilitation agency was interested in whether industrially injured clients who had legal representation in the workers' compensation process were more likely to be satisfied with the outcome of their rehabilitation than those who did not. The researchers kept data on the outcomes of 3,000 cases processed during a calendar year; approximately half of the clients were represented by attorneys and half were not.

   The researchers surveyed the clients 180 days after case closure, asking whether they were gainfully employed, their income level, how satisfied they were with their jobs, and how satisfied they were with the workers' compensation rehabilitation process. Researchers compared the two groups of clients and found that those who had obtained legal representation were no more likely to be gainfully employed; however, those who were employed earned significantly higher incomes and were more satisfied with their jobs than their counterparts without attorneys. Whether employed or not, clients represented by attorneys were more satisfied with the workers' compensation rehabilitation process than clients without attorneys. Based on these results, the researchers recommended that printed informational materials given routinely to all workers' compensation rehabilitation clients should encourage them to seek legal representation.

3. An experiment designed to assess the impact of two different forms of counseling on debilitating test anxiety was carried out in an exclusive, private university on the West Coast. The two forms of counseling compared were rational-emotive therapy (RET) and Rogerian client-centered counseling. The experimenter, a female faculty member at the university, hypothesized that RET would be a more effective form of counseling for anxiety-related problems than client-centered counseling. Participants/clients were recruited through advertisements in the university newspaper and by flyers placed around campus. The flyers and advertisements offered free counseling for test anxiety to anyone who would volunteer to participate in the research project.

When potential clients telephoned, they were told that they would be participating in a study in which two forms of counseling for test anxiety would be compared. Once they had committed to participate in the study, they were randomly assigned to either the client-centered group or the RET group. This procedure was continued until 20 clients had been assigned to each group, at which time the ads and flyers were removed.

Prior to entering treatment, all clients were pretested on the three outcome measures used for the study: an anxiety inventory, a questionnaire concerning beliefs about taking tests, and a rating scale that presented anxiety-arousing testing situations in a hierarchical fashion. The receptionist administered these materials. Participants' GPAs for the two quarters prior to the experiment were also ascertained.

The treatment program consisted of seven counseling sessions during which each client was seen individually by a counselor. The counselor for the RET program was the experimenter. The client-centered therapy was conducted by a male doctoral student in counseling who was aware of the experimenter's hypotheses concerning the effectiveness of rational-emotive versus client-centered counseling.

At the end of the seven sessions, the clients were once again tested on the three outcome measures. As the experimenter had hypothesized, the rational-emotive clients showed significantly more improvement on all measures than did the Rogerian clients. Three months later, the measuring instruments were readministered. Four clients from the rational-emotive group and three clients from the client-centered group could not be located, however. For the clients who were retested, the same results were found; RET was more effective than client-centered counseling. Further, the RET group's mean GPA increased approximately one-half grade point more than did the client-centered group's GPA.

4. Find several research articles in the counseling journals. First, select one with a relatively simple design. Read this article carefully and make a list of any design validity problems you identify as you read it. Make note of (a) why the problem exists, (b) what (if anything) the researchers did about it, and (c) how effective these remedies were.

   Next, consider each of the potential risks to internal and external design validity discussed in Chapter 9 and answer the following questions about the ones you did not already list for this project. Start with bias in group composition as a risk to internal validity if it isn't already on your list. Answer the following questions about this risk:

   a. Is this risk relevant to this project? Why or why not?

   b. If the answer to (a) is yes, does this risk threaten this project's design validity? Why or why not?

   c. What remedies (if any) did this project use as safeguards against this risk?

   d. How effective were these remedies? Explain the basis for your judgment of their effectiveness.

   e. What safeguards against this risk (if any) were clearly not feasible in this project? Why were they infeasible? How would they have helped if they had been feasible?

   f. What feasible remedies (if any) might this project have used as safeguards against this risk but did not use? What do you suspect were the researchers' reasons for not using them? How would they have helped if they had been used?

   g. Review questions (a) through (f) and list any that were difficult to answer because of insufficient information in the project report. What information was missing that would have enabled you to answer any such questions?

   h. Proceed to the next internal or external validity risk you haven't already addressed. Answer questions (a) through (g) with regard to this next risk.

   i. When you have addressed all the internal and external validity risks discussed in Chapter 9 with regard to this project, select another project and repeat the process.

CHAPTER TEN

COLLECTING THE DATA: SAMPLING ISSUES

QUESTIONS TO GUIDE YOUR READING

Populations and Samples
1. When must the issue of representativeness be considered in research projects?
2. Distinguish research populations, research samples, and subpopulations.
3. What are the most difficult issues related to sampling?

Sampling Methods
4. What two concepts underlie all sampling methods?
5. What two criteria define random sampling?
6. Why is the use of a random number table preferred to such methods as rolling dice or drawing numbers from a hat?
7. What two purposes may stratified random sampling serve?
8. How is proportional stratified random sampling conducted?
9. How is systematic sampling conducted? When is systematic sampling likely to yield unrepresentative samples?
10. What is cluster sampling? Why can't results from samples chosen by cluster sampling be interpreted as if participants were chosen individually?
11. For what three reasons is two-phase sampling usually conducted?
12. Why may researchers sometimes rely on convenience sampling? What cautions must be kept in mind when interpreting results from convenience samples?
13. What is time sampling?

Recruitment of Participants
14. What kinds of procedures do researchers use to recruit participants? What problems exist with these procedures with respect to both representativeness of samples and ethical concerns?
15. What two competing sets of factors determine decisions about a research project's sample size?
16. What is meant by the term *precision* with regard to sample size? How does precision differ from representativeness?
17. To what does the term *statistical power* refer? What knowledge is necessary to calculate the power of a statistical significance test?
18. What factors should a researcher consider when deciding whether to conduct a formal analysis to determine a project's sample size?
19. What options are available to researchers if a formal analysis indicates a larger sample should be used than available resources permit?
20. How can knowledge of common practice be helpful when a researcher decides sample size?

Assignment of Participants
21. What purpose does assignment of participants to groups serve in a true experiment?

22. Distinguish captive from sequential assignment.
23. What do the criteria of equal probability and independence imply with respect to random assignment?
24. When may random assignment produce nonequivalent groups?
25. How is block randomization conducted?
26. Why should people other than participants be assigned in experiments? How should they be assigned?

This chapter addresses two major families of issues. The first concerns selecting samples to be representative of the intended populations. A marriage and family counselor, for example, might be interested in doing research with a sample of second generation Hispanic immigrant families that is representative of the population of such families.

The representativeness of samples may apply to any of the research approaches discussed in Chapter 2. It is just as important to have a representative sample of different age groups for a developmental study as it is to have a representative sample of case files for a historical study. When a project involves people in any of several roles, such as participants, clients, judges, teachers, counselors, testers, or administrators of treatment conditions, their selection must also take into consideration the issue of representativeness. As noted in Chapter 8, some but not all projects seek to generalize interpretations to other people, times, places, and circumstances than the ones studied. When such generalization is desired, the issue of representativeness needs to be considered; otherwise it is irrelevant.

The second family of issues concerns assigning people to treatment conditions in experiments or to groups in some descriptive projects.

POPULATIONS AND SAMPLES

Clearly formulated research questions specify the populations to which they refer (for example, abused children, mental health counselors, 9th graders at Harrison High School). Sometimes these populations represent researchers' primary interest; sometimes they result from compromises with feasibility issues. For example, a researcher might be interested in generalizing the results of a survey to all 9th graders in Minneapolis but might have sufficient resources to survey only the 9th graders at Harrison High School. We repeat from Chapter 6 that a research population consists of all "members of any well-defined class of people, events or objects" (Kerlinger, 1973, p. 52) the research question addresses. Populations specified in research questions (such as the 9th graders at Harrison High) are often subpopulations of the populations of the researchers' primary interest (in this example, all 9th graders in Minneapolis).

Subpopulations differ importantly from samples. A sample consists of some members of its population chosen as representative of the population as a whole. For example, a representative sample of Minneapolis 9th graders would undoubtedly be chosen from all high schools in Minneapolis rather than just one. Such representativeness is a necessary but not a sufficient condition for strong external validity, as discussed in Chapter 9. "Representative" means that studying the sample yields approximately the same results as a researcher would get by studying the entire population, if studying the entire population were desirable and feasible. Under certain conditions of sampling, the precision of this approximation can be stated as a predictable and usually small margin of error. Subpopulations, on the other hand, are often atypical of the population as a whole. For example, ethnic minorities are generally atypical of the entire population of U.S. citizens.

Election polls are probably the most familiar use of samples. In such polls, the population of interest is usually the entire electorate of a geographic area, such as a city, state, or nation, at the time of the poll. Studying such populations in their entirety is almost always unnecessarily expensive and time-consuming, if not entirely infeasible. Pollsters therefore study carefully selected samples; they usually achieve acceptably small margins of error. Every election day tests the pollsters' predictive accuracy and provides data they can use to improve their methods for the future.

If a good and complete formulation of the research project has been accomplished, the most difficult decisions related to sampling have already been made:

1. The one or more populations of primary interest to the project's mission have been specified. In studies of counseling process and outcome, these populations include clients and counselors.
2. The one or more populations each research question actually addresses have been identified, based on the populations of primary interest and whatever compromises may be necessary due to feasibility-related constraints.

The populations addressed by the research questions provide the major basis for all subsequent sampling decisions.

SAMPLING METHODS

Several methods are available for selecting samples so that they are appropriately representative of their parent populations. This section discusses random, systematic, stratified, cluster, and double sampling. Last, this section discusses convenience samples, though they are not true samples; Deming (1950) called them **chunks**. Two important concepts underlie all true sampling methods:

- A **pool** comprises all the people, events, or objects available for sampling from any specified population. When people are to be sampled as subjects, the term **subject pool** is often used. When several populations are to be sampled, each has a pool.
- A **sampling frame** is a list of all the members of a pool.

As you might expect, most sampling pools are identical with the populations they represent. However, it is sometimes impossible or infeasible to list all the members of a pool. For example, creating a list of all counseling graduate students in the United States would be extremely difficult. Instead, a researcher could select a number of representative universities and create a list of their counseling graduate students for use as a sampling frame. In such cases, researchers often generalize their findings to the original population of interest (in this example, all counseling graduate students). This generalization is only appropriate, however, if the researchers are certain that the universities selected are truly representative of all universities with counseling graduate programs. If they are not, the **population of primary interest** is all counseling graduate students, but the population addressed by the research question is counseling students at the selected universities at the time of the study.

Regardless of sampling method, approximate sample size (discussed in greater detail later in this chapter) must be decided before sample selection begins.

Random Sampling

An assumption of randomness underlies most, if not all, statistical hypothesis testing. This fact and the relative ease of selecting random samples make this sampling method particularly attractive to researchers. By definition, random sampling fulfills two important criteria:

- **equal probability**—every member of the pool has the same likelihood of being chosen, and
- **independence**—choosing any particular member of the pool does not affect the probability that any other member will be chosen. (There is no connection between choosing one member of the pool and choosing any other member, except as may be caused by the limited size of the frame.)

Computer programs such as SYSTAT can select random samples automatically (Wilkinson, 1987). By hand, the most efficient method of random sampling from a large frame is to number the members of the frame and use a **table of random numbers** to identify the ones to be chosen. (Such a table, along with instructions for its use, is included in Appendix F. If you are unfamiliar with random number tables, we suggest that you turn to Appendix F and review the table and its instructions for use.)

A number of other methods (for example, tossing coins, rolling dice, drawing names from a hat) have sometimes been used as means of random sampling, but we do not recommend such devices. They are unnecessarily laborious when used to select large samples. Even with small samples, they violate either one or both of the equal probability and independence requirements except under a very few special circumstances.

Random sampling applied to the entire frame at once is called **simple or unrestricted random sampling.** In contrast, **stratified random sampling** subdivides the frame according to one or more stratification variables, and then applies simple random sampling to each of the strata separately. With respect to variables with known values for every member of a population (for example, age and gender among a state's licensed drivers), stratified random sampling permits making a sample as closely representative of the population as desired. When population values are unknown, only random sampling permits the degree of precision to be estimated quantitatively with statements typically seen in research reports such as, "The probability is .95 that this sample's mean of 13.4 does not differ from the corresponding population value by more than 2.1 raw score points." The calculations for arriving at such estimates are discussed under the **confidence limits** heading in many statistics texts.

Stratified random sampling. Stratification consists of subdividing a pool into two or more groups according to one or more stratification variables. Stratification variables should be chosen so as to be relevant to the phenomena being investigated; otherwise, the added labor required for stratification is futile. Each of the subgroups created is called a stratum, and a new frame is created for each. Sampling is then carried out from each stratum separately. This method may serve either or both of two purposes:

- to ensure greater representativeness than expected by sampling from the entire pool at once, or
- to enable different strata to be compared.

To serve the first of these purposes, stratification must be proportional. In **proportional stratified sampling,** the number chosen from each stratum is proportional to the representation of that stratum in the entire pool. For example, a researcher divided a university's undergraduate student body into four strata: freshmen, sophomores, juniors, and seniors. Respectively, these strata comprised 42%, 30%, 17%, and 11% of the pool. The researcher therefore chose the following number from each stratum to make up a total sample of 200: freshmen (84), sophomores (60), juniors (34), and seniors (22).

When the only purpose of stratification is to enable the strata to be compared, the most economical procedure is to select the same size sample from each. To enable the strata to be compared and to ensure proportional representation, stratified sampling should be proportional, with sample sizes chosen so that the smallest is large enough to permit meaningful comparisons.

When more than one stratification variable is used simultaneously, the number of strata created is increased. For illustration, undergraduate students might be stratified not only by class level but also by political affiliation:

freshman Republican   freshman Democrat
sophomore Republican   sophomore Democrat

junior Republican junior Democrat
senior Republican senior Democrat

The first four-way stratification produced four strata. Adding a second two-level stratification variable yielded eight strata. To subdivide the pool further by four ethnic groups (Asian, African American, Caucasian, other) would produce 32 strata. The effects of multiple stratification variables on the size and complexity of a project are obvious.

Systematic Sampling

Systematic sampling is probably the least laborious method of selecting a sample by hand from a large frame. First, the number of members of the frame is divided by the intended sample size to yield a sample interval. Next, the members of the frame are numbered sequentially. Then a starting point is chosen at random from the set of numbers beginning with 1 and ending with the sample interval. For example, a sample of 50 and a frame of 1,000 yields a sample interval of 20. The starting point would be any number from 1 to 20 chosen at random. If the starting point is 5, the fifth member in the frame and every 20th member thereafter (25th, 45th, 65th, and so on) would be chosen for the sample.

This method may or may not yield satisfactorily representative samples, depending on the frame arrangement. If the frame is arranged in systematic order (for example, ascending or descending age), biased samples are likely to result. Successive samples with different starting points will differ in predictable ways under such conditions. If a frame is arranged by descending age, a systematic sample with a starting point of 1 will be older than a sample with a starting point of 20. More important, the mean age of a systematic sample from such a frame can be expected to overestimate the corresponding population value if the starting point is a low number (such as 1 or 2), and underestimate the population mean if the starting point is a high number (such as 19 or 20). An alphabetically arranged frame may cause problems if it contains minority subpopulations whose surnames begin with characteristic letters. For example, if the last 19 people in an alphabetically arranged frame (Zymanski, Zytowski, and so on) were all Polish, a sample interval of 20 and a starting point of 1 would exclude all of them from the sample.

In short, we suggest systematic sampling is a reasonable procedure only when both of the following conditions are met:

- No relevant factors underlie the arrangement of members in the frame. ("Relevant" in this context means related to the phenomena the project is investigating.)
- A valuable saving of labor can be achieved over random sampling.

Whenever either of these criteria is in doubt, we recommend random sampling as a safer alternative.

Cluster Sampling

Sometimes it is desirable to apply research procedures to intact groups of participants rather than separating groups to study individuals. For example, a researcher in an elementary school might find it more feasible to conduct experimental procedures with students in their classrooms rather than remove them from their classrooms for this purpose. This choice requires sampling classrooms as a whole rather than sampling individual students. This procedure is known as **cluster sampling.** Each classroom in the school is a cluster for sampling purposes. The researcher can compose a frame by listing all the clusters. The required number of clusters can then be chosen for the sample.

An additional use of cluster sampling was discussed earlier in this chapter in relation to the pool concept. Counseling programs at specified universities (clusters) were chosen from all such university programs in the United States to reduce the pool from unmanageable to manageable size. Students from the selected clusters were then listed individually to form the final frame.

We offer two cautions when samples chosen by cluster sampling are interpreted as if chosen individually. First, a random sample of clusters is not the same as a random sample of individuals. In cluster sampling, individual selections within the same cluster are linked rather than independent. If variables related to the phenomena being studied are related to the grouping of individuals in clusters, cluster sampling can lead to the sample being less representative of the pool than a simple random sample would be. Some characteristics will likely be overemphasized and others underemphasized. For example, if the most unruly students have been assigned to one classroom, a cluster sample will include either all of these students or none of them; a simple random sample of individuals would probably include a few. Second, this risk is intensified if clusters in the pool differ markedly in size, with small clusters having the same likelihood of being chosen as large ones.

Two-Phase Sampling

Two-phase sampling, also sometimes called **double sampling,** involves selecting a subsample from an original sample. After some procedures have been administered to the original sample, additional procedures are applied to the subsample. Here are some examples of two-phase sampling:

- A survey began with a brief questionnaire to a large sample. A small subsample was chosen from the questionnaire respondents; an interviewer explored some of their answers more intensively.
- A culturally diverse school district conducted an experiment involving three methods of teaching cultural awareness. A few students from

each treatment group were interviewed regarding their reactions to the experience.

- Clients in a smoking cessation program kept a diary of their smoking behavior and experiences. From those who reported social pressures to smoke, a sample was selected for special intervention.
- A random sample of closed files in a state rehabilitation agency were examined regarding the length of time spent in the placement phase. Two small subsamples were chosen for follow-up interviews: one from cases closed "rehabilitated" after a very short placement phase, and the other from cases closed "not rehabilitated" after the placement phase had begun.
- Nonrespondents to a mailed questionnaire were contacted by telephone. They were asked why they had not responded and encouraged to do so.

As is evident from these examples, a subsample is sometimes chosen to be representative of the entire original sample, sometimes to represent a specialized subgroup, and sometimes to collect missing data. When a subsample is to represent the entire original sample, the usual reason for double sampling is to reduce the resources (for example, time, effort, money) required to administer the second procedure to the entire original sample. Double sampling for special subgroups addresses research questions related to special subpopulations. In both these situations, principles and procedures regarding selection of the subsample are the same as those discussed earlier in this chapter regarding sample selection generally. Decisions to collect missing data by double sampling need to be made with several cautions in mind. First, nonrespondents often differ from respondents in important respects, such as motivation. Second, the steps to elicit the missing data (encouragement by telephone, for example) may not only induce some people to respond but also change some of their answers. These considerations need to be balanced against alternative possible decisions, such as drawing additional participants from the original pool or not attempting to replace the missing data.

Convenience Sampling

Beginning researchers are often inclined to administer research procedures to the participants conveniently at hand, either overlooking sampling issues entirely or generalizing findings to a population defined to fit these participants and treating this population as the one of primary interest. As noted earlier in this chapter, such groups of participants are often called chunks (Deming, 1950) or convenience samples, although they are not samples in any true sense.

Underlying much of the discussion throughout this chapter is the principle that generalizing sample data to a meaningful population requires that the sample be representative of the population. Without representativeness, external validity is doubtful at best, and convenience samples offer no basis to infer representativeness.

Researchers often face situations in which true sampling procedures are not feasible. Sometimes the participants conveniently at hand are the only ones available. Sometimes it is possible to sample counseling clients but not their counselors. Abandoning the project is rarely if ever a satisfying solution. Data from the participants at hand usually fulfill a project's mission better than no data at all. Redefining the core of a mission to fit the available participants is not a satisfying solution either as this practice puts "the cart before the horse."

For an answer to this dilemma, we turn to a distinction discussed in Chapter 6 and again earlier in this chapter: populations specified in research questions versus populations of primary interest. Feasibility issues often force researchers to specify a different population in research questions than that which was originally the population of primary interest. It is crucial to keep that distinction in mind and not assume that results pertain to the population of primary interest when, in fact, they are only generalizable to the population specified in the research question. Any conclusion regarding the population of primary interest requires an additional logical step based on a premise that the two populations are similar.

Time Sampling

Time sampling is a procedure used in observational studies, especially those employing time series designs. It was noted in the beginning of this chapter that some projects seek to generalize interpretations to other people, times, places, and circumstances than the ones studied; studying the entire population is often not possible. Time sampling, as its name implies, is used to generalize interpretations to times other than the ones studied when continuous observation is impractical.

Most time series designs study only one or a very few participants over a considerable period of time. The dependent variable of interest is often an increase or decrease in specific behaviors in response to the independent variable (usually a treatment program of some sort). Most such studies do not take observations on a participant continually but instead sample from the available times that such observations could be made. Sulzer-Azaroff and Mayer (1991) provide examples in which specific periods each day are chosen for observation. These periods are divided into 15-second intervals, during which the behavior of interest is recorded if it occurs. Time intervals are generally kept quite short to increase the accuracy of recording.

> *Whole-interval time sampling* is used when researchers wish to know whether the behavior of interest persists for the entire time interval. It is generally used for behaviors the researcher hopes to increase (for example, paying attention) through an intervention.

Partial-interval time sampling is used when the researcher wishes to be sure to catch a fleeting instance of a behavior, usually one the researcher wishes to decrease (for example, an obscene gesture). The behavior is recorded if it occurs at any point during the interval.

Momentary time sampling is used for behaviors the researcher wishes to either increase or decrease. It is used primarily when neither whole- nor partial-interval time sampling is practicable, such as when teachers record students' behaviors in a busy classroom or when supervisors record workers' behaviors on a job site. Observers note only whether a behavior is occurring at the end of the specified time interval; their attention is not required for the entire time interval.

RECRUITMENT OF PARTICIPANTS

In many projects, participants must not only be selected but their cooperation must somehow be elicited. People must have a reason for putting some of their efforts into the project's tasks. If we get a questionnaire in the mail, for example, we might answer it immediately, set it aside for later, or send it forthwith to the trash. If we set it aside, the chances that we will get to it before the researcher's deadline are greatly reduced. Our decision will be based on several factors, among them (a) how busy we are at the moment, (b) how much the project arouses our interest, and (c) how much time we estimate it will take us to respond. A transmittal letter accompanying the questionnaire should address points (b) and (c). This letter has the task of arousing our interest and assuring us that the time involved will be worth our efforts.

Similarly, if a researcher wants us to participate as a subject in an experiment, we need to have a reason for doing so. Some projects offer money to their participants; others offer free services of various sorts (for example, free career counseling); others present participation as an interesting experience for participants. Employers who want their employees to serve voluntarily as participants might offer such incentives as preferential parking or longer breaks than for nonparticipants.

Recruitment of participants is usually carried out along with the task of informing them about the project and securing their consent. Telephone, mail, face-to-face contact, posted notices, and help-wanted advertisements have all been used to recruit participants for research projects. Whatever their method and incentives, researchers need to consider the extent to which participants' self-selection might reduce the match between the samples finally used and the populations they presumably represent. People who respond to any recruitment effort are not necessarily representative of the ones to whom the research project is designed to generalize. For example, Taylor, Obitz, and Reich (1982) found significant differences among three groups of participants in an alcoholism treatment program who were solicited to volunteer as research participants: (a) those who signed up as volunteers when asked and kept their appointment, (b) those who signed up but failed to keep their appointment, and (c) those who did not sign up. When recruiting participants, researchers must balance the conflicting demands of ethics and design validity. As discussed in Chapter 5, some issues await further clarification regarding what recruitment activities are ethically acceptable and what constitutes "undue pressure" (Blanck et al., 1992, p. 963).

Determining Sample Size

Typically, decisions about how large a sample to use represent a tradeoff between competing sets of factors: the statistical power and precision desired and practical considerations such as available measurement methods, time, effort, and dollar costs. A project's mission is the best basis for reaching a sound decision about sample size. We know of no set standard.

Sample size can be decided formally or informally. To do so formally, a researcher must first decide whether the project includes one or more statistical tests of significance. If it does, the researcher must:

- decide on the minimum size of difference or relationship he or she wishes to detect,
- decide what is an acceptable risk of failure to achieve statistical significance if the minimum size difference or relationship exists in the populations sampled,
- decide what kind of test to use (for example, *t* test, correlation, analysis of variance) and choose a significance level, and
- know or estimate the population variability (not required for correlations; usually estimated for other kinds of tests).

If the project seeks to draw quantitative estimates of population characteristics (parameters) from one or more samples (that is, determine confidence intervals), a formal decision about sample size requires the researcher to:

- decide what margin of error is acceptable,
- decide what is an acceptable risk of failure to achieve the desired level of precision (that is, risk that the margin of error will be larger than that designated as acceptable), and
- know or estimate the population variability (not required for correlations; usually estimated for other kinds of parameters).

In a formal procedure for deciding minimum sample size, the researcher enters these elements into formulas, either manually or through a computer program such as EX-SAMPLE (Brent, Spencer, & Scott, 1989). To reach a final decision, such calculated minimums are then balanced against available time and resources. Informal decisions apply the same ideas, usually based on the researcher's experience but without precise quantification and with each principle contributing an unknown and uncontrolled weight to the final result. In addition, informal decisions usually consider common practice, that is, sample sizes reported for similar projects in the literature. The next six subsections discuss these principles. Kraemer and Thiemann (1987) provide formulas and tables.

Precision

When a statistical significance test is not involved, **precision** refers to the extent to which sample data agree with corresponding population values (that is, the extent to which the sample's descriptive **statistics** agree with the corresponding population **parameters**). For example, if a researcher is conducting a study with clients of "normal" intelligence, he or she would want the mean IQ of the participants in the sample to be close to 100 because that is the mean IQ of the population in general.

Precision differs from representativeness in that a sample is unrepresentative if systematic factors cause it to be different from the population (for example, a larger proportion of the clients are dyslexic than is found in the general population even though the mean IQ is 100). As noted earlier in this chapter, a random sample is representative within a predictable margin of error (for example, five IQ points on a specified test). This margin of error is predictable because it is known how much repeated samples of the same size from a known population will vary from one another. This knowledge comes from statistical theory and numerous supporting experiments. A representative sample has a high level of precision if this margin of error, due to sampling variation, is small. Large representative samples yield more precise results than do smaller ones; successive small samples differ from one another more widely than large ones do. Unless the degree of bias is known, it is generally useless to estimate precision with biased samples.

This concept is analogous to tolerances in the woodworking and metalworking trades. A cutting error of 1/4 inch, for example, would be unacceptable in fine cabinetry but probably unnoticed in a split-rail fence. Similarly, some projects require more sampling precision than others.

Statistical Power

Statistical power refers to the probability that a significant result will be obtained if a difference or relationship of a given size exists in the populations sampled. For example, a researcher thinks there should be a correlation of at least .20 between first year GPA and the score on a new test in a population of entering freshmen; power is expressed as the probability of a statistically significant correlation in a sample if the population correlation is indeed .20. This usage of power refers only to statistical significance tests. Other things being equal, **significance tests** with large samples are more powerful than the same tests with smaller samples.

The power of a statistical significance test can be calculated from the following:

- the size of difference or relationship the researcher wishes to detect,
- the sample size,
- the kind of test to be used (including significance level),
- the population variability (not required for correlations; usually estimated for other kinds of tests).

As noted earlier in this chapter, a researcher can decide on an acceptable risk of failure (for example, .10); subtracting this probability from 1.00 produces a desired statistical power (.90 in this example). The same formulas are used to calculate power with a sample of known size and to calculate minimum sample size from a desired level of power. Estimates of population variability can be revised as data collection proceeds; in such instances, sample size calculations and sampling plans can be revised accordingly, provided adequate steps are taken to ensure representativeness.

Size of Phenomena to be Detected

Colloquially, this issue is often expressed as, "Is it enough of a difference to make a difference?" As an illustration, Kraemer and Thiemann (1987) suggested a study of Cornell Medical Index (CMI) scores of drinkers and nondrinkers of coffee. The average CMI scores of these groups might need to differ by "perhaps as much as 10 points" to "motivate social and economic strictures on coffee-drinking." Sound research decisions need to be based on both "the researchers' understanding and knowledge of their field, supplemented by the preliminary evidence available," and elements of the project's mission other than the research questions per se. If the researchers who undertook this study of coffee drinkers' CMI scores had other reasons for asking the research question than to "motivate social and economic strictures on coffee-drinking," a difference of less than 10 points might be considered important (p. 24).

Subtle phenomena require larger samples to detect than conspicuous ones. By deciding in the planning phase how large a difference or relationship in the population must be to make a difference, researchers can avoid wasting resources to discover phenomena that turn out to be so small as to be deemed trivial. These observations underscore the importance of good formulation and literature review.

Acceptable Risk of Failure to Detect Phenomena

If the difference or relationship in the populations is large enough to be worth discovering, how important is it that this project achieve a statistically significant result? Colloquially, "How high are the stakes?" If a far-reaching administrative decision rests on a project's results (for example, deciding the qualifications a state's counselors must meet for licensure), researchers will likely choose a higher level of power (lower acceptable risk of failure) than in a study following up a point of idle curiosity.

Similar considerations hold for studies estimating population parameters from samples. For example, a project's mission might be satisfactorily served by estimating the proportion of an electorate who support a school bond issue, with a 10% risk that the margin of error will exceed one percentage point. In such an instance, a larger sample than necessary to achieve this level of precision would represent wasted resources.

These decisions, like so many others that are part of planning, are best based on the project's mission.

Practicalities

The costs of collecting data, in time, effort, and money, often limit the size of researchers' samples. It is, therefore, important to consider any formally computed minimum sample sizes along with the resources available to the project. Three outcomes are possible; two of them call for further formulation work. In some instances, available resources would permit using more participants than needed to achieve the desired level of power and precision. In such instances, we recommend revisiting the triangulation principle discussed in Chapter 6 and considering whether the project might be strengthened or enriched by additional research questions. In other projects, available resources permit using enough participants to achieve the desired level of power and precision but little or no more. Such instances do not necessarily require reconsidering the project's mission.

In the third outcome, limited resources restrict the project to using too few participants to achieve the desired level of power and precision. Compromises must be made. Such situations are probably among the most difficult ones researchers face. When confronted with the need to make such compromises, we recommend asking such questions as these: How many participants would available resources permit using? What level of power and precision would this sample yield? Is this level of power and precision acceptable in view of the mission?

If available resources do not permit a large enough sample to achieve acceptable power and precision, would different design and measurement options solve the problem? For example, choosing a more reliable standardized test than the one planned might sufficiently reduce the number of participants required. Time series experiments usually require fewer participants than traditional group experiments do. A repeated measures design might require a smaller sample than one using independent groups.

If this line of thought is not fruitful, how might the scope of the project's mission be reduced so that acceptable power and precision are feasible with available resources? Alternatively, might the project be deferred until a future time when sufficient resources are expected to be available? Before deciding to make such changes in project plans, researchers need to consider carefully the original mission, particularly the reasons answers to the research questions are being sought.

Formal Analysis or an Informal Decision

Should decisions about a particular project's sample size be based on a formal analysis? The answer is "yes" when both of the following conditions prevail:

- The researcher has reached a considered judgment that a valuable cost saving can be achieved by avoiding either an unnecessarily large sample or a nonsignificant result because the sample is too small. ("Cost" in this context refers to resources in general, including dollars, time, and effort; "saving" refers both to the immediate project and to the uses planned for its results.)
- The researcher has sound bases for the quantities required by the formulas for estimating sample size.

If either of these conditions is absent, a formal analysis is wasteful at best, misleading at worst.

In some projects, circumstances permit little or no cost saving through reduced sample size. For illustration, we offer a fictitious example. A researcher in a public school arranged to have a classroom available on a designated schedule for his project. This room had seating for 40 people. The project's counterbalanced design required all of the periods the room was available. Materials used by each participant consisted of a two-page questionnaire photocopied by the researcher. Entering each participant's answers into a computer required two minutes of clerical time. The principal had asked that enough participants be used so that most of the room's seats were occupied during every scheduled period lest "activist" parents see empty seats and "use them as an excuse to complain" about their children's large classes. In this instance, reducing the sample size would yield a trivial saving (for example, 20 photocopied pages and 20 minutes of clerical time for each 10 participants) and entail a political cost. A larger sample, even if desirable, was administratively infeasible. Under such circumstances, we see no reason to do added work to calculate minimum sample size.

From the discussion on the preceding pages, it is evident that formal decisions about sample size use formulas that require advance decisions. The researcher must be clear about the acceptable level of risk for the project. For example,

- If the populations yielding my samples have means differing by as much as two points, I will accept a 10% risk of getting a nonsignificant result in this project.

- I want my sample to estimate the population mean with 99% likelihood that the margin of error will not exceed one point.
- If the population yielding my sample has a correlation of .30, I will accept a 15% risk of getting a nonsignificant result in this project.
- I want my sample to estimate the proportion of favorable votes in the population with 95% likelihood that the margin of error will not exceed one-half a percentage point.

To the first two of these decisions, the researcher must add estimates of population variability; the last decision in this list requires a rough estimate of the population proportion.

Unless a researcher has data from a preliminary study concerning quantities such as those used as examples here or has some other sound basis for estimating them, a formal calculation of sample size is worthless. The "GIGO" principle is often quoted: garbage in, garbage out. We know of doctoral students who were required to calculate minimum sample sizes, allegedly to strengthen the scientific rigor of their projects, but who arbitrarily decided the quantities to be entered into the formulas. This practice not only wasted the efforts of these researchers but diminished the rigor of these projects because they risked creating a misleading impression that meaningless sample size calculations were sound.

Common Practice

Many published research reports do not state whether sample sizes were decided formally or informally. In our experience, researchers often base their decisions about sample size mainly on practical considerations such as participant availability and time required to collect data.

There is no standard minimum sample size necessary for research to be regarded as sound. Rather, different kinds of studies commonly use different sample sizes. For example, experiments usually use smaller samples than surveys, and national surveys use larger samples than regional or local surveys. Complex experiments with many subgroups usually use more participants than simpler ones. As a rule of thumb, many researchers recommend using at least 12 to 14 participants in each subgroup unless conditions require smaller sizes. A good literature review often reveals sample sizes used in similar projects.

Researchers do not always agree about what size samples to call "large" or "small." Most will agree that 10 participants is a small sample and that 100 participants is a large one for most kinds of studies; the likelihood of disagreement increases as sizes approach the 30 to 50 participant range. A useful standard may be found in sample sizes commonly used in similar projects. A sample of 50, for example, would be very small for a national survey. A sample of 10, however, would be relatively large for a multiple baseline time series experiment.

ASSIGNMENT OF PARTICIPANTS

As noted in Chapter 2, true experiments involving groups of participants require that participants be assigned to groups according to the research plan. Assignment has the purpose of creating comparable groups so as to eliminate **group composition bias** as a threat to design validity.

Random assignment and systematic assignment (similar to random and systematic sampling) are the most common techniques. Some projects assign participants in clusters rather than individually, analogous to cluster sampling. We suggest that readers review these sampling methods before proceeding further with this section. Each method may be used for **captive** or **sequential assignment.**

Captive and Sequential Assignment

Assignment is called captive when all the participants who make up the sample have been identified at the outset. Typically, the researcher has a list of names for the entire sample and makes assignments from this list. Assignment is called sequential when the participants in the sample have not been identified at the beginning; experimental procedures are begun before the researchers know who will be in the sample. For example, a mental health clinic might assign all new nonemergency cases at intake to four experimental conditions until each condition has 25 participants. Both captive and sequential assignment can be carried out with any of the following procedures: random assignment, systematic assignment, or block randomization.

Random Assignment

Like random sampling, random assignment fulfills equal probability and independence criteria. At the outset, each participant must have the same probabilities of being assigned to the various groups. The groups may but need not be the same size. For example, 200 participants might be assigned so that groups A and B have 50 each and group C has 100. In this circumstance, the equal probability criterion requires that every participant must have a 25% chance of assignment to group A, 25% to group B, and 50% to group C.

The independence criterion requires that no participant's assignment probabilities be changed by anyone else's assignment, except as is necessarily so because of the sample size and group sizes. For example, if four participants are assigned by using a random numbers table to equal-size groups X and Y, and the first two go to group X, the last two necessarily go to group Y. In contrast, an alternating assignment procedure might use a random numbers table to choose only the first participant, assigning each successive one to the other group. In this procedure, everyone's assignment is determined when the first participant is assigned to group Y. The independence criterion is fulfilled in the first of these examples, in which every participant is selected via the random number table until one of the groups is full. The alternating assignment procedure is not random because it fails the independence criterion; this procedure represents systematic assignment.

As with random sampling, we recommend referring to a table of random numbers to conduct random assignment. Appendix F includes a random numbers table and instructions for its use. True randomness is often difficult to achieve with other procedures such as tossing coins, rolling dice, or drawing slips of paper from a hat.

Systematic Assignment

Random assignment occasionally produces nonequivalent groups; for example, selection of a certain row or column when using the random number table might produce a situation in which no one is assigned to a given condition (for example, Condition 3) until very late in the assignment process because the number 3 does not happen to appear in the table for a long time. For illustration, suppose that sequential random assignment was being used in a study in which disaster survivors presented themselves for treatment to a mental health clinic in response to an advertisement requesting people with posttraumatic stress disorder. This situation would result in most of the participants in Condition 3 being among those who were the last to present themselves for treatment. Those who are last to present themselves for treatment might differ in systematic ways from those who seek treatment early.

With predictably low (not zero) probabilities, random procedures produce unusual results. Systematic assignment offers an answer to this problem provided no relevant factors underlie the arrangement of participants in the sample. An alternating assignment pattern is a common one. For example, the disaster survivors could be assigned to Conditions 1, 2, 3, 4; 2, 3, 4, 1; 3, 4, 1, 2; and so on to ensure that each group of four people is assigned to one of the four treatment conditions. Note that we do not suggest simply using a 1, 2, 3, 4 pattern. As an example of why such a pattern is unwise, imagine a mental health clinic in which four new clients are scheduled each day at 9 A.M., 11 A.M., 2 P.M., and 4 P.M. Assigning these clients to four groups in a pattern that alternates in only one manner (1, 2, 3, 4) would clearly create groups that differ in the time of day each client is seen. Such biasing factors are not always this blatant; even when the patterns are alternated carefully, subtle biasing factors can exist but go unnoticed until it is too late to avoid them. No matter how carefully alternating patterns are chosen, we recommend that researchers scrutinize their specific situation very carefully from this standpoint before deciding to use systematic assignment.

Block Randomization

Block randomization combines random and systematic features. The list of participants is first divided into blocks, with each block containing one participant for each group. For example, if the entire sample is to be divided into six groups, each block will contain six participants. Within each block, individuals are assigned to groups at random. This procedure reduces the already low risk of atypical groups present in simple random assignment; it also largely avoids biases that systematic procedures such as alternation often introduce. Block randomization can be used for both captive and sequential assignment.

SAMPLING AND ASSIGNING PEOPLE OTHER THAN PARTICIPANTS

In some counseling studies, the people participating as subjects are not the only people sampled or assigned. For example, one might also sample counselors or assign them to treatment conditions according to the research plan, even though their clients are the participants. A well-formulated mission for a counseling process or outcome study includes counselors among its specified populations of primary interest, even when clients are to be the only participants. Under ideal conditions, a sample of counselors can be selected from a pool representative of such a population. Often, however, researchers are limited to convenience samples of counselors, even when clients are selected so as to represent clearly defined populations.

Judges or observers might also be sampled from a pool of available candidates, or assigned to treatment conditions, or both. In some correlational studies, observers or judges must be assigned to groups of participants such as classrooms or teams of employees.

The relationship of such support people to treatment conditions and other variables deserves careful scrutiny so that risks to design validity may be minimized or avoided. Important considerations are discussed in Chapter 9 under several headings, including experimenter bias, demand characteristics, and rater issues. If a pool of good candidates exists from which such support people might be drawn, we recommend making these choices according to a plan (such as random selection) rather than arbitrarily.

In experiments, support people should be assigned so as not to confound their individual characteristics with treatment conditions or classification variables. If several people are available to administer each treatment condition, the researcher might assign them at random. If there are too few for this kind of plan, each support person might administer all treatment conditions, provided experimenter bias can be satisfactorily controlled. Similar considerations hold for observers and judges.

Many descriptive studies investigate differences between groups such as classrooms, work teams, agencies, or companies. Assigning a different judge or observer to each group confounds their individual characteristics with the groups. The data might show one group as different from the others not because the phenomena observed were different but because the judges used different rating standards. In an ideal world, a researcher would be able to randomly sample from a population of judges and randomly assign those judges to the groups to be investigated. The ability to carry out such sampling and assignment is rare however; therefore, researchers usually rely on a convenience sample of judges who have been thoroughly trained in their observational procedures so they are as alike as possible. Those judges are then randomly assigned to the different groups to be studied.

CHAPTER SUMMARY

This chapter addresses two major sets of issues: selecting samples to be representative of a population, and assigning people to treatment conditions in experiments or groups in some descriptive projects. Methods of selection include random, systematic, stratified, cluster, and double sampling. Convenience samples are not true samples. Random sampling fulfills two criteria: equal probability and independence. Except under a limited range of conditions, both are necessary to ensure that the sample is representative of the population of interest. Decisions about how large a sample to use represent a tradeoff between competing sets of factors: the statistical power and precision desired, and practical considerations such as available measurement methods, time, effort, and dollar costs.

Participants are assigned to groups to eliminate bias in group composition. Random assignment fulfills the criteria of equal probability and independence. Systematic assignment is sometimes used to avoid the risk that random assignment might produce nonequivalent groups or because circumstances do not allow random assignment. To maximize design validity, sampling and assignment issues must also be considered for people other than those participating as subjects.

PRACTICAL EXERCISES

1. Imagine that you are a counseling psychologist affiliated with a large, urban medical center. You have decided to conduct an experiment to assess the effects of a communication skills program on the number of times physicians interrupt patients as they describe their symptoms during office visits. Sixty physicians also affiliated with the medical center have volunteered to participate in the experiment. You have decided that you want to select a sample of 40 of these physicians for the research project. Using the random numbers table reproduced in Appendix F, select your sample of 40 physicians. Begin by assuming that physicians are numbered from 1 to 60. Then select your sample by starting with

Row 3/Column 2 of the table. Proceed vertically down each column to the end, then continue at the top of the next column. What are the numbers of the physicians who will be selected for your sample?

2. In practical exercise (1) you were asked to select a sample of 40 physicians from a pool of 60. For this exercise, imagine that you are ready to carry out the next step of the experiment, assigning participants to groups. There will be three groups involved in the experiment. In Group 1, physicians will be told about the proper communication skills and given a handout summarizing the information. In Group 2, physicians will be told about the communication skills and asked to role-play specific patient–doctor interactions. In Group 3, physicians will be asked to communicate as they always have. The 40 physicians must now be assigned to the three experimental groups. Using the random numbers table in Appendix F, assign the physicians to the three groups. Assume the physicians selected for the sample have been renumbered 1 to 40. Because 40 does not divide evenly by 3, assume also that Group 1 will have 14 participants and Groups 2 and 3 will have 13 participants. Begin with Row 4/Column 4 of the table. Proceed horizontally to the end of each row using single digits. At the end of each row, proceed to the beginning of the next. What are the numbers of the physicians in each group?

3. For each of the following examples, decide whether the strategy used is simple random sampling, proportional stratified sampling, systematic sampling, cluster sampling, two-phase sampling, convenience sampling, or time sampling.

   a. College students were surveyed regarding how often they experienced jealous feelings about their "significant other's" interactions with fellow students. When the survey was completed, those students who indicated the most jealous feelings were reinterviewed in depth about their perceived causes of those feelings.

   b. A random numbers table was used to select a sample of 200 juvenile offenders from a pool of approximately 1,000 such offenders who were currently held by the County Juvenile Authority.

   c. A state rehabilitation agency contained files on approximately 8,000 closed cases. Researchers were interested in determining the average time elapsing from case opening to case closure. The case files were arranged alphabetically. The researchers sampled 2,000 of these cases for examination by randomly choosing Case 2 as a starting point and selecting every 4th case thereafter.

   d. A school district was interested in interviewing parents regarding their perception of the extent to which the district's counseling services met their children's needs. The district's ethnic distribution was 57% Hispanic, 16% African American, 12% Anglo, 7% Asian, and 8% "Other." Accordingly, from a sample of 600 parents, district officials chose 342 Hispanic parents, 96 African American parents, 72 Anglo parents, 42 Asian parents, and 48 "Other" parents to interview.

   e. A graduate student in counseling was interested in determining the extent to which entering college students chose majors in the same occupational fields in which one or both parents were employed. During orientation day at the university where she was enrolled as a graduate student, she administered to all incoming freshmen a questionnaire asking parents' occupations and students' planned majors.

f. A couple sought help from a marriage and family counselor because of concern over the behavior of their 3-year-old son. He seemed to have a very difficult time playing cooperatively with other children, and the parents were worried that he would not be allowed to join the neighborhood preschool program. The parents had noticed that their son tended to yell at and hit other children and grab their toys. The counselor recommended accurately assessing these behaviors prior to instituting any form of treatment. He suggested that the parents observe their son carefully during playtime at the park, which was when he usually interacted with other children. The counselor helped the parents develop a form divided into 30-second intervals. He suggested that they observe their son for the first 20 seconds of each interval and record their observations during the last 10 seconds. If the child engaged in hitting, grabbing, or yelling during the 20 seconds, the parents should record an H, G, or Y on the sheet for that interval.

g. A large epidemiological study was conducted to determine whether procedures to reduce the rate of Type A behavior would decrease the number of heart attacks suffered by persons with occluded coronary arteries. The study took place in four cities: New York, Chicago, Los Angeles, and Atlanta. Three representative hospitals were chosen from each city. In each hospital, all patients meeting the project's medical criteria were divided into two groups. One of these groups received instruction on Type A behavior and its reduction in addition to the standard medical information offered to patients with occluded arteries; the other group received only the standard medical information.

4. Examine recent issues of counseling journals to find projects that used sampling and assignment procedures discussed in this chapter. Be prepared to discuss the sampling and assignment procedures in class. Be prepared to answer the following questions:

a. In what ways do sampling and assignment procedures fit the project's mission well or poorly? Do you have any recommendations for improvement? If so, what are they, and how would they help?

b. What, if anything, do you not know about the project's sampling and assignment procedures because the report describes them unclearly or incompletely? If any information was omitted from the report, how much does the omission impair your understanding of the project? (Most project reports omit some procedural details because journal space is limited.)

CHAPTER ELEVEN

COLLECTING THE DATA: MEASUREMENT PRINCIPLES AND SOURCES

Questions to Guide Your Reading

Selection of Measures
1. What are reactive and nonreactive measures? Give examples of each.
2. What two types of reactive effects may occur?
3. How can researchers minimize reactive effects?
4. What is meant by reliability of measuring instruments?
5. What is measurement validity?
6. Briefly define criterion-related, content, construct, factual, and face validity.
7. Why is it inappropriate to say simply that any test or inventory is valid?
8. What can researchers do when relevant validity information is absent or scant?
9. What arguments exist for and against developing a standard battery of instruments for use in a variety of counseling outcome studies?

Instruments
10. What is the difference between tests and inventories?
11. When are tests and inventories considered standardized?
12. Distinguish between questionnaires, interviews, and observation schedules.
13. Distinguish between rating scales, attitude scales, and the semantic differential.
14. What can researchers do to avoid succumbing to the "law of the instrument"?

Physical and Biochemical Measures
15. What physical and biochemical measures are in common use?
16. Why are reports of routine drug screenings often misleading with regard to employees' drug use?

Other Data Sources
17. Why are official records subject to reliability and validity problems?
18. What reactive effects might exist in official records?
19. What is meta-analysis? How does it differ from a literature review?
20. What are physical traces? Is it possible for physical traces to yield reactive measures? Why?

Content Analysis
21. What is content analysis?
22. What kinds of data are amenable to content analysis?

This chapter and the next concern the data collection phase of a research project. This chapter discusses general principles underlying measurement methods and the various sources that can yield research data. Chapter 12 discusses in detail different kinds of instruments (for example, tests, questionnaires, rating scales, interviews) researchers in counseling use to collect data.

Imagine for a moment that you are a counselor for an agency offering services to disaster survivors with posttraumatic stress disorder. Your supervisor has asked you to compare the effectiveness of group versus individual counseling with the agency's clients. Immediately you ask yourself an essential formulation question: What do we mean by effectiveness? Preliminary answers to this question lead to another: How can we measure the effectiveness of these two types of counseling? This second question is part of planning and illustrates the major focus of this chapter and the next.

The measurement issues discussed in these chapters apply not only to dependent variables in experimental studies but also to variables with other roles in the project, including:

- classification variables in studies using any research approach,
- variables in correlational studies, and
- variables used to select subjects.

The first section of this chapter discusses concepts related to the selection of measures; later sections address specific kinds of instruments and other data sources.

SELECTION OF MEASURES

Deciding on the measures to be used is one of the major steps in planning any research project. Usually, this process proceeds from the general to the specific. Early decisions answer these kinds of questions:

- Will participants be administered one or more tests of intelligence, scholastic aptitude, knowledge, physical strength, or some other ability?
- Will participants be administered one or more inventories of interests, personality characteristics, attitudes, or similar variables?
- Will participants be interviewed?
- Will participants be asked to answer one or more questionnaires?
- Will the behavior of participants be recorded by observers?
- Will participants be asked to keep records of their own behavior or experiences?
- Will measures be taken directly from the body or its products, such as body weight or chemical tests of breath, blood, or urine?
- Will measures be based on physical traces of participants' activities, such as dirt and wear on library materials?
- Will measures be based on records of data collected for other purposes than this project, such as school grades or driving records?

Answers to these questions lead to specific choices. For example, if an intelligence test or personality inventory is to be used, which among the many possible tests or inventories will it be? If participants are to be interviewed or are to answer a questionnaire, exactly what will the interview or questionnaire contain?

The term *instrument* is often used to refer generally to any device for collecting data, including tests, inventories, questionnaires, written guides for observing or interviewing, machines that measure (such as polygraphs), and systems for conducting chemical analyses. Sometimes a specific instrument of the chosen type (such as a standardized test or another author's questionnaire) exists that fits the project; sometimes an existing instrument can be modified to fit; sometimes a new instrument must be created for the project. Characteristics to be considered when these decisions are made include reactivity, reliability, **psychometric** validity, and sensitivity. Also included is the idea of establishing a standard battery to recommend for all counseling research. Later sections of this chapter discuss data sources that are not instruments, such as official records, biochemical measures, and physical traces. The last section discusses content analysis as a way of deriving measures from verbal material.

Reactive and Nonreactive Measures

Reactive measures (for example, interviewing, administering tests or questionnaires) give participants something to react to; **nonreactive measures,** such as covert observation and examination of physical traces (for example, number of cigarettes extinguished in an ashtray), do not. Reactive measurement methods sometimes elicit thoughts, feelings, or behavior not otherwise characteristic of participants; people react to measurement stimuli in many ways in addition to those envisioned by researchers. Any such reactions that might distort or confound the intended measurement may be called **reactive effects.** These effects are of two types: those that change the subjects in some way (even if only momentarily) and those that confound the measures, making them less representative of the subjects.

Physical and biological scientists have long been familiar with the idea that measurement processes sometimes change what is being measured. Hawking (1988) argued that you should never assume a measurement process to be totally free from such influences, although these influences are often too small to be of interest. For example, imagine measuring a block of soft foam padding with a steel tape that has a hook at one end. Pulling on the tape compresses the foam, making it temporarily shorter where it is being measured. Pulling very gently might compress it a millimeter or so, an inconsequential amount for purposes of making a mattress; a harder pull might compress the foam enough to cause a problem. As a second example, police officers sometimes use a radar device to measure the speed of a vehicle. If the vehicle has a radar detector, the driver knows that his or her speed is being measured and may slow down. As a third example, a participant's pulse rate might increase because a sexually attractive person is holding the wrist to count heartbeats.

A second type of reactive effect occurs when measurement stimuli introduce extraneous variables that confound the measures, whether or not they also change the variables being measured. For example, some political organizations distribute questionnaires apparently designed to elicit answers supporting the organizations' positions rather than reflecting respondents' true views. Biased questions tend to elicit biased answers, whether or not they change anyone's opinion even temporarily. Anastasi's (1988) discussion of "response sets" and "response styles" is also relevant to this problem. Some respondents have general tendencies to agree, to disagree, to answer in socially typical or atypical ways, or to give socially desirable answers to questionnaires and interviewers. When such respondent tendencies interact with the characteristics of a questionnaire or interview, they can distort the measures it yields. For example, a questionnaire intended to measure political liberalism versus conservatism might consist mainly of yes–no questions with yes responses scored as "liberal." Such a questionnaire would confound response style (an extraneous variable) with the intended measurement.

As an example illustrating both types of reactive effects, participants might be asked to express their feelings toward their spouses in the presence of the spouse rather than alone with an interviewer or on paper. It is a common experience to feel different about another person when with the person than in his or her absence. In addition, respondents may not only feel different because the spouse is present but may also shape their responses according to anticipated consequences for the marital relationship (for example, avoiding or softening expressions likely to evoke emotional pain).

As an additional example, suppose an English-speaking researcher with barely sufficient skill in Spanish interviews undocumented immigrant workers in a Texas border town regarding their views on interethnic relations. This illustration is not representative of usual research practices; rather, we offer it because it contains many possible reactive effects. We list several of both types, without claiming they are the only ones:

- Participants may be afraid that the researcher represents a threat of deportation.
- The researcher's presence might intensify participants' feelings concerning interethnic relations (for example, that they are unjustly treated or have low, subordinate status because of their ethnicity).
- The researcher's questions might raise some participants awareness of ethnic issues they had not previously thought about.
- If poorly constructed, biased questions are contained in the interview, they will likely elicit biased answers not representative of respondents' true views. Such problems are very easy to introduce unknowingly when words in an unfamiliar language have unrecognized shades of meaning.
- Participants might shape their answers according to what they think the researcher expects or wants to hear, even if all questions are unbiased.

Various reactive effects are discussed elsewhere in this book. The phenomenon of participants' shaping their responses according to their expectations of a spouse or interviewer will be readily recognized as demand characteristics (discussed in Chapter 9). Chapter 12 addresses questionnaire construction and the effects of interviewers and observers.

Although the words *reactive* and *nonreactive* in relation to measurement methods suggest otherwise, reactiveness is a matter of degree rather than all or none. Reactive effects, in both their magnitude and their importance, may occupy any point along the entire spectrum from zero to substantial. They need to be considered anew in the planning of each project.

Minimizing Reactive Effects

Reactive effects can often be reduced. Sometimes it is both possible and desirable to substitute or add one or more nonreactive measures. Examples of nonreactive measures include physical traces, official records, and unobtrusive observation. In addition, making measures a routine part of a service program will often eliminate some unwanted reactive effects. For example, in a project with students as participants, tests for research purposes were offered as regular classroom examinations. Although such measures are themselves reactive, some demand characteristics differed from what they would have been if the tests were offered as part of a research project. Administering the tests as classroom examinations increased external validity for generalizing the project's results to the regular classroom environment. (Ethically, this practice is limited to tasks that are in themselves legitimate classroom activities.) In another instance, a project called for data from counseling clients, and the information desired was of a sort that counselors commonly asked for during sessions with clients. Asking the counselors to collect the required data during regular counseling sessions eliminated reactive effects that often occur in special research interviews. Again, external validity is increased if the researcher wishes to generalize results to similar counseling activity.

In both these examples, reactive data collection methods (testing and interviewing) were used in such a way that they were part of the process being studied rather than a separate activity undertaken only for research. Processes studied in counseling research often contain reactive effects of their own, as both these examples illustrate. Such intrinsic reactive effects should not necessarily be eliminated; sometimes they strengthen rather than weaken external validity. In contrast, reactive effects extraneous to the process being studied that nonetheless affect its measurement often weaken design validity. For example, a researcher studying racial attitudes should exercise care that measurement tools such as interviews and questionnaires do not change these attitudes temporarily or distort their expression while measuring them. Such reactive effects should be minimized insofar as possible within existing constraints.

Reliability

In general, **reliability** refers to the consistency of a measure. If a reliable test is administered twice, high pretest scorers will also score high at retest; similarly, moderate and low pretest scorers will not greatly change their standing at retest. Even if practice effect raises everyone's score, this fact does not reduce reliability if the group members' relative standing does not change more than minimally at retest. In contrast, if a test of very low reliability is administered twice, pretest scores poorly predict respondents' standing at retest; many high pretest scorers will score low when retested, and many low pretest scorers will score high. Test–retest is one of several ways to estimate reliability. When measures are susceptible to shifts, such as practice effect or rater drift (discussed in Chapter 9), this matter needs to be considered as a reliability issue. A more detailed discussion of reliability may be found in any good **psychometrics** text, such as Anastasi (1988) or Sax (1989).

Information about the reliabilities of many specific instruments is available in manuals for standardized tests and reports of previous projects. If a planned project is to use instruments for which such information is not available, we recommend evaluating their reliability with a pilot study whenever possible.

Measurement Validity

The term *measurement* distinguishes this kind of validity from design validity as discussed in Chapter 9. Measurement validity has to do with the extent to which a measure can achieve its aims. In short, does it measure what it claims to measure? For example, if a measure purports to assess a respondent's state anxiety (feelings of anxiety at the moment), is that what it really measures? Or does it measure something else, such as trait anxiety (general tendency to experience anxiety) or some variables other than anxiety of any kind? Hadley and Brodwin (1989) noted that scores on speeded tests of ability are influenced by culturally based attitudes toward time. Such effects reduce validity for the abilities measured. Three major types of validity have been distinguished with regard to standardized tests and inventories: criterion-related, content, and construct validity (American Educational Research Association et al., 1985). Face and factual validities are also important in many circumstances.

Criterion-related validity. **Criterion-related validity** refers to a relationship between test or inventory scores and some other measures outside the test or inventory. These other measures are called "criteria" and are chosen to represent what the test or inventory was designed to measure. Academic grades, job performance ratings, reported abstinence from drugs, and expressed satisfaction have been used as criteria in various studies. Criterion-related validity is further subdivided into two subtypes: predictive validity, if one or more predictor variables are measured first to predict one or more criterion variables, and concurrent validity, if no attempt to predict is involved. For example, job aptitude tests have predictive validity for workers' job performance ratings if the workers are tested at the time of hiring and their scores are related to job performance ratings taken later; if they were tested about the time the ratings were made, validity would be concurrent.

Content validity.   An instrument has **content validity** if its **items** fairly represent a defined domain of content. For example, mathematics achievement tests should contain items appropriate to the skills taught in the relevant mathematics curricula; items requiring unrelated mathematical skills or knowledge about other subject matter (such as art) would reduce content validity for these tests.

Construct validity.   **Construct validity** refers to congruence between a test or inventory and a theoretical concept such as intelligence or hostility. This congruence can be assessed in several ways. For example, the construct validity of a standardized intelligence test could be assessed by examining whether it is correlated with other standardized intelligence tests, whether its items require abilities included in commonly accepted definitions of intelligence, whether it predicts grades in school, and whether it predicts whom teachers will select as "most intelligent" among their students or colleagues.

Factual and face validity.   Interviews, questionnaires, and observation techniques are often said to have **factual validity** if they elicit factually truthful answers.

An instrument is said to have **face validity** if respondents see it as measuring what it should. For example, if a test called Plumbing Aptitude Test were administered to potential plumbing school candidates, those candidates would expect to see items having to do with pipes, wrenches, and plumbing systems, not items having to do with pencils, forestry, or airplane parts. Many such respondents would probably resent the latter items as irrelevant, even if the skills required to answer them were important to plumbers' work.

Information about validity.   It is meaningless to state that any measure is valid in general; all meaningful statements of validity say what the measure is valid for and make clear what kind of validity is meant. For example, to say that the Strong Interest Inventory is a "valid interest inventory" and stop there conveys no useful information. A more helpful statement would be that this instrument is valid for predicting respondents' occupations up to 20 years in the future. These considerations apply equally to tests, inventories, and other measures used in research, such as interviews, questionnaires, and observations. Validity information enables a researcher to judge the extent to which an instrument has validity appropriate to its role in the project at hand.

Data from formal validity studies are usually available for standardized tests and inventories but are rarely available for most other kinds of measures. Questionnaires and interview schedules are written anew for most projects that use them, and validity is often assumed. Any existing validity information needs to be carefully considered for its relevance to the project at hand. Strong validity for one measurement purpose does not necessarily imply strong validity for other purposes or with different kinds of respondents. Sometimes validity data exist for instruments similar to but not identical with those being used in the project at hand; relevance to the present project is then a matter of judgment. For example, Mitchell and Krumboltz (1987) found that college students' reports that they had interviewed individuals about their occupations were generally confirmed by those they interviewed. This finding adds support to the validity of similar self-reports for use in a new project.

When relevant validity information is absent or scant, a researcher has several choices. Carrying out an extensive validity investigation in advance of a main study might be the wisest course in some situations; more often, it would use up valuable time and money better reserved for the main study. In some projects, it is possible to achieve a helpful sense of validity by carefully examining the items contained in a planned instrument along with other relevant materials (for example, checking the items on an informal achievement test against a curriculum outline). Sometimes it is possible to include the collection of validity data in a pilot study with little added work. It is often possible to evaluate both validity and reliability in the same pilot study. Although most pilot studies use very few subjects, it is better to have data from small samples than from none. When the content of an instrument is developed directly from the research questions it is designed to answer, satisfactory validity may sometimes be inferred from this fact combined with previous researchers' experience with similar instruments.

The Standard Battery Proposal

Some counseling researchers (Lambert, 1979; Lambert, Masters, & Ogles, 1991; Waskow & Parloff, 1975; Watkins & Schneider, 1991) have argued that one or more standard batteries of outcome instruments should be developed for use in a variety of counseling outcome studies. They point out that such a standard battery would allow more comparison of results between studies and reduce a proliferation of instruments with questionable reliability and validity. These probable benefits need to be weighed against various risks; we list two:

- Researchers might have great difficulty reaching agreement about what to include in any one or more standard batteries.

- Easy access to standard batteries might limit the variety of projects future researchers undertake. For example, researchers might be inclined to study only phenomena to which a standard battery is relevant and be discouraged from investigating new variables not yet envisioned at the time the batteries were developed.

Refer to the cited sources for a more detailed discussion of the issues involved.

INSTRUMENTS

Most instruments used in counseling research are made of paper and ink or electronic impulses recorded on computer-readable media such as diskettes. Other instruments (for example, polygraphs) are made largely of materials such as metal, glass, and plastic. This section and Chapter 12 discuss instruments of the first type. Technical details of the second type of instruments are beyond the scope of this book.

Whatever its components, an instrument is a specific device for collecting data. The following kinds of instruments are discussed very briefly in this section and more fully in Chapter 12: standardized tests and inventories, informal tests, questionnaires, interviews, observation schedules, rating scales, attitude scales, and semantic differentials. We include this brief discussion here to represent the place of these instruments in the larger topic of counseling research measurement and reserve their more detailed discussion for Chapter 12.

Tests and inventories. Most **tests** consist of questions or other tasks on which respondents are instructed or expected to perform at their best, such as tests of intelligence, knowledge, or skill. **Inventories** consist of questions or other types of items calling for respondents' self-report. Many tests are scored by counting the number of correct versus incorrect responses; inventories do not define responses as correct or incorrect. Tests and inventories are **standardized** (Anastasi, 1988) if they have both instructions for uniform administration procedures and norms (results from **norm samples** with known characteristics). Tests lacking either norms or uniform administration instructions are **informal tests.**

Questionnaires, interviews, and observations. **Questionnaires** consist of written questions, sometimes accompanied by other types of items, calling for respondents to write their answers. **Interviews** are conversations carried out by interviewers with respondents. Most research interviews have the purpose of collecting data; some are conducted for other purposes, such as debriefing (discussed in Chapter 5). A written interview guide provides a standard system for conducting the interview and recording responses. **Observation schedules** are written systems for making and recording observations for research purposes.

Scales. Rating scales call for judges to assign numbers or categories (for example, 1 = never, 5 = always) to whatever is being rated: a person, a group, a plan, a document, an idea, a thing, or a set of behaviors, to name a few possibilities. Teachers rate students' performance by assigning A, B, C, D, and F grades. Most **attitude scales** measure attitudes toward a group or kind of people (for example, women, ethnic minorities, people with a penal history, people with disabilities) or a social institution (for example, a church, family life, public schools). Respondents are required to indicate their agreement or disagreement with various statements; answers are combined into a total score.

The **semantic differential** is a form of rating scale calling for respondents to rate a concept (such as school, myself as I am now, myself as I would like to be) on several pairs of opposites (such as good–bad, slow–fast, large–small). Each pair of opposites defines a continuum.

Rating scales and attitude scales are sometimes incorporated into questionnaires and interviews; some interview guides include observation schedules so that both verbal and nonverbal behavior of respondents can be studied.

The Law of the Instrument

Kaplan (1964) introduced the term **the law of the instrument** to represent a principle he summarized like this: "Give a small boy a hammer, and he will find that everything he encounters needs pounding. . . . [A] scientist formulates problems in a way which requires for their solution just those techniques in which he himself is especially skilled" (p. 28). Isaac and Michael (1981) noted that people often become so attached to a particular instrument or procedure that they recommend it as a solution to many more problems than it suits. Many students experience this overreaction as they learn about new instruments and methods; added experience provides a basis for applying these techniques more realistically. A researcher's familiarity with a specific instrument or measurement method, and liking for it, are good points to consider when selecting among possibilities that have all been determined *beforehand* to fit the project's mission. Researchers generally work more effectively and understand their results better with familiar instruments and procedures than with less familiar ones. However, it is never wise to make familiarity more important than a project's mission.

An analogous situation sometimes occurs in counselor education programs when students are asked to plan projects around the use of a particular instrument being studied, such as the MMPI. To guard against the law of the instrument problem, we suggest carefully considering all aspects of each such project's mission. First, the project must meet a class assignment; this is one reason the research questions are being asked. Second, each project must have a set of research questions selected by its planner; different projects usually have different questions. This second aspect of the mission should be examined carefully to ensure that it is well served by the instrument that fulfills the class requirement. These same considerations apply when a counselor plans a project with a view to enhancing his or her familiarity and skills with any instrument.

PHYSICAL AND BIOCHEMICAL MEASURES

Modern technology permits many measures to be made directly from the body or its products. These are too numerous to discuss in detail in this section. We list some common ones, repeating our emphasis on the measures rather than the instruments used for making them:

- A **polygraph** can make a continuous recording on paper (or directly to a computer) of several body functions; among the usual ones are skin temperature, electrical conductance of the skin, heartbeat, breathing, limb volume, muscle tension, and brain electrical activity. A researcher can choose the specific functions to be recorded.
- A small cloth sack of rock salt or alum crystals can be held in a participant's hand while he or she is in a counseling session or performs an assigned task; weighing the sack before and after the session provides a measure of palmar sweating.
- A device can make a continuous photographic recording of eye movements as a participant reads a passage or views a picture.
- A device attached to a bed or chair can make a continuous record of body movements. Such devices have been used frequently in sleep research.
- Several devices can estimate blood-alcohol concentration from a breath sample or ambient air near a participant's face (Dubowski, 1986).
- Urine or blood samples can be analyzed chemically for substances such as glucose, lipids, proteins, neurotransmitters, drugs, and drug metabolites.
- Blood samples can be examined with a microscope to count how many cells of different kinds are present.

Some employers conduct routine drug screening of employees or applicants through chemical tests of urine samples. Although data from such tests in employees' files might be quite useful in evaluating employer–employee relationships, we strongly recommend against naively assuming that these records validly represent employees' drug use.

Sonnenstuhl, Trice, Staudenmeier, and Steele (1987) noted two major technical problems with such drug testing. First, the chemical tests used often yielded false results.

Some laboratories performed very poorly, with false negatives (samples included drugs but tested negative) running as high as 100% on cocaine, amphetamines, codeine and morphine. False positives (samples which were free of drugs but tested positive) ran as high as 37% for amphetamines . . .

> and only one [laboratory] performed acceptably in identifying barbiturates, cocaine, and morphine. (p. 720)

More valid and reliable test procedures were often not used because they cost more. Further, some legally available substances can lead to positive drug test results. For example,

> drinking herbal teas containing coca leaves can cause one to test positively for cocaine, and taking some over-the-counter drugs can cause one to test positively for phenobarbital . . . In some instances, eating poppy-seed cake will cause one to test positively for heroin. (p. 721)

Second, drug abusers and addicts know "how to beat the system; consequently drug screening is more likely to catch less experienced than more experienced users" (p. 720). Drug testing of employees has become more sophisticated and more closely regulated since Sonnenstuhl and colleagues published their report. Nonetheless, these issues still deserve careful attention whenever employers' records are used to study employees' drug use. Further, the Sonnenstuhl et al. report underscores the risks of carelessly chosen chemical tests in any drug study.

Other Data Sources

Official records, **personal documents,** and **physical traces** can provide research data, although they are not instruments. These data sources are all nonreactive in relation to the research project. The researcher does not give participants anything to react to in providing the data. This fact has led some researchers to overlook possible reactive effects. These reactive effects are probable whenever a researcher uses data that were previously collected for other purposes by reactive means; reactive effects are also possible in some other situations.

Official Records

The official files of schools, employers, service agencies, and regulatory bodies contain much information about their students, workers, clients, and licensees. Many research projects have drawn data from such sources.

Validity and reliability.   Our first caution with regard to such data is a point we have seen many beginning researchers overlook: The official status of this information gives it no special claim to either reliability or validity, whatever its administrative importance may be. For example, an employee's personnel file may contain:

- an application form (questionnaire),
- employment interview records,
- qualifying examination (standardized test) results,

- job performance evaluation (ratings),
- grades in two college courses (ratings), and
- results of routine drug tests.

The employer will rely on this file when deciding such major matters as promotion or dismissal. Nonetheless, its data are subject to all the limitations inherent in questionnaires, interviews, standardized tests, ratings, and drug testing.

In addition, records are not always complete, accurate, and up to date. A personnel file may omit some of an employee's training or employment experience if he or she decided to leave it out of the application as irrelevant to the job applied for. If he or she was hired several years ago, some facts correctly reported on the application may have changed in the meantime. In another example, records of the 1936 Olympics represented Korean athlete Sohn Kee-Chung as Japanese under the name Kitei Son. Japan controlled Korea at that time, and he was not allowed to participate as Korean. Records were changed more than 50 years later to reflect his correct name and nationality (S. Kronenthal, personal communication, July 15, 1993). We draw two more examples from hospital experience:

- One patient's diagnosis of mental retardation was misfiled and carried forward to future reports in another patient's chart.
- The first page of a file recorded a "principal diagnosis" the patient had claimed at intake; the second page recorded a later medical examination that *disconfirmed* this diagnosis.

Researchers making longitudinal comparisons based on records cannot safely assume that the rules underlying the records have remained unchanged during the intervening time. If more alcohol-impaired drivers are arrested in a community than previously, does the change mean that there are more drunk drivers on the streets or that the police have become more vigilant, or both? Does a student's increased grade point average reflect improved academic performance or lower faculty grading standards commonly known as "grade inflation," or both? These phenomena do not always threaten design validity; records sometimes permit a historical analysis of such rule changes.

A researcher using records for research purposes should know how data were collected for inclusion in the records and carefully consider this knowledge in light of relevant issues discussed earlier in this chapter. For example, college students' grade records represent ratings (a) made by a number of instructors, (b) based on an uncontrolled mix of informal tests, observations, and other data, and (c) subject to such factors as rater bias, halo effect, and individual instructors' tendencies to emphasize high, low, or moderate grades. It is easy to envision how a researcher without this knowledge about grade records might easily be misled when interpreting results based on these records.

Reactive effects.   Though a personnel file is a nonreactive data source for a research project, most of the data it contains were originally collected through reactive measures. For example, the employee discussed earlier in this section could have shaped some questionnaire and interview responses in service of a wish to be hired. If the employment interview was conducted in an intimidating manner, some responses might have been affected. Job performance ratings are sometimes biased by supervisors' reactions to factors unrelated to employees' work (such as social behavior and preferred clothing styles). We recommend that researchers be alert to such reactive effects whenever data from official records are used.

Access.   Records are a convenient and inexpensive data source for a researcher who has easy access to them. However, access may be limited because of confidentiality or other considerations. Without permission to access the data, a researcher cannot pursue a project involving records. Gaining this access is a planning task (discussed in Chapters 5 and 7).

Personal Documents

In our literate society, many people write copiously in the course of their lives: personal correspondence, diaries, poetry, stories, notes in the family Bible, and records of personal business transactions, to name a few examples. Such records are usually nonreactive. In addition, some methods of counseling and psychotherapy call for clients to create various written materials between sessions. Examples include self-management training (Watson & Tharp, 1992), guided autobiography (Malde, 1988), poetry therapy (Bell, 1984), and some applications of transactional analysis (Jongeward & Scott, 1976). These materials can provide valuable research data. With regard to the researcher, these documents are nonreactive; however, they are reactive in relation to the counseling process. Content analysis, discussed later in this chapter, provides a systematic way to study these materials.

Previous Studies

Chapters 6 and 7 discuss researchers' needs to be familiar with previous related work while formulating and planning a project. Earlier studies can serve a present project not only in this way but also as a data source. For example, Smith and Glass (1977) analyzed the "effect size" of 375 psychotherapy outcome studies. As a second example, Mintz, Mintz, Arruda, and Hwang (1992) found a number of studies that had measured psychiatric patients' capacity to work, both at admission to treatment and when treatment was completed. The collective analysis of data from these studies led to several findings. One of these findings was that depressed patients with symptom remission more fully recovered their capacity to work if they had been treated for longer periods of time rather than more briefly. This analysis was not based entirely on published findings. For example, some studies had used an instrument containing an assessment of work capacity as a component subscale but reported results from the total score only. Mintz et al. (1992) obtained subscale data by contacting the projects' authors. Similarly, Evans and Burck's (1992) analysis of 67 studies found a small positive effect of career education on academic achievement.

Such an analysis of several other projects' results is called a meta-analysis. We emphasize an important difference between a meta-analysis and a literature review. When conducting a literature review, a researcher finds and examines related literature, including the reports of earlier researchers' work. The researcher then considers this literature as a whole to discern its collective meaning. In contrast, a meta-analysis is a new analysis in which data from a number of earlier projects are analyzed collectively. A meta-analysis project includes all six of the steps that make up any research project: formulation, planning, data collection, data analysis, interpretation, and reporting.

We expect that the number of such projects in the counseling research literature will increase substantially if researchers develop and adopt one or more standard batteries. Anticipated advantages and risks of such a battery were discussed earlier in this chapter.

Physical Traces

Sometimes much can be learned from people's direct effects on the physical environment. Wear on the sole of a leg prosthesis indicates it has been used. We would expect to find fewer cigarette butts in ashtrays after an effective antismoking campaign than before. Trash receptacles often contain evidence concerning people's consumption of so-called junk food versus more nutritious items. Files of information about occupations, service programs, and academic majors show signs of dirt and wear with heavy use. Litter provides direct evidence concerning the effectiveness of an antilitter campaign.

Physical traces are probably one of the data sources least vulnerable to reactive effects. However, it is unwise to assume that such effects are absent. For example, suppose cigarette butts in ashtrays are to be used to evaluate a college's antismoking campaign. If students know the campaign is being conducted by the Student Health Service, the researcher would be wise to examine other ashtrays in addition to the ones just outside the Student Health waiting room. If students suspect the ashtrays will be observed to measure the campaign's results, reactive effects are present.

CONTENT ANALYSIS

Content analysis is a major part of much qualitative research. Although it is a means of processing data rather than a data source, we discuss it here because some kinds of data require this step before they are amenable to the statistical analyses discussed in Chapter 13. Examples of data suitable for content analysis include:

- recordings or transcripts of counseling sessions,
- answers to open-ended questionnaire items,
- answers to unstructured or semistructured interviews,
- stated reasons for seeking counseling,
- personal correspondence,
- answers to essay examinations,
- projective test responses,
- answers to written assignments, and
- records of administrative meetings.

Kerlinger (1986) defined content analysis as "a method of studying and analyzing communications in a systematic, objective and quantitative manner to measure variables" (p. 477). Rather than directly observing behavior, or administering tests or scales, a researcher "takes the communications people have produced and asks questions of the communications" (p. 477). Many of the issues discussed in Chapter 12 concerning observation techniques apply equally to content analysis. Kerlinger (1986) discussed several examples of content analysis; Gottschalk (1979) has compiled an anthology of many more.

The Content Analysis Task

The content analysis task usually includes classifying, counting, rating, or some combination of these. A **content analysis system** is a set of rules for carrying out the process. Exactly what must be classified, counted, or rated? What defines the boundaries of the various categories of the variables to be rated? The more explicit these rules are, the more reliably the process will be carried out.

Content analysis obviously entails a judging task, usually a time-consuming one. If judges must be paid, the method can become very expensive. Some applications require much sensitivity and skill to do well; others (such as word counting and time measurement) rather little. If a project's questions and hypotheses include dimensions that require technical knowledge to understand, judges must have this technical knowledge. Two or more judges must examine the same material if the interrater reliability of the analysis process is to be measured; such reliability is essential if the researcher is to have confidence that future judges could apply the same process and expect similar results. The reliability of one judge's work may be studied by asking the same judge to examine the same material on two occasions separated by a long enough time interval that earlier judgments are largely forgotten when later judgments are made. Researchers need to consider such issues as rater bias when deciding whether to do the judging task themselves or assign it to support staff. Project planning needs to provide for a sufficient number of judges who have the necessary time, patience, sensitivity, skill, technical knowledge, and freedom from bias to carry out their task. Judges must be selected and assigned carefully so that their individual characteristics do not become confounded with the variables being studied.

Choosing or Developing a System

Content analysis may be conducted entirely by hand or with the aid of a computer. Because computer-based analyses require very explicit rules, Holsti (1969) recommended, "all content analysis should be designed *as if it were to be done by computer*" (p. 192).

Some projects use content analysis systems developed by prior researchers. If no existing system suits the project at hand, a new system must be developed. To illustrate this development process, we refer to a project one of us coauthored (Hadley & Hadley, 1974). The project's research question was descriptive: What favorable and aversive consequences of drinking are identified by alcoholic clients of the agencies studied? Data were collected through semistructured interviews.

One of the researchers began the content analysis task with 15 to 20 interview records. He read the responses, listed the content categories that occurred to him, wrote definitions of the categories, and assembled them into a judging guide. For illustration, we list some of the "aversive" consequence categories, with illustrative responses in parentheses:

- hangover symptoms (sick headaches every morning),
- other physical illness (liver went bad),
- social loss (divorce, father disowned me),
- arrest or jail,
- economic loss (lost job, always broke), and
- emotional (get depressed, get mad too quickly).

This researcher then reexamined each respondent's record with his new judging guide in hand and noted on a separate sheet of paper all the categories he saw represented in that record. He gave his coworker this judging guide and this same set of responses; she repeated his judging task without seeing his judgments. The researchers then compared notes, discussed the records about which they had differed, and resolved their disagreement about each of these records. Based on their experience doing the judging task, the researchers were able to:

- formulate clearer definitions of some categories,
- add and define a few new categories, and
- decide to continue to do this judging task themselves rather than assign it to others. (They believed they could be sufficiently unbiased because they had no hypothesis about what kinds of results to expect.)

With these refinements in hand, they then independently judged another set of records and again compared notes. They repeated this process until they had judged enough records to estimate reliability of their judgments. They were not satisfied with their first reliability estimates; therefore, they continued to refine their category definitions as they both independently judged new sets of records. When they had achieved satisfactory reliability, they discontinued the double work of independently judging each interview record. Instead, they divided the work and each researcher judged about half of the records; they discussed only the few records they felt doubtful about.

Computer aids. Content analysis is a flexible, widely applicable process that requires much time, effort, and patience to do well. Often, it also requires much skill.

Computers can be used to perform much of the routine work content analysis of verbal materials often entails. The General Inquirer is a set of computer programs designed to support the substantive and statistical aspects of this work; it can be applied to different kinds of research problems (Kerlinger, 1986). Stone, Dunphy, Smith, and Ogilvie (1968) developed a manual, and Holsti (1969) offers a detailed example using General Inquirer and briefly discusses additional computer programs for content analysis. Such computer programs offer researchers an additional benefit—a basis from which to examine and improve their content analysis systems as a whole. Even portions to be done manually can often be improved by specifying them explicitly enough that they could be done by computer.

For additional suggestions regarding development of a content analysis system, see Appendix G and other sources such as Gottschalk (1979), Holsti (1969), Kerlinger (1986), and Stone et al. (1968).

CHAPTER SUMMARY

This chapter addresses principles underlying the selection of measures for research studies in counseling. Every measure must be chosen and used as is, chosen and modified, or developed anew. This process requires much thought and planning with specific attention to the advantages and disadvantages of each possibility for the mission of the research project. General issues to be addressed for the selection of any measures include their reactivity, reliability, and validity. Standardized tests and inventories have the advantages of uniform administration and known norms; most also have reliability and validity data. When no standardized measures meet the purposes of a study, researchers use other measures such as informal tests and inventories, questionnaires, interview guides, rating scales, attitude scales, or observation schedules. Measures are not always applied directly to participants; data may come from sources such as physical traces, official records, personal documents, and earlier projects. Such sources minimize the danger of reactivity, but it should never be assumed that reactivity is totally avoided. Content analysis is a systematic way of measuring variables from verbal material such as counseling sessions, unstructured interview remarks, answers to open-ended questions, or written words.

PRACTICAL EXERCISES

1. In the counseling literature, find a report of a research project that collected data from participants. Identify the kinds of instruments used to collect the data. To the extent that available information permits, state the reasons why the researchers chose (a) each kind of instrument over other possibilities and (b) each specific instrument versus available alternatives of its kind.
2. Imagine that you wish to design a study to compare the effects of two different career counseling approaches. Your participants will be college students who respond to advertisements offering career counseling for students having difficulty choosing a major. You are interested in which career counseling approach is most effective in (a) reducing students' anxiety about making career decisions, (b) increasing students' exploration of available occupations and the majors that lead to them, and (c) increasing the number of students who declare a major. What kinds of measuring instruments would you select to collect these data? Explain your reasons for the selection of the various instruments.
3. Find in the counseling literature a report of a project using content analysis. Gottschalk's (1979) anthology is a possible source if none come to mind that fit your interests. Based on Chapter 11 and Appendix G, answer the following questions regarding the content analysis system and process this project used:
   a. What variables was content analysis used to measure?
   b. What was the universe of content analyzed?
   c. What units were used?
   d. Did the process involve classification, counting, rating, ranking, or physical measurement? Describe each of these procedures used (for example, what was counted?).
   e. How was the project's content analysis system chosen or developed? If the researchers chose an existing system, state the reasons they

chose the one they did. If a new system was developed for this project, describe the procedure used to develop it.

4. Formulate a research question that can be answered by examining physical traces that you can observe where you live, work, or study. Construct a system for observing and recording these traces. Such a system might consist of a record form and a set of written instructions. Express your observing and recording system explicitly enough, and in enough detail, that someone other than you could use it. Next, try out your system by examining and recording the kind of physical traces it calls for, as you observe them. If you experience ambiguities or other difficulties, fine-tune your research question and your observing and recording system as you see fit.

CHAPTER TWELVE

COLLECTING THE DATA: TYPES OF MEASURING INSTRUMENTS

QUESTIONS TO GUIDE YOUR READING

Standardized Tests and Inventories

1. What distinguishes standardized tests and inventories from informal ones?
2. How do tests differ from inventories, according to the terminology used in the text?
3. What advantages do standardized tests and inventories have over informal ones if both types are suitable to a research project's mission?
4. Where can you find information about published tests and inventories?

Informal Tests

5. What advantages and disadvantages does the use of informal tests offer?
6. What options are available to researchers when relevant validity information is absent or scant?
7. What are floor and ceiling effects?
8. What is mean chance expectancy?

Questionnaires

9. Why is the phrase "orally administered questionnaire" usually indefensible?
10. What can researchers do to maximize the rate of return when using questionnaires?
11. What is meant by precise, objective, and efficient language?
12. What two tasks does a transmittal letter need to accomplish? How should a transmittal letter be structured to accomplish these tasks?
13. What purposes are served by conducting one or more pilot studies with a draft form of a questionnaire?
14. What item formats are recommended to avoid discouraging respondents from answering?
15. What are closed-ended and open-ended formats?
16. What are double-barreled items, and why should they be avoided?
17. What suggestions are offered for the arrangement of a questionnaire as a whole?

Interviews

18. In what kinds of projects is interviewing preferable to using questionnaires?
19. What disadvantages does interviewing entail?
20. What are structured, unstructured, and semistructured interviews?
21. What are the advantages and disadvantages of telephone interviewing?
22. What are the advantages and disadvantages of face-to-face interviewing?
23. What are the advantages and disadvantages of group interviews?

Rating Scales

24. What is a category scale? How can such a scale be converted to a numerical format? To a graphic format?

25. What is a forced-choice scale?
26. What is the Likert summated ratings format?
27. What is an attitude scale? How does it differ from other rating scales?
28. What is the semantic differential technique?
29. What recommendations are offered for increasing the reliability of judgments elicited by rating scales?

Observation Systems
30. What dimensions of behavior can be assessed using observation?
31. What is an observation schedule?
32. Distinguish between event and duration recording.
33. Distinguish between whole interval, partial interval, and momentary recording strategies.
34. Why is self-monitoring likely to be highly reactive?

An instrument is a specific device for collecting data. The kinds of instruments discussed in this chapter include standardized tests and inventories, informal tests, questionnaires, interviews, rating scales, attitude scales, semantic differential scales, and observation schedules. Each kind of measure has its own unique features, but most share some features as well. Some of these features present general advantages or disadvantages that differ in importance from project to project. A few features may be advantageous to some projects and disadvantageous to others. A researcher must choose the kind of instrument to be used in a project; once this decision is made, the specific instrument must be used as is, modified, or developed anew.

STANDARDIZED TESTS AND INVENTORIES

A test or inventory is standardized if it has both of the following (Anastasi, 1988):

- instructions for uniform administration and scoring, and
- **norms,** which are results from one or more large samples with known characteristics expressed so that respondents' scores can be compared with them for purposes of interpretation.

Most such instruments have been developed at considerable effort and expense, are copyrighted, and are sold with accompanying manuals that provide important technical data such as administration and scoring instructions, reliability, validity, recommended user qualifications, time required to administer, and norms. Some standardized instruments are published; others are unpublished. In general, published instruments are supported by more extensive development work than are unpublished ones.

Some writers call all standardized psychometric instruments tests. We prefer to reserve this term for those instruments on which respondents are instructed or expected to perform at their best, such as tests of intelligence, aptitude, knowledge, or skill. Many measures of personality, interests, values, and temperament comprise lists of questions calling for true–false or multiple-choice responses that do not have correct or incorrect answers; these instruments are inventories. Most tests permit correct and incorrect responses. Despite this distinction, we accept the semantic choice of any instrument's author who calls it a test. For example, the Thematic Apperception Test presents respondents with pictures and calls for them to tell stories; there are no correct or incorrect answer possibilities.

Standardized tests and inventories offer clear advantages in that the development work has already been done. Such instruments have been tried out and modified, most of them more than once. These repeated modifications usually increase reliability and validity. Technical information is readily available and often extensive. For many projects, these facts mean lower costs and less work than developing a new instrument. One major disadvantage is that the available standardized tests and inventories usually fit a planned project approximately rather than exactly. For example, a researcher might want an inventory of "work values" and note that the only inventory found has technical flaws, or has not been used with the same age group as the planned project's participants, or lacks validity information of the kind wanted. Such disadvantages should be carefully weighed against not only the instrument's advantages but also the advantages and disadvantages of other instruments that might be used instead.

To use standardized tests or inventories in a research project, a researcher should have sufficient training and experience to select them wisely, administer them correctly, and interpret the results validly. This issue was discussed in Chapter 5 as part of counselor-researchers' ethical responsibility to function within their competence.

It is never wise to assume that the name of a test, inventory, or scale completely and correctly represents what it measures. To understand what any standardized test or inventory measures, you must study its manual; many require much additional study. Some instruments, including the Binet and Wechsler intelligence tests and projective measures such as the Rorschach, require special training with supervised practice (American Educational Research Association, 1985). Most publishers of standardized tests have a policy of selling them only to customers with appropriate qualifications.

Several good psychometrics texts discuss the above issues in more detail than is reasonable here. Among them are Anastasi (1988), Cronbach (1984), and Sax (1989). Most large university libraries have the Buros *Mental Measurements Yearbooks* (MMY) and *Tests in Print* (TIP); these sources are updated from time to time and offer much information about many of the available tests and inventories. Goldman and Mitchell (1990) have prepared a dictionary of unpublished experimental mental measures. The Science Directorate of the American Psychological Association has published two relevant pamphlets: *Finding Information on Published Tests* and *Finding Unpublished Tests and Measures*. Publishers' catalogs are another rich information source; although more current than MMY and TIP, these catalogs lack professional reviews such as MMY includes, and their information is presented in a manner designed to sell the instruments. Additionally, you would have to review many catalogs to cover all the tests listed in TIP. For example, an Educational Testing Service brochure alone offers for sale approximately 200 annotated bibliographies in specific subject areas. Finally, Pruitt (1977) discussed evaluation systems based on work samples such as Singer and VALPAR.

INFORMAL TESTS

We use the term *informal test* for any test that does not meet the criteria for standardized tests discussed in the previous section. The most common examples are examinations given in school and college courses. Most instructors write these examinations specifically to cover course content. Researchers have the same option. When no satisfactory standardized test exists covering a knowledge or skill a researcher wants to measure, a test can be written anew for the project. In doing so, the researcher accepts some disadvantages. Very few informal tests have reliability and validity information such as is readily available in the manuals of standardized tests. In addition, most informal tests lack normative data. As noted in Chapter 11, researchers have several choices when relevant validity information is absent or scant:

- Carry out an extensive validity investigation in advance of the main study.
- Derive a sense of content validity from careful examination of the items contained in a planned instrument in conjunction with other relevant materials (for example, checking the items on an informal achievement test against a curriculum outline).
- Collect validity data in a pilot study despite the small sample size.
- Infer construct validity from the way in which the content of an instrument was developed directly from the research questions it was designed to answer combined with previous researchers' experience using similar instruments.

A pilot study is usually necessary for a researcher to be reasonably sure an informal test is well suited to the participants.

Performance Range

It is essential to consider the **performance range** when deciding whether any test is well suited to a project's participants. Ideally, a test should be neither too difficult nor too easy for any of the participants; if it is too difficult or too easy for more than a very few, its performance range is inappropriate. Among other authors, Drew and Hardman (1985) discussed **floor** and **ceiling effects,** which result when a test is too difficult or too easy, offering examples comparing two teaching methods with "mentally retarded" and "nonretarded" students. In one example, the test used to measure the dependent variable was so difficult that the "retarded" participants' scores were all near zero regardless of teaching method. Were the two teaching methods about equally effective with these participants or was there a real difference the test was too difficult to detect? Similarly, if the test was so easy that almost all the "nonretarded" participants had perfect scores regardless of teaching method, a ceiling effect would hide any difference teaching methods might produce with these participants.

With multiple-choice **power tests,** we suggest including **mean chance expectancy** among the issues considered when judging whether a test is too difficult. A power test is untimed or has sufficiently generous time limits that almost all respondents finish. Mean chance expectancy is the average score to be expected if a large group of participants answered every item on the test randomly. For example, if a test consists of 100 items with four answer choices each, with the score being the number of correct answers, it has a mean chance expectancy of 25. An individual score at or near mean chance expectancy usually indicates the test is too difficult for the respondent; when more than a very few of a project's participants score in this region, the test is too difficult for the sample.

Most standardized tests have manuals that offer enough information to enable a researcher to make an informed judgment regarding their suitability for most projects. Some knowledge of a subject pool permits comparisons with populations represented in a test manual. In contrast, a preparer of an informal test cannot dependably judge performance range or other suitability matters (for example, level of language skill required) without trying it out on a sample of participants. When a pilot study shows an informal test to be too easy or too difficult, a researcher can alter the performance range to remedy the problem before beginning the main study. We recommend against modifying a standardized test or inventory in a similar way. Doing so not only loses the advantages of published reliability, validity, and norm data but also invites the risk that readers of the project's report will overlook the modification and misinterpret the results as if the instrument were used in its standardized form. If no standardized test fits a project without modification, an informal test may be constructed.

QUESTIONNAIRES

A questionnaire consists of questions respondents read and to which they write their answers. Questions and answers are usually written on paper. Alternatively, questions may be presented on a computer screen or chalkboard with answers to be written on paper or through a computer keyboard. Occasionally, reports refer to an "orally administered questionnaire." In most circumstances, this expression is a misnomer. To question a research participant orally is to conduct an interview. However, if most of a project's participants read a questionnaire and write their answers while it is read aloud to a few who have impaired vision or limited reading ability, we find it acceptable to say the questionnaire was "administered orally" to these few.

Most questionnaires are written specifically for the projects in which they are used; few have the same quality of validity, reliability, and norm data as standardized tests or inventories. Because questionnaires are very common in survey research, many texts discuss them in a section devoted to surveys. Questionnaires are not limited to survey applications, however, but may be used with any of the research approaches discussed in Chapter 2.

Mode of Delivery

A questionnaire on paper may be delivered in any of several ways. The most common are (a) by mail, to be returned by mail, (b) by hand, to be returned by mail, and (c) by hand, to be returned by hand before the respondent leaves the site where the questionnaire was distributed. It is now possible to administer questionnaires by computer, with answers to be written via the keyboard.

Preparing a Questionnaire

Based on Isaac and Michael (1981), Dillman (1978), and other sources, we offer some recommendations, primarily addressed to maximizing the rate of return. A low rate of return means a biased sample because respondents are likely to differ from nonrespondents in important ways. For example, if a complex questionnaire discourages potential respondents, the researcher will have answers only from people willing to surmount its complexities. See Dillman (1978) for a thorough discussion of questionnaire writing and mailing, but here are some important points to consider when writing a questionnaire:

1. Before beginning to write a questionnaire, have clearly in mind the project's mission and the questionnaire's role in fulfilling that mission.
2. While writing a questionnaire, keep its purposes clearly in mind and its content focused.
3. Never adopt an existing questionnaire without first determining that it is as well suited to the project at hand as a newly written one would be.

4. Bear issues of privacy and confidentiality clearly in mind while writing the questionnaire and accompanying instructions.
5. Keep the questionnaire as short and simple as is consistent with its role in the project.
6. For the questionnaire as a whole and its component items, use the least demanding format consistent with the project's mission.
7. Ensure that every respondent knows what to do with every item.
8. Use precise, objective, and efficient language.
9. While writing a questionnaire, bear in mind the ways answers will be analyzed, and write it so it will elicit answers amenable to the planned analyses.
10. Arrange the material within the questionnaire to maximize response rate.
11. Include an appropriate introduction.
12. By brief, clear, conspicuous instructions, provide a simple way to return completed questionnaires.
13. Write the questionnaire and accompanying instructions to be consistent with a plan for following up nonrespondents.
14. Test a draft form of the questionnaire, including instructions, in a pilot study before it is reproduced in final form for the main study.

In the next subsections, we discuss some of these points in more detail. Format and arrangement have separate sections of their own.

Focus on mission and content.   The idea that a project's mission guides its entire process is often repeated throughout this book. Questionnaire construction is no exception. What research questions are the responses expected to answer? Everything included in a questionnaire should be addressed to eliciting responses that answer the intended research questions. "Avoid fishing expeditions" (Isaac & Michael, 1981, p. 129) and carelessly assembled questions. Include nothing out of idle curiosity. Omit anything unnecessary to the project's mission. Before designing a questionnaire, it is often helpful to explore the views of several potential respondents through unstructured interviews or **focus groups** (Krueger, 1988). This process often helps researchers decide the content, organization, and phrasing of the final questionnaire. For a strictly exploratory purpose ("fishing expedition"), an interview is often more effective than a questionnaire, whether for a pilot study or the main study.

Using existing questionnaires.   If a project is designed to extend an earlier study with a different participant population or under changed conditions, the earlier project's questionnaire may be the best choice. In other situations, however, a literature review rarely reveals an existing questionnaire well suited to the project at hand. More often, an existing questionnaire will be tempting because it already exists, although a better fitting one could be written anew. Yielding to such temptations is false economy, saving the work of writing a questionnaire but getting responses that do not satisfactorily answer the research questions. The best role (if any) for an existing questionnaire is usually as a point of departure or a model for writing a new one.

Ensuring privacy and confidentiality.   Will respondents be asked to identify themselves or invited to answer anonymously? (Underlying ethical issues are discussed in Chapter 5.) In general, anonymous questionnaires elicit higher response rates than if respondents are asked to identify themselves, especially if controversial or sensitive information is also requested. However, the way respondents answer seems little affected by whether the questionnaire is anonymous. Adults tend to answer the same whether anonymously or with identification. Isaac and Michael (1981) noted that anonymous questionnaires require more complex procedures for following up nonrespondents (discussed later in this chapter).

Keeping questionnaires short and simple.   Other things being equal, a questionnaire that demands little time and effort from respondents will elicit a higher response rate than a more demanding one. Complex, excessively demanding questionnaires discourage respondents. "Short" refers primarily to response time, both real and as it appears in potential respondents' first impressions. As a practical matter, "short" also means few words and few pages; most questionnaires that are short in this sense require less time and appear less intimidating than more voluminous ones. "Simple" means keeping to an absolute minimum the time and effort required of respondents to figure out how they should answer.

Ensuring that every respondent knows what to do with every item.   Meeting this requirement depends mostly on the way the items are constructed and arranged (discussed in the format section of this chapter). Clear and complete instructions must bear the remainder of this burden. Instructions must be not only clear and complete but also short and simple, if respondents are not to be discouraged.

Using precise, objective, and efficient language.   Questionnaire instructions, items, and introductory materials (for example, transmittal letters) need to be written in clear, precise, efficient language appropriate to the respondents.

Precise language conveys its intended meanings exactly, literally (not figuratively), and unambiguously. Ambiguous instructions and ambiguous questions get interpreted differently by different readers; researchers therefore have difficulty interpreting their responses. For example, an item that inquires about "income" must make clear what income it refers to: (a) individual or family, (b) earned only or from all sources, (c) weekly, monthly, or annual, (d) before or after deductions. As another example, Sax (1989) pointed out that terms such as *honesty, punctuality,* and *loyalty* have different meanings for different readers.

> One person might equate honesty with obeying the law, but another person might interpret it as telling the truth . . . [however] it is possible to obey the law but not always tell the truth. (p. 164)

Objective language is free from bias and surplus emotional meanings. A questionnaire item that reveals its writer's own opinions will likely elicit biased answers rather than information about respondents' true views. Some questionnaires distributed by political organizations may be deliberately biased in this way. When reported, such biased responses may help a political cause by telling potential voters that an unrealistically large portion of the electorate agrees with the candidate's position. However, seeking biased answers does not fulfill the definition of research as developed in Chapter 1. As the general public continues to become increasingly aware of biased language based on such factors as race, gender, and disability, such biased language in questionnaires will increasingly risk offending prospective respondents and reducing response rates.

Efficient language minimizes the effort readers must use to discern its meaning. Uncommon and excessively long words (including jargon) and needlessly complex sentence structure not only waste readers' efforts but risk being misunderstood, thereby increasing the number of respondents who answer meaninglessly or not at all. Several authors (Hacker, 1989; Hadley, 1992; Lannon, 1982; Pinckert, 1981) have suggested substitutes for overlong expressions. Table 12.1 offers a few examples. It is also important to avoid the other extreme—excessively simple language that leaves respondents feeling talked down to or believing that the questionnaire must be for people less educated than themselves.

Slang compromises all three—precision, objectivity, and efficiency. Slang expressions have different meanings among different subpopulations (for example, geographic areas or age groups); readers aware of more than one meaning may waste time trying to figure out what is meant. Further, slang expressions carry surplus emotional meanings and are likely to offend some potential respondents, leading them not to respond.

Incorporating plans for analysis.   Each item must elicit responses that fit the way these responses are to be analyzed. For example, if the researcher intends to show the percentage of different samples of couples experiencing marital discord, the questionnaire needs to include a clearly discernible item enabling respondents to indicate whether or not they experience such discord. Multiple-choice responses can be analyzed by counting the number of respondents choosing each possible answer. Rating scales, attitude scales, and semantic differential scales permit numerical scoring. In contrast, answers to many open-ended items require content analysis. Such matters need to be borne in mind as each questionnaire item is written.

T A B L E   12.1
Some Long and Shorter Expressions

Long expressions	Shorter expressions
at the present time (2)	now
at present (2)	now
at this time (2)	now
at this point in time	now
in this day and age (4)	today
until such time as (1)	until
in a short period of time (2)	quickly, soon
of limited duration (2)	short, temporary
limited in length (2)	short
multiplicity of (3)	many
as well as (2)	and
bring to a conclusion (4)	conclude
entail a loss of (2)	reduce, sacrifice
to be cognizant (3)	to know
one and the same (4)	the same
each and every (4)	each
any and all (4)	any
undertake the implementation of (2)	begin, establish
reduction of fiscal allocations (2)	budget cuts
due to the fact that (1, 2, 4)	because
for the reason that (1)	because
in spite of the fact that (1, 4)	although
serves as an example of (2)	exemplifies
make inquiry (2)	ask
utilize (3)	use
terminate (3)	end

Note: Numbers in parentheses indicate sources from which examples are quoted: (1) *A Writer's Reference* (p. 98) by D. Hacker, 1989, New York: St. Martin's Press; (2) *Professional Counselor Reporting* (p. 6.27) by R. G. Hadley, 1992, Los Angeles: Author; (3) *Technical Writing* (p. 51) by J. M. Lannon, 1982, Boston: Prentice-Hall; and (4) *The Truth About English* (pp. 36–37) by R. C. Pinckert, 1981, Englewood Cliffs, NJ: Prentice-Hall.

Introducing a questionnaire.   A mailed questionnaire requires a **transmittal letter.** Questionnaires distributed by hand may be accompanied by a brief transmittal letter or an oral explanation, or both. Whatever the vehicle of introduction, the explanation offered should both appeal to prospective respondents and inform them about the purpose of the questionnaire, the auspices under which it is being distributed, the amount of time usually needed to answer it, and when and how it is to be returned. In terms meaningful to respondents, the letter or oral introduction should give them one or more reasons for responding and any instructions necessary in addition to those written on the questionnaire itself. This explanation should be short (letters preferably one page, at most two), and the letterhead and signature should lend prestige and official status. Readers are referred to Dillman (1978) for additional suggestions toward fulfilling the introductory vehicle's ultimate purpose—maximizing the response rate.

Many different appeals have been used to induce prospective respondents to answer questionnaires, including a "sense of professional responsibility, intellectual curiosity, and personal worth" (Isaac & Michael, 1981, p. 136). Dillman (1978) noted that questionnaire researchers have included many kinds of material things to encourage responding, such as lottery tickets, note pads, and money. An offer to send respondents a report of the results is often helpful. However, such a promise should only be made after careful thought, since the researcher is ethically obligated to keep it.

Providing for return.   Having answered the questionnaire, respondents need to know how to return it. The easier it is for them to do so, the more likely they will. Return instructions should be written on the questionnaire form in a conspicuous place, whether or not they are also included in the transmittal letter or oral introduction. Respondents often discard transmittal letters and forget details of oral instructions before they finish answering. Mailed returns need a deadline date and a pre-addressed postpaid envelope or reply card.

Ensuring compatibility with plans for follow-up.   A questionnaire and accompanying instructions need to be written in a manner compatible with follow-up plans. One of the most important decisions in this regard is whether respondents will be asked to identify themselves or invited to answer anonymously. A later section discusses following up nonrespondents to increase response rate.

Conducting a pilot study.   Even if interviews were carried out as a pilot study before the questionnaire writing task was begun, we recommend one or more pilot studies with a draft form of the questionnaire before it is printed in final form for the main study. This process serves three purposes: (a) identifies ambiguous, overly demanding, or redundant items; (b) allows an estimate of time required to respond, and (c) establishes a format that makes the questionnaire as easy as possible to answer and the answers easy to analyze.

Format

Individual items and the questionnaire as a whole both deserve careful attention to ensure that every respondent knows what to do with every item and to maximize response rate.

Item format.   To the extent feasible, questionnaire items should require responses no more complex than check marks or one or two words. Open-ended questions asking respondents to formulate long answers tend to discourage them from answering.

Based primarily on Dillman (1978), we offer this taxonomy of item structures:

- Closed-ended
  - Ordered response choices
  - Unordered response choices
- Partially closed-ended
- Open-ended
  - Short answers of less than one sentence
  - One-sentence answers
  - Answers longer than one sentence

Closed-ended items give respondents a set of answer possibilities from which to choose; respondents are not invited to answer in any other way than choosing among the available alternatives. The multiple-choice items on many familiar aptitude and achievement tests and interest inventories illustrate a closed-ended format. The closed-ended category is subdivided according to whether the available alternatives can be arranged in an obviously meaningful order, such as quantities (for example, number of children, years of experience, salary ranges) or not (for example, academic majors, makes of automobiles, names of an agency's counselors). When a meaningful order underlies the answer possibilities, the format is **ordered,** otherwise it is **unordered.**

Open-ended items call upon respondents to construct their own answers. **Partially closed-ended** items mix these two formats. Respondents have a set of answer possibilities from which to choose and in addition are either invited to add other answers of their own making, if so inclined, or asked to amplify certain of the previously written answer possibilities if these answers are chosen. We have subdivided open-ended items according to the length of response invited. Though this underlying dimension is a continuum, we have arbitrarily chosen division points of longer and shorter than one sentence. Table 12.2 illustrates these item formats. The "travel" item appearing later in this section also illustrates the partially closed-ended format but with unordered answer choices. That item is partially closed-ended because one answer choice ["Other (specify)"] asks respondents choosing this answer to add their own words.

Open-ended questions can be used in two ways. First, they can invite respondents to express themselves freely (for example, "What is the most difficult problem faced by students with physical disabilities on this campus?"). Second, open-ended questions are often used when a closed-ended format would involve an awkwardly large number of possible answers. "What is your major field of study?" can be expressed as a **short-answer,** open-ended item requiring a response of only one or two words. A closed-ended item listing all majors that a university offers might take some respondents longer to read than to answer the open-ended version, and grouping the majors sacrifices some information (for example, the number majoring in psychology versus sociology). "What is your date of birth?"

T A B L E   12.2
Examples of Open-Ended and Closed-Ended Item Formats

Open-ended
What is your major field of study? (If undeclared, write "none") _____

Closed-ended, unordered choices
What is your major field of study?

_____ a social science (e.g., psychology, sociology)

_____ a physical science (e.g., physics, chemistry)

_____ a life science (e.g., biology, botany)

_____ a foreign language (e.g., Chinese, Spanish)

_____ a humanity (e.g., English, history)

_____ a fine art (e.g., music, painting)

_____ other major

_____ undeclared

Closed-ended, ordered choices
Including yourself, how many people in your household are gainfully employed?

_____ None

_____ One

_____ Two

_____ Three

_____ More than three

Partially closed-ended
Including yourself, how many people in your household are gainfully employed?

_____ None

_____ One

_____ Two

_____ Three

_____ More than three (How many? _____)

---

and "In what state or foreign country were you born?" are two other examples of open-ended items with short answers.

Open-ended items that ask for long, involved answers have a serious disadvantage in that they often demand too much of respondents. To answer such a question, respondents must think through not only the substance of a response but also the best way to express it. This effort deters many respondents. Further, respondents write with varying degrees of precision, and unclear answers are difficult to analyze. Word choices, sentence structure, and penmanship all contribute their share of unclarities. A researcher can expect any open-ended item to elicit at least a few illegibly handwritten responses; long answers are more often hard to read than shorter ones. For these reasons, we recommend that researchers consider interviewing as an alternative whenever tempted to write questionnaire items requiring respondents to construct long answers.

In closed-ended and partially closed-ended items, ordered answer choices should always be arranged in either ascending or descending order, never in scrambled order. Deciding how to arrange unordered answer choices usually requires more thought than arranging ordered choices. The arrangement should carefully avoid biasing respondents' answers. For example, we have seen student-written unordered answer choices arranged in order of the writer's own preferences, thus risking bias by suggesting that a continuum of desirability underlies the choices.

Here are some additional suggestions to ensure that every respondent knows what to do with every item. First, **double-barreled** items, which include two questions in one, should be avoided (Sax, 1989). An example of this fault would be to ask teachers, "Do you have excessive absenteeism and tardiness in your classroom?" Double-barreled items do not represent a good way to shorten a questionnaire. Rather, they are likely to confuse some respondents. How should a teacher with excessive tardiness but no absenteeism answer the example in this paragraph?

Second, the answer possibilities for closed-ended items must be inclusive and nonoverlapping. The following example illustrates a problem due to noninclusiveness.

How often do you buy candy from a vending machine on campus?

_____ Once a day

_____ Once a week

_____ Once a month

_____ Never

How should a respondent answer who buys candy six times a day, twice a week, or only on Halloween, for example? One solution to this problem is to include in the instructions a provision such as, "If none of the answers given is exactly right for you, mark the one that comes closest." Alternatively, the answer possibilities might be changed to something like the following:

_____ At least once a day most days

_____ Several times a week

_____ Several times a month

_____ Several times a year

_____ Once or twice a year

_____ Rarely; less than once a year

_____ Never

Admittedly, "several times" is less precise than we might wish. The following version achieves this precision, but at a cost; we suspect it would intimidate some respondents.

On average, how many times a month do you buy candy from a vending machine on campus?

_____ 30 or more

_____ 15–29

_____ 1–14

_____ Occasionally; less than once a month

_____ Never

This version clearly illustrates a nonoverlapping relationship among the answer possibilities. The word "occasionally" in the next to last choice addresses the fact that "never" is less than once a month. The following answer choices illustrate a careless overlapping that should be scrupulously avoided:

_____ 30 or more

_____ 15–30

_____ 1–15

_____ One or less

How should a respondent answer if the correct number is exactly 30, 15, or one?

A third issue also concerns some closed-ended items. Respondents must know whether they should choose only one of the choices offered or mark all that apply. In the above item about buying candy, this point is clear without specific attention to it. Such is not always the case. The following item is ambiguous.

How do you travel to and from school?

_____ Walk

_____ Bus

_____ Own car

_____ By car, riding with others

_____ Bicycle (pedal-powered)

_____ Motorcycle, motor scooter, or motorized bicycle

_____ Other (specify) _____

A better way to phrase this item would be to use one of the two following revisions:

How do you travel to and from school? Mark _all_ the ways you have used so far this term.

_____ Walk

_____ Bus

_____ Own car

_____ By car, riding with others

_____ Bicycle (pedal-powered)

_____ Motorcycle, motor scooter, or motorized bicycle

_____ Other (specify) _____

How do you usually travel to and from school? Mark the *one* way you use *most often*.

_____ Walk

_____ Bus

_____ Own car

_____ By car, riding with others

_____ Bicycle (pedal-powered)

_____ Motorcycle, motor scooter or motorized bicycle

_____ Other (specify) _____

Arrangement of the questionnaire as a whole. Material that logically belongs together should be placed together. Controversial or sensitive material should be placed toward the end. To the extent possible without violating these considerations, items that are easiest to answer should be placed first. Dillman (1978) recommended that the first item should be interesting and applicable to every potential respondent.

Sometimes logical placement involves sections to be answered only by certain respondents. If a questionnaire has some items that do not apply to all respondents, special care may be needed to ensure that everyone knows what to do with every item. For example, single respondents should omit an item that asks whether respondent and spouse share certain household chores. Only respondents with children should answer items about their parenting behavior. One approach to this situation is to divide the questionnaire into sections (for example, one section for everyone, a second section for one sex, and a third for the other); the sections are clearly identified with instructions such as "Men only answer this section; women answer items 10–14 below." This is a good solution unless there are so many sections that the questionnaire becomes forbiddingly complex. A second approach calls for a sentence in the instructions advising respondents to skip any item that does not apply. This solution has the disadvantage of requiring respondents to read items irrelevant to them; some will probably react by deciding to discard the whole questionnaire. We have no recommendation to offer as a perfect solution. Rather, a researcher has the task of making the best choices for each specific project.

Follow-Up

To maximize rate of return, it is necessary to follow up nonrespondents. For mailed questionnaires to be returned by mail, Dillman (1978) recommended the following follow-up plan:

1. At one week after the original mailout, send a postcard reminder to everyone.
2. At three weeks, send a letter and replacement questionnaire to nonrespondents only.
3. At seven weeks, send nonrespondents a letter and replacement questionnaire by certified mail.

Dillman (1978) listed 38 studies using his method with return rates ranging from 50% to 94%. Isaac and Michael (1981) cited a National Education Association study that achieved a 64.3% response rate about 14 days after the original mailing, when a follow-up letter was sent. The return rate increased to 83.6% within the next 14 days, and to 96.8% after a second follow-up letter. A third follow-up elicited no further increase in response rate.

If questionnaire respondents identify themselves, it is easy to compile a list of nonrespondents for follow-up. Anonymous questionnaires make this task more difficult. There are several approaches to this problem. The easiest is to mail follow-up correspondence to everyone, thanking those who have responded and asking those who have not to do so. Cost is one disadvantage of this procedure. A second disadvantage is that some people who receive follow-up correspondence do not remember whether they returned the questionnaire or not. Alternatively, the original mailing can include both an envelope for returning the completed questionnaire and a separate business reply postcard with a message such as "I have returned my questionnaire separately" and provision for the respondent's name.

Some projects put a code number on each copy of the blank questionnaire before it is mailed out; a computer or a clerical worker can use these numbers to compile a nonrespondent mailing list after replies have come in without associating anyone's replies with the person who gave them. Various schemes have been developed for covertly identifying respondents after they were invited to answer anonymously; though this practice may have been common in past decades, it violates current ethical standards.

INTERVIEWS

Many of our recommendations for writing questionnaires also apply to planning interview studies.

- Before beginning to plan an interview, have clearly in mind the project's mission and the interview's role in fulfilling that mission.
- While deciding what to include in an interview, keep its purposes clearly in mind and its content focused.
- Never adopt an existing interview plan without first determining that it is as well suited to the project at hand as a newly developed one would be.
- Bear issues of privacy and confidentiality clearly in mind while planning the interview content and interviewing procedures.

- Make the interview no longer or more demanding for respondents than is necessary to fulfill the project's mission.
- Use precise, objective, and efficient language.
- While planning an interview, bear in mind the ways answers will be analyzed and plan it so it will elicit answers amenable to the intended analyses.
- Arrange the material within the interview to maximize respondent cooperation.
- Include an appropriate introduction.
- Try out planned interview content and procedures in a pilot study before conducting interviews for the main study.

Interviewing is a labor-intensive procedure but is preferable to questionnaires for some projects, such as:

- studies of young children or other respondents who cannot answer questionnaires meaningfully,
- projects with largely exploratory missions, and
- studies in which it is important to observe the environments and behavior of respondents as they answer questions.

It takes more time to prepare and conduct interviews than to prepare and distribute a comparable number of questionnaires. In all but the smallest projects relying primarily on their individual researchers' own efforts, interviewers must be paid; hence, more labor-intensive also means higher cost. For this reason, questionnaires are usually more cost-effective than interviews when either technique would answer the project's research questions equally well.

Demand characteristics represent a second potential disadvantage for interviews. Many factors, such as interviewer race, social status, age, gender, dress, and grooming, can affect responses. Social norms influence how people react to all these factors; in most research projects, these influences represent demand characteristics discussed in Chapter 9.

Rater bias (also discussed in Chapter 9) is a third potential problem. Interviewers' own attitudes may affect their recording of interview data, especially in situations that call for their judgment.

An interview may serve as a project's main instrument or as an exploratory tool for planning a project or as a supplement to other methods (for example, following up unusual or unclear questionnaire responses). An interview may be conducted entirely for research purposes, or research elements may be added to interviews carried out for other purposes, such as counseling or administration. (If unmodified counseling or administrative interviews are used as a data source, the data collection technique is observation or review of records rather than interviewing.)

Interviews differ from one another in many additional ways, including:

- interview structure,
- communication mode,

- individual versus group interviews, and
- recording method.

Regardless of these differences, most interview studies use a written interview guide, sometimes called an interview schedule or interview protocol. This document should never be called a questionnaire; to do so is imprecise and often misleading.

Interview Structure

Structured interviews. A **structured interview** consists of questions read verbatim from the interview guide. Interviewers are free to clarify some points, such as a word unfamiliar to a respondent, although they do not explore any material more deeply than stipulated in the guide. Some structured interviews include questions in multiple-choice format. When such questions have more than two or three answer possibilities, we recommend handing the respondent a card on which these possibilities are written. Many people have difficulty keeping a longer list in mind during oral delivery.

Unstructured interviews. At the other extreme, **unstructured interviews** usually begin with a very general question or probe, such as "Tell me about the experiences that led you to decide to seek counseling." The interviewer is then allowed to explore the topic freely, usually following the respondent's lead. Such unstructured interviews are often very useful in exploratory or pilot studies; we prefer more structure in most main studies.

Semistructured interviews. Many interviews in studies of counseling are **semistructured interviews**; the interview guide stipulates the points to be covered and may include some questions to be read verbatim. Interviewers are free to vary the phrasing of most questions and to explore points more deeply than stipulated in the guide. Such further exploration is also permitted when respondents' initial answers are less clear or less complete than the interviewer believes desirable. Semistructured interviews vary widely in their degree of structuring; some closely approximate structured interviews, others are almost unstructured.

Interviewer requirements. Semistructured and unstructured interviews require more interviewing skill than structured ones. To conduct a structured interview, the interviewer must select questions according to written instructions, read them verbatim to maximize respondent cooperation, and record the answers given. Semistructured and unstructured formats require an interviewer to be sensitive and responsive to the answers given and decide when and how to explore answers further. Any research interviewer must know his or her own biases to minimize their intrusion in the interview and data recording process. This kind of objectivity requires great skill in unstructured interviews and only somewhat less in semistructured interviews. Some studies require interviewers to be specifically trained for the project.

Communication Mode

When planning an interview study, a researcher must decide whether to talk to respondents by telephone or in person. Each method has advantages and limitations. Telephoning has two major advantages. First, the telephone offers greater speed and convenience at less cost than face-to-face interviews. These advantages are enhanced if respondents are most accessible during predictable times, such as evenings and weekends, or if callbacks are required. Second, many respondents feel more at ease on the telephone than with an interviewer in person.

Disadvantages of telephoning include the fact that not everyone has a telephone. In addition, as many as 25% of the intended sample may have unlisted telephones (Isaac & Michael, 1981). A further disadvantage is that some potential respondents may refuse to cooperate with a telephone interviewer because they suspect that the caller who claims to be conducting a research interview has dishonest motives or is trying to sell something.

An advantage of face-to-face interviews is that interviewers can observe respondents' environment and nonverbal behavior during interviews. Most counselors are well practiced in using nonverbal cues to guide exploration of clients' concerns. These cues can be similarly helpful in semistructured and unstructured research interviews and may provide additional data if observational techniques are also used. Telephone interviewers lose these opportunities.

One disadvantage of face-to-face interviews is that they are subject to more demand characteristics. As noted earlier in this section, interview responses can be affected by social norms related to such factors as interviewer race, social status, age, gender, dress, and grooming. Some of these influences (for example, dress and grooming) are totally absent in telephone interviews. Another disadvantage of face-to-face interviews is that personality conflicts arise more often in face-to-face encounters than over the telephone. Skilled interviewing reduces their likelihood, regardless of interview mode.

An important point common to the disadvantages of telephone interviewing is biased sampling. An often-cited example is a 1936 telephone survey predicting that Alf Landon would defeat Franklin Roosevelt by a wide margin in that year's presidential election. Sampling bias was important because the more affluent voters more often had telephones and more often voted Republican. Some of these demographics have changed in the intervening decades; the underlying principles have not. A much larger proportion of the U.S. population now have telephones, and those who don't are an even more unrepresentative group. More important, people who have unlisted numbers are also an unrepresentative group. A study based on directory listings would overlook a disproportionate number of single women, for example.

The fact that a caller's motives may be questioned is important for two reasons. First, sampling may be biased. The study loses any potential respondents who hang up on unknown callers as suspected salespeople or possible burglars. These people probably differ in important ways from others who react differently to unknown callers. Second, respondents are likely to give distorted answers if they fear true answers might be used to support a burglary or an unwanted sales pitch.

Individual versus Group Interviews

Individual interviews are used much more often in counseling research than are group interviews. However, group interviews are much less time-consuming and expensive than individual interviews for the same number of respondents. And they have an additional advantage in that one respondent can introduce an issue and all respondents' ideas about it can then be discussed. For these reasons, group interviews can be particularly useful in exploratory studies. Focus groups (Krueger, 1988; Morgan, 1988) represent one approach. A focus group usually comprises "seven to ten people" and is "designed to obtain perceptions on a defined area of interest in a permissive, nonthreatening environment. . . . [P]articipants share their ideas and perceptions [and] influence each other by responding to ideas and comments in the discussion" (Krueger, 1988, p. 18). Despite their advantages, group interviews introduce many demand characteristics of their own. For example, some respondents may withhold or change the expression of their views in response to group pressure.

Recording Methods

Several possibilities exist for recording interview responses. Respondents' answers can be recorded on paper during the interview. A copy of the interview guide or a separate record form may be used for this purpose. Alternatively, interviews can be recorded electronically and the playback used for posting the answers on paper or entering the data into a computer. Or respondents' answers can be entered directly into a computer as they are given. Easily portable laptop and notebook-size computers expand the range of situations in which this practice is possible.

Each of these options has its advantages and limitations. Making a written record of answers as they are given is much less time-consuming than listening to a playback, although it may divert some of the interviewer's attention away from the respondent. Electronic recording permits more than one person to listen to the answers. This opportunity is valuable if a significant amount of judgment is required to interpret the answers given since it allows reliability of these judgments to be measured.

If a single interviewer makes these judgments from an ongoing interview without an electronic recording, the opportunity to measure their reliability is lost. However, if a researcher relies entirely on an electronic recording, an equipment malfunction can lose whole interviews. Also, some respondents become suspicious of recording equipment. To record an interview without the respondent's knowledge and consent is ethically objectionable. As with just about everything else in a research plan, a method of recording interview data should be selected that best fits the specific project at hand, taking many factors into account. Pilot studies are often very helpful with such decisions.

For additional discussion of research interviewing, see Kvale (1983), McCracken (1988), Mishler (1986), and Spradley (1979).

RATING SCALES

A rating scale is an instrument that requires one or more judges "to assign the rated object to categories or continua" (Kerlinger, 1986, p. 494) that usually have numbers attached to them. The "object" is not necessarily a thing, but may be a person, a group, a plan, a document, a set of behaviors, or an idea, to name a few of many possibilities. The numbers are not always immediately evident to raters; they are often applied afterward by the researcher. Three frequent examples of rating scales are:

- A, B, C, D, and F grades in school,
- public opinion polls asking respondents to rate the performance of elected officials; and
- systems used by employers to rate employees' job performance.

A moment's reflection will probably bring to mind many more.

Rating scales are sometimes used alone as a data source. More often, they are integrated into other methods. Questionnaires and interview record forms often include rating scales. Many observation schedules use rating scales either as their only form of data or in combination with other forms. Studies based on official records or other documents sometimes include ratings in a content analysis process. Ratings are sometimes used to translate physical traces into data amenable to statistical analysis.

Some projects call for participants to make ratings; some call for ratings by the researcher or by other judges. A list of every use to which rating scales have been put would be very long indeed; a few examples are listed here:

- Interviewers rate job applicants' behavior along a passive-assertive-aggressive dimension.
- University students rate the clarity with which their instructor defines course goals and tasks.
- Clients rate the extent to which counseling met their needs.
- Accrediting bodies rate a facility's compliance with established standards.
- A supervisor rates the quality of products made by workers he or she supervises.

- Judges rate the extent to which counseling clients' educational and vocational plans are consistent with measured aptitudes and interests.
- Clients rate their counselors' interview behavior with regard to empathy, warmth, respect, and genuineness.
- University faculty rate administrative officers' supportiveness, helpfulness, and compliance with affirmative-action guidelines.
- An advocacy organization rates various buildings as to ease of access by people with disabilities.
- Employees rate their satisfaction/dissatisfaction with various aspects of their jobs such as pay, advancement opportunity, work tasks, and physical conditions of work.
- Judges review agency files of closed cases and rate parents' cooperativeness/resistiveness in carrying out strategies for disciplining their children in a nonpunitive manner.

The term *rating scale* is sometimes used to refer to one item that asks for a rating and sometimes to a set of such items related by an underlying construct and designed so that responses can be combined into a score. In this chapter, we refer to the first of these meanings unless the second meaning is very clear from context. Many of the examples we listed call for more than one rating scale.

Format

We will discuss eight formats for rating scales: (a) category scales, (b) numerical scales, (c) graphic scales, (d) Likert scales, (e) forced-choice instruments, (f) checklists, (g) nomination procedures, and (h) semantic differential scales.

Category, numerical, and graphic scales.   A category scale is a multiple-choice item such as the following illustration modified from Kerlinger (1986, p. 494):

How careful is she at work? (Check one)
_____ Very careful
_____ Careful
_____ Not careful
_____ Not at all careful.

Adding the numbers 3, 2, 1, 0 or 4, 3, 2, 1 to these answer choices would convert this item to a numerical format. Such numbers create the impression of an equal-interval scale and can be readily analyzed statistically. If participants are asked to rate several people or several dimensions, it is often helpful to use a similar numerical scale for each.

In a **graphic rating scale,** this "careful" item might look like this (adapted from Kerlinger, 1986, p. 495):

| Very | Careful | Not | Not at all |
| careful | | careful | careful |

Respondents are asked to place a check mark anywhere along the line in the position that best describes the person or behavior being rated. For statistical analysis purposes, numbers such as 0, 10, 20, and 30 can be assigned to the vertical markers on this scale and a ruler used to measure the location of each respondent's check mark. Kerlinger (1986) noted that these scales have the advantages of being clear and easy to use and that they suggest equal intervals and a continuum to the observer. He also noted that they can be structured with such variations as vertical segmented lines, continuous lines, and lines broken into marked equal intervals (as above), among other alternatives.

Likert scales. A variation on category scales is provided by the **Likert** summated ratings format. An item employing the Likert summated ratings format is a statement with answer choices reflecting strength of agreement or disagreement and looks like this:

SA A U D SD Students who are hard of hearing should have reserved seats in the front row of every classroom.
SA A U D SD Blind students should be allowed to take notes in Braille during lectures, even though the process is somewhat noisy.
SA A U D SD Colleges should not have to admit students who are so disabled they need special help to do college work.

The letters to the left of each statement represent strongly *agree*, *agree*, *undecided*, *disagree*, and strongly *disagree*. "N" (neutral) or "?" is sometimes used for the middle position rather than "U." Five is the most common number of answer choices. Some scales reduce this number to four by eliminating the middle position; others add "VSA" (very strongly agree) and "VSD" (very strongly disagree) to provide six or seven choices, often with the intent of increasing reliability. Each answer choice is given a score value depending on the position expressed in the item. In the first two of the above three examples, SA, A, U, D, and SD might be assigned score values of 4, 3, 2, 1, and 0 respectively (or 5, 4, 3, 2, and 1); the third item expresses an opposite view, therefore its answer choices would be scored 0, 1, 2, 3, and 4 (or 1, 2, 3, 4, and 5). Omitted items are usually assigned a neutral score. The score values of all responses are then added to yield the respondent's score for the scale.

The Likert summated rating format is the most common category scale used in counseling research, probably because it is so easy to construct and because it is so often used for attitude scales. The "object" of an attitude scale is usually a group or kind of people (such as ethnic minorities, women, people with a penal history, people with disabilities) or a social institution (such as the church, family life, or public schools). Variations on the format are often used. For example, Lam and Chan (1988) asked respondents of limited intellectual ability to express how they felt by pointing to one of five drawn faces ranging from a broad smile to an intense frown.

Forced-choice scales.   A **forced-choice** scale presents respondents with two, three, or four descriptions and asks them to choose which is most characteristic of the person or behavior being rated, for example:

_____ Conscientious about starting times and break periods

_____ Carefully observant of safety rules

_____ Careful about product quality

In some such scales with three or four descriptions, respondents are also asked to indicate the one that is least characteristic. A common practice is to ask them to write "most" and "least" or "M" and "L" in the appropriate places. The forced-choice format differs from the category format in that categories generally represent an underlying dimension, while forced choices do not. The forced-choice technique has been used successfully to reduce problems such as the halo effect and over- or underrating tendencies. However, it often yields less reliable results than most other methods.

Checklists, nominations, and ranking.   A **checklist** is probably the simplest rating format. Respondents are given a list of adjectives or other descriptions and asked to check all those that are true of the person or behavior being rated. **Nomination** procedures are suitable when raters are to make comparisons among several individuals in a group. Raters are given a description and asked to name the one person (sometimes more than one) who best fits it. For example, counselors might be asked, "Among your open cases, who is the client you most enjoy working with?"

We consider ranking a nomination technique; respondents are asked to list all the individuals in the group in rank order according to the degree to which they fit the description. Alternatively, the researcher may list names and ask respondents to assign rank numbers to the names. The "open cases" example would then read as follows: "List all your open cases in rank order according to how much you enjoy working with each client. List in first place the client you most enjoy."

Ranking becomes progressively more difficult as the number of individuals to be ranked increases. Counselors with caseloads of 10 could probably answer the item in this illustration easily, although it would be impractical with counselors who carry open caseloads of 100.

Semantic differential.   Semantic differential is a variety of rating scale that has been used to measure attitudes, but it also has some unique properties. A concept is expressed with one or more words, and respondents are asked to rate it on each of a set of polar adjective pairs. We quote four of six adjective pairs from an example offered by Cohen, Swerdlik, and Smith (1992, p. 438):

Myself

Warm	___ : ___ : ___ : ___ : ___ : ___ : ___ Cold
Tense	___ : ___ : ___ : ___ : ___ : ___ : ___ Relaxed
Optimistic	___ : ___ : ___ : ___ : ___ : ___ : ___ Pessimistic
Frugal	___ : ___ : ___ : ___ : ___ : ___ : ___ Extravagant

In the semantic differential technique, each adjective pair defines a graphic rating scale. The scale positions between the members of each adjective pair are not defined. According to its originator, the number of scale positions should be the same for each adjective pair and should be not less than five nor more than nine, with seven as the optimum number for most purposes (Osgood, Suci, & Tannenbaum, 1957). Respondents may be asked to rate several concepts according to the same set of adjective pairs; in such cases, each concept should be on a new page. The concepts rated need not be abstract ideas, but may be people (for example, myself, my boss), organizations (for example, the American Counseling Association), or ideals (for example, "myself as I would like to be 10 years from now"), to name a few possibilities. Osgood et al. (1957) developed a method for scoring ratings given to a set of adjective pairs to yield scores on three scales: evaluative (such as good–bad), potency (such as hard–soft), and activity (such as fast–slow).

We offer a word of caution: Respondents must think abstractly if this technique is to yield meaningful results. An illustration comes from a student who asked a group of "educable mentally retarded" participants to rate the concept "mother." With regard to the adjective pair "warm–cold," one respondent proudly asked, "Where do you mark 98.6?"

Recommendations to Researchers

In counseling research, the most frequent use of rating scales is to record judgments of people's traits (for example, warmth, hostility, social skill) or their behavior. Used in this manner, a good rating scale will elicit roughly similar ratings from different judges who observe the same people or phenomena. To this end, we offer these recommendations:

- Make the *dimensions* to be rated clear.
- Make clear any *standards* raters are expected to use.
- Make the meaning of answer choices clear.

The following subsections elaborate these points.

Making dimensions clear. Raters need to know what they are looking for. For example, if counseling clients were asked to rate their counselors' "competence," we would expect different people to base their ratings on different factors. One client might give particular weight to whether the counselor had immediate answers to factual questions; another to recognition of the client's emotional concerns; a third to grammar, word usage, and sentence structure; a fourth to a general appearance of emotional comfort in the session. If one is studying the correlates of such "competence" ratings, well and good. But if the ratings are used as measures of counselor performance, "competence" as a dimension is too vague. The "passive-assertive-aggressive" example used earlier in this chapter illustrates another clarity issue. The concept may be very clear to people familiar with the relevant literature. However, if the judges making the ratings do not have this knowledge, the concept must be explained to be clear to them. Clarifying the dimensions to be rated reduces vulnerability to the halo effect and other rater issues discussed in Chapter 9.

Making standards clear.   Words such as "superior," "good," "adequate," and "poor" imply a standard against which the behavior rated is to be compared: Superior to what, adequate for what? Words such as "average" imply a group of people whose behavior is used as a standard of comparison. For example, an instructor might rate a student counselor's clarification responses as "average" compared to experienced professional counselors or "superior" compared to beginning trainees or "above average" in comparison with other trainees at the student's own experience level. If raters are not told what comparison group a researcher wants them to use, they will choose for themselves. When different raters choose different comparison standards, these choices are confounded with the ratings and reliability is reduced. Raters' comparison groups for ratings are analogous to norms of standardized tests and inventories.

Making answer choices clear.   Sometimes this matter is taken care of automatically when the dimension to be rated and the intended comparison standard are clarified, as is usually the case with Likert scales. Because such is not always the case, a researcher should give this matter separate attention. For illustration, we return to the example item in which raters were asked to determine whether someone was "very careful," "careful," "not careful," or "not at all careful" at work. As a rater, you might clearly understand the carefulness dimension and be instructed to use the ratee's co-workers as a comparison standard. Nonetheless, raters must still define for themselves the boundaries between the categories. What kind of behavior should be called "careful" versus "very careful," or "not careful" versus "not at all careful"?

Reliability can be increased if raters are given sample descriptions of behavior illustrating each category, such as is done in the scoring standards for the Wechsler intelligence scales. This increased reliability has its cost. Such sample descriptions lengthen the raters' task, particularly when it includes many ratings. A graphic rating scale is often (but not always) sufficiently clear if only the end points are given sample behavior descriptions and the idea of equal intervals is allowed to carry this burden regarding the intermediate scale points.

Further recommendations. Clearly, constructing a rating scale requires many decisions. How is a beginning researcher to make them? First, do not choose rating scales too quickly, primarily because they seem easy to write. Like any other method, rating scales should be chosen only when they best fit the project at hand. Next, make the raters' task as easy as possible consistent with the needs of the project. Third, carefully address all the rater issues discussed in Chapter 9. Each of these should be considered for its bearing on the various decisions involved in constructing or choosing the project's rating scales. When important decisions still remain, conduct one or more pilot studies; administer possible variations to a few raters and then use semistructured interviews to explore their experience with the task. When rating scales are the method of choice, Kerlinger (1986) recommended that the researcher "study the characteristics of good rating scales, work with painstaking care, and subject rating results to empirical test and adequate statistical analysis" (p. 495). Sax (1989) provides a more detailed treatment of these issues.

Observation Systems

When observation is the method of data collection, a researcher may choose among several kinds of systems for making and recording observations. An observer can (a) *note whether or not* a behavior of a given kind took place, (b) *count* the number of times it occurred, (c) *rate* observed behavior according to one or more rating scales, (d) apply *physical measurement* such as time (for example, from the beginning of a behavior to its end) or distance, or (e) combine two or more of these methods. In exploratory studies, observation is often much less structured than this list implies; observers watch for phenomena and behavior characteristics that strike them as worth studying more systematically. As noted in Chapter 2, this procedure is common in qualitative research. Some qualitative projects begin in this way and then proceed to more systematic study based on the outcomes of this preliminary phase. Numerous examples of systematic observation systems are discussed in Sulzer-Azaroff and Mayer (1991). The more complex an observer's task, the more likely he or she must be specifically trained to do it.

An observation schedule is a written form on which observations are recorded. It may be presented on paper or on a computer screen. Such a schedule and its accompanying instructions make up the instrument that embodies the observation system.

Observers, like raters, must know what behavior they are attending to and how they should record what they observe. We draw from Sulzer-Azaroff and Mayer's (1991) example in which observers tallied a child's incidents of "disruptive" behavior in the classroom. To record such behavior reliably, observers must have clear definitions; a set of such definitions is called a taxonomy. The term *disruptive* requires that several issues must be decided to develop a satisfactory observation schedule; we list a few.

1. What behaviors will be considered disruptive? In Sulzer-Azaroff and Mayer's (1991) example, loud noises, such as screeching, shouting, hitting furniture, and rattling chairs, were chosen for recording. However, these are not the only classroom behaviors most teachers would consider disruptive; others that come to mind are whispering, getting out of seat without permission, and unauthorized physical contact with classmates.

2. Will the behaviors chosen for recording be classified, and if so, how? In this example, disruptive behaviors might be classified as "verbal," "physical," and "nonverbal noise." Whispering is "verbal"; so is shouting a clear verbal message. Shouting an unintelligible sound and screeching are "nonverbal noise"; hitting a classmate and getting out of seat are "physical."

3. How are unclear boundaries between categories to be defined? In this example, should noisily moving a piece of furniture be called "physical" or "nonverbal noise"? Should observers be asked to judge whether movement or noise is the most important feature of each such behavior? Are obscene gestures "verbal" or "physical," since some are regarded as translatable into verbal messages?

4. How should observers treat threatening to do something rather than doing it (in this example, threatening to be disruptive)?

The more clearly these questions are answered, the more likely the project is to have reliable results. Once these questions are answered, an observation schedule must be developed upon which observations can be recorded.

The type of schedule developed depends primarily on the observational systems to be used. The following subsections discuss event recording, duration recording, interval time-sample recording, rating, the mechanics of observing behavior, and self-monitoring.

Event Recording

Event recording, sometimes known as frequency recording, requires simply counting the number of times a behavior or other event (for example, a thought) occurs within a given period of time. The time period chosen might be 10 minutes, an hour, a day, a week, or any other interval. Observation schedules are usually relatively simple for event recording. An observer studying only one or two kinds of behavior might simply make a check mark on a piece of paper each time the behavior being studied occurs, or use wrist or hand counters. Checklists enable a larger variety of behaviors to be counted on the same schedule. Event recording is most suitable for behaviors that have discrete beginning and end points and do not vary greatly in duration (such as spitting).

Duration Recording

To observe not only how often a behavior or other activity occurs but also how long it lasts, duration recording is the observational system of choice. For example, suppose that "tantrumming" was one of the disruptive behaviors of concern. To borrow from an example presented by Sulzer-Azaroff and Mayer (1991), a child might tantrum for three 5-minute periods on Wednesday, but only once on Thursday, even though the Thursday tantrum lasted over an hour. Did tantrumming increase or decrease? Most casual observers would say it increased, but recording a single session of tantrumming on Thursday would suggest a dramatic decrease. When behavior duration is of concern, duration recording can be used to study it. The duration of numerous activities of interest can be recorded: studying, conversations, exercising, crying, and time on task, to name a few. Relatively simple observation schedules can be developed to record such activities; a stopwatch, wristwatch, or other common timepiece can be used to identify elapsed time or starting and ending times. Duration recording is often combined with event recording as in the "tantrumming" example. In contrast, some projects use duration recording alone, such as recording a sheltered workshop client's total time on task during a shift but not the number of work periods or interruptions. A stopwatch is easy to stop and restart repeatedly for this purpose.

Interval Time-Sample Recording

Event and duration recording are appropriate for behaviors that have easily identifiable starting and ending points, known as **discrete** behaviors (Sulzer-Azaroff & Mayer, 1991). Behaviors without clear starting and ending points (such as cooperative play) are called **continuous.** When observing children on a playground, it is easy to identify the beginning and the end of a fist fight, for example, but often extremely difficult to determine when one episode of cooperative play ends and another begins. For studying behaviors that are more or less continuous, interval time-sample recording strategies are extremely useful. To use these strategies, a period of time (for example, 1 hour) is divided into intervals (for example, 60 seconds). The observer usually observes only for the majority of the interval (for example, 45 seconds) and records during the remaining period of the interval. Whether an incident gets recorded depends on the particular time-sampling strategy selected. With whole interval time sampling, the activity of interest must occur throughout the entire interval. For the cooperative play example, the child must be playing cooperatively for the entire 45 seconds for an incidence of cooperative play to be recorded. With partial interval time sampling, only a single instance of the activity is necessary for cooperative play to be recorded. For example, if the child hands another child a toy once during the 45 seconds, cooperative play would be recorded for that interval even if he or she plays alone otherwise. Finally, in momentary time-sampling, the behavior is recorded if it is occurring at the moment the observation interval ends, whether or not it has occurred at other moments during the interval. The time-sampling features of these recording strategies were discussed in more detail in Chapter 10.

A pilot study with multiple observers often helps a researcher test and refine the taxonomy and sampling scheme and estimate its reliability. Reliability is usually estimated by having two or more people simultaneously observe the behaviors of interest for a specified period of time. Interobserver reliability, or percentage of agreement, is then calculated using the formula:

$$\% \text{ agreement} = \frac{A}{(A + D)} \times 100$$

where A = number of agreements and D = number of disagreements.

Sulzer-Azaroff and Mayer (1991) provide an extensive discussion of these observational systems. They are especially widely used in behavioral and cognitive-behavioral counseling but are often used in other approaches as well. Last but not least, the researcher must decide how to analyze the data. Sackett (1978, v. 2) provides a detailed discussion of data collection and analysis issues that can be applied to any observation project, although it was developed in a center for people with developmental disabilities.

Rating

Behaviors can be observed for many other variables than frequency and duration. Intensity is a common one. To return to the "tantrumming" example, much more energy is required to yell and flail the fists than to pout and sulk. Variables such as these can be included in an observational study by incorporating one or more rating scales in the observation schedule. Ratings can be combined with event recording, event and duration recording together, or interval time-sample recording.

Mechanics of Observing Behavior

A researcher can observe behavior as it takes place or watch a tape or film record, or both. Each of these choices has its advantages. Direct observation is not limited to what the camera or tape recorder picks up. However, a tape or film record can be stopped, played back, slowed down, or the like to allow more refined measures than can be carried out reliably with direct observation. A handheld computer can make some tasks of an observer's job easier (Elias, 1984).

Reactive effects also deserve consideration. To what extent and in what ways is the observation process likely to affect the phenomena being studied? Are participants more likely to behave in their usual way with a live observer or a camera present in the room? If a camera is used, the researcher must provide for its operation. An operator represents an additional person in the room unless facilities for remote recording are available. If a counselor or teacher operates this equipment, will this task distract from his or her normal functions?

Haynes and Horn (1982) recommended several strategies for reducing reactive effects. The most common is to provide a period of adaptation for all observational systems. After the schedule is developed and in use, or the equipment is present at the site, a period of adaptation helps to reduce reactive effects as participants grow used to the presence of observers or equipment and revert to their customary behavior.

Self-Monitoring

Clients can be asked to monitor their own experience or behavior, or both, as part of a counseling intervention. In this observation technique, a client is both observer and participant. Barlow, Hayes, and Nelson (1984) noted that this technique can be used with a wide range of clients and a wide range of problems to offer "measures of client progress" (p. 95). As in any observation study, **self-monitoring** requires that specific target behaviors be chosen and defined; "the client then records the occurrences of the selected problems or behaviors as they happen" (p. 95). This target behavior need not be overt physical acts; self-monitoring may also be applied to thoughts and feelings. For example, clients in a smoking cessation program may be asked to record such experiences as intrusive thoughts about smoking and feelings in social situations when others smoke.

Barlow et al. (1984) discuss frequency counts, duration, and self-ratings as kinds of measures that can be used in self-monitoring; this source and Watson and Tharp (1992) give numerous specific examples. Self-monitoring requires a recording system, usually a record form. When constructing a form for recording frequency or duration, you should follow the relevant recommendations discussed earlier in this chapter. Self-ratings require rating scales, also discussed earlier in this chapter.

See Barlow et al. (1984) for ways to enhance compliance with self-monitoring procedures. In addition, this source noted that people usually change any behavior of which they keep careful records. Self-monitoring is very reactive. Therefore, such procedures are best regarded as part of an intervention rather than merely a method for collecting data to evaluate other treatment methods. "If self-monitoring is used, changes cannot be solely attributed to other treatment ingredients" (Barlow et al., 1984, p. 113).

CHAPTER SUMMARY

Instruments used to collect data in counseling research include tests (both standardized and informal), inventories, questionnaires, interview schedules, rating scales, attitude scales, semantic differential, and observation schedules. Each of these kinds of instruments has its special pattern of advantages and limitations, fitting it well to some projects and poorly to others. Whatever kinds a project uses, the specific instruments must be chosen from existing ones and used as is, modified from existing ones, or constructed anew. To make these decisions wisely requires carefully considering many factors, including the project's mission, the kinds of instruments chosen, and prevailing conditions.

PRACTICAL EXERCISES

1. The following items might be presented on a questionnaire. Each item contains one or more flaws likely to confuse respondents. Identify each item's flaws and rewrite the item so it is clearer to respondents.
   a. What is your best estimate of the approximate number of hours per day that your children watch television?
      _____ 4
      _____ 2
      _____ 3
      _____ 1 or less
      _____ 5 or more
   b. Do you allow your children to watch television shows that portray sexually explicit and violent situations?
      _____ Yes, frequently
      _____ Yes, occasionally
      _____ No
   c. How often do you watch television shows with your children?
      _____ Every day
      _____ Once a week
      _____ Once a month
      _____ Never
   d. How many television programs do your children watch per week?
      _____ 0–5
      _____ 5–10
      _____ 10–15
      _____ 15–20
      _____ 20 or more
   e. If you have teenage children, what reading materials do they enjoy?
      _____ fiction books
      _____ nonfiction books
      _____ magazines
      _____ newspapers

2. Appendix H contains a transmittal letter and questionnaire from the Childhood Reflections Project conducted at the University of British Columbia, Canada, in cooperation with the Department of Recreation and Sport in Adelaide, Australia. For this exercise, carefully examine the transmittal letter. Give the questionnaire itself only enough attention to help you respond to the following points about the letter. Determine whether and how respondents are informed about:
   a. the purpose of the questionnaire,
   b. the auspices under which the study is being conducted,
   c. the amount of time needed to respond,
   d. when and how the questionnaire is to be returned, and
   e. the reasons for responding.

   In your opinion, do the organization and the individuals issuing the letter lend prestige and official status? As you read this transmittal letter, do you feel inclined to complete the questionnaire? Can you suggest any improvements for the transmittal letter?

3. For this exercise, examine the Childhood Reflections questionnaire contained in Appendix H. Consider the following questions regarding this questionnaire.
   a. Are respondents' privacy and confidentiality assured? How?
   b. Is the questionnaire short and simple?
   c. Do you think every respondent would know what to do with every item?
   d. Is the language used in the questionnaire precise, objective, and efficient?
   e. Do you believe the questionnaire has been designed with a view toward the planned analysis of the data generated from it?
   f. How have the authors provided for return?
   g. Does the structure follow the suggested guidelines in the text for arrangement of the questionnaire as a whole?
   h. Having read the questionnaire, would you be inclined to complete and return it if it had been sent to you? What suggestions would you offer for changing the questionnaire?

4. Bring a measuring instrument to class and be prepared to discuss its features. The instrument may represent any of the kinds discussed in Chapter 12 (for example, standardized test, interview protocol, attitude scale) or may be a combination of these kinds. Examples of instruments may be found by consulting a published source (such as *Tests in Print*), examining the counseling literature, or consulting with professors in your department who are engaged in research projects. Your discussion should include:
   a. the purpose of the instrument,
   b. examples of the kinds of items used,
   c. your opinion of the instrument's strengths and weaknesses, and
   d. any suggestions you would make to improve the instrument.

CHAPTER THIRTEEN

ANALYZING THE DATA

QUESTIONS TO GUIDE YOUR READING

Nature of the Data

1. In what six ways can data be analyzed?
2. What is the difference between continuous and discrete variables?
3. Describe the properties of identity, order, additivity, and an absolute zero as they relate to numbers.
4. What is a measurement system?
5. Give examples of measurement systems that have the properties of (a) identity only, (b) identity and order only, (c) identity, order, and additivity only, and (d) identity, order, additivity, and an absolute zero. Try to use examples different from those in the text.
6. When should measures be considered almost interval?
7. Why should psychometric scores based on the number of items answered correctly generally be designated as almost interval measures?

Selecting Statistical Tools

8. What two myths are sometimes stated regarding selection of statistical tools? What responses should be offered to these myths?
9. Distinguish descriptive from inferential analysis.
10. What principles should be followed in graphing time series data?
11. How may a functional relationship be indicated when time series data are graphed?
12. What is meant by the terms *mutually exclusive* and *exhaustive* with respect to crosstabulation tables?
13. When would scatter graphs be preferred to frequency tables for bivariate distributions?
14. Define mean, median, and mode.
15. Why is the mean the most frequently used measure of central tendency? When is the median or mode more appropriate?
16. Define range, interquartile range, standard deviation, and variance.
17. Why is it important to construct scatter graphs to visually inspect relationships between variables?
18. What is a respondent's profile? What characteristics may be used to describe a respondent's profile?
19. How do statistical hypotheses differ from research hypotheses?
20. What is a null hypothesis?
21. What is the relationship between level of significance in statistical tests and "errors of Type 1"?
22. What is an "error of Type 2"?
23. What assumptions underlie the use of parametric tests?
24. What are the applications of the *t* test with interval or ratio data?
25. What are the applications of the analysis of variance with interval or ratio data?
26. What are the applications of Chi-square with nominal data?

27. When is the McNemar test used?
28. When is the Median test used?
29. What can researchers do to avoid inflation of probabilities when a project uses several significance tests?
30. What is a confidence interval?

In Chapters 11 and 12 we discussed methods of **data collection** to address research questions. Once data are collected, the next step is to analyze them to answer these research questions.

The material on **data analysis** presented in this chapter was written under the assumption that readers are familiar with descriptive and inferential statistics to the extent usually covered in a one-semester or one-quarter upper division statistics course in education or behavioral science. For those without such a background, several excellent review texts are available, including Mendenhall and Beaver (1994).

Depending on the nature of the data and the questions to which analysis is addressed, data may be analyzed in any one or more of several ways.

The number of people who fulfill stated criteria may be counted, for example, the number of:

- freshmen from different ethnic groups who later graduated,
- clients whose services are (or are not) paid by insurance,
- employees self-referred and supervisor-referred to an employee assistance program (EAP),
- students whose attendance improved after intervention,
- applicants who passed a licensing examination, or
- parents and nonparents who voted for a school bond issue.

The number of times a given kind of event occurred may be counted, for example, the number of times:

- a respondent answered correctly on a test,
- a student interrupted in a classroom,
- a driver was issued traffic citations or had accidents,
- a client made self-references in counseling sessions,
- an employee was absent from work, or
- inmates on a prison ward engaged in fights.

Rating procedures may be applied, for example:

- respondents' WAIS-R Comprehension responses may be scored,
- clients' MMPI-2 profiles may be rated for degree of emotional disturbance,
- the "fit" of clients' career goals with their Strong Interest Inventory profiles may be rated,
- interview replies may be rated for degree of self-disclosure, or
- problem students' records may be classified as improved or not improved after disciplinary intervention.

The distribution of scores or other measures in the sample or samples studied may be statistically described. For example, a researcher may determine:

- the average SAT score of college applicants,
- the range of students' scores on a final examination,
- the average medical benefit utilization costs of employees,
- the median number of tardinesses among students in a classroom, or
- the correlation of clients' satisfaction ratings with age.

Statistical hypotheses about the populations the samples studied represent may be tested with statistical significance tests. Two examples of such hypotheses are:

- Employees' average medical benefit utilization costs will remain the same after EAP services.
- College applicants from magnet schools have the same average SAT scores as other applicants.

Population parameters may be estimated from sample statistics. Such estimates are called **confidence intervals.** Two fictitious examples of such confidence intervals are:

- With 90% probability, we estimate that 48% to 57% of voters favor the bond issue.
- With 99% probability, we estimate that clients receiving counseling services reduced their average medical benefit utilization costs by an amount between $135 and $528 per client.

Counting must often precede other types of analysis. For example, each student's correct answers must be counted before a distribution of class examination scores can be compiled. The number of survey respondents who favor and oppose a bond issue must be counted before the researcher can estimate the likelihood that voters will pass the measure. As noted in Chapter 11, data consisting of verbal responses must often be subjected to content analysis before further analysis can proceed.

In most projects, results of the data analysis are presented in tables or figures in addition to text. It is helpful to plan the layout of these tables and figures as part of planning how the data will be analyzed. Table 13.1 is a **skeleton form** of a table that appears later in this chapter in complete form. Skeleton form means that the table contains no data but is otherwise complete; in Table 13.1:

- the title has been written,
- the kind of data (frequencies and percentages) to be entered has been identified,
- the number of rows and columns has been decided (at least provisionally), and
- rows and columns have been labeled (at least provisionally).

T A B L E   13.1
(Skeleton Form)
Frequency and Percentage of EAP-Referred and
Self-Referred Families Who Reported Various Types of Principal Problems

Problem	Referred by employer's EAP		Self-referred		Total	
	N	%	N	%	N	%
Family relations						
Finances						
Alcohol						
Other drugs						
Other problems						
Total						

In some instances, details of a skeleton table must be decided or revised after data collection has begun. For example, a researcher may plan to devise a system of content analysis based on the replies received, or construct a frequency distribution with grouped data based on the range of scores, neither of which is known until after the data have been collected. As a third example, suppose that the project represented in Table 13.1 unexpectedly yielded a large number of cases with employee–supervisor relations as their principal problem; in this instance, a new row with this label would be added to the table.

NATURE OF THE DATA

Before data analysis can begin, several questions must be asked about the nature of the data. Do the data consist of verbal responses, categories, numbers, or some combination of these? Do numbers represent frequency counts (for example, number of people), scores, or other measures? Do measures represent continuous or discrete variables? Do the measures include very few or many possible values? How much information do the measures carry about the variables they represent? The answers to these questions determine the kinds of data analysis techniques that can be meaningfully used. In the following subsections, we discuss these issues in detail.

Continuous and Discrete Variables

For some variables, known as discrete variables, only certain values (usually whole numbers) are meaningful. For example, a family can have one, two, or no children, but not 1.2 children. A fractional value is meaningless with regard to an individual family, although it may be meaningful as an average of a group of families. Number of children is a discrete variable; only certain values (integers) are meaningful, with intermediate values meaningless. As a second example, the amount of money in your pocket can be $1.00, $1.23, or $1.24, but not $1.236; two-place decimals are meaningful, but not decimals of three or more places, except as averages. A third example is provided by the old adage that a woman cannot be "a little bit pregnant." She is either pregnant or not; pregnancy is not a matter of degree.

In contrast, variables such as length, weight, temperature, and elapsed time can take any value along an entire continuum, whether whole numbers, fractions, or mixed numbers. Fractions, decimals, and mixed numbers are meaningful to whatever level of precision (with decimals, number of places) is justified by the measurement method. Such variables are called continuous variables. The number 1.28 cannot represent the number of children a family has, but it can refer meaningfully to pounds, inches, degrees Celsius, or minutes.

Even with continuous variables, researchers often prefer to work with discrete units for the purpose of data analysis. For example, age (elapsed time since birth) is usually recorded in whole years for adults, and in days, weeks, or months for infants. Sometimes age is classified arbitrarily according to whether one is old enough for some activity, such as to attend school, operate a motor vehicle, vote, purchase alcoholic beverages, or receive Social Security retirement benefits.

The Number of Possible Values

Some data analysis techniques are designed for variables that permit only a few possible values (for example, pregnant versus not pregnant). These techniques must also be used when a classification system has been imposed on a variable with many possible values to reduce the number of possible values to a few (such as people classified by age as children, adolescents, or adults). When underlying variables offer many possible values and those values are actually used, more powerful techniques of analysis are usually possible.

Nominal, Ordinal, Interval, and Ratio Measurement Systems

A **measurement system** is a relationship between a set of numbers or categories and a variable being measured. The variable "age" will serve as an example. Age (elapsed time since birth) is a continuous variable that is usually represented by whole numbers of years for adults. Fractional values are customarily rounded downward (for example, one's age is "20" from the 20th birthday until the 21st birthday). This relationship between numbers and the underlying variable is a measurement system. Sometimes age is represented with different measurement systems, such as expressing infants' ages in whole days, weeks, or months, or classifying people as children, adolescents, or adults according to attained age.

Numbers have the properties of **identity, order, additivity,** and an **absolute zero.** Identity means that each number is different from every other number. The number 4 is different from the number 5, and so on. Order means that numbers hold position with respect to one another. For any three numbers (for example, 2.5, 7, and 15) one is largest, one smallest, and one intermediate between these two. Additivity means that numbers can be added and subtracted to yield sums and differences. An absolute zero means that numbers can be multiplied and divided to yield products and quotients (**ratios**).

Measurement systems have identity, order, additivity, and an absolute zero to the extent that these properties convey meaning about the variable measured. To continue with the example of age as elapsed time in whole years since birth, consider a family in which parents aged 32 and 36 have a 4-year-old son and an 8-year-old daughter. The measurement system has identity because representing each person's age with a different number indicates that everyone's age is different from everyone else's; the son would be considered the same age as a 4-year-old playmate. The measurement system has order because ages have the same order (younger to older or vice versa) as the numbers representing them; the daughter is older than her brother and younger than the parents. The fact that it is meaningful to say that the children's ages (4 and 8) differ by the same amount as the parents' (32 and 36) indicates the measurement system has additivity. The fact that it is meaningful to say that the daughter is twice as old as her brother indicates the measurement system has an absolute zero; zero would indicate no whole years elapsing since birth.

All measurement systems have identity. Order, additivity, and absolute zero may be present or not; the possibilities are:

- identity only;
- identity and order;
- identity, order, and additivity; or
- identity, order, additivity, and absolute zero.

To illustrate a system with identity only, answers to a question about religious affiliation might be coded 3 (Catholic), 2 (Protestant), 1 (Jewish), or 0 (none of these). This system has identity because the numbers represent similarities and differences in religious affiliation (that is, 3 represents Catholics as like other Catholics but different from Protestants, Jews, and others). However, 2 does not represent Protestants as intermediate between Catholics and Jews; therefore the system does not have order. The system also lacks additivity and absolute zero because these properties are impossible without order.

When a measurement system with many possible values is replaced by another with few possible values, some of the information from the original numbers is retained and some is not. To return to our example of age classified into child, adolescent, and adult, identity is maintained in that the category "child" is different from "adolescent," which in turn is different from "adult." This example has order in that the "child" category refers to younger persons than does the "adolescent" category, which in turn refers to younger persons than does the "adult" category. Additivity is present in measurement systems that represent age as numbers of days, weeks, months, or years, but this property is not maintained in the child–adolescent–adult classification system. You can add 10 (a child age) to 16 (an adolescent age) to get 26 (an adult age), but you cannot add child and adolescent to get adult.

A set of categories is called a nominal, ordinal, interval, or ratio scale if they possess the factors of identity, order, additivity, and absolute zero, respectively. The type of scale in turn determines the type of data analysis techniques that may be used. **Nominal** scales have identity only. Classification systems such as married, single, divorced, or widowed are nominal scales. Each category is separate, but there is no inherent order to them. Likewise, diagnostic systems based on categories such as depressed, anxious, and manic-depressive would be considered nominal scales.

Ordinal scales have identity and order. Measurement systems that assign categories such as poor, fair, good, and excellent express an obvious order, as do win, place, and show as used in horse racing. Ranking the children in a classroom as to how disruptively they behave also represents an ordinal scale.

For a measurement system to be considered an interval scale, it must have one property in addition to identity and order. This third property is additivity, which requires that equal intervals between numbers represent equal differences in the variable measured. The most commonly used examples are the Fahrenheit and Celsius temperature scales and calendar time. The **equal interval** characteristic of calendar time is represented by the fact that exactly the same number of hours elapses between noon August 5 and noon August 6 as between midnight January 1 and midnight January 2. All intervals of one day are equal, regardless of the time of year or the time of day an interval begins and ends. By the same token, exactly the same amount of energy is required to raise the temperature of an object from 2 to 3 degrees on the Fahrenheit scale as from 57 to 58 degrees, provided it does not melt or vaporize in the process. Equal intervals between numbers of degrees represent equal differences in temperature. In contrast, a win, place, and show system says nothing about the intervals separating the racehorses. For example, the winner may finish ahead of the place horse by a nose, while the show horse finishes a length behind, or vice versa.

Equal intervals between numbers must represent equal differences in the underlying variable if the numbers in the measurement system are to be meaningfully added and subtracted. You cannot subtract "show" from "win" or "place" (ordinal scale units); even if these terms are replaced with numbers, such as 2, 1, and 3, adding and subtracting them would not yield interpretable results. In contrast, you can meaningfully subtract 17 days from 35 days, or 8 degrees from 50 degrees (equal interval scale units).

The final measurement system category to be discussed, ratio scales, has the properties of identity, order, additivity, and an absolute zero point. Absolute zero means that zero on the measurement scale represents a complete absence of what is being measured. Examples of ratio scales include measures of height and weight, bank balances, and elapsed time. In contrast, equal interval scales, such as those used for temperature, have an **arbitrary zero** point. Zero degrees Fahrenheit does not represent the absence of temperature. That the zero point for interval scales is arbitrary is exemplified by the fact that zero degrees Celsius is 32 degrees Fahrenheit.

Calendar time and elapsed time also illustrate this point. Any calendar date represents elapsed time between that date and an arbitrary event. In the Christian calendar, that event is the presumed birthdate of Christ; dates before and after that event are represented as B.C. and A.D., respectively, equivalent to negative and positive signs. Numerical values are rounded upward; the year 1 represents the first year following the presumed time of Christ's birth, and the end of the year 2000 will mark the end of the 20th century. The Islamic and Chinese calendars follow the same principle but use different events to divide positively from negatively signed dates. Whatever the calendar, the practice of rounding upward eliminates 0 as a date. This fact is not the reason calendar time represents interval rather than ratio measurement; rather, the reason is that different calendars measure time from different events chosen arbitrarily for historical and social reasons that have nothing to do with the inherent nature of time. Different calendars therefore represent the same year with different numbers. Elapsed time, in contrast, represents ratio measurement because zero represents absence of time: absolute simultaneity.

Equal intervals are required for sums and differences to be meaningful with regard to the variable measured; for meaningful products and quotients, the scale must also have an absolute zero point.

Boundaries Between Measurement Categories

The four ordered measurement categories of nominal, ordinal, interval, and ratio have three boundaries: nominal–ordinal, ordinal–interval, and interval–ratio. The first and last of these boundaries are clear and distinct. It is easy to decide whether or not the set of names or numbers a measurement system assigns is an ordered set. "Good" is more like "excellent" than "fair" or "poor" is; however, a baseball player wearing #2 is not necessarily more similar to #1 than is the player wearing #10. Similarly, it is easy to decide whether zero on a measurement scale represents the complete absence of what is being measured. Zero is meaningful in this sense in measures of height, weight, bank balances, and elapsed time. However, a score of zero on a mathematics achievement test usually does not represent absolute mathematical ignorance.

Unlike the nominal–ordinal and interval–ratio boundaries, the ordinal and interval categories are often much more difficult to distinguish. Writers have long debated whether such data as psychometric scores and numerical ratings should be treated as ordinal or interval measures. If a researcher cannot say with confidence that equal differences in scores represent equal differences in the underlying variable, is it justifiable to add scores to compute such statistics as means? For example, a student with an achievement test score of 14 presumably knows more about the subject matter than a classmate with a score of 10; equal intervals, however, mean that two other students with scores 4 points apart (such as 24 and 20) differ in their knowledge by the same amount as do the students with scores of 14 and 10.

We like to think of ordinal and interval as two ends of a continuum rather than as separate and distinct categories. Rank data represent the ordinal end of this continuum. Gold, silver, and bronze medals are awarded to the first three Olympics competitors to finish each race, regardless of the distance separating them at the finish line. "Rank in graduating class" totally ignores the amount by which adjacent grade point averages differ. Fahrenheit and Celsius thermometers represent the interval end of this continuum. Physical evidence attests to the equality of scale intervals; the same amount of heat energy is required to raise the temperature of a kilogram of water one degree, whether from 4 to 5 degrees, from 21 to 22 degrees, or from 89 to 90 degrees.

Many studies of counseling involve measures about which the equal interval property is in doubt; the data are clearly not purely ordinal measures such as ranks, although evidence to support the equal interval idea is lacking. Ratings and psychometric scores, for example, do not ignore the size of differences between adjacent individuals as ranks do, although no clear evidence attests to equality of intervals. Further, many researchers and counselors add subscale scores of tests and inventories to yield total scores and add scores from several Likert items to yield total attitude scores. These examples illustrate a common practice: treating such data *as if* one had true interval measurement despite lack of a basis for confidence that this assumption is correct. However, this assumption of interval scale properties does not seem to do serious damage insofar as the usefulness of the data is concerned. Kirkpatrick and Aleamoni (1983) refer to data of this sort as **almost interval**; when evidence supports the equality of scale intervals, they call the measurement **true interval**.

In addition, most psychometric and rating scale data are distributed in approximately normal fashion when samples are of moderate or larger size. In contrast, rank order data are always distributed rectangularly if there are no ties; one person or object occupies rank #1, another rank #2, a third rank #3, and so on down the list. Although rating scales usually elicit more moderate than extreme ratings, many writers refer to rating scales as ordinal measures because evidence to support equality of intervals is lacking. We prefer Kirkpatrick and Aleamoni's (1983) "almost interval" name for any measures that

- do not ignore the size of differences between adjacent individuals, as ranks do, and
- are distributed more nearly normally than rectangularly, but
- do not have evidence supporting equality of scale intervals.

Most ratings and psychometric scores meet this definition. When the term *interval* is used later in this chapter to refer to a level of measurement, it includes both the almost interval and true interval subcategories (without distinction between them) unless otherwise specified.

A decision-making system. The following guidelines can help you decide whether any particular measurement scale should be called nominal, ordinal, almost interval, true interval, or ratio. Figure 13.1 represents these same ideas in flowchart form.

1. Data can be considered *nominal* when they consist of:
   a. two or more clearly unordered categories (for example, male/female; disabilities classified as motor, sensory, intellectual, or emotional).
   b. numbers that do not allow arrangement into meaningful order (for example, 1 = Hispanic, 2 = African American, 3 = Caucasian).
2. Data can be considered *ordinal* when they consist of categories or numbers that express a meaningful order (such as ranks) and that clearly ignore the magnitude of differences between individuals whom adjacent numbers or categories represent, such as:
   a. 1st, 2nd, 3rd . . . 10th place;
   b. centiles, quartiles, and deciles; or
   c. child, adolescent, adult, whether or not coded numerically (for example, 1 = child, 2 = adolescent, 3 = adult).
3. Data can be considered *almost interval* when they consist of numbers, and adjacent numbers can reasonably be regarded as equally far apart insofar as the variable being measured is concerned even though the idea of equal intervals is not supported by evidence. Examples include:
   a. most psychometric test and inventory scores,
   b. Likert scales, and
   c. grade point averages. (Such averages assume that a change from D to C represents the same amount of improvement as a change from C to B or B to A.)
4. Data can be considered *true interval* when they consist of numbers for which there is evidence (such as energy calibration) that adjacent

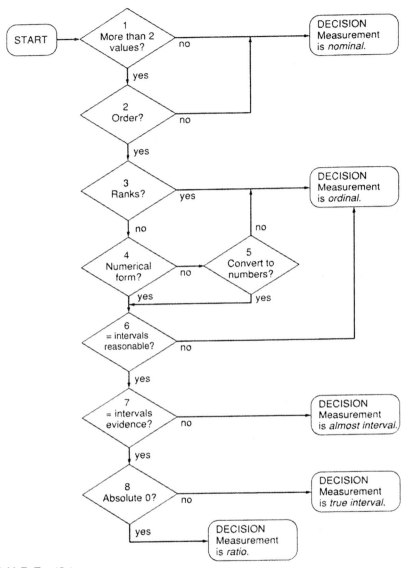

FIGURE 13.1

Flowchart for deciding whether data represent nominal, ordinal, interval, or ratio measurement. Rhombus forms (◇) numbered 1 through 8 refer to the following questions:
1. Does the measurement scale offer *more than two* possible values?
2. Does the measurement scale have *order*?
3. Do the assigned words or numbers represent *ranks*?
4. Are the measures expressed in *numerical form*?
5. Would conversion to numerical form be reasonable and meaningful?
6. Does the *equal intervals* idea reasonably fit the data?
7. Is the *equal intervals* idea supported by evidence?
8. Does the number zero represent *absolute absence* of the trait measured?

numbers represent equal intervals in the variable being measured and the number zero does not represent absolute absence of the trait being measured. Some examples are:
 a. calendar time, and
 b. the Fahrenheit and Celsius temperature scales.
5. Finally, the data can be considered *ratio* when the number zero represents the absolute absence of the trait being measured and the other requirements for true interval measurement are fulfilled. Examples include:
 a. length,
 b. weight,
 c. dollar cost,
 d. number of children,
 e. elapsed time, and
 f. number of absences.

Nominal and ordinal measurements can be expressed with words or numbers; interval and ratio measurements require numbers.

Some clarifications. Three issues deserve some clarification with respect to the above decision-making system. The first concerns the idea of absolute zero. Some students have expressed confusion about whether psychometric scores represent ratio measurement when such scores are based on the number of items answered correctly, since this number has a true zero point. If such a score is considered only as a measure of the number of items answered correctly, it represents ratio measurement. However, such is rarely the case. Usually, such scores are regarded as measures of traits; since zero items answered correctly does not necessarily represent complete absence of the trait, the measurement of the trait does not represent a ratio scale. For most such scores, we regard almost interval as the best designation.

The second issue concerns ordinal measurement scales with very few categories. Sometimes considerations of convenience lead researchers to apply a gross classification system to an underlying interval or ratio variable even though some information is lost in this process. An illustration exists in an example to which we have referred before: classifying people as children (under age 13), adolescents (age 13–17), or adults (age 18 and over). This system clearly has order, since adolescents are younger than adults yet older than children. Scale intervals are clearly not equal, since adolescents represent a much smaller age range than either children or adults. This measurement system, therefore, is ordinal; an ordinal scale has been imposed on an underlying ratio variable. Because there are only three categories, however, most researchers would choose statistical methods usually applied to nominal data. The imposed measurement system does not lose the property of order (which it would have to do to become truly nominal) merely because it is very gross. Nonetheless, such grossness of measurement often leads researchers to choose analysis methods *as if* the data were nominal. Such choices do not represent errors but rather are a conservative response to very gross measurement.

The final issue concerns changes that take place in the data as analysis proceeds. Earlier in this chapter, it was noted that counting or rating procedures must often precede further analysis. These procedures often but not always change the nature of the data. For example, the correctness or incorrectness of a respondent's answer to one test item represents a nominal measure with two possible values. Counting the number of his or her correct answers yields a score with a larger number of possible values; most such scores are almost interval measures. Similarly, counting the number of days a student was absent from class during a semester begins with a nominal measure with two possible values (present versus absent on each day), and derives a ratio measure with many possible values. If judges rank participants' MMPI-2 profiles according to degree of emotional disturbance indicated, the several almost interval measures constituting the profile are converted to one ordinal measure. In contrast, counting people who fit one or more categories (such as Republicans versus Democrats who voted for or against a ballot proposition) does not change the nominal character of the data.

SELECTING STATISTICAL TOOLS

The remainder of this chapter addresses the selection of statistical tools for analyzing a project's data. This selection depends on both the project's mission and the kinds of data to be analyzed. These tools provide a link between the raw data and the statements the researcher must make to fulfill that mission.

Kirkpatrick and Aleamoni (1983) stated two myths regarding selection of statistical tools:

Myth 1: "No matter what kind of data a research project yields, there is some statistical test which can be used to analyze the results satisfactorily" (p. 74).

Myth 2: "There is one and only one statistical test which will accomplish the end results needed by the researcher" (p. 74).

We offer two analogies to these myths from counseling practice. First, imagine a college student who has been taking a few courses at a time over several years and has never sought academic advisement nor declared a major. Course selections were based on whatever looked interesting and was taught at a convenient time. After accumulating more than 186 quarter units (the number required to graduate), the student asks a counselor to "find a major for me so I can graduate with what I have taken." Myth 1 is as unrealistic as this student's expectation of the counselor. Wise students who plan to graduate select courses with degree requirements in mind; wise researchers consider statistical analysis tools during the planning phase, *before* data are collected.

An analogy to Myth 2 is the idea that there is one and only one right occupational choice for every career counseling client. Just as there are many possible occupations for every person, there are generally several suitable analyses for every data set. To continue the analogy, a client might find some kinds of work preferable to others for various reasons, such as less specialized preparation, higher potential income, or more job stability; some statistical choices are preferable to other possibilities for such reasons as higher precision, more power, or less computational labor. (The concepts of precision and power were discussed in Chapter 10.)

Analysis by Computer

Among other considerations, choices of statistical analysis rest on the resources available to carry out the process. Increasingly, research projects use computers for this purpose. Computers perform computations much more rapidly, with much less labor, and with fewer errors than human operators with desk calculators. These advantages make a computer the tool of choice for most large research projects. Even with a small project, a computer may be the best choice if the researcher has easy access to appropriate hardware and software (generally the case in college and university settings) and is already familiar with their use. Without this familiarity and easy access, it often requires less time and labor to analyze the data from a small project by hand than to gain access to a computer and an appropriate software program and learn how to use them. A computer cannot wisely decide what kind of analysis should be used for any project.

We recommend deciding in the planning phase whether to analyze the data by computer or by hand. If by computer, the machine and the program to be used must also be decided. The program must be able to carry out the kinds of analysis the project requires, and the computer must have the capacities required by the program. These matters cause fewer problems now than they once did for two major reasons. First, a number of statistical software packages that formerly required mainframe systems now have versions for personal computers. For example, the Statistical Package for the Social Sciences (SPSS) can be used with both mainframe and personal computers and can perform all of the analyses discussed in this chapter and many more. Second, capacities of personal computers have risen sharply in the last few years.

Whatever computer and program are to be used, data must usually be entered by hand, although some kinds of systems (such as polygraphs and SCANTRONs) can enter data directly from a mechanical measuring device into a computer. In either case, data must be entered in a form and layout accessible to the program. Failing to provide for such matters during planning usually means much wasted time and effort later.

Occasionally researchers forgo the analysis techniques regarded as ideal for a project's mission. Simpler techniques are chosen instead because the ideal ones would require excessive computational labor to perform by hand and appropriate computer hardware and software are unavailable, too difficult to learn, or too costly.

Conversely, a computer's capacity to rapidly perform many different kinds of analysis occasionally tempts an inexperienced researcher to conduct many more analyses than necessary to answer his or her research questions. The researcher must then sort a bewildering stack of printouts and judge their value for the project. A planning task has been deferred until after data analysis has been completed, wasting both researcher effort and computer time. To draw a metaphor from weaponry, a shotgun is used when a carefully aimed rifle would be more effective. We are reminded of beginning counselors who ask their clients to complete many irrelevant tests and inventories because the counselors resist the more difficult task of exploring the problems presented. Analyses should be planned before data are collected.

Descriptive and Inferential Analysis

The distinction between descriptive and inferential analysis underlies the choice of statistical tools for any project. The purpose of descriptive analysis is to describe the features of a set of data. Inferential analysis uses data from samples to answer questions about the populations these samples represent; descriptive statistics alone do not suffice for this purpose. Descriptive analysis is often carried out to provide a basis for inferential analysis, however. The next two major sections discuss various descriptive and inferential analysis possibilities.

DESCRIPTIVE ANALYSIS

Even among experienced researchers, very few people can examine a large body of raw data and reliably infer what the data mean without some kind of analysis. Descriptive statistical tools can translate a bewildering mass of data into a much smaller number of interpretable statistics.

Descriptive analysis may yield numbers of people or events, facts about the distribution of scores or other measures, or both. Such results are usually presented in tables or graphs in addition to narrative text. The analysis is usually undertaken to answer research questions about the individuals studied (for example, in time series designs) or the groups studied (for example, in traditional group designs). Such questions generally concern the

T A B L E   13.2
Number of Persons with Various Diagnoses

Diagnosis	Number of persons
Situational disorder	26
Anxiety neurosis	32
Manic-depression	28
Clinical depression	14
Personality disorder	8
Total	108

T A B L E   13.3
Frequency Distribution of Participants' Grade Point Averages

Grade point average	Number of students
3.51–4.00	25
3.01–3.50	41
2.51–3.00	65
2.01–2.50	72
1.51–2.00	35
1.01–1.50	8
0.51–1.00	2
0.00–0.50	0
Total	248

characteristics of the groups (such as gender, age, or educational level) or whether certain events or behaviors are typical of these individuals or groups.

Frequency Counts

With nominal data, frequency counts are often the only kind of analysis that will yield interpretable results. Ordinal, interval, and ratio data permit other choices, although frequency counts are sometimes best even with these other kinds of data for the particular question at hand. Further, frequency counts are usually the first step in the descriptive analysis of all types of data other than time series data when additional analyses are planned. In counseling research, frequency counts are most commonly organized into **frequency distributions, crosstabulations** (also called **crossbreaks** [Kerlinger, 1986]), or **scatter diagrams.**

In graph or tabular form, a frequency distribution presents the number of cases belonging to each level of a variable. Table 13.2 presents fictitious data in which most of the cases occupy a very few possible values on the underlying variable. When many possible values on the underlying variable are represented in the data, it is common practice to present grouped data to simplify the frequency distribution. Table 13.3 illustrates this practice with fictitious data.

T A B L E   13.4
Frequency and Percentage of EAP-Referred and
Self-Referred Families Who Reported Various Types of Principal Problems

Problem	Referred by employer's EAP		Self-referred		Total	
	N	%	N	%	N	%
Family relations	10	12	36	28	46	22
Finances	15	17	31	25	46	22
Alcohol	31	36	18	14	49	23
Other drugs	20	23	19	15	39	19
Other problems	10	12	23	18	33	15
Total	86	100	127	100	213	100

Note: Percentages may not add to exactly 100% due to rounding.

Several decisions are required in compiling such a frequency distribution from ungrouped data in which many values are represented. Among these are how many groups to use, how wide the score intervals should be, and exactly where these intervals should be divided. Most good introductory statistics texts discuss these and related points in detail.

Sometimes the percentage of cases at each level of the underlying variable is shown in addition to the number of cases. This practice is particularly helpful when frequency distributions of two or more samples of unequal size are to be compared.

Crosstabulations classify cases according to two or more variables simultaneously and show the frequency or percentage of cases in each of the categories so created. This kind of analysis often provides an easy basis for studying the relations between the variables. It may be used with nominal, ordinal, interval, or ratio data. As an example, Table 13.4 presents a two-variable crosstabulation based on fictitious data of a sort that might come from a clinic offering counseling services to families. The two variables are *type of problem* and *source of referral*. (This is the same table as that shown in skeleton form as Table 13.1.)

The data of Table 13.4 might be further subdivided according to a third variable, such as request for short-term (ST) versus long-term (LT) counseling. Table 13.5 illustrates how such a crosstabulation might be presented, showing only the first two rows from Table 13.4.

Based primarily on Kerlinger (1986), here are several guidelines for constructing crosstabulation (crossbreak) tables. First, categories should be based on the research questions the data are to answer.

Second, the categories represented by the rows should be mutually exclusive and exhaustive; likewise, so should the categories represented by the columns. Mutually exclusive means that the categories do not overlap. In Table 13.4, for example, "arguing with spouse over money" would not be classified as both "finances" and "family relations." Neither would inability

TABLE 13.5
Frequency and Percentage of EAP-Referred and Self-Referrred Families who Reported
Various Types of Principal Problems and Requested Short-Term or Long-Term Counseling

	Referred by employer's EAP				Self-referred				Total			
	ST		LT		ST		LT		ST		LT	
Problem	N	%	N	%	N	%	N	%	N	%	N	%
FR	06	07	04	05	24	19	12	09	30	14	16	08
FI	10	11	05	06	16	13	15	12	26	12	20	10

Note: FR = Family relations; FI = Finances; ST = Short-term; LT = Long-term.

to pay for a child's orthodontia. We would probably classify the first of these as "family relations" and the second as "finances." It is possible to create tables where persons or events are represented more than once, however. For example, a family might have separate and distinct problems with both finances and alcohol. If both problems are to be used in classification, a footnote is necessary to point out that the same family might have more than one problem and thus be represented more than once in the table. If the data are not to be subjected to a statistical significance test (Chi-square would be the appropriate test in this instance), the footnote is satisfactory for this purpose. However, if a Chi-square test is desired, the table should include each subject only once, such as in Table 13.4 where families are classified by "principal" problem. Exhaustive means that no subjects are omitted from the table. The row labeled "other problems" in Table 13.4 provides a way to meet this requirement without adding many rows with few people in them.

Third, when percentages are used to express the results of experiments, the number of cases in each treatment condition (defined by the independent variable) should be used as the basis for calculating the percentage in each outcome classification (defined by the dependent variable). To illustrate this rule, Table 13.6 presents fictitious results from an experiment involving college students who were randomly assigned to immediate versus two-week delayed appointments after they were first notified they were on academic probation for low grades. It is more germane to this project's mission to calculate what proportion of the "immediate appointment" group qualified for good standing (44%) than what proportion who qualified for good standing were in the "immediate appointment" group (70%). The direction of causal influence in the research question is from type of appointment to future grade improvement, not from grades to type of appointment.

And finally, when percentages are used to express the extent to which a predictor variable predicted a criterion variable, percentages are calculated from the predictor to the criterion in the same manner as from the independent variable to the dependent variable in experiments.

Tables 13.4 and 13.5 illustrate crosstabulations with nominal data. In Table 13.6, one nominal variable (immediate versus delayed appointment) is paired

T A B L E   13.6
Frequency and Percentages of First-Time Probationary Students with
Immediate and Delayed Appointments Whose Grades Improved the Following Term

Status at following term	Immediate appointment		Delayed appointment		Total	
	N	%	N	%	N	%
Grades improved; qualified for "good standing"	93	44	40	20	133	32
Grades improved; still on probation	66	31	50	25	116	28
Grades not improved	45	21	83	41	128	31
Not enrolled following term	8	4	28	14	36	9
Totals	212	100	201	100	413	100

T A B L E   13.7
Students' Science and Mathematics Grades

Science grade	Mathematics grade					
	A	B	C	D	F	Total
A	10	12	8	2	0	32
B	12	16	10	7	1	46
C	8	14	21	10	5	58
D	4	9	13	12	8	46
F	0	2	5	9	10	26
Totals	34	53	57	40	24	208

Note: Each cell represents the number of students with the indicated mathematics and science grades.

with an almost interval variable (improvement in grades) grouped into a few categories. To illustrate crosstabulation with two almost interval variables, Table 13.7 shows the relationship between the science and mathematics grades of a fictitious sample of students. Tables 13.4, 13.6, and 13.7 represent **bivariate** frequency distributions; frequencies at the various levels of two variables are tabulated jointly. Table 13.5 presents a three-variable crosstabulation. In Table 13.7, each of the two variables has five possible values; the resulting table has 25 cells, 10 marginal totals, and one grand total: 36 numbers in all. It is readily apparent that such a tabular presentation of a bivariate distribution can be quite unwieldy if the variables have a large number of possible values. Grouping the data is one possible solution, at a cost of some lost precision. Instead, we recommend **scatter graphs** for presenting bivariate distributions when both variables represent interval or ratio data with many possible values.

A scatter graph, often called a scattergram or scatter diagram, graphically presents the relationship between two variables. One variable is represented on the horizontal axis (**X axis** or abscissa), the other on the vertical axis

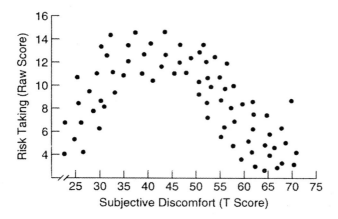

F I G U R E 13.2
A scatter graph illustrating a curvilinear bivariate distribution of subjective discomfort and risk-taking scores in a fictitious sample of participants.

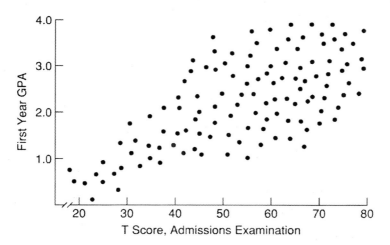

F I G U R E 13.3
A scatter graph illustrating a fan-shaped bivariate distribution of admissions examination scores and first-year grade point averages in a fictitious sample of students.

(**Y axis** or ordinate). Figures 13.2 and 13.3 provide illustrations based on fictitious data. Figure 13.2 represents the relationship of subjective discomfort with risk-taking scores, and Figure 13.3 represents the relationship of students' first-year grade point average with admissions examination scores. In a scatter graph, each participant is represented by a dot placed so that it shows his or her score on both variables (for example, a participant with an admissions examination score of 50 and a GPA of 2.0 would be represented by a dot placed directly above the number 50 and directly to the right of the number 2.0). The curvilinear and fan-shaped features of Figures 13.2 and 13.3 are discussed later in this chapter.

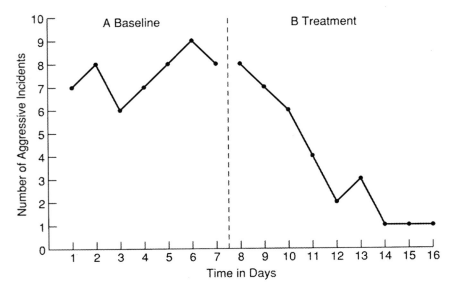

FIGURE 13.4
Fictitious data showing number of aggressive incidents as a function of parental attention.

Graphing Time Series Data

As discussed in Chapter 8, most time series experiments study one or a few participants intensively over a period of weeks or months. Data from most such experiments are analyzed descriptively by examining data points plotted on a graph. Graphs serve two functions in such experiments: first as an analysis tool and later as a way of reporting findings to consumers. This section discusses graphing for analyzing time series data; Chapter 14 discusses additional issues regarding graphs for reporting a project.

To provide an example, Figure 13.4 repeats the graph from Figure 8.1, showing data from a fictitious experiment in which parents treated a young girl's aggressive behavior toward her sibling by giving her their attention when she was not behaving aggressively and removing her to her room when she was. This graph follows principles offered by several authors (for example, Sulzer-Azaroff & Mayer, 1991):

- The horizontal axis displays the passage of time and the vertical axis displays the variable of interest, in this case, "aggressive incidents." Both axes are clearly labeled.
- A vertical dashed line indicates each change in conditions or treatment phases; treatment phases or conditions are clearly labeled.
- Lines connect data points within each phase; data points are not connected between phases.

We noted in Chapter 8 that the graphed data should be examined carefully for indication of a functional relationship between the treatment (independent) variable and the outcome (dependent) variable (in this example, parental attention and aggressive incidents, respectively). This interpretation process is discussed in Chapter 14. Such a functional relationship may take several forms (Sulzer-Azaroff & Mayer, 1991) as indicated by the graph in Figure 13.4 produced from the data:

> *The level of the line may change.* In this example, the number of aggressive incidents did not change much immediately but decreased sharply later.
>
> *The slope of the line may change.* The slope could accelerate or decelerate more rapidly or more slowly. In this example, the number of aggressive incidents changed to a sharply declining pattern.
>
> *The line may indicate a change in the variability of the data.* The dependent variable may vary more widely from day to day or become more consistent. In this example, the number of aggressive incidents per day varied no more than 2 points from one day to the next.

In an experiment involving more than two phases, the graph needs to be described at each phase change.

Interpreting and reporting time series data are discussed in Chapter 14. For further information on graphing time series data, see Barlow and Hersen (1984) or Sulzer-Azaroff and Mayer (1991).

Descriptive Statistical Measures

The previous subsection discussed frequency distributions based on counting the cases at each level of one or more variables. This subsection addresses descriptive statistical measures that can be derived from the data to describe a distribution of scores. These measures include measures of central tendency, measures of variability, and measures of relationship. These are the measures counseling researchers will most probably find useful. Because these measures describe distributions of numbers, it is important to keep in mind that they

- are not useful with nominal data,
- require that data be in numerical form, and
- are one step further removed from the raw data than frequency counts.

Formulas and calculation procedures for these measures are satisfactorily covered in most good statistics texts.

Measures of central tendency.   There are three commonly used measures of central tendency: the mean, the median, and the mode. The mean is the arithmetic average of a set of scores or other numbers (the sum of the scores divided by the number of scores). The mode is the most common score in the distribution, and the median is the 50th **percentile** (the point at which the distribution of scores is divided into two equal parts).

With interval and ratio data, the mean is the most commonly reported measure of central tendency in the counseling research literature. This measure has several advantages; two major ones are:

1. The mean is a more precise statistic than the median or mode. As discussed in Chapter 9, "more precise" means that sample values usually more closely approximate the corresponding population parameter.
2. The most frequently used tests of statistical hypotheses about central tendencies (the *t* **test** and the **analysis of variance,** discussed later in this chapter) refer to differences between means.

However, the mean is sensitive to extreme values in a distribution. If a small sample contains a few atypically high or low values, these values will affect the mean more than the median or mode. If extreme values are present in the data, a researcher must judge whether this sensitivity presents a problem regarding the choice of measures of central tendency. Sometimes the mean, median, and mode are all reported. The mean, median, and mode are identical in a normal distribution.

With ordinal data, the median is probably the most defensible measure of central tendency. Use of the mean with ordinal data has been criticized on the basis that sums are not meaningful when a measurement system ignores the size of differences between adjacent individuals. When the median and mode are markedly different, we recommend reporting both median and mode. When a distribution has more than one mode, we recommend reporting all modes and the median.

Measures of variability. Variability is the extent to which scores in a distribution are dispersed from one another. Measures of variability include **range, interquartile range, standard deviation,** and **variance.** With ordinal data, the range and interquartile range are the most defensible measures of variability in most instances. **Centiles** are an exception; their interquartile range is always 25–75 and their range is always 1–99 or similar, depending on the number of cases. Unless ranks are coupled with a nonrank measure of the same variable (such as scores), the range and interquartile range provide no added information about the distribution.

The range is the difference between the highest and lowest scores in a distribution. Sometimes the highest and lowest scores are reported; sometimes the lowest is subtracted from the highest to yield a single number. Reporting the range is often helpful to consumers who must judge the applicability of a project's results to their own situation. Quartiles are points that divide distributions into equal fourths. The interquartile range (the difference between the score values that bound the middle 50% of scores) is often helpful to report if the distribution is noticeably asymmetrical (skewed) or otherwise different from normal in form. For example, a researcher might say, "Participants ranged in age from 23 to 67 years, with a mean of 35 and a median of 31. The middle 50% of the sample ranged from 27 to 40."

When the mean is computed en route to inferential statistics, the corresponding standard deviation, or the extent to which the scores cluster around the mean, must be computed to the same end and is therefore usually reported. Variance (the square of the standard deviation) is usually reported only when it must be computed as part of inferential statistics, such as in the analysis of variance. Standard deviations are commonly reported only with interval or ratio data; objections to these statistics with ordinal data are the same as noted in the preceding subsection with regard to means.

Measures of relationship.   Measures of relationship include the Pearson correlation, multiple correlations, rank correlation, and point biserial correlation. To measure the relationship between two variables when both are represented with interval or ratio data, we recommend the **Pearson correlation** (r). When two or more predictor variables are combined to predict a criterion variable (for example, scholastic aptitude and high school GPA to predict first-semester GPA of incoming freshmen), a **multiple correlation** (R) expresses the degree of relationship. When two variables are both expressed with ordinal data, the Spearman rank-order correlation (*rho*) is generally used with samples larger than 10, and Kendall's Tau with smaller samples. The *phi* coefficient expresses the relationship between two **binary** (that is, having two possible values each) nominal variables. The relationship of a binary nominal variable with an interval or ratio variable may be expressed with the point biserial correlation.

A scatter graph presents visually a relationship a correlation coefficient expresses in a single number. For this reason, we like to construct scatter graphs for any correlational relationships in a project unless the number of correlations is so great as to make prohibitive the labor of graphing them all. Among the kinds of situations a scatter graph can reveal are a curvilinear relationship and a fan-shaped relationship. In Chapter 6, we cited Shedler and Block's (1990) results illustrating a curvilinear relationship. Their participants with moderate levels of subjective distress used less marijuana than either the most distressed or the least distressed. Sometimes retest findings illustrate a fan-shaped relationship; that is, participants with low pretest scores show little variability in their scores on retest while participants scoring high at pretest vary more widely on retest. Figure 13.2 is a scatter graph with a curvilinear distribution. Figure 13.3 shows a fan-shaped distribution.

A correlation coefficient alone does not reveal such situations; instead, it measures the relationship between the variables assuming they are related in a straight-line form. Without a scatter graph, a researcher might mistakenly infer from a zero correlation that the variables are unrelated when in fact they have a curvilinear relationship. If two variables are related in a fan-shaped fashion, this fact is particularly important to know when one variable is to be used to predict the other. In such cases, the predictive value of a respondent's score on the predictor variable depends how high or low it is. In Figure 13.3, low test scores more reliably predicted grade point averages than high test scores did.

Profiles.   Many instruments used in counseling assessment and research yield several scores for each respondent. Such a set of scores for one respondent is his or her **profile**. When a group's mean is computed on each scale of such an instrument, the resulting means constitute the group's mean profile. A few tests and inventories that yield profiles are:

- California Test of Basic Skills (CTBS),
- Career Assessment Inventory (CAI),
- General Aptitude Test Battery (GATB),
- Minnesota Multiphasic Personality Inventory (MMPI-2),
- Strong Interest Inventory (SII), and
- Wechsler Adult Intelligence Scale (WAIS-R).

Any individual profile may be described according to any one or more of several characteristics. Among these are:

Elevation, usually expressed as the mean of all scores in the profile. (It is essential to distinguish this idea from mean profiles. An elevation is one mean based on all scores in the individual profile of one respondent; a mean profile consists of several means, each representing one scale and based on all individuals in a group.)

Scatter, the variability among the scores in the profile, often expressed as a range or standard deviation. Profiles with little variability are often called "flat" (Hansen, 1984).

Pattern, the specific high, low, and moderate scores in the profile. Profiles can be classified into categories as Dahlstrom, Welsh, and Dahlstrom (1972) and others have done with the MMPI.

The extent to which it differs from another profile. The **D statistic** (Cronbach & Gleser, 1953) combines elevation and pattern to express the difference between two profiles by a single number. For example, this statistic might be used to test whether clients' "self" ratings on the semantic differential were more similar to their "ideal self" ratings after counseling than before. As a second example, this statistic might be used to measure the differences between group therapy clients' individual profiles and their group mean profile.

INFERENTIAL ANALYSIS

Descriptive analysis describes the data at hand. Inferential analysis enables researchers to use data from samples to make inferences about the populations that the samples represent. The inferences often concern questions such as these:

- Do the samples at hand represent populations with the same mean?
- Given the sample data, is the researcher's hypothesis about the population reasonable?
- How closely do the descriptive measures from a sample estimate the corresponding population values?

In most projects using samples, corresponding population values are unknown.

If the data at hand represent a sample, descriptive analysis yields statistics; analogous results from an entire population are called parameters. For example, a sample mean is a statistic; a population mean is a parameter. Additional statistics (such as t) may be calculated from sample data to draw inferences from descriptive statistics to their corresponding parameters. Populations, samples, and representativeness were discussed in Chapter 10; you may find it helpful to review this discussion before proceeding with the present section.

Inferential statistics include significance tests and confidence intervals. A significance test is a test of a statistical hypothesis; confidence intervals estimate population parameters from sample data. The statistical hypotheses underlying significance tests are different from research hypotheses (discussed in Chapter 6). Briefly stated, the difference is that research hypotheses consist of ideas about what a project's results will be; statistical hypotheses concern the one or more populations represented by the project's sample or samples. All statistical hypothesis testing seeks answers to the question "Given the sample data at hand, how reasonable is an idea (hypothesis) about the populations from which the samples were randomly drawn?"

The statistical hypotheses most frequently tested in counseling research are null hypotheses such as these:

- The research sample came from a population with a correlation of zero between the two variables of interest.
- The research samples represent populations with the same mean.
- The research sample represents a population with a mean pretest–posttest difference of zero.

The term *null* refers to a hypothesis of no difference or no relationship in the populations represented by the project's samples.

We choose a question about the relationship between two variables as a first example. Suppose a company's management wanted to know whether a given aptitude test would predict productivity among newly hired employees. The test was administered to 100 new employees, and the results were hidden from all who might influence the employees' job performance or its evaluation. Six months later, every employee had a productivity record. A Pearson correlation of .46 was calculated between productivity and aptitude test score.

If the researcher had stopped here, the result would represent only a descriptive analysis referring to the specific employees tested. However, the company management wanted to use the results to help decide whether to administer this test to future job applicants as part of a selection process. Such a decision would be irresponsible if the .46 figure could reasonably be regarded as a result of random sampling from a population with zero correlation between productivity and aptitude test scores. Therefore, the researcher looked up the obtained value of .46 in a table and found it "significant" at a chosen probability level (in counseling research, traditionally .05

or .01). "Significant" in this context means that sample correlations this large occur only rarely in random samples of this size from a population wherein the correlation is zero. Rather than believe the .46 figure at hand arose from such a rare sampling accident, the personnel officer preferred to regard the sample as having come from a population with a correlation greater than zero. If the sample correlation were not statistically significant, management would have concluded that the sample might reasonably have come from a population wherein the correlation was zero, in which case the test would have no predictive value for employee productivity. It is important to remember that "might reasonably have come" does *not* mean the same as "came."

A research question about a difference between two populations will serve as a second example. In the fictitious project underlying Table 13.6, suppose the researcher wanted to test a hypothesis regarding the mean grade point average (GPA) earned by the two groups in the following term. The *t* test for independent samples would be the statistic of choice. Suppose, further, that the *t* test was "significant." The researcher would likely conclude that the treatment difference probably caused a difference in mean GPA. The researcher's underlying statistical logic proceeds roughly as follows:

> If my two samples were drawn *at random from populations with the same mean*, a value of *t* this large would be a very rare sampling event (probability less than .05 if significant at the .05 level). Rather than believe the data at hand represent such a rare event, I prefer to believe that my samples came from *populations with different means.* I cannot know for certain.

The statistical reasoning stops here. The inference that "the treatment . . . probably caused a difference" requires in addition that all the applicable risks to design validity discussed in Chapter 9 were adequately addressed.

A nonsignificant result usually leads to statistical logic such as the following:

> If my two samples represent populations with the same mean, a value of *t* this large is a relatively common sampling event. Therefore, the null hypothesis (that population means are the same) remains one among many plausible possibilities given this result. Because the null hypothesis is plausible, the data do not support a conclusion that the treatment difference probably caused a difference in mean GPA.

"The data *do not support* a conclusion that the treatment difference probably caused . . . " is *not* the same as "The data support a conclusion that the treatment difference *probably did not cause* . . ."

In response to errors we have frequently encountered from students, we emphasize the following points:

> The null hypothesis is *never* about a sample; it is *always* about the parent populations from which the study samples were drawn at random.
> The null hypothesis is *never* proven or disproven. A significant result means that the data at hand represent a rare sampling event *if* the

null hypothesis is correct. A nonsignificant result means that the data at hand represent a reasonably common sampling event *if* the null hypothesis is correct.

Significance Levels

To conduct a statistical significance test, a researcher must choose a **significance level**. How large must a result be to be called "statistically significant" versus "not significant"? As noted earlier in this chapter, .05 and .01 are the levels most commonly found in the counseling research literature. Such numbers refer to *the probability that random sampling from a population (or populations) for which the null hypothesis is correct will produce results such as those at hand.* The level of significance refers to the probability of committing what statisticians call a **Type 1 error:** finding a statistically significant result when the null hypothesis is true. Significance at the .01 level requires a larger correlation or a larger difference than does significance at the .05 level. Requiring a larger result to claim significance reduces the risk of committing a Type 1 error.

This method of reducing the risk of a Type 1 error has a cost: increasing the risk of getting a *non*significant result even though the null hypothesis is false (Type 2 error). A **Type 2 error** consists of failing to find evidence in support of the phenomena being studied, when these phenomena in fact exist. Risk of a Type 2 error is the obverse of statistical power (discussed in Chapter 10): higher risk of a Type 2 error is the same as lower power. Statistical power can be increased, without increasing the risk of a Type 1 error, by increasing the sample size.

Parametric and Nonparametric Tests

When the *t* test, analysis of variance (**ANOVA**), and significance tests involving the Pearson correlation were derived mathematically, the derivations included assumptions about parameters of the populations from which the samples were drawn. Therefore these tests, among others, are called **parametric tests.** Tests not based on such assumptions, such as Chi-square and the **median test,** are called **nonparametric tests.** When the data sufficiently fulfill the conditions for parametric tests, these tests are preferred over their nonparametric alternatives because most parametric tests are more powerful in the sense discussed in Chapter 10. This matter requires careful attention during planning.

Our discussion of these conditions is based on Kirkpatrick and Aleamoni (1983) and other sources. Assumptions underlying most parametric tests include:

- The means being compared represent interval or ratio measurement.
- The one or more samples represent normally distributed populations.

- When two or more samples are being compared, their parent populations have the same variance.

Because a researcher can never know population characteristics from sample data, it is helpful to understand the consequences of violating these assumptions in practice. To this end, computers have been used to conduct sampling experiments with specially constructed populations (Boneau, 1960; Havlicek & Peterson, 1974; Norton, cited by Lindquist, 1953).

Trachtman, Giambalvo, and Dippner (1978) found that violating the interval measurement assumption posed "a serious problem" in interpreting results of parametric tests. According to Kirkpatrick and Aleamoni (1983), almost interval measurement fulfills this assumption satisfactorily.

Under a wide range of practical conditions, violating the normal distribution or equal variance assumption makes little difference with most parametric tests. Serious problems (Kirkpatrick & Aleamoni, 1983) ensue, however, when all of the following conditions coexist for a test with more than one sample, or conditions 1 and 4 coexist for a one-sample test:

1. Samples are small. Statisticians disagree about the definition of "small." Kirkpatrick (1981) had few qualms with samples larger than 30 but serious doubts about samples smaller than 20. As a conservative guideline, we suggest regarding small samples as a possible problem if any sample has fewer than 30 cases.
2. Two or more samples of unequal size are being compared.
3. Two or more samples are being compared and their parent populations have markedly different variances.
4. One or more parent populations have seriously non-normal distributions (for example, rectangular, bimodal, markedly skewed).

The one-sample t test, for example, should not be used when the sample is small and the population seriously non-normal (conditions 1 and 4 coexisting); a nonparametric alternative such as the median test should be substituted. Large samples of equal size represent one way of avoiding these problems. Kirkpatrick and Aleamoni (1983) noted that unequal sample sizes can be equalized, with some loss of data, by randomly eliminating cases from the larger sample. This loss of data results in some loss of statistical power. When circumstances limit a project to small samples of unequal size, the normality and equal variances assumptions can be tested with preliminary procedures offered by Glass and Stanley (1970); when results of these tests suggest conditions 3 and 4 both prevail, we recommend using nonparametric techniques to test the significance of central tendencies even though the data represent interval or ratio measurement.

The Pearson correlation satisfactorily expresses the degree of relationship between two variables when both variables represent interval or ratio measurement and are related in a rectilinear (straight line) rather than curvilinear fashion. This descriptive use refers only to the data at hand and does not involve inferring from sample data to the population the sample represents. Parametric assumptions become important when a sample correlation is to be tested for statistical significance or when two correlations are to be tested for the significance of their difference. These significance tests rely on an assumption that each sample represents a population wherein the variables are distributed in "bivariate normal" fashion (that is, a three-dimensional, perfect bell shape) (Glass & Stanley, 1970).

Parametric Tests

The t test. With interval or ratio data, applications of the *t* test include comparing the mean of *one sample* with a specified population mean, comparing the means of *two independent samples,* or comparing *two correlated means.* Correlated means comparisons are made by comparing *repeated measures* of the same variable from the same sample, comparing the same variable in *related samples,* or by comparing two commensurately measured variables (such as different scales on the same interest inventory) in the same sample (*within-group comparison*).

In counseling research, the most common application of the one-sample *t* test appears to be to test whether a sample fairly represents a known population. For example, the *t* test might be used to compare the mean of a group of college students who sought career counseling with that of the entire student body on an interval or ratio variable, such as grade point average, age, or number of units enrolled in the current term. A statistically significant result would probably be interpreted to mean that seeking career counseling introduced a sampling bias such that those students differed from the remainder of the student body in some systematic way.

Among the common applications of the independent-samples *t* test is the posttest-only control group design with one dependent variable. This design was discussed in detail in Chapter 8. This same test can also be used in descriptive projects to compare two samples (such as males and females) with regard to one interval or ratio variable. This test requires that the two samples are entirely independent (that is, that they contain none of the same people and that membership in one sample did not affect membership in the other, as is the case with husbands and their wives).

All three applications of the correlated means *t* test require the same calculations. Longitudinal developmental studies comparing the same variable on two occasions in the same sample represent a common repeated-measures application. For example, clients' self-effectiveness ratings at intake and after the first counseling session might be compared. Comparing the average mathematics and language achievement test scores of the same group of students exemplifies a within-group application. A related-samples *t* test might compare a sample of college students with their fathers to determine whether they significantly differ in mean ratings regarding the value of education.

A warning is in order when the correlated means *t* test is used for within-group comparisons. Such comparisons are meaningful only when both variables are measured on the same scale (measured in commensurate units). For example, scores on different subtests of the same achievement test (such as mathematics and language) are usually expressed in the same units. However, comparing mathematics achievement scores with IQs would not be meaningful because the scores are expressed in different units. Usually, the same units requirement is fulfilled if both measures are expressed in a system such as the standard scores offered by most standardized tests and inventories that have more than one scale. Most such systems are designed so that all scales yield the same mean and standard deviation in one norm sample when scores are expressed as standard scores. Interpretable within-group comparisons require that the norm sample used to develop the standard score system must be different from the sample in which comparisons are made. A thorough discussion of standard scores may be found in most good psychometrics texts (for example, Anastasi, 1988; Sax, 1989).

Analysis of variance. In counseling research, the analysis of variance (ANOVA) has been applied to data from standardized tests and inventories, informal tests, rating scales, physical measures, and frequencies of specified behaviors, to name a few. The simplest application of ANOVA extends the independent-samples *t* test to test whether three or more samples represent populations with the same mean. Additional one-dimensional applications represent extensions of the *t* test for correlated means: (a) three or more repeated measures of the same variable in one sample, (b) the same variable in three or more related samples, and (c) the same sample's three or more measures (a profile, as discussed earlier in this chapter). These applications extend the analogous uses of the correlated means *t* test.

ANOVA is also recommended when factorial or mixed designs (discussed in Chapter 8) are used with interval or ratio data. Mixed designs are often used to compare two or more samples' mean profiles or changes in their mean profiles over time.

When a mixed design ANOVA is used to analyze profiles from a standardized test or inventory, we recommend expressing all scores as **standard scores** based on the same standard score system. As noted above regarding within-group comparisons with the *t* test, the standard score system must be based on a norm sample different from the samples used in the ANOVA. Centiles should not be used because they are ordinal data (ranks). Grade equivalents, often used to report results of educational achievement tests, have been criticized on several bases, including inconsistent variabilities from scale to scale (Cronbach, 1984). **T scores** are among the most common standard scores encountered in counseling research and practice. Some tests, such as the WAIS-R, GATB, and College Entrance Examination Board tests, use special standard score systems of their own. Most tests and inventories have manuals with tables that make conversion to standard scores a routine clerical task. Most commercial scoring services report standard scores either routinely or by special request.

The number of statistical significance tests in any ANOVA increases sharply with the complexity of the design. A one-dimensional ANOVA addresses one primary research question and involves one **statistical test.** As noted in Chapter 8, a two-dimensional factorial or mixed design addresses three questions, and a three-dimensional design, seven questions. Each of these questions requires its own significance test. If any of these tests is **statistically significant,** it may be followed up with a separate analysis to identify specific cell differences contributing to the significant results. With multiple tests, inflation of probabilities becomes an issue. This is discussed later in this chapter.

Nonparametric Tests

Chi-square and the Fisher test.   With nominal data, the Chi-square test is used in counseling research to test the plausibility of a hypothesis regarding the proportional representation of various categories (for example, males and females) in a sample's parent population: a one-dimensional application. The Chi-square test is also used to test the significance of differences between or among independent samples with regard to the proportional representation of various categories in the samples' parent populations (that is, to test the null hypothesis that these categories are distributed alike in all these populations): a two-dimensional application. This application begins with a crosstabulation table. Other applications of Chi-square, such as its use with the McNemar test and the median test, are discussed later in this chapter.

As an example of a one-dimensional application, suppose a university researcher solicited volunteers as participants and wanted to test the plausibility of the hypothesis that the resulting volunteer sample represented a population with the same proportional distribution of the five most common academic majors as the entire student body. University records contained the proportion of the entire student body who had declared each major. Chi-square could compare the distribution of majors in the sample with the corresponding distribution in the entire student body (population). A statistically significant result would probably be interpreted to mean that the solicitation of volunteers introduced a sampling bias, with students in some majors more likely to volunteer than students in other majors.

To illustrate a two-dimensional application of Chi-square, suppose a representative of a fraternity wanted to test the influence of a persuasive communication designed to recruit new freshmen into his fraternity. He randomly divided a sample of incoming freshmen into two groups and delivered his persuasive communication to one group but not the other. At midterm, he counted the number of students from each of these groups who belonged to each of the five fraternities on his campus. Chi-square could be used to test the significance of the difference between these two samples with regard to their fraternity membership. We do not recommend Chi-square with crosstabulation tables containing more than two dimensions because the results are too difficult to interpret. Rather, it is often possible to conduct several two-dimensional tests, bearing in mind the inflation of probabilities issue.

When any cell of a crosstabulation table has an "expected frequency" lower than 5 to 10 ("5 to 10" because statisticians disagree), Chi-square should not be used. Sometimes it is possible to combine categories so that all cells contain enough cases. For illustration, suppose that the fraternity project found many students in the Alpha and Beta fraternities but few in Gamma, Delta, and Epsilon. These latter three could be combined into an "other" category for purposes of Chi-square analysis. With four-cell (2×2) crosstabulation tables, the **Fisher exact probability test** may be used when cell frequencies are too low for Chi-square; it requires much computational labor with moderate-sized or large samples.

Chi-square and the Fisher test require that no cases be represented in more than one cell of the frequency table. For example, if the data in Tables 13.4 and 13.5 had been organized so that families who presented more than one problem were represented in more than one cell of the table, Chi-square could not be used to test the data for significance. As an answer to this situation, we organized the data so that each family's *principal* problem was recorded; the tables thus permit Chi-square analysis. This situation underscores the importance of careful attention to analysis during the planning phase; if this were an actual study with the data to be tested for statistical significance, data would need to be collected in such a way that each participant's principal problem could be identified, even if the distinction between "principal" and other problems were otherwise irrelevant to the project's mission.

McNemar test. The **McNemar test** is used in repeated-measures, related-samples, and within-group situations to test the significance of differences in a nominal variable having two possible values. Such situations include testing the difference between two occasions with one sample, testing the difference between two related samples (such as husbands and wives), or testing differences between two commensurate measures with one sample. We illustrate these applications with two fictitious examples:

A counselor wanted to test whether clients in a counseling group represented a population in which people were equally likely to speak spontaneously (without being specifically addressed) in the first session as in the second session. The two occasions and the nominal variable of interest allowed clients to be classified into four groups:

- Spoke spontaneously in both sessions,
- Spoke spontaneously in first session only,

- Spoke spontaneously in second session only, and
- Spoke spontaneously in neither session.

A large employer surveyed its workforce, finding that it included both partners of about 150 married couples. The employer engaged a career counselor on a consultancy basis who planned several sessions of a presentation on two-career family issues. Twenty-five couples chosen at random were invited to the first session. The counselor wanted to test the hypothesis that husbands and wives, in the entire population of 150 couples, were equally likely to attend. Although husbands and wives are different people, the fact that they are joined requires that they be treated as related samples rather than as independent samples. To that end, the couples invited to the first session were classified into four groups:

- Both partners were present,
- Wife *only* was present,
- Husband *only* was present,
- Both partners were absent.

A special formula leads to a value of Chi-square.

While it would be possible to arrange the frequencies of these categories into a 2 × 2 crossbreak table, we decided against that form of presentation lest you confuse the McNemar test with the Chi-square test comparing independent samples. Computational procedures in these two applications are different.

The median test. With ordinal data (ranks), we recommend the nonparametric median test to test the difference between samples in the kinds of situations in which the one-sample and independent-samples *t* tests are used with interval and ratio data. In the one-sample application, the numbers of cases in the sample above and below the known population median are counted; Chi-square is then used to compare these observed frequencies with their corresponding expected frequencies, half of the sample above the median and half below. In the two-sample application, the two samples are first combined to yield a common median; the numbers in each sample above and below this common median are then entered into a fourfold crossbreak table and Chi-square applied to this table. The sign test and Wilcoxon matched-pairs signed ranks test can be used in repeated-measures or related-samples comparisons with ordinal data.

A Decision-Making Guide

With regard to nominal, ordinal, interval, and ratio measurement, we recommend using methods suited to nominal data whenever:

- the data represent two or more *unordered* categories (truly nominal data), or

- a gross classification system produces a *very few* categories, even though the data may truly represent a higher level of measurement.

Use methods suited to ordinal data when the data represent ranks. Distinguish ranks from ratings.

Use methods suited to interval data when the data represent scores, even though the equality of scale intervals may be in doubt because they are unsupported by evidence. Likert scale ratings are often treated as scores. Parametric statistical methods may be applied to data qualifying as almost interval, true interval, or ratio. Tables 13.8, 13.9, and 13.10 summarize our recommendations regarding statistical significance tests for nominal, ordinal, and interval or ratio data, respectively.

T A B L E   13.8
Recommended Applications of Statistical Significance Tests for
Category Distributions of Frequencies and Proportions: Nominal Data

Application	*Significance test*
1 sample and hypothesized population values	Chi-square
1 sample with 2 measures or 2 related samples	McNemar test
2 samples, moderate or large Ns	Chi-square
2 samples, small Ns	Fisher exact probability
3 or more samples, moderate or large Ns	Chi-square
3 or more samples, small Ns	Chi-square or Fisher (must first combine some cells to make larger samples)

Notes: Methods suited to nominal data should be used whenever the data represent two or more unordered categories or a gross classification system produces very few categories, even though the data may truly represent a higher level of measurement. McNemar and Fisher tests may be used with binary variables only.

T A B L E   13.9
Recommended Applications of Statistical
Significance Tests for Medians: Ordinal Data

Application	*Sample statistics*	*Significance test*
1 sample and hypothesized population median	1 median	Median test
1 sample with 2 measures or 2 related samples	2 medians	Sign test or Wilcoxon matched-pairs
2 independent samples	2 medians	Median test or Mann-Whitney U
3 or more samples	3 or more medians	ANOVA by ranks

T A B L E   13.10
Recommended Applications of Statistical Significance Tests for Interval or Ratio Data

Application	Sample statistics	Significance test
Measure: Central Tendency		
1 sample and hypothesized population value	1 mean	One-sample *t* test
1 sample with 2 measures, or 2 related samples, one measure each	2 means	*t* test for correlated means
2 independent samples, one measure each	2 means	*t* test for independent samples
2 or more independent samples with 2 or more repeated or different measures each	4 or more means	ANOVA, mixed design
3 or more independent samples, 1 factor	3 or more means	ANOVA, simple
4 or more independent samples, 2 or more factors	4 or more means	ANOVA, factorial design
2 or more independent sets of related samples	4 or more means	ANOVA, mixed design
1 sample with multiple measures, or multiple related samples, one measure each	3 or more means	ANOVA, randomized block design
Measure: Correlation		
1 sample and hypothesized zero population value	Pearson r	Direct reference to probability table
2 samples	Pearson r	r-to-z transformation

Beginning researchers should expect to experience some confusion in their efforts to choose analyses appropriate to their projects. To that end, more experienced faculty members are expected to help students in the selection of data analysis strategies, as statistical consultants or specialists often help other researchers. However, beginning researchers should participate in decisions regarding data analysis and should inform themselves as much as possible regarding applicable analyses.

Multiple Tests and Inflation of Probabilities

When one statistical test is conducted, the probability of a Type 1 error is equal to the significance level chosen: .05 or .01 in most counseling research. However, when a project includes several tests, the probability of at least one Type 1 error increases dramatically, approaching certainty when more than 50 tests are conducted at the .05 significance level (Parker & Szymanski,

1992). Alternatively stated, a researcher who conducts enough statistical tests can be virtually assured of a few significant results even if the null hypothesis is true for every test. Whether such statistically significant results have any significance for research questions is increasingly dubious as the number of tests increases. This problem is compounded by some researchers' and publishers' practices of reporting and publishing only projects with statistically significant results.

Parker and Szymanski (1992) offered several practical suggestions:

- Limit the number of statistical tests to those that are most relevant to the project's mission.
- When choosing significance levels for a study involving several statistical tests, consider using adjustments such as discussed by Cohen (1988), Marascuilo and Serlin (1988), and Rosenthal and Rubin (1984).
- Report the significance level for each test in the methodology section; when inflation of probabilities occurs, report it in the limitations section.
- Replicate research projects.

Determining Confidence Intervals

The technique of determining confidence intervals is directed toward questions such as: "I found a correlation of .58 in my sample. Within what limits might I expect it to deviate from its corresponding population value?" The calculations include the use of sample size and, for substantially nonzero correlations, the r-to-z transformation table (found in most statistics texts). These calculations yield a maximum and minimum value with a stated probability of including the population correlation between them. A researcher might report this result in language such as, "The 90% confidence interval for the population correlation was found to be .42–.65."

Confidence intervals can also be applied to results concerning comparisons. For example, a sample of employees might have been found to cost their firm an average of $15 per month less for medical benefits after smoking cessation and stress management interventions. The company president wants to know how much this figure might be expected to deviate from its corresponding population value. Suppose the Research Division reports a 95% confidence interval of $12–$18. This result means that the president has a 95% chance of being right in expecting the population value to be within this range.

CHAPTER SUMMARY

Data analysis may include descriptive procedures such as counting, rating, and description of distributions as well as inferential procedures such as significance tests and confidence intervals. Before data analysis can begin, the researcher must decide whether data (a) are continuous or discrete,

(b) allow only a few or many possible values, and (c) represent nominal, ordinal, almost interval, true interval, or ratio measurement.

The purpose of descriptive analysis is to describe the features of a set of data. Descriptive tools include graphing, frequency counts, and descriptive statistics. Frequency counts with two or more variables are generally presented in crosstabulation tables. Descriptive statistical procedures may yield measures of central tendency (mean, median, and mode), measures of variability (range, interquartile range, standard deviation, and variance), measures of relationship (various correlation coefficients), and profiles.

The purpose of inferential analysis is to answer questions about populations from sample data. A significance test is based on a statistical hypothesis, usually the null hypothesis, that asserts no difference or no relationship in the one or more populations represented by the project's samples. To conduct a significance test, a researcher must choose (a) between parametric and nonparametric procedures, and (b) a level of significance. Parametric procedures require that the data meet certain assumptions about the parameters of the populations from which the samples were drawn; nonparametric procedures do not. If those assumptions can be satisfactorily met, parametric procedures are to be preferred because they have more statistical power. Commonly used parametric tests include the t test (one sample, two independent samples, and correlated means applications) and the analysis of variance. Commonly used nonparametric tests include Chi-square, the Fisher test, the McNemar test, and the median test. Confidence intervals yield maximum and minimum values with a stated probability of embracing population parameters.

PRACTICAL EXERCISES

1. For each of the following studies or articles drawn from the counseling literature, determine whether the measures discussed should be considered nominal, ordinal, almost interval, true interval, or ratio.
    a. Vacc and Loesch (1993) used content analysis to analyze 383 opinions about the National Counselor Examination. The opinions were written by candidates for national certification who had just completed the exam. The content analysis involved counting the numbers of words that indicated satisfaction and dissatisfaction with the exam's overall content, examination process, and professional value.
    b. Lyddon, Bradford, and Nelson (1993), in an article reviewing measuring instruments for assessing adolescent and adult attachment, reviewed an instrument called The Inventory of Parent and Peer Attachment (IPPA) (Armsden & Greenberg, 1987). The inventory was composed of two subscales, one relating to attachment to peers (25 items) and the other to attachment to parents (28 items). Participants were asked to mark whether each item was "almost always true," "often true," "seldom true," "sometimes true," or "almost never true."
    c. Thoreson, Shaughnessy, Cook, and Moore (1993) reported a survey

of a national sample of male counselors and counselor educators. One of the major purposes of the survey was to determine what percentage of male counselors engaged in sexual contact with clients during and after the professional relationship. Accordingly, respondents were asked to indicate, among other things, the number of times they had been sexually involved with either clients, students under supervision, or students not under supervision.

d. Quintana and Kerr (1993) assessed the extent of depressive complaints in 87 students (mean age equaled 19 years) in introductory psychology courses as part of a larger study. Depressive complaints were assessed via the IPAT-D, an instrument developed by the Institute for Personality and Ability Testing. An illustrative item for the IPAT-D is:

I get into moods when I feel low and depressed.
a. often (2)   b. occasionally (1)   c. never (0)

The number to the right of each possible response indicates how that response is scored to produce a total depression score.

2. Imagine that a time series study was conducted to determine the impact of teacher praise on the rate at which students raise their hands before answering questions aloud in class. For a five-day baseline period the teacher was requested not to change his practice of allowing students to answer questions whether or not they raised their hands. For a two-hour block per day, an observer in the classroom recorded the number of students who blurted out answers to questions before being called upon. On the sixth day, the teacher was requested to ignore those students who blurted out answers and to respond with praise only to students who raised their hands to be called upon. For an additional ten days the observer then recorded the number of students per day (during the two-hour block) who blurted out answers. For the 15 days of the study, the numbers of students who blurted out answers were as follows: 24, 26, 22, 25, 23, 24, 18, 13, 3, 2, 2, 4, 2, 1, 2. Graph these time series data and examine the line for changes in level, slope, and variability. Report your impressions.

3. Imagine that you are a counselor at a large public university that has conducted a survey to determine the major reasons the incoming freshman class reports for having chosen to enter college. You elect to use the American Council on Education–UCLA Cooperative Institutional Research Program's Freshman Survey (Astin, Dey, Korn, and Riggs, 1991), which allows students to check one or more of five possible reasons for attending college: (1) learn more about things, (2) get a better job, (3) prepare for grad school, (4) general education, and (5) make more money. Results reported by the American Council on Education allow you to compare your freshman students' responses to the answers given by students at comparable four-year public universities and at all four-year public universities. The percentages of freshman students from these three groups, respectively, selecting Reason 1 were 26%, 18%, and 12%; Reason

2, 33%, 19%, and 27%; Reason 3, 17%, 27%, and 19%; Reason 4, 20%, 23%, and 25%; and Reason 5, 4%, 13%, and 17%. Arrange these data into a crosstabulation table.

4. For each of the fictitious studies discussed below, choose an appropriate inferential statistical analysis. First, determine whether parametric or nonparametric statistical tests would be appropriate. Then decide which specific tests of the chosen type would be most suited to the data.

   a. Counselors at a junior high school were extremely concerned about the large number of 7th grade boys who were referred, usually more than once per week, to disciplinary staff for misbehavior. A study was conducted to determine the impact of participation in "self-esteem groups" on 7th grade boys' referrals to disciplinary staff. Forty 7th grade boys were randomly selected to participate in the groups, which met once a week for six weeks. From the end of the six weeks until the end of the term, the average number of referrals for discipline of the selected boys was compared to the average number of referrals for discipline of all other 7th grade boys in the school.

   b. A longitudinal study was conducted to assess the degree to which people who reported experiencing childhood sexual abuse felt the abuse affected their adult lives. Participants were asked to indicate the effect of the reported abuse at age 20 and again at age 30 by responding on a scale from 1 to 9, with 1 indicating "no discernible effect" and 9 indicating "still affects my life on a daily basis."

   c. An experiment was designed to determine which of two treatments, participant modeling or assertiveness training, was more effective in helping shy people initiate interactions in social settings. Each client experienced both treatments. Half of the clients experienced assertiveness training first and participant modeling second, while the other half experienced the treatments in the reverse order. Clients were asked to keep self-report records of the number of contacts they initiated in social situations for a total of 12 weeks.

   d. Counselors at a mandatory court-referred treatment program for people arrested for driving under the influence were interested in comparing the effects of a 12-week inpatient versus a 12-week outpatient alcoholism recovery program. Fifty incoming clients were randomly divided into two groups, one to receive the inpatient and one to receive the outpatient program. One year after completion of the treatment programs, clients were categorized into two groups: those who had been arrested again for driving under the influence and those who had not.

5. Examine the counseling literature for studies using any of the methods of data analysis discussed in Chapter 13. Try to find one study relying on purely descriptive analysis and one that used inferential statistics in the analysis. Bring the articles reporting the studies to class and be prepared to discuss the analyses used, especially with regard to how well the methods of analysis fit the projects' mission and their data.

CHAPTER FOURTEEN

Drawing Inferences and Reporting the Project

QUESTIONS TO GUIDE YOUR READING

Interpretation According to a Project's Mission

1. What conditions should be met to ensure that the interpretation process leads to sound conclusions?
2. What is the implication for a research hypothesis if the data indicate statistical significance in the expected direction?
3. What are the implications of a nonsignificant result?
4. Under what conditions is a research hypothesis contradicted or disconfirmed?
5. What procedures should be followed when interpreting results of theory-based projects? Applied projects?
6. What procedures should be followed when a project's data fail to support a research hypothesis?
7. Why is it important to examine the results of a project for implications that extend beyond the immediate mission?
8. What major questions need to be asked to determine whether risks to design validity compromise a project's results?
9. What kinds of social influences can lead researchers to overlook plausible interpretations or to misinterpret findings?

Reporting the Project

10. Why do original decisions (from the planning phase) about the reporting process often need revisiting after the results have been interpreted?
11. What portions of a project's process should be expressed in writing?
12. What points must a researcher have in mind to make sound decisions about the reporting process?
13. Why must a researcher have a clear idea of who a report's consumers will be?
14. Why do researchers sometimes need to prepare more than one report of a project's results?
15. What content should all research reports include?
16. What information should reports addressed to other researchers ideally include?
17. How should researchers decide whether or not to omit material from a report because of stakeholder interests?
18. What plan of organization for research reports is prescribed by the *Publication Manual of the American Psychological Association*?
19. After constructing a table, what can beginning researchers do to ensure that the table is understandable to readers?
20. What kinds of graphs are typically used in counseling research reports?
21. What suggestions are offered for making circle graphs clear to readers?
22. When should vertical bars be used in bar graphs? When are horizontal bars preferred?
23. A line graph may display the relationship between what kinds of variables?
24. When is it appropriate to construct scatter graphs?

25. What general recommendations are offered for constructing all line, bar, and scatter graphs?
26. What principles of language and writing style guide all good research reporting? Briefly describe each.

After data have been collected and analyzed, researchers must say what they mean and convey these interpretations to consumers to fulfill the project's mission. Further, results often have implications for theory and practice beyond those envisioned in the original mission. Interpretation and reporting are the last two of the six steps that make up the research process. Interpretation consists mainly of thinking, although writing down thoughts often helps clarify them, and some writing is usually necessary to enable all those thoughts to be retrieved when needed later. In the reporting phase, material from the previous five steps must be selected and expressed in speech or writing. This chapter addresses the tasks of deciding what the results mean and communicating about the project and its findings to consumers.

INTERPRETATION ACCORDING TO A PROJECT'S MISSION

Interpretation of results according to a project's mission is a rather straightforward process if several important conditions are met:

- The researcher has a thorough understanding of the body of theory and practice that gave rise to the project.
- The mission has been clearly formulated, including the research questions and the reasons for seeking answers to the research questions.
- The project has been carefully and correctly planned to fulfill its mission.
- A pilot study was conducted, if relevant and feasible, and any indicated changes in the project's plan have been made.
- All applicable risks to design validity have been satisfactorily addressed in the plan.
- Data were carefully collected and analyzed according to plan.
- Unanticipated events have not affected the project so severely as to cloud the meaning of its results.

Failure to meet any one of these seven conditions can make this interpretation process very difficult and its conclusions dubious if not wrong. Typically, a researcher's time and thought invested in careful formulation and planning will pay handsome returns when the data must be interpreted.

Research Hypotheses

Most projects using statistical significance tests have research hypotheses set in opposition to one or more null hypotheses. "Opposition" in this context means that if the result is statistically significant in the expected direction (that is, the null hypothesis is not plausible), the research hypothesis is supported.

As noted in Chapter 13, a nonsignificant result means that the null hypothesis remains among the many tenable possibilities; such a result *fails to support* (not contradicts or disconfirms) the research hypothesis. One of these tenable possibilities is that the hypothesized difference or relationship is present but so weak that a significant result would be unlikely under the conditions (such as sample sizes and measurement methods) of the present project. Occasionally a project yields statistically significant results in the opposite direction to that expected; then and only then is the research hypothesis contradicted or disconfirmed.

Interpretation often begins with a decision about one or more research hypotheses. Do the findings support, fail to support, or contradict each one? But good interpretations do not stop there.

Linking Findings to the Mission

Whether or not the project's mission involves hypotheses, the researcher must say what answer the data give to each research question. Some complex research questions comprise several parts, and therefore may require several answers from the data. These answers, in turn, must be linked to the other part of every project's mission: the reasons answers to the research questions were sought.

When interpreting results of theory-based projects, the researcher must first answer the specific research questions, then say what these answers mean for the larger body of theory. Drew and Hardman (1985) cogently recommended that the entire larger body of theory be held "in storage" as the findings are brought to bear on the parts of the theory to which they are relevant, one part at a time. After this phase of the interpretation task has been completed, the parts can be drawn together to link the findings to the theory as a whole. This process will not proceed smoothly unless the formulation phase has adequately addressed what the theory means in behavioral terms.

Applied projects have research questions related to practice; answers to these questions are sought for practical reasons, usually as an aid to decision making. A good interpretation not only uses the project's findings to answer its research questions but also links these answers to the decisions that need to be made and usually also recommends action. Such recommendations need to be based soundly on the project's findings and also need to be realistic in view of the agency context in which they are to be carried out. To offer an absurd example, it would be futile to recommend that state rehabilitation agencies across the United States offer every client a course of psychoanalytically oriented individual psychotherapy. Even if results supported such a recommendation, these agencies could not follow it within their budgets. Further, it would meet much opposition from the administrators expected to carry it out.

Whenever a project's data disconfirm or fail to support a research hypothesis, the researcher's interpretation task includes seeking to understand why. This quest represents a search for plausible possibilities rather than definitive answers. Sometimes these possibilities represent hypotheses to be tested in future projects. Approach this quest with the intent to understand what took place and why without assuming that anything was done wrong. Perhaps mistakes will be discovered, perhaps not. If they are, view them as opportunities for learning rather than causes for guilt or self-reproach. Such reactions impair the open-mindedness necessary for this task. Carefully review the entire research process up to this point, including but not necessarily limited to all of the following:

- the body of theory or practical experience (or both) giving rise to each research hypothesis;
- the logic leading from this theory or experience to each research hypothesis;
- the treatment conditions (if any) and measures chosen to represent the variables specified in each hypothesis;
- the populations of persons yielding the data;
- the samples used, if any, as representative of these populations;
- the procedures used to select and recruit participants;
- potential design validity problems and safeguards used against them;
- the procedures by which data were analyzed; and
- any social influences likely to have shaped the interpretation process.

Depending on the reporting outlet, this quest may be discussed fully, partially, or not at all in the project report. Nonetheless, it is an essential part of the interpretation phase whenever results do not confirm a research hypothesis.

INTERPRETING BEYOND THE MISSION

Results often have implications that extend beyond the project's research questions and the reasons these questions were asked. For example, Pajak and Blase (1984) studied public school teachers who were drinking in bars; the researchers related their findings to ways the usual public school social environments might be changed to meet teachers' social and emotional needs better. Among other possible additional applications, we think their results have clear implications for programs designed to help alcohol-impaired professionals (including but not limited to teachers) recover from their dependence. As another example, Abramson's (1990) study of secrecy in relation to AIDS sought to help social workers provide more effective service to clients who have this condition. We think her results have much broader implications. Not only are the same issues faced by other professionals who serve people with AIDS, but the general social psychology of disability includes concealment (Wright, 1983) among its major concerns.

Some reporting outlets do not want reports to discuss implications beyond the project's original mission. Students sometimes ask why a researcher should be concerned with such implications if they are not to be included in the project's report. Research findings often have additional importance beyond that originally envisioned when the project was formulated; to limit your thinking arbitrarily to that original vision reduces the potential value of the results. Further reports, in addition to those originally planned, may be suggested as additional implications of the results are considered.

We add two notes of caution. First, implications are not conclusions. The further removed an interpretation is from the data on which it is based, the more tenuous it is. Though this fact is important when researchers link their findings with reasons why answers to the research questions were sought, it is even more important for implications beyond the mission. For example, implications of Pajak and Blase's (1984) findings for treating alcohol-impaired professionals other than teachers must assume some similarities between these professionals and the teachers this project studied who were not necessarily alcohol-impaired. Such similarities may be drawn from sources outside the project, such as professional experience or other researchers' findings. Sometimes implications beyond a project's mission are best regarded as hypotheses to be investigated through future research.

Second, as new implications of the findings are explored, it is essential to remember the project's original mission. Sometimes these new implications are experienced as much more intriguing than the original mission, particularly if the researcher's interest in that mission has been dulled by a long history of much hard work and many difficult obstacles. When results are disappointing, the effects of such a history are compounded.

At its best, the interpretation phase of any project includes all three steps:

- applying the results to answer the research questions,
- relating these answers to the reasons why they were sought, and
- exploring additional meanings the results may have.

The first two of these are essential to fulfill any project's mission; the third is a highly desirable addition that often enriches the project's contribution.

COMPROMISES AND CAVEATS

A research report needs to discuss the project's "important strengths and limitations" (Pyrczak & Bruce, 1992, p. 76). As noted in Chapter 9, it is seldom if ever possible to remedy all threats to design validity simultaneously. Research planning involves compromises as some of these threats are accepted to permit procedures that guard against others viewed as more important to the particular project. For example, laboratory studies permit careful control of many factors affecting internal validity, although external validity is at risk when results of such studies are generalized to other contexts, such as counseling offices or classrooms. Conducting the project in a counseling office or classroom answers this risk to external validity, although internal validity is weakened if desirable controls are impractical. Another important compromise that appears in many projects comes from the differences between the populations of primary interest and the populations represented by the project's samples, as discussed in Chapter 10. Considerations such as these often lead researchers to use such phrases as "should be interpreted with caution" in their reports.

Although "should be interpreted with caution" may suffice for some kinds of reports, this phrase without further elaboration does not meet the need to take design validity compromises into account when interpreting results. Interpretation needs to consider the extent and manner in which each of these compromises is likely to have affected the results or their meaning. To beginning researchers, we recommend a systematic procedure for approaching this part of the interpretation task one step at a time: Start with a list of risks to design validity (such as the one in Chapter 9) and address the following questions to *each risk in turn*:

1. Is this risk to design validity relevant to this project?
    a. If not, explain why not, and skip questions 2 through 4 for this risk; proceed to the next risk on the list.
    b. If it is relevant, describe the risk and the situation or procedures that created it.
2. What did the project do about this risk to design validity?
    a. If the project included a procedure that dealt with this risk, list it.
    b. How effectively did this procedure solve the problem posed by this risk? State the basis for your judgment.
    c. If the project did not include a procedure that dealt with this risk, say so.
3. Is there anything you think should have been done about this risk, but was not done?
    a. If there is, say what should have been done differently and how it would have helped.
    b. If there were no such omissions, say so.
4. Considering all the procedures you listed in answer to #2, do you think this risk affects the answers the findings offer to any of the project's research questions? A risk to design validity may affect the conclusions if nothing was done to address it or if it was addressed incompletely. If the procedures undertaken fully answer this risk, it does not affect the conclusions. In some projects, these procedures represent a special strength.
    a. If this risk does not affect the answers to any of the research questions, say so and state the basis for your judgment.
    b. If it does affect one or more answers, express each affected answer in a manner that takes into account the effects of this risk.
    c. Decide whether procedures addressed to this risk represent one

of the project's important strengths, and state the basis for your judgment.

    d. Proceed to the next risk in the list. Defer answering #5 and #6 until you have completed questions 1 through 4 for all the relevant risks on the list.

5. Review your answers to questions 1 through 4 for all risks on the list.

    a. Examine the answers given to all of the project's research questions. Express each answer so as to *consider all the risks to design validity that affect it.*

    b. To what extent, if any, do these issues of design validity affect the capacity of the project's conclusions to fulfill its mission?

6. If you have identified implications that transcend the project's original mission, review these implications and express them to take into account all risks to design validity.

Many of these ideas are included in the practical exercises for Chapter 9. We recommend writing responses to the above six steps on scrap paper or a word processor. A good interpretation process yields many more thoughts than are suitable to include in most project reports. Nonetheless, writing your thoughts during the interpretation phase is a good way to clarify them and make them available when needed later. Then the material appropriate to each report can be selected for inclusion. For example, a thesis or dissertation should discuss most if not all of these matters in considerable detail; a journal article need only highlight the most important ones.

SOCIAL INFLUENCES AFFECTING INTERPRETATION

Chapter 5 noted that scientific misconduct often stems from social influences, such as an employer's desire that results turn out a particular way or journal editors' policies of publishing only positive results. Appelbaum (1970) has cautioned counselors not to let their interpretations of client behavior be unduly shaped by such factors as needs to agree or disagree with colleagues. Similar social forces can lead researchers to misinterpret findings, particularly to overlook rival interpretations that may be plausible in addition to favored ones.

Some further possible influences on researchers' interpretations are more subtle. Students' interpretations of published results are often shaped by their views of their own competence as compared with that of published authors. We see this problem as an example of a larger one that was discussed in a program presented by the Canadian Broadcasting Corporation (1987) on the relationship between humans and the planet. It was noted that scientists, like other humans, *interpret what they see according to their expectations.* For example, a singing blackbird had been interpreted as making territorial claims even though other rival hypotheses were equally compatible with the bird's behavior and circumstances. Denmark, Russo, Frieze, and Sechzer

(1988) pointed out that gender bias and other social stereotypes can impair any phase of a research project: formulation, planning, data collection, data analysis, interpretation, or reporting.

Researchers' expectations are often shaped by "the power of those working at the core of a discipline over maverick scientists" (Dewsbury, 1993, p. 869). The people wielding this power encourage some ideas and discourage others, at least partly because it is difficult to distinguish "the creative innovator" from "the crackpot . . . in the early stages of development" (p. 869). Anthropology students are repeatedly cautioned not to project their own culture into their ethnographies. Counselors need to be alert to a similar risk when they interpret clients' statements and behavior. We encourage counselor-researchers to be aware of ways their interpretations of results are likely to be shaped by their own expectations and the views prevalent in their social surroundings and to expand their thinking beyond these influences. For example, a researcher in a psychoanalytically oriented mental health clinic might produce findings all of his or her colleagues interpret in terms of transference, overlooking equally reasonable interpretations in terms of behavior shaped by social reinforcement.

This section concerns thinking in contrast to expressing thoughts. Chapters 4 and 5 include the idea that expressing yourself on a controversial topic can elicit criticism and controversy from the social and professional environment. Our recommendation here is that counselor-researchers think beyond traditional limits when interpreting results. It is often helpful to discuss findings with colleagues representing several different theoretical orientations. Having done so, you can deliberately decide how much of the resulting thoughts to express in the environments at hand.

Like other research skills, interpreting results is best learned through practice. Practical Exercise 2 at the end of this chapter is designed to provide a start to such practice.

REPORTING THE PROJECT

A research project is not complete until it has been reported. Its final product is a report, not a set of results hidden in a file at risk of being forgotten. The only exceptions to this rule are instances in which the researcher is also the project's only consumer. Though such instances are probably common in simple household situations (such as conducting a behavior modification regimen to reduce a child's whining at bedtime), they are rare in counseling research. Consumers must know about the project and its results for its mission to be fulfilled. Chapter 7 discussed deciding the intended outlet for a project's report as part of the planning phase. As noted earlier in this chapter, additional reporting possibilities sometimes come to mind during the interpretation phase because interpretations outside a project's original mission point to other consumers who should know about the findings.

After the results have been interpreted, the original reporting decisions need a second look. Sometimes editorial policies, acceptance rates, and other facts about an outlet change while a long-term project is under way. Results often differ from anticipations; sometimes reporting plans need to be changed. Further, some stakeholder interests may change or new interests emerge while the project is under way. Whether the original outlet decisions are kept or changed, we recommend routinely asking whether any additional dissemination plans are in order.

The Reporting Task

In Chapter 7 we suggested that various portions of a project's process be expressed in writing while it is under way including:

- the research questions, both as originally conceived and in final form after problem distillation,
- reasons for seeking answers to the research questions,
- linkages between these reasons and the research questions,
- a substantive summary of the literature review and its relationship to both the project's mission and the research plan,
- bibliographic data on each source in the literature review,
- the research plan expressed in sufficient detail to guide collecting and analyzing the data, and
- records of the day-to-day data collection process.

Most proposals for theses or dissertations and many proposals for grant-funded projects are expected to include the first six of these components. Fulfilling this requirement accomplishes much of the work of preparing the project report. The extent to which these materials must be changed for the final report depends on the reporting outlet. A thesis or dissertation, for example, will include most if not all of the literature review; in a journal article this information may need to be limited to one or two typed pages.

We recommend making a separate copy of all these materials as a point of departure for preparing the report, leaving the original version intact. When more than one report is to be prepared, a separate copy should be made for each report. With a word processor, each report should have a different file. The existing materials can then be edited as needed for each report. For example, verb tenses regarding procedures can be changed from future (in the plan) to past (for the report). If new literature emerged while the project was under way, it can be added to the literature review. Exact figures can be substituted for quantities estimated in the proposal, such as sample sizes. Findings can be inserted into tables originally prepared in skeleton form. Such editing and revising require much less time and effort than preparing these parts of a report anew.

The narrative describing the results and interpreting the findings (*results* and *discussion* sections, respectively, in journal articles) must be prepared entirely anew after the data analysis is complete. Pyrczak and Bruce (1992) discuss many good reporting suggestions that are beyond the scope of this book.

A researcher who has been closely and personally involved with all previous phases of a subject, from formulation through interpretation, will be better prepared to write the project report than one who has delegated large portions of this work to others. Even very thorough records rarely record every detail needed for a good report; personal experience with the project often fills such gaps.

The writing process usually takes more time and work than you at first expect, and rarely goes smoothly. There are times when you will feel the need to sit and think; an applicable metaphor is allowing tea to steep. Ideas may then flow well for a while, only to come to a frustrating halt long before the task is done. This experience is made worse by the pressure of deadlines or by self-critical internal messages of a sort counselors often help clients overcome. Struggling to produce ideas only makes the blockage feel worse. Beginning and experienced writers alike have such blockages from time to time. Experienced writers have one advantage; they know that past blockages were temporary. Therefore, the current one can be expected to come to an end. The following poem (Hadley, 1992, p. 1.12) arose from just such an episode while writing this book.

Writer's Block

I sat and stared at the computer screen in vain.
In search of one, just one exact, elusive word
I drudged to mine the empty caverns of my brain
Until I stopped to listen idly to a bird,
And watch a wisp of cloud waft past my windowpane.

I saw a flock of sparrows come, then disappear
And soon return to perch on branches of a tree.
As I forgot about the clock and my career,
The clouds and birds caressed my thoughts and set them free
To make some vague and evanescent meanings clear.

The idea that striving blocks the mind from intended results has a long history in Asian thought.

Two temptations we strongly advise against are procrastinating the writing task and internally resisting it. Procrastination increases later deadline pressures, and internally resisting any task makes it more difficult and aversive than it would otherwise be. When a block results from not knowing how best to express an idea you have or where to put it in the report's organization, write it now as best you can; revise its wording and decide its placement later.

To prepare a report on any topic, a researcher must decide what material to include, organize this content, and compose the sentences and paragraphs that make up the report. Sound reporting decisions require that a researcher have several points clearly in mind:

- Who are the intended *consumers* of information about the project?
- What information do these consumers *need*?
- How are these consumers expected to *use* the reports?
- What other *stakeholder interests* (if any) need to be considered?
- What are each reporting outlet's *requirements and procedures*?

While considering these points, we recommend carefully reviewing the project's original mission with regard to reasons for seeking answers to the research questions. What is each report's role in fulfilling this mission? If not addressed to this original mission, what is it expected to accomplish? To prepare a good report, you must know why it is to be produced. Clarity on these points makes these decisions much easier than they might otherwise be:

- What reports are to be prepared?
- What material is to be included in each report?
- How long and detailed will each report be?
- How will each report be organized?
- How are interpretations to be expressed?
- What editorial style will each report follow?

Determining the Consumers

Who are the people expected to receive the report? Possibilities include other counselors, other researchers, students, administrators, accrediting bodies, legislators, and the general public. A report needs to be prepared to maximize the likelihood that its intended consumers will receive it and use it in a way consistent with its mission. To do so, a researcher must know who these consumers are and what they are likely to want from the report.

Information Needs

Various consumer groups have very different information needs. For example, other researchers need to know many procedural details the general public would not understand and that many administrators and counselors would react to with impatience. Counselors need to know how they might apply the findings in their work with clients. Administrators need knowledge relevant to the decisions they must make. Reports should be prepared to minimize the amount of irrelevant material any consumer has to read or hear to get the needed information. "Irrelevant" in this context refers specifically to material outside that consumer's needs and interest. Perhaps there are several consumer groups whose information needs vary so widely that more than one report should be issued. For example, a researcher might prepare one or more journal articles, a monograph, a newsletter article, a memorandum to his or her department head, a letter to a legislative committee, an address to the local chamber of commerce, and a conference poster session, all based on the same project. The specific content and the degree of detail in each report should be based on the information needs of its receivers.

Some reporting outlets can be expected to reach several consumer groups with one report. For example, most professional counseling journals are read by counselors, researchers, counseling program administrators, and counselor education students. Attendees at professional conferences in counseling usually include these same groups.

To provide for the fact that most journals' page limitations do not allow "full documentation" of some projects (particularly qualitative ones), Polkinghorne (1991) recommended preparing two reports: one of monograph length and one of six to eight pages for journal publication. Meeting various consumer groups' information needs is a good reason to prepare multiple reports from the same project. Chapter 5 noted an unethical reason some researchers do so: solely to lengthen their lists of publication credits.

Intended Uses of the Report

Researchers are wise to think clearly about the ways they hope consumers will use a report. Is it intended to stimulate other researchers, suggest ways to improve counselors' work with clients, justify an administrative decision, support a recommended action, increase its author's chances for promotion, or enhance an agency's credibility to a credentialing body or potential customer? Chapters 3 and 5 discuss additional issues having to do with unintended effects that might be anticipated from some reports. In the project's formulation and planning phases, all these matters needed to be considered. Now, they need to be revisited in light of all that has taken place while the project was under way and borne in mind as each report is prepared. A report may explicitly express such intended uses, or not, according to its preparer's judgment.

Content and Degree of Detail

As Pyrczak and Bruce (1992) noted, all research reports need to

- state the research questions the project sought to answer,
- say how the data were collected and analyzed,
- say what results were obtained, and
- use the results to answer the research questions.

Beyond these basic points, the specific content and the degree of detail in any report should be based on the information needs of its consumers and the ways its preparer hopes these consumers will use the report. For example, some reports also develop the linkages between the research questions and the project's reasons for seeking answers. Some discuss additional implications suggested by the results.

Everything included in a research report should be relevant to the research problem (Kerlinger, 1986). This problem may include not only the project's original mission but also additional implications identified during the interpretation phase. Even experienced researchers sometimes get sidetracked from this focus, particularly in large, complex projects (Kerlinger, 1986).

As an *ideal* for reports addressed to other researchers, Kerlinger (1986) suggested that a report should provide enough information that another investigator could replicate the project from reading it. Space limitations in most books and journals prohibit including enough detail to meet this ideal, as do time limits in oral presentations. Nonetheless, reports for other researchers should approximate this ideal as closely as possible within prevailing limits. Other consumers' interests and needs usually require much less detail.

Occasionally, a researcher will decide to omit material from a report because of stakeholder interests. As an extreme example, scientists' employers prohibited them from reporting some of their findings regarding the Alaska and Persian Gulf oil spills (Wheelwright, 1991). As another example, Dewsbury (1993) noted some journal editors' reluctance to publish material they regard as controversial. When there is a realistic risk that disclosing results may work against the interests of one or more important stakeholders, the decision to report or withhold results often requires careful thought. This thought needs to include, but not be limited to, ethical issues discussed in Chapter 5.

Organization

Organizing any report includes two kinds of decisions: grouping and sequencing. **Grouping** refers to deciding what material is to go together in the report's various sections. In this book, for example, most of the content about reporting is in this chapter, although some reporting material related to program evaluation, ethics, and planning is in Chapters 4, 5, and 7, respectively. **Sequencing** refers to choosing the order in which material is to appear in the report. In this chapter, for example, we discuss *degree of detail* after *uses* and before *organization*.

It is important to know the requirements and customs of the reporting outlet for which one is writing. Most counseling journals require research manuscripts to follow the organization plan prescribed by the *Publication Manual of the American Psychological Association* (1983). Sulzer-Azaroff and Reese (1982) developed a checklist with a task analysis for a report's various sections. See these sources and Pyrczak and Bruce (1992) for more detail than the following summary offers.

The main text of an article is preceded by a title page and an **abstract.** An abstract is a brief, concise summary, usually in 100 to 150 words. The main text comprises four major sections: introduction, method, results, and discussion. Each of these sections is introduced by a heading (sometimes omitted for the introduction). The method section is divided into subsections with each introduced by its own subheading. The other sections may be so subdivided or not, according to their length and complexity. A list of references follows the main text. This list includes every source cited in the text, and only those sources. If certain detailed information would be helpful to readers but would be distracting or otherwise inappropriate in the main text (for example, a detailed description of a complex apparatus), it may be placed in an appendix. An appendix is rare in journal articles but much more common in longer reports.

In reports substantially longer than journal articles (such as theses, dissertations, monographs, funded projects' reports to granting agencies), these sections may appear as chapters. Each chapter is usually divided into its own major sections, and each section of a chapter may be further subdivided. Most theses and dissertations include a much more extensive literature review than is usually possible in a journal article; a whole chapter is often devoted to this literature and its role in shaping the project's mission.

Except as required by the reporting outlet, no specific organization plan needs to be slavishly followed. Variations abound in the literature. One example is Kerlinger's (1986, pp. 645–651) suggested outline:

  I. Problem
    1. Theory, hypotheses, definitions
    2. Previous research; the literature
 II. Methodology—Data Collection
    1. Sample and sampling method
    2. How hypotheses were tested . . . procedures, instrumentation
    3. Measurement of variables
    4. Methods of analysis, statistics
    5. Pretesting and pilot studies
III. Results, Interpretation, and Conclusions

Existing organization plans are often helpful as a point of departure from which to develop your own.

Regardless of length and specific organization plan, any written report should be organized to lead readers quickly and easily along the course of the writer's thinking. This principle applies equally to every chapter, section, subsection, and paragraph.

Constructing Tables and Graphs

Chapter 13 recommends preparing graphs and tables in skeleton form as an aid to deciding what data analysis steps to carry out. This section discusses the role of tables and graphs in a research report and some of the mechanics of preparing them.

Quantitative data in a table or graph can often be read and understood more quickly and easily than the same data presented in narrative prose. Similarly, a table sometimes enhances the presentation of qualitative material, as exemplified by Tables 13.8, 13.9, and 13.10. Such is the purpose of these forms of presentation. The narrative needs to refer consumers (readers or listeners) to tables or graphs containing material under discussion but should *not* slavishly repeat every detail contained in any table or graph. The narrative should "describe the main conclusions to be reached . . . and point out highlights that the reader may otherwise overlook" (Pyrczak & Bruce, 1992, p. 70).

The manner of arranging tables and graphs with the text depends on the type of report. In a manuscript to be typeset by a publisher (such as a journal article or book), each table or graph must be on a separate page with the approximate place of insertion indicated in the text (APA, 1983). This arrangement allows the compositor to place these materials where they fit best. When a report is to be reproduced from typed or computer-printed originals, tables and graphs are usually integrated into the narrative, although it is permissible to place them at the end when they are so large or so numerous that integrating them would make the narrative difficult to read. In an oral presentation, tables and graphs may be projected onto a screen or reproduced on paper and distributed as handouts.

Although a table or graph supplements the narrative and is an integral part of the report, it should be understandable independently of the narrative. Much has been done toward fulfilling this requirement if all of the following are clear:

- the title,
- the heading of every row and column of a table, and
- the label of each axis, line, bar, and sector present in a graph.

Sometimes clarity requires one or more explanatory notes. The *Publication Manual of the American Psychological Association* (1983) discusses preparation of tables and graphs in much more detail than we find reasonable to include in this chapter. We recommend having this source at hand when preparing any table or graph for inclusion in a research report.

Tables. The *Publication Manual* (APA, 1983) offers detailed instructions for the preparation of tables, illustrated with many examples. Most such instructions have to do with clarity; it is wise to observe these whenever they are applicable. A few instructions (double spacing, for example) are specific to manuscripts and can be ignored when preparing reports to be reproduced directly from computer-printed or typed copy. Chapter 13 includes several examples of tables. Others may be found in the literature search for any new research project. A researcher may use any or all of these as models when preparing his or her own tables.

Some beginning researchers are tempted to construct tables so complex that readers have difficulty understanding them. A very complex table may seem perfectly clear to a researcher who is intimately familiar with the project but be much less so to readers lacking this familiarity. Tables are used to convey data efficiently to readers. If readers must spend a long time studying a table's layout to figure out what it means, its purpose is undermined. To avoid this problem, we suggest to beginning researchers:

- Ask one or more people unfamiliar with the project to read each table in draft form and comment on it before the report is completed.
- If any table is difficult to understand because it is too complex, consider dividing it into two or more tables.

Each table should be numbered and identified by number when discussed in the narrative.

Graphs. Graphs used in counseling research reports include circle graphs (also called **pie graphs** or **pie charts**), line graphs, bar graphs, and scatter graphs (also called scattergrams). We will provide illustrations of the various kinds of graphs in the following pages. Our recommendations throughout the remainder of this section are based largely on the *Publication Manual* (APA, 1983), Kerlinger (1986), and Larsen (1989).

Circle graphs, as illustrated in Figure 14.1, usually represent the frequency distribution of a nominal variable; sometimes circle graphs are used for an ordinal, interval, or ratio variable for which values have been classified into categories (for example, children, adolescents, and adults as age groups). Other uses of circle graphs include showing the distribution of an agency's income (for example, client fees, grants, contracts, insurance) and expenses

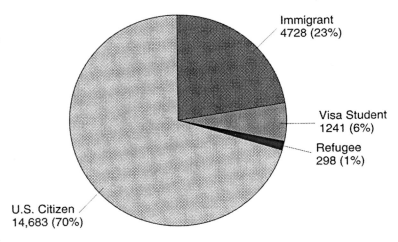

F I G U R E 14.1
Sample circle graph: distribution of a state university's student body by citizenship status.
SOURCE: *Cal State L.A. Facts*, #7, Office of Public Affairs and Analytical Studies, California State University, Los Angeles, 1992.

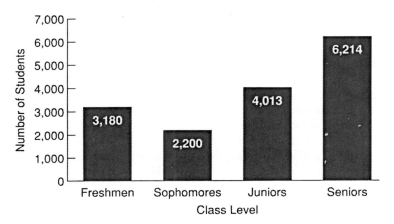

F I G U R E   14.2
Sample bar graph showing the frequency distribution of class standing in a university's undergraduate student body.
SOURCE: *Cal State L.A. Facts #7*, Office of Public Affairs and Analytical Studies, California State University, Los Angeles, 1992.

(for example, salaries, fringe benefits, office rent, supplies, mileage). Circle graphs show proportions more prominently and directly than any other type of graph. They are ideally suited to this purpose, less so to others. For example, consider a frequency distribution of a variable that has order, such as students' class standing (freshman, sophomore, junior, senior). A circle graph shows this order feature less clearly than a **bar graph,** as illustrated in Figure 14.2.

Several precautions need to be borne in mind to avoid making a circle graph confusing to readers:

- Too many sectors make a circle graph hard to read. Kerlinger (1986) recommended using a bar graph instead whenever the number of categories exceeds five.
- Distinguishing sectors by shading makes the graph easier to read.
- The graph needs to be large enough that the label for every sector is easy to read and easy to identify with the correct sector.
- It is usually best that the sector labels include numbers showing the percentage or proportion in each sector. Further, an idea of absolute size should be conveyed in either of two ways: by reporting the number in each sector, as in Figure 14.1, or by stating the size of the entire sample in the caption.
- Sometimes it is desirable to put more than one circle graph in the same figure (for example, to show similarities and differences in the distributions of two samples). The circles should be the same size in such cases, even if one sample is larger than the other. When differently sized circles are used to represent different sample sizes, readers are often confused.

Bar, line, and scatter graphs have their space defined by a pair of **axes**: a horizontal and a vertical line that intersect at right angles. Another name for these axes is **coordinates**. The horizontal axis is called the **abscissa;** the vertical axis, the **ordinate.** Both axes are quantitative in line and scatter graphs; one axis may represent qualitative classifications in bar graphs. Each bar, line, and scatter graph in the following figures is drawn approximately two-thirds as high as it is wide. Scale units on the two axes are set so the graphs use most of the space defined by these axes.

Bar graphs are useful not only for frequency distributions but may be used to compare subsamples with regard to any quantitative variable. For example, a bar graph such as the one in Figure 14.2 might compare the freshman, sophomore, junior, and senior classes with regard to their average number of units per term or their average income earned working off campus or the proportion living in dormitories. Figure 14.3 illustrates this point by showing money received through grant-funded proposals by the various schools within a large state university. This figure shows an additional possibility with bar graphs: bars of different shading enable the graph to show the variable represented on the ordinate (dollars) in relation to two other variables (school and year) at the same time. Since school is a nominal variable, the schools are arranged on the abscissa in arbitrary order.

Most bar graphs in counseling research use vertical bars. However, the labels for the bars are sometimes so long that they cannot be placed under vertical bars without being made difficult to read. In such instances, it is

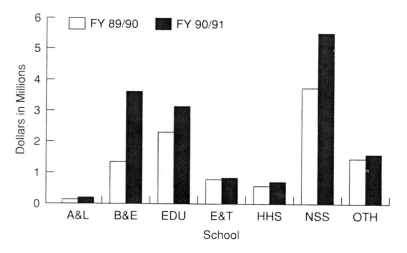

FIGURE 14.3

Sample bar graph showing grant funds received by a university's six schools and other offices during fiscal years 1990/91 and 1989/90. The "school" abbreviations represent, respectively: Arts & Letters, Business & Economics, Education, Engineering & Technology, Health & Human Services, Natural & Social Sciences, and other offices.

SOURCE: *Sponsored Program News*, California State University, Los Angeles, Summer, 1991, p. 13.

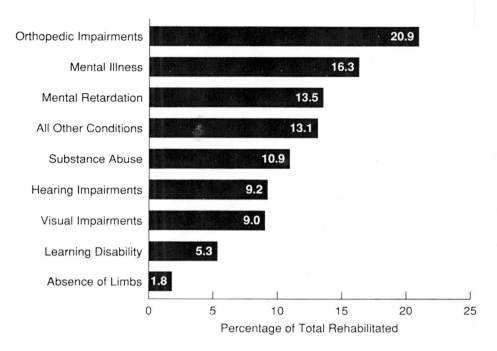

F I G U R E   14.4

Sample bar graph with horizontal bars to accommodate long labels for the bars. The graph shows the percentage distribution of disabilities among 220,408 people rehabilitated by the state–federal rehabilitation system in fiscal year 1989.

SOURCE: U.S. Department of Education, Rehabilitation Services Administration (1990), pp. 245–246.

permissible to use horizontal bars as in Figure 14.4. This figure shows the percentage distribution of disability categories among 220,408 people rehabilitated by the state–federal rehabilitation system in fiscal year 1989. Because the distribution is shown in percentages rather than frequencies, the total number of cases is given in the caption.

A **line graph** presents the relationship between two variables. Both must be continuous (as in Figure 14.5) or, if discrete, have many possible values. An example of a discrete variable with many possible values is "monthly income." It is discrete because differences of less than one cent are impossible, although one-cent increments are so small relative to variations in monthly income that the variable may be treated as if it were continuous. Connecting two data points with a line implies that all the values along the line are meaningful for both variables. For example, Figure 14.5 includes data points for blood-alcohol level two hours and three hours after a dose of alcohol. Connecting these data points with a line implies that blood-alcohol level between these times was between the two plotted values, even if not directly represented in the data. This idea is both meaningful and reasonable in this instance. In contrast, data points are *not* connected with lines in

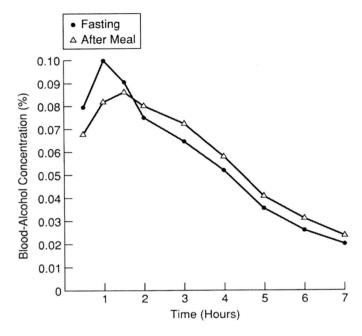

F I G U R E 14.5
Sample line graphs (two on the same pair of axes) showing mean blood-alcohol concentration during seven hours after a dose of alcohol administered under two conditions:
10-hour fasting and 15 minutes after a meal. Data are fictitious.

Figure 14.3; a point between "Business & Economics" and "Education," for
example, would be meaningless.

It is important to distinguish fundamentally discrete variables from continuous variables to which a discrete measurement system has been applied. This distinction was discussed in Chapter 13. A line graph is often
appropriate when the underlying variables are continuous although
measured with systems offering few possible values. For example, the
Wechsler tests' subscale standard scores are integers with a mean of 10 and
a standard deviation of 3, even though the abilities they measure are assumed
to be continuous variables. Therefore, a line graph might be used to chart
an individual's changing scores through a series of retests. As a second example, line graphs are used in Figures 8.1, 8.2, 8.3, 8.4, and 13.4, even though
"number of incidents" has only integer values from zero to nine. In each
of these graphs, "number of incidents" is assumed to represent an underlying continuous variable, such as the participant's inclination to the unwanted behavior. Similarly, time is a continuous variable, although these
graphs measure time in whole days. This idea makes values between data
points meaningful, even when these points involve differences of one day
or one incident. In contrast, the various schools in a university (Figure 14.4)
represent a discrete variable, as does the number of children a family has.

A scatter graph can be used to show the relationship between two quantitative variables when each participant is measured on both. In Chapter 13, we recommend constructing scatter graphs when correlation coefficients are used to analyze data so that unusual situations such as unanticipated curvilinear relationships may be discovered. Each axis of a scatter graph represents one of the variables, and each participant is represented by a dot placed according to his or her scores on both variables. In Figure 13.3, for example, a participant whose admissions examination score is 50 and whose grade point average (GPA) is 2.0 would be represented by a dot placed directly above the 50 point on the abscissa and directly to the right of the 2.0 point on the ordinate. Figure 13.3 follows the custom of representing the predictor variable (admissions examination score) with the abscissa and the criterion variable (GPA) with the ordinate. The double slash (//) at the point where the two axes meet (called the **origin**) calls readers' attention to the fact that neither axis begins at zero.

For easy reference, here is a summary of our major recommendations from the previous discussion, plus a few additional ones:

1. Construct every graph and its caption so that they can be understood without reading the accompanying narrative.
2. Use a circle graph to present the frequency distribution of a variable represented by categories whenever
   a. it is desirable to emphasize the proportions in the categories,
   b. there are five or fewer categories, and
   c. the categories represent a *nominal* variable and therefore do not have a meaningful order, or showing this order in the graph is unimportant.
3. Use a bar graph for a frequency distribution of a variable represented by categories whenever
   a. there are more than five categories, or
   b. it is desirable to show the *order* of the categories.
4. When graphing a distribution showing the proportions of a sample in various categories, supplement the graph with either the number of cases in each category or the number of cases in the entire sample.
5. When a bar graph presents two or more sets of data as in Figure 14.3, distinguish them by shading the bars differently. Provide a legend showing the meaning of each shading pattern.
6. Ordinarily, draw bar graphs with vertical bars. If labels for the bars are so long as to be awkward under vertical bars, use horizontal bars as in Figure 14.4.
7. Use a line graph only if the variables represented are continuous (or, if discrete, have many possible values). If values intermediate between the data points are *not* meaningful, use a bar graph instead.
8. With line and scatter graphs, assign variables to horizontal and vertical axes appropriately:

    a. In an experiment, represent the independent variable with the abscissa and the dependent variable with the ordinate.

    b. When one of the variables was used to predict the other, represent the predictor variable with the abscissa and the criterion variable with the ordinate. Also, follow this rule if the report recommends *future* use of one of the variables to predict the other, even if the project at hand made no such predictions.

    c. In a study showing changes in a variable over time (as in Figure 14.5), represent time with the abscissa.

9. When graphing the same pair of continuous variables in more than one group or under more than one condition, as in Figure 13.4, draw more than one line graph (but not more than four) on the same pair of axes. The *Publication Manual* (APA, 1983, p. 96) offers an alternative to too many lines on the same graph: an illustration shows four similar pairs of axes in one figure with two graphs on each pair of axes.

    a. To distinguish the lines, use a different shape (for example, circles, stars, squares, triangles; solid and hollow figures) for plotting data points on each line rather than solid versus dotted lines.

    b. Provide a legend clearly indicating the meaning of each shape.

10. Make a line, bar, or scatter graph *approximately* two-thirds as tall as it is wide. Set the scale units on the two axes so that the graph uses most of the full height and width of these axes unless doing so would misleadingly exaggerate a weak relationship.

11. Clearly label *each* axis of a line, bar, or scatter graph.

    a. Name the variable each axis represents; state the unit of measurement unless it is otherwise clear (for example, "blood-alcohol concentration (%)" in Figure 14.5).

    b. Use grid marks and numbers on the axes to indicate units of measurement (both axes on line and scatter graphs, one axis on bar graphs).

    c. Unless the point where the two axes meet (called the *origin*) represents zero on *both* in a line or scatter graph, indicate the discontinuity with a double slash (//) at the origin. In a bar graph, use the double slash if the axis representing the length of the bars does not begin at zero.

12. Clearly label each sector on a circle graph and each bar on a bar graph. Distinguish sectors on a circle graph by shading.

    Additional helpful suggestions and examples may be found in the *Publication Manual* (APA, 1983) and in Larsen (1989).

Language and Writing Style

This subsection is addressed to the task of composing the sentences and paragraphs that comprise a research report. A main guiding principle of good research reporting, underlying all the others developed later in this sub-section, is the idea that a research report has a fundamental purpose to *interpret and inform:* to interpret the results of the project and inform con-sumers about those results. In some but not all research reports, "interpret" includes recommending action and influencing some consumers to act ac-cordingly. Although we regard reporting as a creative task, it differs from what is commonly called "creative writing"; research reports do *not* seek to create a mood, entertain, or offer social commentary as some other forms of writing do. The following principles guide all good research reporting:

- objectivity,
- precision,
- efficiency,
- correct mechanics, and
- interest value.

Hadley (1992) has developed these principles in greater detail than is reason-able in this chapter. An overview is presented here to guide your report preparation.

Objectivity. The principle of objectivity includes the idea that inter-pretations, impressions, opinions, and recommendations are expressed with language that treats them openly and obviously as what they are and does not disguise them as facts. Words such as "seem," "appear," and "impres-sion" convey impressions. Explicitly deriving an interpretation from its fac-tual basis makes clear which is which. Expressions such as "in our view" designate opinions.

Language used to link interpretations with the facts on which they are based correctly expresses the degree of support these facts provide. Tenuous support is acknowledged as such rather than exaggerated. Strong support is not discounted with **weasel words** (Hollis & Donn, 1979) such as "may suggest."

Attempts to influence action are based entirely on reasoning, not emo-tional appeal. The researcher's feelings and attitudes are either not evident in the report or are expressed openly and acknowledged as his or her own. Any that are expressed serve the report's underlying goal of informing its consumers and interpreting results. For example, feelings experienced while a project was under way may have influenced decisions as to its course, such as Gordon and Shontz (1990) reported. Words and phrases carrying surplus emotional meaning (such as "confined to a wheelchair") are absent except as direct quotations.

Social commentary is absent except as it pertains to conditions under-lying the project's mission. For example, a report might refer to ethnic biases in an agency's recruitment policies and recommend changing these policies based on the project's findings; it would not criticize ethnic bias in the society at large. Bias based on social stereotypes is absent. The following are a few of the characteristics on which such stereotypes are based:

race	disability
national origin	religion
language spoken	gender
age	marital status
occupation	sexual orientation
social class	living arrangements (such as homeless)

Other biases (such as covertly favoring one theoretical orientation over others) are absent. Slang and colloquialisms are also avoided, except as direct quotations. Such expressions usually carry surplus emotional meanings. The *Publication Manual* (APA, 1983, pp. 45–49) offers detailed guidelines for "nonsexist writing"; Hadley and Brodwin (1988) and Kailes (1985) discuss language about people with disabilities.

Precision.   Precise language expresses its author's meanings exactly, unambiguously, exclusively, and literally. Careless substitutions such as calling drunkenness "alcoholism" (and vice versa) are avoided. So are euphemisms such as "get sick" to mean "vomit" and exaggerations such as "starved" to refer to a level of hunger such as might come from delaying a meal for an hour or two. Every pronoun has a clear antecedent. For example, "When Joe went to the races with his brother, he borrowed money from him" does not make clear who was the borrower and who the lender. Words that have more than one definition are used very carefully if at all so that their intended meanings will not be confused with alternate possibilities even if quoted out of context. For example, it is better to refer to decreased abusive behavior as a "desired" change rather than a "positive" change; in mathematical parlance, a decrement is a negative change. Pyrczak and Bruce (1992) noted that it is unclear to call the same variable by different names to avoid repetition or in different parts of a report.

Efficiency.   Efficient language conveys its intended meanings quickly and correctly to its readers or listeners, requiring minimal effort on their part. Further, it uses no more words than necessary to achieve this end while complying with editorial style requirements. To this end, organize the material and provide linkages between ideas to lead readers or listeners through the flow of thought with minimal effort on their part. Avoid **jargon** unless (a) all consumers will readily understand it and (b) more words would be needed to express the intended meanings with equal precision and objectivity in ordinary English. Avoid **windyfoggery** (Bernstein, 1977); do not use unusual, sophisticated sounding words when simpler, more common words will convey the intended meanings equally well. Research reports need to inform their consumers about the project and interpret its results, not arouse in them the awe sought by Reginald Bunthorne in Gilbert and Sullivan's *Patience:*

> If this young man expresses himself in terms too deep for me,
> Why, what a very singularly deep young man this deep young man must be.

Replace unnecessarily long expressions with shorter ones of equivalent meaning (for example, *now* for *at the present time*, *short* or *temporary* for *of limited duration*, *because* for *due to the fact that*). A longer list of such expressions was offered in Table 12.1. Avoid redundancies. For example, "He is a male nurse" contains no more information than "He is a nurse"; therefore "male" is redundant in this sentence. Further, it impairs objectivity because it represents gender bias. A second example is "Participants were people who . . . "; "people who" is redundant unless the context leaves some doubt that they might represent some other species.

When editing and revising drafts, look for opportunities to express the same ideas more efficiently. Writing concisely while maintaining precision and objectivity is a skill normally mastered only through long practice.

Mechanics. Mechanics refers to (a) correct grammar, spelling, and word usage and (b) compliance with the reporting outlet's editorial style requirements. Editorial style includes:

- capitalization, punctuation, and placement (for example, center, left margin, or paragraph indentation) of headings and subheadings;
- manner of citing references in the text and listing them to link the citations with the listings;
- spacing (for example, single versus double) and margins; and
- numbering tables and figures and placement of their captions.

Most journals rigidly prescribe these matters to maintain consistency among articles; inconsistencies are esthetically undesirable and risk confusing readers. Most counseling journals use the *Publication Manual* (APA, 1983) for this purpose. This source also offers guidelines regarding correct grammar and other qualities of effective writing. These guidelines are helpful even when writing for an outlet that does not prescribe editorial style. Research reports are expected to meet a much higher standard of grammar than most informal communication does. For example, "they" appears often as a singular pronoun of unspecified gender in ordinary conversation as in, "A student is penalized if they submit their homework late" (Hadley, 1992, p. 6.9). Although many people do not notice the grammatical error, this usage is unacceptable in research reports.

Interest value. To transmit ideas to readers or listeners, any report needs to maintain readers' interest rather than challenge their ability to remain awake. An alert brain receives and retains ideas more effectively than a sleepy one. Most consumers of research reports approach them with at least some interest in their content; good reports enhance this interest rather than reduce it through a plodding, tedious style of expression. Whether the report is to be presented orally or in writing, approach the tasks of preparing and delivering it with the attitude that you have something important to convey to consumers. If you undertake these tasks with the view that they are boring, burdensome obligations that you would prefer to avoid, you will probably transmit these qualities to the product. Better that you endow it with your interest and enthusiasm instead.

Maintain objectivity. Objective writing need not be dull. Vary the length and structure of sentences. Avoid repeating the same word many times when synonyms convey the intended meanings equally well. We regard the litany as a poor model for research writing. Express action directly with verbs rather than indirectly with verbal nouns. For example, "Participants were assigned . . . " is more effective than "Assignment of participants was . . . " Unless otherwise necessary for clarity or to meet editorial requirements, refer to yourself or the research team with personal pronouns such as *I* or *we* rather than impersonally with such expressions as *the experimenter.* Do not use the editorial "we" when you mean "I."

Review the draft of the report looking for ways to improve its interest value before issuing the final copy. Whether the report is to be delivered orally or in writing, pay attention to how it would sound if read aloud (Lanham, 1980). And when delivering an oral report, do *not* read it verbatim from copy. Instead, maintain eye contact with the audience, using notes only as necessary. Even if a report prepared in advance is to appear in published proceedings, most conferences do not require that oral presentations match such copy word for word.

Chapter Summary

After a project's data have been analyzed, the researcher must decide what the results mean, both as answers to the research questions and in relation to the reasons these questions were asked. The interpretation of results should discuss the project's strengths and weaknesses, including any compromises or unanticipated events that may have affected design validity. Unless the researcher is to be the project's only consumer, the project must be reported to fulfill its mission. Many projects yield more than one report. Each report must take into account its consumers' information needs; good reports contain the information needed and no more. By organizing and linking ideas, a good report leads consumers through the author's train of thought. Research reports use language that is objective, precise, efficient, correct, and interesting to consumers. The editorial requirements of reporting outlets must be met.

Practical Exercises

1. Find examples of line graphs, bar graphs, pie charts, and scatter graphs in the research literature. Evaluate the graphs you find against the recommendations listed in Chapter 14.
2. This exercise is modified from a similar one suggested by Drew and Hardman (1985). In the literature, find a research report on a topic of which

you have some prior knowledge through reading or experience. Scan the report sufficiently to establish that the project has a relatively simple design. Then use paper clips and a blank sheet of paper to cover up the author's interpretation of the results; "discussion" is a common title for this portion of a report. Carefully read the article up to your cover sheet. Then write your own interpretation of the results. Because the point of this exercise is to provide practice in interpretation (mostly thinking) rather than to produce a finished written product, focus your attention on getting the main ideas down even if you express them awkwardly. Include the following points in your interpretation:

a. Use the results to answer each of the project's research questions.
b. Link these answers to the reasons the research questions were asked. In applied projects, these linkages usually lead to recommendations for action. (If the article does not make clear why its research questions were asked, you may need to infer these reasons from what is expressed.)
c. Identify implications the results may have for theory or practice beyond the project's stated mission.
d. Using the list of questions in the Compromises and Caveats section of this chapter and the list of risks to design validity in Chapter 9, judge how much the project is susceptible to each internal and external validity risk.

Now remove the cover sheet and compare your interpretation with the author's. What ideas are in the author's interpretation but not in yours? What ideas did you express that are not in the original article? Use your judgment to account for any differences. For example, did space limitations in the reporting outlet leave too little room to discuss some of the issues you identified? Do you have reason to suspect that social influences such as those discussed in this chapter have affected either your interpretations or the author's, or both? Never automatically assume that any differences represent your ignorance or misjudgment in contrast with a published author's greater wisdom. Although such an assumption will sometimes be correct, the reverse situation is true more often than most of us, students and experienced researchers alike, find comfortable. Therefore, we suggest that you think carefully about all such differences and the issues that underlie them. When faced with questions you cannot resolve for yourself, consult a colleague or an instructor.

When you have finished this exercise with one article and had time to think about and digest the experience, repeat it with another. As you gain experience and skill, try it with increasingly complex projects.

Appendix A

Potential Literature Sources

Databases

The following databases include references to sources relevant to studies of counseling. The EAPA entry is from *EAP Association Exchange*, May 1991 (vol. 21, #5, p.14). The "Test Collection" entry is from an Educational Testing Service brochure. The other addresses listed were taken from *Directory of Online Databases*, published quarterly by Cuadra/Elsevier and available in most university libraries. Additional databases relevant to specific projects may be found in this source.

Most university libraries offer searches of these and other databases as a service to students and faculty. Users may also access such databases via the Internet. Such access requires appropriate computer software and hardware and knowledge of user-interface tools such as Gopher or TechInfo, navigators such as Gopher, WAIS, or WorldWideWeb, and navigator servers and their data such as archie, VERONICA, or Usenet. Smith (1993) provides helpful information for navigating the Internet.

Family Resources
National Council on Family Relations
Family Resource & Referral Center
1910 W. County Road B, Suite 147
St. Paul, MN 55113

Rehabdata
National Rehab Information Center
Catholic University of America
4407 8th Street NE
Washington, DC 20017
(202) 635-5822 or (800) 346-2742

ERIC
National Institute of Education
ERIC Processing & Referral Facility
4833 Rugby Avenue, Suite 301
Bethesda, MD 20814
(301) 871-9422

EAPA
Resource Center
Employee Assistance Professionals Association
4601 N. Fairfax Drive, Suite 1001
Arlington, VA 22203
(Searches may be ordered from a menu that is expanded from time to time.)

PsyINFO
American Psychological Association
1400 N. Uhle Street
Arlington, VA 22201
(800) 374-2721

Test Collection Database
Test Collection
Educational Testing Service
Princeton, NJ 08541
(609) 921-9000

ABSTRACTS AND INDEXES

The following abstracts and indexes contain references to professional literature relevant to various specializations in counseling.

Business Periodicals Index
Child Development Abstracts & Bibliography
Current Index to Journals in Education
DSH Abstracts (deafness, speech, hearing)
Education Index
Educational Administration Abstracts
Exceptional Child Education Abstracts
Human Resources Abstracts
Personnel & Management Abstracts
Psychological Abstracts
Resources in Education
Women's Studies Abstracts
Work Related Abstracts

Until 1983, the *Journal of Studies on Alcohol* (and its predecessor, the *Quarterly Journal of Studies on Alcohol*) published abstracts of the world literature on alcohol and alcoholism. However, this journal has discontinued this service.

ANNUAL REVIEWS

The following annual reviews may be useful sources of research literature on various counseling topics.

Advances in Clinical Rehabilitation
Annual Review of Addictions Research & Treatment
Annual Review of Gerontology & Geriatrics
Annual Review of Psychology
Annual Review of Rehabilitation (published 1980–86; superseded in 1987
    by *Advances in Clinical Rehabilitation*)
Evaluation Studies Review Annual

JOURNALS

Numerous professional journals publish articles relevant to counseling. We
list some of them, plus a few related to program evaluation.

Addictive Behaviors
Administrative Science Quarterly
Advances in Behaviour Research & Therapy
AIDS Education and Prevention
Alcohol Alert (published by NIAAA)
Alcohol Health and Research World
American Counselor
American Education Research Journal
American Journal of Community Psychology
American Journal of Orthopsychiatry
American Journal of Psychiatry
American Psychologist
Applied and Preventive Psychology
Applied Measurement in Education
Archives of Sexual Behavior
Behavioral and Brain Sciences
Behavioral Health Management
Behavior Therapy
Behaviour Research and Therapy
Biofeedback and Self-Regulation
Brain and Cognition
Brain and Language
Brain, Behavior, and Immunity
British Journal of Clinical Psychology
British Journal of Developmental Psychology
British Journal of Medical Psychology
British Journal of Psychology
British Journal of Social Psychology
Child Assessment News
Clinical Gerontologist
Cognitive Psychology
Cognitive Therapy and Research

Consciousness and Cognition
Contemporary Educational Psychology
Cross Cultural Research (formerly *Behavior Science Research*)
Developmental Review
Development and Psychopathology
Disability Studies Quarterly
Drug Abuse Services Research Series
EAPA Exchange (formerly the ALMACAN)
EAP Digest
Educational Psychology Quarterly
Educational Researcher
Employee Assistance
Evaluation Practice
Evaluation Review
Health Psychology
Hormones and Behavior
International Journal of Addictions
International Journal of Psychoanalytic Psychotherapy
Journal of Abnormal Psychology
Journal of Applied Behavior Analysis
Journal of Applied Behavioral Science
Journal of Applied Psychology
Journal of Applied Rehabilitation Counseling
Journal of Behavior Therapy and Experimental Psychiatry
Journal of Clinical Child Psychology
Journal of Clinical Psychology
Journal of Consulting and Clinical Psychology
Journal of Counseling and Development (formerly *Personnel & Guidance Journal*)
Journal of Cross Cultural Psychology
Journal of Educational Psychology
Journal of Health and Social Behavior
Journal of Human Stress
Journal of Learning Disabilities
Journal of Nervous and Mental Disease
Journal of Occupational & Organizational Psychology
Journal of Organizational Behavior Management
Journal of Private Sector Rehabilitation
Journal of Psychosomatic Research
Journal of Rehabilitation
Journal of Studies on Alcohol (formerly *Quarterly Journal of Studies on Alcohol*)
Journal of Substance Abuse Treatment
Journal of the Experimental Analysis of Behavior
Journal of Vocational Behavior
Journal of Vocational Rehabilitation

NIDR Forum (published by the National Institute for Dispute
  Resolution)
Organizational Behavior & Human Decision Processes
Professional Counselor
Professional Psychology
Psychoanalytic Psychology
Psychosomatic Medicine
Psychology of Addictive Behaviors
Psychology of Women Quarterly
Psychotherapy: Theory, Research & Practice
Rehabilitation Counseling Bulletin
Rehabilitation Psychology
The Arts in Psychotherapy
The Behavior Analyst
The Behavior Therapist
The Counseling Psychologist
The Personnel Administrator
The School Counselor
Training and Development Journal

CONFERENCES

Encyclopedia of Associations, edited by K. Gruber, lists dates and locations
of conferences scheduled by various organizations. This source is issued
annually by Gale Research Company. You can also contact directly the
organizations listed below to ask about dates and content of past and future
conferences.

ORGANIZATIONS

Many professional organizations are concerned with counseling or its various
specialties. We offer a partial list, *not* representative of the counseling profession as a whole.

American Counseling Association (ACA): ACA (formerly the American
  Association of Counseling and Development) is a national organization
  with many divisions, each relating to a different counseling specialty,
  and statewide affiliates in many states.
  5999 Stevenson Avenue
  Alexandria, VA 22304
  (800) 545-2223
American Educational Research Association (AERA): AERA is a national
  organization with many divisions. Division E (Counseling and Human
  Development) is most relevant to counselors, but the activities of Divi-

sions D (Measurement and Research Methodology) and H (School Evaluation and Program Development) may also be of interest to counselors.

    1230 17th Street NW
    Washington, DC 10036-3078
    (202) 223-9485

American Psychological Association (APA): APA has many divisions, several of which are relevant to counseling, and many statewide and local affiliates.

    1200 17th Street NW
    Washington, DC 20036
    (800) 374-2721

Association for Advancement of Behavior Therapy (AABT): AABT was founded to rapidly communicate news and the discussion of current issues in behavior therapy via its journal, newsletter, and annual conference.

    15 East 36th Street
    New York, NY 10018
    (212) 279-7970

Association for Behavior Analysis (ABA): ABA was founded to promote the experimental, theoretical, and applied analysis of behavior. They have many state and international chapters.

    Western Michigan University
    258 Wood Hall
    Kalamazoo, MI 49008-5052
    (616) 387-4494

Board for Rehabilitation Certification (BRC): BRC is a national organization that certifies work adjustment and vocational evaluation specialists, rehabilitation counselors, and insurance rehabilitation specialists.

    1835 Rohlwing Road, Suite E
    Rolling Meadows, IL 60008
    (312) 394-2104

Employee Assistance Professionals Association (EAPA): Formerly Association of Labor, Management, Administrators, and Consultants on Alcoholism (ALMACA). EAPA is the major professional organization for people who administer or evaluate employee assistance programs (EAPs) or work as EAP counselors. For several years, the organization has had a much broader focus than alcoholism; this focus is reflected in its 1989 name change.

    4601 N. Fairfax Drive
    Alexandria, VA 22203
    (703) 522-6272

National Association of Rehabilitation Professionals in the Private Sector (NARPPS): NARPPS is primarily concerned with insurance-supported rehabilitation. It holds annual conferences and publishes a newsletter.

    P. O. Box 870
    Twin Peaks, CA 92391

National Clearinghouse of Rehabilitation Materials
    Oklahoma State University
    115 Old USDA Building
    Stillwater, OK 74078
    (405) 624-7650
National Rehabilitation Association (NRA): NRA has divisions relating to
    rehabilitation administration, rehabilitation counseling, job placement,
    and vocational evaluation and work adjustment.
    633 South Washington Street
    Alexandria, VA 22314
    (703) 620-4404
Professional Rehabilitation Association
    P. O. Box 772
    Lindenhurst, NY 11757-0772
Rehabilitation International
    25 East 21st Street
    New York, NY 10010
    (212) 420-1500

Appendix B

Sample Goal and Objectives

The goal and objectives quoted (with editorial revisions) on this and the following pages are drawn from a proposal submitted to the National Institute of Alcohol Abuse and Alcoholism in 1981. This particular mission statement was strengthened by organizing outcome and process objectives into separate sections and distinguishing between them by a numbering system. Each number begins in "O" or "P" respectively, representing an outcome or a process objective.

Goal

To develop a demonstration program that will improve the quality, availability, and utilization of services to people with alcohol problems who also have other disabilities. These services include both those addressed to recovery and those addressed to rehabilitation.

Outcome Objectives

Measurement of outcome objectives will be based primarily on interview and questionnaire data collected by Regional Rehabilitation Coordinators (RRCs), who will be responsible for the execution of project activities within an assigned geographic region. RRCs will make at least one visit per year to each agency involved with this three-year project. Comparison between agency replies to the same inquiries on these occasions will form the basis for evaluation of the degree to which outcome objectives are met. Before the first visit to any agency by an RRC, the evaluation specialist will develop (a) interview guides for the RRCs' use in collecting the needed data; (b) record forms for convenient recording and storage of these data; and (c) procedures for storage and retrieval of these data that meet legal and ethical requirements concerning confidentiality.

Objective O-1
By the end of the second project year, to increase by at least 15% the number of people being served in a manner appropriate to their existing combination of alcohol problems and problems arising from other disabilities.

Data gathered. Number of clients served by agencies providing alcoholism services who have other disabilities, services received by each client from that and other agencies, number of clients served by agencies providing services to people with other disabilities who have alcohol problems, scope of services received by such clients.

Objective O-2
To increase the receptiveness of alcoholism service facilities toward clients who also have other disabilities.

Data gathered. Facility's willingness to serve people with other disabilities, reasons for reluctance to serve people with other disabilities, presence or absence of architectural barriers, availability of assistive services such as readers and interpreters.

Objective O-3
To increase the extent to which alcoholism service facility staff have basic knowledge required to serve people with other disabilities (for example, psychological, social, and medical aspects of disability; relatedness between certain disabilities and alcohol; sources of help).

Data gathered. Information held by staff on such topics as medical aspects of disabilities, psychological and social aspects of disablement, relatedness of alcohol to certain disabilities, and sources of services for people with disabilities.

Objective O-4
To increase the frequency with which alcoholism service facilities make appropriate referrals when unable to service disabled clients because of factors beyond their immediate control, such as major architectural barriers.

Data gathered. Incidents remembered by staff in which disabled clients or applicants were discharged or refused services because of disability, reasons why the disability led to this decision, and referrals made, if any.

Objective O-5
To change the attitudes of staff in facilities serving disabled people toward greater acceptance of people with drinking problems. "Acceptance" in this context refers to willingness to consider each case individually as opposed to an inclination to reject automatically any client or applicant who has a drinking problem.

Data gathered. Attitudes expressed by staff toward working with clients who have alcohol problems.

Objective O-6
To increase the knowledge of staff concerning drinking problems and what can be done about them.

Data gathered. Information known by staff about (a) cues that a drinking problem probably exists, (b) common behaviors among persons with drinking problems, (c) relatedness of certain disabilities to alcohol, and (d) sources of help for people seeking to gain or maintain sobriety.

Objective O-7
By the end of the third project year, to increase by 15% the frequency with which facilities serving disabled people identify and address drinking problems among their clients.

Data gathered. Incidents remembered by staff covering the previous 12 months in which a client had a drinking problem; nature of agency's response to such incidents.

Objective O-8
By the end of the third project year, to increase by at least 20% the number of established referral relationships between alcoholism service facilities and facilities serving disabled people generally.

Data gathered. Nature of referral relationships reported by facilities serving disabled people and by alcoholism service providers.

PROCESS OBJECTIVES

Process objectives will be evaluated largely through a record of the project's activities. Each RRC will gather the data specified for each objective and subobjective.

Objective P-1
To develop a network of relationships with individuals, service facilities, and other organizations that will enable the project to:

a. seek out, identify, visit, and (when appropriate) refer people with disabilities who may be abusing alcohol but who are not receiving services appropriate to the existing combination of disability and alcohol problems.

Data gathered. For each potential client visited: descriptive data (such as age, gender, ethnicity), nature of alcohol problem, nature of other disabilities, previous experience with service providers, current service needs, referrals made, results of follow-up contacts, dates of visit.

b. provide information to staff of alcoholism provider services concerning such matters as:
   1. 1973 Rehabilitation Act requirements
   2. psychological and social aspects of disability generally
   3. relatedness of alcohol to certain disabilities
   4. special needs of certain disability groups, such as blind, deaf, and spine injured
   5. community resources to meet those needs

Data gathered. Name of agency, names of staff attending staff development sessions covering topics above, topics discussed, date.

c. provide information to staff of disability provider services concerning matters such as:

1. signs that suggest increased likelihood that a client has a drinking problem
2. special characteristics of alcohol abusers as a disability group
3. ways to evaluate whether client drinking constitutes a problem that merits referral
4. ways to deal with client drinking that interferes with the rehabilitation process (for example, constructive confrontation, Addiction Research Foundation, 1979)
5. community resources to which clients with other disabilities may be referred for help with alcohol problems

Data gathered. See Objective P-1-b.

d. consult with staff of alcoholism provider services and disability provider services concerning emergent problems of individual clients (and potential clients) who have disabilities other than addiction and who also drink abusively.

Data gathered. For each consultation: name of agency, names of staff with whom consulted, topics discussed, dates of consultation and follow-up contact, results of follow-up.

e. consult with government granting and contracting agencies concerning ways in which definitions of billable services might be changed to allow contractors to improve services to people with disabilities other than addiction who also drink abusively.

Data gathered. For each consultation: names of agencies and people consulted, type of billable services discussed, reason change believed desirable, recommendations made, dates of consultation and follow-up contact, results of follow-up.

Objective P-2

To offer information about people with alcohol problems who also have other disabilities to the general public and to relevant professions through such means as conference presentations, information booths at conferences, and free public talks.

Data gathered. Nature of each dissemination activity, location, dates, names of cooperating organizations.

Objective P-3

To develop materials that may be used for purposes of training and consultation with staff, education of students, and dissemination of information to the general public concerning people with alcohol problems who also have other disabilities. These materials will include, but not necessarily be limited to

a. a directory of service providers with information concerning ability and willingness to serve people with alcohol problems who also have other disabilities, including limitations that apply to some disabilities but not others, such as architectural barriers.
b. training guides and accompanying materials such as brochures, booklets, filmstrips, and posters.

Data gathered. Verification that materials (directory, training guides, and so forth) were developed, ratings of value of these materials from potential users.

Appendix C

Documents Pertinent to Ethical Research Practices

Organizations That Publish Ethical Guidelines for Research

American Association of Marriage & Family Therapists
American Counseling Association
American Educational Research Association
American Psychological Association
Association for Behavior Analysis
Commission on Rehabilitation Counselor Certification
Employee Assistance Certification Commission
National Association of Rehabilitation Professionals in the Private
  Sector
National Board for Certified Counselors
National Career Development Association

Note: These organizations may have state and regional affiliates that also publish documents related to ethical research.

A GENERIC FORM FOR OBTAINING INFORMED CONSENT

You are invited to participate in a study conducted by [insert name and affiliation]. We hope to learn more about [state the subject of the study]. You were selected to participate in this study [explain how client/participant was selected]. Participants will be involved as follows: [describe what will be expected of participants and explain any risks, discomforts, inconveniences, and benefits they may experience].

If you do not wish to participate in this study, you may receive counseling services similar to those offered in the study by [explain how they may receive similar services].

All information gathered in this study will remain confidential and will be disclosed only with your permission or as required by law. If you give us your permission by signing this consent form, we promise to protect your confidentiality so that no reports that result from this study will identify you as having been a participant.

Your decision to participate or not to participate will not influence your [academic, client, professional] status at [name of sponsoring agency]. If you decide to participate, you are free to withdraw from the study at any time without prejudice.

The [human subjects at risk committee] has reviewed this study and approved the present research. If you have any concerns, however, please call [name and telephone number] where you may report your concerns anonymously if you wish.

If you have any questions about this research, please call [name and telephone number of researcher], who will be happy to answer them.

By signing the consent form below, you indicate that you have read the form and that you are voluntarily agreeing to participate in the study.

_____   _____
Signature of Participant   Date

_____
Signature of Parent or Guardian (if applicable)

An Ethical Issues Checklist
for Research Projects in Counseling

Planning the Project

_____ Ethical standards of pertinent professional organizations and certifying bodies have been obtained and thoroughly reviewed.

_____ Ethical requirements of the agencies or educational institutions sponsoring the project have been obtained and thoroughly reviewed.

_____ The project has been designed in accordance with these ethical standards.

_____ The costs and benefits of the project to the participants/clients, the researcher, the sponsoring agencies, and the larger community have been considered.

_____ The project has been designed to eliminate or minimize any procedures that may place research participants at risk of harm. All the following are absent or have been minimized:

    _____ deception

    _____ mental stress, including subjection to public embarrassment, social criticism, or reduced self-esteem

    _____ humiliation

    _____ physical or emotional discomfort

    _____ irritation or harassment

    _____ hypnosis

    _____ sensory deprivation

    _____ sleep deprivation

    _____ injection

    _____ inhalation or ingestion of possibly toxic materials, including all alcohol, other drugs, or placebos

    _____ strenuous physical exertion

    _____ use of physical stimuli in abnormal amounts (for example, shock, heat, cold, light)

    _____ violation of anonymity or confidentiality of participants and data

    _____ observations recorded about individuals that, if made public, could produce civil or criminal action against the participant or harm the participant's financial or employment status

    _____ violation of any civil rights

_____ Consideration has been given to *whether, when,* and *from whom* participant consent must be obtained.

_____ Consideration has been given to how project staff will respond if any participant shows evidence of intent to commit violence.

_____ A decision has been made as to whether a debriefing procedure is to be used.

Data Collection

_____ Procedures have been developed (unless deemed unnecessary), preferably including the construction of a written consent form, to ensure informed consent of all clients/participants.

_____ A written consent form, if utilized, is written in language as clear and simple as possible, and includes:

    _____ the name and affiliation of the researchers

    _____ the purpose of the study

    _____ any expected benefits or possible harm to the clients/participants, and a description of alternative procedures available to them

    _____ a description of how and when any proposed compensation, monetary or otherwise, will be offered

    _____ an assurance of confidentiality, within such limits as may exist

    _____ an assurance that participation will in no way affect the client's/participant's status with the sponsoring agency

    _____ a statement that the appropriate review committee, if such a committee exists, has reviewed the research procedures

    _____ an assurance that the client/participant is free to withdraw from the research project at any time without prejudice

    _____ a name and telephone number to contact anonymously if the client/participant wishes to report any deviation from these procedures

    _____ a place for a signature indicating that the consent form has been read and consent is given or not given to participate in the research project

_____ If the research project involves administration of a counseling intervention, such intervention is within the professional competence of the person administering it.

_____ All people administering research procedures have been thoroughly trained in the use of any equipment involved and emergency procedures for dealing with unusual client reactions.

_____ Susceptible participants (such as people with heart conditions) who should be screened out of the study have been deleted.

_____ All clients/participants requiring debriefing have been debriefed, preferably immediately after the research procedure.

_____ Procedures are in place to remediate any undesirable consequences clients/participants may have experienced as a result of the research procedures.

Data Analysis

_____ Provisions have been made to ensure that only research project staff with legitimate access to information revealing clients'/participants' identities have such access.

Reporting

_____ Only research results that are sufficiently clear, interpretable, and useful to the readership are reported.

_____ The social consequences of reporting possibly controversial results have been anticipated and considered.

_____ Care has been taken to ensure that reporting of research results is not misleading.

_____ Authorship of the reporting document has been fairly determined based on the actual contribution to the research project and the document.

_____ In the reporting document, ideas and information drawn from the work of others are appropriately credited.

_____ Care has been taken to ensure the confidentiality of all clients/participants in the reporting document.

_____ Similar articles about the project are not submitted simultaneously to two or more similar journals.

_____ Appropriate credit is given in the written document to any people, other than the authors, who have made contributions of note to the research project or report.

Appendix D

Suggestions for Managing Literature Review Materials

Information found in a literature review must be recorded, evaluated, and stored so as to be readily available when needed to pursue leads to further relevant sources, plan the project, and prepare the project report. Here are some practical suggestions toward this end based on four expectations from our experience:

- Many more sources will be identified than are eventually used.
- Some sources will at first appear irrelevant and later be found useful.
- Different sources will bear on different aspects of the project (for example, some may concern theoretical issues, some design, some sampling, some measurement methods, some counseling techniques, some statistical analysis, some several of these aspects).
- The final report will require an alphabetized list of references.

Record each source on a separate card or sheet when making notes from literature by hand. We find 5 × 8 cards, or similar size paper, easiest to use. For convenience, we refer to these sheets or cards as "reference cards." Reference cards can be sorted into categories, resorted as the need arises, and later arranged alphabetically and photocopied to make a rough copy of a reference list. When you identify a reference in a book, article, abstract, or other source, make a reference card for it. Assemble those you have yet to look up in a way that will make this next task easy.

With a word processor, use a separate "document." Several computer manufacturers now offer laptop models small and light enough to carry easily into a library. Entering material from a literature search directly onto a diskette can save much redundant work of copying and recopying as the project report is prepared. If you use a word processor for making notes of literature sources, put these notes on a separate document with its own file name rather than on the document you are using to write the project report. You can use a *move text* function to arrange your sources according to category as you are writing, and then rearrange them in alphabetical order for the final reference list. A *copy* function will enable you to copy material from your notes into the text of your report. To ensure against loss of information by accidental damage to a diskette, it is wise to (a) print your list of sources from time to time as it grows and (b) make a backup disk and revise it each time you add new sources. Clearly dating each sheet of these printed lists helps prevent confusing earlier versions with later ones.

Record complete bibliographic data from the start.   "Complete bibliographic data" means all the information you will need to include about this source in the list of references if you list it. Follow a guide such as the *Publication Manual of the American Psychological Association* (1983) with regard to what to include. If you locate a source through an abstract or another author's reference list, note complete bibliographic information at that time, then check it for accuracy when you get the primary source. It is tempting to make such shortcuts as omitting the volume number of a periodical or the publisher of a book. However, saving minutes or seconds in this way can waste hours when you must later track down the missing information.

Follow a standard format.   When noting bibliographic data, follow the standard format you will probably use when you compile a reference list for your final report. You will then be able to arrange your reference cards in alphabetical order, overlap them to reveal bibliographic data only, and photocopy them to create a draft of your reference list.

Make note of where you first found a reference to this source.   If you first found the reference in an abstract, computerized database, or other author's reference list, make note of the page number or keyword through which you found it. This step is insurance against the possibility that you make an error transcribing the bibliographic data (for example, transpose digits in a number or misspell a name). You will not have difficulty finding the primary document later if you have this information at hand.

Record call numbers for library books.   If you should need to go back to a book later, you will save time if you have kept its call number and general location (for example, third floor) in the library. If you are using several libraries, keep track of which one you got each book from; the same book may have different call numbers in different libraries.

Record page numbers for quotes.   If you find a direct quotation you think you might use in your final report, note its page numbers on your reference card. Most editors and many instructors require page numbers for all direct quotations.

Conspicuously identify aspects of the project each source addresses.   For example, if some sources concern theoretical issues, some design, some sampling, some measurement methods, some counseling techniques, and some statistical analysis, a different color might be assigned to each aspect of the project and a corner of each reference card marked with the appropriate color.

American Psychological Association (1983). *Publication manual.* Washington, DC: Author.

Baumrind, D. (1985). Research using intentional deception. *American Psychologist, 40,* 165–174.

Cochran, W.G. (1965). *Sampling techniques.* New York: Wiley.

F I G U R E D.1
A method of stacking reference cards to photocopy only the bibliographic data.

Include both substantive and methodological material in your notes. Do not limit the notes on your reference card to the author's conclusions. Make note of such matters as the mission of the reported project, hypotheses (if any), sampling procedures, subjects, measurement methods, tasks subjects performed (if any), statistical procedures used, findings, solutions to design validity problems, and any significant flaws. Exhibit D.1 provides a model of how a reference source may be summarized in such a manner. Making thorough summaries of reference sources provides for the possibility that you later become aware of methodological problems that you did not notice at first.

Photocopy. Make duplicates of the citations on your reference cards, except perhaps those relating to articles you have photocopied in their entirety. It will usually be possible to copy several citations on a page by stacking the cards to reveal the bibliographic data for each source and hide the remainder of your notes, as illustrated in Figure D.1. Keep the photocopies in a safe place, separate from your original cards. This step is insurance against having to start from scratch if the originals get lost or stolen. When you photocopy pages from a book, periodical, or other document, be sure you have complete bibliographic data on your copy.

EXHIBIT D.1
Sample Summary of a Reference Source

McKenna, A. E., & Ferrero, G. W. (1991). Ninth-grade students' attitudes toward nontraditional occupations. *The Career Development Quarterly, 40*(2), 168–181.

Mission: to discern the attitudes of 9th grade students in Pennsylvania toward vocational education, nontraditional occupations, and sources of information on careers.

Hypotheses: none. Research questions: (1) What are the most and least significant factors (job security, job prestige, remuneration, or interest in the work) considered by 9th graders when choosing an occupation? (2) Are there differences in the relative helpfulness of selected factors as sources of occupational information? Does the relative helpfulness of the factors differ by student characteristics (sex, grade, or occupational preference)? (3) Where do students prefer to go for occupational information? (4) What jobs do 9th graders consider entering when they begin working? (5) Would 9th graders consider registering for a nontraditional vocational education program? If not, why not?

Sampling procedures: Systematic sampling of one-fourth of Pennsylvania's 501 school districts; 85 of the 128 school districts contacted participated in the study.

Participants: 5,937 9th grade students, 2,934 girls and 3,003 boys.

Measurement methods: A three-part questionnaire focusing on career awareness, nontraditional occupations, and vocational education.

Tasks performed: Filling out questionnaire.

Statistical procedures: Calculation of frequencies and percentages.

Findings: (1) Most significant factor in choosing an occupation was interest in the work. (2) Students find same sex parent primary source of career information. (3) Students prefer to talk to workers and counselors as occupational information sources. Some variation by gender, but minor. (4) 45.2% of girls and 77.2% of boys would prefer to select a traditional occupation; the least appealing nontraditional vocational programs for girls were bricklaying, plumbing, and heating and air-conditioning; for boys, the least appealing programs were cosmetology, nursing, and secretarial work. (5) Majority of students were either uninterested in nontraditional occupations or preparation for the nontraditional occupation of choice was not offered in Pennsylvania.

Flaws: limited external validity: (1) sample limited to Pennsylvania; (2) one-third of school districts did not answer questionnaire.

Solutions: larger sample (nationwide?) and double sampling or more persuasive techniques for encouraging nonrespondents to reply.

APPENDIX E

SAMPLE TIME LINES

A time line may be presented verbally or graphically. Which format is best depends on the particular project. Some projects present the time line in both formats.

Our first sample represents a *verbal* presentation and is quoted from a project proposal designed to bring veterans' representatives from state employment service offices to a training site as "participants" in groups of 30. Each group would experience a five-day training program scheduled for eight hours daily. Each repetition of this training program, with a new group of participants, was called a "session." Fifteen sessions were planned for the project.

Note that some of the material in Exhibit E.1 is expressed in telegraphic style. In some proposals, telegraphic style is not acceptable; rather, all material must be expressed in complete sentences.

Our second sample time line uses a *graphic* format, as shown in Exhibit E.2. This sample time line is quoted from the same proposal as the goal and objectives in Appendix B.

EXHIBIT E.1
Time Line in Verbal Format

Project Time Line

October through December, 1986: Development phase. Staff hired, curriculum developed, curriculum materials prepared for first session; arrangements made for trainees' travel and lodging; first session's trainees identified.

January 5–8, 1987: First session.

January 12–23, 1987: Second session.

February through June, 1987: Sessions 3 through 15 will be conducted during alternate weeks to provide for revision of curriculum materials and instructional arrangements before each session begins. Evaluation data will be collected from trainees after each session.

June through September, 1987: Follow-up evaluation data collected. Final project report prepared and distributed.

EXHIBIT E.2
Sample Time Line in Graphic Format

Phase-In Time Table

Month ——	1	2	3	4	5	6	7	8	9	10	11	12
Hire program director	—											
Post jobs using P.O. box	——											
Establish physical facilities					——							
Hire administrative secretary	—											
Establish telephone, utilities, equipment	——											
Hire five regional rehabilitation coordinators (RRCs)							—					
Train & orient staff									——————			
Interstaff workshops: exchange interregional information								————————————————→				
Develop media materials												
Initial brochure	—————————————————											
Workshop materials			————————————————————									
News/journal articles for public information	——————————————————————————————→											
RRCs develop regional advisory/ volunteer committees	——————————————————————————————→											

EXHIBIT E.2
Sample Time Line in Graphic Format (*continued*)

Month ——	1	2	3	4	5	6	7	8	9	10	11	12
Train volunteers								—————————————————————→				
RRCs develop networks:												
Alcoholism provider service								—————————————————————————→				
Disability provider service								—————————————————————→				
RRCs maintain network											—————→	
RRCs develop and receive referrals of target population											————→	
Evaluation specialist												
Develops interview guides & record forms		————————————————										
Trains staff in use				———								
Develops evaluation reports											—————————	

Note: Arrows represent activities that continue past the 12th month.

APPENDIX F

RANDOM NUMBER TABLES AND INSTRUCTIONS FOR THEIR USE

The best way to ensure random selection of subjects from a pool and random assignment of subjects to groups is with random number tables such as the one reproduced in Table F.1. Procedures for their use differ slightly depending on whether the goal is selection or assignment of subjects.

USE OF RANDOM NUMBER TABLES TO SELECT SUBJECTS

The first step in using a random number table to select subjects from a pool is to number all subjects sequentially (a pool of 50 subjects would be numbered from 1 to 50). An arbitrary starting point, which can be any row and column, is then selected from the random number table. To illustrate, let us select Row 16/Column 5 (which contains the number 67) from Table F.1 as our starting point. We can then proceed either horizontally or vertically in the table to select a sample of subjects from our pool.

Suppose we would like to select a sample of 30 subjects from our pool of 50. If we proceed vertically and go straight down the column, the first number is 17, the second is 36, the third is 50, and the fourth is 51. The first three numbers tell us we should select Subjects 17, 36, and 50 from our pool for inclusion in our sample. The last number, 51, does not belong to any of the members of our pool, because we have only 50 subjects. Therefore, we will ignore it and go on to the next number. If we move to the top of the next column, Column 6, and move down vertically, we must ignore the numbers until we get to Row 5 because they are all higher than 50. The number 16 in Row 5 tells us that Subject 16 should be included in our sample. When we reach the top of Column 7, we skip the number 50 because we have already selected Subject 50 for the sample based on Column 5 and Row 19. This procedure is followed until we have selected all 30 subjects.

Table F.1 is laid out in columns of two digits, but it could be used equally well with a pool of any size from which a sample of any size was desired. For example, suppose we have a pool of 400 from which we want to choose 280 subjects. We could simply use both numbers from any column and the first number from the column next to it to create three-digit numbers. For illustration, let us select Column 2/Row 1 as our starting point. If we use the first digit of the next column to create our third digit, our first subject would be Subject 275, the next would be Subject 214, the next Subject 151, and so on until our sample was complete.

T A B L E F.1
Table of Random Numbers

Rows	Columns									
	1	2	3	4	5	6	7	8	9	10
1	10	27	53	96	23	71	50	54	36	23
2	28	41	50	61	88	64	85	27	20	18
3	34	21	42	57	02	59	19	18	97	48
4	61	81	77	23	23	82	82	11	54	08
5	61	15	18	13	54	16	86	20	26	88
6	91	76	21	64	64	44	91	13	32	97
7	00	97	79	08	06	37	30	28	59	85
8	36	46	18	34	94	75	20	80	27	77
9	88	98	99	60	50	65	95	79	42	94
10	04	37	59	87	21	05	02	03	24	17
11	63	62	06	34	41	94	21	78	55	09
12	78	47	23	53	90	34	41	92	45	71
13	87	08	62	15	43	53	14	36	59	25
14	47	60	92	10	77	88	59	53	11	52
15	56	88	87	59	41	65	28	04	67	53
16	02	57	45	86	67	73	43	07	34	48
17	31	54	14	13	17	48	62	11	90	60
18	28	50	16	43	36	28	97	85	58	99
19	63	29	62	66	50	02	63	45	52	38
20	45	65	58	26	51	76	96	59	38	72

SOURCE: Taken from Random Numbers Table of Fisher & Yates, *Statistical Tables for Biological, Agricultural and Medical Research,* published by Longman Group UK Ltd., 1974. Reprinted by permission of the Literary Executor of the late Sir Ronald A. Fisher, F.R.S. and Dr. Frank Yates, F.R.S.

USE OF RANDOM NUMBERS TABLES TO ASSIGN SUBJECTS

Assigning subjects to two or more groups can be accomplished in a somewhat similar manner. Suppose we have a sample of 64 subjects who must be assigned to four groups of equal size. Such assignment would be accomplished by once again selecting an arbitrary starting point in the random number table. Let us choose Row 6/Column 3 for our purposes. We need only examine one digit at a time, since only the numbers 1–4 concern us. If we move horizontally across the table, the first number is 2, telling us that the first subject goes into Group 2. The second is 1, so the second subject is assigned to Group 1. The remaining numbers tell us that Subjects 3, 4, 5, and 6 go into Group 4, Subject 7 into Group 1, and so on. As before, numbers larger than the number needed, in this case 4, are ignored. After any group is full, that group's number is ignored. In our example, suppose Group 2 is the first to reach its quota of 16 subjects; thereafter, we would pay attention to only the numbers 1, 3, and 4, ignoring the number 2. When all groups but the last one are full, all the remaining subjects are assigned to this last group.

We could also have chosen to move vertically down the columns rather than horizontally across rows; other aspects of the procedure would not change.

Appendix G

Suggestions for Developing
a Content Analysis System

This material supplements the discussion of content analysis systems in Chapter 11.

Universe

First, a researcher must define the *universe* of content to be analyzed. This universe might be:

- tape recordings of specified counseling sessions (for example, initial and final) taking place during a specified time period in a specified agency,
- answers to specified open-ended questions from interviews or questionnaires,
- prospective clients' stated reasons for seeking counseling during a specified time period in a specified agency,
- a couple's personal correspondence to each other during a specified time period,
- students' answers to the final examination in a specified course,
- clients' responses to the Thematic Apperception Test,
- students' analyses of case data in a written assignment, or
- transcripts of staff meetings in a specified agency during a specified time period.

The researcher's questions or hypotheses usually lead to decisions about what aspects of this universe are to be considered. For example, a researcher might choose to examine tape recordings of counseling sessions with regard to (a) relative emphasis on content versus affect, (b) clients' assignment of responsibility to self versus others, or (c) number of different issues discussed. Ordinarily, these definition tasks should be part of the formulation phase.

Unit of Analysis

Next, a researcher must define the unit of analysis. Kerlinger (1986) listed five: "words, themes, characters, items, and space-and-time measures" (p. 479).

The smallest and probably simplest units are *words*. For example, a researcher might count the number of nouns or verbs or adjectives or feeling words. Nouns might be subdivided according to whether they refer to people, places, things, or abstract ideas. Based on ideas from neurolinguistic programming (Dills, Grinder, Bandler, & DeLozier, 1980), a researcher might count the number of visual, auditory, and kinesthetic words. Schulman's (1991) two-dimensional system classifies words (a) as relating to oneself or others and (b) as directing, thought, evaluative, or qualifying-conditional.

Another possible unit is a single utterance made by a counselor or client during a session.

A **theme** is a proposition, thesis, statement, or assertion, usually about one or more people, places, things, or ideas. A simple theme often consists of one sentence; a complex theme may comprise several related sentences. For example, a researcher might note (a) clients' statements of self-reference, (b) supervisors' beliefs about the best way to respond to employees' tardiness, or (c) teachers' classroom statements about causes of racial tension.

A **character** is an individual, usually but not necessarily in a literary work. In this context, "literary work" should be very broadly construed to include not only such productions as novels, plays, stories, and poems but also material written for course assignments, as part of a counseling or psychotherapy process, or in response to tasks like the Thematic Apperception Test. For example, a researcher might note the age and sex of the protagonist in a story and rate the relative importance of this person's victim, persecutor, and rescuer roles. As a nonliterary example, a researcher might examine the various people clients introduce into the discussion during counseling sessions.

An *item* is a whole production, such as a student's term paper, a reporter's news story, a television program, or a client's account of an event as reported in a counseling session. In a study of autobiographies, the whole autobiography is an item (Kerlinger, 1986). In a study of Thematic Apperception Test responses, a researcher might regard an individual story or one respondent's entire set of stories as an item. In an analysis of questionnaire and interview data, an item might be an answer to one question or all of one respondent's answers.

Physical *space-and-time measures* can be applied to the record of a communication (for example, inches of space on the page, or minutes or seconds on a tape recording). For example, a counseling session might be examined for the proportion of time each participant speaks.

MECHANICS

Five possible quantification methods are classification, counting, rating, ranking, and physical measurement. When a unit of analysis has been chosen (words, themes, characters, items), each such unit can be classified. We list some examples:

1. Words: first person (I, me, we, us), second person (you), and third person (he, she, him, her, they, them) pronouns.
2. Themes: clients' self-references involving the self as cause, as effect, as both cause and effect, or as neither.
3. Characters: people mentioned in clients' problem statements, classified according to age, gender, and their superior, subordinate, or peer relationship with the client.
4. Items: each client's presenting problem, classified as alcohol/drug, finances, marital, legal, social relationships on the job, other social relationships, or "other."

Counting is sometimes but not always a possible and meaningful sequel to classification. In the above examples, a researcher could count the number of:

1. first person, second person, and third person words a client or counselor used in a session.
2. times each client referred to the self as cause, effect, both, neither.
3. adult men and adult women in superior, subordinate, and peer relationships with the client.
4. types of problem presented by each client, or clients with each type of presenting problem.

Some projects include ratings. For example, the "presenting problems" in Example 4 might be rated for their severity; the people in Example 3 might be rated for their importance as contributors to the client's presenting problems. As an alternative to rating, ranking might be used to measure the severity of problems presented by any client with more than one type (for example, marital problems most severe, alcohol/drug next, financial third).

APPENDIX H

CHILDHOOD REFLECTIONS PROJECT TRANSMITTAL LETTER AND QUESTIONNAIRE

Department of
Recreation and Sport

Recreation SA
Level 9 Citi Centre
11 Hindmarsh Square
Adelaide SA 5000

Postal Address:
GPO Box 1865
Adelaide SA 5001

Dear

The CHILDHOOD REFLECTIONS project is an attempt to recall the play experience of people during their childhood years. Enclosed is a questionnaire developed by Dr. Gary Pennington who is currently working in conjunction with the Playgrounds Unit. The intention is to gather information about play experiences of children in order to establish an idea of how play may have changed over time.

We hope to gather the folklore of children's play within the family context. We expect the questionnaire will take about 30–40 minutes to complete. Having tested the questionnaire ourselves we feel that the contents may well stimulate some wonderful recollections as the family shares in childhood memories.

We would appreciate you completing the questionnaire during the Christmas season. We know this is a very busy time for most people but it is also one of the times when families gather together to share special moments, and it is these moments we feel will contribute significantly to the value of this project.

Please do not feel limited by what you should or shouldn't include and by all means write on the back of the page or use additional paper if you need more space.

We would appreciate the questionnaire being returned by no later than Friday the 15th of January 1993. Please address the envelope as follows:

Richard McConaghy, Playgrounds Unit,
Recreation S.A., Department of Recreation & Sport
G.P.O. Box 1865, ADELAIDE, 5001

We trust that you will enjoy reliving the imaginative aspects of your childhood as well as evoking treasured memories about play from older members of the family who lived in such different times.

Many thanks for your contribution,

Richard McConaghy,
Project Officer

Gary Pennington,
Associate Professor, UBC

Childhood Reflections: A Study of the
Folklore of Children's Play

The CHILDHOOD REFLECTIONS PROJECT is an attempt to recall the play experiences of people during their childhood years. As one phase of this project we are asking individuals to provide information and anecdotes about their own play from earliest recollections up to about the age of twelve years. Questions have been suggested by friends in the fields of play leadership, child development, and early childhood education. We hope these questions will evoke vivid images about play from people's past. The intent of our project is to determine how the play of children has changed over the generations.

Stories of childhood by children have been largely overlooked in the folk history of Western countries. We would like to help remedy this and begin to fill in some of the gaps in our history and our understanding about children's play. Findings will be used to facilitate better play opportunities for children in schools and communities. We hope that you will help us in this "playful task." Results of the study will be made available to interested parties.

Please think back to your childhood and tell us about your playtime experiences and the feelings you had as a young boy or girl. Answer questions as candidly and fully as possible. We have found thinking about our childhood a very pleasant experience and trust you will as well.

A unique feature of this study is that we are asking friends and colleagues to help us in extending our network of contacts in order to gather data. We are particularly interested to gather childhood reflections on play from people in the same family. A number of people who have done this already have found the experience of sharing their recollections of early childhood to be very rewarding. We hope that you will not only complete a questionnaire yourself but that you will also consider asking friends and family members to take part in our study as a piece of family history.

PLEASE RETURN COMPLETED QUESTIONNAIRES TO:

Richard McConaghy, Playgrounds Unit,
Recreation S.A., Dept. of Recreation & Sport
G.P.O. Box 1865, Adelaide, 5001

WE WOULD APPRECIATE THE RETURN OF THE FORMS BY:

Friday 15th January 1993

If you would like extra copies of the "CHILDHOOD REFLECTIONS" questionnaire for family or friends please contact the above address indicating the number of forms you require and a mailing address.

WE SINCERELY THANK YOU FOR YOUR HELP

PERSONAL DETAILS

Name (Optional) _____

Address (Optional) _____

_____ Phone _____

In what country did you live as a child? _____

In what country were your parents brought up? _____

Do you belong to, or identify with, any particular cultural or ethnic group? If

so, what is it? _____

As a child did you live mainly in the city, suburbs, or country?

_____

Were you a child during (Tick one):

1. [ ] pre 1900   2. [ ] 1900–1909   3. [ ] 1910–1919
4. [ ] 1920–1929   5. [ ] 1930–1939   6. [ ] 1940–1949
7. [ ] 1950–1959   8. [ ] 1960–1969   9. [ ] 1970–1979

How many brothers did you have? [ ]   How many sisters? [ ]

Are you:

1. [ ] the youngest child   2. [ ] the oldest child
3. [ ] an only child   4. [ ] other _____

Did you have a TV at home when you were a child? _____

If yes, how many hours per week did you watch? _____

What were your favorite programs? _____

_____

Did you play video games as a child? _____

If so, how many hours per week? _____

Would you be willing to give a personal interview about your playtime experi-

ences as a youngster? _____

Do you have any photographs of your childhood which might be of help to

our project? _____

QUESTIONS ABOUT YOUR PLAY AS A CHILD

1. CLUBS/GROUPS/LANGUAGE.   Did you and your friends form any special clubs or groups as children? If so, what were they? Were there any rituals or special rules involved? Did you use any special language or passwords? Please elaborate.

2. CHANTS/RHYMES/SINGING GAMES.   As a child, were there things that you and your friends used to sing, chant, or say that were fun? If yes, what were they? Can you explain why they were so enjoyable?

3. COLLECTIONS/GIFTS.   What things, if any, did you collect as a child? How did you usually get them? What was the best gift you received as a youngster?

4. PLAYTHINGS/PETS.   When you were young what playthings did you like best?

5. PLAY SPACES.   Where did you like to play as a child? What were your favorite places or what was your most special place? Why?

6. NATURE.   Did you make any playthings (toys, musical instruments, etc.) out of things which you found in nature? Were there other things in nature that you particularly enjoyed?

7. ADVENTURE/RISKS.   What "Great Adventures," if any, did you have when playing as a child? Things that really gave you a thrill and which you recall vividly?

(Use back of page if you require more space)

8. FAVORITE PASTIME. What did you most like to do or play as a child? Things that you did in your free time, either alone or with friends, that were special? Why were they so important?

9. GAMES. Were there formal or informal games that you played a lot? What were they?

10. PRETENDING/FANTASY/DAYDREAMS. A common expression among children is "Let's pretend we are . . .". Did you and your friends do this? If so, what were some of the things you pretended to be? Do you remember what you used to daydream or fantasize about? What did you think about when you were alone in your room, your hideaway, your cubby, or your special place? What was your special place?

11. FUN/HAPPINESS. What was the thing that made you happiest as a child? What, to you, was the most fun?

12. ADULTS. Did adults have any significant part in your playworld? If so, who were they and how did they help or hinder your play?

13. STORIES. What else can you tell us about your childhood in terms of play? Anecdotes? Issues? Ironies? Earliest remembrances? Special friendships? Anything at all that may help us understand the child's world of your generation.

14. QUESTIONS. Please let us know of any additional questions which you feel need to be asked about play and childhood (and your answers as well).

15. FAMILY/OTHERS. Are there other members of your family and/or friends you suggest that we should contact concerning this project? If so, indicate names and addresses on the back of this form, or make a copy of this form and pass it on to them.

THANK YOU AGAIN FOR YOUR HELP WITH OUR PROJECT

CHILDHOOD REFLECTIONS

WHAT DO YOU REMEMBER ABOUT YOUR CHILDHOOD, PARTICULARLY YOUR PLAYTIME EXPERIENCES? The following words and phrases are intended to serve as "triggers" to help you remember the things which were important in your childhood years.

first dream
first joke
best laughs
favorite toys
favorite gifts
mishaps
likes
dislikes
favorite outings and visits
favorite visitors
holidays
best birthday
best Christmas
favorite holidays
parent(s) help with play
parent(s) hindrance of play
playing with parent(s)
playing with grandparent(s)
play with brothers
play with sisters
playing with other relatives
favorite playspace
playing alone
memorable times
water play
sand or mud play
make-believe play
dress-up times
very best times
worst times
hideaways/cubbies/tree houses
climbing tree
tricks, puzzles, magic

first games
first team
school yard
community playground
first friends
playleaders
first drawings
first writing
special songs, rhymes, chants
passwords, special sayings
special childhood language
favorite games
best friends, playmates
most fun
braveries
television likes
radio likes
favorite treats
biggest surprise
pet hates, dislikes
nicknames
biggest adventures, risks, thrills
daydreams
things you made, built
heros, heroines
favorite books
stories, fairy tales, legends
special secrets
animals, pets
collections
special things in nature
best finds
good luck charms, lucky pieces

Gary Pennington
University of British Columbia

GLOSSARY

ABAB design   A time series design that administers the *A* and *B* phases twice, using the principle of withdrawal or reversal to demonstrate a functional relation between the independent and dependent variables.

AB design   The simplest time series design, with A and B referring to phases. This design is considered weak because a number of extraneous variables could be confounded with the introduction of the experimental treatment. Because of this weakness, the AB design represents a quasi-experiment and is rarely used.

abscissa   The horizontal axis of a graph.

absolute zero   A property of measurement systems involving numbers; zero represents absolute absence of the trait being measured.

abstract   A brief, concise summary of a report, usually 100 to 150 words.

accelerating curve   A graph's curve steeper at high than at low levels of one of the variables: the predictor variable or independent variable, when one exists.

accountability   A service program's responsibility to furnish data to others regarding its operations, results, and costs.

accountability evaluation   Program evaluation in which a service program collects data about itself to influence decisions by others or to meet external requirements.

action research   One of the major research approaches discussed in this book; its mission includes developing new skills or new methods for doing something, or improving existing ones. In a counseling agency, this "something" is usually delivering service to clients.

additivity   A property of measurement systems involving numbers; numbers can be added and subtracted to yield meaningful sums and differences. Equal intervals are required for additivity.

almost interval   Having the measurement system properties of identity, order, arbitrary zero, and probably also the property of equal intervals, although the latter is not supported by evidence (Kirkpatrick & Aleamoni, 1983).

analogue research   Research studying questions about specific aspects of counseling by using laboratory procedures carefully contrived to represent those aspects (Heppner, Kivlighan, & Wampold, 1992). The laboratory procedures (such as scripted materials, client surrogates, or tape recordings of counseling interactions) are considered analogous to the counseling phenomena of interest.

analysis of variance   A test for the significance of differences among three or more means.

ANOVA   Abbreviation for analysis of variance.

A phase   The first phase in a time series experiment and any subsequent phase in which like conditions are administered; observations are usually taken but no intervention is administered.

applied research   Research conducted to solve practical problems, whether or not the findings have any relevance to theory.

arbitrary zero   A property of measurement systems involving numbers: zero does not represent absolute absence of the trait being measured.

assignment   Allocating subjects to groups according to a research plan. Instead of assigning subjects, some projects use existing groups composed before the research planning begins.

attitude scale   An instrument usually consisting of a set of statements with which respondents express their agreement or disagreement. Some scales also ask respondents to indicate the intensity of their position; others do not. The "object" of an attitude scale is usually a group or kind of people (such as ethnic minorities, women, people with a penal history, people with disabilities) or a social institution (such as the church, family life, or public schools).

audit   A thorough, multifaceted evaluation of some aspects of an organization's activity; several research questions are included. The application of this term in program evaluation is derived from its customary use in accounting.

authority   Any official permission that may be needed to collect and analyze the data for a research project and report the project according to plan.

axis   One of two lines (horizontal and vertical) that define the space for a line, bar, or scatter graph.

bar graph   A graph that represents quantities with vertical or horizontal bars.

baseline period   In a time series experiment, an initial A phase in which observations are taken but no intervention administered to change the behavior of the subjects.

basic research   Research conducted to answer questions drawn from theory, whether or not the findings have any practical application.

bibliographic data   Information about a literature source that must be given when listing it as a reference. Included are author, title, and date of publication for all sources and journal name, volume number, and pages for articles.

binary   Having exactly two possible values. For example, gender is a binary variable.

bivariate   Representing two variables simultaneously.

block randomization   An assignment method that combines random and systematic features. The list of subjects is first divided into blocks, with each block containing one subject for each group. Within each block, individuals are assigned randomly to groups.

B phase   The second phase in a time series experiment and any subsequent phase in which like conditions are administered; observations are usually taken while an intervention is administered.

calibration   Tendency of raters or mechanical measuring devices to become more strict or more lenient in their standards as they are involved in a project over a period of time (Drew & Hardman, 1985). Such changes in raters are usually inadvertent. When confounded with the phenomena being studied, calibration changes weaken internal validity.

captive assignment   Assignment when all the subjects who make up the sample have been identified at the outset. Typically, the researcher has a list of names for the entire sample and assigns from this list.

case study   One of several descriptive research approaches. Its purpose is to study intensively a given social unit such as an individual, group, institution, school, workplace, or community.

causal-correlational   A research approach that seeks to answer questions of cause by examining a systematic set of relationships between variables.

causal path analysis   See *path analysis.*

ceiling effect   Limitation of the range of possible scores when an instrument's performance range is too low for the respondents (for example, a test is too easy).

centile   The percentage of cases in a norm sample who scored below a specified level. Also called percentile.

character   In content analysis, an individual represented in written or oral communication. Examples of such communications include poems, novels, plays, personal documents, material written for course assignments, Thematic Apperception Test responses, and clients' discussion during counseling sessions.

checklist   An instrument that gives respondents a list of adjectives or other descriptions and asks them to check all those that are true of the person or behavior being rated.

chunk   See *convenience sample* (Deming, 1950).

CIPP model   A conceptual model whereby research questions of program evaluation projects are classified as context, input, process, product, or some combination of these.

circle graph   A graph consisting of a circle divided into sectors, with each sector representing the size of one category in the data.

classification variable   A preexisting characteristic (such as age, gender, or intelligence scores) on the basis of which a researcher deliberately compiles subject groups so that they differ as specified by the research plan. Sometimes subjects are assigned to such groups based on preexisting data before the project's new data are collected. Alternatively, subjects may be divided according to a classification variable after the data collection is fully or partially completed.

client A person served by a counselor or service program.

client pathway The sequence of client services and decision points in a service program that serves clients.

closed-ended Giving respondents a set of answer possibilities from which to choose; respondents are not invited to answer in any other way than choosing among the available alternatives that have been written. Includes multiple-choice, which refers to three or more answer possibilities per item.

cluster sampling A procedure in which intact groups rather than individuals are sampled, such as entire classrooms rather than individual students in a school district.

cohort design A design for developmental studies based on independent-group comparisons among samples who have reached different stages of development at the time the study is conducted. For example, a researcher might compare samples of people of different ages: 20, 30, 40, 50, and 60, then from these comparisons draw inferences about the course of development. Each age group is called a "cohort."

conceptual utilization Use of program evaluation results to "influence thinking about issues in a general way. These uses range from simply sensitizing persons and groups about current and emerging social problems to influencing program and policy development by examining the results of a series of evaluations together" (Rossi & Freeman, 1989, p. 455).

confidence interval An interval estimated from a sample, expressing the degree of precision with which a statistic approximates its corresponding parameter. For example: "The probability is .95 that this sample's mean of 13.4 does not differ from the corresponding population value by more than 2.1 raw score points."

confidence limits The boundaries of a confidence interval.

confidentiality An ethical principle that holds that information from and about clients and research participants may not be disclosed to others except as required by law or expressly authorized in advance by the client or research participant, unless his or her identity is fully protected.

confound To blend one or more extraneous variables with one or more variables under study so that it is impossible to know to what extent each contributed to the results.

constructed controls People experiencing the control conditions in a traditional group quasi-experiment; they are "selected by nonrandom methods to be comparable in crucial respects" (Rossi & Freeman, 1989, p. 310) to the groups given the experimental treatments.

construct validity Congruence between a measure and a theoretical concept. Examples of such concepts include intelligence, self-efficacy, and hostility.

consumers   (1) People who learn about a research project and its results and may or may not use this knowledge. Consumers may learn about a project through formal or informal channels: (a) its written or oral report, (b) secondary sources, or (c) informal communication. (2) Actual or potential users of services. This definition represents expansion of a usage found in the current rehabilitation literature: people with disabilities, as actual or potential users of rehabilitation services. This definition substantially overlaps two other terms: an agency's clients are actual (not potential) users of its services; its targets are the people it intends to serve, whether or not they become clients. *Targets* emphasizes the perspective of the agency; *consumers*, that of the people served.

content analysis   "A method of studying and analyzing communications in a systematic, objective and quantitative manner to measure variables" (Kerlinger, 1986, p. 477).

content analysis system   A set of rules for carrying out the content analysis process (Holsti, 1969).

content validity   The extent to which the items of a test or inventory represent a defined domain of content. For example, the items on a mathematics achievement test may well or poorly represent the material taught in a school's curriculum.

context evaluation   One of the CIPP model's four components. This kind of program evaluation seeks to answer questions concerning needs to be served by a service program and the nature of the organizational and community context in which the planned program is to operate (Stufflebeam & Shinkfield, 1985).

continuous   Having values that are meaningful at any point along an entire continuum; not discrete. Variables such as length, weight, temperature, and elapsed time are continuous.

control   (1) Prevent one or more extraneous variables from being confounded with the phenomena being studied and therefore clouding the meaning of a project's results. (2) An aspect of a research plan by which #1 is accomplished. (3) Used for purposes of (a) comparison with an experimental treatment or (b) accomplishing control (definition #1).

control condition   The condition experienced by control subjects, in contrast to the experimental treatment administered to experimental subjects in an experiment.

control variable   A preexisting characteristic used by a researcher to deliberately compose subject groups so that they are alike insofar as possible according to this characteristic. For example, two groups might be composed to contain exactly the same proportion of males and females and the same distribution of previous professional experience.

convenience sample   A set of individuals studied in a research project chosen because they are conveniently available, without regard to whether they are representative of a population; not a true sample.

coordinates   In graphing, the horizontal and vertical axes of a graph.

correlated-measures comparison   Comparison of measures that may be correlated; includes related-groups, repeated-measures, and within-group comparisons.

correlational   One of several descriptive research approaches. Correlational studies investigate relationships among the variables studied.

correlation coefficient   A statistical measure expressing the relationship between two variables (or among more than two) with a single number between -1.00 and 1.00, inclusive.

cost–benefit analysis   Considering together the observed or expected benefits (desired outcomes) and costs (including unwanted effects) of an action or service program. Definitions #1 and #2 below represent formal and informal cost–benefit analysis, respectively. (1) Efficiency assessment that quantifies both desired outcomes and costs of a service program in the same terms, usually monetary (Rossi & Freeman, 1989). For example, dollar costs of operating a public rehabilitation agency are balanced against taxes its rehabilitated clients pay and welfare payments they do not collect because they are employed. (2) Examining both benefits and costs to reach a decision without necessarily quantifying costs or benefits.

cost-effectiveness analysis   Efficiency assessment that quantifies both desired outcomes and costs of a service program, but not in the same terms (Rossi & Freeman, 1989). For example, a cost-effectiveness analysis might yield an average dollar cost per contact hour or per rehabilitated client.

cost-offset ratio   A ratio expressing the relationship between a service program's earnings and its costs. For example, Smith and Mahoney's (1989) EAP evaluation yielded a cost-offset ratio of 4:1, indicating that the EAP's results saved the parent company four times the program's costs.

counterbalance   In an experiment with own-control design, to schedule treatment conditions so that the same number of subjects experience each treatment condition in every sequence position (for example, first, second, third).

coverage accountability   Accountability to show the extent to which a service program reaches the people it is intended to serve and provides the intended services to them. What are the number and characteristics of the people served, partially served, and not served? (Rossi & Freeman, 1989)

criterion-related validity   A relationship between one measure (such as test scores) and some other measures of the same variables. For example, job aptitude test scores predict workers' job performance ratings.

criterion variable   A variable being studied in a correlational project, regarding the extent to which it is correctly predicted by one or more predictor variables.

crossbreak   See *crosstabulation* (Kerlinger, 1986).

cross-lagged panel correlations   A technique for seeking answers to questions of cause from correlational data, relying on repeated measures of the variables being studied: at least two variables measured at least twice. Inference about a causal relationship between two variables is based on the idea that if Variable A influences Variable B (but not the reverse), A will show higher correlations with later than with earlier measures of B (Cook & Campbell, 1979).

cross-sectional design Another name for cohort design.

crosstabulation (1) A procedure whereby cases are classified according to two or more variables simultaneously to show the frequency or percentage of cases in each of the categories so created. (2) The arrangement of data resulting from #1.

curvilinear Not rectilinear. The graph of a curvilinear relationship is a curve.

data analysis The fourth phase of the six-phase model of the research process. In this phase, the project's data are analyzed for interpretation and reporting.

database A body of information maintained so as to be accessible by computer. Some databases may be accessed directly by users; others require staff assistance.

data collection The third phase of the six-phase model of the research process. In this phase, data are collected for the project's data analysis, interpretation, and reporting.

debrief To conduct a session with one or more research participants after data have been collected to provide information about the nature of the study and remove any misconceptions that may have arisen.

decelerating curve A graph's curve that is steeper at low than at high levels of one of the variables: the predictor variable or independent variable, when one exists.

degree of relationship Strength of relationship. In a strong relationship, almost all instances follow the indicated trend; contrary examples, if any, are few. If the degree of relationship is low (weak relationship), contrary examples are many. Correlation coefficients near 1.00 or -1.00 represent a high degree of relationship; coefficients near zero, a low degree of relationship.

demand characteristics Influences on subjects' behavior based on the various social norms and standards our society and its subcultures offer for the social situation that participation in the research project represents. Subjects are usually willing to give a researcher what they think he or she wants.

dependent variable A variable that is observed or measured in an experiment to determine whether it is affected by an independent variable.

descriptive (1) One of the major research approaches discussed in this book; descriptive studies seek to tell what is without the idea of cause included in the research questions. Subcategories of descriptive approaches include surveys, case studies, developmental studies, trend studies, process studies, correlational studies, and follow-up studies. (2) When applied to statistics: describing the frequency distribution of a sample; includes measures of central tendency, variability, and relationship, among others.

design That aspect of a research project's plan that specifies (a) what subjects are to be used; (b) the number of variables considered, and the role of each variable in the project (for example, independent, dependent, control, classification, stratification, predictor, criterion); (c) whether and how subjects are divided into groups to be studied; (d) the choice and timing of measurements taken on subjects; and (e) the general type of analysis to be applied. The design of experiments includes three additional aspects of the project's plan that do not apply to other research approaches: (f) the number of experimental (treatment) and control conditions; (g) the sequence and timing of experimental and control conditions; and (h) the method of assigning experimental and control conditions to subjects.

design validity Technical soundness of a project's design as it relates to fulfillment of the project's mission. Includes both internal and external validities.

developmental One of several descriptive research approaches. Developmental studies investigate change over time.

developmental variable In developmental studies, usually time or the course of development.

differential treatment control Comparing two or more different treatments in an experiment rather than a treatment with its absence.

direct relationship A relationship in which high, moderate, and low values on one variable are associated with high, moderate, and low values (respectively) on the other. For example, most studies of scholastic aptitude tests show a direct relationship with grades. The term *direct relationship* refers only to this characteristic; it says nothing about the strength of relationship. A positive correlation coefficient (between zero and 1.00) represents a direct relationship.

direct utilization Use of program evaluation results to influence service program decisions (Rossi & Freeman, 1989).

discrete Not continuous. Only certain values are meaningful, with intermediate values meaningless. For example, a family can have one child, two children, or none, but not 1.2 children; the number 1.28 can refer to the number of dollars but not to the number of cents in your pocket.

documents Existing written sources such as case files, official records, correspondence, books, and periodicals.

double-barreled Including two questions in one item. Said of items on questionnaires, inventories, and tests.

double-blind Controlling for the placebo effect in experiments when different treatments are being compared; subjects do not know what treatment they are being given, nor do the staff who administer it to them. Double-blind designs are most common in medical experiments.

double sampling See *two-phase sampling.*

D statistic A measure that expresses the difference between two profiles with a single number (Cronbach & Gleser, 1953).

efficiency accountability A service program's accountability to show how the impacts of the entire program and its component elements are related to costs (Rossi & Freeman, 1989).

efficiency assessment Evaluation that quantifies both a service program's desired outcomes and its costs; one of two components of program utility assessment. In turn, efficiency may be measured in two ways: cost–benefit and cost-effectiveness analyses (Rossi & Freeman, 1989).

employee assistance program An employer-based service program providing assessment and referral services to employees with problems that adversely affect job performance. Some programs also offer counseling, usually brief.

equal intervals A property of measurement systems involving numbers; throughout the range of possible values, adjacent numbers represent equal differences with regard to the variable measured.

equal probability One of two criteria necessary for randomness. In random sampling, every member of the *pool* has the same likelihood of being chosen. In random assignment, each subject at the outset has the same probabilities of being assigned to the various groups. In random responding to multiple-choice items, each answer possibility has the same likelihood of being chosen.

ethical accountability Accountability to show the extent to which a service program meets its ethical responsibilities, particularly those not codified in law or specified by contract.

ethnographic Similar to anthropologists' descriptive field studies of ethnic groups.

evaluability assessment "Pre-evaluation" to systematically take stakeholders' interests into account when planning program evaluation projects to "maximize the utility of the evaluation" (Rossi & Freeman, 1989, pp. 151, 114); may include one or more pilot studies.

ex-ante efficiency analysis Efficiency analysis in advance to anticipate probable outcomes in relation to costs, usually undertaken as part of program planning (Rossi & Freeman, 1989).

experiment A research approach (or a project using this approach) in which the researcher manages or manipulates at least one variable and observes or measures at least one variable. This term includes both true experiments and quasi-experiments.

experimental group A set of subjects to whom a project applies one or more experimental treatments or conditions; some projects use one or more control groups to estimate what the experimental groups would have done without the experimental treatments.

experimental mortality Changes in the samples originally selected for a research project because people withdraw from the project while it is being conducted. To the extent that the study groups lose subjects in different proportions or for different reasons, internal validity is weakened. If lost subjects make samples less representative of the populations toward which generalizability is desired, external validity is weakened.

experimental treatment A procedure administered to create a treatment condition in an experiment.

experimenter bias Extraneous influences on subjects' behavior based on the manner in which services or experimental treatments are administered. Such effects are more often inadvertent than deliberate. One of the most frequent is a preconceived idea about the results desired or expected. When confounded with the phenomena being investigated, such bias weakens internal validity.

exploratory When applied to research, seeking to furnish data helpful in generating hypotheses or other ideas, usually in the formulation phase of a future project.

ex post facto A research approach that uses descriptive data to explore possible cause and effect relationships among the variables studied.

external phenomena study One of three kinds of passive studies of cause questions; phenomena outside the researcher's control (such as earthquakes and new laws) are studied as possible causes.

external validity Generalizability of results to other people, times, places, and circumstances than those studied, as relevant to the project's mission.

extraneous variable A variable that is not being studied or specifically controlled and therefore might influence results in unplanned and unknown ways.

face validity Respondents' sense of the validity of a test, inventory, or similar instrument.

factorial design A design that includes only independent-group comparisons and simultaneously investigates (a) more than one independent variable with the same dependent variables, (b) an independent variable and one or more classification variables with the same dependent variables, or (c) a descriptive variable with two or more classification variables.

factual validity The extent to which respondents' answers correspond to objective fact.

feedback evaluation Program evaluation in which a service program collects data about itself for use in its internal decision making.

fine-tune Make changes (usually small) in a research plan as indicated by pilot data and emergent events, usually before data collection for the main study begins; additional emergent events requiring further fine-tuning may occur throughout the duration of the project.

fiscal accountability Accountability regarding use of funds (Rossi & Freeman, 1989). How much do services provided cost per client? What does each kind of service cost? If service levels were to be increased or decreased, how much would such changes raise or lower costs? How much do costs vary as a function of such factors as program site, time of year, and introduction of any competing programs?

Fisher exact probability test A significance test for 2×2 crossbreak tables representing two independent samples. It is recommended for small samples, unwieldy for large ones.

floor effect Limitation of the range of possible scores when an instrument's performance range is too high for the respondents (for example, a test is too difficult).

focus group A semistructured group interviewing procedure "designed to obtain perceptions on a defined area of interest in a permissive non-threatening environment. . . . [P]articipants . . . share their ideas and perceptions [and] influence each other by responding to ideas and comments in the discussion." Groups usually comprise "seven to ten people" (Krueger, 1988, p. 18).

follow-up (1) One of several descriptive research approaches. This term refers to descriptive studies of outcome. These studies examine the people who have experienced a process such as education, counseling, or medical treatment. The measures taken refer to their behavior or experience, or both, after the process has been completed. (2) In an extended posttest design, referring to additional data collected later than the posttest immediately following a treatment or control condition. (3) In projects using mailed questionnaires, a procedure for contacting nonrespondents to encourage them to respond.

forced-choice Offering respondents two, three, or four descriptions and asking them to choose which is most characteristic. The descriptions are often unrelated to each other. This term may apply to rating scales or to items on questionnaires or inventories.

formal mission statement A written document expressing a service program's goals and the objectives related to each goal.

formulation The first phase of the six-phase model of the research process. In this phase, the project's mission is chosen and carefully defined.

free agent adult A person of legal age who is mentally and emotionally able to decide on his or her own behalf whether to participate in a research project and has legal authority to do so (Keith-Spiegel, 1976).

frequency A quantity determined by counting.

frequency distribution A characteristic of a sample or a population: the number of times each value of a variable appears.

functional relation A relationship between independent and dependent variables in which changes in the dependent variable occur when, and only when, changes are introduced in the independent variable (Sulzer-Azaroff & Mayer, 1991).

goal A broad, general statement of a desired outcome from a service program. From each goal, several objectives are usually derived.

Greco-Latin square A plan similar to a Latin square, which simultaneously counterbalances treatment conditions for two variables.

graphic rating scale   A rating scale expressed in graphic form. Usually, each item has a straight or segmented line along which respondents mark their position.

grounded theory   Theory derived from holistic descriptive data gathered through naturalistic inquiry (Patton, 1987).

group   A set of people or other subjects studied in a research project, not necessarily a group in any social sense; such groups often comprise strangers who do not communicate with each other in any way.

group composition bias   Nonequivalence of treatment groups at the outset of an experiment; internal validity is weakened.

group experiment   An experiment that involves one or more groups or samples, with each group or sample comprising a number of subjects. Some projects compare two or more differently treated groups; others compare results from the same groups under different conditions.

grouping   A type of decision that relates to preparing a report: What material is to go together in each section and subsection?

historical   One of the major research approaches. Historical studies seek to reconstruct the past.

hold constant   To control one or more extraneous variables by assuring that all experimental and control groups, and experimental and control conditions, are alike with respect to these variables.

hypothesis   A statement that expresses a prediction about what the answer to a research question will be or an idea about the phenomena being studied.

identity   A property of measurement systems; one number or label may be the same as or different from another.

impact accountability   Accountability to show the extent to which a service program brings about the desired changes in the target population (Rossi & Freeman, 1989).

impact assessment   Evaluation of "the extent to which a program causes changes in the desired direction" (Rossi & Freeman, 1989, p. 49); one of two components of program utility assessment.

independence   One of two criteria necessary for randomness. In random sampling, choosing any particular member of the pool does not affect the probability that any other member will be chosen, except as may be caused by the limited size of the frame. In random assignment, no subject's assignment probabilities are changed by anyone else's assignment, except as is necessarily so because of the sample size and group sizes.

independent groups comparison   Comparison of the same measures taken from groups comprising different subjects; "independent" in this context means that the composition of any one group did not determine the composition of any other group. Students in two different classrooms, for example, represent independent groups in this sense; husbands and their wives do not.

independent variable   A variable that is managed or manipulated in an experiment to determine whether it affects a dependent variable.

informal test   A test that is not standardized. Most classroom examinations are informal tests.

informed consent   An ethical principle that holds that prospective participants in research projects have a right to (a) correctly understand the risks and tasks involved in their participation before deciding whether to participate, (b) freely choose, without coercion, whether to accept these risks and tasks, and (c) be free to discontinue their participation at any time.

input evaluation   One of the CIPP model's four components. This kind of program evaluation seeks to answer questions concerning resources a service program has at its disposal and the "barriers" and "constraints" in the "environment . . . to be considered in the process of activating the program" (Stufflebeam & Shinkfield, 1985, p. 173).

instrument   A specific device for collecting data or presenting stimuli. "Device" is construed broadly, including (in addition to mechanical ones) those made of paper and ink or electronic impulses transmitted through a computer.

instrumentation   (1) Collectively, all the instruments used in a project. (2) A threat to internal validity from changes in instruments while a project is being conducted (for example, machines that present stimuli or measure responses); a threat to both internal and external validity if instruments are poorly designed, chosen, or administered.

intensive experiment   An experiment that studies one or a very few subjects intensively over a long period of time (usually weeks or months).

interaction   The influence of one variable on the relationship (whether causal or not) between two or more others. For example, suppose a project found female counselors elicited more self-disclosure from clients with personal-social problems than did their male counterparts, but the reverse difference was observed among clients with vocational problems. These findings would represent an interaction between counselor gender and type of client problem with regard to client self-disclosure.

internal validity   An aspect of design validity: the extent to which all extraneous variables are controlled, enabling results to be interpreted unambiguously regarding the people, settings, and occasions studied.

interpretation   The fifth phase of the six-phase model of the research process. In this phase, the researcher decides what the results mean for the project's mission and perhaps also for other features of the project. When results have implications extending beyond this mission, these wider implications may also be considered.

interquartile range   A measure of variability of a frequency distribution: the range occupied by the middle 50% of the cases.

interview   A conversation conducted by one or more interviewers with one or more respondents carried out according to a plan for a specific purpose. Research interviews are conducted by members of the research team for purposes of data collection.

interview guide   A written plan for conducting interviews and recording responses.

interview protocol   See *interview guide.*

interview schedule   See *interview guide.*

inventory   A self-report instrument, usually containing questions or other kinds of items calling for true–false or multiple-choice responses, with no answers defined in advance as correct or incorrect. Many measures of personality, interests, values, and temperament are inventories.

inverse relationship   A relationship in which high, moderate, and low values on one variable are associated with low, moderate, and high values on the other, respectively. For example, adults' performance on many speeded ability tests is inversely related to age; young adults perform best on the average, old people worst, and middle-aged people at intermediate levels. A negative correlation coefficient (between zero and -1.00) represents an inverse relationship.

item   (1) A part of a test, inventory, scale, or questionnaire, usually bearing an item number and calling for a response. (2) In content analysis, a "whole production," such as a student's term paper, a reporter's news story, a television program, or a client's account of an event as reported in a counseling session. In a study of autobiographies, "the whole autobiography" is an item (Kerlinger, 1986, p. 480). In a study of Thematic Apperception Test results, a researcher might regard an individual story or one respondent's entire set of stories as an item. In an analysis of open-ended questionnaire and interview data, an item might be an answer to one question or all of one respondent's answers.

jargon   Specialized vocabulary of a particular profession, professional specialty, or theoretical orientation.

Latin square   A matrix in which any number (k) of letters of the alphabet are arranged in a square with k rows and k columns so that each letter appears once and only once in each row and in each column. It is often used as a plan for counterbalancing treatment conditions in an experiment with an own-control design.

law of the instrument   The fact that people often become so attached to a particular instrument or procedure as to recommend it as a solution to almost every problem (Isaac & Michael, 1981).

legal accountability   Accountability to show the extent to which a service program meets legal responsibilities such as informed consent, protection of privacy, community representation on decision-making boards, equity in provision of services, and cost sharing (Rossi & Freeman, 1989).

Likert   Consisting of one or more statements with closed-ended answer choices reflecting strength of agreement or disagreement (for example, strongly agree, agree, undecided, disagree, strongly disagree).

line graph   A graph on which data points are connected with a line.

literature review (1) A careful search, study, and analysis of the professional literature on a topic. It may be carried out as part of the formulation and planning phases of a research project or as a separate activity. (2) A written or oral report of #1, whether or not as part of a research project report.

longitudinal design A developmental design that studies the same people at different times; inferences about the developmental variable are based on repeated-measures comparisons.

management information system (MIS) A system, usually computerized, for collecting and analyzing service delivery and outcome information on an ongoing basis and providing timely access to this information as required to meet management needs. Ideally, it provides both managers and evaluators with needed program information.

McNemar test A statistical test for correlated-measures comparisons based on a binary variable.

mean The average value of a variable in a sample or a population.

mean chance expectancy The average score to be expected from a large group of subjects answering every item randomly on a closed-ended test, inventory, or scale.

measure (1) Representation of a variable by a set of numbers or other labels. For example, achievement test scores are measures of knowledge. (2) To apply a measurement system.

measurement system A relationship between a set of numbers or other labels and a variable being measured.

median The middle value in a frequency distribution. Half of the cases are above the median, half below.

median test A nonparametric significance test of the difference between two medians.

MIS Abbreviation for management information system.

mission (1) The goal or purpose of a research project, including (a) the specific questions to which answers are sought from the data, and (b) reasons for seeking answers to these questions. (2) A service program's goals and objectives.

mixed design A design for a group experiment or descriptive project that includes both independent-groups comparisons and correlated-measures comparisons and simultaneously investigates (a) more than one independent variable with the same dependent variables, (b) an independent variable or (c) one or more classification variables with the same dependent variables, or one or more descriptive variables with one or more classification variables.

mode The most frequently occurring value of a variable in a sample or a population.

multiple baseline design A time series design composed of a number of AB designs with baselines of varying lengths. The functional relation is demonstrated if the dependent variable changes whenever the independent variable is introduced. This design may study (a) multiple subjects, (b) multiple behaviors of the same subject, or (c) the same behavior of the same subject in multiple situations.

multiple correlation A correlation representing the relationship between one variable and a combination of two or more other variables.

N = 1 experiment See *single-subject experiment.*

naturalistic Based on phenomena as they occur naturally, without any attempt to change them for purposes of study as would be required in an experiment.

needs assessment Context evaluation that seeks data to answer questions about needs so that effective program planning can proceed.

nominal Having the measurement system property of identity only.

nomination A rating procedure that gives raters a description and asks them to name the one or more persons who best fit it.

nonparametric test A statistical test based only on mathematical derivations that do not include assumptions about parameters of populations from which the samples were drawn. Chi-square, the median test, and the Fisher exact probability test are nonparametric.

nonreactive measure A measurement method that does not give subjects something to react to (Isaac & Michael, 1981). Examples are covert observation and examination of physical traces.

norms Results from one or more large samples with known characteristics with which individual respondents' results may be compared.

norm sample A sample used for providing norms.

no-treatment control The simplest version of the control group idea: an experimental treatment is administered to one group of subjects and withheld from the other.

null hypothesis A statistical hypothesis of "no difference" or "no relationship" in the populations represented by the samples yielding the data. A hypothesis of "no difference" asserts that the samples being compared came from populations that do not differ from one another with regard to the measure being compared, usually that these populations have the same mean, or the same median, or the same proportional distribution. A hypothesis of "no relationship" asserts that the variables being examined are unrelated to each other (that is, have a correlation of zero) in the population represented by the study sample.

objective (1) A statement of a specific desired outcome from a service program. Several objectives are usually derived from each of the program's goals and are usually much narrower than their parent goal. Most good statements of objectives specify the data by which their attainment can be measured. (2) Free from bias. (3) When referring to psychometric instruments: calling for responses requiring little or no human judgment for scoring (for example, multiple-choice tests).

observation schedule A written form on which observations are to be recorded. It may be presented on paper or on a computer screen.

one-shot evaluation Program evaluation carried out one time only, usually (a) as part of planning or establishing a new program, or (b) "in response to a perceived crisis or particularly difficult policy situation" (Franklin & Thrasher, 1976, p. 27).

open-ended Calling for respondents to answer in their own words rather than choosing among answer possibilities already written. This term usually refers to items in tests, interviews, or questionnaires.

opportunity costs Opportunities forgone because of service program activities (Rossi & Freeman, 1989).

order A property of measurement systems; if any three numbers or labels all differ from one another, one is intermediate between the other two. For example, numbers have order; academic majors do not.

ordered Able to be arranged in an obviously meaningful sequence, such as quantities (for example, number of children, years of experience, salary ranges). Used to describe answer possibilities for closed-ended items on tests, inventories, or questionnaires.

ordinal Having the measurement system properties of identity and order.

ordinate The vertical axis of a graph.

origin In graphing, the point where the ordinate and abscissa meet.

outcome study A study that addresses what happens after the entire counseling process or some specified part of it is completed.

own-control design An experimental design that administers all treatment conditions to every subject rather than each treatment to a different group of subjects.

parameter A characteristic of the frequency distribution (whether or not known) of a population. Parameters describe populations in the same manner as descriptive statistics describe samples.

parametric test A statistical test based on mathematical derivations that include assumptions about parameters of populations from which the samples were drawn. The t test, ANOVA, and tests involving the Pearson correlation are parametric.

partially closed-ended Mixing open-ended and closed-ended formats; respondents have a set of answer possibilities from which to choose, and in addition are either (a) invited to add other answers of their own making if inclined to do so, or (b) asked to amplify certain of the previously written answer possibilities if these answers are chosen.

participant A person who is a subject in a research project or part of a group (such as a family or work group) serving as a subject. Unless this specialized meaning is clear from context, the ordinary meaning of this word (one who participates) is usually intended.

participant observer A person who is both studying a process as an observer and at the same time participating in it.

passive Said of studies in which the researcher does not administer treatment conditions to manipulate variables (Cook & Campbell, 1979).

path analysis A technique for seeking answers to questions of cause by constructing a model of causal relationships among three or more variables being studied and comparing expected correlations based on the model with observed correlations after data are collected (Cook & Campbell, 1979).

payback period An estimate of the time required for a service program's expected benefits to recover its costs; usually calculated as part of a formal cost–benefit analysis.

Pearson correlation A type of correlation suitable for two interval or ratio variables.

percentile See centile.

performance range The range within which an instrument measures a variable. A test that is too difficult or too easy has an inappropriate performance range.

periodic evaluation Program evaluation carried out recurrently at regular intervals (Franklin & Thrasher, 1976).

personal documents Written materials created for personal purposes. Sometimes they are later used for research. Some examples are personal correspondence, diaries, poetry, stories, notes in the family Bible, records of personal business transactions, and various written materials counseling clients may be asked to create between sessions.

persuasive utilization Use of program evaluation results by someone other than evaluators or sponsors, usually to support or attack a political position (Rossi & Freeman, 1989). For example, the Reagan administration defended cutting social programs by noting that evaluations of major social programs failed to produce clear findings of desirable impact.

phase One of two or more time periods in which observations are taken in a time series experiment.

phenomenology The study of people's internal experiences, usually through their verbal reports of these experiences.

physical traces Direct effects on the physical environment. For example, wear on the sole of a leg prosthesis indicates it has been used.

pie chart See *circle graph.*

pie graph See *circle graph.*

pilot study A small research project carried out during planning of a much larger project, usually employed to try out tools or procedures being considered for the main study. Sometimes a pilot study is carried out to help the researcher decide whether to conduct the main study, modify its mission, or abandon it.

placebo A pharmacologically inert substance given as a medication.

placebo effect Psychosocial influences on people's reactions to a treatment based on such factors as researchers' statements of what effects to expect.

When these are confounded with the effects of treatment, internal validity is weakened.

planning The second phase of the six-phase model of the research process. In this phase, detailed plans are developed for the project's data collection, data analysis, interpretation, and reporting.

polygraph A mechanical instrument that makes a continuous recording on paper (or directly to a computer) of several body functions such as skin temperature, electrical conductance of the skin, heartbeat, breathing, limb volume, muscle tension, and brain electrical activity. A researcher can choose the specific functions to be recorded.

pool All the individuals available for sampling from any specified population. The individuals may be people, events, or objects. Most but not all pools are identical with the populations they represent.

population The entire set of individuals of interest to a project, such as all freshman college students in the United States, all dentists practicing in Ohio, or all 3rd grade arithmetic texts published in English from 1985 through 1989. Usually, it is not possible to study all members of the population of interest; therefore researchers use samples.

population of primary interest The population about which a researcher would like to answer questions before feasibility issues are confronted during the formulation phase. As a compromise with this ideal, a more limited population may be chosen for the research question if sampling from the population of primary interest is too difficult, too expensive, or otherwise infeasible.

posttest-only control-group design A group experimental design in which subjects are assigned to two groups: one group is administered an experimental treatment, the other a control condition, before the dependent variable is measured.

power test A test that is untimed or has a sufficiently generous time limit that almost all respondents finish.

practice effect Influences of learning when subjects perform tasks more than once. Many measures of dependent variables in research projects are based on learnable tasks. This learning threatens internal validity when the effects of practice are confounded with a treatment effect or developmental variable, such as in pre–post and time series designs without adequate controls.

precision (1) The extent to which a sample's descriptive statistics agree with the corresponding population's parameters. (2) A characteristic of oral or written expression; intended meanings are conveyed exactly, literally, and unambiguously.

predictor variable A variable being studied in a correlational project regarding the extent to which it correctly predicts one or more criterion variables. For example, aptitude test scores (predictor variables) are often used to predict people's grades in school or performance at work (criterion variables). When a project studies a relationship between variables, with neither variable predicting the other, predictor and criterion are best avoided as imprecise terms.

pretest–posttest control-group design   A design for a group experiment that uses two groups of subjects; the dependent variable is measured, then one group experiences an experimental treatment and the other a control condition, then the dependent variable is measured again.

principal author   See *senior author.*

process evaluation   One of the CIPP model's four components. This kind of program evaluation seeks to answer questions concerning a service program's day-to-day operations. Are activities being carried out as planned? Are they on schedule? Are unforeseen obstacles or delays being encountered? (Stufflebeam & Shinkfield, 1985)

process study   One of several descriptive research approaches. Most process studies of counseling address what takes place during sessions with clients.

product development   One of the major research approaches discussed in this book. Product development projects bring diverse data together to bring forth a tangible product such as a new or improved test or inventory. The mission of this research is much like that of engineers who develop new and improved automobiles and household appliances.

product evaluation   One of the CIPP model's four components. This kind of program evaluation seeks to answer questions concerning the extent to which a service program's objectives are being achieved. Product evaluation is carried out "to measure, interpret and judge the attainments of a program" (Stufflebeam & Shinkfield, 1985, p. 176).

profile   A set of scores for one respondent derived from the same instrument or battery of related instruments.

program evaluation   Applied research carried out to make or support decisions about a service program.

program utility assessment   Product evaluation that studies how effectively, and at what cost, a service program accomplishes what it sets out to do. It comprises two components: impact assessment and efficiency assessment (Rossi & Freeman, 1989).

proportion   A ratio expressing the relationship between a frequency in a sample or population and the size of the entire sample or population. For example, if a sample of 72 people contains 36 males, the frequency of males is 36 and the proportion of males is one-half or 50%.

proportional stratified sampling   Stratified sampling in which the number chosen from each subdivision is proportional to the representation of that subdivision in the entire pool.

psychometric   Pertaining to the measurement of one or more psychological variables.

psychometrics   (1) A field of study involving characteristics, construction, and modification of psychometric instruments and analysis and interpretation of data derived from them. (2) In a case record, data derived from psychometric instruments.

publication lag The length of time that elapses after a journal or other print source receives a manuscript, before material is published.

qualitative Without quantities or numbers.

quantitative Involving quantities or numbers.

quasi-experiment An experiment in which satisfactory control of extraneous variables is not feasible under prevailing conditions, although a true experiment would ideally suit the project's mission.

questionnaire An instrument consisting of written questions to which respondents are expected to write their answers. It may be presented on paper or by computer.

random Fulfilling both of two criteria: equal probability and independence.

random assignment Assignment of subjects or participants so that both the criteria of equal probability and independence are fulfilled. Usually accomplished by using a table of random numbers.

randomization Random selection or assignment. This tactic is the easiest way to control any extraneous variables a researcher cannot explicitly identify as well as many factors that can be identified.

range A measure of variability of a frequency distribution: (1) the highest and lowest values, or (2) the difference between these values.

rater bias Bias of ratings from raters' knowledge about subjects, such as which subjects belong to an experimental group and which to a control group, or subjects' pretest scores. Despite raters' best intentions to be objective, any knowledge that might bias their ratings can be expected to do so to some extent. When confounded with the phenomena being studied, rater bias weakens internal validity.

rater drift Change in raters' approach to their task (for example, rating standards, vigilance) over time as a project progresses (Hill, 1991). When confounded with the phenomena being studied, rater drift weakens internal validity.

rating scale An instrument that requires one or more judges "to assign the rated object to categories or continua" (Kerlinger, 1986, p. 494) that usually have numbers attached to them. The "object" is not necessarily a thing, but may be a person, a group, a plan, a document, a set of behaviors, or an idea, among other possibilities. The numbers are not always immediately evident to raters; they are often applied afterward by the researcher.

ratio (1) A quantity produced when one number can be meaningfully divided by another. (2) Having the properties of identity, order, equal intervals, and absolute zero.

reactive effects Subjects' extraneous reactions to measurement procedures; such reactions may (a) temporarily change the variables being measured, (b) confound the intended measurement, or (c) do both.

reactive measure A measurement method that gives subjects something to react to (Isaac & Michael, 1981). Examples are tests, questionnaires, and interviews.

recruitment   Eliciting the participation of a project's prospective subjects.

rectilinear   Approximating a straight line; not curvilinear.

related-groups comparison   Comparison of the same measures taken from groups comprising different subjects; the composition of the groups is not independent. Husbands and wives represent related groups.

reliability   The general consistency of a measure.

repeated-measures comparison   Comparison of measures of the same variables taken at two or more different times from the same subjects (in single-subject projects, the same person).

replicate   To repeat a research project that has been conducted before to determine whether similar results will be obtained.

reporting   The last phase of the six-phase model of the research process. In this phase, the researcher communicates to consumers the project's mission, methods, results, and interpretations.

representative   Similar to what is represented. Studying a representative sample yields approximately the same results as would studying the entire population, were studying the entire population desirable and feasible. Under certain conditions of sampling, the precision of this approximation can be stated as a predictable and usually small margin of error.

research   (1) A human activity that seeks to increase knowledge by systematically collecting, analyzing, and interpreting data to answer carefully formulated questions about publicly observable phenomena. (2) Research reports, collectively.

research approach   A basis for classifying research projects, based primarily on their missions, secondarily on methods. The major research approaches discussed in this book are descriptive, historical, action, product development, passive causal, and experimental.

research hypothesis   A statement that expresses a prediction about the answer to a research question.

research industry   All research activity being carried out by the society as a whole or any part of it; "industry" is used similarly in such expressions as "insurance industry" and "health care industry."

research process   The process by which each research project moves from beginning to end: formulation, planning, data collection, data analysis, interpretation, and reporting.

research product   The extensive body of formal and informal records resulting from research activity: the professional literature and a cumulative collective experience among researchers.

research program   A set of related projects that have some aspects of their missions in common. The program as a whole has a mission, which in turn forms part of each individual project's mission.

research question   A question a research project seeks to answer as part of its mission. A well-formulated research question specifies what populations and what variables are to be studied and what kinds of answers are sought (for example, qualitative descriptions, proportions, averages, comparisons, or relationships between variables).

retrospective design A developmental design that asks participants for responses under two sets of instructions: (a) in the usual way, representing present time, and (b) by remembering a previous time so as to answer as they think they would have then. This design is used when a longitudinal design is desirable but not practical because time and resources are insufficient to study the participants over a long time period.

reversal In a phase of a time series experiment, actively attempting to reverse the behavior change brought about in a previous phase. Some past writers have used this term to refer to withdrawal; this usage is now obsolete (Sulzer-Azaroff & Mayer, 1991).

review board See *review committee.*

review committee A committee, usually within a large organization, that evaluates research proposals before the organization grants financial support or permission to carry out each project.

rigor Control of all factors in a research project that might reduce the clarity with which its results answer the research questions. This term includes, but is not limited to, internal validity.

sample (1) A set of the members of a population chosen so as to be representative of the population. (2) Select the individuals to be included in one or more samples.

sampling frame A list of all the members of a pool.

scatter graph A graph that presents a bivariate distribution showing the relationship between two quantitative variables. One of the variables is represented with the horizontal axis and the other with the vertical axis; each case is represented with a dot or other symbol that represents the individual's standing on both variables. Scatter graphs are also referred to as scatter diagrams or scattergrams.

scientific method Seeking answers to questions with data. Questions are carefully formulated; data are systematically collected, analyzed, and interpreted according to a plan to maximize the clarity with which the interpretations answer the questions asked in the project's mission.

scientist-practitioner model The idea that practitioners have training in research methods and that their professional activities include both research and direct client service.

self-fulfilling prophecy The tendency of people's actions to fulfill their expectations, whether deliberately or inadvertently. Includes both rater bias and experimenter bias.

self-monitoring An observation technique in which people are asked to monitor and record their own experience or behavior, or both. The same person is both observer and subject.

semantic differential An instrument consisting of one or more concepts that respondents rate on each of a set of polar adjective pairs. Each adjective pair represents a graphic rating scale.

semistructured interview An interview in which an interview guide stipulates the points to be covered. It may include some questions to be read verbatim, although interviewers are free to vary the phrasing of most questions and often to explore points more deeply than stipulated in the guide or presented in initial answers.

senior author The first author listed for a research report having more than one author; usually the author who made the greatest contribution to the project in the formulation, planning, interpretation, and reporting phases, considered collectively.

sequencing A type of decision that relates to preparing a report: In what order is the material to be presented?

sequential assignment Assignment when the subjects in the sample have not been identified at the beginning; procedures are begun before the researchers know who will be in the sample. For example, a mental health clinic might assign all new nonemergency cases at intake to four experimental conditions until each condition has 25 subjects.

service delivery accountability Accountability to show the extent to which a service program operates according to plans, with services delivered by appropriately qualified staff (Rossi & Freeman, 1989).

service program A set of service activities; it can be any size, from very large (for example, the entire federal–state public rehabilitation system) to very small (for example, a small community agency's activities with a few local high school students who have special needs, or even one counselor's work with one client).

shadow controls "Expert and participant judgments" used in some program evaluation projects in lieu of controls when even constructed controls are impracticable (Rossi & Freeman, 1989, p. 310).

short-answer Calling for respondents to formulate answers of few words (on questionnaires, usually one or two words).

significance level The probability that random sampling from populations for which the null hypothesis is correct will produce results such as those at hand.

significance test See *test* (definition #3).

simple random sampling Random sampling applied to the entire frame at once.

single-blind Controlling for the placebo effect in experiments when different treatments are being compared; subjects do not know what treatment they are being given or why it is expected to be effective. Contrasted with double-blind, in which this information is withheld from both subjects and people administering the treatment.

single case experiment See *single-subject experiment*.

single-subject experiment A time series experiment using one subject.

skeleton form A preliminary version of a table or graph; it contains no data but is otherwise complete. The title has been written; the kind of data to be entered (such as means, percentages) has been identified; explanatory notes (if any) have been written. For a table, the number of rows and columns has been decided; rows and columns have been labeled. For a graph, the general type (for example, line, bar, pie) has been decided; axes have been labeled; the number of lines, bars, or sectors has been decided at least provisionally and they have been labeled; a legend, if needed, has been written.

Solomon four-group design A design for a group experiment; it combines the posttest-only and pretest–posttest control-group design features and includes four groups of subjects: pretested experimental, pretested control, unpretested experimental, and unpretested control.

stakeholders People with vested interests in a research project or its results. An evaluation project's stakeholders also include people with vested interests in the service program being evaluated (Rossi & Freeman, 1989).

standard deviation A measure of variability of a frequency distribution: the square root of its variance.

standardized Having both (a) instructions for uniform administration procedures and (b) norms (Anastasi, 1988). This term is usually applied to tests and inventories, sometimes to other instruments such as questionnaires.

standard score A score transformed according to a system whereby scores from each of several instruments or subscales have the same mean and standard deviation in a norm sample.

statistic A measure calculated from data from one or more samples.

statistical analysis Analysis of quantitative data for interpretation and reporting; may include tabulation, graphing, descriptive statistics, tests of significance, or any combination of these.

statistical hypothesis A hypothesis about the populations represented by the samples studied in a research project.

statistically significant Of a magnitude rarely obtained by random sampling from populations for which the null hypothesis is true.

statistical power The probability that a statistically significant result will be obtained if a difference or relationship of a given size exists in the populations sampled.

statistical regression A statistical artifact whereby groups of people chosen for their atypically high or low scores usually have more moderate mean scores when retested. This phenomenon occurs because at least part of the reason they scored at the extreme ends of the scale was due to chance factors that favored high scorers or depressed the scores of low scorers. When confounded with the phenomenon being studied, statistical regression weakens internal validity.

statistical test See *test* (definition #3).

stratification variable A variable used to subdivide a population for purposes of selecting a stratified sample.

stratified random sampling Stratified sampling in which the principles of random sampling are applied separately to each subdivision.

stratified sampling A method of sampling in which the population is subdivided according to one or more stratification variables before the sample is selected. Each subdivision of the population is represented by a corresponding subdivision in the sample. See *stratified random sampling* and *proportional stratified sampling.*

structured interview An interview consisting of questions read verbatim from an interview guide. Interviewers are free to clarify some points such as a word unfamiliar to a respondent, although they do not explore any material more deeply than stipulated in the guide.

subject A person or other entity upon whom (or which) a research project makes observations or measures.

subject pool A pool consisting of people or other kinds of subjects to be sampled.

subpopulation A part of a population, usually defined by special characteristics; usually atypical of the population as a whole, such as ethnic minorities; not representative and therefore not a sample. For example, clients supported by one insurance company are a subpopulation, not a sample, of insurance-supported clients as a whole.

support people People other than researchers or subjects who contribute their efforts or other support to a project. Examples include observers, raters, judges, cooperating counselors whose clients are subjects, and agency administrators.

survey One of several descriptive research approaches. Most surveys seek to describe defined sets of people according to the variables stipulated by the research questions. Instead of people, a survey might study sets of things, organizations, animals, curriculum topics, or documents, among other possibilities.

systematic assignment Assignment according to a nonrandom pattern established in advance. An alternating pattern is a common one. For example, subjects could be assigned to four treatment conditions in the order 1, 2, 3, 4; 2, 3, 4, 1; 3, 4, 1, 2; and so forth.

systematic sampling Sampling by selecting individuals from a frame at regular intervals. For example, a sample of 50 might be chosen from a frame of 1,000 by choosing the first individual at random from the first 20 members, and thereafter selecting every 20th member.

systematic variation A method of controlling explicitly identified potentially confounding variables in an experiment by ensuring that two or more groups in each experimental and control condition differ with respect to these variables as specified in the research plan; influences of these variables can be identified statistically in the data analysis.

table of random numbers A table comprising numbers chosen randomly.

targets (1) The people a service program is intended to serve. (2) People, groups, ideas, practices, or objects toward whom (or which) feelings or attitudes are directed.

test (1) A psychometric instrument that (a) calls upon respondents to perform at their best (such as tests of intelligence, aptitude, knowledge, or skill) or (b) is called a "test" by its author (for example, the Thematic Apperception Test). We recommend against carelessly calling inventories "tests." (2) A procedure for determining whether a specified substance or condition exists in the body or its products or to determine the amount of such a substance present. (3) A statistical procedure (statistical test) for evaluating the reasonableness of a statistical hypothesis. (4) To administer a test (definition #1) to one or more persons or to conduct a test (definition #2 or #3).

theme   In content analysis, a proposition, thesis, statement, or assertion, usually about one or more people, places, things, or ideas (Kerlinger, 1986). A simple theme often consists of one sentence; a complex one may comprise several related sentences. For example, one might note may comprise several related sentences. For example, one might note (a) clients' statements of self-reference, (b) supervisors' beliefs about the best way to respond to employees' tardiness, or (c) teachers' classroom statements about causes of racial tension.

time line   A written expression of the sequence and timing of a research project's activities, usually developed in planning. May be in text or graphic form.

time sampling   A procedure used in observational studies, especially those employing time series designs; samples are taken from the available times that observations could be made (Sulzer-Azaroff & Mayer, 1991).

time series experiment   An experiment, usually using one or a very few subjects, that seeks to make inferences about causality by carefully managing the time sequence in which treatment conditions are administered.

traditional group experiment   See *group experiment.*

transmittal letter   A letter accompanying and introducing a questionnaire or other materials, whether mailed or delivered by hand.

treatment condition   A condition administered to one or more subjects as determined by the independent variable in an experiment. An experiment may involve one or more treatment conditions. Most experiments also include one or more control conditions; some compare two or more conditions without designating any as "control."

trend study   One of several descriptive research approaches. Trend studies examine the same variables over a period of time, including the present, to predict at least one of these variables in the future.

triangulation   The principle that a project with a well-chosen set of related research questions will likely offer a richer payoff for the researcher's efforts than a project with only one. Collecting the data for one question answers one question only, while adding the data for a carefully chosen second question may also permit a third to be answered with little further work.

true experiment   An experiment in which potentially confounding variables are satisfactorily controlled, usually by (a) random assignment of participants to experimental conditions or (b) sequencing of experimental conditions.

true interval   Having the measurement system properties of identity, order, arbitrary zero, and equal intervals, with the latter supported by evidence (Kirkpatrick & Aleamoni, 1983).

T score   A standard score with a mean of 50 and a standard deviation of 10 in a norm sample.

t **test**   A statistical test for the difference between two means.

two-phase sampling   Selecting a subsample from an original sample. Usually, some research procedures are administered to the original sample, and additional procedures are later applied to the subsample.

Type 1 error   Obtaining a statistically significant result when the null hypothesis is true.

Type 2 error   Obtaining a statistically nonsignificant result even though the null hypothesis is false.

unit of analysis   The element of a communication chosen for content analysis. Kerlinger (1986, p. 479) listed five: "words, themes, characters, items, and space-and-time measures."

unordered   Not able to be arranged in an obviously meaningful sequence (for example, academic majors, makes of automobiles, counselors' names). Said of answer possibilities for closed-ended items on tests, inventories, or questionnaires.

unrestricted random sampling   See *simple random sampling.*

unstructured interview   An interview that usually begins with a very general question or probe; the interviewer is then allowed to explore the topic freely, usually following the respondent's lead.

utilization evaluation   Assessment of the extent to which research results are used: (a) the extent to which a program evaluation project's reports served their intended purposes, usually expressed through consumers' decisions based on the project's results, or (b) the extent and manner in which program decisions use existing results. When program evaluation results are underutilized or not utilized, it is important to identify barriers to satisfactory utilization (Rossi & Freeman, 1989).

validity   See *design validity, content validity, criterion-related validity, construct validity, face validity,* and *factual validity.*

variable   A characteristic of people, environments, physical objects, tasks, behavior, or anything else in which a researcher is interested.

variance   A measure of variability of a frequency distribution: the average squared difference between each case and the mean.

wait-control design   A design for a group experiment in which all participants are treated; control is achieved by requiring some participants to wait longer than others. The immediate-treatment group is pretested, treated, and posttested. The wait group is pretested, required to wait, posttested, and then treated. In some projects, both groups are post-tested again after the wait group has been treated.

weasel words   Words that express more tentativeness than is justified (Hollis & Donn, 1979).

windyfoggery   Unusual, sophisticated sounding words used when simpler language would convey the intended meanings equally well (Bernstein, 1977).

withdrawal   In the second A phase of a time series experiment, discontinuing the intervention that was introduced in the first B phase; in an ABAB design this intervention is reintroduced in the second B phase (Sulzer-Azaroff & Mayer, 1991).

within-group comparison   Comparison of measures from the same group on two or more different variables (for example, language achievement and mathematics achievement), whether at the same or different times.

X axis   The abscissa of a graph.

Y axis   The ordinate of a graph.

REFERENCES

Abramson, M. (1990). Keeping secrets: Social work and AIDS. *Social Work, 35,* 169–173.

Adair, J. G., Dushenko, T. W., & Lindsay, R. C. (1985). Ethical regulations and their impact on research practice. *American Psychologist, 40,* 59–72.

Addiction Research Foundation. (1979). *Report of the Task Force on Employee Assistance Programs.* Toronto, Ontario: Author.

Adler, T. (1991). Cancer patients helped by therapy, study finds. *The APA Monitor, 22*(2), 9.

American Association for Marriage and Family Therapy. (1991). *AAMFT Code of ethical principles for marriage and family therapists.* Washington, DC: Author.

American Counseling Association. (1988). Ethical standards of the American Association for Counseling and Development (3rd revision). *Journal of Counseling and Development, 67,* 4–8.

American Counseling Association. (1993). ACA proposed standards of practice and ethical standards. *Guidepost, 36*(4), 15–22.

American Educational Research Association, American Psychological Association, & National Council on Measurement in Education. (1985). *Standards for educational and psychological testing.* Washington, DC: American Psychological Association.

American Psychological Association. (1973). *Ethical principles in the conduct of research with human participants.* Washington, DC: Author.

American Psychological Association. (1982). *Ethical principles in the conduct of research with human participants.* Washington, DC: Author.

American Psychological Association. (1983). *Publication manual of the American Psychological Association.* Washington, DC: Author.

American Psychological Association (1990). Ethical principles of psychologists (amended June 2, 1989). *American Psychologist, 45,* 390–395.

American Psychological Association. (1992). Ethical principles of psychologists and code of conduct. *American Psychologist, 47,* 1597–1628.

Anastasi, A. (1988). *Psychological testing* (6th ed.). New York: Macmillan.

Anderson, D. (1992). A case for standards of counseling practice. *Journal of Counseling and Development, 71*(1), 22–26.

Anderson, W. P., & Heppner, P. P. (1986). Counselor applications of research findings to practice: Learning to stay current. *Journal of Counseling and Development, 65,* 152–155.

Appelbaum, P. S., & Rosenbaum, A. (1989). Tarasoff and the researcher: Does the duty to protect apply in the research setting? *American Psychologist, 44,* 885–894.

Appelbaum, S. A. (1970). Science and persuasion in the psychological test report. *Journal of Consulting and Clinical Psychology, 35,* 349–355.

Armsden, G. C., & Greenberg, M. T. (1987). The inventory of parent and peer attachment: Individual differences and their relationship to psychological well-being in adolescence. *Journal of Youth and Adolescence, 16,* 427–453.

Ary, D., Jacobs, L. C., Razavieh, A. (1985). *Introduction to research in education* (3rd ed.). New York: Holt, Rinehart & Winston.

Astin, A., Dey, E., Korn, W., & Riggs, E. (1991). *The American Council on Education–UCLA Cooperative Institutional Research Program Freshman Survey.* Los Angeles: Higher Education Research Institute, UCLA.

Babbie, E. R. (1973). *Survey research methods.* Belmont, CA: Wadsworth.

Backer, T., & Trotter, M. W. (1986). *RRN innovation directory: Computer applications.* Los Angeles: Human Interaction Research Institute.

Bandura, A. (1969). *Principles of behavior modification.* New York: Holt, Rinehart, & Winston.

Bandura, A. (1977). Self-efficacy: Toward a unifying theory of behavioral change. *Psychological Review, 84*(2), 191–215.

Barlow, D. H., Hayes, S. C., & Nelson, R. O. (1984). *The scientist practitioner.* New York: Pergamon Press.

Barlow, D. H., & Hersen, M. (1984). *Single case experimental designs: Strategies for studying behavior change* (2nd ed.). Elmsford, NY: Pergamon Press.

Barnette, E. L. (1989). A program to meet the emotional and social needs of gifted and talented adolescents. *Journal of Counseling and Development, 67,* 525–528.

Bauer, B. G., & Anderson, W. P. (1989). Bulimic beliefs: Food for thought. *Journal of Counseling and Development, 67,* 416–419.

Beck, A. T. (1976). *Cognitive therapy and the emotional disorders.* New York: International Universities Press.

Bell, G. L. (1984). Poetry therapy: A focus on moments. *Arts in Psychotherapy, 11*(3), 177–185.

Bernstein, T. M. (1977). *Dos, don'ts & maybes of English usage.* New York: Time Books.

Bersoff, D. N. (1978). Legal and ethical concerns in research. In L. Goldman (Ed.), *Research methods for counselors: Practical approaches in field settings* (pp. 363–400). New York: Wiley.

Best, J. W., & Kahn, J. V. (1989). *Research in education* (6th ed.). Englewood Cliffs, NJ: Prentice Hall.

Bishop, J. B., & Trembley, E. L. (1987). Counseling centers and accountability: Immovable objects, irresistible forces. *Journal of Counseling and Development, 65,* 491–494.

Blanck, P. D., Bellack, A. S., Rosnow, R. L., Rotheram-Borus, M. J., & Schooler, N. R. (1992). Scientific rewards and conflicts of ethical choices in human subjects research. *American Psychologist, 47,* 959–965.

Blume, S. B. (1987). *Confidentiality of patient records in alcoholism and drug treatment programs.* New York: National Council on Alcoholism.

Bolk, L. R. (1983). Adolescents' reactions to bereavement. *Personnel and Guidance Journal, 61*(9), 547–553.

Boneau, C. A. (1960). The effects of violations of assumptions underlying the *t* test. *Psychological Bulletin, 57,* 49–64.

Boor, M. (1986). Suggestions to improve manuscripts submitted to professional journals. *American Psychologist, 41,* 721–722.

Borders, L. D., & Drury, S. M. (1992a). Comprehensive school counseling programs: A review for policymakers and practitioners. *Journal of Counseling and Development, 70,* 487–495.

Borders, L. D., & Drury, S. M. (1992b). *Counseling programs: A guide to evaluation.* Newbury Park, CA: Corwin Press.

Boschen, K. A. (1984). Issues in evaluating vocational rehabilitation programs. *Rehabilitation Psychology, 29,* 37–48.

Bracht, G. H., & Glass, V. V. (1968). The external validity of experiments. *American Educational Research Journal, 5,* 437–474.

Brent, E. E., Spencer, J. C., & Scott, J. K. (1989). EX-SAMPLE: An expert system program to assist in determining sample size. *Social Science Computer Review, 7*(3), 314–319.

Brooks, N. A. (1983). Using field research to gain subjective insights. In N. M. Crewe & I. K. Zola (Eds.), *Independent living for physically disabled people* (pp. 292–310). San Francisco: Jossey-Bass.

Bryans, C. H. (1983). *Dream stuff & such.* Los Angeles: Author.

Buchler, J. (1966). *Charles Pierce's empiricism.* New York: Octagon Books.

Burrello, L. C., & Reitzug, U. C. (1993). Transforming context and developing culture in schools. *Journal of Counseling and Development, 71,* 669–677.

Byck, R. (1987). The effects of cocaine on complex performance in humans. *Alcohol, Drugs, and Driving, 3,* 9–12.

Byrd, K., Williamson, W., Byrd, D. (1986). Literary characters who are disabled. *Rehabilitation Counseling Bulletin, 30,* 57–61.

California State University, Los Angeles. (1991, Summer). *Sponsored Program News.* Los Angeles: Author.

Campbell, D. C., & Stanley, J. C. (1966). *Experimental and quasi-experimental designs for research.* Chicago: Rand-McNally.

Canadian Broadcasting Corporation (Producer). (1987). *Subdue the Earth* [Television Broadcast]. Toronto, Ontario, Canada: CBC Educational Sales.

Claiborn, C. D. (1987). Science and practice: Reconsidering the Pepinskys. *Journal of Counseling and Development, 65,* 286–288.

Cohen, J. (1988). *Statistical power analysis for the behavior sciences* (3rd ed.). New York: Academic Press.

Cohen, R. J., Swerdlik, M. E., & Smith, D. K. (1992). *Psychological testing and assessment: An introduction to tests and measurement* (2nd ed.). Mountain View, CA: Mayfield Publishing Co.

Coffler, D. B., & Hadley, R. G. (1973). The residential rehabilitation center as an alternative to jail for chronic drunkenness offenders. *Quarterly Journal of Studies on Alcohol, 34,* 1180–1186.

Comings, D. E. (1991). The genetics of addictive behaviors: The role of childhood behavioral disorders. *Addiction and Recovery, 11*(6), 13–16.

Cook, T. D., & Campbell, D. T. (1979). *Quasi-experimentation: Design & analysis issues for field settings.* Boston: Houghton-Mifflin.

Couch potato physique. (1989, September). *Psychology Today,* p. 8.

Coursey, R. D., Ward-Alexander, L. W., & Katz, B. (1990). Cost-effectiveness of providing insurance benefits for posthospital psychiatric halfway house stays. *American Psychologist, 45*(10), 1116–1126.

Critelli, J. W., & Neumann, K. F. (1984). The placebo: Conceptual analysis of a construct in transition. *American Psychologist, 39,* 32–39.

Cronbach, L. J. (1984). *Essentials of psychological testing.* New York: Harper & Row.

Cronbach, L. J., & Gleser, G. C. (1953). Assessing similarity between profiles. *Psychological Bulletin, 50,* 456–473.

Dahlstrom, W. G., Welsh, G. S., & Dahlstrom, L. E. (1972). *An MMPI handbook* (Vol. 1) Clinical interpretation. Minneapolis: University of Minnesota Press.

Dalai Lama (Speaker). (1984). Untitled remarks at the Inner Science Conference, Amherst College, MA. San Jacinto, CA: Insight Recordings.

Deal, T. W., & Kennedy, A. A. (1982). *Corporate cultures.* Reading, MA: Addison-Wesley.

Debord, J. B. (1989). Paradoxical interventions: A review of the recent literature. *Journal of Counseling and Development, 67*(7), 394–398.

Deming, W. E. (1950). *Some theory of sampling.* London: John Wiley & Sons.

Denmark, F., Russo, N. F., Frieze, I. H., & Sechzer, J. A. (1988). Guidelines for avoiding sexism in psychological research. *American Psychologist, 43,* 582–585.

Denton, D. E. (1981). Understanding the life of the counselor. *Personnel and Guidance Journal, 59,* 596–599.

Denzin, N. K. (1978). The logic of naturalistic inquiry. In N. K. Denzin (Ed.), *Sociological methods: A sourcebook* (pp. 6–29). New York: McGraw-Hill.

Deutsch, S. J., & Alt, F. B. (1977). The effect of Massachusetts gun control law on gun-related crimes in the city of Boston. *Evaluation Quarterly,* 543–568.

Dewsbury, D. A. (1993). On publishing controversy: Norman R. F. Maier and the genesis of seizures. *American Psychologist, 48,* 869–877.

Diener, E., & Crandall, R. (1978). *Ethics in social and behavioral research.* Chicago: University of Chicago Press.

Dillman, D. A. (1978). *Mail and telephone surveys: The total design method.* New York: Wiley.

Dills, R., Grinder, J. Bandler, R., & DeLozier, J. (1980). *Neuro-linguistic programming.* Cupertino, CA: Meta Publications.

Drew, C. J., & Hardman, M. L. (1985). *Designing and conducting behavioral research.* Elmsford, NY: Pergamon Press.

Dubowski, K. M. (1986). Recent development in alcohol analysis. *Alcohol, Drugs, and Driving: Abstracts and Reviews, 2*(2) 13–46. Published by Alcohol Information Service, Neuropsychiatric Institute, UCLA.

Eaton, W. J. (1994, April 1). Nicotine study suppressed, Waxman says. *Los Angeles Times,* p. A20.

Einstein, A. (1954). *Ideas and opinions.* New York: Bonanza Books.

Elias, M. F. (1984). Handheld computers for recording timed behavior observations. *Ethology and Sociobiology, 5*(1), 59–60.

English, P. T. (1987). The use of isolation time-out with a disabled adult in a regular work setting: A case study. *Journal of Rehabilitation, 53,* 67–70.

Evans, J. H., Jr., & Burck, H. (1992). The effects of career education intervention on academic achievement: A meta-analysis. *Journal of Counseling and Development, 71,* 63–68.

Fairchild, T. N., & Zins, J. E. (1986). Accountability practices of school counselors: A national survey. *Journal of Counseling and Development, 65,* 196–199.

Fielding, N. G., & Fielding, J. L. (1986). *Linking data.* Beverly Hills, CA: Sage.

Filstead, W. J. (Ed.) (1970). *Qualitative methodology: Firsthand involvement with the social world.* Chicago: Markham.

Fleming, I., & Baum, A. (1987). Stress: Psychobiological assessment. *Journal of Organizational Behavior Management, 8*(2), 117–140.

Flynn, R. J., Glueckauf, R. L., Langill, G. F., & Schacter, G. (1984). Program evaluation in Canadian rehabilitation facilities for physically disabled persons: A national survey. *Rehabilitation Psychology, 29,* 11–20.

Forsyth, D. R., & Strong, S. R. (1986). The scientific study of counseling and psychotherapy: A unificationist view. *American Psychologist, 41*(2), 113–119.

Fowler, F. J., Jr. (1984). *Survey research methods.* Beverly Hills, CA: Sage.

Franklin, J. L., & Thrasher, J. H. (1976). *An introduction to program evaluation.* New York: Wiley.

Froehle, T. C., & Rominger, R. L. (1993). Directions in consultation research: Bridging the gap between science and practice. *Journal of Counseling and Development, 71,* 693–699.

Gay, L. R. (1987). *Educational research: Competencies for analysis and action* (3rd ed.). Columbus, OH: Merrill.

Gelso, C. J. (1979). Research in counseling: Methodological and professional issues. *The Counseling Psychologist, 8*(3), 7–35.

Gladstein, G. A. (1969). Client expectations, counseling experience, and satisfaction. *Journal of Counseling Psychology, 16,* 476–481.

Gladue, B. A. (1994, March/April). Making the case for basic research. *Psychological Science Agenda,* p. 8.

Glaser, B. G., & Strauss, A. L. (1967). *The discovery of grounded theory: Strategies for qualitative research.* Chicago: Aldine.

Glass, G. V., & Stanley, J. C. (1970). *Statistical methods in education and psychology.* Englewood Cliffs, NJ: Prentice-Hall.

Gleick, J. (1987). *Chaos: Making a new science.* New York: Penguin.

Goldman, B. A., & Mitchell, D. F. (1990). *Dictionary of unpublished experimental mental measures* (Vol. 5). Dubuque, IA: William C. Brown.

Gordon, J., & Shontz, F. C. (1990). Living with the AIDS virus: A representative case. *Journal of Counseling & Development, 68,* 287–292.

Gottfriedson, G. D. (1984). A theory-ridden approach to program evaluation. *American Psychologist, 39,* 1101–1112.

Gottschalk, L. A. (1979). *The content analysis of verbal behavior.* New York: SP Medical and Scientific Books, Spectrum.

Grantham, R. J. (1973). Effects of counselor sex, race, and language style on black students in initial interviews. *Journal of Counseling Psychology, 20,* 553–559.

Greenberg, D. (1987, June 8). Publish or perish—or fake it. *U.S. News & World Report, 102*(22), pp. 72–73.

Grisso, T., Baldwin, E., Blanck, P. D., Rotheram-Borus, M. J., Schooler, N. R., & Thompson, T. (1991). Standards in research: APA's mechanism for monitoring the challenges. *American Psychologist, 46,* 758–766.

Gysbers, N. C., Hughey, K. F., Starr, M., & Lapan, R. T. (1992). Improving school guidance programs: A framework for program, personnel, and results evaluation. *Journal of Counseling & Development, 70,* 565–570.

Hacker, D. (1989). *A writer's reference.* New York: St. Martin's Press.

Hackett, G. (1985). The role of mathematics self-efficacy in choice of math-related majors of college men and women: A path analysis. *Journal of Counseling Psychology, 32,* 47–56.

Hadley, P. A., & Hadley, R. G. (1970). Moral issues in using ethnic identification as a group counseling tool with American Indian alcoholics. Paper presented at the annual convention of the Western Psychological Association, Los Angeles, CA.

Hadley, R. G. (1972). Ethical aspects of research in service settings. *Proceedings of the 80th Annual Convention of the American Psychological Association, 7,* 585–586.

Hadley, R. G. (1992). *Professional counselor reporting.* Los Angeles, CA: Author.

Hadley, R. G., & Brodwin, M. G. (1988). Language about people with disabilities. *Journal of Counseling & Development, 67,* 147–149.

Hadley, R. G., & Brodwin, M. G. (1989). Interpreting timed and untimed test performance. *Journal of Private Sector Rehabilitation, 4,* 101–105.

Hadley, R. G., & Hadley, P. A. (1974). A behavioral conflict perspective on alcoholics in treatment. Paper presented at the 20th International Institute on the Prevention and Treatment of Alcoholism, Manchester, England.

Hadley, R. G., & Hadley, P. A. (1983). Rehabilitation of people with alcohol problems. *Annual Review of Rehabilitation, 3*, 121–177.

Hansen, J. C. (1984). *User's Guide for the SVIB-SCII.* Stanford, CA: Stanford University Press.

Haring-Hidore, M., & Vacc, N. (1988). The scientist-practitioner model in training entry-level counselors. *Journal of Counseling and Development, 66*, 286–288.

Havlicek, L. L., & Peterson, N. L. (1974). Robustness of the *t* test: A guide for researchers on effect of violations of assumptions. *Psychological Reports, 34*, 1095–1114.

Hawking, S. (1988). *A brief history of time.* New York: Bantam Books.

Haynes, S. N., & Horn, W. F. (1982). Reactivity in behavioral observation: A review. *Behavioral Assessment, 4*, 369–385.

Heppner, P. P., & Anderson, W. P. (1985). On the perceived non-utility of research in counseling. *Journal of Counseling and Development, 63*, 545–547.

Heppner, P. P., Kivlighan, D. M., Jr., & Wampold, B. E. (1992). *Research design in counseling.* Pacific Grove, CA: Brooks/Cole.

Hill, C. E. (1991). Almost everything you ever wanted to know about how to do process research on counseling and psychotherapy but didn't know who to ask. In C. E. Watkins, Jr. & Lawrence J. Schneider (Eds.), *Research in counseling* (pp. 85–118). Hillsdale, NJ: Lawrence Erlbaum Associates.

Holland, J. L. (1966). *The psychology of vocational choice.* Waltham, MA: Blaisdell.

Holland, J. L. (1973). *Making vocational choices: A theory of careers.* Englewood Cliffs, NJ: Prentice-Hall.

Hollis, J. W., & Donn, P. A. (1979). *Psychological report writing.* New York: Accelerated Development.

Holsti, O. R. (1969). *Content analysis for the social sciences and humanities.* Reading, MA: Addison-Wesley.

Holzman, D. (1991, April 29). Honesty's litmus test in the lab. *Insight, 7*(17), 48–50.

Hoshmand, L. T., & Polkinghorne, D. E. (1992). Redefining the science-practice relationship and professional training. *American Psychologist, 47*, 55–66.

Hunnisett, R. (1986). Developing phenomenological method for researching lesbian existence. *Canadian Journal of Counseling, 20*, 255–286.

Ireland, C. (1992, October). The politics of nutrition. *Vegetarian Times*, pp. 54–63.

Isaac, S., & Michael, W. B. (1981). *Handbook in research and evaluation.* San Diego: EdITS.

Jones, L. K., Gorman, S., & Schroeder, C. G. (1989). A comparison between the SDS and the Career Key among career undecided college students. *The career development quarterly, 37*(4), 334–344.

Jongeward, D., & Scott, D. (1976). *Women as winners.* Reading, MA: Addison-Wesley.

Kailes, J. (1985). Watch your language, please! *Journal of Rehabilitation, 51*, 68–69.

Kaplan, A. (1964). *The conduct of inquiry.* San Francisco: Chandler Publishing Company.

Kaufman, R., & Thomas, S. (1980). *Evaluation without fear.* New York: New Viewpoints.

Keith-Spiegel, P. (1976). Children's rights as participants in research. In G. P. Koocher (Ed.), *Children's rights and the mental health professions* (pp. 53–81). New York: Wiley.

Keppel, G., & Zedeck, S. (1989). *Data analysis for research designs: Analysis of variance and multiple regression/correlation approaches.* New York: W. H. Freeman.

Kerlinger, F. N. (1964). *Foundations of behavioral research* (1st ed.). New York: Holt, Rinehart & Winston.

Kerlinger, F. N. (1973). *Foundations of behavioral research* (2nd ed.). New York: Holt, Rinehart & Winston.

Kerlinger, F. N. (1986). *Foundations of behavioral research* (3rd ed.). New York: Holt, Rinehart & Winston.

Kirkpatrick, J. S. (1981). Nonparametric statistics: Useful tools for counselors. *Personnel and Guidance Journal, 59,* 627–630.

Kirkpatrick, J. S., & Aleamoni, L. M. (1983). *Experimental research in counseling.* Springfield, IL: Charles C Thomas.

Kohlberg, L. (1963). Development of children's orientations toward a moral order. *Vita Humana, 6,* 11–36.

Kraemer, H. C., & Thiemann, S. (1987). *How many subjects? Statistical power analysis in research.* Newbury Park, CA: Sage.

Krishnamurti, J. (1968). *Talks and dialogs.* New York: Avon Books.

Krueger, R. A. (1988). *Focus groups: A practical guide for applied research.* Newbury Park, CA: Sage.

Kuhn, T. (1962). *The structure of scientific revolutions.* Chicago: University of Chicago Press.

Kvale, S. (1983). The qualitative research interview. *Journal of Phenomenological Psychology, 14,* 171–196.

Laing, J. (1988). Self-report: Can it be of value as an assessment technique? *Journal of Counseling and Development, 67,* 60–61.

Lam, C. S., & Chan, F. (1988). Job satisfaction of sheltered workshop clients. *Journal of Rehabilitation, 54*(3), 51–54.

Lambert, M. J. (1979). *The effects of psychotherapy* (Vol. 1). Montreal, Quebec: Eden Press.

Lambert, M. J., Masters, K. S., & Ogles, B. M. (1991). Outcome research in counseling. In C. E. Watkins, Jr. & L. J. Schneider (Eds.), *Research in counseling* (pp. 51–83). Hillsdale, NJ: Lawrence Erlbaum Associates.

Lanham, R. A. (1980). *Revising business prose.* New York: Charles Scribner & Sons.

Lannon, J. M. (1982). *Technical writing.* Boston: Prentice-Hall.

Larsen, G. H. (1989). *Mastering Harvard graphics.* San Francisco: Sybex.

Lauver, P. J., Kelley, J. D., & Froehle, T. C. (1971). Client reaction time and counselor verbal behavior in an interview setting. *Journal of Counseling Psychology, 18,* 26–30.

LeShan, L. (1992). Creating a climate for self-healing: The principles of modern psychosomatic medicine. *Advances, 8*(4), 20–27.

Lewis, J. A., & Lewis, M. D. (1986). *Counseling programs for employees in the workplace.* Pacific Grove, CA: Brooks/Cole.

Lyddon, W. J., & Adamson, L. A. (1992). Worldview and counseling preference. *Journal of Counseling and Development, 71*(1), 41–47.

Lyddon, W. J., Bradford, E., & Nelson, J. P. (1993). Assessing adolescent and adult attachment: A review of current self-report measures. *Journal of Counseling and Development, 71*(4), 390–395.

Malde, S. (1988). Guided autobiography: A counseling tool for older adults. *Journal of Counseling & Development, 66,* 290–293.

Marascuilo, L., & Serlin, R. (1988). *Statistical methods for the social and behavioral sciences* (2nd ed.). Pacific Grove, CA: Brooks/Cole.

Martin, J. (1988). A proposal for researching possible relationships between scientific theories and the personal theories of counselors and clients. *Journal of Counseling and Development, 66,* 261–265.

Martin, J. (1992). Scholarship and professionalism: A personal narrative. *Journal of Counseling & Development, 70,* 563–564.

Matkin, R. E., & Riggar, T. F. (1986). The rise of private sector rehabilitation and its effects on training programs. *Journal of Rehabilitation, 52*(2), 50–58.

McCracken, G. D. (1988). *The long interview.* Newbury Park, CA: Sage.

McKenna, A. E., & Ferrero, G. W. (1991). Ninth-grade students' attitudes toward nontraditional occupations. *The Career Development Quarterly, 40*(2), 168–181.

McKenzie, V. M. (1986). Ethnographic findings on West-Indian American clients. *Journal of Counseling and Development, 65,* 40–44.

Meara, N. M. (1990). Paradigmatic shifts: Science, applications, and policies: A response to Gordon and Shontz. *Journal of Counseling & Development, 69,* 67–69.

Mendenhall, W., & Beaver, R. J. (1994). *Introduction to probability and statistics.* Belmont, CA: Duxbury Press.

Milgram, S. (1963). Behavioral study of obedience. *Journal of Abnormal and Social Psychology, 67,* 371–378.

Milgram, S. (1974). *Obedience to authority.* New York: Harper & Row.

Mintz, J., Mintz, L. I., Arruda, M. J., & Hwang, S. S. (1992). Treatments of depression and the functional capacity to work. *Archives of General Psychiatry, 49,* 761–768.

Mishler, E. G. (1986). *Research interviewing: Context and narrative.* Cambridge, MA: Harvard University Press.

Mitchell, L. K., & Krumboltz, J. D. (1987). The effects of cognitive restructuring and decision-making training on career indecision. *Journal of Counseling and Development, 66*(4), 171–174.

Moore, R. A. (1977). Ten years of inpatient programs for alcoholic patients. *American Journal of Psychiatry, 134–135,* 542–545.

Morgan, D. L. (1988). *Focus groups as qualitative research.* Newbury Park, CA: Sage.

Moss, S., & Butler, D. C. (1978). The scientific credibility of ESP. *Perceptual and Motor Skills, 46,* 1063–1079.

Murray, P. V., Levitov, J. E., Castenell, L., & Joubert, J. H. (1987). Qualitative evaluation methods applied to a high school counseling center. *Journal of Counseling and Development, 65,* 259–261.

Myers, D. W. (1984). *Establishing and building employee assistance programs.* Westport, CT: Quorum Books.

Naisbitt, J. & Auburdene, P. (1990). *Megatrends two thousand: Ten new directions for the 1990s.* New York: Avon.

Orne, M. T. (1962). On the social psychology of the psychological experiment: With particular reference to demand characteristics and their implications. *American Psychologist, 17,* 776–783.

Osgood, H. E. (1989). Methods of improving self-report as an assessment technique. *Journal of Counseling & Development, 68,* 58–60.

Osgood, C. E., Suci, G. J., & Tannenbaum, P. H. (1957). *The measurement of meaning.* Urbana, IL: University of Illinois Press.

Pace, C. R., Barahona, D., & Kaplan, D. (1985). *The credibility of student self-reports.* Los Angeles: Center for the Study of Evaluation.

Pajak, E. F., & Blase, J. J. (1984). Teachers in bars: From professional to personal self. *Sociology of Education, 57,* 164–173.

Parker, R. M., & Szymanski, E. M. (1992). Fishing and error rate problem. *Rehabilitation Counseling Bulletin, 36,* 66–69.

Patton, M. Q. (1987). *How to use qualitative methods in evaluation.* Newbury Park, CA: Sage.

Pepinsky, H. B., & Pepinsky, P. N. (1954). *Counseling: Theory and Practice.* New York: Ronald Press.

Phi Delta Kappa National Study Committee on Education. (1971). *Educational evaluation and decision making.* Itasca, IL: F. E. Peacock.

Philips, S. D., Friedlander, M. L., Kost, P. P., Spectermas, R. V., & Robbins, E. S. (1988). Personal versus vocational focus in career counseling: A retrospective outcome study. *Journal of Counseling and Development, 67*(3), 169–173.

Piaget, J. (1952). *The origins of intelligence in children.* New York: International University Press.

Piaget, J. (1972). *The child's conception of the world.* Totowa, NJ: Littlefield, Adams.

Pinckert, R. C. (1981). *The truth about English.* Englewood Cliffs, NJ: Prentice-Hall.

Polkinghorne, D. E. (1991). Qualitative procedures for counseling research. In C. E. Watkins, Jr. & L. J. Schneider (Eds.), *Research in counseling* (pp. 163–204). Hillsdale, NJ: Lawrence Erlbaum Associates.

Ponterotto, J. G., & Casas, J. M. (1991). *Handbook of racial/ethnic minority counseling research.* Springfield, IL: Charles Thomas.

Pope, K. S., Vetter, V. A. (1992). Ethical dilemmas encountered by members of the American Psychological Association. *American Psychologist, 47,* 397–411.

Popper, K. R. (1982). *The open universe.* Totowa, NJ: Rowman & Littlefield.

Pruitt, W. A. (1977). *Vocational work evaluation.* Menomenie, WI: W. Pruitt Associates.

Pyrczak, F., & Bruce, R. R. (1992). *Writing empirical research reports.* Los Angeles: Pyrczak Publishing.

Quintana, S. M., & Kerr, J. (1993). Relational needs in late adolescent separation-individuation. *Journal of Counseling and Development, 71*(3), 349–354.

Robinson, S. E., & Gross, D. R. (1986). Counseling research: Ethics and issues. *Journal of Counseling and Development, 64,* 331–333.

Roethlisberger, F. J., & Dickson, W. J. (1939). *Management and the worker.* Cambridge, MA: Harvard University Press.

Rogers, C. R., & Dymond, R. F. (Eds.). (1954). *Psychotherapy and personality change.* Chicago: University of Chicago Press.

Roman, P. M. (1992). Program evaluation: The right approach. *Employee Assistance, 5*(3), 6–8.

Rosenthal, R., & Jacobson, L. F. (1968). *Pygmalion in the classroom: Teachers' expectations and pupils' intellectual development.* New York: Holt, Rinehart & Winston.

Rosenthal, R., & Rubin, D. (1984). Multiple contrasts and ordered Bonferroni procedures. *Journal of Educational Psychology, 76,* 1028–1034.

Rossi, P. H., & Freeman, H. E. (1985). *Evaluation: A systematic approach* (3rd ed.). Beverly Hills, CA: Sage.

Rossi, P. H., & Freeman, H. E. (1989). *Evaluation: A systematic approach* (4th ed.). Newbury Park, CA: Sage.

Royce, J. E. (1989). *Alcohol problems and alcoholism: A comparative survey.* New York: Free Press.

Rubin, S. E., & Rice, J. M. (1986). Quality and relevance of rehabilitation research: A critique and recommendations. *Rehabilitation Counseling Bulletin, 30,* 33–42.

Sackett, G. P. (Ed.). (1978). *Observing behavior* (Vol. 1). Baltimore: University Park Press.

Sackett, G. P. (Ed.). (1978). *Observing behavior, Vol. 2, Data collection and analysis methods.* Baltimore: University Park Press.

Sampson, J. P., Jr. (1991). The place of the computer in counseling research. In C. E. Watkins, Jr. & L. J. Schneider (Eds.), *Research in counseling* (pp. 261–284). Hillside, NJ: Lawrence Erlbaum Associates.

Sax, G. (1989). *Principles of educational and psychological measurement and evaluation* (3rd ed.). Belmont, CA: Wadsworth.

Scarr, S. (1988). Race and gender as psychological variables: Social and ethical issues. *American Psychologist, 43,* 56–59.

Schaie, K. W. (1965). A general model for the study of developmental problems. *Psychological Bulletin, 64,* 92–107.

Schaie, K. W. (1988). Internal validity threats in studies of adult cognitive development. In M. L. Howe & C. E. Brainerd (Eds.), *Cognitive development in adulthood: Progress in cognitive development research* (pp. 241–272). New York: Springer-Verlag.

Schaie, K. W. (1993). Ageist language in psychological research. *American Psychologist, 48,* 49–51.

Schaie, K. W., & Strother, C. R. (1968). A cross-sectional study of age changes in cognitive behavior. *Psychological Bulletin, 70,* 671–680.

Schulman, E. D. (1991). *Intervention in human services* (4th ed.). New York: Merrill.

Shedler, J., & Block, J. (1990). Adolescent drug use and psychological health. *American Psychologist, 45,* 612–630.

Sheehan, J. G., Hadley, R. G., & Gould, E. (1967). The impact of authority on stuttering. *Journal of Abnormal Psychology, 72,* 290–293.

Shepherd, L. J. (1993). *Lifting the veil: The feminine face of science.* Boston: Shambhala Publications.

Shore, J. H., Tatum, E. L., & Vollmer, W. M. (1986). Psychiatric reactions to disaster: The Mount St. Helens experience. *American Journal of Psychiatry, 143*(5), 590–595.

Sieber, J. E., & Stanley, B. (1988). Ethical and professional dimensions of socially sensitive research. *American Psychologist, 43,* 49–55.

Skinner, B. F. (1953). *Science and human behavior.* New York: MacMillan.

Skinner, B. F. (1956). A case history in scientific method. *American Psychologist, 11,* 221–233.

Skinner, B. F. (1972). *Cumulative record* (3rd ed.). New York: Appleton-Century-Crofts.

Skovholt, T. M., & Ronnestad, M. H. (1992). Themes in therapist and counselor development. *Journal of Counseling and Development, 70,* 505–515.

Smith, D., & Mahoney, J. (1989). McDonnell Douglas Corporation's EAP produces hard data. *The ALMACAN, 19*(8), 18–26.

Smith, M. L. (1981). Naturalistic research. *Personnel and Guidance Journal, 59,* 585–589.

Smith, M. L., & Glass, G. V. (1977). Meta-analysis of psychotherapy outcome studies. *American Psychologist, 32,* 752–760.

Smith, R. (1993). *Navigating the Internet.* Indianapolis, IN: Sams.

Sobell, M. B., & Sobell, L. K. (1973). Alcoholics treated by individualized behavior therapy. One-year treatment outcome. *Behaviour Research and Therapy, 11,* 599–618.

Solomon, R. (1949). An extension of control group design. *Psychological Bulletin, 46,* 137–150.

Sonnenstuhl, W. J., Trice, H. M., Staudenmeier, W. J., & Steele, P. (1987). Employee assistance and drug testing: Fairness and injustice in the workplace. *Nova Law Review, 11,* 709–731.

Spradley, J. P. (1979). *The ethnographic interview.* New York: Holt, Rinehart & Winston.

Stanley, B., Sieber, J. S., & Melton, G. B. (1987). Empirical studies of ethical issues in research: A research agenda. *American Psychologist, 42,* 735–741.

Stolberg, S. (1994, April 1). Feeling betrayed by science. *Los Angeles Times,* pp. A1, A22.

Stone, P. J., Dunphy, D. C., Smith, M. S., & Ogilvie, D. M. (1968). *User's manual for the General Inquirer.* Cambridge, MA: MIT Press.

Strong, S. R. (1991). Science in counseling psychology: Reply to Gelso (1991) and Patton and Jackson (1991). *Journal of Counseling Psychology, 38,* 217–218.

Stufflebeam, D. L., McCormick, C. H., Brinkerhoff, R. O., & Nelson, C. O. (1985). *Conducting educational needs assessments.* Boston: Kluwer-Nijhoff.

Stufflebeam, D. L., & Shinkfield, A. J. (1985). *Systematic evaluation: A self-instructional guide to theory and practice.* Boston: Kluwer-Nijhof.

Sulzer-Azaroff, B., & Mayer, G. R. (1991). *Behavior analysis for lasting change.* San Francisco: Holt, Rinehart & Winston.

Sulzer-Azaroff, B., & Reese, E. P. (1982). *Applying behavior analysis.* Chicago, IL: Holt, Rinehart & Winston.

Taylor, W. F., Obitz, F. W., & Reich, J. W. (1982). Experimental bias resulting from using volunteers in alcoholism research. *Journal of Studies on Alcohol, 43,* 240–251.

Tennyson, W. W., Miller, G. D., Skovholt, T. M., & Williams, P. C. (1989). How they view their role: A survey of counselors in different secondary schools. *Journal of Counseling and Development, 67*(7), 399–403.

Thoreson, R. W., Shaughnessy, P., Cook, S. W., & Moore, D. (1993). Behavioral and attitudinal correlates of masculinity: A national survey of male counselors. *Journal of Counseling and Development, 71*(3), 337–342.

Tomlinson, M. (Producer). (1992). *Can you believe TV ratings?* [Film]. Films for the Humanities.

Tracey, T. J. (1991). Counseling research as an applied science. In C. E. Watkins, Jr. & Lawrence J. Schneider (Eds.), *Research in counseling* (pp. 3–31). Hillsdale, NJ: Lawrence Erlbaum Associates.

Trachtman, J. N., Giambalvo, V., & Dippner, R. S. (1978). On the assumptions concerning the assumptions of the *t* test. *Journal of General Psychology, 99,* 107–116.

U.S. Department of Education, Rehabilitation Services Administration. (1990). *Annual report to the President and to the Congress. Fiscal year 1990, on federal activities related to the Rehabilitation Act of 1973 as amended.* Washington, DC: U.S. Government Printing Office.

Vacc, N. A., & Loesch, L. C. (1993). A content analysis of opinions about the National Counselor Examination. *Journal of Counseling and Development, 71*(4), 418–421.

Van Dalen, D. B. (1979). *Understanding educational research.* New York: McGraw-Hill.

Walz, G. R., Bleuer, J. C., & Maze, M. (1989). *Counseling software guide.* Alexandria, VA: American Counseling Association.

Waskow, I. E., & Parloff, M. B. (1975). *Psychotherapy change measures* (DHEW) Publica tion No. ADM 74-20). Washington, DC: U.S. Government Printing Office.

Watkins, C. E., Jr., & Schneider, L. J. (1991). Research in counseling: Some concluding thoughts and ideas. In C. E. Watkins, Jr. & L. J. Schneider (Eds.), *Research in counseling* (pp. 287–299). Hillsdale, NJ: Lawrence Erlbaum Associates.

Watson, D. L., & Tharp, R. G. (1992). *Self-directed behavior: Self-modification for personal adjustment.* Pacific Grove, CA: Brooks/Cole.

Wheelwright, J. (1991, April 2). Muzzling science. *Newsweek*, p. 10.

Wilkins, W. (1986). Placebo problems in psychotherapy research. *American Psychologist, 41,* 551–556.

Wilkinson, L. (1987). SYSTAT: The system for statistics. Evanston, IL: SYSTAT, Inc.

Wilkinson, T., & Rainey, J. (1990, January 19). Tapes of children decided the case for most jurors. *Los Angeles Times*, pp. A1, A22.

Winer, B. J., Brown, D. R., & Michels, K. M. (1991). *Statistical principles in experimental design.* New York: McGraw-Hill.

Wolpe, J. (1958). *Psychotherapy by reciprocal inhibition.* Stanford University Press.

Wright, B. (1983). *Physical disability—a psychosocial approach.* New York: Harper & Row.

Wright, R. M., & Strong, S. R. (1982). Stimulating therapeutic change with directives: An exploratory study. *Journal of Counseling Psychology, 29,* 199–202.

Index

TO THE OWNER OF THIS BOOK:

We hope that you have found *Counseling Research & Program Evaluation* useful. So that this book can be improved in a future edition, would you take the time to complete this sheet and return it? Thank you.

School and address: ─────────────────────────────────

Department: ──────────────────────────────────────

Instructor's name: ───────────────────────────────────

1. What I like most about this book is: ──────────────────────

──

──

2. What I like least about this book is: ──────────────────────

──

──

3. My general reaction to this book is: ──────────────────────

──

4. The name of the course in which I used this book is: ─────────────

──

5. Were all of the chapters of the book assigned for you to read? ────────

   If not, which ones weren't? ──────────────────────────

6. In the space below, or on a separate sheet of paper, please write specific suggestions for improving this book and anything else you'd care to share about your experience in using the book.

──

──

──

──

Optional:

Your name: _____ Date: _____

May Brooks/Cole quote you, either in promotion for *Counseling Research & Program Evaluation*, or in future publishing ventures?

Yes: _____ No: _____

Sincerely,

Robert G. Hadley
Lynda K. Mitchell

FOLD HERE

- -

BUSINESS REPLY MAIL

FIRST CLASS   PERMIT NO. 358   BELMONT, CA

POSTAGE WILL BE PAID BY ADDRESSEE

ATT: *Hadley/Mitchell* _____

Brooks/Cole, Cengage Learning
20 Davis Drive
Belmont, CA 94002